everything's an argument

with readings

Third Edition

EVERYTHING'S AN
argument
with readings

Andrea A. Lunsford
Stanford University

John J. Ruszkiewicz
University of Texas at Austin

Keith Walters
University of Texas at Austin

BEDFORD/ST. MARTIN'S
BOSTON ■ NEW YORK·

For Bedford/St. Martin's

Developmental Editor: Stephanie Carpenter
Production Editor: Bernard Onken
Senior Production Supervisor: Nancy Myers
Art Director: Lucy Krikorian
Text Design: Anna George
Copy Editor: Alice Vigliani
Indexer: Riofrancos & Co. Indexes
Photo Research: Alice Lundoff
Cover Design: Lucy Krikorian
Cover Photos: Barbie doll: the first Barbie doll produced in 1959, Barbie Doll
    Museum, Palo Alto. Photo © Neema Frederic/CORBIS; Seal of the President/
    United States. Photo Joseph Sohm/Photo Researchers. White Dove: Photo ©
    Roger Tidman/CORBIS; 4×4 on Road: Photo Getty Images/Antonio M. Rosario;
    Mobile phone keypad (digital enhancement): Getty Images/Rick Rusing.
Composition: Monotype Composition Company, Inc.
Printing and Binding: R.R. Donnelley & Sons Company

President: Joan E. Feinberg
Editorial Director: Denise B. Wydra
Editor in Chief: Nancy Perry
Director of Marketing: Karen Melton Soeltz
Director of Editing, Design, and Production: Marcia Cohen
Managing Editor: Erica T. Appel

Library of Congress Control Number: 2003107543

Copyright © 2004 by Bedford/St. Martin's

Manufactured in the United States of America.
9 8 7 6 5 4
f e d c b a

For information, write:
Bedford/St. Martin's
75 Arlington Street
Boston, MA 02116   (617-399-4000)

ISBN: 0-312-40724-6

ACKNOWLEDGMENTS

Acknowledgments and copyrights appear at the back of the book on pages 890–898, which constitute an extension of the copyright page.

PREFACE

In this third edition, *Everything's an Argument with Readings* remains a labor of love for us, a lively introduction to rhetoric drawn directly from our experiences teaching persuasive writing. The chapters still practically write themselves, and we take special pleasure in discovering fresh new arguments or provocative visual images that illuminate the ways we all use language to assert our presence in the world. Apparently, the book continues to strike a chord with many students and instructors who have made *Everything's an Argument with Readings* a top-seller in its field since its debut. We offer now a third edition, thoroughly revised to reach more students and instructors and to account for changes we see in the way arguments are framed and circulated throughout the world.

The purposefully controversial title of this text sums up two key assumptions we share. First, language provides the most powerful means of understanding the world and of using that understanding to help shape lives. Second, all language—including the language of visual images or of symbol systems other than writing—is persuasive, pointing in a direction and asking for response. From the morning news to the presidential seal, from the American flag to the Mercedes three-pointed star, from the latest hip-hop hit to the brand identity of Pepsi, texts everywhere beckon for response. People walk, talk, and breathe persuasion very much as they breathe the air: *everything* is a potential argument.

So our purpose in *Everything's an Argument with Readings* is to present argument as something that's as natural and everyday as an old pair of jeans, as something we do almost from the moment we are born (in fact, an infant's first cry is as poignant a claim as we can imagine), and—because of its ever-present nature—as something worthy of careful attention and practice. In pursuing this goal, we try to use ordinary language whenever possible and to keep our use of specialized terminology to a minimum. But we also see argument, and want students to see it, as a craft both delicate and powerful. So we have designed *Everything's an Argument with Readings* to be itself an argument for argument, with a voice that aims to appeal to readers cordially but that doesn't hesitate to make demands on them when appropriate.

We also aim to balance attention to the critical *reading* of arguments (analysis) with attention to the writing of arguments (production). Moreover, we have tried to demonstrate both activities with lively—and realistic—examples, on the principle that the best way to appreciate an argument may be to see it in action. Indeed, we have worked hard to enhance the power of the examples selected for this third edition, expanding the range of texts we present and including works more deliberately oriented toward the concerns of college students in all their diversity.

In the previous edition, we broadened the context of argument to include visual media and the public spaces and electronic environments that students now inhabit so much of the time. We've intensified that effort in this latest edition, with every chapter presenting new images and fresh argumentative situations. We also offer more about that remarkably useful ancient way of approaching arguments called "stasis theory," integrating its principles across several key chapters. In addition, this third edition offers more advice about rhetorical analysis and then goes on to show students how to write an analysis of their own, since such assignments are increasingly common in courses on argument. Based on advice from teachers and students using this text and from reviewers, we have expanded both our general chapter on logical arguments (Chapter 7) and our more specialized chapter on Toulmin reasoning (Chapter 8) so that writers can choose what sort of approach to take toward reasoning. As a result, the Toulmin chapter not only includes more helpful explanations and diagrams but also shows how Toulmin's concepts operate in extended arguments, illustrating the point by focusing on a lively essay by Alan M. Dershowitz on speech codes. To help students better understand the increasingly complicated world of intellectual property and to show them how to avoid plagiarism, we've expanded Chapter 20 on intellectual property to offer more examples of situations familiar to students. We've also carefully revised the prose throughout *Everything's an Argument with Readings* to make our discussions livelier and clearer. We use fewer abstract subjects, fewer passive verbs, more lively images, and many more examples in some chapters. We hope the new book is even more engaging to read than the first two editions.

In selecting texts for the anthology in this revised edition, we've tried to choose topics of interest and concern to today's students. Rather than focusing on abstract notions of gender rights, we've included a cluster of arguments about the very real and continuing debates over Title IX and its consequences on campuses nationwide. We've added a new cluster of readings on the ways in which sports in America often stands in as a proxy for politics, whether the topic is the Augusta National Golf Club or the costs of college sports, especially basketball and football. In light of September 11 and the war on Iraq, we've included new clusters of readings about the definition of patriotism and the limits of privacy and civil liberties in general. As debates about the role of religion in American public life continue to heat up, we've expanded the readings that treat matters of faith or religion, always trying to demonstrate the complexity of such issues. Rather than offering a series of pro/con debates on bilingual education, we've provided a new cluster of readings on what it means to be bilingual in America at a time when the country has more immigrants than at any time in its past (though immigrants make up a far lower percentage of the population than they did a century ago). We believe these issues will be familiar to students—they have certainly surfaced in discussions with the students we teach—and we trust the readings included here will give rise to arguments worth having, worth writing about, and worth reading. Finally, in response to instructors who have asked for more extended, more complex arguments, we have increased the average length of selections, offering students a balance of shorter pieces and more sustained arguments. We continue to reproduce these texts as they were originally published, as much as possible. This "look," after all, is an important part of the arguments the readings make, as Marshall McLuhan insisted when he said that "the medium is the massage" or as Demosthenes argued when he said that the three most important parts of any message were "delivery, delivery, and delivery."

In pursuing all the above goals, we've tried hard to keep this book easy to use. Designed as two books in one, with the rhetoric chapters up front and the anthology in the back, the book offers instructors a great degree of flexibility. You can focus on the elements of argumentation, supplementing with readings from the anthology, or you can focus on real arguments, referring back to the explanations in the front as necessary. To help you work with the two parts of the book, we have included links in the margins throughout, pointing out helpful examples of the rhetorical elements found in the readings as well as useful explanations found in the rhetoric.

Key Features

- Two books in one, neatly linked. Up front is a full guide to argument; in back is a thematically arranged anthology of readings. The two parts of the book are linked by cross-references in the margins, leading students from the argument chapters to specific examples in the readings and from the readings to appropriate rhetorical instruction.

- A unique and winning approach, going beyond pro/con assumptions to show that argument is everywhere—in essays, news articles, scholarly writing, poems, advertisements, cartoons, posters, bumper stickers, billboards, Web sites, Web logs, and other electronic environments.

- Fresh and important topics, selected because they encourage students to take up complex positions. Readings on topics such as "Stereotypes in Media and Pop Culture," "What's Public, What's Private?," and "Being Bilingual in the United States" demand that students explore the many sides of an issue.

- A real-world design—with readings presented much as they were in the original publication. Newspaper articles look like newspaper text, complete with callouts and original illustrations; writing from the Web looks like plain Web text; essays appear in a conventional format—helping students recognize and think about the effect design and visuals have on written arguments.

- Student-friendly explanations in simple, everyday language; many brief examples; and a minimum of technical terminology.

- Eleven sample essays, including six by student writers, annotated to show rhetorical features. Most of these essays are new to the third edition.

- Unique, full chapters on visual argument, argument in electronic environments, spoken argument, and humor in argument.

- Extensive coverage of the use of sources in argument, with full chapters on assessing and using sources, documenting sources in up-to-date MLA and APA styles, and intellectual property.

New to This Edition

- Forty-four new readings on timely topics, including such stimulating selections as "Globalization of Beauty Makes Slimness Trendy" by Norimitsu Onishi, "The Homeland Security State: How Far Should We Go?" by Matthew Brzezinski, "Football Is a Sucker's Game" by Michael Sokolove, and "Tee Time for Equality" by Deborah Rhode.

- Four unique and provocative new topic clusters — "Privacy and Civil Liberties After September 11," "Is Sports Just a Proxy for Politics?," "Being Bilingual in the United States," and "Will the Real American Patriot Please Stand Up?" — presenting multifaceted issues that students will want to discuss and write about. Updated selections in *all* chapters complement the previous edition's successful, classroom-tested readings.

- A greater number of longer selections in response to instructor feedback from across the country. By providing students with a balance of shorter pieces and more extended arguments, the book more realistically represents what argument is and offers more diverse models for student writing.

- Greater integration of visual arguments in every chapter throughout the book so that students can recognize and respond to a more diverse range of arguments.

- Expanded coverage of analyzing arguments in Chapter 2 to improve students' critical thinking and help them form their own arguments. Analyses of both a visual and a written text demonstrate this process for students.

- An expanded intellectual property chapter within a trio of chapters on using sources that helps students understand the larger issues surrounding intellectual property and addresses the concerns about avoiding plagiarism that students face daily in their college courses.

- More help in understanding Toulmin argument through a sample Toulmin analysis of a full argument and more diagrams to explain the relationships among claims, reasons, warrants, and qualifiers. These additional aids help students analyze arguments and develop and test their own ideas. Additional extended examples of how to use the stasis questions during invention show students how this ancient theory can help them in their own writing.

- Livelier prose and a greater range of examples to make the third edition more engaging than ever.

Acknowledgments

We owe a debt of gratitude to many people for making *Everything's an Argument with Readings* possible. Our first thanks must go to the students we have taught in our writing courses for more than two decades, particularly first-year students at The Ohio State University, Stanford University, and the University of Texas at Austin. Almost every chapter in this book has been informed by a classroom encounter with a student whose shrewd observation or perceptive question sent an ambitious lesson plan spiraling to the ground. (Anyone who has tried to teach claims and warrants on the fly to skeptical first-year students will surely appreciate why we have qualified our claims in the Toulmin chapter so carefully.) But students have also provided the motive for writing this book. More than ever, students need to know how to read and write arguments effectively if they are to secure a place in a world growing ever smaller and more rhetorically challenging.

We are grateful to our editors at Bedford/St. Martin's who contributed their talents to our book, beginning with Joan Feinberg and Nancy Perry, who have enthusiastically supported the project and provided us with the resources and feedback needed to keep us on track. Most of the day-to-day work on the project has been handled by the remarkably patient and perceptive Stephanie Carpenter. She prevented more than a few lapses of judgment yet understands the spirit of this book—which involves, occasionally, taking risks to make a memorable point. We have appreciated, too, her advice about pop culture issues, which begin to escape us, and her uncanny ability to focus our attention where it mattered.

We are similarly grateful to others at Bedford/St. Martin's who contributed their talents to our book: Bernard Onken, Steve Scipione, Alice Lundoff, Anita Duckwith, Nicholas Wolven, Lucy Krikorian, Nancy Myers, Nick Carbone, and especially Anna George, whose design contributes so much to the book's appeal and accessibility. Thanks also to Karen Melton Soeltz and Brian Wheel for their superb marketing.

We'd also like to thank the astute instructors and students who reviewed the third edition: Petia Dimitrova Alexieva, University of South Carolina; Darlene Anderson, University of South Carolina; Cathryn Best, Grand Rapids Community College; Thomas Bonfiglio, Arizona State University; Joyce Brownell, Ferris State University; Terri-Ann Burack, Iowa State University; Jennifer R. Bush, Pennsylvania State University; Alison Cable, North Carolina State University; Patrick Clauss, Butler University; Michelle Comstock, University of South Alabama; Lauren Coulter, University of Tennessee–Chattanooga; Jane Fife, University of Tennessee–Chattanooga; Kenneth Hawley, University of Kentucky; Mary Hocks, Georgia State University; Janice Hudley, United States Military Academy–West Point; Priscilla Kanet, Clemson University; Lindsay Lightner, Pennsylvania State University; Amy Lister, Louisiana State University; Rachel Lutwick-Deaner, North Carolina State University; Aimee Mapes, Louisiana State

University; Kristine V. Nakutis, United States Military Academy – West Point; Richard Ogle, University of Tennessee – Chattanooga; Darrel Jesse Peters, University of North Carolina – Pembroke; Malea Powell, University of Nebraska – Lincoln; Catherine E. Ross, The University of Texas at Tyler; Stephen Schneider, Pennsylvania State University; Carol Severino, University of Iowa; Lee S. Tesdell, Iowa State University; Alex Vuilleumier, Oregon State University; Anne Wiegard, SUNY – Cortland; the excellent group of teaching assistants at The University of Texas who shared their ideas early in the revision; and the students of Cassie Armstrong's English 141 class at the University of Colorado – Colorado Springs.

Thanks, too, to our graduate assistants whose work made this new edition and its ancillaries possible. Jodi Egerton contributed in important ways to the selection of new readings for the anthology and to the Web site for the book, while John Kinkade helped us greatly with the rhetoric portion of the text. Jodi and John prepared the instructor's guides for this third edition, building on the earlier work of Michal Brody and Ben Feigert, who also did excellent work on the Web site and text exercises, respectively. We thank them all for their contributions to this and earlier editions of *Everything's an Argument with Readings*. Finally, we are especially grateful to the undergraduate students whose fine argumentative essays appear in our chapters.

We hope that *Everything's an Argument with Readings* responds to what students and instructors have said they want and need. And we hope readers of this text will let us know how we've done: please share your opinions and suggestions with us at www.bedfordstmartins.com/everythingsanargument.

Andrea A. Lunsford
John J. Ruszkiewicz
Keith Walters

CONTENTS

PART 5   CONVENTIONS OF ARGUMENT   365

18. What Counts as Evidence   367

19. Fallacies of Argument   384

> A TALL, THIN woman. Yeah! That's
> what I want. 5'8" to 6'2", fun, pretty,
> seeking long-term relationship. I'm
> 6', muscular, grey and green, 40s,
> intelligent, V.I.P. businesses. Country
> life, boating, camping to limousine
> trips, dinners, tours.

PART 6   ARGUMENTS   455

23. Mirror, Mirror . . . Images and the Media   457

Who's the Fairest of Them All?   459

If the media function as a mirror that reflects "the fairest of us all," what sorts of bodies appear there, what sorts don't, and what might the consequences of this situation be?

Stereotypes in Media and Pop Culture 494

What are the implications of a bilingual Chihuahua selling tacos? Of Jar Jar Binks having dreads? Of the fact that father rarely knows best on TV sitcoms? This cluster of arguments invites you to decide whether media stereotypes matter and why.

24. What's Public? What's Private? 513

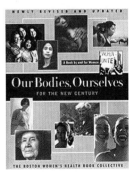

26. Who Owns What?   643

Who Owns the Body and Its Parts and Who Owns Life?   645

Have you ever thought of your body as property—or considered that your genes, embryos, organs, and remains can be bought, sold, patented, and traded? As this cluster of readings makes clear, the question of who owns the body is anything but simple.

Who Owns Words and Ideas?   673

Can words and ideas be "owned"? If so, who owns "I Have a Dream"? And how do you feel knowing that someone else could own *your* next good idea?

27. Language(s) and Identities   700

Being Bilingual in the United States   739

What's life like for Americans who live in two languages? What similarities and differences exist among them? And between them and monolinguals? As the number of bilingual Americans continues to grow, we all need to understand.

28. Beliefs and Stances   774

Religious Beliefs in the Public Arena   776

It's clear that many Americans understand the First Amendment to guarantee freedom of religion—not freedom *from* religion. But what roles should faith and religious belief play in American public life?

Will the Real American Patriot Please Stand Up? 826

What does it mean to be a patriot? To be patriotic? How have the events of September 11, 2001, framed that question anew for all Americans? These arguments challenge you to think about how and why you define patriotism as you do now.

everything's an argument

with readings

INTRODUCING argument

Everything Is an Argument

"Best Breakfast Anywhere!" proclaims a sign in the window of a diner.

A professor interrupts a lecture to urge her students to spend less time on Instant Messaging and more in the company of thick, old books.

A senator tells a C-SPAN caller that recent legislation, such as the Homeland Security Bill, does not reduce citizens' constitutional rights or their privacy.

A nurse assures a youngster eyeing an approaching needle, "This won't hurt one bit."

A sports columnist blasts a football coach for passing on fourth down and two in a close game—even though the play produces a touchdown.

Sign found on a teenager's bedroom door:

Bumper sticker sighted in November 2002:

"Please let me make it through this chem exam!" a student silently prays.

■ ■ ■

These visual and verbal messages all contain arguments. In fact, it's hard to go more than a few minutes without encountering some form of argument in our culture. From the clothes you wear to the foods you choose to eat to the groups you decide to join—all of these everyday activities make nuanced, sometimes implicit, arguments about who you are and what you value. Thus an argument can be any text—whether written, spoken, or visual—that expresses a point of view. Sometimes arguments can be aggressive, composed deliberately to change what readers believe, think, or do. At other times your goals may be more subtle, and your writing may be designed to convince yourself or others that specific facts are reliable or that certain views should be considered or at least tolerated.

In fact, some theorists claim that language is itself inherently persuasive (even when you say "hi, how's it going?" for instance, you are in one sense arguing that your hello deserves a response) and hence *every* text is also an argument, designed to influence readers. For example, a poem that observes what little girls do in church may indirectly critique the role religion plays in women's lives, for good or ill:

> **I worry for the girls.**
> **I once had braids,**
> **and wore lace that made me suffer.**

> I had not yet done the things
> that would need forgiving.
>   –Kathleen Norris, "Little Girls in Church"

To take another example, observations about family life among the poor
in India may suddenly illuminate the writer's life and the reader's experience, forcing comparisons that quietly argue for change:

> I have learned from Jagat and his family a kind of commitment, a form
> of friendship that is not always available in the West, where we have
> become cynical and instrumental in so many of our relationships to
> others.
>   –Jeremy Seabrook, "Family Values"

Even humor makes an argument when it causes readers to become aware—
through bursts of laughter or just a faint smile—of the way things are
and how they might be different. Take a look, for example, at an excerpt
from the introduction to Dave Barry's latest book, *Dave Barry Hits Below the
Beltway*, along with its cover, which also makes a humorous argument:

> To do even a halfway decent book on a subject as complex as the
> United States government, you have to spend a lot of time in Wash-
> ington, D.C. So the first thing I decided, when I was getting ready to
> write this book, was that it would not be even halfway decent.

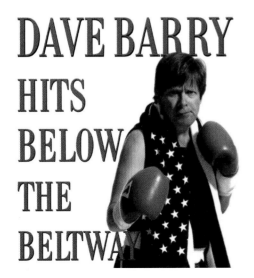

FIGURE 1.1 DAVE BARRY'S
HUMOROUS ARGUMENT
BEGINS ON HIS BOOK'S COVER.

More obvious as arguments are those that make a claim and present evidence to support it. Such writing often moves readers to recognize problems and to consider solutions. Suasion of this kind is usually easy to recognize:

> Discrimination against Hispanics, or any other group, should be fought and there are laws and a massive apparatus to do so. But the way to eliminate such discrimination is not to classify all Hispanics as victims.
>
> –Linda Chavez, "Towards a New Politics of Hispanic Assimilation"

> [W]omen unhappy in their marriages often enter full-time employment as an escape. But although a woman's entrance into the workplace does tend to increase the stability of her marriage, it does not increase her happiness.
>
> –The Popular Research Institute, Penn State University

> Resistance to science is born of fear. Fear, in turn, is bred by ignorance. And it is ignorance that is our deepest malady.
>
> –J. Michael Bishop, "Enemies of Promise"

ARGUMENT ISN'T JUST ABOUT WINNING

Deborah Kovach Caldwell's examination of Hindu culture in the United States is a good example of an argument to explore.

··LINK TO P. 789

If in some ways all language has an argumentative edge that aims to make a point, not all language use aims to win out over others. In contrast to the traditional Western concept of argument as being about fighting or combat, communication theorists such as Sonja Foss, Cindy Griffin, and Josina Makau describe an *invitational* argument, which aims not to win over another person or group but to invite others to enter a space of mutual regard and exploration. In fact, as you'll see, writers and speakers have as many purposes for arguing as for using language, including—in addition to winning—to inform, to convince, to explore, to make decisions, even to meditate or pray.

Of course, many arguments *are* aimed at winning. Such is the traditional purpose of much writing and speaking in the political arena, in the business world, and in the law courts. Two candidates for office, for example, try to win out over each other in appealing for votes; the makers of one soft drink try to outsell their competitors by appealing to public tastes; and two lawyers try to defeat each other in pleading to a judge and jury. In your college writing, you may also be called on to make an argument that appeals to a "judge" and/or "jury" (your instructor and classmates). You might, for instance, argue that peer-to-peer file-sharing is protected under the doctrine of fair use. In doing so, you may need to defeat your unseen opponents—those who oppose such file-sharing.

At this point, it may be helpful to acknowledge a common academic distinction between argument and persuasion. In this view, the point of argument is to discover some version of the truth, using evidence and reasons. Argument of this sort leads audiences toward conviction, an agreement that a claim is true or reasonable, or that a course of action is desirable. The aim of persuasion is to change a point of view or to move others from conviction to action. In other words, writers or speakers argue to find some truth; they persuade when they think they already know it.

Argument (discover a truth) ⟶ conviction

Persuasion (know a truth) ⟶ action

In practice, this distinction between argument and persuasion can be hard to sustain. It is unnatural for writers or readers to imagine their minds divided between a part that pursues truth and a part that seeks to persuade. And yet, you may want to reserve the term *persuasion* for writing that is aggressively designed to change opinions through the use of both reason and other appropriate techniques. For writing that sets out to persuade at all costs, abandoning reason, fairness, and truth altogether, the term *propaganda,* with all its negative connotations, seems to fit. Some would suggest that *advertising* often works just as well.

But, as we have already suggested, arguing isn't always about winning or even about changing others' views. In addition to invitational argument, another school of argument—called Rogerian argument, after the psychotherapist Carl Rogers—is based on finding common ground and establishing trust among those who disagree about issues, and on approaching audiences in nonthreatening ways. Writers who follow Rogerian approaches seek to understand the perspectives of those with whom they disagree, looking for "both/and" or "win/win" solutions (rather than "either/or" or "win/lose" ones) whenever possible. Much successful argument today follows such principles, consciously or not.

Some other purposes or goals of argument are worth considering in more detail.

Arguments to Inform

You may want or need to argue with friends or colleagues over the merits of different academic majors. But your purpose in doing so may well be to inform and to be informed, for only in such detailed arguments can you come to the best choice. Consider how Joan Didion uses argument to inform readers about the artist Georgia O'Keeffe:

> This is a woman who in 1939 could advise her admirers that they were missing her point, that their appreciation of her famous flowers was merely sentimental. "When I paint a red hill," she observed coolly in the catalogue for an exhibition that year, "you say it is too bad that I don't always paint flowers. A flower touches almost everyone's heart. A red hill doesn't touch everyone's heart."
>
> –Joan Didion, "Georgia O'Keeffe"

By giving specific information about O'Keeffe and her own ideas about her art, Didion in this passage argues that readers should pay closer attention to the work of this artist.

Less subtle and more common as informative arguments are political posters featuring the smiling faces of candidates and the offices they are

FIGURE 1.2 GEORGIA O'KEEFFE'S *WHITE FLOWER ON RED EARTH, #1* (1943)

seeking: "Honda in 2002," "Lujan for Mayor." Of course, these visual texts are usually also aimed at winning out over an unmentioned opponent. But on the surface at least, they announce who is running for a specific office.

Arguments to Convince

If you are writing a report that attempts to identify the causes of changes in global temperatures, you would likely be trying not to conquer opponents but to satisfy readers that you've thoroughly examined those causes and that they merit serious attention. As a form of writing, reports typically aim to persuade readers rather than win out over opponents. Yet the presence of those who might disagree is always implied, and it shapes a writer's strategies. In the following passage, for example, Paul Osterman argues to convince readers of the urgency surrounding jobs for all citizens:

> Among employed 19- to 31-year-old high school graduates who did not go to college, more than 30 percent had not been in their position for even a year. Another 12 percent had only one year of tenure. The pattern was much the same for women who had remained in the labor force for the four years prior to the survey. These are adults who, for a variety of reasons — a lack of skills, training, or disposition — have not managed to secure "adult" jobs.
> —Paul Osterman, "Getting Started"

Osterman uses facts to report a seemingly objective conclusion about the stability of employment among certain groups, but he is also arguing against those who find that the current job situation is tolerable and not worthy of concern or action.

Arguments to Explore

Many important subjects call for arguments that take the form of exploration, either on your own or with others. If there's an "opponent" in such a situation at all (often there is not), it is likely the status quo or a current trend that — for one reason or another — is puzzling. Exploratory arguments may be deeply personal, such as E. B. White's often-reprinted essay "Once More to the Lake." Or the exploration may be aimed at addressing serious problems in society. James Fallows opens such an argument by explaining the process of exploration he went through:

> Over the past few months I interviewed several dozen people about what could be expected in Iraq after the United States dislodged

Saddam Hussein. . . . The people I asked were spies, Arabists, oil-company officials, diplomats, scholars, policy experts, and many active-duty and retired soldiers. They were from the United States, Europe, and the Middle East. Some firmly supported a pre-emptive war against Iraq; more were opposed. As of late summer, before the serious domestic debate had begun, most of the people I spoke with expected a war to occur.

–James Fallows, "The Fifty-First State?"

Perhaps the essential argument in any such piece is the writer's assertion that a problem exists (in this case, whether or not to go to war with Iraq) and that the writer or reader needs to solve it. Some exploratory pieces present and defend solutions. Others remain more open-ended, as is the case with Fallows's essay, which concludes with a form of meditation:

It has become a cliché in popular writing about the natural world that small disturbances to complex systems can have unpredictably large effects. The world of nations is perhaps not quite as intricate as the natural world, but it certainly holds the potential for great surprise. Merely itemizing the foreseeable effects of a war with Iraq suggests reverberations that would be felt for decades. If we can judge from past wars, the effects we can't imagine when the fighting begins will prove to be the ones that matter most.

Arguments to Make Decisions

Charles C. Mann challenges us to explore the definition of intellectual property and its consequences in our daily lives in his essay "Who Will Own Your Next Good Idea?"

···················· LINK TO P. 675

Closely allied to argument that explores is that which aims at making good, sound decisions. In fact, the result of many exploratory arguments may be to argue for a particular decision, whether that decision relates to the best computer for you to buy or to the "right" person for you to choose as your life partner. For college students, choosing a major is a major decision, and one way to go about making that decision is to argue your way through several alternatives. By the time you have examined the pros and cons of each alternative, you should be at least one step closer to a good decision. In the following paragraphs, history major Jessica Cohen reasons her way toward a momentous decision, asking should she, or should she not, become an egg donor for a wealthy couple:

Early in the spring of last year a classified ad ran for two weeks in the *Yale Daily News*: "EGG DONOR NEEDED." The couple [Michelle and David] that placed the ad was picky, and for that reason was offering $25,000 for an egg from the right donor. . . .

> I kept dreaming about all the things I could do with $25,000. I had gone into the correspondence [with David and Michelle] on a whim. But soon, despite David's casual tone and the optimistic attitude of all the classifieds and information I read, I decided that this process was something I didn't want to be part of. I understand the desire for a child who will resemble and fit in with the family. But once a couple starts choosing a few characteristics, shooting for perfection is too easy—especially if they can afford it. The money might have changed my life for a while, but it would have led to the creation of a child encumbered with too many expectations.
> —Jessica Cohen, "Grade A: The Market for a Yale Woman's Eggs"

Arguments to Meditate or Pray

Sometimes arguments can take the form of intense meditations on a theme, or of prayer. In such cases, the writer or speaker is most often hoping to transform something in him- or herself or to reach a state of equilibrium or peace of mind. If you know a familiar prayer or mantra, think for a moment of what it "argues" for and of how it uses quiet meditation to accomplish that goal. Such meditations do not have to be formal prayers, however. Look, for example, at the ways in which Michael Lassell's poetry uses a kind of meditative language to reach understanding for himself and to evoke meditative thought in others:

> Feel how it feels to
> hold a man in your arms
> whose arms are used to holding men.
> Offer God anything to bring your brother back.
> Know you have nothing God could possibly want.
> Curse God, but do not
> abandon Him.
> —Michael Lassell, "How to Watch Your Brother Die"

Another sort of meditative argument can be found in the stained-glass windows of churches and other public buildings. Dazzled by a spectacle of light, people pause to consider a window's message longer than they might were the same idea conveyed on paper. The window engages viewers with a power not unlike that of poetry. (See Figure 1.3.)

As these examples suggest, the effectiveness of argument depends not only on the purposes of the writer but also on the context surrounding the plea and the people it seeks most directly to reach. Though we'll examine arguments of all types in this book, we'll focus chiefly on the kinds made in professional and academic situations.

FIGURE **1.3**   STAINED-GLASS WINDOW PORTRAYING THE PRODIGAL SON LEAVING HIS FATHER'S HOUSE

OCCASIONS FOR ARGUMENT

Another way of thinking about arguments is to consider the public occasions that call for them. In an ancient textbook of rhetoric, or the art of persuasion, the philosopher Aristotle provides an elegant scheme for classifying the purposes of arguments, one based on issues of time—past, future, and present. His formula is easy to remember and helpful in suggesting strategies for making convincing cases. But because all classifications overlap with others to a certain extent, don't be surprised to encounter many arguments that span more than one category—arguments about the past with implications for the future, arguments about the future with bearings on the present, and so on.

Arguments about the Past

Debates about what has happened in the past are called forensic arguments; such controversies are common in business, government, and academia. For example, in many criminal and civil cases, lawyers interrogate witnesses to establish exactly what happened at an earlier time: *Did the defendant sexually harass her employee? Did the company deliberately ignore evidence that its product was deficient? Was the contract properly enforced?*

The contentious nature of some forensic arguments is evident in this brief excerpt from a letter to the editor of *The Atlantic Monthly*:

> Kenneth Brower's review of "Ansel Adams at 100," in your July/August issue, is misguided and inaccurate. . . . [In fact, Adams] worked seven days a week, never taking vacations, until he was eighty. It is impossible to imagine such activity in a person of "compromised health." Ditto for the notion of "delicate since childhood."
>
> –William A. Turnage

In replying to this letter, the author of the review, Kenneth Brower, disputes Turnage's statements, introducing more evidence in support of his original claim. Obviously, then, forensic arguments rely on evidence and testimony to re-create what can be known about events that have already occurred.

Forensic arguments also rely heavily on precedents—actions or decisions in the past that influence policies or decisions in the present—and on analyses of cause and effect. Consider the ongoing controversy over Christopher Columbus: Are his expeditions to the Americas events worth celebrating, or are they unhappy chapters in human history? No simple exchange of evidence will suffice to still this debate; the effects of Columbus's actions beginning in 1492 may be studied and debated for the next five hundred years. As you might suspect from this example, arguments about history are typically forensic.

Forensic cases may also be arguments about character, such as when someone's reputation is studied in a historical context to enrich current perspectives on the person. Allusions to the past can make present arguments more vivid, as in the following text about Ward Connerly, head of an organization that aims to dismantle affirmative action programs:

> Despite the fact that Connerly's message seems clearly opposed to the Civil Rights Movement, some people are fond of pointing out that the man is black. But as far as politics goes, that is irrelevant. Before black suffrage, there were African Americans who publicly argued against their own right to vote.
>
> –Carl Villarreal, "Connerly Is an Enemy of Civil Rights"

Such writing can be exploratory and open-ended, the point of argument being to enhance and sharpen knowledge, not just to generate heat or score points.

Martin Luther King Jr. uses a forensic argument when he invokes Abraham Lincoln and Lincoln's era in his famous "I Have a Dream" speech: "Five score years ago, a great American, in whose symbolic shadow we stand, signed the Emancipation Proclamation. This momentous decree came as a great beacon light of hope to millions of Negro slaves who had been seared in the flames of withering injustice."

LINK TO P. 811 ·······································

Arguments about the Future

Debates about the future are a form of deliberative argument. Legislatures, congresses, and parliaments are called deliberative bodies because they establish policies for the future: *Should Social Security be privatized? Should the United States build a defense against ballistic missiles?*

Because what has happened in the past influences the future, deliberative judgments often rely on prior forensic arguments. Thus, deliberative arguments often draw on evidence and testimony, as in this passage:

> **The labor market is sending a clear signal. While the American way of moving youngsters from high school to the labor market may be imperfect, the chief problem is that, for many, even getting a job no longer guarantees a decent standard of living. More than ever, getting ahead, or even keeping up, means staying in school longer.**
> **–Paul Osterman, "Getting Started"**

But since no one has a blueprint for what is to come, deliberative arguments also advance by means of projections, extrapolations, and reasoned guesses — *if X is true, Y may be true; if X happens, so may Y; if X continues, then Y may occur:*

> **In 2000, according to a World Health Organization assessment, 1.1 billion people worldwide had no regular access to safe drinking water, and 2.4 billion had no regular access to sanitation systems. Lack of access to clean water leads to four billion cases of diarrhea each year. Peter Gleick, an expert on global freshwater resources, reveals that even if we reach the United Nations' stated goal of halving the number of people without access to safe drinking water by 2015, as many as 76 million people will die from water-borne diseases before 2020.**
> **–Pacific Institute for Studies in Development, Environment, and Security**

Arguments about the Present

Arguments about the present are often arguments about contemporary values — the ethical premises and assumptions that are widely held (or contested) within a society. Sometimes called epideictic arguments or ceremonial arguments because they tend to be heard at public occasions, they include inaugural addresses, sermons, eulogies, graduation speeches, and civic remarks of all kinds. Ceremonial arguments can be passionate and eloquent, rich in anecdotes and examples. Martin Luther King Jr. was a master of ceremonial discourse, and he was particularly adept at finding affirmation in the depths of despair:

> Three nights later, our home was bombed. Strangely enough, I accepted the word of the bombing calmly. My experience with God had given me a new strength and trust. I know now that God is able to give us the interior resources to face the storms and problems of life.
> –Martin Luther King Jr., "Our God Is Able"

King argues here that the arbiter of good and evil in society is, ultimately, God. But not all ceremonial arguments reach quite so far.

More typical are values arguments that explore contemporary culture, praising what is admirable and blaming what is not. Andrew Sullivan, for example, examines what he considers a national craving for often-unjustified self-esteem. Yet he concludes by arguing that achieving a strong self-image is still "surely worth the effort":

> Self-esteem isn't all that it's cracked up to be. In fact . . . it can be a huge part of the problem. New research has found that self-esteem can be just as high among D students, drunk drivers and former Presidents from Arkansas as it is among Nobel laureates, nuns and New York City fire fighters. In fact, according to research performed by Brad Bushman of Iowa State University and Roy Baumeister of Case Western Reserve University, people with high self-esteem can engage in far more antisocial behavior than those with low self-worth. . . . Racists, street thugs and school bullies all polled high on the self-esteem charts. And you can see why. If you think you're God's gift, you're particularly offended if other people don't treat you that way. So you lash out or commit crimes or cut ethical corners to reassert your preeminence. After all, who are your moral inferiors to suggest that you could be doing something, er, wrong? What do they know? . . . Of course, in these therapized days, reality can be a touchy subject. It's hard to accept that we may not be the best at something or that we genuinely screwed up or that low self-esteem can sometimes be fully justified. But maintaining a robust self-image while being able to absorb difficult criticism is surely worth the effort.
> –Andrew Sullivan, "Lacking in Self-Esteem: Good for You!"

As in many ceremonial arguments, Sullivan here reinforces common values of modesty and fair play.

KINDS OF ARGUMENT

Yet another way of categorizing arguments is to consider their status or stasis—that is, the kinds of issues they address. This categorization system is called stasis theory. In ancient Greek and Roman civilizations, rhetoricians defined a series of questions by which to examine legal cases. The questions would be posed in sequence, because each depended on the question(s) preceding it. Together, the questions helped determine the point of contention in an argument, the place where disputants could focus their energy and hence what kind of an argument to make. A modern version of those questions might look like the following:

- Did something happen?
- What is its nature?
- What is its quality?
- What actions should be taken?

Here's how the questions might be used to explore a "crime."

Did Something Happen?

Yes. A young man kissed a young woman against her will. The act was witnessed by a teacher and friends and acquaintances of both parties. The facts suggest clearly that something happened. If you were going to write an argument about this event, this first stasis question proves not very helpful, since there's no debate about whether the act occurred. If the event were debatable, however, you could develop an argument of fact.

What Is Its Nature?

The act might be construed as "sexual harassment," defined as the imposition of unwanted or unsolicited sexual attention or activity on a person. The young man kissed the young woman on the lips. Kissing people who aren't relatives on the lips is generally considered a sexual activity. The young woman did not want to be kissed and complained to her teacher. The young man's act meets the definition of "sexual harassment." Careful analysis of this stasis question could lead to an argument of definition.

What Is Its Quality?

Both the young man and young woman involved in the action are six years old. They were playing in a schoolyard. The boy didn't realize that kissing girls against their will was a violation of school policy; school sexual harassment policies had not in the past been enforced against first-graders. Most people don't regard six-year-olds as sexu-

Is Ebonics a separate language, a dialect of English, or something else? David D. Troutt's "Defining Who We Are in Society" and John Rickford's "Suite for Ebony and Phonics" offer slightly different answers, basing their claims on different kinds of evidence.

·································· LINK TO PP. 718 AND 723

ally culpable. Moreover, the girl wants to play with the boy again and apparently doesn't resent his action. Were you to decide on this focus, you would be developing an argument of evaluation.

What Actions Should Be Taken?

The case has raised a ruckus among parents, the general public, and some feminists and anti-feminists. The consensus seems to be that the school overreacted in seeking to brand the boy a sexual harasser. Yet it is important that the issue of sexual harassment not be dismissed as trivial. Consequently, the boy should be warned not to kiss girls against their will. The teachers should be warned not to make federal cases out of schoolyard spats. And with this stasis question as your focus, you would be developing a proposal argument.

As you can see, each of the stasis questions explores different aspects of a problem and uses different evidence or techniques to reach conclusions. You can use stasis theory to help you explore the aspects of any topic you are considering. In addition, studying the results of your exploration of the stasis questions can help you determine the major point you want to make and thus identify the type of argument that will be most effective.

Arguments of Fact—Did Something Happen?

An argument of fact usually involves a statement that can be proved or disproved with specific evidence or testimony. Although relatively simple to define, such arguments are often quite subtle, involving layers of complexity not apparent when the question is initially posed.

For example, the question of pollution of our oceans—Is it really occurring?—would seem relatively easy to settle. Either scientific data prove that the oceans are being polluted as a result of human activity, or they don't. But to settle the matter, writers and readers would first have to agree on a number of points, each of which would have to be examined and debated: *What constitutes pollution? How will such pollution be measured? Over what period of time? Are any current deviations in water quality unprecedented? How can one be certain that deviations are attributable to human action?*

Nevertheless, questions of this sort can be disputed primarily on the facts, complicated and contentious as they may be. But should you choose to develop an argument of fact, be aware of how difficult it can sometimes be to establish "facts." (For more on arguments based on facts, see Chapter 7.)

Arguments of Definition — What Is the Nature of the Thing?

Just as contentious as arguments based on facts are questions of definition. An argument of definition often involves determining whether one known object or action belongs in a second — and more highly contested — category. One of the most hotly debated issues in American life today involves a question of definition: *Is a human fetus a human being?* If one argues that it is, then a second issue of definition arises: *Is abortion murder?* As you can see, issues of definition can have mighty consequences — and decades of debate may leave the matter unresolved.

Writer Jan Morris defines a condition, homesickness, she assumes is familiar to almost everyone, but she works with shades of meaning to explain what homesickness is for her:

> Homesickness is the most delicious form of nostalgia, if only because, generally speaking, it really can be gratified. We cannot return to the past, but we can go home again. In my case homesickness is related to something the Welsh language calls *hiraeth*. This over-worked word (the Welsh are big on emotions) means literally "longing," "nostalgia," or sometimes plain "grief." It has come to signify, however, something even less exact: longing, yes, but for nothing definite; nostalgia, but for an indeterminate past; grief without cause or explanation. *Hiraeth!*— an insidious summation of all that is most poetical, most musical, most regretful, most opaque, most evasive, most extinguishable, in the character of Wales.
>
> –Jan Morris, "Home Thoughts from Abroad"

Bob Costas, eulogizing Mickey Mantle, a great baseball player who had many universally human faults, advances his assessment by means of an important definitional distinction:

> In the last year, Mickey Mantle, always so hard upon himself, finally came to accept and appreciate the distinction between a role model and a hero. The first he often was not, the second he always will be.
>
> –Bob Costas, "Eulogy for Mickey Mantle"

But arguments of definition can be less weighty than these, though still hotly contested: *Is video game playing a sport? Is Madonna an artist? Is ketchup a vegetable?* To argue such cases, one would first have to put forth definitions, and then those definitions would have to become the foci of debates themselves. (For more about arguments of definition, see Chapter 9.)

Arguments of Evaluation — What Is the Quality of the Thing?

Arguments of definition lead naturally into arguments of quality — that is, to questions about quality. Most auto enthusiasts, for example, would not be content merely to inquire whether the Corvette is a sports car. They'd prefer to argue whether it is a *good* sports car or a better sports car than, say, the Viper. Or they might wish to assert that it is the best sports car in the world, perhaps qualifying their claim with the caveat *for the price*. Arguments of evaluation are so common that writers sometimes take them for granted, ignoring their complexity and importance in establishing people's values and priorities. The stasis question "what is the quality of the thing" is at the heart of attempts to understand the nuclear capability of North Korea. Those working to develop U.S. policy toward North Korea need to use this stasis question to develop a compelling argument of evaluation.

Consider how Rosa Parks assesses Martin Luther King Jr. in the following passage. Though she seems to be defining the concept of "leader," she is measuring King against criteria she has set for "*true*" leader," an important distinction:

> Dr. King was a true leader. I never sensed fear in him. I just felt he knew what had to be done and took the leading role without regard to consequences. I knew he was destined to do great things. He had an elegance about him and a speaking style that let you know where you stood and inspired you to do the best you could. He truly is a role model for us all. The sacrifice of his life should never be forgotten, and his dream must live on.
>
> —Rosa Parks, "Role Models"

Parks's comments represent a type of informal evaluation that is common in ceremonial arguments; because King is so well known, she doesn't have to burnish every claim with specific evidence. (See p. 14 for more on ceremonial arguments.) In contrast, Molly Ivins in praising Barbara Jordan makes quite explicit the connections between her claim and the evidence:

> Barbara Jordan, whose name was so often preceded by the words "the first black woman to . . ." that they seemed like a permanent title, died Wednesday in Austin. A great spirit is gone.
>
> The first black woman to serve in the Texas Senate, the first black woman in Congress (she and Yvonne Brathwaite Burke of California were both elected in 1972, but Jordan had no Republican opposition), the first black elected to Congress from the South since Reconstruction, the first black woman to sit on major corporate boards, and so on. Were it not for the disease that slowly crippled her, she probably

Pondering the prospect of cosmetic surgery for her husband, Angela Neustatter writes an evaluative argument: "Yet I couldn't and wouldn't condemn it or him because no way do I want to join the band of puritans who deify their wrinkles and castigate, for their failure to age naturally, anyone who so much as has a collagen implant, because puritanism is a far nastier vice than narcissism."

LINK TO P. 483

would have been the first black woman on the Supreme Court—it is known that Jimmy Carter had her on his short list.

And long before she became "the first and only black woman to . . ." there was that astounding string of achievements going back to high school valedictorian, honors at Texas Southern University, law degree from Boston University. Both her famous diction and her enormous dignity were present from the beginning, her high school teachers recalled. Her precise enunciation was a legacy from her father, a Baptist minister, and characteristic of educated blacks of his day. Her great baritone voice was so impressive that her colleagues in the Legislature used to joke that if Hollywood ever needed someone to be the voice of the Lord Almighty, only Jordan would do.

–Molly Ivins, "Barbara Jordan: A Great Spirit"

An argument of evaluation advances by presenting criteria and then measuring individual people, ideas, or things against those standards. Both the standards and the measurement can be explored argumentatively. And that's an important way to think of arguments—as ways to expand what is known, not just to settle differences. (For more about arguments of evaluation, see Chapter 10.)

Proposal Arguments — What Actions Should Be Taken?

Arguments may lead to proposals for action when writers have succeeded in presenting problems in such a compelling way that readers ask: *What can we do?* A proposal argument often begins with the presentation of research to document existing conditions. Thus if you are developing an argument about rising tuition costs at your college, you could use all of the stasis questions to explore the issue and to establish that costs are indeed rising. But the last question—"What actions should be taken?"— will probably be the most important, since it will lead you to develop concrete proposals to address the rise in fees. Knowing and explaining the status quo enable writers to explore appropriate and viable alternatives and then to recommend one preferable course of action. In examining a nationwide move to eliminate remedial education in colleges, John Cloud considers one possible proposal to avoid such action:

Students age 22 and over account for 43% of those in remedial classrooms, according to the National Center for Developmental Education. [. . . But] 55% of those needing remediation must take just one course. Is it too much to ask them to pay extra for that class or take it at a community college?

–John Cloud, "Who's Ready for College?"

Where a need is already obvious, writers may spend most of their energies describing and defending the solution. John Henry Newman, for example, assumes the need for strong higher learning in proposing a new form of liberal education in the nineteenth century. Here, he enumerates the benefits his preferred solution will bring to society:

> [A] university education is the great ordinary means to a great but ordinary end; it aims at raising the intellectual tone of society, at cultivating the public mind, at purifying the national taste, at supplying true principles to popular enthusiasm and fixed aims to popular aspiration, at giving enlargement and sobriety to the ideas of the age, at facilitating the exercise of political power, and refining the intercourse of private life.
> –John Henry Newman, "The Idea of a University"

Americans in particular tend to see the world in terms of problems and solutions; indeed, many Americans expect that any difficulty can be overcome by the proper infusion of technology and money. So proposal arguments seem especially appealing, even when quick-fix attitudes may themselves constitute a problem. (For more about proposal arguments, see Chapter 12.)

CULTURAL CONTEXTS FOR ARGUMENT

If you want to communicate effectively with people across cultures, then you need to try to learn something about the norms in those cultures—and to be aware of the norms guiding your own behavior.

- Be aware of the assumptions that guide your own customary ways of arguing a point. Remember that most of us tend to see our own way as the "normal" or "right" way to do things. Such assumptions guide your thinking and your judgments about what counts—and what "works"—in an argument.

- Keep in mind that if your own ways seem inherently right, then even without thinking about it you may assume that other ways are somehow less than right. Such thinking makes it hard to communicate effectively across cultures.

- Remember that ways of arguing are influenced by cultural contexts and that they differ widely across cultures. Pay attention to the ways people from cultures other than your own argue, and be flexible and open to the many ways of thinking you will no doubt encounter.

(continued)

- Respect the differences among individuals within a given culture; don't expect that every member of a community behaves — or argues — in just the same way.

The best advice, then, might be *don't assume.* Just because you think wearing a navy blazer and a knee-length skirt "argues" that you should be taken seriously as a job candidate at a multinational corporation, such dress may be perceived differently in other settings. And if in an interview a candidate does not look you in the eye, don't assume that this reflects any lack of confidence or respect; he or she may intend it as a sign of politeness.

STASIS QUESTIONS AT WORK

Suppose you have an opportunity to speak at a student conference on the issue of global warming, which has been a particularly hot topic on your campus. The Campus Young Republicans are sponsoring the conference, but they have made a point of inviting students with varying perspectives to speak. You are concerned about global warming and are tentatively in favor of making changes to industrial pollution standards aimed at reducing global warming trends. You decide that you'd like to learn a lot more by investigating the issue more fully and preparing to speak on it. You use the stasis questions to get started.

- **Did something happen?** Does global warming exist? The Bush administration, on the one hand, is skeptical, so much so that the President refused to sign an international agreement aimed at reducing global warming. Environmentalists, on the other hand, argue that the phenomenon does exist, that it has reached very serious proportions, and that it must be addressed as soon as possible. In coming to your own conclusion about global warming, you will weigh the factual evidence very carefully, making sure that you can support your answers to the question "Does it exist?" and that you can point out problems associated with counterarguments.
- **What is the nature of the thing?** Looking for definitions of global warming also reveals great disagreement. The Bush administration defines the phenomenon as naturally occurring, while environmentalists base their definition on industry-related causes. Thus you begin to consider competing definitions very carefully: How do the

(continued)

definitions they choose to use foster the goals of each group? Who gets to say what definition is acceptable? What is at stake for industry in promoting its definition of global warming? What is at stake for environmentalists in putting forth their definition? Exploring this stasis question will help you understand how the context of an argument shapes the claims that the argument makes.

- **What is the quality of the thing?** This question will lead you to examine claims that global warming is — or is not — harming our environment. Again, you quickly find that these charges are hotly contested. The pro-industry stance of the Bush administration shapes its analysis, leading to a dismissal of claims that the phenomenon is causing great environmental harm. Exploring these arguments will allow you to ask who or what entities are providing evidence in support of their claim and who stands to gain in this analysis. Turning to the environmentalist arguments, you ask the same questions: Where does evidence for the dangers of global warming come from? Who stands to gain if the dangers are accepted as real and present, and who stands to lose if they are not?

- **What actions should be taken?** In this case as well, you find wide disagreement. If global warming is a naturally occurring phenomenon, then it is at least arguable that nothing needs to be done, that the problem will correct itself in time. Or perhaps those in the administration who have made these arguments will decide to recommend a new study of global warming, in an effort to prove once and for all that their understanding of global warming and its effects is the correct one. If, on the other hand, global warming is a clear and present threat to the quality of the atmosphere, as the environmentalists argue, then they are bound to recommend implementing appropriate and effective responses to such danger (although not everyone agrees on precisely what such responses should be). You quickly discover that the goals and definitions being used directly shape the actions that each side recommends. As you investigate the proposals being made and the reasons that underlie them, you come closer and closer to developing your own argument.

Using the stasis questions as a way to get into the topic of global warming adds up to a crash course on the subject. As you sort through the claims and counterclaims associated with each of the questions, you move toward identifying your own stance on global warming — and toward the claim you want to make about it for the student con-

(continued)

ference. You come to the conclusion that global warming does exist and that it does present a serious danger. Yet given the audience for the conference, you know that you still have quite a bit of work to do. Since many will not agree with your conclusion, you begin to gather the most fair and evenhanded research available to make your case, and you begin working to establish your own credibility and to consider how best you can present your case to your specific audience.

IS EVERYTHING AN ARGUMENT?

In a world where argument is as abundant as fast food, everyone has a role to play in shaping and responding to arguments. Debate and discussion are, after all, key components of the never-ending conversation about our lives and the world that is sometimes called academic inquiry. Its standards are rigorous: Take no claim at face value, examine all evidence thoroughly, and study the implications of your own and others' beliefs. Developing an inquiring turn of mind like this can serve you well now and into the future. It might even lead you to wonder, with healthy suspicion, whether *everything* really is an argument.

RESPOND●

1. Can an argument really be any text that expresses a point of view? What kinds of arguments—if any—might be made by the following items?

> the embossed leather cover of a prayer book
>
> a Web site's home page
>
> a New York Yankees cap
>
> the label on a best-selling rap CD
>
> the health warning on a bag of no-fat potato chips
>
> a belated birthday card
>
> the nutrition label on a can of soup
>
> the cover of a science fiction novel
>
> a colored ribbon pinned to a shirt lapel
>
> a Rolex watch

2. Decide whether each of the following items is an example of *argument, persuasion,* or *propaganda.* You'll likely have a variety of responses among your classmates, so be prepared to explain your categorization.

   a proof in a calculus textbook

   a banner proclaiming "Halt Globalization Now!" at a World Trade Organization protest

   a U.S. president's State of the Union address

   a lawyer's opening statement at a jury trial

   a movie by American film director Martin Scorsese

   the television show *Jackass*

   a lecture on race in an anthropology class

   a marriage proposal

   an environmental ad by a chemical company

3. Write short paragraphs describing times in the recent past when you've used language to inform, to convince, to explore, to make decisions, and to meditate or pray. Be sure to write at least one paragraph for each of these purposes. Then decide whether each paragraph describes an act of argument, persuasion, or both, and offer some reasons in defense of your decisions.

   In class, trade paragraphs with a partner, and decide whether his or her descriptions accurately fit the categories to which they've been assigned. If they do not, work with your partner to figure out why. Is the problem with the descriptions? The categories? Both? Neither?

4. In a recent newspaper or periodical, find three editorials—one that makes a ceremonial argument, one a deliberative argument, and one a forensic argument. Analyze the arguments by asking these questions: Who is arguing? What purposes are the writers trying to achieve? To whom are they directing their arguments?

   Then consider whether the arguments' purposes have been achieved in each case. If they have, offer some reasons for the arguments' success.

5. If everything really is an argument, then one should be able to read poetry through the same lens, and with the same methods, as one reads more obviously argumentative writing. This means considering the occasions, purposes, and stasis of the poem—a process that may seem odd but that might reveal some interesting results.

   Find a poem that you like and that seems completely *nonargumentative* (you might even pick one that you have written). Then read it as a rhetorician, paying attention to the issues in this chapter, searching for claims, thinking about audience, and imagining occasions and purposes. Write a few paragraphs explaining why the poem is an argument.

Next, for balance (and to make this a good argument), write a paragraph or two explaining why the poem is not an argument. Make sure you give good reasons for your position. Which of the two positions is more persuasive? Is there a middle ground—that is, a way of thinking about the poem that enables it both to be an argument and not to be an argument?

6. Work with one or two other members of your class to examine the front and back covers of this textbook. What arguments do you find being made there? How do these arguments shape your understanding of this text's purposes? What other kinds of images or words might have been used to achieve this purpose more effectively?

chapter two

Reading and Writing Arguments

Do you love your sport utility vehicle? Unless you live in New York City, you or someone you know likely owns one of these tall, rugged-looking, luggage-toting, off-road-capable (for the most part) trucks—maybe a Tahoe or a Liberty or full-dress Excursion almost nineteen feet long. They load it up with stuff, crank up the stereo, and hit the highway, head and shoulders above more mundane traffic, two tons or more of metal and plastic cushioning them from other drivers.

Well, Keith Bradsher, for one, doesn't love SUVs, and he's not shy about staking his claim:

> [T]he proliferation of SUVs has created huge problems. Their safe image is an illusion. They roll over too easily, killing and injuring occupants at an

alarming rate, and they are dangerous to other road users, inflicting catastrophic damage to cars that they hit and posing a lethal threat to pedestrians. Their "green" image is also a mirage, because they contribute far more than cars to smog and global warming. Their gas-guzzling designs increase American dependence on imported oil at a time when anti-American sentiment is prevalent in the Middle East.

–Keith Bradsher, *High and Mighty: SUVs—The World's Most Dangerous Vehicles and How They Got That Way*

FIGURE 2.1   CRITICS CLAIM THAT 95% OF SUVS NEVER VENTURE OFF ROAD.

Bradsher wants the government to make gasoline taxes so high that people couldn't afford to drive SUVs or to legislate them out of existence by instituting tough new standards for fuel economy or exhaust emission. He argues his case in a nearly 500-page book thick with statistics and footnotes. You may agree with Bradsher, a reporter for the *New York Times,* or you may be handcuffing yourself to your Explorer, daring Hillary Clinton and Tom Daschle to take it away. But an argument has been made, a claim advanced, and the national machinery of deliberation is rolling on this and a thousand other matters, big and small, that affect your life in one way or another.

The fact is that there are people out there—good, well-intentioned, soft-spoken, well-organized citizens—ready to defend a woman's right to an abortion or to fight for the life of the unborn. There are people out there who want marijuana to be as legal as Coors beer, and others who argue passionately that the American League should dump the designated hitter. Some want the government to run the health care industry; others think the government should abandon the postal business. Still others want reparations paid to African Americans for centuries of slavery. Lots of Americans argue over the way college football chooses its national champion, and a few wonder whether we should keep the electoral college to choose presidents. Do you think adults age eighteen to twenty who can sign contracts and defend their country should also be able to drink alcohol legally? You'd better prepare to defend this because others aren't so sure. Do you like burgers and fries? Groups are gearing up to make them as politically incorrect as cigarettes.

You can, of course, kick back and pretend you don't care. After all, you're just one person and one vote. But so is Keith Bradsher, and *he's* gunning for your SUV. Sooner or later—and more than likely this week—you will be affected by an argument someone is making. Maybe it's a classmate pressuring a professor for an extension on a research project. Maybe it's a faculty committee arguing for an increase in student parking fees or a student group choosing campus speakers for next term. Maybe it's a secretary of defense wondering whether it's time to revive the draft. You need to be involved, ready to make and defend claims on your own. To do that, you need a sense of how to make an argument.

But given the variety of arguments (see Chapter 1) and all the different readers and occasions they serve, we can't outline a simple process for writing a convincing argument. Nor can we offer you simple formulas because there aren't many. But in this chapter we can draw your attention to six key issues that readers and writers routinely face when dealing with arguments:

- connecting as a reader or writer (Chapter 3)
- understanding lines of argument (Chapters 4–7)
- making a claim (Chapter 8)
- giving an argument shape (Chapters 9–13)
- giving an argument style (Chapters 14–17)
- managing the conventions of argument (Chapters 18–22)

As this list indicates, each of these matters is discussed in one or more chapters in this book. But because you'll be called upon to read and write arguments before you've finished the entire book, it's a good idea to get an overview of what's involved. In effect, this chapter provides a short lesson on strategies of argument and a quick look at dozens of topics you'll meet in more detail later on.

CONNECTING AS READER OR WRITER

Just as "know thyself" is the philosopher's touchstone, "know thy *audience*" has long been the watchword among people who are interested in persuasion. If you use Amazon.com, you know the company records what you browse and buy on the site so that it can offer you recommendations for your next purchases. Advertisers and TV producers also use demographic studies to target their customers, studying their consumers' likely ages, preferences, and habits. Stores even survey the way their customers shop so that they can create sales environments that make people eager to empty their wallets. Fortunately, understanding audiences isn't just a matter of discovering the age, income levels, reading preferences, and favorite colors of those whom you expect to reach. Connecting entails far more, whether you are a reader or a writer.

You won't be shocked to learn that American society is divided by markers of race, gender, ethnicity, class, intelligence, religion, age, sexuality, ability, and so on. To some extent, who we are and where we come from — culturally, socially, even geographically — determine what and how we'll write. We make assumptions, too, about the people who will read our arguments, slotting them into categories based on our own life experiences and, sometimes, the stereotypes we've developed. But our guesses are often wrong. Life would be much less interesting if they weren't.

In fact, relationships between readers and writers shift like clouds in a blustery wind. As you read, you'll likely notice when a writer who doesn't share your race, gender, or credit card limit sees the world differently than you do. When you write a particular piece, your own religion, sexual orientation, or age — alone or in combination with other factors — may play a part in how you present an idea. Even subjects that seem relatively neutral to some readers do not to others. What, for example, could SUVs have to do with gender or class? More than you suspect, maybe.

In short, as you read or write arguments, you must be aware of points of contact between readers and writers — some friendly, others more troubled. And, of course, any writer or reader exploring a new subject should be willing to learn that territory. Readers should ask what motivates writers to make a case — what credentials or experiences they bring to the table. And writers must consider how (and whether) to tell readers who they are. Consider how Catherine Crier, a former lawyer turned judge and then TV host, opens her book-length attack on the legal profession by introducing herself to readers:

From the time I was a little girl, I wanted to be a lawyer. I was obsessed by the notion of justice. Like the boy who became a marine biologist after witnessing his goldfish being flushed down the toilet, I had my reasons. My heroes were the great trial lawyers of our time, like Clarence Darrow, as portrayed by Spencer Tracy in *Inherit the Wind,* and Atticus Finch, as portrayed by Gregory Peck in *To Kill a Mockingbird.* Those were the characters who convinced me I wanted a career in the law. Now, if you'd asked my mother, she'd tell you I'd argue with a post and had to find a profession that would pay me to do that. Nevertheless, I like my story, and I'm sticking to it.

–Catherine Crier, *The Case Against Lawyers*

Connecting means learning to identify with a writer or a reader, imagining yourself in someone else's shoes or helping others to slip into yours. Writers who fail to see much beyond their own noses—who haven't considered alternative views and opinions—may seem unyielding and bigoted. If you're reading an argument that strikes you as narrow, you might ask yourself: *What is the writer missing? Who is he or she excluding from the audience, deliberately or not?*

As a writer, you may sometimes want to connect with readers who share your own concerns. It's natural to look for allies. For example, Anthony Brandt, an author who wonders whether nonreligious parents like himself should provide religious training for their children, aims his deliberative argument directly at parents in his own situation, addressing them familiarly as *us* and *we*:

> For those of us without faith it's not so easy. Do we send our kids to Sunday school when we ourselves never go to church? Do we have them baptized even though we have no intention of raising them as religious?
>
> –Anthony Brandt, "Do Kids Need Religion?"

Brandt's technique illustrated here is just one of many ways to build an author-reader relationship. Yet some readers might find his appeal too overt or aimed more at self-justification than at connecting with an audience. As we said, there are no formulas.

Another bond between readers and writers involves building trust. In reading arguments, you should look for signals that writers are sharing accurate, honest information. You may find such reassurance in careful documentation of facts, in relevant statistics, or in a style that is moderate, balanced, and civil. Also look for indications of a writer's experience with the subject. For example, if you read comic books devotedly, you'd probably want to be sure that someone writing a serious book about them

In her editorial "We Should Relinquish Some Liberty in Exchange for Security," Mona Charen signals her intention right up front to exclude readers with certain points of view. In the second sentence of her article, her use of the phrase "the left has pitched fits" signals this intention.

LINK TO P. 540

really knew what he was talking about. Chances are you'd trust an author who introduced his study of popular culture this way:

> **Superhero comic books do strange and wonderful things when exposed to literary and psychoanalytic theory. No kidding. For years I read poetry and poetic theory in school, and I read superhero comics for fun. After a while I started having a hard time separating the two activities. This book is what I learned from that juxtaposition.**
> –Geoff Klock, *How to Read Superhero Comics and Why*

After all, before you agree with an argument, you want to be sure its author knows what he or she is talking about. And, as a writer of arguments, you have to pay attention to the very same issues—and do it right from the start of the writing process.

In short, connecting to an audience also means gaining authority over your subject matter—earning the right to write and be read. (For more about connecting, see Chapter 3.)

UNDERSTANDING LINES OF ARGUMENT

When you encounter an argument, you should immediately ask questions: *What is this piece up to? On what assumptions is it based? How good is its evidence? Am I being manipulated?* Likewise, when you write an argument, you must find strategies of your own to build a case. Consider these four tried and true appeals, or lines of argument:

- arguments from the heart
- arguments based on values
- arguments based on character
- arguments based on facts and reason

Discovering appeals that will work is called a process of *invention*. Aristotle described it as finding "all the available means of persuasion." You can return to the following four sections whenever you're given an argumentative assignment, asking yourself as you consider each of them which sort of appeals—to the heart, values, character, or reason—might make your case especially persuasive and powerful. People making arguments too often settle on the first or second idea that comes to mind, or they approach an issue from one direction only. These sections, like the four points of a compass, will help you navigate all the terrain your subject encompasses and give your arguments depth and perspective.

Finding Arguments from the Heart

Arguments from the heart appeal to readers' emotions and feelings. You've probably been told to watch out for emotions because they can lead to bad judgments. And indeed, some emotional appeals are, in fact, just ploys to win you over with a pretty face.

But emotions can also make readers think more carefully about what they do. So you need to consider which emotional appeals legitimately support a claim you want to make. For example, persuading people not to drink and drive by making them fear death, injury, or arrest seems like a fair use of an emotional appeal. That's exactly what the Texas Department of Transportation did in 2002 when it created a memorable ad campaign (see Figure 2.2) featuring the image of a formerly beautiful young woman horribly scarred in a fiery accident caused by an SUV driver who had too much to drink. The headline above the gut-wrenching image was simple: "Not everyone who gets hit by a drunk driver dies."

An argument you are developing may not require quite so powerful an appeal, but you should ask yourself what legitimate emotions might serve your cause: anger? sympathy? fear? happiness? envy? love? For instance, you might find strong scientific reasons for restricting logging in certain areas of the Northwest, but reminders of nature's beauty and fragility might also persuade a general audience. And, of course, the two appeals can work together. Or, if you wanted the argument to move the other way, you might make an audience resent government intrusions onto their land, provoking in them feelings of anger or fear.

In analyzing an argument that is heavy on emotional appeals, you'll always want to question exactly how the emotions generated support the claims a writer makes. Is there even a connection between the claim and the emotional appeal? Sometimes there isn't. Most readers have seen advertisements that promise an exciting life and attractive friends if only they drink the right beer or wear the best clothes. Few are fooled when they think about such ads. But emotional appeals often distract people from thinking just long enough to make a bad choice—and that's precisely the danger.

Finally, though people may not always realize it, humor, satire, and parody are potent forms of emotional argument that can make ideas or individuals seem foolish or laughable. (For more about emotional arguments, see Chapter 4.)

Consider how Martin Luther King Jr. uses arguments from the heart in his powerful "I Have a Dream" speech.

LINK TO P. 811 ···

FIGURE **2.2** IMAGES AND WORDS COMBINE TO CREATE AN UNFORGETTABLE EMOTIONAL APPEAL.

Finding Arguments Based on Values

Arguments that appeal to core values resemble emotional appeals, but they work chiefly within specific groups of people—groups as small as families or as large as nations. In such appeals, writers usually either (1) ask others to live up to higher principles, respected traditions, or even new values, or (2) complain that they have not done so. Here, for example, is social critic Michael Moore, famous for his anti-GM documentary *Roger and Me,* decrying the outcome of the 2000 presidential election, portraying it as an assault on fundamental American values and the resulting Bush administration as a *junta,* an illegitimate government:

> **We are now finally no better than a backwater banana republic. We are asking ourselves why any of us should bother to get up in the morning to work our asses off to produce goods and services that only serve to make the junta and its cohorts in Corporate America (a separate, autonomous fiefdom within the United States that has been allowed to run on its own for some time) even richer. Why should we pay our taxes to finance their coup? Can we ever send our sons off into battle to give their lives defending "our way of life"—when all that really means is the lifestyle of the gray old men holed up in the headquarters they have seized by the Potomac?**
>
> –Michael Moore, *Stupid White Men . . . And Other Sorry Excuses for the State of the Nation*

Moore's argument will succeed or fail depending on how readers react to his charge that the events that put Bush in the White House were, in fact, an assault on core American principles.

Appeals based on values take many forms—from the Nike swoosh on a pair of basketball shoes to the peal of a trumpet playing taps at a military funeral. Such appeals can support various kinds of claims, especially ceremonial arguments, which, in fact, define or celebrate the ideals of a society (see Chapter 1). Writers hoping to argue effectively need a keen sense of the values operating within the communities they are addressing.

As you consider making an argument, you should ask yourself who you want to persuade and what values that audience claims. Without compromising the beliefs you have or the claims you intend to make, you need to consider how to align your arguments with the values your readers likely hold. Consider, for instance, how difficult it might be to persuade many college students that reducing the drinking age to eighteen would be a bad idea. What values could you appeal to in this audience to accept such an argument? You might not find many, but even such a conclusion would be useful as you develop your case: you realize that you'll have to rely on other appeals to overcome a significant difference in values between you and your readers. (For more on arguments based on values, see Chapter 5.)

Finding Arguments Based on Character

Character matters when you read arguments, even when you don't know who the authors are. Readers tend to believe writers who seem honest, wise, and trustworthy. In examining an argument, you should look for evidence of these traits. Does the writer have authority to write on this subject? Are all claims qualified reasonably? Is evidence presented in full, not tailored to the writer's agenda? Are important objections to the author's position acknowledged and addressed? Are sources documented?

As a writer of arguments, expect readers to make the same demands of you. Realize, too, that everything you do in an argument sends signals to readers. Language that is hot and extreme (such as Michael Moore's in the preceding section) can mark you as either passionate or loony. Organization that is tight and orderly can suggest that you are in control. Confusing or imprecise language can make you seem incompetent; technical terms and abstract phrases can characterize you as either knowledgeable or pompous.

Yet arguments based on character reach well beyond the shape and structure of a piece itself. Readers respond powerfully to the people behind arguments, to the experience and power they bring to their work. Listen to the late Edward Abbey, novelist and environmentalist, introducing a collection of his work, explaining what it means to be a writer in a troubled world:

> **In such a world, why write? How justify this mad itch for scribbling? Speaking for myself, I write to entertain my friends and exasperate our enemies. I write to record the truth of our time, as best I can see it. To investigate the comedy and tragedy of human relationships. To resist and sabotage the contemporary drift toward a technocratic, militaristic totalitarianism, whatever its ideological coloration. To oppose injustice, defy the powerful, and speak for the voiceless.**
> **–Edward Abbey, *The Best of Edward Abbey***

Of course, not everyone can write with Abbey's hubris. But neither can writers ignore the power their own voices may have within an argument. (For more about arguments based on character, see Chapter 6.)

Where an argument appears also has a bearing on how seriously it is received. Not every such judgment will be fair, but it is hard to deny that a writer who is published in the *New Yorker* or *Commentary* or even *Newsweek* will be more respected than one who writes for a local paper or a supermarket tabloid. An argument that appears in a scholarly book thick with footnotes and appendices may seem more estimable than one that is offered in a photocopied newsletter handed out on the street corner. Likewise, facts and figures borrowed from the congressional Web site Thomas <thomas.loc.gov> will carry more weight than statistics from Jason's Gonzo Home Page.

Finding Arguments Based on Facts and Reason

In judging most arguments, you'll have to decide whether a writer has made a plausible claim and offered good reasons for you to believe it. You'll also need to examine links between the claim and any supporting reasons.

Claim	Federal income taxes should be cut . . .
Reason	. . . because the economy is growing too slowly.
Links	Tax cuts will stimulate the economy.
	A slow-growing economy is unhealthy.

Then you'll have to assess the evidence presented to support each part of the argument. In this case, you'd probably expect proof that the economy is, in fact, growing too slowly for the good of the country, as well as evidence from history that tax cuts do stimulate economic growth. In other words, you should always read arguments critically, testing every assumption, claim, fact, and source. (For more on arguments based on facts and reason, see Chapter 7.)

When you compose an argument, you should write with an equally skeptical reader in mind (think of the most demanding teacher you have ever had). Offer logical arguments backed with the best evidence, testimony, and authority you can find. To find potential logical arguments, nothing beats a good brainstorming session. Just list every argument, however implausible, that might support your case; jot down, too, any types of evidence that would really help your case if you could find them. Don't be too critical at this stage. You just want ideas to work with. Even those you eventually discard might help you anticipate objections to your stronger arguments. (For more about logical arguments, see Chapter 8.)

Many logical appeals rely heavily on data and information from reliable sources. Knowing how to judge the quality of sources is more important now than ever because the electronic pathways where increasing numbers of writers find their information are clogged with junk. The computer terminal may have become the equivalent of a library reference room in certain ways, but the sources available on-screen vary much more widely in quality. As a consequence, both readers and writers of arguments today must know the difference between reliable, firsthand, or fully documented sources and those that don't meet such standards. (For more on using and documenting sources, see Chapters 21 and 22.)

Note how the Pew Global Attitudes Project uses statistics as reliable evidence to support its conclusions about the role of religion in the United States.

LINK TO P. 778

MAKING A CLAIM

Not every argument you read will package its claim in a neat sentence or thesis. A writer may tell a story from which you have to infer the claim: think of the way many films make a social or political statement by dramatizing an issue, whether it be political corruption, government censorship, or economic injustice. But in conventional arguments, the kind you might find on the editorial page of a newspaper, arguments may be as plain as nails. Writers stake out a claim and then offer the reasons you should buy it. Here are two such examples. The first is a feisty opening paragraph previewing the contents of an entire book; the second occurs nearer the conclusion of a lengthy article defending the car against its many snobbish critics:

> Political "debate" in this country is insufferable. Whether conducted in Congress, on the political talk shows, or played out at dinners and cocktail parties, politics is a nasty sport. At the risk of giving away the ending: It's all liberals' fault.
> –Ann H. Coulter, *Slander: Liberal Lies about the American Right*

> But even if we do all the things that can be done to limit the social costs of cars, the campaign against them will not stop. It will not stop because so many of the critics dislike everything the car stands for and everything society constructs to serve the needs of its occupants.
> –James Q. Wilson, "Cars and Their Enemies"

Cartoons are especially good at making claims implicitly. Check out, for example, "It Begins" to see P. Byrnes's commentary on body image issues.

LINK TO P. 461

Think of claims as vortices of energy in an argument—little dust devils stirring up trouble. You need to decide on a claim early on in writing an argument. You'll spend the remainder of your time testing and refining that claim or thesis.

A lengthy essay may contain a series of claims, each developed to support an even larger point. Indeed, every paragraph in an argument may develop a specific claim. In reading arguments you need to keep track of all these separate propositions and the relationships among them. Likewise, in drafting an argument you must be sure that readers always know how to get from one point to another. Treat transitional words and phrases as guideposts to mark the trail you are building.

Yet a claim itself is not really an argument until it is attached to the reasons that support it and the premises that uphold it. Consider this claim from an article by Lynne Cheney, former head of the National Endowment for the Arts, who is writing about undergraduate education:

There are many reasons to be silent rather than to speak out on campuses today.

–Lynne Cheney, *Telling the Truth*

The sentence makes a point, but it doesn't offer an argument yet. That comes when the claim is backed by reasons that the author will then have to support. To show the connection, we've inserted a *because* between the two sentences Cheney actually wrote:

> **There are many reasons to be silent rather than to speak out on campuses today. [because] Undergraduates have to worry not only about the power of professors to determine grades, but also about faculty members' ability to make the classroom a miserable place for the dissenting student.**

Now the author has a case she can set out to prove and a reader can test. When you read an argument, you'll always want to look for such claims and reasons, perhaps underlining them or marking them in some other way. Then you can weigh the argument against its claims—*Is the case based on reasonable assumptions and values readers would share? Does the writer provide sufficient evidence to prove the claim?*

When you are the one writing, you may find it necessary to change a claim you like but can't defend with good reasons or evidence. That process is called *education*. (For more on making and developing claims, see Chapter 8.)

GIVING AN ARGUMENT SHAPE

Most arguments have a logical structure. Aristotle carved the structure of argument to its bare bones when he observed that it had only two parts:

- statement
- proof

You could do worse, in reading an argument, than just to make sure that every claim a writer makes is backed by sufficient evidence. When you can do so, underline every major statement in an article and then look for the data offered to support it. Weigh those various claims, too, against the conclusion of the essay to determine whether the entire essay makes sense.

Most arguments you read and write will, however, be more than mere statements followed by proofs. Writers will typically offer some background information for readers who may not know precisely what's at stake. They'll qualify the arguments they make, too, so they don't bite off more than they can chew. Smart writers will even admit that other points of view are plausible, though they might spend more than a few paragraphs undercutting them.

Arguments may also contain various kinds of evidence. Some may open with anecdotes or incorporate whole narratives that, in fact, constitute the argument itself. Or the claim may be buttressed with charts, tables of statistics, diagrams, or photographs. Even sounds and short movies can now be incorporated into arguments when they appear on the World Wide Web, thanks to the capacity of computers to handle many types of media.

In any argument you write, all these elements must be connected in ways readers find logical and compelling. (For more about structuring arguments, see Chapters 8–13.)

GIVING AN ARGUMENT STYLE

Even a well-shaped and coherent argument flush with evidence may not connect with readers if it is dull, inappropriate, or offensive. You probably judge the credibility of writers yourself in part by how stylishly they make their cases — though you might not know exactly what *style* is. Consider how these simple, blunt sentences from the opening of an argument shape your image of the author and probably determine whether you are willing to continue to read the whole piece:

> **We are young, urban and professional. We are literate, respectable, intelligent and charming. But foremost and above all, we know what it's like to be unemployed.**
> **–Julia Carlisle, "Young, Privileged and Unemployed"**

Now consider how you would approach an argument that begins like the following, responding to a botched primary election in Florida following the electoral disaster of 2000:

> **The question you're asking yourself is: Does South Florida contain the highest concentration of morons in the entire world? Or just in the United States?**
> **The reason you're asking this, of course, is South Florida's performance in Tuesday's election. This election was critical to our image, because of our performance in the 2000 presidential election — the**

one that ended up with the entire rest of the nation watching, impatiently, as clumps of sleep-deprived South Florida election officials squinted at cardboard ballots, trying to figure out what the hell the voters were thinking when they apparently voted for two presidents, or no presidents, or part of a president, or, in some cases, simply drooled on the ballot.

–Dave Barry, "How to Vote in 1 Easy Step"

Both styles probably work, but they signal that the writers are about to make very different kinds of cases. Style alone tells you what to expect.

Manipulating style also enables writers to shape readers' responses to their ideas. Devices as simple as repetition and parallelism can give sentences remarkable power. Consider this selection from Andrew Sullivan, who argues for greater tolerance of homosexuals in American culture:

Homosexuals in contemporary America tend to die young; they sometimes die estranged from their families; they die among friends who have become their new families; they die surrounded by young death and by the arch symbols of cultural otherness. Growing up homosexual was to grow up normally but displaced; to experience romantic love, but with the wrong person; to entertain grand ambitions, but of the unacceptable sort; to seek a gradual self-awakening, but in secret, not in public.

–Andrew Sullivan, "What Are Homosexuals For?"

The style of this passage asks readers to pay attention and perhaps to sympathize. But the entire argument can't be presented in this key without exhausting readers—and it isn't. Style has to be modulated almost like music to keep readers tuned in.

Many writers prefer to edit for style after they've composed full drafts of their arguments. That makes sense, especially if you're a writer who likes to get to lots of ideas on the page first. But the tone and spirit of an argument are also intimately related to subject matter, so style should not be a last-minute consideration. Often, how you express a thought can be as important as the thought itself. (For more about the style of arguments, see Chapters 14–17.)

MANAGING THE CONVENTIONS OF ARGUMENT

Persuasive writers know how to use sources well. They know how to present tables or graphs, how to document borrowed material, how to select and introduce quotations, how to tailor quotations to the grammar of surrounding sentences, how to shorten quoted passages, and so on. (For more about the conventions of argument, see Chapters 18–22.)

New conventions for argument are evolving in electronic environments. Just since the last edition of this book, Web logs, or *blogs,* have become one of the more potent forms of political discussion in the United States, proving what was only speculation a few years ago — that new environments and media will foster new tools of persuasion. That means that you will have to learn new ways to connect ideas and, in particular, to merge visual arguments with verbal ones. The prospects are quite exciting. (For more about visual and electronic arguments, see Chapters 15 and 16.)

COMPOSING A RHETORICAL ANALYSIS

As you now have seen, arguments have many twists, but how exactly do they work? Why does a Bose ad make you want to buy new speakers or an op-ed piece in the *Washington Post* suddenly change your thinking about school vouchers? A rhetorical analysis might help you understand. You perform a rhetorical analysis by analyzing how well the components of an argument work together to persuade or move an audience. You can study arguments of any kind — advertisements, for example, or editorials, political cartoons, perhaps even movies or photographs. (If everything really is an argument, then just about any communication can be opened up rhetorically.) And you can examine many different aspects of a piece to discover how it does its work.

Because arguments have so many components, you may need to be selective when you try your hand at a rhetorical analysis. You could begin by exploring issues such as the following raised in our first two chapters:

- Who is the audience for this argument? How does the argument connect with its audience?

- What is the purpose of this argument? What does it hope to achieve?

- What are the contexts — social, political, historical, cultural — for this argument? How does the argument fit into the world? Whose interests does it serve? Who gains or loses by it?

- What appeals does the argument use?

- What emotional arguments or techniques does it use?

- What values does it invoke or count on?

- What authorities does the argument rely on or appeal to? Who is making the argument, and are they trustworthy?

- What facts are used in the argument? What logic? What evidence? How is the evidence arranged and presented?

- What claims are advanced in the argument? What issues are raised and which are ignored or, perhaps, silenced?

- What shape does the argument take? How are arguments presented or arranged? What media do the argument use?

- How does the language or style of the argument work to persuade an audience?

Such questions should help you think about an argument. But a rhetorical analysis will be a persuasive piece itself: you'll need to make a claim about the item or article you are studying to explain how or how well it works. That's important because just summarizing what is "in" an argument usually isn't helpful and would be no more enlightening than describing Mona Lisa as a woman with a curious mouth or attributing the appeal of a BMW to its kidney-shaped grille. In performing a rhetorical analysis, you have to show how the key elements in an argument actually contribute to its success or mark it for failure, at least for some audiences. You need to show how the parts work together or, perhaps, work at odds with each other. If the argument startles audiences, or challenges them, or makes them angry or patriotic or lulls them into complacency, you need to explain, as best you can, how that happens.

You can usually do an adequate job by thinking first about the purpose and audience of a piece and then looking at the various appeals it uses. For example, to do a rhetorical analysis of the Texas Department of Transportation ad and poster on p. 34 of this chapter, you might begin by brainstorming its most compelling features and strategies.

- The poster has been created to reduce the incidence of drunk driving. The point it clearly supports is "Don't drink and drive," a claim stated in bold type at the bottom of the ad.

- The argument is probably aimed at a broad audience, but the fact that the drunk driving victim is only twenty-four years old probably will have an impact on younger drivers. The ad also aims to reach those who might dismiss the consequences of drunk driving.

- The poster is primarily a visual argument, dominated by two pictures of Jacqueline Saburido, a small one before her collision with a drunk driver and a much larger one taken four years later. The contrast between the two images will shock most readers, and the larger image may offend some. But they provide testimony that cannot be ignored or softened.

- The poster likely generates strong emotions: sympathy for Saburido and fear for the consequences of drunk driving. A person viewing the ad does not want to become either the victim of a drunk driver or the cause of such horrendous suffering.

- The few words in the ad, deliberately understated, reinforce the potent emotional appeal. A headline in bold type makes a point that might be reassuring if it weren't posed above Saburido's image: *Not everyone who gets hit by a drunk driver dies.* Two short sentences under the dominant image state the facts of Saburido's case simply and make an implicit argument: the consequences of drunk driving don't end with the accident it might cause.

- There are no words under the smaller image. None are needed.

- Many value arguments are implied in the poster. A young woman's life has been shattered by someone else's irresponsible choice. She can never recover the life she had. Yet she is showing enormous courage in allowing her image to be used on a poster to perhaps prevent others from enduring what she has suffered.

- The poster draws on the authority of the Texas Department of Transportation, which sponsors a "Save a Life" program and offers a Web site. Other public safety groups add their endorsement to the poster in small letters at the bottom. They also benefit from the argument that the ad makes. They seem less like meddlesome public agencies warring against social drinking when the consequences of alcohol abuse are made so powerfully clear.

Beginning with such a list, you would be prepared to show in considerable detail how the Texas Department of Transportation ad works by relying primarily upon dramatic visual elements to deliver an unforgettable emotional blow to anyone who might shrug off the consequences of drunk driving. (You probably know such drivers.)

Perhaps you might draw other conclusions from your study of the poster. Or find other elements in it omitted from our list. We have, for example, barely touched on the technical elements in the dominant photograph of Saburido: how she is posed, lighted, dressed. The more you look at the way arguments are composed, the more you will see. This principle holds for written arguments as well. Words, for example, have as much texture and color as pictures—though you might have to work harder to describe how they achieve their effects.

Then you could start writing, providing reasons and evidence to support whatever claims you decide to make about the argument you are analyzing. Following is an argument written by Derek Bok, followed by student Milena Ateyea's rhetorical analysis.

Protecting Freedom of Expression at Harvard

DEREK BOK

For several years, universities have been struggling with the problem of trying to reconcile the rights of free speech with the desire to avoid racial tension. In recent weeks, such a controversy has sprung up at Harvard. Two students hung Confederate flags in public view, upsetting students who equate the Confederacy with slavery. A third student tried to protest the flags by displaying a swastika.

These incidents have provoked much discussion and disagreement. Some students have urged that Harvard require the removal of symbols that offend many members of the community. Others reply that such symbols are a form of free speech and should be protected.

Different universities have resolved similar conflicts in different ways. Some have enacted codes to protect their communities from forms of speech that are deemed to be insensitive to the feelings of other groups. Some have refused to impose such restrictions.

It is important to distinguish between the appropriateness of such communications and their status under the First Amendment. The fact that speech is protected by the First Amendment does not necessarily mean that it is right, proper, or civil. I am sure that the vast majority of Harvard students believe that hanging a Confederate flag in public view—or displaying a swastika in response—is insensitive and unwise because any satisfaction it gives to the students who display these symbols is far outweighed by the discomfort it causes to many others.

I share this view and regret that the students involved saw fit to behave in this fashion. Whether or not they merely wished to manifest their pride in the South—or to demonstrate the insensitivity of hanging Confederate flags, by mounting another offensive symbol in return—they must have known that they would upset many fellow students and ignore the decent regard for the feelings of others so essential to building and preserving a strong and harmonious community.

To disapprove of a particular form of communication, however, is not enough to justify prohibiting it. We are faced with a clear example of the conflict between our commitment to free speech and our desire to foster a community founded on mutual respect. Our society has wrestled with this problem for many years. Interpreting the First Amendment, the Supreme Court has clearly struck the balance in favor of free speech.

While communities do have the right to regulate speech in order to uphold aesthetic standards (avoiding defacement of buildings) or to protect the public from disturbing noise, rules of this kind must be applied across the board and cannot be enforced selectively to prohibit certain kinds of messages but not others.

Under the Supreme Court's rulings, as I read them, the display of swastikas or Confederate flags clearly falls within the protection of the free-speech clause of the First Amendment and cannot be forbidden simply because it offends the feelings of many members of the community. These rulings apply to all agencies of government, including public universities.

Although it is unclear to what extent the First Amendment is enforceable against private institutions, I have difficulty understanding why a university such as Harvard should have less free speech than the surrounding society—or than a public university.

One reason why the power of censorship is so dangerous is that it is extremely difficult to decide when a particular communication is offensive enough to warrant prohibition or to weigh the degree of offensiveness against the potential value of the communication. If we begin to forbid flags, it is only a short step to prohibiting offensive speakers.

I suspect that no community will become humane and caring by restricting what its members can say. The worst offenders will simply find other ways to irritate and insult.

In addition, once we start to declare certain things "offensive," with all the excitement and attention that will follow, I fear that much ingenuity will be exerted trying to test the limits, much time will be expended trying to draw tenuous distinctions, and the resulting publicity will eventually attract more attention to the offensive material than would ever have occurred otherwise.

Rather than prohibit such communications, with all the resulting risks, it would be better to ignore them, since students would then have little reason to create such displays and would soon abandon them. If this response is not possible—and one can understand why—the wisest course is to speak with those who perform insensitive acts and try to help them understand the effects of their actions on others.

Appropriate officials and faculty members should take the lead, as the Harvard House Masters have already done in this case. In talking with students, they should seek to educate and persuade, rather than resort to ridicule or intimidation, recognizing that only persuasion is likely to produce a lasting, beneficial effect. Through such effects, I believe that we act in the manner most consistent with our ideals as an educational institution and most calculated to help us create a truly understanding, supportive community.

A Curse and a Blessing

MILENA ATEYEA

In 1991, when Derek Bok's essay "Protecting Freedom of Expression at Harvard" was first published in the Boston Globe, I had just come to America to escape the oppressive Communist regime in Bulgaria. Perhaps my background explains why I support Bok's argument that we should not put arbitrary limits on freedom of expression. Bok wrote the essay in response to a public display of Confederate flags and a swastika at Harvard, a situation that created a heated controversy among the students. As Bok notes, universities have struggled to achieve a balance between maintaining students' right of free speech and avoiding racist attacks. When choices must be made, however, Bok argues for preserving freedom of expression.

Connects article to personal experience to create ethical appeal

Provides brief overview of Bok's argument

States Bok's central claim

In order to support his claim and bridge the controversy, Bok uses a variety of rhetorical strategies. The author first immerses the reader in the controversy by vividly describing the incident: two Harvard students had hung Confederate flags in public view, thereby "upsetting students who equate the Confederacy with slavery" (51). Another student, protesting the flags, decided to display an even more offen-

Transition sentence

Examines the emotional appeal the author establishes through description

sive symbol--the swastika. These actions provoked heated discussions among students. Some students believed that school officials should remove the offensive symbols, whereas others suggested that the symbols "are a form of free speech and should be protected" (51). Bok establishes common ground between the factions: he regrets the actions of the offenders but does not believe we should prohibit such actions just because we disagree with them.

The author earns the reader's respect because of his knowledge and through his logical presentation of the issue. In partial support of his position, Bok refers to U.S. Supreme Court rulings, which remind us that "the display of swastikas or Confederate flags clearly falls within the protection of the free-speech clause of the First Amendment" (52). The author also emphasizes the danger of the slippery slope of censorship when he warns the reader, "If we begin to forbid flags, it is only a short step to prohibiting offensive speakers" (52). Overall, however, Bok's work lacks the kinds of evidence that statistics, interviews with students, and other representative examples of controversial conduct could provide. Thus, his essay may not be strong enough to persuade all readers to make the leap from this specific situation to his general conclusion.

Throughout, Bok's personal feelings are implied but not stated directly. As a lawyer who was president of Harvard for twenty years, Bok knows how to present his opinions respectfully without offending the feelings of the students. However, qualifying phrases like "I suspect that," and "Under the Supreme Court's rulings, as I read them" could weaken the effectiveness of his position. Furthermore, Bok's attempt to be fair to all seems to dilute the strength of his proposed solution. He suggests that one should either ignore the insensitive deeds in the hope that students might change their behavior, or talk to the offending students to help them comprehend how their behavior is affecting other students.

Nevertheless, although Bok's proposed solution to the controversy does not appear at first reading to be very strong, it may ultimately be effective. There is enough flexibility in his approach to withstand various tests, and

Links author's credibility to use of logical appeals

Reference to First Amendment serves as warrant for Bok's claim

Comments critically on author's evidence

Examines how Bok establishes ethical appeal

Identifies qualifying phrases that may weaken claim

Analyzes author's solution

Raises points that suggest Bok's solution may work

Bok's solution is general enough that it can change with the times and adapt to community standards.

In writing this essay, Bok faced a challenging task: to write a short response to a specific situation that represents a very broad and controversial issue. Some people may find that freedom of expression is both a curse and a blessing because of the difficulties it creates. As one who has lived under a regime that permitted very limited, censored expression, I am all too aware that I could not have written this response in 1991 in Bulgaria. As a result, I feel, like Derek Bok, that freedom of expression is a blessing, in spite of any temporary problems associated with it.

Returns to personal experience in conclusion

Work Cited

Bok, Derek. "Protecting Freedom of Expression on the Campus." Current Issues and Enduring Questions. Eds. Sylvan Barnet and Hugo Bedau. 6th ed. Boston: Bedford, 2002. 51-52. Rpt. of "Protecting Freedom of Expression at Harvard." Boston Globe 25 May 1991.

RESPOND●

1. Describe a persuasive moment you can recall from a speech, an article, an editorial, an advertisement, or your personal experience. Alternatively, research one of the following famous moments of persuasion and then describe the circumstances of the appeal: what the historical situation was, what issues were at stake, and what made the address memorable.

   Abraham Lincoln's "Gettysburg Address" (1863)

   Elizabeth Cady Stanton's draft of the "Declaration of Sentiments" for the Seneca Falls Convention (1848)

   Franklin Roosevelt's inaugural address (1933)

   Winston Churchill's addresses to the British people during the early stages of World War II (1940)

   Martin Luther King Jr.'s "Letter from Birmingham Jail" (1963)

   Ronald Reagan's tribute to the *Challenger* astronauts (1986)

   Toni Morrison's speech accepting the Nobel Prize (1993)

   George Bush's speech to Congress following the 9/11 terrorist attack (2001)

2. Working in a small group, make a list of some of the issues brought to your attention in a given week by people or groups engaged in political or social kinds of persuasion. What methods do they use to make you aware of their issues? How successful are they in engaging your attention? Do you worry about any of these issues or the groups advocating them? Why or why not?

3. Before class, find an editorial argument in a recent newspaper or periodical. Analyze this argument with regard to the six components summarized in this chapter: write a few sentences describing and evaluating the author's success at

> connecting to his or her readers
>
> arguing from the heart, values, character, and facts
>
> making a claim
>
> giving the argument shape
>
> giving the argument style
>
> managing the conventions of argument

In class, exchange editorials with a partner and analyze the one you've just been given along the same lines. Compare your analysis with your partner's: Have you responded similarly to the editorials? If not, how do you account for the differences?

4. At one point, the chapter text poses this question: "What . . . could SUVs have to do with gender or class?" Take a stab at answering the question, based upon a day or two of examining SUVs, both the vehicles and the drivers. Summarize your observations in a fully developed paragraph that makes a claim about SUVs. Don't hesitate to add other categories to your analysis if they seem appropriate: age, race, sexual orientation, religion, physical size, academic major, and so on.

5. Browse a magazine, newspaper, or Web site to find an example of a powerful emotional argument made visually. Then, in a paragraph, defend a claim about how the argument works. For example, does an image itself make a claim, or does it draw you in to consider a verbal claim? What emotion does the argument generate? How does that emotion work to persuade you?

6. Review all the major examples in this chapter—from Bradsher, Crier, Brandt, Klock, Moore, Abbey, Coulter, Wilson, Cheney, Carlisle, Barry, and Sullivan—and try to draw some conclusions about style. Write a paragraph explaining how (if at all) style makes a writer powerful or appealing.

chapter three

Readers
and Contexts
Count

Note how artist and cartoonist Charles Schulz tackles the task of announcing his retirement—the end of the long-running hit comic "Peanuts." In this strip (see Figure 3.1), Schulz addresses his readers directly with "Dear Friends" and goes on to talk about the difficult decision to discontinue the comic that had been the "fulfillment of [his] childhood ambition." Schulz is careful to explain his reasoning to his readers and to acknowledge the contributions others have made to this strip, thereby addressing not only the readers of the comic strip but those who have worked on it as well. In fact, Schulz also appears to be writing partially to himself, as the last sentence ends unfinished: "Charlie Brown, Snoopy, Linus, Lucy . . . how can I ever forget them. . . ." Moreover, Schulz's letter suggests that he has been mulling over the

FIGURE 3.1 FINAL PEANUTS STRIP

way his readers will respond to and interpret his decision, and it raises the question of whether readers will ever forget these characters as well.

■ ■ ■

In the same way that this cartoon makes an argument (that Schultz's decision to retire was appropriate) and anticipates response, so all arguments call for *response*, for the voices of others. Even in thinking through a choice you have to make—for example, whether to major in psychology or in international affairs—you will want to give some response to yourself as you weigh the pros and cons of each choice. And because argument is (at least) a two-way street, thinking hard about the people your argument will engage is crucial to communicating clearly and effectively. This kind of thinking is complicated, however, because those in a position to respond to your arguments or to join you in the argument are always individually complex and varied. In fact, if you can count on any one thing about people, it may be that they are infinitely varied—so varied that it is dangerous to make quick assumptions about what they do or do not think, or to generalize about what will or will not appeal to them. Quick assumptions about your readers are especially troubling in our electronic age, when a click on "send" can convey your message literally around the world.

MAPPING THE TERRITORY OF READERS

Readers or audiences for argument exist across a range of possibilities—from the flesh-and-blood person sitting right across the table from you, to the "virtual" participants in an online conversation, to the imagined ideal readers a written text invites. The sketch in Figure 3.2 may help you think about this wide range of possible readers or audiences.

FIGURE 3.2 READERS AND WRITERS IN CONTEXT

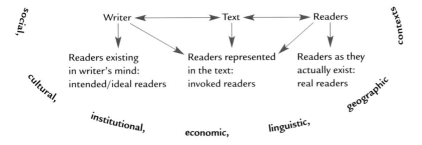

As you consider your argument and begin to write, you will almost always be addressing an intended reader, one who exists in your own mind. As we write this textbook, we are certainly thinking of those who will read it: you are our intended reader, and ideally you know something about and are interested in the subject of this book. Though we don't know you personally, a version of you exists very much in us as writers, for we are *intending* to write for you. In the same way, the writer bell hooks indicates in an essay that she carries intended readers within her:

> The most powerful resource any of us can have as we study and teach in university settings is full understanding and appreciation of the richness, beauty, and primacy of our familial and community backgrounds.
>
> –bell hooks, "Keeping Close to Home: Class and Education"

This sentence reflects hooks's intention of talking to a certain "us"—those who "study and teach in university settings."

But if texts—including visual texts—have intended readers (those the writer consciously intends to address), they also have invoked readers (those who can be seen represented in the text). Later in this chapter, "you" are invoked as one who recognizes the importance of respecting readers. For another example, look at the first paragraph of Chapter 1; it invokes readers who are interested in the goals of argument, whether those goals are overt or subtle. And bell hooks's text also invokes or inscribes a particular reader within its lines: an open, honest person who regards education as what hooks calls the "practice of freedom" and is willing to build bridges to others without losing the ability to think critically. As she says, "It is important that we know who we are speaking to, who we most want to hear us, who we most long to move, motivate, and touch with our words." To invoke the readers hooks wants, her text uses the pronouns *us* and *we* throughout.

But this device can be dangerous: those who read hooks's text (or any text) and do not fit the mold of the reader invoked there can feel excluded from the text—left out and thus disaffected. Such is the risk that Christopher Hitchens takes in a review of a book on animal rights:

> **Without condescension but with a fine contempt [the author] introduces us to "canned hunting": the can't-miss virtual safaris that charge a fortune to fly bored and overweight Americans to Africa and "big game" destinations on other continents for an air-conditioned trophy trip and the chance to butcher a charismatic animal in conditions of guaranteed safety.**
> **–Christopher Hitchens, "Political Animals"**

The words *bored*, *overweight*, and *butcher*, in particular, invoke readers who will agree with Hitchens's implicit condemnation of such people and the actions they take. Those who do not agree are not invited into this piece of writing; there is little space made for them there.

In addition to intended readers and the readers invoked by the text of the argument, any argument will have "real" readers—and these real people may not be the ones intended or even the ones that the text calls forth. You may pick up a letter written to someone else, for instance, and read it even though it is not intended for you. Even more likely, you will read email not sent to you but rather forwarded (sometimes unwittingly) from someone else. Or you may read a legal brief prepared for a lawyer and struggle to understand it, since you are neither the intended reader nor the knowledgeable legal expert invoked in the text. As these examples suggest, writers can't always (or even usually) control who the real readers of any argument will be. As a writer, then, you want to think carefully about these real readers and to summon up what you do know about them, even if that knowledge is limited.

When Julia Carlisle wrote an op-ed article for the *New York Times* about being "young, urban, professional, and unemployed," she intended to address readers who would sympathize with her plight; her piece invokes such readers through the use of the pronoun *we* and examples meant to suggest that she and those like her want very much to work at jobs that are not "absurd." But Carlisle ran into many readers who felt not only excluded from her text but highly offended by it. One reader, Florence Hoff, made clear in a letter to the editor that she did not sympathize with Carlisle at all. In fact, she saw Carlisle as self-indulgent and as asking for entitlement to one kind of job while rejecting others—the jobs that Hoff and others like her are only too glad to hold. In this instance, Carlisle needed to think not only of her intended readers or of the readers her text invited in, but also of all the various "real" readers who were likely to encounter her article in the *Times*.

CONSIDERING CONTEXTS

No consideration of readers can be complete without setting those readers in context. In fact, reading always takes place in what you might think of as a series of contexts—concentric circles that move outward from the most immediate context (the specific place and time in which the reading occurs) to broader and broader contexts, including local and community contexts, institutional contexts (such as school, church, or business), and cultural and linguistic contexts. Julia Carlisle's article, for instance, was written at a specific time and place (in New York City in 1991), under certain economic conditions (increasing unemployment of the kind currently seen across the United States in urban areas, particularly in the high-tech industry), and from the point of view of white, college-educated, and fairly privileged people. As we have seen, such broader contexts always affect both you as a writer of arguments and those who will read and respond to your arguments. As such, they deserve your careful investigation. As you compose arguments of your own, you need to think carefully about the contexts that surround your readers—and put your topic in context as well.

ESTABLISHING CREDIBILITY

Because readers are so variable and varied, and because the contexts in which arguments are made are so complex, it's almost impossible to guarantee that readers will always find you credible. Nevertheless, you can work toward establishing credibility by listening closely to those you want to reach, by demonstrating to readers that you are knowledgeable, by highlighting shared values, by referring to common experiences related to the subject at hand, by using language to build common ground, by respecting readers—and by showing that you are trying hard to understand them. (See also Chapter 6, "Arguments Based on Character.")

Demonstrate Knowledge

One good way to connect with readers is by demonstrating that you know what you are talking about—that you have the necessary knowledge to make your case. Notice how Lisa Takeuchi Cullen uses examples and statistics to demonstrate her claims to knowledge and to bolster her argument that white-collar workers are economically hard hit:

> It has come to this. White-collar workers are joining the jobless ranks in record numbers, tossed aside by the same companies that not long ago lavished them with signing bonuses and free lattes. Although the Labor department announced last week that overall unemployment fell slightly to 5.6% in September, the number of white-collar workers who are jobless has doubled from two years ago. Professionals, managers and technical and administrative workers now make up 43% of the unemployed, according to the government.
> —Lisa Takeuchi Cullen, "Will Manage for Food"

Highlight Shared Values

Even though all your readers will be somewhat different from you, they will not all be completely different. As a result, you can benefit from thinking about what values you hold and what values you may share with your readers. Jack Solomon is very clear about one value he hopes readers will share with him—the value of "straight talk":

> There are some signs in the advertising world that Americans are getting fed up with fantasy advertisements and want to hear some

straight talk. Weary of extravagant product claims and irrelevant associations, consumers trained by years of advertising to distrust what they hear seem to be developing an immunity to commercials.
   –Jack Solomon, "Masters of Desire: The Culture of American Advertising"

Anthony Brandt faces a different kind of challenge in "Do Kids Need Religion?" for he assumes that his real readers will include those who would answer that question in very different ways. Because he wants to be attended to by readers on all sides of this issue, he highlights a widely shared value: the love for one's children and the wish for a good life for them. "I hope my children find a straighter road than I've found," he says near the end of the essay, concluding, "The longing for meaning is something we all share." To the extent that readers do share such a longing, they may be more receptive to Brandt's argument. (For more about arguments based on values, see Chapter 5.)

CULTURAL CONTEXTS FOR ARGUMENT

Listening well is an essential element of effective argument. When you are arguing a point with people from cultures other than your own, make a special effort to listen for meaning: What is it that they're *really* saying? Misunderstandings sometimes occur when people hear only the words and not the meaning.

- Ask people to explain or even repeat a point if you're not absolutely sure you understand what they're saying.
- Take care yourself to be explicit about what you mean.
- Invite response—ask if you're making yourself clear. This kind of back-and-forth is particularly easy (and necessary) in email.

A recent misunderstanding among a professor and two students helps to make these points. The issue was originality: the professor told the students to be more "original." One student (who was from the Philippines) thought this meant going back to the original and then relating her understanding of it in her own essay. The other student (who was from Massachusetts) thought it meant coming up with something on her own. The professor (who was French) had another definition altogether: he wanted students to read multiple sources and then come up with a point of their own about those sources. Once the students understood what he meant, they knew what they were supposed to do.

Refer to Common Experiences

In their "Statement of Conscience," the organization Not
In Our Name draws on common
experience to connect with
their audience, saying, "We too
watched with shock the horrific
events of September 11, 2001.
We too mourned the thousands
of innocent dead . . . ."

···LINK TO P. 864

In her article "The Signs of Shopping," Anne Norton draws on an experience common to many in her analysis of the ways symbolic messages are
marketed to consumers: "A display window of Polo provides an embarrassment of semiotic riches. Everyone, from the architecture critic at the
New York Times to kids in the hall of a Montana high school, knows what
Ralph Lauren means."

In a very different kind of essay, Susan Griffin draws on a common
experience among men to build credibility with readers: "Most men can
remember a time in their lives when they were not so different from girls,
and they also remember when that time ended." Such references assume
that readers have enough in common with the writer to read on and to
accept—at least temporarily—the writer's credibility.

Build Common Ground

We've already mentioned the ways in which the use of pronouns can
include or exclude readers and define the intended audience. Writers who
want to build credibility need to be careful with pronouns and, in particular,
to make sure that *we* and *our* are used accurately and deliberately. In her
essay entitled "In Search of Our Mothers' Gardens," Alice Walker's use of
pronouns reveals her intended audience. She uses first-person singular and
plural pronouns in sharing recollections of her mother and demonstrating
the way her heritage led her to imagine generations of black women and
the "creative spark" they pass down. When she refers to "our mothers and
grandmothers," she is primarily addressing other black women. This
intended audience is even more directly invoked when she shifts to the second person: "Did you have a genius of a great-great-grandmother who died
under some ignorant and depraved white overseer's lash?" Through this
rhetorical direct address, Walker seeks solidarity and identification with her
audience and builds her own credibility with them.

Respect Readers

Another very effective means of building credibility and of reaching readers comes through a little seven-letter word made famous by Aretha
Franklin: *respect*. Especially when you wish to speak to those who may disagree with you, or who may not have thought carefully about the issues

you wish to raise, respect is crucial. In introducing an article on issues facing African American women in the workplace, editor-in-chief of *Essence* Diane Weathers considers the problems she faced with respecting all her readers:

> We spent more than a minute agonizing over the provocative cover line for our feature "White Women at Work." The countless stories we had heard from women across the country told us that this was a workplace issue we had to address. From my own experience at several major magazines, it was painfully obvious to me that Black and White women are not on the same track. Sure, we might all start out in the same place. But early in the game, most sisters I know become stuck—and the reasons have little to do with intelligence or drive. At some point we bump our heads against that ceiling. And while White women may complain of a glass ceiling, for us, the ceiling is concrete.
>
> So how do we tell this story without sounding whiny and paranoid, or turning off our White-female readers, staff members, advertisers and girlfriends? Our solution: Bring together real women (several of them highly successful senior corporate executives), put them in a room, promise them anonymity and let them speak their truth.
>
> –Diane Weathers, "Speaking Our Truth"

Of course, writers can also be deliberately *dis*respectful, particularly if they want to be funny or if they are very angry. Garrison Keillor, of the radio show "Prairie Home Companion," saddened by the untimely death of Minnesota senator Paul Wellstone and outraged at the election of Wellstone's opponent, Norman Coleman, wrote a fairly blistering attack on Coleman, addressed to readers who would be sure to include many of Coleman's supporters:

> Republicans don't like my criticism? Too bad. They have to answer for Norm Coleman's campaign, which exploited 9/11 in a way that was truly evil.
>
> The hoots and cackles of Republicans reacting to my screed against Norman Coleman, the ex-radical, former Democratic, now compassionate conservative senator-elect from Minnesota, was all to be expected, given the state of the Republican Party today. Its entire ideology, top to bottom, is We-are-not-Democrats, We-are-the-unClinton, and if it can elect an empty suit like Coleman, on a campaign as cheap and cynical and unpatriotic as what he waged right up to the moment Paul Wellstone's plane hit the ground, then Republicans are perfectly content. They are Republicans first and Americans second.
>
> –Garrison Keillor, "Minnesota's Shame"

Ed Madden expects some resistance from his readers in his "Open Letter to My Christian Friends," in which he describes the pain and difficulty he had in his home and church as a gay youth. He treats his audience with great respect, saying, "Regardless of what you think about homosexuality, please remember that you know homosexuals and lesbians, whether you are aware of them or not. . . . We are your invisible sons and daughters, your invisible brothers and sisters. Please at least think about that."

LINK TO P. 794 ···

Note that *hoots* and *cackles* carry negative connotations and that Keillor addresses Republican readers as *they* rather than *you*, thus further distancing himself from those he seeks to chastise. How do you think Keillor's message was received?

THINKING ABOUT READERS AND CONTEXTS

The following questions may help you craft an argument that will be compelling to your readers:

- How could (or do) you describe your intended readers? What characterizes the group of people you most want to reach? What assumptions do you make about your readers—about their values, goals, and aspirations?

- How does your draft represent or invoke readers? Who are the readers that it invites into the text, and who are those that it may exclude? What words and phrases convey this information?

- What range of "real" readers might you expect to read your text? What can you know about them? In what ways might such readers differ from you? From one another? What might they have in common with you? With one another?

- Whether readers are intended, invoked, or "real," what is their stance or attitude toward your subject? What are they likely to know about it? Who will be most interested in your subject, and why?

- What is your own stance or attitude toward your subject? Are you a critic, an advocate, an activist, a detached observer, a concerned consumer or citizen? Something else? In what ways may your stance be similar to or different from that of your readers?

- What is your stance or attitude toward your readers? That of an expert giving advice? A subordinate offering recommendations? A colleague asking for support? Something else?

- What kinds of responses from readers do you want to evoke?

- Within what contexts are you operating as you write this text? College course? Workplace? Community group? Local or state or national citizenry? Religious or spiritual group? Something else?

- What might be the contexts of your readers? How might those contexts affect their reading of your text?

- How do you attempt to establish your credibility with readers? Give specifics.

Considering and connecting with readers inevitably draws you into understanding what appeals—and what does not appeal—to them, whether they are imagined, invoked, or "real." Even though appeals are as varied as readers themselves, it is possible to categorize those that have been traditionally and most effectively used in Western discourse. These appeals are the subject of Part 2, "Lines of Argument."

RESPOND.

1. Find an example of one of the following items. Explain the argument made by the piece and then describe, as fully as you can, the audience the text is designed to address or invoke.

   a request for a donation by a charitable group

   a poster for the latest hit film

   an editorial in a newspaper or magazine

   the cover of a political magazine or journal (such as *The Onion, New Republic, Nation,* or *Mother Jones*)

   a bumper sticker

2. What common experiences—if any—do the following objects, brand names, and symbols evoke, and for what audiences in particular?

   a USDA organic label

   the Nike swoosh

   the golden arches

   a dollar bill

   a can of Coca-Cola

   Sleeping Beauty's castle on the Disney logo

   Oprah Winfrey

   the Vietnam memorial

   the World Trade Towers

   the Sean John label, as seen on its Web site (see next page):

3. Carry out an informal demographic study of the readership of a local newspaper. Who reads the paper? What is its circulation? What levels of education and income does the average reader have? Are readers politically conservative, moderate, or liberal? How old is the average reader? You'll likely have to do some research—phone calls, letters, follow-ups—to get this information, and some of it might be unavailable.

   Then select an article written by one of the paper's own reporters (not a wire-service story), and analyze it in terms of audience. Who seem to be its intended readers? How does it invoke these readers? Does it seem addressed to the average reader you have identified?

4. Choose a chapter in this textbook and read it with a special eye for how it addresses its readers: Does the chapter follow the guidelines offered here—that is, does it demonstrate knowledge, highlight shared values, build common ground, and respect readers? How does the chapter use pronouns to establish a relationship between the writers of the text and its readers? What other strategies for connecting with readers can you identify?

PART 2

LINES OF argument

chapter four

Arguments from the Heart

What makes you glance at a magazine ad long enough to notice a product? These days, it's probably an image or design promising pleasure (a Caribbean beach), excitement (bikers at Moab), beauty (a model in low-rise jeans), security (a kindly physician), or good health (more models). In the blink of an eye, ads can appeal to your emotions, intrigue you, perhaps even seduce you. Look closer and you might find good reasons in the ads themselves for buying a product or service. But would you have even gotten there without an emotional tug to pull you into the page?

FIGURE 4.1 THIS IMAGE PARODIES ADS THAT EXPLOIT ONE OF THE MOST POWERFUL OF EMOTIONAL APPEALS.

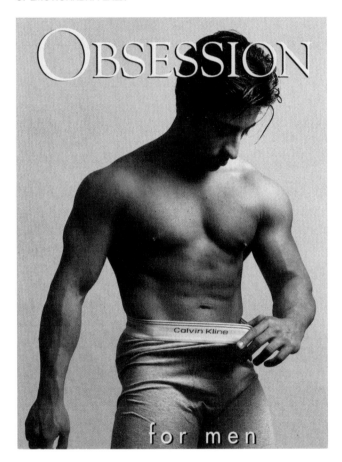

■ ■ ■

Emotional appeals (sometimes called appeals to *pathos*) are powerful tools for influencing what people think and believe. We all make decisions — even important ones — based on our feelings. We rent broken-down apartments or buy zonked-out cars because we fall in love with some small detail. On impulse, we collect whole racks of ties or blouses we're later too embarrassed to wear. We date, maybe even marry, people everyone else seemed to know are wrong for us—and sometimes it works out just fine.

That may be because we're not computers who use cost/benefit analyses to choose our friends or make our political decisions. Feelings belong in our lives. There's a powerful moment in Shakespeare's *Macbeth* when the soldier Macduff learns that his wife and children have been executed by the power-mad king. A well-meaning friend urges Macduff to "dispute it like a man." Macduff responds, gruffly, "But I must also feel it as a man" (*Macbeth*, 4.3.219–21). As a writer, you must learn like Macduff to appreciate legitimate emotions, particularly when you want to influence the public. When you hear that formal or academic arguments should rely solely on facts, remember that facts alone often won't carry the day, even for a worthy cause. The civil rights struggle of the 1960s is a particularly good example of a movement that persuaded people equally by means of the reasonableness and the passion of its claims.

But one doesn't have to look hard for less noble campaigns peppered by emotions such as hatred, envy, and greed. Democracies suffer when people use emotional arguments (and related fallacies such as personal attacks and name-calling) to drive wedges between groups, making them fearful and hateful. For that reason, writers can't use emotional appeals casually. (For more about emotional fallacies, see Chapter 19.)

UNDERSTANDING HOW EMOTIONAL ARGUMENTS WORK

You already know that words, images, and sounds can arouse emotions. In fact, the stirrings they generate are often physical. You've likely had the clichéd "chill down the spine" or felt something in the "pit of the stomach" when a speaker (or photograph or event) hits precisely the right note, as George W. Bush did when he unexpectedly took up a megaphone to assure rescue workers at the site of the 9/11 terrorist act (see Figure 4.2): "I can hear you. The rest of the world hears you. And the people who knocked down these buildings will hear all of us soon." Now, if writers and speakers can find the words and images to make people feel certain emotions, they might also move their audiences to sympathize with ideas they connect to those feelings, and even to act on them. Make people hate an enemy, and they'll rally against him; help people to imagine suffering, and they'll strive to relieve it; make people feel secure or happy, and they'll buy products that promise such good feelings.

FIGURE 4.2 PRESIDENT GEORGE W. BUSH STIRRED THE EMOTIONS OF MANY AMERICANS WITH HIS WORDS AT THE SITE OF THE WORLD TRADE CENTER ATTACK. HE WAS IN NEW YORK CITY ON SEPTEMBER 14, 2001.

Arguments from the heart probably count more when you are persuading than when you are arguing. When arguing, you might use reasons and evidence to convince readers something is true—for instance, that preserving wetlands is a worthy environmental cause. When persuading, however, you want people to take action, actually to join an environmental boycott, contribute money to an organization dedicated to wetlands protection, or write a well-researched op-ed piece for the local paper about a local marsh threatened by development.

Argument (discover a truth) ———▶ conviction

Persuasion (know a truth) ———▶ action

The practical differences between being convinced and acting on a conviction can be enormous. Your readers may agree that contributing to charity is a noble act, but that conviction may not be enough to persuade them to part with their spare change. You need a spur sharper than logic, and that's when emotion might kick in. You can embarrass readers into contributing to a good cause ("Change a child's life for the price of a pizza") or make them feel the impact of their gift ("Imagine the smile on that little child's face") or tell them a moving story ("In a tiny village in Central America . . ."). Doubtless, you've seen such techniques work.

USING EMOTIONS TO BUILD BRIDGES

You may sometimes want to use emotions to connect with readers, to assure them that you understand their experiences or, to use a famous political line, "feel their pain." Such a bridge is especially important when you are writing about matters that readers regard as sensitive. Before they will trust you, they'll want assurances that you understand the issues in depth. If you strike the right emotional note, you'll establish an important connection.

That's what presidential advisor Condoleezza Rice did while teaching a Sunday School class at the National Presbyterian Church, arguing that communities of faith should play a role in American politics. To reinforce her point, Rice lets us peer into her own experiences with religion, one of the most sensitive of all subjects:

> I think people who believe in a creator can never take themselves too seriously. I feel that faith allows me to have a kind of optimism about the future. You look around you and you see an awful lot of pain and suffering and things that are going wrong. It could be oppressive. But when I look at my own story or many others that I have seen, I think, "How could it possibly be that it has turned out this way?" Then my only answer is it's God's plan. And that makes me very optimistic that

this is all working out in a proper way if we all stay close to God and pray and follow in His footsteps.

I really do believe that God will never let you fall too far. There is an old gospel hymn, "He knows how much you can bear." I really do believe that.

–Condoleezza Rice, "Walking in Faith"

In no obvious way is Rice's recollection an actual argument. But it prepares her audience to accept the case she will make, because she seems to be teaching from an authentic experience with religion.

A more obvious way to build an emotional tie is simply to help readers identify with your experiences. If, like Georgina Kleege, you were blind and wanted to argue for more sensible attitudes toward blind people, you might ask readers in the very first paragraph of your argument to confront their prejudices. Here Kleege, a writer and college instructor, makes an emotional point by telling a story:

I tell the class, "I am legally blind." There is a pause, a collective intake of breath. I feel them look away uncertainly and then look back. After all, I just said I couldn't see. Or did I? I had managed to get there on my own—no cane, no dog, none of the usual trappings of blindness. Eyeing me askance now, they might detect that my gaze is not quite focused. . . . They watch me glance down, or towards the door where someone's coming in late. I'm just like anyone else.

–Georgina Kleege, "Call It Blindness"

Given the way she narrates the first day of class, readers are as likely to identify with the students as with Kleege, imagining themselves sitting in a classroom, facing a sightless instructor, confronting their own prejudices about the blind. Kleege wants to put them on edge emotionally.

Let's consider another rhetorical situation: How do you win over an audience when the logical claims you are making are likely to upset what many passionately believe? Once again, a slightly risky appeal to emotions on a personal level may work. That's the tack Dinesh D'Souza takes in trying to make the case that the evils of European colonialism may be exaggerated. He turns to his own experiences to meet the objections head on:

Much as it chagrins me to admit it—and much as it will outrage many third-world intellectuals for me to say it—my life would have been much worse had the British never ruled India.

How is that possible? Virtually everything that I am, what I do, and my deepest beliefs, all are the product of a worldview that was brought to India by colonialism. I am a writer, and I write in English. My ability to do this, and to reach a broad market, is entirely thanks to the British. My understanding of technology, which allows me, like so many Indians, to function successfully in the modern world, was largely the product of a Western education that came to India as a result of the British. So also my beliefs in freedom of expression, in self-government, in equality of rights under the law, and in the universal principle of human dignity—they are all the products of Western civilization.

—Dinesh D'Souza, "Two Cheers for Colonialism"

Although D'Souza's claims are, strictly speaking, logical, based on his own observations, he acknowledges that they will *outrage* most third-world intellectuals and many academics in the United States as well. But perhaps D'Souza is hoping his willingness to reveal personal background will build an emotional bridge among readers who respect someone willing to challenge intellectual orthodoxies. The strategy may have an unpredictable result (it can backfire), but it is also remarkably common.

USING EMOTIONS TO SUSTAIN AN ARGUMENT

You can also use emotional appeals to make logical claims stronger or more memorable. That is, in fact, the way photographs and other images add power to arguments. In a TV attack ad, the scowling black-and-white photograph of a political opponent may do as much damage as the claim that his bank laundered drug money. Or the attractive skier in a spot for lip balm may make us yearn for dry, chafing winter days. The technique is tricky, however. Lay on too much emotion—especially those like outrage, pity, or shame, which make people uncomfortable—and you may offend the very audiences you hoped to convince. But sometimes a strong emotion such as anger adds energy to a passage, as it does when Susan Faludi accuses writer Katie Roiphe of minimizing the significance of date rape:

Roiphe and others "prove" their case [that date rape is exaggerated] by recycling the same anecdotes of false accusations; they all quote the same "expert" who disparages reports of high rape rates. And they never interview any real rape victims. They advise us that a feeling of victimization is no longer a reasonable response to sexual violence; it's a hallucinatory state of mind induced by witchy feminists who cast a spell on impressionable co-eds. These date-rape revisionists claim to be liberating young women from the victim mind-set. But is women's sexual victimization just a mind trip—or a reality?

—Susan Faludi, "Whose Hype?"

Here, the threat in Faludi's sarcasm becomes part of the argument: if you make the kind of suggestion Roiphe has, expect this sort of powerful response.

In the same way, writers can generate emotions by presenting logical arguments in their starkest terms, stripped of qualifications or subtleties. Readers or listeners are confronted with core issues or important choices and asked to consider the consequences. It is hard to imagine an argument more serious than a debate about war and peace or one more likely to raise powerful feelings. Here is Andrew Sullivan on his Web log (commonly known as a *blog*) in late summer 2002, inviting opponents of a proposed American invasion of Iraq to put their cards on the table. That he favors military action is clear in the sharp and emotional way he outlines the consequences of the decision. We have italicized his more emotionally charged words and phrases:

> So far, very few have had the *cojones* to take such a stand [opposing action against Iraq], especially in Congress. (There are some honorable, principled exceptions among traditional pacifists, leftists and hard-core foreign policy 'realists.') But soon, even Howell Raines [editor of the *New York Times*] will have to take responsibility for backing a *passive policy of leaving America and our allies vulnerable to massive destruction.* Far from *ducking* this *vital* debate, those of us who believe our *national security is at stake* should *embrace* the discussion enthusiastically. And each side should be held accountable for the difficult and *unknowable* consequences of our respective stands. After all, what is at issue is the possible *future murder of thousands* of American citizens, *nuclear blackmail* from a *rogue state,* or *chemical warfare waged in American cities* by agents in close contact with the *Iran-Iraq-Syria-Saudi* axis. It's hard to think of a *graver moment in recent American history.*
> –Andrew Sullivan, <andrewsullivan.com>

You might imagine how an opponent of war might respond at this point: Would a more reasoned approach work, or would the reply have to be just as stirring as Sullivan's challenge, listing the potential consequences of ill-considered action? Or is this an opportunity to suggest alternatives to an either/or choice between war and peace?

It is possible, of course, for feelings to be an argument in themselves when they are powerfully portrayed. Here, for example, is the incomparable Camille Paglia hammering Harvard psychologist William Pollack for his view that American boys ought to be raised with greater, almost feminine, sensitivity. Again, the phrases with emotional kick are italicized.

> Specifically, I reject Pollack's position that mothers shouldn't *push growing boys away* and discourage displays of *weakness, fear and tears.*

Everywhere, I see the opposite problem: white, upper-middle-class mothers *clinging too much to their whiny sons* and turning them into companion daughters or substitute spouses. Boys are not girls: *the mocking epithets "sissy" (i.e., "sister") and "mollycoddle" do describe something real*—a stalling in the evolution of masculine identity, which requires boys to *leave the maternal nest* and make their way as independent adults.

Perhaps because of his background, Pollack overestimates the power of words in most men's lives. His program privileges female values and *simply cuts boys down to pliable ciphers* in a family matriarchy. It's actually a perfect recipe for *producing obedient office-workers, happy eunuchs in the corporate food chain.*

–Camille Paglia, "Guns and Penises"

As you can see, it is difficult to gauge how much emotion will work in a given argument. Some issues—such as date rape, abortion, gun control—provoke strong feelings and, as a result, are often argued on emotional terms. But even issues that seem deadly dull—such as funding for Medicare and Social Security—can be argued in emotional terms when proposed changes in these programs are set in human terms: Cut benefits and Grandma will have to eat cat food; don't cut benefits and the whole health care system will go broke, leaving nothing for aging baby boomers. Both alternatives might scare people into paying enough attention to take political action.

Patricia Hampl uses her emotional interactions with her mother to sustain her argument in "Other People's Secrets."

LINK TO P. 528 ···

USING HUMOR

Humor has great power. Some days after terrorists attacked the World Trade Center and the Pentagon on September 11, 2001, comedian David Letterman, whose TV show originates in New York City, returned to the air. It was a memorable, emotionally riveting performance, with Letterman choking up during tributes to police and firefighters. But there were a few gibes and a few laughs, most of them at the expense of guest Regis Philbin. With remarkable grace that night, Letterman helped Americans to find themselves again.

Humor has always played an important role in argument, sometimes as the sugar that makes the medicine go down. You can certainly slip humor into an argument to put readers at ease, thereby making them more open to a proposal you have to offer. It is hard to say "no" when you're laughing. Humor also makes otherwise sober people suspend their judgment and even their prejudices, perhaps because the surprise and naughtiness of wit are combustive: they provoke laughter or smiles, not reflection. That may be why TV sitcoms like *All in the Family* or *Will and Grace* have been able to reach mainstream audiences, despite their some-times controversial subjects. Similarly, it is possible to make a point through humor that might not work at all in more sober writing. Consider the gross stereotypes about men that humorist Dave Barry presents here, tongue in cheek, explaining why people don't read the instructions that come with the products they buy:

> **The third reason why consumers don't read manuals is that many consumers are men, and we men would no more read a manual than we would ask directions, because this would be an admission that the person who wrote the manual has a bigger . . . OK, a bigger grasp of technology than we do. We men would rather hook up our new DVD player in such a way that it ignites the DVDs and shoots them across the room—like small flaming UFOs—than admit that the manual-writer possesses a more manly technological manhood than we do.**
> **–Dave Barry, "Owners' manual Step No. 1: Bang head against the wall"**

Our laughter testifies to a kernel of truth in Barry's observations and makes us more likely to agree with his conclusions.

A writer or speaker can use laughter to deal with especially sensitive issues. For example, sports commentator Bob Costas, given the honor of eulogizing the great baseball player Mickey Mantle, couldn't ignore well-known flaws in Mantle's character. So he argues for Mantle's greatness by admitting the man's weaknesses indirectly through humor:

> **It brings to mind a story Mickey liked to tell on himself and maybe some of you have heard it. He pictured himself at the pearly gates, met by St. Peter who shook his head and said "Mick, we checked the record. We know some of what went on. Sorry, we can't let you in. But before you go, God wants to know if you'd sign these six dozen baseballs."**
> **–Bob Costas, "Eulogy for Mickey Mantle"**

Similarly, politicians use humor to admit problems or mistakes they couldn't acknowledge in any other way. Here, for example, is President Bush at the annual Radio & TV Correspondents Dinner discussing his much-mocked intellect: "Those stories about my intellectual capacity do get under my skin. You know, for a while I even thought my staff believed it. There on my schedule first thing every morning it said, 'Intelligence briefing.'"

Not all humor is well intentioned. In fact, among the most powerful forms of emotional argument is ridicule—humor aimed at a particular target. Lord Shaftesbury, an eighteenth-century philosopher, regarded humor as a serious test for ideas, believing that sound ideas would survive prodding. In our own time, comedians poke fun at politicians and their ideas almost nightly, providing an odd barometer of public opinion. Even bumper stickers can be vehicles for succinct arguments:

Vote Republican: It's easier than thinking.
Vote Democrat: It's easier than working.

But ridicule is a two-edged sword that requires a deft hand to wield it. Humor that reflects bad taste discredits a writer completely, as does ridicule that misses its mark. Unless your target deserves assault and you can be very funny, it's usually better to steer clear of humor. (For more on humorous arguments, see Chapter 13.)

USING ARGUMENTS FROM THE HEART

You don't want to play puppetmaster with people's emotions when you write arguments, but it's a good idea to spend some time early in your writing or designing process thinking about how you want readers to feel as they consider your persuasive claims. Would readers of your editorial about campus traffic policies be more inclined to agree with you if you made them envy faculty privileges, or would arousing their sense of fairness work better? What emotional appeals might persuade meat eaters to consider a vegan diet—or vice versa? Would sketches of stage props on a Web site persuade people to buy a season ticket to the theater, or would you spark more interest by featuring pictures of costumed performers?

Consider, too, the impact that telling a story can have on readers. Writers and journalists routinely use what are called "human interest stories" to give presence to issues or arguments. You can do the same, using a particular incident to evoke sympathy, understanding, outrage, or amusement. Take care, though, to tell an honest story.

In his essay "Counterpoint: Paranoid Privacy Hawks Don't Realize How Good They've Got It," Roahn Wynar uses ridicule to make a point about a certain kind of person: "Privacy freaks are mild conspiracy theorists who think someone is watching them. Get over it."

LINK TO P. 515

RESPOND●

1. To what specific emotions do the following slogans, sales pitches, and maxims appeal?

    "Just do it." (ad for Nike)

    "Think different." (ad for Apple Computers)

"Reach out and touch someone." (ad for a long-distance phone company)

"In your heart, you know he's right." (1964 campaign slogan for U.S. presidential candidate Barry Goldwater, a conservative)

"It's the economy, stupid!" (1992 campaign theme for U.S. presidential candidate Bill Clinton)

"By any means necessary." (rallying cry from Malcolm X)

"When the going gets tough, the tough get going." (maxim used by many coaches)

"You can trust your car to the man who wears the star." (slogan for Texaco)

"We bring good things to life." (slogan for GE)

"Know what comes between me and my Calvins? Nothing!" (tag line for Calvin Klein jeans)

"Don't mess with Texas!" (antilitter campaign slogan)

2. Bring a magazine to class and analyze the emotional appeals in as many full-page ads as you can. Then classify those ads by types of emotional appeal and see whether you can connect the appeals to the subject or target audience of the magazine. Compare your results with those of your classmates and discuss your findings. For instance, do the ads in newsmagazines like *Time* and *Newsweek* appeal to different emotions and desires than ads in publications such as *Cosmo*, *Rolling Stone*, *Sports Illustrated*, *Automobile*, and *National Geographic*?

3. It's important to remember that argument—properly carried out—can be a form of inquiry: rather than a simple back-and-forth between established positions, good argument helps people discover their positions and modify them. Arguments from the heart can help in this process, as long as they are well tempered with reason.

   With this goal of inquiry in mind, as well as an awareness of the problems associated with emotional arguments, imagine how another Indian (or anyone who has lived in a former British colony) might respond to Dinesh D'Souza's argument that his life is probably better because the British once ruled his native land.

   You might also do this as a group exercise. Over several days, one group might read the entire D'Souza article, originally published in the *Chronicle of Higher Education* (May 10, 2002), while another examines the responses of his critics in the same journal (June 14, 2002). Then the groups could meet together to discuss the issues raised and the emotions evoked.

4. How do arguments from the heart work in different media? Are such arguments more or less effective in books, articles, television (both news and entertainment shows), films, brochures, magazines, email, Web sites, the theater, street protests, and so on? You might focus on a single medium, exploring how it handles emotional appeals, or compare different media. For example, why do Internet news groups seem to encourage angry outbursts? Are newspapers an emotionally colder source of information than television news programs? If so, why?

chapter five

Arguments
Based on Values

Some people would argue that beauty pageants should be a thing of the past in a country just an election cycle or two from putting a woman in the Oval Office. But every September, amid much pomp and publicity, a new Miss America is crowned in Atlantic City. How does a beauty pageant survive in a society that seems committed to equality between men and women? Very nicely, thanks to a continuing adjustment of pageant values by the organization sponsoring the event, which now describes itself as the "world's leading provider of scholarships for young women." If good looks were enough of a qualification for a contestant in the early decades, women competing today for the title of Miss America must meet different standards. "Contestants at all levels of the Miss America program," say the competition's

FIGURE 5.1 IN 1921, MARGARET GORMAN BECAME THE FIRST MISS AMERICA.

rules, "are required to clearly define a social issue to which they are sincerely committed and for which each will be an activist during her year of service." So crowning a Miss America is really an argument about contemporary values, the person selected supposedly representing a contemporary ideal of womanhood. Of course, critics of the pageant complain that the competition is still out of step with the times. And they, too, are making an argument based on values.

Arguments like these usually occur within or between groups—in this case the 280 million people who describe themselves as Americans. Most groups are much smaller. But they stay together because, consciously or not, their members share core beliefs about issues such as politics, religion, ethics, art, work, or family. You shouldn't be surprised if arguments based on values often involve other sorts of claims. For instance, writing about love of country as a value might stir emotional memories or lead to passionate claims about character—*she is a real patriot; he's a traitor.* But appeals based on value are powerful in their own right because they ask people to look inside themselves. Thus it is only common sense to try to find out all you can about the beliefs of people you want to persuade. That also means you need to be aware of how your own core values shape your view of the world.

UNDERSTANDING HOW VALUES ARGUMENTS WORK

Sometimes the values shared by members of a group are clearly spelled out in a statement of principles, a platform, a creed, or a document such as the Declaration of Independence. Here's how the Knighthood of BUH, a college group dedicated to creative humor, rather seriously defines its counterculture values:

> Among its members . . . the Knighthood is about more than just comedy. It is about being an individual, and thinking for yourself. A lot of the time, it is easier to feel the way a movie wants us to . . . than it is to generate our own emotions. It seems the world is a place for being the guy next to you. The Knighthood is about being you, about thinking for yourself, and about believing what you have decided is believable, not simply what your parents or your pastor told you. It is about creativity, but not creativity as your third grade teacher meant it, which is to say bright colors and lots of glitter, but creativity in the true and not-so-easy-to-have sense of the word—divergent thinking.
> –The Knighthood of BUH

At other times, the beliefs evolve as part of the history and traditions of a club or movement or political party; for example, what it means to be a traditional Navajo, a committed feminist, or an environmentalist may never be entirely clear, but it is always somehow understood. Moreover, many groups prefer to keep their principles a little blurred around the edges so they can attract new members or change with the times. Arguments about principles may be, in fact, what help many groups evolve. Sharon Clahchischilliage, a Navajo woman from New Mexico, faced such a conflict of values when she decided to run for Secretary of State, as a news report from the *Washington Times* explains:

FIGURE 5.2
SHARON CLAHCHISCHILLIAGE

> By placing her face on billboards around the state and publicizing her justcallmesharon.com Web site, she is bucking tribal customs. Navajos as a rule do not stare people in the eyes, nor ask for money or boast about their capabilities.

> "I'm going against the norms of my culture," she admits, "just by
> being a candidate."
> > –Julia Duin, "Navajo Woman Vies for Political Distinction"

Because principles do change, appeals to values typically involve a
comparison between *what is* and *what ought to be*:

- A person or group does not live up to current values.
- Past values were better or nobler than current ones.
- Future values can be better or worse than current ones.

USING VALUES TO DEFINE

You will likely find appeals to values whenever members of a group disagree about who belongs in the group or what its core principles are. *What
does it mean to be an American? A faithful Muslim? A good Christian? A true
Texan? A patriot? A concerned liberal?* Everyone who belongs to such a group
likely has an answer—as do people who stand outside—and their opinions might generate plenty of talk.

How, for instance, would you define an American? Here is Hector St.
Jean de Crèvecoeur, a Frenchman, trying in 1782 to do exactly that, speaking in the imagined voice of an American:

> We are a people of cultivators, scattered over an immense territory,
> communicating with each other by means of good roads and navi-
> gable rivers, united by the silken bands of mild government, all
> respecting the laws without dreading their power, because they are
> equitable. We are all animated with the spirit of industry which is
> unfettered and unrestrained, because each person works for himself.
> > –Hector St. Jean de Crèvecoeur, "What Is an American?"

Crèvecoeur lived in a different era (few Americans are farmers now), but
the core values he describes might still stir a mainstream crowd on the
Fourth of July: limited government, fair laws, hard work, self-reliance.
Appeals to such shared (and flattering) principles are so common that
even advertisers exploit them. In Texas, for example, one truck manufacturer used to advertise its products as "Texas tough," making the assumption that Texans like to think of themselves as rugged.

But let's consider an entirely different way of imagining American values, one far less idealistic (and perhaps parodic). This time the writer is
Dana Cloud, an associate professor of Communication Studies writing to

a student newspaper to applaud a California federal court's decision (later suspended) forbidding public schools from using the phrase "one nation, under God" as part of the Pledge of Allegiance. Cloud's version of America is less comforting than Crèvecoeur's and much different from that in the familiar Pledge of Allegiance, which she parodies:

> My daughter, who is 11, and I were delighted at the California court decision omitting the words "under God" from the Pledge of Allegiance. She and I have always been uncomfortable saying the pledge, not only because of the religious imposition, but because it seems very strange to pledge loyalty to a scrap of cloth representing a corrupt nation that imposes its will, both economic and military, around the world by force. So she inspired me to rewrite the Pledge.

> Imagine schoolchildren every day reciting the following:

> *I pledge allegiance to all the ordinary people around the world,*
> *to the laid off Enron workers and the WorldCom workers*
> *the maquiladora workers*
> *and the sweatshop workers from New York to Indonesia,*
> *who labor not under God but under the heel of multinational corporations; I*
>   *pledge allegiance*
> *to the people of Iraq,*
> *Palestine and Afghanistan,*
> *and to their struggles to survive and resist*
> *slavery to corporate greed,*
> *brutal wars against their families,*
> *and the economic and environmental ruin wrought by global capitalism; I*
>   *pledge allegiance*
> *to building a better world*
> *where human needs are met*
> *and with real liberty, equality and justice for all.*

> The original pledge does not include or represent us godless radicals. The backlash against the California decision shows just how thin our democracy is.

> –Dana Cloud, *The Daily Texan*

You can imagine the local backlash to Cloud's letter to the editor, but her words were also soon sprinting across the Internet, where they were the subject of both denunciation and praise on various Web logs. Are Crèvecoeur's "silken bands of mild government" in any way compatible with Cloud's "heel of multinational corporations"? Can both of these views represent an authentic version of American values? As a writer, you may find that any real America exists in the turbulence between such conflicting views—in the arguments about values that you, like Crèvecoeur and Cloud, may help to shape.

EMBRACING OR REJECTING VALUES

You can often make a strong argument by connecting your own beliefs and values to core principles that are better established and more widely respected. This strategy is particularly effective when your position seems to threaten traditional values. For example, when Terry Tempest Williams is arrested for protesting nuclear weapons testing, she claims her action represents an American value as old and honorable as the Boston Tea Party:

> I crossed the line at the Nevada Test Site and was arrested with nine other Utahns for trespassing on military lands. They are still conducting nuclear tests in the desert. Ours was an act of *civil disobedience.* (emphasis added)
> –Terry Tempest Williams, "The Clan of One-Breasted Women"

By linking her own arrest to the respected tradition of civil disobedience, she makes an argument in defense of her entire cause. Similarly, advocates of abortion rights and school vouchers—people usually on different ends of the political spectrum—both claim to favor "choice," a value fundamental to any democracy.

But appeals to core values of a culture can cut in different ways. What happens when principles of equality lead to new kinds of discrimination? For instance, some argue that Title IX of a 1972 federal education act barring gender discrimination compels colleges and universities to shut down men's sports teams when the number of men playing sports exceeds their proportion of the school's population. Does an ideal of equity conflict, then, with a related value of fairness? Welch Suggs, a writer for the *Chronicle of Higher Education*, explores exactly that question:

> Why should courts and administrators presume that men's interests in competing in college sports are being met simply by providing them with opportunities proportional to their enrollment at a university? Curt A. Levey, a lawyer for the Center for Individual Rights . . . says that athletics is the only area in education where quotas are permitted.
>
> Should a university's nursing school, he wonders, be forced to enroll men in numbers proportional to their overall enrollment at the university?

As you might guess, there's another side to the argument that also appeals to principles of fairness. Suggs continues his report on the controversy:

> **Sports programs are different, responds Mary Frances O'Shea, who oversees Title IX compliance in athletics for the U.S. Department of Education's Office for Civil Rights.**
>
> **"Athletic programs are the only programs wherein schools can establish [teams] set aside for men and women," Ms. O'Shea says. "You can't have Algebra I-A for boys and Algebra I-B for girls, but in athletics, because of the nature of the program, you can." As such, rules must be in place to ensure that men and women are treated equitably in athletic programs, Ms. O'Shea says.**
>
> — Welch Suggs, "Colleges Consider Fairness of Cutting Men's
> Teams to Comply with Title IX"

Conflicts about core values keep courts and newspaper editorialists very busy.

COMPARING VALUES

Many arguments based on values involve comparisons. Something is faulted for not living up to an ideal, or the ideal is faulted for not reaching far enough, or one value is presented as preferable to another or in need of redefinition. It would be hard to find an argument based on values more clearly stated than the following example from a book by Stephen Carter that explores what he sees as a trend toward intolerance of religion among America's legal and political elites:

> **The First Amendment guarantees the "free exercise" of religion but also prohibits its "establishment" by the government. There may have been times in our history when we as a nation have tilted too far in one direction, allowing too much religious sway over politics. But in late-twentieth-century America, despite some loud fears about the weak and divided Christian right, we are upsetting the balance afresh by tilting too far in the other direction—and the courts are assisting in the effort.**
>
> — Stephen Carter, *The Culture of Disbelief*

In this case, Carter makes his argument by appealing to the balance between "free exercise" and "establishment" of religion guaranteed by the First Amendment to the U.S. Constitution. If readers share his interpretation of the First Amendment, they also likely agree with him that disrupting this equilibrium would be bad. Carter's argument is relatively easy to make because most Americans do have a high—almost religious—regard for the First Amendment. He doesn't have to defend it. But consider how much tougher it would be to get the same consensus for the Second Amendment's protection of the right to bear arms. It provides a shakier premise for arguments, one that requires more backing. (See Chapter 8 for more on using evidence.)

Adrienne Rich, a poet and writer, provides a clear example of a second type of value comparison, one in which a current value—in this case, power—is redefined for a different group so that it can be embraced in a new way. Notice especially how she unpacks the meaning of power:

> The word *power* is highly charged for women. It has been long associated for us with the use of force, with rape, with the stockpiling of weapons, with the ruthless accrual of wealth and the hoarding of resources, with the power that acts only in its own interest, despising and exploiting the powerless—including women and children. . . . But for a long time now, feminists have been talking about redefining power, about that meaning of power which returns to the root—*posse, potere, pouvoir*: to be able, to have the potential, to possess and use one's energy of creation—transforming power.
> —Adrienne Rich, "What Does a Woman Need to Know?"

As you can see, arguments based on values are challenging and sophisticated. That's because they often take you right into the heart of issues.

USING ARGUMENTS BASED ON VALUES

Knowing your audience is a key to arguing successfully. The more you know about the values your readers hold dear, the better you will be at selecting the options available to you for making an argument. Corporations and political organizations do massive demographic studies to figure out who their consumers and constituencies are and what they want. Companies that track what you buy or even what you browse on their Web sites are doing a similar kind of audience study. But you don't have to be quite so intrusive. Although you want to influence readers, you need not do that by violating your own principles. Instead, you should study the values of others to appreciate the ways they differ from you and, when possible, to find common ground. Precisely because people are so complicated and because their values can change, you are in a position as a writer to explore values in ways that can make a difference.

Check out the many different value arguments made by the different speakers in the National Public Radio piece "Schoolchildren Debating What It Means to Be a Patriot."

LINK TO P. 828 ·

RESPOND

1. Listed here are groups whose members likely share some specific interests and values. Choose a group you recognize (or find another special interest group on your own), research it on the Web or in the library, and, in a paragraph, explain its core values for someone less familiar with the group.

   parrotheads

   Harley Davidson owners

   Trekkies

   Log Cabin Republicans

   PETA members

   hip-hop fans

   survivalists

2. A number of selections in this chapter deal with specifically American values. Can you list 30 values—core values—associated with the people of the United States? 100? 200? List as many as you can, and then ask yourself when the list stops being representative of core values. Why does this problem arise? (If you are not from the United States, you might instead list the core values of your home country or another country you know well.)

   Now make a list of core values for a small group—the members of your college's English department, for instance, or a church philanthropy committee, or an athletic team. Any small group will do. How many core values can you list? How does the list compare to the list you generated for the people of the United States?

3. Using the list of core values you've developed for the smaller group, write a paragraph arguing that a public figure—such as Jesse Jackson, Jennifer Lopez, or Serena Williams—meets the standards of that group.

4. Several years ago, a group of animal rights activists raided a mink "ranch" and released several thousand animals from their cages. Many of the minks died during and after their release. Soon thereafter, other animal rights groups criticized this action, arguing that it did not represent the values of true animal rights activists.

   What might these values be? And how would those responsible for the release characterize their own values? Write a statement from one of the other groups, using arguments based on values to express your disapproval of the release. Then write a statement from the releasing group, explaining why its actions were consonant with the values of true animal lovers. In each of these letters, you'll have to decide whether you're writing to a public audience or directly to the opposing group; the values you refer to might change, depending on the audience.

5. A contestant in the Miss America competition is now expected to demonstrate "a commitment to a social issue." Study the pageant's Web site at <missamerica.org> to get a sense of the organization's values. Then make a list of social issues the most contestants would likely avoid. Be prepared to explain why these issues might be controversial or even contrary to the values of the pageant.

chapter six

Arguments Based on Character

In the introduction to his book about men, Dave Barry tries to explain the difference between *men* and *guys*. Naturally, in making such a distinction, he makes readers wonder how he will define each term. Here is what he has to say about the second:

> **And what, exactly, do I mean by "guys"? I don't know. I haven't thought much about it. One of the major characteristics about guyhood is that guys don't spend a lot of time pondering our deep innermost feelings.**
>
> **—Dave Barry, "Guys vs. Men"**

If you know that Barry is a famous humorist (there was even a TV sitcom based on his life), you understand just how to take his self-deprecating remarks. He's not writing a serious piece, a fact he stresses in the very first line of his introduction:

> This is a book about guys. It's not a book about men. There are already way too many books about men and most of them are way too serious.

But imagine for a moment that you've never heard of Dave Barry and have somehow missed all the comedy in his introduction. What might you think of a writer who confessed, "I don't know. I haven't thought much about it," it being the subject of his book? Chances are you'd close the volume and choose another by someone smarter.

That's because in argument, as in politics, character matters. Readers usually won't consider an argument unless they trust the person or group offering it. You earn a reader's trust by seeming to know what you are talking about and demonstrating your authority.

You must also seem honest — and sometimes, likable — if you are to persuade an audience. Opponents of Richard Nixon, the controversial thirty-sixth president of the United States, once raised doubts about his integrity by asking a single ruinous question: *Would you buy a used car from this man?* Put that question under the photograph of any controversial politician, and you've composed a powerful visual argument about their *ethos*, or character. Being smart doesn't matter if you aren't perceived as honest.

In composing an argument, you have to convey both authority and honesty through an appeal based on character — what the ancient Greeks called *ethos*. You can do so in various ways, both direct and subtle.

FIGURE 6.1 PUBLIC FIGURES TRY TO CONTROL THEIR IMAGES FOR OBVIOUS REASONS. WOULD YOU BUY A USED CAR FROM ANY OF THESE DISTINGUISHED MEN AND WOMEN?

UNDERSTANDING HOW ARGUMENTS BASED ON CHARACTER WORK

Because life is complicated, we often need shortcuts to help us make choices; we can't weigh every claim to its last milligram or trace every fragment of evidence to its original source. And we have to make such decisions daily: *Which college or university should I attend? For whom should I vote in the next election? Which reviewers of* The Matrix Reloaded *will I believe? What pain reliever will get me through the 10K race?*

To answer the more serious questions, people typically rely on professionals for wise, well-informed, and honest advice: a doctor, lawyer, teacher, pastor. But people look to equally trustworthy individuals to guide them in less momentous matters as well: a coach, a friend, maybe even a waitperson (*Is the fish really fresh?*). Depending on the subject, an *expert* can be anyone with knowledge and experience, from a professor of nuclear physics at a local college to a short-order cook at the local diner.

Readers give people (or companies) they know a hearing they might not automatically grant to a stranger or to someone who hasn't earned their respect or affection. That indicates the power of arguments based on character and accounts for why people will trust the opinion of the "car guy" in their neighborhood more than the reviews in *Consumer Reports*. And they'll take *Consumer Reports* more seriously than the SUV ads in *People*.

CLAIMING AUTHORITY

When you read an argument, especially one that makes an aggressive claim, you have every right to wonder about the writer's authority: *What does he know about the subject? What experiences does she have that make her especially knowledgeable? Why should I pay attention to this writer?*

When you offer an argument yourself, you have to anticipate pointed questions exactly like these and be able to answer them, directly or indirectly. Sometimes the claim of authority will be bold and uncompromising, as it is when writer and activist Terry Tempest Williams attacks those who poisoned the Utah deserts with nuclear radiation. What gives her the right to speak on this subject? Not scientific expertise, but gut-wrenching personal experience:

> **I belong to the Clan of One-Breasted Women. My mother, my grandmothers, and six aunts have all had mastectomies. Seven are dead.**

The two who survive have just completed rounds of chemotherapy and radiation.

I've had my own problems: two biopsies for breast cancer and a small tumor between my ribs diagnosed as a "borderline malignancy."

–Terry Tempest Williams, "The Clan of One-Breasted Women"

We are willing to listen to her claims because she has lived with the nuclear peril she will deal with in the remainder of her essay.

But just as often, writers make claims of authority in other and more subtle ways. We may not have lords and dukes in the United States, but it seems everyone has a job title that confers some clout. When writers attach such titles to their names, they are saying "This is how I've earned the right to be heard"—they are medical doctors or have law degrees or have been board certified to work as psychotherapists. Similarly, writers can assert authority by mentioning who employs them—their institutional affiliations—and how long they have worked in a given field. Bureaucrats often identify themselves with government agencies, and professors always mention what schools they represent. As a reader, you'll likely pay more attention to an argument about global warming if it's offered by a professor of atmospheric and oceanic science at the University of Wisconsin, Madison, than by your Uncle Sid who sells tools at Sears. But you'll prefer your uncle to the professor when you need advice about a reliable rotary saw.

When your readers are apt to be skeptical of both you and your claim—as is usually the case when your subject is controversial—you may have to be even more specific about your credentials. That's exactly the strategy Richard Bernstein uses to establish his right to speak on the delicate subject of teaching multiculturalism in American colleges and universities. At one point in a lengthy argument, he challenges those who make simplistic pronouncements about non-Western cultures, specifically "Asian culture." But what gives a New York writer named *Bernstein* the authority to write about Asian peoples? Bernstein tells us in a sparkling example of an argument based on character:

The Asian culture, as it happens, is something I know a bit about, having spent five years at Harvard striving for a Ph.D. in a joint program called History and East Asian Languages and, after that, living either as a student (for one year) or a journalist (six years) in China and Southeast Asia. At least I know enough to know there is no such thing as the "Asian culture."

–Richard Bernstein, *Dictatorship of Virtue*

Clearly, Bernstein understates the case when he says he knows "a bit" about Asian culture and then mentions a Ph.D. program at Harvard and years of living in Asia. But the false modesty may be part of his argumentative strategy, too.

Bjørn Lomborg, an associate professor of statistics and author of *The Skeptical Environmentalist*, faces a problem much like Bernstein's. Lomborg claims that many environmental threats to the natural world have been exaggerated, sometimes wildly. But what, one might ask, does a statistician know about topics such as global warming, deforestation, or water pollution? Lomborg anticipates that question in the introduction to his book, where he explains what a statistician can add to the discussion (emphasis added):

> *I teach statistics* **at the University of Aarhus and basically my skills consist in knowing how to handle international statistics. Normally you associate statistics with a boring run-through of endless rows of numbers—a problem I must every semester convince new students is not necessarily true. Actually, statistics can be thoroughly exciting because** *it confronts our myths with data and allows us to see the world more clearly.*

You need not agree with Lomborg's conclusions, but it makes sense for him to defend his credentials this way. His expertise may make it possible to understand the facts better.

When you write for readers who trust you and your work, you may not have to make such an open claim to authority. But you should know that making this type of appeal is always an option. A second lesson is that it certainly helps to know your subject when you are making a claim.

Even if an author does not make an explicit effort to assert authority, authority can be conveyed through tiny signals that readers may pick up almost subconsciously. Sometimes it comes just from a style of writing that presents ideas with robust confidence. For example, years ago when Allan Bloom wrote a controversial book about problems in American education, he used tough, self-assured prose to argue for what needed to be done. We've italicized the words that convey his confident ethos:

> *Of course,* **the only** *serious* **solution [to the problems of higher education] is the one that is almost universally rejected: the** *good old* **Great Books approach. . . . I am** *perfectly aware* **of, and actually agree with, the objections to the Great Books Cult. . . . But** *one thing is certain:*

> wherever the Great Books make up a central part of the curriculum, the students are excited and satisfied.
>
> —Allan Bloom, *The Closing of the American Mind*

Bloom's "of course" seems arrogant; his concession—"I am perfectly aware"—is poised; his announcement of truth is unyielding—"one thing is certain." Writing like this can sweep readers along; the ideas feel carved in stone. Bloom was a professor at the University of Chicago, respected and knowledgeable and often able to get away with such a style even when his ideas provoked strong opposition. Indeed, there is much to be said for framing arguments directly and confidently, as if you really mean them. (And it helps if you do.)

In an essay reflecting on her life as a lesbian rabbi, La Escondida makes a powerful claim of authority: "I am a Jew. I am a woman. I am a rabbi. I am a lesbian."

LINK TO P. 799 ···

CULTURAL CONTEXTS FOR ARGUMENT

In the United States, students writing arguments are often asked to establish authority by drawing on certain kinds of personal experience, by reporting on research they or others have conducted, and by taking a position for which they can offer strong evidence and support. But this expectation about student authority is by no means universal. Indeed, some cultures regard student writers as novices who can most effectively make arguments by reflecting back on what they have learned from their teachers and elders—those who hold the most important knowledge, wisdom, and, hence, authority. Whenever you are arguing a point with people from cultures other than your own, therefore, you need to think about what kind of authority you are expected to have:

- Whom are you addressing, and what is your relationship with him or her?

- What knowledge are you expected to have? Is it appropriate or expected for you to demonstrate that knowledge—and if so, how?

- What tone is appropriate? If in doubt, always show respect: politeness is rarely if ever inappropriate.

ESTABLISHING CREDIBILITY

Writers with authority seem smart; those with credibility seem trustworthy. As a writer you usually want to convey both impressions, but sometimes, to seem credible, you have to admit limitations: *This is what I know; I won't pretend to fathom more.* Readers pay attention to writers who are willing to be honest and who appear modest about their claims.

Imagine, for instance, that you are the commencement speaker at a prestigious women's college. You want the graduates to question all the material advantages they have enjoyed. But you yourself have enjoyed many of the same privileges. How do you protect your argument from charges of hypocrisy? The poet Adrienne Rich defuses this very conflict simply by admitting her status:

> **And so I want to talk today about privilege and tokenism and about power. Everything I can say to you on this subject comes hard-won from the lips of a woman privileged by class and skin color, a father's favorite daughter, educated at Radcliffe.**
> **–Adrienne Rich, "What Does a Woman Need to Know?"**

Candor is a strategy that can earn writers immediate credibility. It's a tactic used by people as respected in their fields as was the late biologist Lewis Thomas, who in this example ponders whether scientists have overstepped their bounds in exploring the limits of DNA research:

> **Should we stop short of learning some things, for fear of what we, or someone, will do with the knowledge? My own answer is a flat no, but I must confess that this is an intuitive response and I am neither inclined nor trained to reason my way through it.**
> **–Lewis Thomas, "The Hazards of Science"**

When making an argument, many people would be reluctant to write "I suppose" or "I must confess," but those are the very concessions that might increase a reader's confidence in Lewis Thomas. Note, too, how Thomas's honesty differs from the giddy celebration of ignorance in Dave Barry's comic piece on guys that opened this chapter.

You can invite readers to see you as honest in other ways, too. Nancy Mairs, in an essay entitled "On Being a Cripple," wins the attention and maybe the respect of her readers by facing her disability with a riveting directness:

> **First, the matter of semantics. I am a cripple. I choose this word to name me. I choose from among several possibilities, the most common of which are "handicapped" and "disabled." I made the choice a number of years ago, without thinking, unaware of my motives for doing so. Even now, I am not sure what those motives are, but I recognize that they are complex and not entirely flattering. People— crippled or not—wince at the word "cripple," as they do not at "handi-**

capped" or "disabled." Perhaps I want them to wince. I want them to see me as a tough customer, one to whom the fates/gods/viruses have not been kind, but who can face the brutal truth of her existence squarely. As a cripple, I swagger.

–Nancy Mairs, "On Being a Cripple"

The paragraph takes some risks because the writer is expressing feelings that may make readers unsure how to react because Mairs herself doesn't completely understand her own feelings and motives. Yet the very uncertainty helps her to build a bridge to readers.

Thus a reasonable way to approach an argument—especially an academic or personal one—is to be honest with your readers about who you are and what you do and do not know. If it is appropriate to create a kind of dialogue with readers, as many writers do, then you want to give readers a chance to identify with you, to see the world from your perspective, and to appreciate why you are making specific claims.

In fact, a very powerful technique for building credibility is to acknowledge outright any exceptions, qualifications, or even weaknesses in your argument. Making such concessions to objections that readers might raise, called *conditions of rebuttal*, sends a strong signal to the audience that you've scrutinized your own position with a sharp critical eye and can therefore be trusted when you turn to arguing its merits. W. Charisse Goodman, arguing that the media promote prejudice against people who aren't thin, points out that some exceptions do exist:

Television shows . . . occasionally make an effort. Ricki Lake, who has since lost weight, was featured in the defunct series *China Beach*; Delta Burke once co-starred in *Designing Women* and had her own series; and Roseanne's show has long resided among the Top 10 in the Nielsen ratings. Although these women are encouraging examples of talent overcoming prejudice, they are too few and far between. At best, TV shows typically treat large female characters as special cases whose weight is always a matter of comment, rather than integrating women of all sizes and shapes into their programs as a matter of course.

–W. Charisse Goodman, "One Picture Is Worth a Thousand Diets"

Notice how pointing out these exceptions helps build Goodman's credibility as a critic. Conceding some effort on the part of television shows allows her to make her final judgment more compellingly.

You can also use language in other ways to create a relationship of trust with readers. Speaking to readers directly, using *I* or *you*, for instance, enables you to come closer to them when that strategy is appropriate.

Using contractions will have the same effect because they make prose sound more colloquial. Consider how linguist Robert D. King uses such techniques (as well as an admission that he might be wrong) to add a personal note to the conclusion of a serious essay arguing against the notion that language diversity is endangering the United States (emphasis added):

> *If I'm wrong*, then the great American experiment will fail—not because of language but because it no longer means anything to be an American; because we have forfeited that "willingness of the heart" that F. Scott Fitzgerald wrote was America; because we are no longer joined by Lincoln's "mystic chords of memory."
>
> We are not even close to the danger point. *I suggest* that we relax and luxuriate in our linguistic richness and our traditional tolerance of language differences. Language does not threaten American unity. Benign neglect is a good policy for any country when it comes to language, and *it's a good policy* for America.
>
> –Robert D. King, "Should English Be the Law?"

On the other hand, you may find that a more formal tone gives your claims greater authority. Choices like these are yours to make as you search for the ethos that best represents you in a given argument.

Another fairly simple way of conveying both authority and credibility is to back up your claims with evidence and documentation—or, in an electronic environment, to link your claims to sites with reliable information. Citing trustworthy sources and acknowledging them properly shows that you have done your homework.

Indeed, any signals you give readers to show that you have taken care to present ideas clearly and fairly will help your credibility. A helpful graph, table, chart, or illustration may carry weight, as does the physical presentation of your work (or your Web site, for that matter). Even proper spelling counts.

In his op-ed essay "If Only We All Spoke Two Languages," Ariel Dorfman establishes credibility for his argument about the methods of teaching English to immigrants in the United States by stating, "Both methods can work. I should know. I have endured them both. But my experience was unquestionably better with bilingual education."

LINK TO P. 704

USING ARGUMENTS FROM CHARACTER

A number of studies over the years have shown that tall, thin, good-looking people have an advantage in getting a job or getting a raise. Apparently, employers respond to their attractive appearance and make assumptions about their competence that have no basis in fact. You probably act the same way in some circumstances, even if you resent the practice. So you might recall these studies when you make an argument, knowing that like it or not, readers and audiences are going to respond to how you present yourself as a person. Fortunately, you need not add inches to your height or character to your cheekbones to be persuasive in writing. What you do need is to sound confident, knowledgeable, and honest. Sounding friendly may help too, though many persuasive writers manage without that trait.

Be sure that your writing also conveys competence visually. Choose a medium that shows you at your best. Some writers love the written text, garnished with quotations, footnotes, charts, graphs, and bibliography. Others can make a better case online or in some purely visual form. Design arguments that tell readers they can trust you.

RESPOND•

1. Consider the ethos of each of the following figures. Then describe one or two public arguments, campaigns, or products that might benefit from their endorsements as well as several that would not.

   Eminem—rap artist

   Ricki Lake—TV talk-show host

   Jesse Ventura—former governor of Minnesota and professional wrestler

   Katie Holmes—actress featured on *Dawson's Creek*

   Donald Rumsfeld—secretary of defense in the Bush administration

   Jesse Jackson—civil rights leader

   Queen Latifah—actress and rap artist

   Dave Barry—humorist and columnist

   Jeff Gordon—NASCAR champion

   Madeleine Albright—secretary of state in the Clinton administration

   Bill O'Reilly—TV news show host

   Marge Simpson—sensible wife and mother on *The Simpsons*

   Ozzy Osbourne—rock personality

2. Voice is a choice. That is, writers modify the tone and style of their language depending on who they want to seem to be. In the excerpts from this chapter, Allan Bloom wants to appear poised and confident;

his language aims to convince us of his expertise. Terry Tempest Williams wants to appear serious, knowledgeable, and personally invested in the problems of radiation poisoning; the descriptions of her family's illness try to convince us. In different situations, even when writing about the same topics, Bloom and Williams would adopt different voices. (Imagine Williams explaining "The Clan of One-Breasted Women" to a young girl in her family—she might use different words, a changed tone, and simpler examples.)

Rewrite the Williams passage on p. 90, taking on the voice—the character—of someone speaking to a congressional committee studying nuclear experiments in Utah. Then rewrite the selection in the voice of someone speaking to a fourth-grade class in New Hampshire. You'll need to change the way you claim authority, establish credibility, and demonstrate competence as you try to convince different audiences of your character.

3. Create your own version of the famous "Would you buy a used car from this man?" argument aimed against Richard Nixon when he was a candidate for political office. Begin by choosing an intriguing or controversial person or group and finding an image online. Download the image into a word-processing file. Create a caption for the photo modeled after the question asked about Nixon—*Would you give this woman your email password? Would you share a campsite with this couple? Would you eat lasagna this guy prepared?* Finally, write a serious 300-word argument that explores the character flaws (or strengths) of your subject(s).

FIGURE 6.2 WOULD YOU BUY LONG-DISTANCE SERVICE FROM CARROT TOP?

4. A well-known television advertisement from the 1980s featured a soap-opera actor promoting a pain relief medication. "I'm not a doctor," he said, "but I play one on TV." Likewise, Michael Jordan trades on his good name to star in Nike advertisements. Actress Susan Sarandon uses the entertainment media to argue for political causes. One way or another, each of these cases relies on arguments based on character.

Develop a one-page print advertisement for a product or service you use often—anything from soap to auto repair to cell phone service. There's one catch: Your advertisement should rely on arguments based on character, and you should choose as a spokesperson someone who would seem the least likely to use or endorse your product or service. The challenge is to turn an apparent disadvantage into an advantage by exploiting character.

chapter seven

Arguments Based on Facts and Reason

"Logic and practical information do not seem to apply here."

"You admit that?"

"To deny the facts would be illogical, Doctor."

–Spock and McCoy, "A Piece of the Action"

When the choice is between logic and emotion, a great many of us are going to side with *Star Trek*'s Dr. McCoy rather than the stern Spock. Most of us respect logical appeals—arguments based on facts, evidence, reason, and logic—but, like the good doctor, we are inclined to test the facts against our feelings and against the character and values of those making the appeal. As McCoy observes in another *Star Trek* episode, "You can't evaluate a man by logic alone."

The fact is that human beings aren't computers and most human issues don't present themselves like problems in geometry. When writers need to persuade, they usually try their best to give readers or listeners good reasons to believe them or to enter into a conversation with them. Not infrequently, they will tell a story to make their point, dramatizing their case by showing how an issue affects the lives of individuals or a community. Sometimes these well-reasoned cases get listened to sympathetically; at other times, even the most reasonable efforts to persuade fail. Then people try harder—perhaps by strengthening their good reasons with stronger appeals to the heart or to their personal credibility. (For more on these types of appeals, see Chapters 4 and 6.)

Still, when you argue logically, you've got plenty of resources to draw upon—far too many to list in a text this brief. Here we can only summarize some ways of arguing logically. Aristotle, one of the first philosophers to write about persuasion, gives us a place to begin. He divided logical proofs into two kinds: those based on what we'd call *hard evidence* (what Aristotle called *inartistic appeals*—facts, clues, statistics, testimonies, witnesses) and those based upon *reason and common sense* (what Aristotle called *artistic appeals*). Though these categories overlap and leak (what, after all, is *common sense?*), they are useful even today. For instance, when lawyers in a trial question witnesses, judges usually restrict them to questions about evidence and fact. But when the same lawyers make their closing arguments to juries, they can draw on those facts and testimony to raise broader questions of guilt or innocence. They can speak more openly about motives, mitigating circumstances, and reasonable doubt. In other words, they can *interpret* the hard evidence they have assembled (as at the O.J. Simpson trial when Simpson was asked to try on a bloody glove)

FIGURE 7.1   DURING HIS TRIAL FOR THE MURDER OF HIS EX-WIFE, O. J. SIMPSON WAS ASKED TO TRY ON A PAIR OF BLOODY GLOVES SAID TO BE HIS. THEY DIDN'T FIT.

to urge conviction or exoneration (in Johnnie Cochran's words, *If it does not fit, you must acquit*). We'll examine both types of logical appeals in this chapter.

HARD EVIDENCE

It wasn't so in Aristotle's time, but people today probably prefer arguments based on facts and testimony to those grounded in reason. In a courtroom as well as in the popular media, for example, lawyers or reporters look for the "smoking gun"—that piece of hard evidence that ties a defendant or politician to a crime. It might be an audiotape, a fingerprint, a stained dress, or, increasingly, a videotape or DNA evidence. Popular crime shows such as *CSI: Crime Scene Investigation* focus intensely on gathering this sort of "scientific" support for a prosecution. Less dramatically, the factual evidence in an argument might be columns of data carefully collected over time to prove a point about climate change or racial profiling or the effects of Title IX on collegiate sports. After decades of exposure to science and the wonders of technology, audiences today have more faith in claims that can be counted, measured, photographed, or analyzed than in those that are merely defended with words. If you've ever been ticketed after a camera caught you running a red light, you know what hard evidence means.

Factual evidence, however, comes in many forms. Which ones you use will depend on the kind of argument you are writing. In fact, providing accurate evidence ought to become a habit whenever you write an argument. The evidence makes your case plausible; it may also supply the details that make writing interesting. Just recall Aristotle's claim that all arguments can be reduced to two components:

Statement + Proof

Here's another way of naming those parts:

Claim + Supporting Evidence

When you remember to furnish evidence for every important claim you make, you go a long way toward understanding how to argue responsibly. The process can be remarkably straightforward. In a scholarly article, you can actually see this process occurring in the text and in the notes. As an example, we reprint a single page from a much-cited review of Michael Bellesiles's *Arming America: The Making of America's Gun Culture* by James Lindgren published in the *Yale Law Review*. Bellesiles had used evidence gathered from eighteenth-century documents to argue that gun ownership in frontier America was much rarer than advocates of the right to bear arms believed. Upon publication, *Arming America* was hailed by gun critics for weakening the claim of gun advocates today that the ownership of weapons has always been a part of American culture. But Lindgren, as well as many other critics and historians, found so many evidentiary flaws in Bellesiles's arguments that questions were soon raised about his scholastic integrity. Lindgren's review of *Arming America* runs for more than 50 meticulous pages (including an appendix of errors

FIGURE 7.2 THIS SELECTION FROM JAMES LINDGREN'S REVIEW OF MICHAEL BELLE-SILES'S *ARMING AMERICA* FIRST APPEARED IN THE *YALE LAW REVIEW*, VOL. 111 (2002).

LINDGRENFINAL.DOC   APRIL 26, 2002 4/26/02 12:34 PM

2002]   *Arming America*   2203

B. *How Common Was Gun Ownership?*

The most contested portions of *Arming America* involve the book's most surprising claim, that guns were infrequently owned before the mid-1800s. As I show below, the claim that colonial America did not have a gun culture is questionable on the evidence of gun ownership alone. Compared to the seventeenth and eighteenth centuries, it appears that guns are not as commonly owned today. Whereas individual gun ownership in every published (and unpublished) study of early probate records that I have located (except Bellesiles's) ranges from 40% to 79%; only 32.5% of households today own a gun.[44] This appears to be a much smaller percentage than in early America—in part because the mean household size in the late eighteenth century was six people,[45] while today it is just under two people.[46] The prevailing estimate of 40% to 79% ownership differs markedly from Bellesiles's claim that only about 15% owned guns.[47] In the remainder of this Section, I explain why.

1. *The Gun Censuses*

Bellesiles bases his claims of low gun ownership primarily on probate records and counts of guns at militia musters.[48] He also discusses censuses of all guns in private and public hands, but on closer examination, none of these turns out to be a general census of all guns.

The trend is set in Bellesiles's first count of guns in an American community—the 1630 count of all the guns in the Massachusetts Bay Colony of about 1000 people. Bellesiles's account is quite specific: "In 1630 the Massachusetts Bay Company reported in their possession: '80 bastard musketts, . . . [10] Fowlinge peeces, . . . 10 Full musketts . . . .' There were thus exactly one hundred firearms for use among seven towns

---

44. This results from my analysis of the March 2001 release of the National Opinion Research Center's *General Social Survey, 2000* [hereinafter 2000 NORC GSS]. The data are also available at Nat'l Opinion Research Ctr., General Social Survey, *at* http://www.icpsr.umich.edu/GSS/ (last visited Apr. 8, 2002). According to the survey, 32.5% of households owned any gun, 19.7% owned a rifle, 18.6% owned a shotgun, and 19.7% owned a pistol or revolver. 2000 NORC GSS, *supra*. Only 1.2% of respondents refused to respond to the question. *Id.*

45. Inter-Univ. Consortium for Political & Soc. Research (ICPSR), Census Data for the Year 1790, http://fisher.lib.virginia.edu/cgi-local/censusbin/census/cen.pl?year=790 (last visited Aug. 10, 2001).

46. 2000 NORC GSS, *supra* note 44.

47. BELLESILES, *supra* note 3, at 445 tbl.1.

in Bellesiles's work) and contains 212 footnotes. You can see a factual argument in action just by looking at how Lindgren handles evidence on a single page. You may never write an argument as detailed as Lindgren's review, but you should have the same respect for evidence.

Facts

"Facts," said John Adams, "are stubborn things," and so they make strong arguments, especially when readers believe they come from honest sources. Gathering such information and transmitting it faithfully practically defines what we mean by journalism in one realm and scholarship in another. We'll even listen to people we don't agree with when they overwhelm us with evidence. Here, for example, a reviewer for the conservative journal *National Review* praises the work of William Julius Wilson, a liberal sociologist, because of how well he presents his case (emphasis added):

> **In his eagerly awaited new book, Wilson argues that ghetto blacks are worse off than ever, victimized by a near-total loss of low-skill jobs in and around inner-city neighborhoods. In support of this thesis, he** *musters mountains of data, plus excerpts from some of the thousands of surveys and face-to-face interviews that he and his research team conducted among inner-city Chicagoans.* **It is a book that deserves a wide audience among thinking conservatives.**
> –John J. Dilulio Jr., "When Decency Disappears"

Here, the facts are trusted even above differences in political thinking.

When your facts are compelling, they may stand on their own in a low-stakes argument, supported by little more than a tag that gives the source of your information. Consider the power of phrases such as "reported by the *New York Times*," "according to CNN," or "in a book published by Oxford University Press." Such sources gain credibility if they have, in readers' experience, reported facts accurately and reliably over time. In fact, one reason you document the sources you use in an argument is to let the credibility of those sources reflect positively on you—one important reason to find the best, most reliable authorities and evidence to support your claims.

But arguing with facts also sometimes involves challenging claims made by reputable sources. You don't have to look hard to find critics of the *Times* or CNN. Web loggers (commonly known as *bloggers*) particularly enjoy pointing out the biases or factual mistakes of major media outlets. Here, for example, is blogger Andrew Sullivan charging that a headline of a story in the *New York Times*, his favorite target, distorts the facts reported in a poll:

THE TIMES AND POLLS: It's gotten to the point now that I always check the actual poll when reading the *New York Times'* version. This particular story is from the AP, so I'm not sure where the bias lies. But the *Times* headline is a complete distortion of the poll numbers. The *Times'* story reads: "Poll: Support For Iraq Action Drops." The poll itself shows that on the generic question of supporting military action against Iraq, those supporting it numbered 59 percent in June and 64 percent today. Those opposing it dropped from 34 percent to 21 percent. Lies, damned lies, and the *New York Times*!

–Andrew Sullivan, <andrewsullivan.com>

In an ideal world, good information would always drive out bad. But you'll soon learn that such is not always the case. That's why as a reader and researcher, you should look beyond headlines, scrutinizing any facts you collect before using them yourself, testing their reliability and reporting them with all the needed qualifiers. As a writer, you have to give your readers not only the facts but where they came from and what they may mean.

Statistics

Let's deal with a cliché right up front: *figures lie and liars figure*. Like most clichés, it contains a grain of truth. It is possible to lie with numbers, even those that are accurate. Anyone either using or reading statistics has good reason to ask how the numbers were gathered and how they have been interpreted. Both factors bear on the credibility of statistical arguments.

However, the fact remains that contemporary culture puts great stock in tables, graphs, reports, and comparisons of numbers. People use such numbers to understand the past, evaluate the present, and speculate about the future. These numbers almost always need writers to interpret them. And writers almost always have agendas that influence their interpretations.

For example, you might want to herald the good news that unemployment in the United States stands just a little over 5 percent. That means 95 percent of Americans have jobs, a figure much higher than that of most other industrial nations. But let's spin the figure another way. In a country as populous as the United States, unemployment at 5 percent means that millions of Americans are without a daily wage. Indeed, *one out of every twenty adults* who wants work can't find it. That's a remarkably high number. As you can see, the same statistics can be cited as a cause for celebration or shame.

We don't mean to suggest that numbers are meaningless or untrustworthy or that you have license to use them in any way that serves your

FIGURE 7.3 *USA TODAY* IS FAMOUS FOR THE TABLES, PIE CHARTS, AND BAR GRAPHS
IT CREATES TO PRESENT STATISTICS AND POLL RESULTS. WHAT CLAIMS MIGHT THE
EVIDENCE IN THIS CHART SUPPORT? HOW DOES THE DESIGN OF THE ITEM INFLUENCE
YOUR READING OF IT?

purposes. Quite the contrary. But you do have to understand the role you
play in giving numbers a voice and a presence.

Consider the matter we mentioned earlier about using cameras at
highway intersections to catch drivers who run red lights. The cameras
may intrude a little into our privacy, but they are an effective way to deal
with a serious traffic hazard, aren't they? Well, no, not according to
former House Majority Leader Dick Armey. In an article on his Web site
entitled "The Truth about Red Light Cameras," Armey uses numbers and
statistics to raise doubts about the motives that cities and police forces
have for installing cameras at traffic lights. We've highlighted his use of
figures:

> Safety was never the primary consideration [for installing traffic light
> cameras in San Diego]. In fact, none of the devices were placed at any
> of San Diego's *top-ten most dangerous intersections.* Instead, the docu-
> ments tell us how the camera operators consciously sought out mis-
> timed intersections as locations for new red light cameras.
>
> Yellow signal time at intersections turns out to be directly related
> to "red light running." Simply put, when the yellow light is short, more
> people enter on red. Inadequate yellow time causes a condition where
> individuals approaching an intersection are unable either to come to a
> safe stop or [to] proceed safely before the light turns red.

Though dangerous, this condition also turns out to be very profitable. Each time someone ends up in an intersection on red in San Diego, *the city collects $271*. And $70 of that fine is paid as bounty to the city's private contractor. Combine hefty fines with mistimed signals and you've found the formula for big money. A single camera brought the city *$6.8 million in just 18 months*. . . .

Consider the intersection of Mission Bay Drive and Grand Avenue in San Diego. With *a yellow time of 3 seconds*, the intersection produced about *2,300 violations every month*.

Documents show that the *yellow time was increased to 4.7 seconds* at that particular intersection on July 28, 2000. Immediately after the change, *red light entries dropped 90 percent*—and they stayed down.

The simple and inexpensive step of adding a little over a second to the yellow time produced a significant safety benefit. Did the city tell the world of its success? Did the city refocus its efforts to correct signal timing at other intersections? No. That's because this "success" *cost the City of San Diego $3 million* in yearly revenue it would have otherwise collected from the mistimed signal.

Red light entries similarly dropped about 70 percent in Mesa, Arizona, after the city increased yellow times at its intersections in response to motorist complaints. The problem subsided so dramatically that their camera program turned into a big money loser. The incredible truth about Mesa, however, is that the city had to break its contract with the camera operators to achieve this safety benefit.

Inadequate yellows are more dangerous, but they are also more profitable. It's hard to conceive another explanation for a contract that prevents engineering safety measures that could dilute profits.

–Dick Armey, "The Truth About Red Light Cameras"

This is hardly the last word on traffic light cameras. Proponents (including insurance companies) might cite different numbers and studies that report reductions in collisions after cameras were installed or savings on insurance claims. Perhaps a compromise is possible—longer yellow signals *and* traffic light cameras?

Surveys, Polls, and Studies

Surveys and polls produce statistics. These measures play so large a role in people's political and social lives that writers, whether interpreting them or fashioning surveys themselves, need to give them special attention.

Surveys and polls provide persuasive appeals when they verify the popularity of an idea or proposal because, in a democracy, majority opinion offers a compelling warrant: *a government should do what most people want.* Polls come as close to expressing the will of the people as anything short of an election—the most decisive poll of all. (For more on warrants, see Chapter 8, p. 129.)

However, surveys, polls, and studies can do much more than help politicians make decisions. They can also provide persuasive reasons for action or intervention. When studies show, for example, that most American sixth-graders can't locate France or Wyoming on the map, that's an appeal for better instruction in geography. When polls suggest that consumer confidence is declining, businesses may have reason to worry about their bulging inventories. By this point, you should appreciate the responsibility to question any study or report. It always makes sense to ask who is reporting the results and numbers and what stake the source has—financial, political, ethical—in the outcome.

Consider how the Pew Hispanic Center/Kaiser Family Foundation's "2002 National Survey of Latinos" uses surveys and polls in order to argue about the changing role of Latinos in United States society.

················LINK TO P. 744

Are we being too suspicious? No. In fact, this sort of scrutiny is exactly what you should anticipate from your readers whenever you use such material to frame an argument. Especially with polls and surveys, you should be confident that you or your source surveyed enough people to be accurate, that the people you chose for the study were representative of the selected population as a whole, and that you chose them randomly—not selecting those most likely to say what you hoped to hear.

Surveys and polls can be affected, too, by the way questions are asked or results are reported. Professional pollsters generally understand that their reputations depend on asking questions in as neutral a way as possible. But some researchers aren't above skewing their results by asking leading questions. There's even a term for using polls to sway the people being polled rather than to survey public opinion: *push polling.* Consider how differently people might respond to the following queries on roughly the same subject:

Do you support cuts in Medicare to help balance the federal budget?

Do you support adjustments in Medicare to keep the system solvent?

Do you support decisive action to prevent the bankruptcy of Medicare?

You must also read beyond the headlines to be sure you understand the claims made in a poll. A recent headline on a Gallup poll was potentially confusing: "Fewer Americans Favor Private Investment of Social Security Taxes." Fewer than what? Does the headline mean that a majority of Americans oppose privatizing Social Security or that support for the idea has declined? Fortunately a subheading clarified the matter: "Proposal still gets majority approval." A less honest pollster might have omitted that important line. The simple lesson here is to use polls, surveys, and other studies responsibly.

Testimonies, Narratives, and Interviews

We don't want to give the impression that numbers and statistics make the only good evidence. Indeed, writers support arguments with all kinds of human experiences, particularly those they or others have lived or reported. The testimony of reliable witnesses counts in almost any situation in which a writer seeks to make a case for action, change, or sympathetic understanding.

In a court, for example, decisions are often based upon detailed descriptions of what happened. Following is a reporter's account of a court case in which a panel of judges decided, based on the testimony presented, that a man had been sexually harassed by another man. The narrative, in this case, supplies the evidence:

> The Seventh Circuit, in a 1997 case known as Doe v. City of Belleville, drew a sweeping conclusion allowing for same-sex harassment cases of many kinds. Title VII was sex-neutral, the court ruled; it didn't specifically prohibit discrimination against men or women. Moreover, the judges argued, there was such a thing as gender stereotyping, and if someone was harassed on that basis, it was unlawful. This case, for example, centered on teenage twin brothers working a summer job cutting grass in the city cemetery of Belleville, Ill. One boy wore an earring, which caused him no end of grief that particular summer—including a lot of menacing talk among his co-workers about sexually assaulting him in the woods and sending him "back to San Francisco." One of his harassers, identified in court documents as a large former marine, culminated a verbal campaign by backing the earring-wearer against a wall and grabbing him by the testicles to see "if he was a girl or a guy." The teenager had been "singled out for this abuse," the court ruled, "because the way in which he projected the sexual aspect of his personality"—meaning his gender—"did not conform to his co-workers' view of appropriate masculine behavior."
>
> –Margaret Talbot, "Men Behaving Badly"

Personal experience carefully reported can also support a claim convincingly, especially if a writer has earned the trust of readers. In the following excerpt, Christian Zawodniak describes his experiences as a student in a first-year college writing course. Not impressed by his instructor's performance, Zawodniak provides specific evidence of the instructor's failings:

My most vivid memory of Jeff's rigidness was the day he responded to our criticisms of the class. Students were given a chance anonymously to write our biggest criticisms one Monday, and the following Wednesday Jeff responded, staunchly answering all criticisms of his teaching: "Some of you complained that I didn't come to class prepared. It took me five years to learn all this." Then he pointed to the blackboard on which he had written all the concepts we had discussed that quarter. His responses didn't seem genuine or aimed at improving his teaching or helping students to understand him. He thought he was always right. Jeff's position gave him responsibilities that he officially met. But he didn't take responsibility in all the ways he had led us to expect.

–Christian Zawodniak, "Teacher Power, Student Pedagogy"

Zawodniak's portrait of a defensive instructor gives readers details by which to assess the argument. If readers believe Zawodniak, they learn something about teaching. (For more on establishing credibility with readers, see Chapter 6.)

Shifting from personal experience to more distanced observations of people and institutions, writers move into the arena of ethnographic observation, learning what they can from the close study of human behavior and culture. Ethnography is a specific discipline with clearly defined methods of studying phenomena and reporting data, but the instinct to explore and argue from observation is widespread. Notice that instinct in play as English professor Shelby Steele assembles evidence to explain why race relationships on college campuses may be deteriorating:

To look at this mystery, I left my own campus with its burden of familiarity and talked with black and white students at California schools where racial incidents had occurred: Stanford, UCLA, and Berkeley. I spoke with black and white students—not with Asians and Hispanics—because, as always, blacks and whites represent the deepest lines of division, and because I hesitate to wander into the complex territory of other minority groups. A phrase by William H. Gass—"the hidden internality of things"—describes, with maybe a little too much grandeur, what I hoped to find. But it is what I wanted to find, for this is the kind of problem that makes a black person nervous, which is not to say that it doesn't unnerve whites as well. Once every six months or so someone yells "nigger" at me from a passing car. I don't like to think that these solo artists might soon make up a chorus, or worse, that this chorus might one day soon sing to me from the paths of my own campus.

–Shelby Steele, "The Recoloring of Campus Life"

Steele's method of observation also includes a rationale for his study, giving it both credibility and immediacy. Chances are, readers will pay attention to what he discovers. It may be worth noting that personal narratives and ethnographic reports can sometimes reach into the "hidden internality of things" where more scientific approaches cannot inquire so easily or reveal so much.

As you can see, with appropriate caution and suitable qualifications you can offer personal experiences and careful observations as valid forms of argument.

See Sherman Alexie's poem "The Exaggeration of Despair" for a good example of the use of testimony in the genre of poetry.

LINK TO P. 504 ┈┈┈┈┈┈┈┈┈┈┈┈┈┈┈┈┈

REASON AND COMMON SENSE

"Facts are stupid things," Ronald Reagan once misspoke, delighting his critics with what they thought was evidence of his lack of sophistication. But Reagan was right in at least one sense. In and of themselves, facts can be mute. They need to be interpreted. Or, in the absence of reliable facts, claims must be supported with other kinds of reasoning.

The *Washington Times* made precisely such a distinction between facts and reasoning in reporting on an argument raging in Washington, D.C., in September 2002 over whether Osama bin Laden was dead or alive, describing the dilemma in terms Aristotle might have admired (emphasis added): "An increasing number of government analysts believe Osama bin Laden is dead, but *the assessment is based on rational deduction, not hard evidence.*" Because bin Laden's body had not been found and no reliable witnesses had confirmed his death, the paper offered a list of good reasons (rather than cold facts) for believing that the leader of Al Qaeda — not seen in public for months — might, in fact, be deceased:

- *Bin Laden has an enormous ego*, and with it, a need to appear in public. . . . "He has too big an ego to stay quiet this long," said a senior military officer. . . .

- *It is easier to hide bin Laden's death than his life.* . . . If bin Laden were alive, he must be talking to Al Qaeda members at some point, who in turn talk to other followers. Those conversations would surface in communications "chatter" and be picked up by U.S. intelligence. . . .

- *Al Qaeda supporters have put out videotapes of anti-Western speeches by bin Laden, claiming that they are new.* U.S. analysts say all tapes since December [2001] are old. Some surmise that Al Qaeda is putting out phony tapes to cover up bin Laden's death.

Lacking a smoking gun (or, in this case, a cold corpse), government officials were falling back on probabilities and likelihoods, drawing their inferences from the scant knowledge about bin Laden they did have. Yet the process is one we all use when we can't speak with certainty about an issue—and that's the case most of the time. When we argue about matters that are unsettled or unknown, we use reason to give voice to the facts we do possess. In short, evidence and reason work hand in hand.

Logic is the formal study of principles of reasoning, but few people—except perhaps mathematicians and philosophers—present their arguments using formal logic; the extent of what most people know about it is the most famous of all syllogisms (a vehicle of formal deductive logic):

> **All human beings are mortal.**
>
> **Socrates is a human being.**
>
> **Therefore, Socrates is mortal.**

Fortunately, even as gifted a logician as Aristotle recognized that most people could argue very well using informal logic (some might say common sense). Consciously or not, people are constantly stating propositions, drawing inferences, assessing premises and assumptions, and deriving conclusions whenever they read or write. Mostly, we rely on the cultural assumptions and habits of mind we share with readers or listeners.

In the next chapter, we describe a system of informal logic you may find useful in shaping credible arguments—Toulmin argument. Here, we want to examine the way informal logic works in people's daily lives.

Once again, we begin with Aristotle, who used the term *enthymeme* to describe a very ordinary kind of sentence, one that includes both a claim and a reason.

> **Enthymeme = Claim + Reason**

Enthymemes are logical statements that everyone makes almost effortlessly. The following sentences are all enthymemes:

> **We'd better cancel the picnic because it's going to rain.**
>
> **Flat taxes are fair because they treat everyone in the same way.**
>
> **I'll buy a Honda Civic because it's cheap and reliable.**
>
> **Barry Bonds will be in the baseball Hall of Fame because he's already accomplished more than most players already there.**

Enthymemes are persuasive statements when most readers agree with the assumptions within them. Sometimes the statements seem so commonsensical that readers aren't aware of the inferences they are drawing in accepting them. Consider the first example:

> **We'd better cancel the picnic because it's going to rain.**

When a person casually makes such a claim, it's usually based on more specific information, so let's expand the enthymeme a bit to say what the speaker really means:

> **We'd better cancel the picnic this afternoon because the weather bureau is predicting a 70 percent chance of rain for the remainder of the day.**

Embedded in this argument are all sorts of assumptions and bits of cultural information that help make it persuasive, among them:

> **Picnics are ordinarily held outdoors.**

> **When the weather is bad, it's best to cancel picnics.**

> **Rain is bad weather for picnics.**

> **A 70 percent chance of rain means that rain is more likely to occur than not.**

> **When rain is more likely to occur than not, it makes sense to cancel picnics.**

> **The weather bureau's predictions are reliable enough to warrant action.**

You'd sound ridiculous if you drew out all these inferences just to suggest that a picnic should be canceled because of rain. For most people, the original statement carries all this information on its own; it is a compressed argument, based on what audiences know and will accept.

But what if a claim isn't so self-evident? Compare these examples:

> **You'd better stop driving. The oil level in your engine is very low.**

> **You'd better stop driving. The oil level in your engine is very high.**

Most drivers know that not having enough oil in the crankcase of an engine can damage a vehicle, so the first enthymeme doesn't need much explanation or defense. But what happens when a crankcase has too much oil? Is that condition harmful enough to require a driver to do something immediately? Most people don't know whether too much oil can also damage an engine (it can, though not as quickly as too little oil), so you'd have to do some technical backfilling to support the second enthymeme. Otherwise, readers might not understand the assumption on which it is based. But even when readers get the assumption, you may still have to prove that a particular claim is true—for example, that the weather bureau has actually predicted bad weather for the day of the picnic or that the dipstick does in fact show that the oil level is low. In other words, to be persuasive, you have to make reasonable claims based upon assumptions your readers accept and then provide whatever evidence your readers need.

Cultural Assumptions

Some of the assumptions in an argument will be based on culture and history. In the United States, for example, few arguments work better than those based on principles of fairness and equity. Most Americans believe that all people should be treated in the same way, no matter who they are or where they come from. That principle is announced in the Declaration of Independence: all men are created equal.

Because fairness is culturally accepted, in American society enthymemes based on equity ordinarily need less support than those that challenge it. That's why, for example, both sides in debates over affirmative action programs seek the high ground of fairness: Proponents claim that affirmative action is needed to correct enduring inequities from the past; opponents suggest that the preferential policies should be overturned because they cause inequity today. Here's Linda Chavez drawing deeply on the equity principle:

> **Ultimately, entitlements based on their status as "victims" rob Hispanics of real power. The history of American ethnic groups is one of overcoming disadvantage, of competing with those who were already here and proving themselves as competent as any who came before. Their fight was always to be treated the same as other Americans, never to be treated as special, certainly not to turn the temporary disadvantages they suffered into permanent entitlement. Anyone who thinks this fight was easier in the earlier part of this century when it was waged by other ethnic groups does not know history.**
> –Linda Chavez, "Towards a New Politics of Hispanic Assimilation"

Chavez expects Hispanics to accept her claims because she believes they do not wish to be treated differently than other ethnic groups in the society.

Naturally, societies in other times and places have operated from very different premises—they may have privileged a particular race, gender, religion, or even aristocratic birth. Within particular organizations, you

Aisha Khan appeals to our sense of fairness as she argues for equal treatment and understanding as she follows Muslim traditions and rituals.

LINK TO P. 823

may see such powerful assumptions operating. Understanding such core cultural assumptions is a key to making successful arguments.

STRUCTURES FOR ARGUMENTS

Some types of argument seem less tightly bound to particular cultural assumptions. They work on their own to make a plausible case that readers can readily comprehend — even when they don't necessarily agree with it. In the second part of this book we examine in detail some structures of arguments we use almost daily: *arguments of definition, evaluative arguments, causal arguments,* and *proposal arguments.* Although we present them individually, you'll cross boundaries between types of arguments all the time when you make a case on your own. Arguments should be consistent, but they need not follow a single pattern.

In fact, there are many types of logical arguments to draw on — structures that your readers will recognize without the need for much explanation. Arguments about *greater or lesser* are of this type. In the novel *The Fountainhead,* novelist Ayn Rand asks the question: "If physical slavery is repulsive, how much more repulsive is the concept of servility of the spirit?" Most readers understand immediately the point she intends to make about mental slavery because they already appreciate the cruelty of physical slavery. Rand may still have to offer evidence that "servility of the spirit" is, in fact, worse than bodily servitude, but she has begun with a structure readers can understand. This type of argument can be made in many forms and in many circumstances:

- If I can get a ten-year warranty on a humble Hyundai, shouldn't I get the same or better treatment from Mercedes or BMW?

- The widespread benefits to be derived from using human stem cells in research will outweigh the largely theoretical ethical qualms of harvesting the cells from fetuses.

- Better a conventional war now than a nuclear confrontation later.

Analogies offer another structure of argument that people understand intuitively. They usually involve explaining something that is not well known by comparing it to something much more familiar. We reject or accept such analogies, depending on the quality of the comparison. Here, for example, is a controversial analogy that Maryland governor Kathleen Kennedy Townsend used during her campaign, comparing affirmative

See how Charles Mann, in his article "Who Will Own Your Next Good Idea?" sets up a false analogy about a friend's writing being plagiarized in order to frame his argument.

·············LINK TO P. 675

action to other race-based activities. The question, of course, is whether her analogy makes affirmative action seem like the desirable policy she believes it is.

> He [her Republican opponent, Robert Erhlich] opposes affirmative action based on race. Slavery was based on race. Lynching was based on race. Discrimination was based on race. Jim Crow was based on race. Affirmative action should be based on race.
>
> –Kathleen Kennedy Townsend

Townsend demonstrates that analogies can be slippery types of arguments, but they do have power when readers believe that a comparison works. And analogies aren't the only type of argument of similarity. Consider a claim like the following:

> If motorists in most other states can pump their own gas safely, surely the state of New Jersey can trust its own drivers to be as capable. It's time for New Jersey to permit self-service gas stations.

You can probably think of dozens of arguments that follow a similar pattern.

Arguments from precedent are related to arguments of analogy and similarity in that they both involve comparisons. But precedents deal with issues of time: *We did it before; we can do it again.* Cases in court are routinely argued this way. What previous courts have decided often determines how courts will rule on a similar issue. Even parents will use precedents in dealing with their children: *We never let your older sister date while she was in high school, so we're not about to let you go to the prom either.* It is easy to see the appeal in overturning precedents, particularly in a society as fond of rebellious stances as American culture. But there is no denying that you can support a claim effectively by showing that it is consistent with previous policies, actions, or beliefs.

You'll encounter additional kinds of logical structures as you create your own arguments. You'll find some of them in the following chapter on Toulmin argument and still more in Chapter 19, "Fallacies of Argument."

USING LOGICAL ARGUMENTS

Nothing might seem more obvious than to enter an argument by listing all the reasons you can think of both for and against your claim. In some cases you'll be gathering statistics, testimonies, and studies right from the start. And you'll certainly want to put into words—preferably complete sentences — the good reasons people might have for believing you as well as the respectable reasons people might have for dissenting from your view.

When you've done that, you can begin arranging your evidence and thoughts strategically, looking for relationships and sequences. Inevitably, some arguments will seem more persuasive than others. When some of those strong arguments are on the other side of your claim, deal with them honestly. Quite often, you'll want to modify or moderate your own opinions to reflect what you've learned when you open your mind to different points of view. All the while, keep your audience in mind as you shape an argument.

RESPOND•

1. Discuss whether the following statements are examples of hard evidence or rational appeals. Not all cases are clear-cut.

     "The bigger they are, the harder they fall."

     Drunk drivers are involved in more than 50 percent of traffic deaths.

     DNA tests of skin found under the victim's fingernails suggest that the defendant was responsible for the assault.

     Polls suggest that a large majority of Americans favor a constitutional amendment to ban flag burning.

     A psychologist testified that teenage violence could not be blamed on computer games.

     Honey attracts more flies than vinegar.

     Historical precedents demonstrate that cutting tax rates usually increases tax revenues because people work harder when they can keep more of what they earn.

     "We have nothing to fear but fear itself."

     Air bags ought to be removed from vehicles because they can kill young children and small-framed adults.

2. We suggest in this chapter that statistical evidence becomes useful only when responsible authors interpret the data fairly and reasonably. As an exercise, go to the *USA Today* Web site or to the newspaper itself and look for the daily graph, chart, or table called the "*USA Today* snapshot." (On the Web site, you'll have a series of these items to choose from.) Pick a snapshot and use the information in it to support at least three different claims. See if you can get at least two of the

claims to make opposing or very different points. Share your claims with classmates.

We don't mean to suggest that you learn to use data dishonestly, but it is important that you see firsthand how the same statistics can serve a variety of arguments.

3. Testimony can be just as suspect as statistics. For example, movie reviews are often excerpted by advertising copywriters for inclusion in newspaper ads. A reviewer's stinging indictment of a shoot-'em-up film — "This summer's blockbuster will be a great success at the box office; as a piece of filmmaking, though, it is a complete disaster" — could be reduced to "A great success."

    Bring to class a full review of a recent film that you enjoyed. (If you haven't enjoyed any films lately, select a review of one you hated.) Using testimony from that review, write a brief argument to your classmates explaining why they should see that movie (or why they should avoid it). Be sure to use the evidence from the review fairly and reasonably, as support for a claim that you are making.

    Then exchange arguments with a classmate and decide whether the evidence in your peer's argument helps convince you about the movie. What is convincing about the evidence? If it does not convince you, why not?

4. Choose an issue of some consequence, locally or nationally, and then create a series of questions designed to poll public opinion on the issue. But design the questions to evoke a range of responses. See if you can design a reasonable question that would make people strongly inclined to favor or approve an issue, a second question that would lead them to oppose the same proposition just as intensely, a third that tries to be more neutral, and additional questions that provoke different degrees of approval or disapproval. If possible, try out your questions on your classmates.

PART 3

WRITING
arguments

chapter eight

Structuring Arguments

Even if you aren't a political junkie, you've probably tuned in to cable TV talk shows to watch hosts like Bill O'Reilly and Greta Van Susteren on FOX or James Carville and Tucker Carlson on CNN turn discussions of political and social issues into WWE Smackdowns. In the heart of prime time, they duke it out with their guests on matters from war in the Middle East to the cultural sway of Eminem. In these shows argument becomes entertainment, just a bit more civilized than hair-pulling and head-butting. Yet these people do know how to think on their feet. Quick as NBA guards, they offer claims, counterclaims, rebuttals, and apologies in about the time it takes viewers to pop open a can of Coke.

But these highly paid pundits can hardly claim to have invented political debate in the United States. From the earliest days of the American revolution, spirited citizens have been engaged in serious argument about the welfare of the state. You probably remember Tom Paine, the ardent revolutionary who wrote pamphlets to keep the American Revolution alive, his most famous words today probably being those that open *The American Crisis* (1776):

> **THESE are the times that try men's souls. The summer soldier and the sunshine patriot will, in this crisis, shrink from the service of their country; but he that stands it now, deserves the love and thanks of man and woman. Tyranny, like hell, is not easily conquered; yet we have this consolation with us, that the harder the conflict, the more glorious the triumph. What we obtain too cheap, we esteem too lightly.**

Then, just a decade later, Alexander Hamilton shares the nom de plume "Publius" with James Madison and John Jay to produce *The Federalist Papers* (1787–88), a series of influential political pamphlets written to rally support for the proposed new United States Constitution. The pace of Hamilton's eighteenth-century prose in this excerpt may not be to your taste, but read carefully and you'll hear the voice of a skilled writer and politician moving you to think favorably about the new Constitution.

> **Yes, my countrymen, I own to you that, after having given it an attentive consideration, I am clearly of opinion it is your interest to adopt it.**

FIGURE 8.1 BILL O'REILLY

> I am convinced that this is the safest course for your liberty, your dignity, and your happiness. I affect not reserves which I do not feel. I will not amuse you with an appearance of deliberation when I have decided. I frankly acknowledge to you my convictions, and I will freely lay before you the reasons on which they are founded. The consciousness of good intentions disdains ambiguity. I shall not, however, multiply professions on this head. My motives must remain in the depository of my own breast. My arguments will be open to all, and may be judged of by all. They shall at least be offered in a spirit which will not disgrace the cause of truth.
> –Alexander Hamilton, *Federalist No. 1*

As you might guess, Publius had to face crossfire from opponents, who produced pamphlets now collectively know as the *Anti-Federalist Papers*.

Following ratification of that Constitution (1789), the country would spend half a century arguing the monumental issue of slavery, culminating (verbally at least) in the famous Lincoln-Douglas Debates in Illinois (1858). Here is Abraham Lincoln from the first debate with Stephen A. Douglas on August 21, 1858:

> This declared indifference, but, as I must think, covert real zeal for the spread of slavery, I cannot but hate. I hate it because of the monstrous injustice of slavery itself. I hate it because it deprives our republican example of its just influence in the world — enables the enemies of free institutions, with plausibility, to taunt us as hypocrites — causes the real friends of freedom to doubt our sincerity, and especially because it forces so many really good men amongst ourselves into an open war with the very fundamental principles of civil liberty — criticizing the Declaration of Independence, and insisting that there is no right principle of action but self-interest.

All of these examples of argument appear in environments stirring with controversy and political ideas. The participants are engaged with important issues and capable of generating complex and richly developed arguments: *The Federalist Papers* ended up as a series of 85 pamphlets; Lincoln and Douglas talked for hours before large crowds in seven different cities during their famous competition for the Illinois Senate seat. (Douglas won.) Yet contemporary issues are no less complex or important.

We won't pretend that learning how to make (or analyze) an argument is easy. Nor will we offer you any foolproof guidelines for being persuasive because arguments are as complicated and different as the people who make them. Five-step plans for changing minds or scoring big on *The O'Reilly Factor* won't work. But making effective arguments isn't a mystery either. As you'll see shortly, you understand, almost intuitively, most of the basic moves in effective logical arguments. But it helps to give them names and to appreciate how they work. When you can recognize a reasonable claim, you can make one of your own. When you know that claims need to be supported with both sound reasons and reliable evidence, you'll expect to see both in what you read and what you write yourself. You'll also see that all arguments rest on assumptions, some far more controversial than others. And when you do, you'll be prepared to air your differences with some degree of confidence.

TOULMIN ARGUMENT

To look at argument, we'll borrow some of the key terms and strategies introduced by British philosopher Stephen Toulmin in *The Uses of Argument* (1958). Toulmin was looking for a method that accurately described the way people make convincing and reasonable arguments. Because Toulmin argument takes into account the complications in life—all those situations when we have to qualify our thoughts with words such as *sometimes*, *often*, *presumably*, *unless*, and *almost*—his method isn't as airtight as formal logic, that is, the kind that uses syllogisms (see Chapter 7). But for exactly that reason, Toulmin logic has become a powerful and, for the most part, practical tool for shaping argument in the real world.

You'll find Toulmin argument especially helpful as a way to come up with ideas and test them. Moreover, it will help you understand what goes where in many kinds of arguments. The method won't predict the shape of every possible line of reasoning, and it may not help you out in a late-night dorm-room squabble. But then again, it just might—because you'll acquire good critical thinking habits when you think in Toulmin's terms.

Making Claims

In the Toulmin model, arguments begin with claims, which are statements or assertions you hope to prove. With a claim, you stake out a position others will likely find controversial and debatable. Notice that in this model the arguments depend on conditions set by others—your audience or readers. *It's raining* might be an innocent statement of fact in one situation; in another, it might provoke a debate: *No, it's not. That's sleet.* And so an argument begins, involving a question of definition.

FIGURE 8.2 CLAIM

Claim

Claims worth arguing tend to be controversial; there's no point worrying about points on which most people agree. For example, there are assertions in the statements *Twelve inches make a foot* and *Earth is the third planet from the sun*. But except in unusual circumstances, such claims aren't worth much time.

Claims should also be debatable; they can be demonstrated using logic or evidence, the raw material for building arguments. Sometimes the line between what's debatable and what isn't can be thin. You push back your chair from the table in a restaurant and declare, *That was delicious!* A debatable point? Not really. If you thought the meal was appetizing, who can challenge your taste, particularly when your verdict affects no one but yourself?

But now imagine you're a restaurant critic working for the local newspaper, leaning back from the same table and making the same observation. Because of your job, your claim about the restaurant's cannelloni would have different status and wider implications. People's jobs might be at stake. *That was delicious!* suddenly becomes a claim you have to support, bite by bite.

Many writers stumble when it comes to making claims because facing issues squarely takes thought and guts. A claim is your answer to the sometimes-hostile question: *So what's your point?* Some writers would rather ignore the question and avoid taking a stand altogether. But when you make a claim worth writing about, you step slightly apart from the crowd and ask that it notice you.

Is there a danger that you might oversimplify an issue by making too bold a claim? Of course. But making that sweeping claim is a logical first step toward eventually saying something more reasonable and subtle. Here are some fairly simple, undeveloped claims:

The Electoral College has outlived its usefulness.

It's time to lower the drinking age.

NASA should launch a human expedition to Mars.

Vegetarianism is the best choice of diet.

New York City is the true capital of the United States.

Note that these claims are statements, not questions. There's nothing wrong with questions per se; in fact, they're what you ask to reach a claim:

> ***Questions*** What should NASA's next goal be? Should the space agency establish a permanent moon base? Should NASA launch more robotic interstellar probes? Should NASA send people to Mars or Venus?

> ***Statement*** NASA should launch a human expedition to Mars.

Don't mistake one for the other.

Good claims—those that lead toward arguments people want to hear—often spring from personal experience. Almost all of us know enough about something to merit the label *expert*—though we don't always realize it. If you are a typical first-year college student, for example, you're probably an expert about high school. You could make trustworthy claims (or complaints) about a range of consequential issues, from competency testing to the administration of athletic programs. And if you aren't a typical college student, what makes you different—perhaps your experiences at work, in the military, or with a family—should make claims sprout like crabgrass. Whether you are a typical or nontypical college stu-

---

CULTURAL CONTEXTS FOR ARGUMENT

In the United States, many people (especially those in the academic and business worlds) expect a writer to "get to the point" as directly as possible and to articulate that point efficiently and unambiguously. Student writers are typically expected to make their claims explicit, leaving little unspoken. Such claims usually appear early on in an argument, often in the first paragraph. But not all cultures take such an approach. Some prefer that the claim or thesis be introduced subtly and indirectly, expecting that readers "read between the lines" to understand what is being said. Some even save the thesis until the very end of a written argument. Here are a couple of tips that might help you think about how explicitly you should (or should not) make your points:

- What general knowledge does your audience have about your topic? What information do they expect or need you to provide?

- Does your audience tend to be very direct, saying explicitly what they mean? Or are they more subtle, less likely to call a spade a spade? Look for cues to determine how much responsibility you have as the writer and how you can most successfully argue your points.

dent, you might also know a lot about music or urban living or retail merchandising, or inequities in government services and so on—all of them fertile ground for authoritative, debatable, and personally relevant claims.

Offering Data and Good Reasons

A claim is a lonely and unpersuasive statement until it is accompanied by some data and good reasons. You can begin developing a claim simply by drawing up a list of reasons to support it or finding evidence that backs up the point. In doing so, you'll likely generate still more claims in need of more support; that's the way arguments work.

FIGURE 8.3 CLAIM, DATA, REASON

Data & Reason(s) ⟶ <u>So</u> Claim

One student writer, for instance, wanted to gather good reasons in support of an assertion that his college campus needed more space for motorcycle parking. He had been doing some research—gathering statistics about parking space allocation, numbers of people using particular parking lots, and numbers of motorcycles registered on campus. Before he went any further with this argument, however, he decided to list the primary reasons he had identified for more motorcycle parking:

- *Personal experience*: At least three times a week for two terms, he had been unable to find a parking space for his bike.
- *Anecdotes*: Several of his best friends told similar stories; one had even sold her bike as a result.
- *Facts*: He had found out that the ratio of car to bike parking spaces was 200 to 1, whereas the ratio of cars to bikes registered on campus was 25 to 1.
- *Authorities*: The campus police chief had indicated in an interview with the college newspaper that she believed a problem existed for students trying to park motorcycles.

On the basis of his preliminary listing of possible reasons in support of the claim, this student decided that his subject was worth still more research. He was on the way to amassing a set of good reasons sufficient to support his claim.

In some arguments you read, claims might be widely separated from the reasons offered to support them. In shaping your own arguments, try putting claims and reasons together early in the writing process to create what Aristotle called *enthymemes*, or arguments in brief. Think of these enthymemes as test cases or even as topic sentences:

> **The Electoral College has outlived its usefulness because it gives undue power to small and mid-sized states in presidential elections.**
>
> **It's time to lower the drinking age because I've been drinking since I was fourteen and it hasn't hurt me.**
>
> **NASA should launch a human expedition to Mars because Americans need a unifying national goal.**
>
> **Vegetarianism is the best choice of diet, the only one that doesn't require the suffering of animals.**

As you can see, attaching a reason to a claim often spells out the major terms of an argument. In rare cases, the full statement is all the argument you'll need:

> **Don't eat that mushroom—it's poisonous.**
>
> **We'd better stop for gas because the gauge has been reading empty for more than thirty miles.**

Justice Antonin Scalia presents a definitional argument to make his claim, in "God's Justice and Ours," that the Constitution is an enduring rather than a living, evolving document.

·· LINK TO P. 816

More often, your work is just beginning when you've put a claim together with its supporting reasons and data. If your readers are capable—and you should always assume they are—they will then begin to question your statement. They might ask whether the reasons and data you are offering really are connected to the claim: *Should the drinking age be changed simply because you've managed to drink since you were fourteen? Should the whole state base its laws on what's worked for you?* They might ask pointed questions about your data: *Exactly how do small states benefit from the Electoral College?* Eventually, you've got to address both issues: quality of assumptions and quality of evidence. The connection between claim and reason(s) is a concern at the next level in Toulmin argument. (For more on enthymemes, see Chapter 7, p. 112.)

Determining Warrants

Crucial to Toulmin argument is appreciating that there must be a logical and persuasive connection between a claim and the reasons and data supporting it. Toulmin calls this connection the *warrant*; it answers the question *How exactly do I get from the claim to the data?* Like the warrant in legal situations (a search warrant, for example), a sound warrant in an argument gives you authority to proceed with your case.

FIGURE 8.4 CLAIM, REASON, WARRANT

It tells readers what your assumptions are—for example, that no states should have undue influence on presidential elections or that what works for you ought to work for them as well. If readers accept your warrant (as they might in the first case), you can then present specific evidence to develop your claim.

FIGURE 8.5 EXAMPLE OF CLAIM, REASON, WARRANT

But if readers dispute your warrant (as they might in the second instance), you'll have to defend it before you can move on to the claim itself.

FIGURE 8.6 EXAMPLE OF CLAIM, REASON, WARRANT

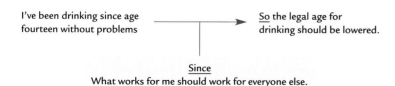

When you state a warrant accurately, you sometimes expose a fatal flaw in an argument.

However, stating warrants can be tricky because they can be phrased in various ways. What you are looking for is the general principle that enables you to justify the move from a reason to a specific claim, the bridge connecting them. The warrant is the assumption that makes the claim seem plausible. It is often a value or principle you share with your readers. Let's demonstrate this logical movement with an easy example.

> **Don't eat that mushroom—it's poisonous.**

The warrant supporting this enthymeme can be stated in several ways, always moving from the reason ("it's poisonous") to the claim ("Don't eat that mushroom"):

> **That which is poisonous shouldn't be eaten.**
>
> **If something is poisonous, it's dangerous to eat.**

Here is the relationship, diagrammed:

FIGURE 8.7 EXAMPLE OF CLAIM, REASON, WARRANT

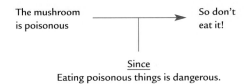

Perfectly obvious, you say? Exactly—and that's why the statement is so convincing. If the mushroom in question is indeed a death angel or toad-stool (and you might still need expert testimony to prove that's what it is), the warrant does the rest of the work, making the claim it supports seem logical and persuasive.

Let's look at a similar example, beginning with the argument in its basic form:

> **We'd better stop for gas because the gauge has been reading empty for more than thirty miles.**

In this case, you have data so clear (a gas gauge reading empty) that the reason for getting gas doesn't even have to be stated: the tank is almost empty. The warrant connecting the data to the claim is also compelling and pretty obvious:

> **If the fuel gauge of a car has been reading empty for more than thirty miles, that car is about to run out of gas.**

Since most readers would accept this warrant as reasonable, they would also likely accept the statement the warrant supports.

Naturally, factual information might undermine the whole argument—the fuel gauge might be broken, or the driver might know from previous experience that the car will go another fifty miles even though the fuel gauge reads empty. But in most cases, readers would accept the warrant.

Let's look at a third easy case, one in which stating the warrant confirms the weakness of an enthymeme that doesn't seem convincing on its own merits:

> **Grades in college should be abolished because I don't like them!**

Moving from stated reason to claim, we see that the warrant is a silly and selfish principle:

> **What I don't like should be abolished.**

Most readers won't accept this assumption as a principle worth applying generally. It would produce a chaotic or arbitrary world, like that of the Queen of Hearts in *Alice in Wonderland*. ("Off with the heads of anyone I don't like!")

So far, so good. But how does understanding warrants make you better at writing arguments? The answer is simple: warrants tell you what arguments you have to make and at what level you have to make them. If your warrant isn't controversial, you can immediately begin to defend your claim. But if your warrant is controversial, you must first defend the warrant—or modify it or look for better assumptions on which to support it. Building an argument on a weak warrant is like building a house on a questionable foundation. Sooner or later, the structure will crack.

Let's consider how stating and then examining a warrant can help you determine the grounds on which you want to make a case. Here's a political enthymeme of a familiar sort:

> **Flat taxes are fairer than progressive taxes because they treat all taxpayers in the same way.**

Warrants that follow from this enthymeme have power because they appeal to a core American value—equal treatment under the law:

Treating people equitably is the American way.

All people should be treated in the same way.

You certainly could make an argument on these grounds. But stating the warrant should also raise a flag if you know anything about tax policy. If the principle is so obvious and universal, why are federal income taxes progressive, requiring people at higher levels of income to pay at higher tax rates than people at lower income levels? Could it be that the warrant isn't as universally popular as it might seem at first glance? To explore the argument further, try stating the contrary argument and warrant:

Progressive taxes are fairer than flat taxes because they tax people according to their ability to pay.

Taxing people according to their ability to pay is the American way.

Now you see how different the assumptions behind opposing positions really are. In a small way, we've stated one basic difference between political right and political left, between Republicans and Democrats. If you decided to argue in favor of flat taxes, you'd be smart to recognize that some members of your audience might have fundamental reservations about your position. Or you might even decide to shift your entire argument. After all, you aren't obligated to argue any particular proposition. So you might explore an alternative rationale for flat taxes:

Flat taxes are preferable to progressive taxes because they simplify the tax code and reduce the likelihood of fraud.

Here you have two stated reasons, supported by two new warrants:

Taxes that simplify the tax code are desirable.

Taxes that reduce the likelihood of fraud are preferable.

As always, you have to choose your warrant knowing your audience, the context of your argument, and your own feelings. Moreover, understanding how to state a warrant and how to assess its potential makes subsequent choices better informed.

Offering Evidence: Backing and Grounds

As you might guess, claims and warrants provide only the skeleton of an argument. The bulk of a writer's work—the richest, most interesting part—still remains to be done after the argument has been outlined. Claims and

Consider Johnny Hart's *B.C.* cartoons, which address matters of faith from a Christian perspective. The warrant underlying these cartoons might be that the teachings of Jesus should be taken to heart.

LINK TO P. 786

warrants clearly stated do suggest the scope of the evidence you have yet to assemble.

An example will illustrate the point. Here's an argument in brief — suitably debatable and controversial, if somewhat abstract:

NASA should launch a human expedition to Mars because Americans need a unifying national goal.

Here's the warrant that supports the enthymeme, at least one version of it:

What unifies the nation ought to be a national priority.

To run with this claim and warrant, a writer needs, first, to place both in context because most points worth arguing have a rich history. Entering an argument can be like walking into a conversation already in progress. In the case of the politics of space exploration, the conversation has been a lively one, debated with varying intensity since the launch in 1957 of the Soviet Union's *Sputnik* satellite (the first man-made object to orbit the earth) and sparked again recently after the *Columbia* disaster. A writer stumbling into this dialogue without a sense of history won't get far. Acquiring background knowledge (through reading, conversation, inquiry of all kinds) is the price you have to pay to write on the subject. Without a minimum amount of information on this — or any comparable subject — all the moves of Toulmin argument won't do you much good. You've got to do the legwork before you're ready to make a case. (See Chapter 6 for more on gaining authority.)

If you want examples of premature argument, just listen to talk radio or C-SPAN phone-ins for a day or two. You'll soon learn that the better callers can hold a conversation with the host or guests, fleshing out their basic claims with facts, personal experience, and evidence. The weaker callers usually offer a claim supported by a morsel of data. Then such callers begin to repeat themselves, as if saying over and over again that "Republicans are starving our children" or "Democrats are scaring our senior citizens" will make the statement true.

If you are going to make a claim about the politics of space exploration, you need to defend both your warrant and your claim with authority, knowledge, and some passion (see Chapters 4–7), beginning with the warrant. Why? Because there is no point defending any claim until you've satisfied readers that any questionable warrants the claim is based on are, in fact, defensible. Evidence you offer to support a warrant is called *backing*.

Warrant

> What unifies the nation ought to be a national priority.

Backing

> On a personal level, Americans want to be part of something bigger than themselves. (Emotional claim)

> A country as regionally, racially, and culturally diverse as the United States of America needs common purposes and values to hold its democratic system together. (Ethical claim)

> In the past, enterprises such as westward expansion, World War II, and the Apollo moon program enabled many—though not all— Americans to work toward common goals. (Logical claim)

Once you are confident that most readers will agree with your warrant, you can move on to demonstrate the truth of your claim. Evidence you offer in support of your claim is sometimes called the *grounds*—the specific data that supports your point. Toulmin himself doesn't make this distinction between backing and grounds in *The Uses of Argument*, but you might find it helpful simply as a reminder that you'll need evidence for every questionable claim you make.

Argument in brief (Enthymeme)

> NASA should launch a human expedition to Mars because Americans need a unifying national goal.

Grounds

> The American people are politically divided along lines of race, ethnicity, religion, gender, and class. (Factual claim)

> A common challenge or problem often unites people to accomplish great things. (Emotional claim)

> Successfully managing a Mars mission would require the cooperation of the entire nation—financially, logistically, and scientifically. (Logical claim)

> A human expedition to Mars would be a valuable scientific project for the nation to pursue. (Logical claim)

Notice that you would likely have to do research to flesh out the backing or grounds, finding out more about the space program than you know now. After all, uninformed opinion doesn't have much status in argument.

Note, too, that you can draw from the full range of argumentative appeals to provide support for your arguments. Appeals to values and emotions might be just as appropriate as appeals to logic and facts, and all such claims will be stronger if a writer presents a convincing ethos. Although one can study such appeals separately, they work together in arguments, reinforcing each other. (See Chapter 6 for more on ethos.)

Finally, understand that arguments can quickly shift downward from an original set of claims and warrants to deeper, more basic claims and reasons. In a philosophy course, for example, you might dig many layers deep to reach what seem to be first principles. In general, however, you need to pursue an argument only as far as your audience demands, always presenting readers with adequate warrants and convincing evidence. There comes a point, as Toulmin himself acknowledges, at which readers have to agree to some basic principles or else the argument becomes pointless.

Miriam Marquez, in "Why and When We Speak Spanish in Public," defends her decision to speak in her native tongue when out in public with her family or Spanish-speaking friends. What's her enthymeme? Her warrant? Her backing and grounds?

LINK TO P. 751 ···

Using Qualifiers

What makes Toulmin's system work so well in the real world is that it acknowledges that *qualifiers*—words and phrases that place limits on claims such as *usually*, *sometimes*, *in many cases*—play an essential role in arguments. By contrast, formal logic requires universal premises: *All men are mortal*, for example. Unfortunately, politics and life don't lend themselves well to many such sturdy truths. If we could argue only about these types of sweeping claims, we'd be silent most of the time.

Toulmin logic, in fact, encourages you to limit your responsibilities in an argument through the effective use of qualifiers. You can save time if you qualify a claim early in the writing process. But you might not figure out how to limit a claim effectively until after you have explored your subject or discussed it with others.

FIGURE 8.8 CLAIM, REASON, WARRANT, QUALIFIER

FIGURE 8.9 EXAMPLE OF CLAIM, REASON, WARRANT, QUALIFIER

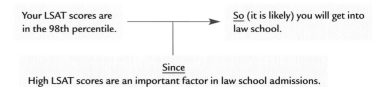

Your LSAT scores are in the 98th percentile. → So (it is likely) you will get into law school.

Since
High LSAT scores are an important factor in law school admissions.

One way to qualify an argument is by spelling out the terms of the claim as precisely as possible. Never assume that readers understand the limits you have in mind. You'll have less work to do as a result, and your argument will seem more reasonable. In the following examples, the first claim in each pair would be much harder to argue convincingly and responsibly—and tougher to research—than the second claim.

> **People who don't go to college earn less than those who do. (Unqualified claim)**
>
> *In most cases,* **people who don't go to college earn less than those who do. (Qualified claim)**

> **Welfare programs should be cut. (Unqualified claim)**
>
> *Ineffective federal* **welfare programs should be** *identified, modified,* **and,** *if necessary, eliminated.* **(Qualified claim)**

Experienced writers cherish qualifying expressions because they make writing more precise and honest.

Check out the effects that Welch Suggs creates in his article about the fairness of cutting men's teams when he uses the phrases "almost everyone," "almost everybody," and "everyone."

LINK TO P. 590

QUALIFIERS

few	it is possible
rarely	it seems
some	it may be
sometimes	more or less
in some cases	many
in the main	routinely
most	one might argue
often	perhaps
under these conditions	possibly
for the most part	if it were so

Notice that the second qualified claim above does not use terms from this list but instead specifies and limits the action proposed.

Understanding Conditions of Rebuttal

There's a fine old book on writing by Robert Graves and Alan Hodges entitled *The Reader over Your Shoulder* (1943), in which the authors advise writers always to imagine a crowd of "prospective readers" hovering over their shoulders, asking questions. At every stage in Toulmin argument—making a claim, offering a reason, or studying a warrant—you might converse with those nosy readers, imagining them as skeptical, demanding, even a bit testy. They may well get on your nerves. But they'll likely help you foresee the objections and reservations real readers will have regarding your arguments.

In the Toulmin system, potential objections to an argument are called *conditions of rebuttal*. Understanding and reacting to these conditions are essential not only to buttress your own claims where they are weak, but also to understand the reasonable objections of people who see the world differently. For example, you may be a big fan of the Public Broadcasting Service (PBS) and the National Endowment for the Arts (NEA) and prefer that federal tax dollars be spent on these programs. So you offer the following claim:

> *Claim*   The federal government should support the arts.

Of course, you need reasons to support this thesis, so you decide to present the issue as a matter of values:

> *Argument in Brief*   The federal government should support the arts because it also supports the military.

Now you've got an enthymeme and can test the warrant, or the premises of your claim:

> *Warrant*   If the federal government can support the military, it can also support other programs.

But the warrant seems frail—something is missing to make a convincing case. Over your shoulder you hear your skeptical friends wondering what wouldn't be fundable according to your very broad principle. They restate your warrant in their own mocking fashion: *Because we pay for a military, we should pay for everything!* You could deal with their objection in the body of your paper, but revising your claim might be a better way to parry the objections. You give it a try:

> *Revised Argument*   If the federal government can spend huge amounts of money on the military, it can afford to spend moderate amounts on arts programs.

Now you've got a new warrant, too:

> **Revised**   **A country that can fund expensive programs can also afford**
> **Warrant**   **less expensive programs.**

This is a premise you feel more able to defend, believing strongly that the arts are just as essential to the well-being of the country as a strong military. (In fact, you believe the arts are more important; but remembering those readers over your shoulder, you decide not to complicate your case by overstating it.) To provide backing for this new and more defensible warrant, you plan to illustrate the huge size of the federal budget and the proportion of it that goes to various programs.

Although the warrant seems solid, you still have to offer strong grounds to support your specific and controversial claim. Once again you cite statistics from reputable sources, this time comparing the federal budgets for the military and the arts; you break them down in ways readers can visualize, demonstrating that much less than a penny of every tax dollar goes to support the arts.

But once more you hear those voices over your shoulder, pointing out that the "common defense" is a federal mandate; the government is constitutionally obligated to support a military. Support for public television or local dance troupes is hardly in the same league. And the nation still has a huge federal debt.

Hmmm. You'd better spend a paragraph explaining all the benefits the arts provide for the very few dollars spent, and maybe you should also suggest that such funding falls under the constitutional mandate to "promote the general welfare." Though not all readers will accept these grounds, they will at least see that you haven't ignored their point of view. You gain credibility and authority by anticipating a reasonable objection.

As you can see, dealing with conditions of rebuttal is a natural part of argument. But it is important to understand rebuttal as more than mere opposition. Anticipating objections broadens your horizons and likely makes you more open to change. One of the best exercises for you or for any writer is to learn to state the views of others in your own favorable words. If you can do that, you're more apt to grasp the warrants at issue and the commonalities you may share with others, despite differences.

Fortunately, today's wired world is making it harder to argue in isolation. Newsgroups and Web logs on the Internet provide quick and potent responses to positions offered by participants in discussions. Email and instant messaging make cross-country connections feel almost like face-to-face conversations. Even the links on Web sites encourage people to

John Leo attacks George Lucas's use of stereotypes in *Star Wars Episode I: The Phantom Menace.* But look for moments when he concedes Lucas's talents or offers other explanations for the apparent stereotypical characters.

·LINK TO P. 496

think of communication as a network, infinitely variable, open to many voices and different perspectives. Within the Toulmin system, conditions of rebuttal—the voices over the shoulder—remind us that we're part of this bigger world. (For more on arguments in electronic environments, see Chapter 16.)

A TOULMIN ANALYSIS

You might wonder how Toulmin's method works when applied to a full-length argument, not just to a few sentences. Do real arguments work the way Toulmin predicts? Such an exercise can be both revealing and a bit embarrassing. Knowledgeable readers often won't agree even on what the core claim in a piece is, let alone its warrants, stated or implied. Yet such an analysis can be rewarding because it can't help but raise basic questions about purpose, structure, quality of evidence, and rhetorical strategy. The following short argument by Alan Dershowitz, a professor of law, provides an interesting opportunity for applying Toulmin's terms and method to a challenging piece. Here, Dershowitz is responding to a proposal by Harvard Law School in late 2002 to impose a speech code on its students.

Testing Speech Codes

ALAN M. DERSHOWITZ

We need not resort to hypothetical cases in testing the limits of a proposed speech code or harassment policy of the kind that some students and faculty members of Harvard Law School are proposing. We are currently experiencing two perfect test cases.

The first involves Harvard's invitation to Tom Paulin to deliver a distinguished lecture for which it is paying him an honorarium. Paulin believes that poetry cannot be separated from politics, and his politics is hateful and bigoted.

He has urged that American Jews who make aliya to the Jewish homeland and move into the ancient Jewish quarters of Jerusalem or Hebron "should be shot dead." He has called these Jews "Nazis" and has expressed "hatred" toward "them." "Them" is many of our students and graduates who currently live on land captured by Israel during the defensive war in 1967 or who plan to move there after graduation.

The Jewish quarters of Jerusalem and Hebron have been populated by Jews since well before the birth of Jesus. The only period in which they were Judenrein was between 1948 and 1967, when it was under Jordanian control, and the Jordanian government destroyed all the synagogues and ethnically cleansed the entire Jewish populations.

Though I (along with a majority of Israelis) oppose the building of Jewish settlements in Arab areas of the West Bank and Gaza, the existence of these settlements—which Israel has offered to end as part of an overall peace—does not justify the murder of those who believe they have a religious right to live in traditional Jewish towns such as Hebron.

Paulin's advocacy of murder of innocent civilians, even if it falls short of incitement, is a paradigm of hate speech. It would certainly make me uncomfortable to sit in a classroom or lecture hall listening to him spew his murderous hatred. Yet I would not want to empower Harvard to censor his speech or include it within a speech code or harassment policy.

Or consider the case of the anti-Semitic poet Amiri Baraka, who claims that "neo-fascist" Israel had advance knowledge of the terrorist attack on the World Trade Center and warned Israelis to stay away. This lie received a standing ovation, according to *The Boston Globe*, from "black students" at Wellesley last week. Baraka had been invited to deliver his hate speech by Nubian, a black student organization, and [was] paid an honorarium with funds provided by several black organizations. Would those who are advocating restrictions on speech include these hateful and offensive lies in their prohibitions? If not, would they seek to distinguish them from other words that should be prohibited?

These are fair questions that need to be answered before anyone goes further down the dangerous road to selective censorship based on perceived offensiveness. Clever people can always come up with distinctions that put their cases on the permitted side of the line and other people's cases on the prohibited side of the line.

For example, Paulin's and Baraka's speeches were political, whereas the use of the "N-word" is simply racist. But much of what generated controversy at Harvard Law School last spring can also be deemed political. After all, racism is a political issue, and the attitudes of bigots toward a particular race is a political issue. Paulin's and Baraka's poetry purports to be "art," but the "N-word" and other equally offensive expressions can also be dressed up as art.

The real problem is that offensiveness is often in the eyes and experiences of the beholder. To many African Americans, there is nothing more offensive than the "N-word." To many Jews, there is nothing more offensive than comparing Jews to Nazis. (Ever notice that bigots never compare Sharon to Pinochet, Mussolini, or even Stalin, only to Hitler!)

It would be wrong for a great university to get into the business of comparing historic grievances or experiences. If speech that is deeply offensive to many African Americans is prohibited, then speech that is deeply offensive to many Jews, gays, women, Asians, Muslims, Christians, atheists, etc. must also be prohibited. Result-oriented distinctions will not suffice in an area so dominated by passion and historical experience.

Unless Paulin's and Baraka's statements were to be banned at Harvard—which they should not be—we should stay out of the business of trying to pick and choose among types and degrees of offensive, harassing, or discriminatory speech. Nor can we remain silent in the face of such hate speech. Every decent person should go out of his or her way to condemn what Tom Paulin and Amiri Baraka have said, just as we should condemn racist statements made last spring at Harvard Law School.

The proper response to offensive speech is to criticize and answer it, not to censor it.

Analysis

Dershowitz uses an inverted structure for his argument, beginning with his evidence—two extended examples—and then extracting lessons from it. Indeed, his basic claim occurs, arguably, in the final sentence of the piece, and it is supported by three major reasons—although the third reason might be seen as an extension of the second:

The proper response to offensive speech is to criticize and answer it, not to censor it [because]

- **Clever people can always come up with distinctions that put their cases on the permitted side of the line and other people's cases on the prohibited side of the line.**

- **It would be wrong for a great university to get into the business of comparing historic grievances or experiences.**

- **[W]e should stay out of the business of trying to pick and choose among types and degrees of offensive, harassing, or discriminatory speech.**

Dershowitz opens the essay by focusing on two lengthy examples that provide evidence or data for the arguments he offers near the end of the essay. As Dershowitz presents them, the cases of Tom Paulin and Amiri Baraka suggest that smart people can always find reasons for defending the legitimacy of their offensive speech.

The closest Dershowitz gets to stating a warrant for his argument may be in the following sentence:

> **The real problem is that offensiveness is often in the eyes and experiences of the beholder.**

He doesn't want individuals dictating the limits of free speech because if they did, freedom would likely be restrained by the "eyes and experiences" of specific people and groups, not protected by an absolute and unwavering principle. Dershowitz doesn't actually offer such a warrant, perhaps because he assumes that most readers will understand that protecting free speech is a primary value in American society.

Dershowitz establishes his ethos by making it clear that although he is powerfully offended by the speech of both Paulin and Baraka, he would not censor them—even though Paulin especially says things offensive to him. An implicit claim is that if Dershowitz is willing to allow such hate speech to be experienced on his own campus, surely the university itself should be able to show such tolerance toward its students.

BEYOND TOULMIN

Can all arguments be analyzed according to Toulmin's principles? The honest answer is no, if you expect most writers to express themselves in perfectly sequenced claims or warrants. You might not think of Toulmin's terms yourself as you build arguments. Once you are into your subject, you'll be too eager to make a point to worry about whether you're qualifying a claim or finessing a warrant.

That's not a problem if you appreciate Toulmin argument for what it teaches:

- *Claims should be stated clearly and qualified carefully.* If you expect to find a single claim neatly stated in most arguments in magazines or newspapers, you'll be disappointed. Skilled writers often develop a single point, but to make that point they may run through a complex series of claims. They may open with an anecdote, use the story to raise the issue that concerns them, examine alternative perspectives on the subject, and then make a half-dozen related claims only as they move toward a conclusion. Even so, you can enter an argument through any of its separate claims, examining what they say exactly and studying the connections between them, working backward through the essay if necessary. You have the same freedom to develop your own arguments, as long as you know how to make clear and reasonable claims.

- *Claims should be supported with data and good reasons.* Remember that a Toulmin analysis provides just the framework of an argument. Real arguments are thick with ideas and with many different kinds of evidence. You may not think of photographs or graphs as evidence, but they can serve that purpose. So can stories, even those that go on for many paragraphs or pages. A tale may not look like "data," but if it supports an author's claim, it is. Once you acquire the habit of looking for reasons and data, you will be able to separate real supportive evidence from filler, even in arguments offered by professional writers. When you write arguments, you'll discover that it is far easier to make claims than to back them up.

- *Claims and reasons should be based on assumptions readers will likely accept.* Toulmin's focus on warrants confuses a lot of people, but that's because it forces readers and writers to think about their assumptions—something they would often just as soon skip. It is tough for a writer, particularly in a lengthy argument, to be consistent about warrants. At one point a writer might offer arguments based on warrants that make "free speech" a first principle. But later he might rail against those who contribute too much money to political campaigns, making democracy a higher value than free speech. Because most people read at the surface, they may not detect the discrepancy. Toulmin pushes you to probe into the values that support any argument and to think of those values as belonging to particular audiences. You can't go wrong if you are both thoughtful and aware of your readers when you craft an argument.

- *All parts of an argument need the support of solid evidence.* Arguments come in all shapes and sizes, including massive studies produced by federal departments and full-length articles in scholarly journals. But it's hard to deny that much political and social argument in the most influential media rarely runs more than a few pages, screens, or columns. Thus any writer wanting to make a convincing argument had better know how to find and present the best possible evidence succinctly and powerfully—and often visually.

Alan Dershowitz presents a complete Toulmin argument that the United States should adopt a national ID card program.

LINK TO P. 556

- *Effective arguments anticipate objections readers might offer.* Argument seems more partisan than ever today. In fact, the term *spin* describes a kind of political advocacy that makes any fact or event, however unfavorable, serve a politician's purpose. Yet there's still plenty of respect for people who can make a powerful, even passionate case for what they believe without dismissing the objections of others as absurd or idiotic. They are also willing to admit the limits of their own knowledge. Toulmin argument appreciates that any claim can crumble under certain conditions, so it encourages a complex view of argument, one that doesn't demand absolute or unqualified positions. It is a principle that works for many kinds of successful and responsible arguments.

It takes considerable experience to write arguments that meet all these conditions. Using Toulmin's framework brings them into play automatically; if you learn it well enough, constructing good arguments can become a habit.

CULTURAL CONTEXTS FOR ARGUMENT

As you think about how to organize your writing, remember that cultural factors are at work: the patterns that you find satisfying and persuasive are probably ones that are deeply embedded in your culture. The organizational patterns favored by U.S. engineers in their writing, for example, hold many similarities to the system recommended by Cicero some two thousand years ago. It is a highly explicit pattern, leaving little or nothing unexplained: introduction and thesis, background, overview of the parts that follow, evidence, other viewpoints, and conclusion. If a piece of writing follows this pattern, Anglo-American readers ordinarily find it "well organized."

In contrast, writers who are accustomed to different organizational patterns may not. Those accustomed to writing that is more elaborate or that sometimes digresses from the main point may find the U.S. engineers' writing overly simple, even childish. Those from cultures that value subtlety and indirectness tend to favor patterns of organization that display these values instead.

When arguing across cultures, think about how you can organize material to convey your message effectively. Here are a couple of points to consider:

- Determine when to state your thesis—at the beginning? At the end? Somewhere else? Not at all?

- Consider whether digressions are a good idea, a requirement, or an element that is best avoided.

RESPOND●

1. Following is a claim followed by five possible supporting reasons. State the warrant that would support each of the arguments in brief. Which of the warrants would need to be defended? Which would a college audience likely accept without significant backing?

   > We should amend the Constitution to abolish the Electoral College
   >
   > —because a true democracy is based on the popular vote, not the votes of the usually unknown electors.
   >
   > —because under the Electoral College system the votes of people who have minority opinions in some states end up not counting.
   >
   > —because then Al Gore would have won the 2000 election.
   >
   > —because the Electoral College is an outdated relic of an age when the political leaders didn't trust the people.
   >
   > —because the Electoral College skews power toward small and mid-size states for no good reason.

2. Claims aren't always easy to find—sometimes they are buried deep within an argument, and sometimes they are not present at all. An important skill in reading and writing arguments is the ability to identify claims, even when they are not obvious.

   Collect a sample of eight to ten letters to the editor of a daily newspaper (or a similar number of argumentative postings from a political Web log). Read each item and try to reduce it to a single sentence, beginning with "I believe that . . ."—this should represent the simplest version of the writer's claim. When you have compiled your list of claims, look carefully at the words the writer or writers use when stating their positions. Is there a common vocabulary? Can you find words or phrases that signal an impending claim? Which of these seem most effective? Which seem least effective? Why?

3. At their simplest, warrants can be stated as *X is good* or *X is bad*. Consider the example from page 130, *Don't eat that mushroom—it's poisonous*. In this case, the warrant could be reduced to *Poison is bad*. Of course, this is an oversimplification, but it may help you to see how warrants are based in shared judgments of value. If the audience members agree that poison is bad (as they are likely to do), they will accept the connection the writer makes between the claim and the reason.

   As you might expect, warrants are often hard to find, relying as they do on unstated assumptions about value. Return to the letters to the editor or Web log postings that you analyzed in exercise 2, this time looking for the warrant behind each claim. As a way to start, ask yourself these questions: *If I find myself agreeing with the letter writer, what assumptions about the subject matter do I share with the letter writer?*

If I disagree, what assumptions are at the heart of that disagreement? The list of warrants you generate will likely come from these assumptions.

4. Toulmin logic is a useful tool for understanding existing arguments, but it can also help you through the process of inventing your own arguments. As you decide what claim you would like to make, you'll need to consider the warrants, different levels of evidence, conditions of rebuttal, and qualifiers. The argument about federal support for the arts provides a good illustration of the Toulmin system's inventional power. By coming to terms with the conditions of rebuttal, you revised your claim and reconsidered the evidence you'd use.

   Using a paper you are writing for this class—it doesn't matter how far along you are in the process—do a Toulmin analysis of the argument. At first, you may struggle to identify the key elements, and you might not find all the categories easy to fill. When you're done, see which elements of the Toulmin scheme are represented. Are you short of evidence to support the warrant? Have you considered the conditions of rebuttal?

   Next, write a brief revision plan: How will you buttress the argument in the places where your writing is weakest? What additional evidence will you offer for the warrant? How can you qualify your claim to meet the conditions of rebuttal? Having a clearer sense of the logical structure of your argument will help you revise more efficiently.

   It might be instructive to show your paper to a classmate and have him or her do a Toulmin analysis, too. A new reader will probably see your argument in a very different way than you do and suggest revisions that may not have occurred to you.

5. You can find transcripts of TV talk/news programs at CNN.com, MSNBC.com, and FOXNews.com. Locate one such transcript (you may have to look under the site for a particular program), and then find a segment where several guests discuss one particular issue—perhaps between commercials. Do a Toulmin analysis of the section, trying to identify as many specific claims, reasons or data, warrants, evidence, and qualifiers as possible. Note in particular how often—or more likely, how rarely—you find a fully developed argument in one of these segments. What might the transcript suggest about the differences between oral and written arguments?

chapter nine

Arguments of Definition

A traffic committee must define what a small car is in order to enforce parking restrictions in a campus lot where certain spaces are marked "Small Car Only!" Owners of compact luxury vehicles, light trucks, and motorcycles have complained that their vehicles are being unfairly ticketed.

A panel of judges must decide whether computer-enhanced images will be eligible in a contest for landscape photography. At what point is an electronically manipulated image no longer a photograph?

A scholarship committee must decide whether the daughter of two European American diplomats, born while her parents were assigned to the U.S. embassy in Nigeria, will be eligible to apply for grants designated specifically for "African American students." The student claims that excluding her from consideration would constitute discrimination.

A priest chastises some members of his congregation for being "cafeteria Catholics" who pick and choose which parts of Catholic doctrine they will accept and follow. A member of that congregation responds to the priest in a letter explaining her view of what a "true Catholic" is.

A young man hears a classmate describe hunting as a "blood sport." He disagrees and argues that hunting for sport has little in common with "genuine blood sports" such as cock fighting.

A committee of the student union is accused of bias by a conservative student group, which claims that the committee has brought a disproportionate share of left-wing speakers to campus. The committee defends its program by challenging the definition of "left wing" used to classify its speakers.

■ ■ ■

UNDERSTANDING ARGUMENTS OF DEFINITION

Vandalism happens all the time. It's no big deal when someone spray paints a slogan on a billboard. Or is it? On November 29, 2002, <Instapundit .com>, a Web log (or blog) run by University of Tennessee professor of law Glenn Reynolds, posted an image of a defaced billboard in St. Paul congratulating Minnesota senator-elect Norm Coleman. Coleman's contest with former vice president Walter Mondale (following the death of the incumbent, Senator Paul Wellstone) had attracted enormous press coverage and significant national attention because much was at stake in the election: Coleman's victory tilted the U.S. Senate from Democratic to Republican control.

On the billboard, someone had painted swastikas on Coleman's forehead and lapel and scrawled "Newest Member of the SS" under the words "Congratulations Senator Norm Coleman." In his Web entry, Reynolds labels this vandalism a *hate crime*. What would move the graffiti into this serious category?

Is it enough that the vandal is implying that Coleman is a Nazi, a diatribe the political Left hurls against conservatives about as often as Republicans brand liberals Socialists? Or is it the more specific charge that Coleman is a member of the SS—Hitler's elite henchmen? If that's a

FIGURE 9.1   A VANDALIZED BILLBOARD IN MINNESOTA BECOMES AN ARGUMENT OF DEFINITION NATIONWIDE WHEN IT ATTRACTS A BLOGGER'S ATTENTION.

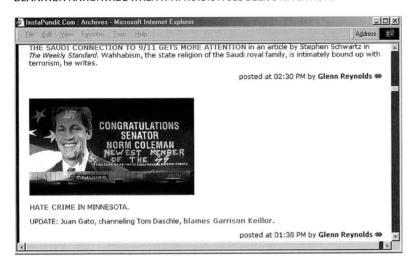

political comment, it clearly crosses the line, but hate crimes usually involve an attack on a person as a member of an ethnic or cultural group. This is where the argument for a hate crime turns: Norman Coleman is a Jew. Blind political rage or malicious vandalism changes to something different when the motive for an attack shifts from the political to the personal. In effect, the act has moved from one category to another and taken on a different name. What you call something matters. That's what arguments of definition are about.

Even in the biblical book of Genesis when Adam names the animals, he gains authority over them because to name things is, partly, to control them. That's why arguments of definition are so important and so very contentious. They can be about the power to say what someone or something is or can be. As such, they can also be arguments that include or exclude: A creature is an endangered species or it isn't; an act is harassment or it isn't; a person is a homicide bomber or, perhaps, a freedom fighter.

Another way of approaching definitional arguments, however, is to think of what comes between is and is *not*. In fact, the most productive definitional arguments probably occur in this murky realm. Consider the controversy over how to define human intelligence. Some might argue that human intelligence is a capacity measured by tests of verbal and mathematical reasoning. In other words, it's defined by IQ and SAT scores. Others might define intelligence as the ability to perform specific practical tasks. Still others might interpret intelligence in emotional terms, as a competence in relating to other people. Any of these positions could be defended reasonably, but perhaps the wisest approach would be to construct a definition of intelligence rich enough to incorporate all three perspectives—and maybe more.

In fact, it's important to realize that many political, social, and scientific definitions are constantly "under construction," reargued and reshaped whenever they need to be updated for the times. Writing for a campus newsletter, Katherine Anundson, for instance, revisits the definition of *eco-terrorism* in light of other world events and enumerates its characteristics: "Eco-terrorism is terrorism, plainly put. It is the moral equivalent to the September 11th attacks: Innocent people are hurt, expenses are incurred, and property is destroyed." Similarly, just a few weeks after the attacks of 9/11, Peter Ferrara, a law professor at George Mason University, thought it was appropriate to refine the meaning of the word *American* in response to a call in Pakistan to kill all people of that nationality. Here are the opening and conclusion of what proved to be an "extended definition" of the term— a lengthy exploration of the many dimensions of the word, some of which people might have not considered earlier:

> You probably missed it in the rush of news last week, but there was actually a report that someone in Pakistan had published in a newspaper there an offer of a reward to anyone who killed an American, any American.
>
> So I just thought I would write to let them know what an American is, so they would know when they found one.
>
> An American is English . . . or French, or Italian, Irish, German, Spanish, Polish, Russian or Greek. An American may also be African, Indian, Chinese, Japanese, Australian, Iranian, Asian, or Arab, or Pakistani, or Afghan.
>
> An American is Christian, or he could be Jewish, or Buddhist, or Muslim. In fact, there are more Muslims in America than in Afghanistan. The only difference is that in America they are free to worship as each of them choose.
>
> An American is also free to believe in no religion. For that he will answer only to God, not to the government, or to armed thugs claiming to speak for the government and for God. . . .
>
> So you can try to kill an American if you must. Hitler did. So did General Tojo and Stalin and Mao Tse-Tung, and every bloodthirsty tyrant in the history of the world. But in doing so you would just be

killing yourself. Because Americans are not a particular people from a particular place. They are the embodiment of the human spirit of freedom. Everyone who holds to that spirit, everywhere, is an American.
–Peter Ferrara, "What Is an American?"

Clearly, Ferrara's definition is in fact an argument in favor of American values and principles. The definition makes an unabashed political point.

In case you are wondering, you usually *can't* resolve important arguments of definition by consulting dictionaries. (Ferrara certainly wouldn't have found any of his definitions of an American in *Webster's*.) Dictionaries themselves just reflect the way particular groups of people used words at a specified time and place. And, like any form of writing, these reference books mirror the prejudices of their makers—as shown, perhaps most famously, in the entries of lexicographer Samuel Johnson (1709–1784), who gave the English language its first great dictionary. Johnson, no friend of the Scots, defined *oats* as "a grain which in England is generally given to horses, but in Scotland supports the people." (To be fair, he also defined *lexicographer* as "a writer of dictionaries, a harmless drudge.") Thus it is quite possible to disagree with dictionary definitions or to regard them merely as starting points for arguments.

KINDS OF DEFINITION

Because there are different kinds of definitions, there are also different ways to make a definition argument. Fortunately, identifying a particular type of definition is less important than appreciating when an issue of definition is at stake. Let's explore some common definitional issues.

Formal Definitions

Formal definitions are what you find in dictionaries. Such definitions involve placing a term in its proper genus and species—that is, first determining the larger class to which it belongs and then identifying the features that distinguish it from other members of that class. That sounds complicated, but a definition will help you see the principle. A minivan might first be identified by placing it among its peers—light trucks. Then the formal definition would go on to identify the features necessary to distinguish minivans from other light trucks—sliding side doors, enclosed luggage area, six- to nine-passenger capacity, family-friendly interior.

People can make arguments from either part of a formal definition, from the genus or the species, so to speak. Does the object or idea really belong to the larger class to which it is traditionally assigned? *Are all minivans really light trucks, or are some of them just gussied-up station wagons?* That's the genus argument. Maybe the object doesn't have all the features required to meet the definition. *Is a Pacifica roomy enough to be a respectable minivan?* That's the species argument.

QUESTIONS RELATED TO GENUS

- What is a minivan?
- Is tobacco a drug or a crop?
- Should hate speech be a criminal offense?
- Is *On the Record with Greta Van Susteren* a news program? A tabloid? Both?

QUESTIONS RELATED TO SPECIES

- Is a Pacifica or an FX45 really a minivan?
- Is tobacco a harmless drug? A dangerously addictive one? Something in between?
- Is using a racial epithet always an instance of hate speech?
- Do tabloids report the news or sensationalize it?

John Rickford's essay "Suite for Ebony *and* Phonics" provides a good example of a definitional argument of species, considering the question of whether Ebonics is a dialect of English.

LINK TO P. 723

Operational Definitions

Operational definitions identify an object not by what it is so much as by what it does or by the conditions that create it: *A line is the shortest distance between two points; Sexual harassment is an unwanted and unsolicited imposition.* You'll get arguments that arise from operational definitions when people debate the conditions that define something and whether these conditions have been met. (See also the discussion of "stasis theory" in Chapter 1, p. 15.)

QUESTIONS RELATED TO CONDITIONS

- Must sexual imposition be both unwanted and unsolicited to be considered harassment?
- Can institutional racism occur in the absence of individual acts of racism?
- Is a volunteer who is paid still a volunteer?
- Does someone who ties the record for home runs in one season deserve the title *Hall of Famer?*

QUESTIONS RELATED TO FULFILLMENT OF CONDITIONS

- Was the act really sexual harassment if the accused believed the interest was mutual?

- Has the institution supported traditions or policies that might lead to racial inequities?

- Was the compensation given to volunteers really "pay" or just "reimbursement" for expenses?

- Has a person actually tied a home-run record if the player has hit the same number of homers in a long season that someone else has hit in a shorter season?

Definitions by Example

Resembling operational definitions are definitions by example, which define a class by listing its individual members. For example, one might define planets by listing all nine major bodies in orbit around the sun, or true American sports cars by naming the Corvette and the Viper.

Arguments of this sort focus on who or what may be included in a list that defines a category: great movies, great presidents, groundbreaking painters. Such arguments often involve comparisons and contrasts with the items most readers would agree from the start belong in this list. One might, for example, wonder why planet status is denied to asteroids, when both planets and asteroids are bodies in orbit around the sun. A comparison between planets and asteroids might suggest that size is one essential feature of the nine recognized planets that asteroids don't meet.

Similarly, you might define great English novelists simply by listing Jane Austen, Emily Brontë, Charlotte Brontë, and Virginia Woolf. Does Iris Murdoch belong in this company? You could argue that she does if she shares the qualities that place the other writers indisputably in this select group.

QUESTIONS RELATED TO MEMBERSHIP IN A NAMED CLASS

- Is any rock artist today in a class with Chuck Berry, Elvis, the Beatles, Madonna, or Aretha Franklin?

- Is the Mustang a Viper-class sports car?

- Who are the Madame Curies or Albert Einsteins of the current generation?

- Does Washington, D.C., deserve the status of a state?

Other Issues of Definition

Many issues of definition cross the line between the types described here and some other forms of argument. For example, if you decided to explore whether banning pornography on the Internet violates First Amendment guarantees of free speech, you'd first have to establish a definition of free speech—either a legal one already settled on by, let's say, the Supreme Court, or another definition closer to your own beliefs. Then you'd have to argue that types of pornography on the Internet are (or are not) in the same class or share (or do not share) the same characteristics as free speech. In doing so, you'd certainly find yourself slipping into an evaluative mode because matters of definition are often also questions of value. (See Chapter 10.)

When exploring or developing an idea, you shouldn't worry about such slippage—it's a natural part of the process of writing. But do try to focus an argument on a central issue or question, and appreciate the fact that any definition you care to defend must be examined honestly and rigorously. Be prepared to explore every issue of definition with an open mind and with an acute sense of what will be persuasive to your readers.

See the second cluster of readings in Chapter 28 for various essays in which the authors present and challenge definitions of "patriotism."

LINK TO P. 826

DEVELOPING A DEFINITIONAL ARGUMENT

Definitional arguments don't just appear out of the blue; they evolve out of the occasions and conversations of daily life, both public and private. You might get into an argument over the definition of "ordinary wear and tear" when you return a rental car with some battered upholstery. Or you might be asked to write a job description for a new position to be created in your office: you have to define the position in a way that doesn't step on anyone else's turf on the job. Or maybe someone in your family has to deal with a government agency trying to define farm property they own as "wetlands." Or someone derides one of your best friends as "just a typical fratboy." In a dozen ways every day, you encounter situations that turn out to be issues of definition. They are so frequent and indispensable that you barely notice them for what they are.

In his essay "Divinity and Pornography," Dennis Prager develops a definitional argument around the invented term *hetero-phobia* in defense of a Harvard dean who was fired for having pornographic images on his office computer.

LINK TO P. 519

Formulating Claims

In addressing matters of definition, you'll likely formulate tentative claims—declarative statements that represent your first response to such situations. Note that these initial claims usually don't follow a single definitional formula.

CLAIMS OF DEFINITION

- A person paid to do public service is not a volunteer.
- Institutional racism can exist—maybe even thrive—in the absence of overt civil rights violations.
- A wetland is just a swamp with powerful friends.
- A municipal fee is often the same darn thing as a tax.
- The District of Columbia has nothing in common with states and ought not to be one.
- It is more accurate to call a suicide bomber a homicide bomber.

None of the claims listed here could stand on its own. Such claims often reflect first impressions and gut reactions. That's because stating a claim of definition is typically a starting point, a moment of bravura that doesn't last much beyond the first serious rebuttal or challenge. Statements of this sort aren't arguments until they're attached to reasons, data, warrants, and evidence. (See Chapter 8.)

Finding good reasons to support a claim of definition usually requires formulating a general definition by which to explore the subject. To be persuasive, the definition must be broad and not tailored to the specific controversy:

- A volunteer is . . .
- Institutional racism is . . .
- A wetland is . . .
- A tax is . . .
- A state is . . .
- A terrorist is . . .

Now consider how the following claims might be expanded with a general definition in order to become full-fledged definitional arguments:

ARGUMENTS OF DEFINITION

- Someone paid to do public service is not a volunteer because volunteers are people who . . .
- Institutional racism can exist even in the absence of overt violations of civil rights because, by definition, institutional racism is . . .
- A swampy parcel of land becomes a federally protected wetland when . . .
- A municipal fee is the same darn thing as a tax. Both fees and taxes are . . .

- Washington, D.C., ought not to be considered eligible for statehood because states all . . . —and the District of Columbia doesn't!
- Someone who straps on a bomb with the intention to kill other people differs from the suicide victim who intends to kill no one but herself.

Notice, too, that some of the issues here involve comparisons between things: swamp/wetland; fees/taxes.

Crafting Definitions

Imagine that you decide to tackle the concept of "paid volunteer" in the following way:

> **Participants in the federal AmeriCorps program are not really volunteers because they are paid for their public service. Volunteers are people who work for a cause without compensation.**

In Toulmin terms, the argument looks like this:

Claim	Participants in AmeriCorps aren't volunteers . . .
Reason	. . . because they are paid for their service.
Warrant	People who are compensated for their services are, ordinarily, employees.

As you can see, the definition of *volunteers* will be crucial to the shape of the argument. In fact, you might think you've settled the matter with this tight little formulation. But now it's time to listen to the readers over your shoulder (see Chapter 8) pushing you further. Do the terms of your definition account for all pertinent cases of volunteerism—in particular, any related to the types of public service AmeriCorps volunteers might be involved in?

Consider, too, the word *cause* in your original statement of the definition:

> **Volunteers are people who work for a cause without compensation.**

Cause has political connotations that you may or may not intend. You'd better clarify what you mean by *cause* when you discuss its definition in your paper. Might a phrase such as "the public good" be a more comprehensive or appropriate substitute for "a cause"?

And then there's the matter of compensation in the second half of your definition:

> **Volunteers are people who work for a cause without compensation.**

Aren't people who volunteer to serve on boards, committees, and commissions sometimes paid, especially for their expenses? What about members of the so-called all-volunteer military? They are financially compensated for their years of service, and they enjoy substantial benefits after they complete their tour of duty.

As you can see, you can't just offer up a definition as part of your argument and assume that readers will understand or accept it. Every part of the definition has to be weighed, critiqued, and defended. That means you'll want to investigate your subject in the library, on the Internet, or in conversation with others. You might then be able to present your definition in a single paragraph, or you may have to spend several pages coming to terms with the complexity of the core issue.

Were you to get involved in an environmental case involving the meaning of *wetlands*, for instance, you might have to examine a range of definitions from any number of sources before arriving at the definition you believe will be acceptable to your readers. Here are just three definitions of wetlands we found on the Internet, suggesting the complexity of the issue:

> In general terms, wetlands are lands where saturation with water is the dominant factor determining the nature of soil development and the types of plant and animal communities living in the soil and on its surface.
>
> –U.S. Fish and Wildlife Service

> WETLANDS are lands transitional between terrestrial and aquatic systems where the water table is usually at or near the surface or the land is covered by shallow water.
>
> –U.S. Fish and Wildlife Service

> [Wetlands are] land where the water table is at, near, or above the land surface long enough to promote the formation of hydric soils or to support the growth of hydrophytes, and shall also include types of wetlands where vegetation is lacking and soil is poorly developed or absent as a result of frequent drastic fluctuations of surface water levels, wave action, water flow, turbidity or high concentration of salts or other substances in the substrate. Such wetlands can be recognized by the presence of surface water or saturated substrate at some [time] during each year and their location within, or adjacent to vegetated wetland or deepwater habitats.
>
> –California Department of Fish and Game

The definitions, taken together, would help you to distinguish the conditions that are *essential* and *sufficient* for defining whether a given plot of land is wetlands. *Essential conditions* are elements that must be part of a definition but that—in themselves—aren't enough to define the term.

What would be sufficient conditions for intellectual property to belong in the public domain? Four pieces in Chapter 26 argue about a court case that will decide whether Martin Luther King Jr.'s "I Have a Dream" speech should belong to the public.

·······································LINK TO PP. 694–99

Clearly, a wetland needs water and land in proximity, but it isn't a sufficient condition since a riverbank or beach might meet that condition without being a wetland.

A *sufficient condition* is any element or conjunction of elements that is enough to define a term. The sufficient condition for wetlands seems to be a combination of land and water sufficient to form a regular (if sometimes temporary) ecological system.

One might add *accidental conditions* to a definition as well—elements that are often associated with a term but are not present in every case or sufficient to identify it. An important accidental feature of wetlands, for example, might be specific forms of plant life or species of birds.

After conducting research of this kind, you might be in a position to write an extended definition well enough informed to explain to your readers what you believe makes a wetland a wetland, a volunteer a volunteer, a tax a tax, and so on. At the end of this chapter, writer Lynn Peril provides just such a definition of the mind-set she claims is imposed on women in this country, what she calls "Pink Think."

Matching Claims to Definitions

Once you've formulated a definition readers will accept—a demanding task in itself—you might need to look at your particular subject to see if it fits that general definition, providing evidence to show that

- it is a clear example of the class defined,
- it falls outside the defined class,
- it falls between two closely related classes,

  or

- it defies existing classes and categories and requires an entirely new definition.

It's possible that you might have to change your original claim at this point if the evidence you've gathered suggests that qualifications are necessary. It is amazing how often seemingly cut-and-dry issues of definition become blurry—and open to compromise and accommodation—when you learn more about them. That has proved to be the case as various campuses across the country have tried to define hate speech or sexual harassment—very tricky matters. And even the Supreme Court has never quite been able to say what "pornography" is. Just when matters seem settled, new legal twists develop. Should virtual child pornography created with software be as illegal as the real thing? Is a virtual image—even a lewd one—an artistic expression protected like other works of art by the First Amendment? That's an issue of definition the Court may have to decide someday soon. (See Chapter 8.)

KEY FEATURES OF DEFINITIONAL ARGUMENTS

In writing an argument of definition of your own, consider that it is likely to include the following parts:

- a claim involving a question of definition
- a general definition of some key concept
- a careful look at your subject in terms of that general definition
- evidence for every part of the argument
- a consideration of alternative views and counterarguments
- a conclusion, drawing out the implications of the argument

It is impossible, however, to predict what emphasis each of those parts might receive or what the ultimate shape of an argument of definition will be.

Whatever form an argument takes, the draft should be shared with others who can examine its claims, evidence, and connections. It is remarkably easy for a writer in isolation to think narrowly—and not to imagine that others might define *volunteer* or *institutional racism* in a completely different way than they do. Thus it is important to keep a mind open to criticism and suggestions. Look very carefully at the terms of any definitions you offer. Do they really help readers distinguish one concept from another? Are the conditions offered sufficient or essential? Have you mistaken accidental features of a concept or object for more important features?

Don't hesitate to look to other sources for comparisons with your definitions. You can't depend on dictionaries to offer the last word about any disputed term, but you can at least begin there. Check the meaning of terms in encyclopedias and other reference works. And search the Web intelligently to find how your key terms are presented there. (In searching for the definition of *wetland*, for example, you could type *wetland definition* into a search engine like Google and get a limited number of useful hits.)

Finally, be prepared for surprises in writing arguments of definition. That's part of the delight in expanding the way you see the world. "You're not a terrier; you're a police dog," exclaims fictional detective Nick Charles after his fox terrier, Asta, helps him solve a case. Such is the power of definition.

Finding a Topic

You are likely entering an argument of definition when you

- formulate a controversial definition: *Discrimination is the act of judging someone on the basis of unchangeable characteristics.*
- challenge a definition: *Judging someone on the basis of unchangeable characteristics is not discrimination.*
- try to determine whether something fits an existing definition: *Affirmative action is/is not discrimination.*

Look for issues of definition in your everyday affairs—for instance, in the way jobs are classified at work; in the way key terms are described in your academic major; in the way politicians characterize the social issues that concern you; in the way you define yourself or others try to define you. Be especially alert to definitional arguments that may arise whenever you or others deploy adjectives such as *true, real, actual,* or *genuine: a true Texan, real environmental degradation, actual budget projections, genuine rap music.*

Researching Your Topic

You can research issues of definition by using the following sources:

- college dictionaries and encyclopedias
- unabridged dictionaries
- specialized reference works and handbooks, such as legal and medical dictionaries
- your textbooks (check their glossaries)
- newsgroups and listservs that focus on particular topics

Be sure to browse in your library reference room. Also, use the search tools of electronic indexes and databases to determine whether or how often controversial phrases or expressions are occurring in influential materials: major online newspapers, journals, and Web sites.

Formulating a Claim

After exploring your subject, begin to formulate a full and specific claim, a thesis that lets readers know where you stand and what issues are at stake. In moving toward this thesis, begin with the following types of questions of definition:

- questions related to genus: *Is assisting in suicide a crime?*

- questions related to species: *Is tobacco a relatively harmless drug or a dangerously addictive one?*

- questions related to conditions: *Must the imposition of sexual attention be both unwanted and unsolicited to be considered sexual harassment?*

- questions related to fulfillment of conditions: *Has our college kept in place traditions or policies that might constitute racial discrimination?*

- questions related to membership in a named class: *Is any rock artist today in a class with Elvis, Dylan, the Beatles, or the Rolling Stones?*

Your thesis should be an actual statement. In one sentence, you need to make a claim of definition and state the reasons that support your claim. In your paper or project itself, you may later decide to separate the claim from the reasons supporting it. But your working thesis should be a fully expressed thought. That means spelling out the details and the qualifications: *Who? What? Where? When? How many? How regularly? How completely?* Don't expect readers to fill in the blanks for you.

Examples of Definitional Claims

- Assisting a gravely ill person to commit suicide should not be considered murder when the motive behind the act is to ease a person's suffering, not to do harm or to benefit from the death.

- Although tobacco is admittedly addictive and ultimately harmful to health, it should not be classified as a dangerous drug because its immediate effects are far less damaging to the individual and society than those of heroin, marijuana, and cocaine.

- Flirting with the waitstaff in a restaurant should be considered sexual harassment when the activity is repeated, obviously offensive, unsolicited, and unappreciated.

- Giving college admission preference to children of alumni is an example of class discrimination because most such policies privilege families that are rich and already advantaged.

Preparing a Proposal

If your instructor asks you to prepare a proposal for your project, here's a format you might use.

State your thesis completely. If you are having trouble doing so, try outlining it in Toulmin terms:

> Claim:
>
> Reason(s):
>
> Warrant(s):

Explain why this argument of definition deserves attention. What is at stake? Why is it important for your readers to consider?

Explain whom you hope to reach through your argument and why this group of readers would be interested in it.

Briefly discuss the key challenges you anticipate in preparing your argument: Defining a key term? Establishing the essential and sufficient elements of your definition? Demonstrating that your subject will meet those conditions?

Determine what strategies you will use in researching your definitional argument. What sources do you expect to consult: Dictionaries? Encyclopedias? Periodicals? The Internet?

Consider what format you expect to use for your project: A conventional research essay? A letter to the editor? A Web page?

Thinking about Organization

Your argument of definition may take various forms, but it is likely to include elements such as the following:

- a claim involving a matter of definition: *Pluto ought not to be considered a genuine planet.*

- an attempt to establish a definition of a key term: *A genuine planet must be a body in orbit around the sun, spherical (not a rock fragment), large enough to sustain an atmosphere, and . . .*

- an explanation or defense of the terms of the definition: *A planet has to be large enough to support an atmosphere in order to be distinguished from lesser objects within the solar system . . .*

- an examination of the claim in terms of the definition and all its criteria: *Although Pluto does orbit the sun, it may not in fact be spherical or have sufficient gravity to merit planetary status . . .*

- evidence for every part of the argument: *Evidence from radio telescopes and other detailed observations of Pluto's surface suggest . . . , and so . . .*
- a consideration of alternative views and counterarguments: *It is true, perhaps, that Pluto is large enough to have a gravitational effect on . . .*

Getting and Giving Response

All arguments benefit from the scrutiny of others. Your instructor may assign you to a peer group for the purpose of reading and responding to each other's drafts; if not, make the effort yourself to get some careful response. You can use the following questions to evaluate a draft. If you are evaluating someone else's draft, be sure to illustrate your points with examples. Specific comments are always more helpful than general observations.

The Claim

- Is the claim clearly an issue of definition?
- Is the claim significant enough to interest readers?
- Are clear and specific criteria established for the concept being defined? Do the criteria define the term adequately? Using this definition, could most readers identify what is being defined and distinguish it from other related concepts?

Evidence for the Claim

- Is enough evidence furnished to explain or support the definition? If not, what kind of additional evidence is needed?
- Is the evidence in support of the claim simply announced, or are its significance and appropriateness analyzed? Is a more detailed discussion needed?
- Are all the conditions of the definition met in the concept being examined?
- Are any objections readers might have to the claim, criteria, or evidence, or to the way the definition is formulated, adequately addressed?
- What kinds of sources are cited? How credible and persuasive will they be to readers? What other kinds of sources might be more credible and persuasive?
- Are all quotations introduced with appropriate signal phrases (such as "As Himmelfarb argues,") and blended smoothly into the writer's sentences?

Organization and Style

- How are the parts of the argument organized? Is this organization effective, or would some other structure work better?

- Will readers understand the relationships among the claim, supporting reasons, warrants, and evidence? If not, what could be done to make those connections clearer? Are more transitional words and phrases needed? Would headings or graphic devices help?

- Are the transitions or links from point to point, paragraph to paragraph, and sentence to sentence clear and effective? If not, how could they be improved?

- Is the style suited to the subject? Is it too formal? Too casual? Too technical? Too bland?

- Which sentences seem particularly effective? Which ones seem weakest, and how could they be improved? Should some short sentences be combined, or should any long ones be separated into two or more sentences?

- How effective are the paragraphs? Do any seem too skimpy or too long?

- Which words or phrases seem particularly effective, vivid, and memorable? Do any seem dull, vague, unclear, or inappropriate for the audience or the writer's purpose? Are definitions provided for technical or other terms that readers might not know?

Spelling, Punctuation, Mechanics, Documentation, Format

- Are there any errors in spelling, punctuation, capitalization, and the like?

- Is an appropriate and consistent style of documentation used for parenthetical citations and the list of works cited or references? (See Chapter 22.)

- Does the paper or project follow an appropriate format? Is it appropriately designed and attractively presented? If it is a Web site, do all the links work?

RESPOND•

1. Briefly discuss the criteria you might use to define the italicized terms in the following controversial claims of definition. Compare your definitions of the terms with those of your classmates.

   Burning a nation's flag is a *hate crime*.

   The Bushes have become America's *royal family*.

   Matt Drudge and Larry Flynt are legitimate *journalists*.

   College sports programs have become *big businesses*.

   Plagiarism can be an act of *civil disobedience*.

   Satanism is a *religion* properly protected by the First Amendment.

   Wine (or beer) is a *health food*.

   Campaign contributions are acts of *free speech*.

   The District of Columbia should have all the privileges of an American *state*.

   Committed gay and lesbian couples should have the legal privileges of *marriage*.

2. This chapter opens with sketches of six rhetorical situations that center on definitional issues. Select one of these situations, and write definitional criteria using the strategy of formal definition. For example, identify the features of a photograph that make it part of a larger class (art, communication method, journalistic technique). Next, identify the features of a photograph that make it distinct from other members of that larger class.

   Then use the strategy of operational definition to establish criteria for the same object: What does it do? Remember to ask questions related to conditions (*Is a computer-scanned photograph still a photograph?*) and questions related to fulfillment of conditions (*Does a good photocopy of a photograph achieve the same effect as the photograph itself?*).

3. In an essay at the end of this chapter entitled "Pink Think," Lynn Peril makes a variety of claims about a concept she identifies as *pink think*, which she defines in part as "a set of ideas and attitudes about what constitutes proper female behavior." After reading this selection carefully, consider whether Peril has actually defined a concept that operates today. If you think "pink think" still exists, prove it by showing how some activities, behaviors, products, or institutions meet the definition of the concept. Write, too, about the power this concept has to define behavior.

Alternatively, define a concept of your own that applies to a similar kind of stereotypical behavior—for example, *jock think* or *frat think* or *theater think* or *geek think*. Then argue that your newly defined concept does, in fact, influence people today. Be sure to provide clear and compelling examples of the concept in action as it shapes the way people act, think, and behave.

TWO SAMPLE ARGUMENTS OF DEFINITION

Creating a Criminal

....

MICHAEL KINGSTON

In reaction to the Vietnamese American practice of raising canines for food, Section 598b of the California Penal Code was recently amended to read as follows:

> (a) Every person is guilty of a misdemeanor who possesses, imports into this state, sells, buys, gives away, or accepts any carcass or part of any carcass of any animal traditionally or commonly kept as a pet or companion with the sole intent of using or having another person use any part of that carcass for food.

The California Penal Code defines what actions constitute a misdemeanor.

> (b) Every person is guilty of a misdemeanor who possesses, imports into this state, sells, buys, gives away, or accepts any animal traditionally or commonly kept as a pet or companion with the sole intent of killing or having another person kill that animal for the purpose of using or having another person use any part of the animal for food.

This is a fascinating new law, one that brings up a complex set of moral, political, and social questions. For example: What constitutes a "pet"? Do pets have special "rights" that other animals aren't entitled to? How should these "rights" be balanced with the real political rights of the human populace? How do we define the civil rights of an ethnic minority whose actions reflect cultural values that are at odds with those of the majority? Section 598b does not mention these issues. Rather, it seems to simply walk around them, leaving us to figure out for ourselves whose interests (if any) are being served by this strange new law.

All the questions Kingston raises here arise from an issue of definition: What is a pet?

Michael Kingston wrote "Creating a Criminal" while he was a student at the University of California, Riverside. Kingston argues that a law banning the consumption of animals regarded as pets targets specific immigrant groups. Key to the argument are definitions of *pet* and *racial discrimination*.

The first thing one might wonder is whether the purpose of Section 598b is to improve the lot of pets throughout California. What we do know is that it seeks to prevent people from eating animals traditionally regarded as pets (dogs and cats). But for the most part, the only people who eat dogs or cats are Vietnamese Americans. Furthermore, they don't consider these animals "pets" at all. So, pets aren't really being protected. Maybe Section 598b means to say (in a roundabout manner) that *all* dogs and cats are special and therefore deserve protection. Yet, it doesn't protect them from being "put to sleep" in government facilities by owners who are no longer willing to have them. Nor does it protect them from being subjected to painful, lethal experiments designed to make cosmetics safe for human use. Nor does it protect them from unscrupulous veterinarians who sometimes keep one or two on hand to supply blood for anemic pets of paying customers. No, the new law simply prevents Vietnamese Americans from using them as food.

Kingston compares the ostensible purpose of the new statutes with what he regards as their real purpose.

Is the consumption of dogs or cats so horrible that it merits its own law? One possible answer is that these practices pose a special threat to the trust that the pet-trading network relies upon. Or in other words: that strange man who buys one or more of your puppies might just be one of those dog-eaters. But this scenario just doesn't square with reality. A Vietnamese American, canine-eating family is no more a threat to the pet-trading industry than is a family of European heritage that chooses to raise rabbits (another popular pet) for its food. Predictably, there is a loophole in Section 598b that allows for the continued eating of pet rabbits. Its circular logic exempts from the new law any animal that is part of an *established* agricultural industry.

The case for prejudice can be built on a loophole in the law's definition of pet — *one that favors the culinary habits of the European American majority.*

It seems as though Vietnamese Americans are the only ones who can't eat what they want, and so it is hard not to think of the issue in terms of racial discrimination. And why shouldn't we? After all, the Vietnamese community in California has long been subjected to bigotry. Isn't it conceivable that latent xenophobia and racism have found their way into the issue of dog-eating? One needs only to look at the law itself for the answer. This law protects animals "traditionally . . . kept as a pet." Whose traditions? Certainly not the Vietnamese's.

The meaning of traditions now becomes a key issue.

Of course, the typical defense for racially discriminatory laws such as this one is that they actually protect minorities by forcing assimilation. The reasoning here is that everything will run much smoother if we can all just manage to fall in step with the dominant culture. This argument has big problems. First, it is morally bankrupt. How does robbing a culture of its uniqueness constitute a protection? Second, it doesn't defuse racial tensions at all. Racists will always find reasons for hating the Vietnamese. Finally, any policy that seeks to label minorities as the cause of the violence leveled against them is inherently racist itself.

A counterargument is considered and refuted.

Whatever the motives behind Section 598b, the consequences of the new law are all too clear. The government, not content with policing personal sexual behavior, has taken a large step toward dictating what a person can or cannot eat. This is no small infringement. I may never have the desire to eat a dog, but I'm rankled that the choice is no longer mine, and that the choice was made in a climate of racial intolerance. Whatever happened to the right to life, liberty, and the pursuit of happiness?

In this paragraph, Kingston draws on emotional and ethical appeals.

Unfortunately, we may suffer more than just a reduction in personal choice. Crimes such as dog-eating require a certain amount of vigilance to detect. More than likely, the police will rely upon such dubious measures as sifting through garbage left at curbside, or soliciting anonymous tips. Laws that regulate private behavior, after all, carry with them a reduction in privacy.

The threat the new law poses to privacy rights adds an emotional kick to the conclusion.

We sure are giving up a lot for this new law. It's sad that we receive only more criminals in return.

Pink Think

LYNN PERIL

From the moment she's wrapped in a pink blanket, long past the traumatic birthday when she realizes her age is greater than her bust measurement, the human female is bombarded with advice on how to wield those feminine wiles. This advice ranges from rather vague proscriptions along the lines of "nice girls don't chew gum/swear/wear pants/fill-in-the-blank," to obsessively elaborate instructions for daily living. How many women's lives, for example, were enriched by former Miss America Jacque Mercer's positively baroque description of the proper way to put on a bathing suit, as it appeared in her guide *How to Win a Beauty Contest* (1960)?

> [F]irst, roll it as you would a girdle. Pull the suit over the hips to the waist, then, holding the top away from your body, bend over from the waist. Ease the suit up to the bustline and with one hand, life one breast up and in and ease the suit bra over it. Repeat on the other side. Stand up and fasten the straps.

Instructions like these made me bristle. I formed an early aversion to all things pink and girly. It didn't take me long to figure out that many things young girls were supposed to enjoy, not to mention ways they were supposed to behave, left me feeling funny—as if I was expected to pound my square peg self into the round hold of designated girliness. I didn't know it at the time, but the butterflies in my tummy meant I had crested the first of many hills on the roller coaster ride of femininity—or, as I soon referred to it, the other f-word. Before I knew what was happening, I was hurtling down its track, seemingly out of control, and screaming at the top of my lungs.

After all, look what I was up against. The following factoids of femininity date from the year of my birth (hey, it wasn't *that* long ago):

- In May of 1961, Betsy Martin McKinney told readers of *Ladies' Home Journal* that, for women, sexual activity commenced with intercourse and was completed with pregnancy and childbirth. Therefore, a woman who used contraceptives denied "her own creativity, her own sexual role, her very femininity." Furthermore, McKinney asserted that "one of the most stimulating predisposers to orgasm in a woman may be childbirth followed by

---

Lynn Peril is the publisher of the 'zine *Mystery Date*. This essay is excerpted from the introduction to *Pink Think*, a book that examines the influence of the feminine ideal.

several months of lactation." (Mmm, yes, must be the combination of episiotomy and sleep deprivation that does it.) Politely avoiding personal examples, she neglected to mention how many little McKinneys there were.

- During the competition for the title of Miss America 1961, five finalists were given two questions to answer. First they were asked what they would do if "you were walking down the runway in the swimsuit competition, and a heel came off one of your shoes?" The second question, however, was a bit more esoteric: "Are American women usurping males in the world, and are they too dominant?" Eighteen-year-old Nancy Fleming, of Montague, Michigan, agreed that "there are too many women working in the world. A woman's place is in the home with her husband and children." This, along with her pragmatic answer to the first question ("I would kick off both shoes and walk barefooted") and her twenty-three-inch waist (tied for the smallest in pageant history), helped Nancy win the crown.

- In 1961, toymaker Transogram introduced a new game for girls called Miss Popularity ("The True American Teen"), in which players competed to see who could accrue the most votes from four pageant judges — three of whom were male. Points were awarded for such attributes as nice legs, and if the judges liked a contestant's figure, voice, and "type." The prize? A special "loving" cup, of course! Who, after all, could love an unpopular girl?

These are all prime examples of "pink think." Pink think is a set of ideas and attitudes about what constitutes proper female behavior; a groupthink that was consciously or not adhered to by advice writers, manufacturers of toys and other consumer products, experts in many walks of life, and the public at large, particularly during the years spanning the mid-twentieth century — but enduring even into the twenty-first century. Pink think assumes there is a standard of behavior to which all women, no matter their age, race, or body type, must aspire. "Femininity" is sometimes used as a code word for this mythical standard, which suggests that women and girls are always gentle, soft, delicate, nurturing beings made of "sugar and spice and everything nice." But pink think is more than a stereotyped vision of girls and women as poor drivers who are afraid of mice and snakes, adore babies and small dogs, talk incessantly on the phone, and are incapable of keeping secrets. Integral to pink think is the belief that one's success as a woman is grounded in one's allegiance to such behavior. For example, a woman who fears mice isn't necessarily following the dictates of pink think. On the other hand, a woman who isn't afraid of mice but pretends to be because she thinks such helplessness adds to her appearance of femininity is toeing the pink think party line. When you hear the words "charm" or "personality" in the context of successful womanhood, you can almost always be sure you're in the presence of pink think.

While various self-styled "experts" have been advising women on their "proper" conduct since the invention of the printing press, the phenomenon defined here as pink think was particularly pervasive from the 1940s to the 1970s. These were fertile years for pink think, a cultural mindset and consumer behavior rooted in New Deal prosperity yet culminating with the birth of women's liberation. During this time, pink think permeated popular books and magazines aimed at adult women, while little girls absorbed rules of feminine behavior while playing games like the aforementioned Miss Popularity. Meanwhile, prescriptions for ladylike dress, deportment, and mindset seeped into child-rearing manuals, high school home economics textbooks, and guides for bride, homemaker, and career girl alike.

It was almost as if the men and women who wrote such books viewed proper feminine behavior as a panacea for the ills of a rapidly changing modern world. For example, myriad articles in the popular press devoted to the joys of housewifery helped coerce Rosie the Riveter back into the kitchen when her hubby came home from the war and expected his factory job back. During the early cold war years, some home economics texts seemed to suggest that knowing how to make hospital corners and a good tuna casserole were the only things between Our Way of Life and communist incursion. It was patriotic to be an exemplary housewife. And pink-thinking experts of the sixties and seventies, trying to maintain this ideal, churned out reams of pages that countered the onrushing tide of both the sexual revolution and the women's movement. If only all women behaved like our Ideal Woman, the experts seemed to say through the years, then everything would be fine.

You might even say that the "problem with no name" that Betty Friedan wrote about in *The Feminine Mystique* (1963) was a virulent strain of pink-thinkitis. After all, according to Friedan, "the problem" was in part engendered by the experts' insistence that women "could desire no greater destiny than to glory in their own femininity"—a pink think credo.

The pink think of the 1940s to 1970s held that femininity was necessary for catching and marrying a man, which was in turn a prerequisite for childbearing—the ultimate feminine fulfillment. This resulted in little girls playing games like Mystery Date long before they were ever interested in boys. It made home economics a high school course and college major, and suggested a teen girl's focus should be on dating and getting a boyfriend. It made beauty, charm, and submissive behavior of mandatory importance to women of all ages in order to win a man's attention and hold his interest after marriage. It promoted motherhood and housewifery as women's only meaningful career, and made sure that women who worked outside the home brought "feminine charm" to their workplaces lest a career make them too masculine.

Not that pink think resides exclusively alongside antimacassars and 14.4 modems in the graveyard of outdated popular culture: Shoes, clothing, and movie stars may go in and out of style with astounding rapidity, but attitudes have an unnerving way of hanging around long after they've outlived their usefulness—even if they never had any use to begin with.

chapter ten

Evaluations

"We don't want to go *there* for Tex-Mex. Their tortillas aren't fresh, their quesadillas are mush, and they get their salsa from New York City!"

After a twenty-two-year stint, the president of a small liberal arts college decides to retire. After the announcement a committee is formed to choose a new leader, with representatives from the faculty, administration, alumni, and student body. The first task the group faces is to describe the character of an effective college president in the twenty-first century.

A senior is frustrated by the "C" he received on an essay written for a history class, so he makes an appointment to talk with the teaching assistant who graded the paper. "Be sure to review the assignment sheet first," she warns.

The student notices that the sheet, on its back side, includes a checklist of requirements for the paper; he hadn't turned it over before.

"We have a lousy home page," a sales representative observes at a district meeting. "What's wrong with it?" the marketing manager asks. "Everything," she replies, then quickly changes the subject when she notices the manager's furrowed brow. But the manager decides to investigate the issue. Who knows what an effective Web site looks like these days.

You've just seen *Citizen Kane* for the first time and want to share the experience with your roommate. Orson Welles's masterpiece is playing at the Student Union for only one more night, but *Die Hard X: The Battery* is featured across the street in THX sound. Guess which movie Bubba wants to see? You intend to set him straight.

■ ■ ■

UNDERSTANDING EVALUATIONS

Kristin Cole has a problem. The holiday break is approaching, she is headed out of town, and she still has not found a pet-sitter for Baldrick, her lovable cockatiel. When her first email appeal to colleagues in a large academic department fails to turn up a volunteer, she tries a second, this one more aggressively singing the praises of her companion:

> Apologies for all duplications, folks! Since nobody's stepped forward to birdsit for me from 15–30 or 31 December, I must repeat my plea.
>
> Please take my bird for this time. I'll pay. If you have other pets, all I ask is that your little darlings can't get at my little darling.
>
> And let me repeat that Baldrick could be the poster child for birds: he's quiet, loves people, and couldn't be happier than to sit on your shoulder while you go about your day. He'll whistle and make kissy noises in your ear, since he's a huge flirt. I must admit that he loves to chew paper and pens, but that's controllable. And he loves feet—that can be positive, negative, or neutral, depending on you.
>
> He is much easier than a cat or dog—no litter boxes, walks, or poop in the yard. And his food smells like candy. He's pretty much allergy-free, and the mess he makes is easily vacuumable with the dustbuster I will lend you. He just needs contact with people and a fair amount of supervised out-of-cage time per day.

Please do let me know if you can help me out. He's a great pet—he converted me, who had always thought a proper pet needed fur and four legs!

–Kristin

In just a few lines, Kristin offers about a half-dozen reasons for birdsitting Baldrick, many of them based on the evaluative claim "he's a great pet." The petition deploys several different lines of argument, including appeals to the heart ("he's a huge flirt"), the head ("I'll pay"), and even values ("he converted me, who had always thought a proper pet needed fur and four legs"). About the only potential device Kristin misses is a visual argument—for example, a photo of Baldrick, which she might have attached to the email easily enough.

Kristin makes Baldrick seem lovable and charming for a reason: to persuade someone to board the cockatiel over the holidays. In this respect her strategy is typical of many arguments of evaluation. They are written to clarify or support other decisions in our lives: what to read, whom to hire, what to buy, which movies to see, for whom to vote. (In case you are wondering, Kristin's email worked.)

Evaluations are everyday arguments. By the time you leave home in the morning, you've likely made a dozen informal evaluations. You've selected dressy clothes because you have a job interview in the afternoon with a law firm; you've chosen low-fat yogurt and shredded wheat over artery-clogging eggs and bacon; you've clicked the remote past cheery

FIGURE 10.1 BALDRICK—THE POSTER CHILD FOR BIRDS

Katie Couric for what you consider more adult programming on C-SPAN. In each case, you've applied criteria to a particular problem and then made a decision.

Some professional evaluations require much more elaborate standards, evidence, and paperwork (imagine what an aircraft manufacturer has to do to certify a new jet for passenger service), but such work doesn't differ structurally from the simpler choices that people make routinely. And, of course, people do love to voice their opinions, and always have: a whole mode of ancient rhetoric—called the ceremonial, or epideictic— was devoted entirely to speeches of praise and blame. (See Chapter 1.)

Today, rituals of praise and blame are part of American life. Adults who'd choke at the very notion of debating causal or definitional claims will happily spend hours appraising the Miami Hurricanes or the Fighting Irish. Other evaluative spectacles in our culture include awards shows, beauty pageants, most-valuable-player presentations, lists of best-dressed or worst-dressed celebrities, "sexiest people" magazine covers, literary prizes, political opinion polls, consumer product magazines, and—the ultimate formal public gesture of evaluation—elections. Indeed, making evaluations is a form of entertainment in America—one that generates big audiences (think of *American Idol*) and revenues.

FIGURE 10.2 *PEOPLE* DEDICATES AN ISSUE EVERY YEAR TO CHOOSING THE SEXIEST MAN. CRITERION? THE WINNERS ARE ALMOST ALWAYS ACTORS.

CRITERIA OF EVALUATION

Whether arguments of evaluation produce simple rankings and winners or lead to more profound decisions about our lives, they involve standards. The particular standards we establish for judging anything—whether an idea, a work of art, a person, or a product—are called *criteria of evaluation*. Sometimes criteria are pretty self-evident. You probably know that a truck that gets ten miles per gallon is a gas hog or that a steak that's charred and rubbery should be returned. But criteria are often more complex when a potential subject is more abstract. *What makes a politician or a teacher effective? What features make a film a classic? How do we measure a successful foreign policy or college education?* Struggling to identify such difficult criteria of evaluation can lead to important insights into your values, motives, and preferences.

Why make such a big deal about criteria when many acts of evaluation seem almost effortless? Because we should be most suspicious of our judgments precisely when we start making them carelessly. It's a cop-out simply to think that everyone is entitled to an opinion, however stupid and uninformed it might be. Evaluations always require reflection. And when we look deeply into our judgments, we sometimes discover important "why" questions that typically go unasked:

- You may find yourself willing to challenge the grade you received in a course, but not the practice of grading itself.

- You argue that Miss Alabama would have been a better Miss America than the contestant from New York, but perhaps you don't wonder loudly enough whether such competitions make sense at all.

- You argue passionately that a Republican Congress is better for America than a Democratic alternative, but you fail to ask why voters get only two choices.

- You can't believe people take Britney Spears seriously as a singer, but you never consider what her impact on young girls might be.

Push an argument of evaluation hard enough, and even simple judgments become challenging and intriguing.

In fact, for many writers, grappling with criteria is the toughest step in producing an evaluation. They've got an opinion about a movie or book or city policy, but they also think that their point is self-evident and widely shared by others. So they don't do the work they need to do to specify the criteria for their judgments. If you know a subject well enough to evaluate

When is reality no longer reality? When it's Reality TV. Caryn James argues that the plastic surgery reality television show "Extreme Makeover" crosses the lines of both reality and good taste, while offering a frightening insight into contemporary American perceptions of beauty.

LINK TO P. 480

it, your readers should learn something from you when you offer an opinion. Do you think, for instance, that you know what makes a grilled hamburger good? The following criteria offered on the *Cooks Illustrated* Web site will probably make you more thoughtful the next time you maul a Big Mac:

> I'll admit it: I have, at times, considered becoming a vegetarian. I could give up steaks and pork chops and leg of lamb, but when I bite into a juicy grilled hamburger with all the trimmings, I'm back with the carnivores.
>
> I'm not talking about one of those pasty, gray "billions served" or "have it your way" specimens. And I'm not talking about the typical backyard barbecue burger, either. You know the one I mean, because we've all made them. This burger is tough, chewy, and dry, and, after one flip with a spatula, more of its crust—if it formed one at all—sticks to the grill than to the patty. And of course there's the shape—domed, puffy, and round enough to let all the condiments slide right off. The ideal grilled burger, however, is altogether different: moist and juicy, with a texture that's tender and cohesive, not dense and heavy. Just as important, it's got a flavorful, deeply caramelized, reddish brown crust that sticks to the meat, and a flat shape to hold the goodies.
> —Adam Ried and Julia Collin, "Grilling Great Hamburgers"

We've all eaten burgers, but have we thought about them this much? If we intend to evaluate them convincingly, we'd better. It's not enough to claim merely that a good burger is juicy or tasty. It's also not very interesting.

Criteria of evaluation aren't static either. They will differ according to time and audience. Much market research, for example, is designed to find out what particular consumers want now and in the future—what their criteria for buying a product are. Consider what the researchers at Honda discovered when they asked Y-generation men—a targeted demographic of consumers who generally don't consider Honda products—what they wanted in a new car. The answer, reported in the *New York Times*, was surprising:

> The Honda group found that young adults wanted a basic, no-nonsense vehicle with lots of space—and they didn't seem to care much about the exterior style. "We found that vehicles, in this generation, were not the top priority," Mr. Benner said. "They're the means, not the end. The car is a tool." . . .
>
> What distinguishes younger buyers, all car companies seem to agree, is that they don't seem to care as much about cars as young people used to—putting more stock in the style of their cellphones or P.D.A.'s than in the style of what they drive.
> —Phil Patton, "Young Man, Would You Like That in a Box?"

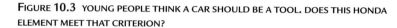

FIGURE 10.3 YOUNG PEOPLE THINK A CAR SHOULD BE A TOOL. DOES THIS HONDA ELEMENT MEET THAT CRITERION?

Such an evaluation of criteria actually led Honda to build the Element, a boxy—some would say homely—truck with swing-out side doors and an easily reconfigurable interior designed to be a "place" more than a vehicle. Its success would depend on how well the designers understood the values of their target audience and how well their vehicle met those criteria.

CHARACTERIZING EVALUATION

One way of understanding evaluative arguments is to consider the types of evidence they use. A distinction we explored in Chapter 7 between hard evidence and arguments based on reason is helpful here. You may recall that we defined hard evidence as facts, statistics, testimony, and other kinds of arguments that can be measured, recorded, or even found—the so-called "smoking gun" in a criminal investigation. Arguments based on reason are those shaped by language, using various kinds of logic.

We can study arguments of evaluation the same way, looking at some as *quantitative* and others as *qualitative*. Quantitative arguments of evaluation rely on criteria that can be measured, counted, or demonstrated in some mechanical fashion—something is taller, faster, smoother, quieter, more powerful than something else. In contrast, qualitative arguments rely on criteria that must be explained through words, relying on such matters as values, traditions, and even emotions: something is more ethical, more beneficial, more handsome, more noble. Needless to say, a claim of evaluation might be supported by arguments of both sorts. We separate them below merely to present them more clearly.

Check out the way Angela Neustatter supports her argument that it should be acceptable for men to get face lifts, liposuction, and other cosmetic procedures.

LINK TO P. 483 ⋯⋯⋯⋯⋯⋯⋯⋯

Quantitative Evaluations

At first glance, quantitative evaluations would seem to hold all the cards, especially in a society as enamored of science and technology as our own. Once you have defined a quantitative standard, making judgments should be as easy as measuring and counting—and in a few cases, that's the way things work out. *Who is the tallest or heaviest or loudest person in your class?* If your colleagues allow themselves to be measured, you could find out easily enough, using the right equipment and internationally sanctioned standards of measurement: the meter, the kilo, or the decibel.

But what if you were to ask, *Who is the smartest person in class?* You could answer this more complex question quantitatively too, using IQ tests or college entrance examinations that report results numerically. In fact, almost all college-bound students in the United States submit to this kind of evaluation, taking either the SAT or ACT to demonstrate their verbal and mathematical prowess. Such measures are widely accepted by educators and institutions, but they are also vigorously challenged. What do they actually measure? They predict likely success in college, which is not the same thing as intelligence.

Like any standards of evaluation, quantitative criteria must be scrutinized carefully to make sure that what they measure relates to what is being evaluated. For example, in evaluating a car, you might use 0–60 mph times as a measure of acceleration, 60–0 mph distances as a measure of braking capability, skidpad numbers (0.85) as a measure of handling ability, and coefficient of drag (0.29) as a test of aerodynamic efficiency. But all these numbers are subject to error. And even when the numbers are gathered accurately and then compared, one vehicle with another, they may not tell the whole story, because some cars generate great test numbers and yet still feel less competent than vehicles with lower scores. The same disparity between numbers and feel occurs with other items—compact disc recordings, for example. CDs can produce awesome sonic accuracy numbers, but some listeners feel the music they produce may lack aural qualities important to listening pleasure. Educators, too, acknowledge that some students test better than others, which doesn't necessarily indicate greater intelligence.

We don't mean to belittle quantitative measures of quality, only to offer a caveat: even the most objective measures have limits. They have been devised by fallible people looking at the world from their own inevitably limited perspectives. Just a few decades ago, teachers hoped that they might figure out how to measure quality of writing by applying quantitative measures relating to "syntactical maturity." The endeavor now seems almost comical because the more complex the human activity, the more it resists quantification. And writing is very complicated.

Yet experts in measurement assert with confidence that quantitative measures are almost always more reliable than qualitative criteria—no matter what is being evaluated. It is a sobering claim, and one not easily dismissed.

Qualitative Evaluations

Many issues of evaluation closest to people's hearts simply aren't subject to quantification. *What makes a movie great?* If you suggested a quantitative measure like length, your friends would probably hoot. Get serious! But what about box office receipts, especially if they could be adjusted to reflect inflation? Would films that made the most money—an easily quantifiable measure—really be the "best pictures"? In that select group would be movies such as *Star Wars, The Sound of Music, Gone with the Wind, Titanic,* and *Harry Potter and the Sorcerer's Stone.* An interesting group of films, but the best? To argue for box office revenue as a criterion of film greatness, you'd have to defend the criteria vigorously because many people in the audience would express doubts about it—major ones.

More likely, then, in defining the criteria for "great movie," you would look for standards to account for the merit of films widely respected among serious critics. For example, the American Film Institute, which ranks the top hundred American films of the past century (see <AFI.com/tv/movies.asp>), lists the following as its top ten:

1. *Citizen Kane* (1941)

2. *Casablanca* (1942)

3. *The Godfather* (1972)

4. *Gone with the Wind* (1939)

5. *Lawrence of Arabia* (1962)

6. *The Wizard of Oz* (1939)

7. *The Graduate* (1967)

8. *On the Waterfront* (1954)

9. *Schindler's List* (1993)

10. *Singin' in the Rain* (1952)

You might consider the qualities common to such respected movies, exploring such elements as their societal impact, cinematic technique, dramatic structures, casting, and so on. Most of these markers of quality could be defined with some precision, but not measured or counted. Lacking hard numbers, you would have to convince the audience to accept your standards and make your case rhetorically. As you might guess, a writer using qualitative measures could spend as much time defending criteria of evaluation as providing evidence that these standards are present in the film under scrutiny.

But establishing subtle criteria is what can make arguments of evaluation so interesting. They require you, time and again, to challenge conventional wisdom. Look at the way Nick Gillespie in *reasononline* celebrates MTV on the occasion of its twentieth anniversary not so much for the music it has presented but for the new openness it has fostered in American culture. As you'll see, most of Gillespie's selection is about his criterion of evaluation—which may be as controversial as MTV itself.

Most rock-and-roll purists have never liked MTV, arguing that the channel is relentlessly, blandly commercial and that the music-video form inevitably swings the spotlight away from uncompromising artistes and shines it on good-looking posers whose only musical bona fides are perfect hair and teeth. On MTV, goes this line of thinking, strategically coifed divas like Christina Aguilera rule and raw punk priestesses like Ani DiFranco need not apply.

Such critics make some valid points. MTV has certainly never been avant garde and much of its programming is mediocre and unmemorable (anyone remember *Austin Stories?*). But these critics miss the larger contribution that the cable channel has made, both to pop music and to pop culture: MTV has been an exceptionally vital force in the growth of the wide variety of new and ever-shifting identities that characterize our times. It has been perhaps the premier showcase—in the nation's living rooms no less—for what anthropologist Grant McCracken calls "plenitude," or the "quickening speciation of social groups, gender types, and lifestyles that characterizes our times."

> From the start, MTV has been an unending and gloriously attractive parade of freaks, gender-benders, and weirdos who push the boundaries of good taste and break down whatever vestiges of mainstream sensibilities remain. Can anyone forget just how awesomely odd bands like Devo, Eurythmics, and Culture Club seemed to us once upon a time? Or how totally normal they now look?
>
> In the years since video killed the radio star, America has become a much looser place. We're less uptight with difference and we're more interested in customized experiences, whether we're talking about 50 types of coffee, special-blend whiskeys—or highly individualized ways of dress, sexuality, and being in the world.
>
> That trend may bother some, but for most of us, it has been both liberating and exciting.
>
> To the extent that MTV has contributed to it, may its next 20 years be as rich as its first two decades.
>
> —Nick Gillespie, "Happy Birthday, MTV"

As Gillespie acknowledges, not everyone will agree that America is a better place because it now accepts a "parade of freaks, gender-benders, and weirdos." But we do understand why he values MTV. His evaluation makes sense, given the criterion he has offered and defended.

DEVELOPING AN EVALUATIVE ARGUMENT

Developing an argument of evaluation can seem like a simple process, especially if you already know what your claim is likely to be:

Citizen Kane is the finest film ever made by an American director.

Having established a claim, you would then explore the implications of your belief, drawing out the reasons, warrants, and evidence that might support it.

Claim	Citizen Kane is the finest film ever made by an American director . . .
Reason	. . . because it revolutionizes the way we see the world.
Warrant	Great films change viewers in fundamental ways.
Evidence	Shot after shot, Citizen Kane presents the life of its protagonist through cinematic images that viewers can never forget.

The warrant here is, in effect, a statement of criteria—in this case, the quality that defines "great film" for the writer.

In developing an evaluative argument, you'll want to pay special attention to criteria, claims, and evidence.

Formulating Criteria

Most often neglected in evaluations is the discussion of criteria. Although even thoughtless evaluations ("The band stinks!") might be traced to reasonable criteria, most people don't bother defending their positions until they are challenged ("Oh yeah?"). Yet when writers address audiences whom they understand well or with whom they share core values, they don't defend most of their criteria in detail. One wouldn't expect a film critic like Roger Ebert to restate all his principles every time he writes a movie review. Ebert assumes his readers will—over time—come to appreciate his standards.

Still, the criteria can make or break the piece. In an essay from *Salon.com*'s series of evaluative arguments called "Masterpieces," writer Stephanie Zacharek can barely contain her enthusiasm for the Chrysler Building in downtown Manhattan:

> Architects, who have both intuition and training on their side, have some very good reasons for loving the Chrysler Building. The rest of us love it beyond reason, for its streamlined majesty and its inherent sense of optimism and promise for the future, but mostly for its shimmery, welcoming beauty—a beauty that speaks of humor and elegance in equal measures, like a Noel Coward play.
>
> How can a mere building make so many people so happy—particularly so many ornery New Yorkers, who often pretend, as part of their act, not to like anything? There may be New Yorkers who dislike the Chrysler Building, but they rarely step forward in public. To do so would only invite derision and disbelief.

Certainly it may seem odd to suggest that one measure of a great building is that it makes people happy. And so the writer has a lot to prove. She's got to provide evidence that a building can, in fact, be delightful. And she seems to do precisely that later in the same essay when she gives life even to the windows in the skyscraper:

> Looking at the Chrysler Building now, though, it's hard to argue against its stylish ebullience, or its special brand of sophisticated cheerfulness. . . . Particularly at night, the crown's triangular windows—lit up, fanned out and stacked high into the sky—suggest a sense of movement that has more in common with dance than with architecture: Those rows of windows are as joyous and seductive as a chorus line of Jazz Age cuties, a bit of sexy night life rising up boldly from an otherwise businesslike skyline.

Personal ads present evaluation criteria distilled and condensed. W. Charisse Goodman quotes the following ad in her essay about weight prejudice in the United States: "Be any race, be yourself, but be beautiful."

LINK TO P. 466

FIGURE 10.4   WHY DOES THIS BUILDING MAKE PEOPLE HAPPY?

The criteria Zacharek uses lead to an inventive and memorable evalua-tion, one that may teach readers to look at buildings a whole new way.

Don't take criteria of evaluation for granted. If you offer vague, dull, or unsupportable principles, expect to be challenged. You are most likely to be vague about your beliefs when you haven't thought enough about your subject. So push yourself at least as far as you imagine the readers will. Imagine the readers looking over your shoulder, asking difficult questions.

Say, for example, that you intend to argue that serious drivers will obvi-ously prefer a 5-Series BMW to an E-Class Mercedes. What standards would serious drivers apply to these sedans? Razor-sharp handling? But what does that mean? Perhaps it's the ability to hold the road in tight curves with minimal steering correction. That's a criterion you could defend. Serious drivers would likely expect precise braking, too. Might that mean that the brake pedal should be firm, responding linearly to driver input? Are such standards getting too technical? Or do you need to assert such sophisticated criteria to establish your authority to write about the subject? These are appropriate questions to ask.

Making Claims

Claims can be stated directly or, in rare instances, strongly implied. For most writers the direct evaluative claim probably works better, with the statement carefully qualified. Consider the differences between the following claims and how much less the burden of proof would be for the second and third ones:

John Paul II was the most important leader of the twentieth century.

John Paul II may have been one of the three or four most influential leaders of the twentieth century.

John Paul II may come to be regarded as one of the three or four most influential spiritual leaders of the twentieth century.

The point of qualifying a statement is not to make evaluative claims bland, but to make them responsible and manageable. Consider how sensitively Christopher Caldwell frames his claim in the eulogy he writes for former Beatle George Harrison. (A eulogy is a very important kind of evaluative argument.)

Leaving aside the screaming Beatlemaniacs in thrall to the idiosyncrasies of sex appeal, there were never any George People or Ringo People. But George Harrison's death from cancer Thursday at the age of 58 reminds us that there ought to have been. If any of the four could be called "typical" of the group, the most Beatley Beatle, the heart of the Fab Four, the means of bridging Paul's appeal and John's, and thus the glue that held the band together, it was George.
–Christopher Caldwell, "All Things Must Pass"

Caldwell will have to prove this claim, offering evidence that George contributed in important ways to a musical group dominated by John Lennon and Paul McCartney. But he doesn't have to show that George was the most important Beatle, just the group's binding element. And that's a much more manageable task.

Of course, claims themselves might be more responsible if they were always written after a sober study of facts and evidence. But most people don't operate that way. They start with an opinion and then look for reasons and evidence to support it. If people are honest, though, they'll at least modify their claims in the face of contrary evidence.

In fact, bringing strongly held claims to the table can work well in situations where different opinions collide. That's what makes discussions on listservs so potentially exciting: people with different values make contradictory claims and then negotiate their differences, sometimes over days and weeks. Committees and study groups can work in this way, too. For example, imagine Congress contemplating alternatives to the current federal income tax system. A committee assigned to explore better systems of taxation would likely work best if it included people willing to champion the merits of different plans, everything from a flat tax to the current progressive income tax. Each of these positions, well argued, would broaden the scope of what the committee knew and might help the group move toward consensus. Or it might not.

Presenting Evidence

The more evidence the better in an evaluation, provided that the evidence is relevant. For example, in evaluating the performance of two computers, the speed of their processors would certainly be important, but the quality of their keyboards or the availability of service might be less crucial, perhaps irrelevant.

Just as important as relevance in selecting evidence is presentation. Not all pieces of evidence are equally convincing, nor should they be treated as such. Select evidence most likely to impress your readers, and arrange the paper to build toward your best material. In most cases, that best material will be evidence that is specific, detailed, and derived from credible sources. Look at the details in these paragraphs by David Plotz evaluating rapper, producer, and entertainer Sean "Puffy" Combs:

> **Combs is a Renaissance man, but only by the standards of a P.T. Barnum world. Rarely has someone become so famous by being so mediocre at so many things—a boy wonder without any wonder. Puffy is a famous rapper who can't rap, and he's becoming a movie actor who can't act. He's a restaurateur who serves ho-hum food; a magazine publisher whose magazine was immediately forgettable (*Notorious*—see, you've forgotten already); a music producer whose only talents are stealing old songs and recycling the work of his dead friend the Notorious B.I.G.**
>
> **Combs can be seen as the inverse of the past century's great Renaissance man, Paul Robeson, a truly wonderful singer, actor, athlete, and political activist. Puffy has none of that talent, but unlike the Communist Robeson, he has a profound understanding of capitalism. Puffy has thrived because he has achieved his mediocrity with immense panache, with bling-bling hoopla and PR genius. Puffy is the Sam Glick of hip-hop—a man without wit, talent, charm, or convictions, but so full of drive that he made $230 million anyway.**
> **–David Plotz, "Sean Combs: Why Is Puffy Deflating?"**

The details are rich enough to make the case that Sean Combs lacks the talent of a real artist or genius. But notice that Plotz admits what's obvious to anyone aware of the man's fame: he's a success by contemporary standards. Combs's income can't be ignored in this argument.

However, don't be afraid to concede such a point when evidence goes contrary to the overall claim you wish to make. If you are really skillful, you can even turn a problem into an argumentative asset, as Bob Costas does in acknowledging the flaws of baseball great Mickey Mantle in the process of praising him:

> **None of us, Mickey included, would want to be held to account for every moment of our lives. But how many of us could say that our best moments were as magnificent as his?**
> –Bob Costas, "Eulogy for Mickey Mantle"

For a discussion of who's a better sitcom dad—Homer Simpson or Ray Romano—see John Levesque's article "Sitcom Dads Rarely Know Best, Study of TV Laments."

LINK TO P. 506

KEY FEATURES OF EVALUATIONS

In drafting an evaluation, you should consider three basic elements:

- an evaluative claim that makes a judgment about a person, idea, or object
- the criterion or criteria by which you'll measure your subject
- evidence that the particular subject meets or falls short of the stated criteria

All these elements will be present in one way or another in arguments of evaluation, but they won't follow a specific order. In addition, you'll often need an opening paragraph to explain what you are evaluating and why. Tell readers why they should care about your subject and take your opinion seriously.

Nothing adds more depth to an opinion than letting others challenge it. When you can, use the resources of the Internet or more local online networks to get responses to your opinions. It can be eye-opening to realize how strongly people react to ideas or points of view that you regard as perfectly normal. When you are ready, share your draft with colleagues, asking them to identify places where you need additional support for your ideas, either in the discussion of criteria or in the presentation of evidence.

Finding a Topic

You are entering an argument of evaluation when you

- make a judgment about quality: Citizen Kane *is probably the finest film ever made by an American director.*
- challenge such a judgment: Citizen Kane *is vastly overrated by most film critics.*
- construct a ranking or comparison: Citizen Kane *is a more intellectually challenging movie than* Casablanca.

Issues of evaluation arise daily—in the judgments you make about public figures or policies; in the choices you make about instructors and courses; in the recommendations you make about books, films, or television programs; in the preferences you exercise in choosing products, activities, or charities. Be alert to evaluative arguments whenever you read or use terms that indicate value or rank: *good/bad, effective/ineffective, best/worst, competent/incompetent, successful/ unsuccessful.* Finally, be aware of your own areas of expertise. Write about subjects or topics about which others regularly ask your opinion or advice.

Researching Your Topic

You can research issues of evaluation using the following sources:

- journals, reviews, and magazines (for current political and social issues)
- books (for assessing judgments about history, policy, etc.)
- biographies (for assessing people)
- research reports and scientific studies
- books, magazines, and Web sites for consumers
- periodicals and Web sites that cover entertainment and sports
- Web logs for exploring current affairs

Surveys and polls can be useful in uncovering public attitudes: *What books are people reading? Who are the most admired people in the country? What activities or businesses are thriving or waning?* You'll discover that Web sites, newsgroups, and Web logs thrive on evaluation. Browse these public forums for ideas and, when possible, explore your own topic ideas there.

Formulating a Claim

After exploring your subject, begin to shape a full and specific claim, a thesis that lets readers know where you stand and on what criteria you will base your judgments. Look for a thesis that is challenging enough to attract readers' attention, not one that merely repeats views already widely held. In moving toward this thesis, you might begin with questions of this kind:

- What exactly is my opinion? Where do I stand?
- Can I make my judgment more specific?
- Do I need to qualify my claim?
- According to what standards am I making my judgment?
- Will readers accept my criteria, or will I have to defend them, too?
- What major reasons can I offer in support of my evaluation?

Your thesis should be a complete statement. In one sentence, you need to make a claim of evaluation and state the reasons that support your claim. Be sure your claim is specific enough. Anticipate the questions readers might have: *Who? What? Where? Under what conditions? With what exceptions? In all cases?* Don't expect readers to guess where you stand.

Examples of Evaluative Claims

- Though they may never receive Oscars for their work, Sandra Bullock and Keanu Reeves deserve credit as actors who have succeeded in a wider range of film roles than most of their contemporaries.
- Many computer users are discovering that Mac OS X is a more intuitive, stable, robust, and elegant operating system than anything currently available on PC platforms.
- Jimmy Carter has been highly priaised as an ex-president of the United States, but history may show that even his much-derided term in office laid the groundwork for the foreign policy and economic successes now attributed to later administrations.
- On a hot day, nothing tastes better than a scoop of ice cream rich in butter fat, expertly blended, creatively concocted, and free of off-putting preservatives, emulsifiers, and artificial flavors.
- Because knowledge changes so quickly and people switch careers so often, an effective education today is one that trains people *how to learn* more than it teaches them *what to know*.

Preparing a Proposal

If your instructor asks you to prepare a proposal for your project, here's a format you might use.

State your thesis completely. If you are having trouble doing so, try outlining it in Toulmin terms:

Claim:

Reason(s):

Warrant(s):

Explain why this issue deserves attention. What is at stake?

Specify whom you hope to reach through your argument and why this group of readers would be interested in it.

Briefly discuss the key challenges you anticipate. Defining criteria? Defending them? Finding quantitative evidence to support your claim? Developing qualitative arguments to bolster your judgment?

Determine what research strategies you will use. What sources do you expect to consult?

Consider what format you expect to use for your project. A conventional research essay? A letter to the editor? A Web page?

Thinking about Organization

Your evaluation may take various forms, but it is likely to include elements such as the following:

- a specific claim: *Most trucks are unsuitable for the kind of driving most Americans do.*

- an explanation or defense of the criteria (if necessary): *The overcrowding and pollution of American cities and suburbs might be relieved if more Americans drove small, fuel-efficient cars. Cars do less damage in accidents than heavy trucks and are also less likely to roll over.*

- an examination of the claim in terms of the stated criteria: *Most trucks are unsuitable for the kind of driving Americans do because they are not designed for contemporary urban driving conditions.*

- evidence for every part of the argument: *Trucks get very poor gas mileage; they are statistically more likely than cars to roll over in accidents . . .*

- consideration of alternative views and counterarguments: *It is true, perhaps, that trucks make drivers feel safer on the roads and give them a better view of traffic conditions . . .*

Getting and Giving Response

All arguments benefit from the scrutiny of others. Your instructor may assign you to a peer group for the purpose of reading and responding to each other's drafts; if not, make the effort yourself to get some careful response. You can use the following questions to evaluate a draft. If you are evaluating some-one else's draft, be sure to illustrate your points with examples. Specific comments are always more helpful than general observations.

The Claim

- Is the claim clearly an argument of evaluation? Does it make a judgment about something?

- Does the claim establish clearly what is being evaluated?

- Is the claim too sweeping? Does it need to be qualified?

- Will the criteria used in the evaluation be clear to readers? Do the criteria need to be defined more explicitly or precisely?

- Are the criteria appropriate ones to use for this evaluation? Are they controversial? Does evidence of their validity need to be added?

Evidence for the Claim

- Is enough evidence provided to ensure that what is being evaluated meets the criteria established for the evaluation? If not, what kind of additional evidence is needed?

- Is the evidence in support of the claim simply announced, or are its significance and appropriateness analyzed? Is a more detailed discussion needed?

- Are any objections readers might have to the claim, criteria, or evidence adequately addressed?

- What kinds of sources are cited? How credible and persuasive will they be to readers? What other kinds of sources might be more credible and persuasive?

- Are all quotations introduced with appropriate signal phrases (for instance, "As Will argues,") and blended smoothly into the writer's sentences?

Organization and Style

- How are the parts of the argument organized? Is this organization effective, or would some other structure work better?

- Will readers understand the relationships among the claims, supporting reasons, warrants, and evidence? If not, what could be done to make those connections clearer? Are more transitional words and phrases needed? Would headings or graphic devices help?
- Are the transitions or links from point to point, paragraph to paragraph, and sentence to sentence clear and effective? If not, how could they be improved?
- Is the style suited to the subject? Is it too formal? Too casual? Too technical? Too bland?
- Which sentences seem particularly effective? Which ones seem weakest, and how could they be improved? Should some short sentences be combined, or should any long ones be separated into two or more sentences?
- How effective are the paragraphs? Do any seem too skimpy or too long?
- Which words or phrases seem particularly effective, vivid, and memorable? Do any seem dull, vague, unclear, or inappropriate for the audience or the writer's purpose? Are definitions provided for technical or other terms that readers might not know?

Spelling, Punctuation, Mechanics, Documentation, Format

- Are there any errors in spelling, punctuation, capitalization, and the like?
- Is an appropriate and consistent style of documentation used for parenthetical citations and the list of works cited or references? (See Chapter 22.)
- Does the paper or project follow an appropriate format? Is it appropriately designed and attractively presented? If it is a Web site, do all the links work?

RESPOND •

1. Choose one item from the following list that you understand well enough to evaluate. Develop several criteria of evaluation you could defend to distinguish excellence from mediocrity in the area. Then choose another item from the list, this time one you do not know much about at all, and explain the research you might do to discover reasonable criteria of evaluation for it.

   fashion designers

   Navajo rugs

   action films

   hip-hop music

   American presidents

   NFL quarterbacks

   contemporary painting

   professional journalists

   TV sitcoms

   fast food

   rock musicians

2. Review Kristin Cole's appeal for a pet-sitter for Baldrick (see p. 175), and then write an email of your own in which you try to persuade friends to care for someone or something while you are away. Be sure that the argument includes strong elements of evaluation. Why should friends be eager to pamper your pit bull Killer, care for your fragile collection of tropical orchids, or baby-sit your ten-year-old twin siblings Bonnie and Clyde?

3. In the last ten years, there has been a proliferation in awards programs for movies, musicians, sports figures, and other categories. For example, before the Oscars are handed out, a half-dozen other organizations have given prizes to the annual crop of films. Write a short opinion piece assessing the merits of a particular awards show or a feature such as *People*'s annual "sexiest man" issue. What should a proper event of this kind accomplish? Does the event you are reviewing do so?

4. Local news-and-entertainment magazines often publish "best of" issues or articles that list readers' and editors' favorites in such categories as "best place to go on a first date," "best softball field," and "best dentist." Sometimes the categories are very specific: "best places to say, 'I was retro before retro was cool,'" or "best movie theater

seats." Imagine that you are the editor of your own local magazine and that you want to put out a "best of" issue tailored to your hometown. Develop ten categories for evaluation. For each category, list the evaluative criteria you would use to make your judgment.

Next, consider that because your criteria are warrants, they are especially tied to audience. (The criteria for "best dentist," for example, might be tailored to people whose major concern is avoiding pain, to those whose children will be regular visitors, or to those who want the cheapest possible dental care.) For several of your evaluative categories, imagine that you have to justify your judgments to a completely different audience. Write a new set of criteria for that audience.

5. Develop an argument using (or challenging) one of the criteria of evaluation presented in this chapter. Among the criteria you might explore are the following:

    A car should be a tool.

    Buildings should make people happy.

    Great films change viewers in fundamental ways.

    Good pets need not have fur and four legs.

    Great burgers need just the right shape and texture.

6. For examples of powerful evaluation arguments, search the Web or library for obituaries of famous, recently deceased individuals. Try to locate at least one such item and analyze the types of claims it makes about the deceased. What criteria of evaluation are employed? What kinds of evidence does it present?

TWO SAMPLE EVALUATIONS

Why I Hate Britney

NISEY WILLIAMS

I'm afraid of having children. Not because of labor pains, but because of the odds that I may actually have a girl. Today, efficiently raising a daughter is almost impossible because of pop culture's persistent emphasis on sex. It's rare to watch MTV or BET and not be bombarded with images of women's bare midriffs, protruding cleavage and round rumps. Bellies, breasts and booties. I can't imagine how much more difficult it will be to protect my daughter from this in 15 years when she'd be approaching puberty.

And for my fear of motherhood, I blame Britney Spears.

The thesis is stated clearly and emphatically.

Well, in all fairness, Britney's not the only one to influence our youth. There is a growing group of sexualized, so-called entertainers who seem to be multiplying like roaches: Britney Spears, Destiny's Child, Christina Aguilera, 3LW, Mariah Carey, Shakira, Jessica Simpson, Pink, J.Lo, etc.—hereafter known as Britney et al. Daily, these destructive divas serve young girls with an earful and eyeful of sex, tempting children to mimic their musical heroes. So much so that the media has coined such phrases as "Baby Britneys," "Teeny Christinees," and "Junior J.Los." Still, while there are other female artists who also discourage the healthy development of our youth—most

When she wrote this paper Nisey Williams was a senior at the University of Texas, Austin, an African American Studies and Cultural Anthropology major who plans on teaching honors English to high school students. Although she enjoys all realms of creative writing, her passion is poetry. She hopes to publish poetry and short stories.

"Why I Hate Britney" is her response to an assignment that asked for an argument with a personal voice suitable for publication in a newspaper or magazine. Sources were to be documented in the paper itself, not through formal documentation.

recently J.Lo with her serial marrying/divorcing practices—Britney remains the most culpable.

A *Dallas Morning News* reporter claims it's "always convenient to blame the sinister influence of Britney," but it's much more than "convenient"—it's practical. *Forbes* magazine voted Britney as the most powerful celebrity of 2002, beating such influential personalities as Steven Spielberg and Oprah Winfrey. With such recognition comes responsibilities. It's undeniable that Britney is at the forefront of this sex-crazed phenomenon and I, like many others, hold her accountable. On a website called *Pax Vobiscum*, one concerned father of two teenage daughters refers to Britney as "the chief apostlette for the sexualization of our little girls" with her "revealing clothing and 'come-hither' image." This couldn't be more accurate.

Evidence suggests that Spears is responsible for influencing young women.

While she says she hopes to save her virginity for marriage, she also wears see-through outfits and dances like a stripper on the MTV Video Music Awards. Actions speak louder than words; her chastity claim falls short beside her sleazy image. Britney's marketing management is pimping her and she's without the dignity or strength to step off the street corner and hail a cab from Lolita Lane to Respectable Road.

Several other female artists don't sell their bodies in order to sell their music. Among them is Avril Lavigne, one of Arista's latest signers, who openly criticizes Britney for her confusing and contradictory image. In a recent interview with *Chart Attack*, Avril explains that: "The clothes I wear onstage are the clothes I would wear to school or to go shopping. Britney Spears goes up onstage and dresses like a showgirl. She's not being herself. I mean, the way she dresses . . . would you walk around the street in a bra? It's definitely not what I'm going to do." And so far, Avril hasn't had to compromise herself to be a success. Her first album, *Let Go*, debuted at No. 8 on the Billboard charts and has since gone double platinum. She was also awarded Best New Artist at the 2002 MTV Video Music Awards. Avril is known as the "Anti-Britney" because, as AskMen.com explained, she "stands out in the current sea of female teen vocalists as a distinctly unmanufactured artist whose

An alternative to Spears's approach to success is offered.

success can be directly linked to her musical talent." Can't say the same for Miss Spears.

It's amazing how Britney ignores her influence on children. In *Rolling Stone*, her response to critics judging her clothing style was a reference to her younger days of playing dress-up in her mother's closet—within the confines of her home. She explained: "We put on our mom's clothes and we dressed up. It was our time to daydream and fantasize." Does she seriously think wearing Mom's clothes is the same as having your own and flaunting them at the mall or in the classroom?

Then in an *In Style* interview, she says she has no patience for those who criticize her skin-baring. In her words: "I mean, I'm a girl! Why not?" Great message for the kiddies, Brit: if you got it, flaunt it. And what about those girls who don't "got it"? Britney basically tells girls that body image is of primary importance—a difficult problem for many young females. Some girls who feel this constant pressure to attain unrealistic goals end up with destructive behaviors such as eating disorders and low self-esteem. Many girls who strive to be Britney look-alikes do not realize they lack her resources, such as makeup artists, silicone enhancements, and millions of dollars.

Spears does not live up to criteria for responsible behavior —given her role as a model for young girls.

The main argument against those like me who bash Britney is that it's up to parents—not celebrities—to teach their children morals and appropriate behavior. While I agree with elements of that claim, there is only so much a parent can do. Sexual material is so intertwined in pop culture that even cautious parents have a hard time keeping their children away from it. In the *Milwaukee Journal Sentinel*, one psychiatrist explains that parents "often don't even think about it [keeping children away from pop culture] because it's an overwhelming task," while another equated "trying to insulate a child from sexual material" with "fighting a tornado."

An alternative perspective is explored and rejected.

During the crucial years of adolescence, popular opinion sometimes overrides that of parents. In the same Milwaukee article, one mother reports that her daughter threw a fit in the department store when she refused to buy her thongs. The mother was completely baffled by her

Numerous examples enforce the claim that children are being sexualized too early by "Britney et al."

child's reaction until the 12-year-old admitted that the other girls in the locker room teased her for wearing bikini underwear instead of thongs. Many kids will do anything to fit in because peer approval is so necessary to a child learning her place in school.

Experts are torn on the long-term effects our sex-heavy pop culture may have on children, but many agree that there are likely negative consequences. According to Diane Levin, an education professor who has studied the effects of media on children's development for over 20 years, our sex-saturated culture will rub off on children in the most undesired ways. On *ABCNews.com*, Levin explains that "the kind of increased sexual images that children are seeing parallel with when they get a little older. They start becoming sexually active earlier." Currently, the Alan Guttmacher Institute reports that two out of ten girls and three out of ten boys have had sexual intercourse by age 15, while there are also several widespread reports of increased sexual activity—including oral sex—among middle-school students. How much worse will these statistics be by the time my daughter reaches the age of 15?

Although there is no documented evidence of how pop culture's over-sexualization affects children, an August 14th taping of *Good Morning, America,* entitled "From Oshkosh to Oh My Gosh," revealed some startling reactions. The show divided the children by sex and then interviewed the two groups separately about issues surrounding pop culture. The result was a roomful of shocked parents who had no idea the word *sexy* was such a frequent and familiar part of their children's vocabulary. When the girls' group watched a Jennifer Lopez video, the relationship between the mature concept of sexiness and popular music became obvious. After one young girl predicted the video's ending was J.Lo removing her shirt, another girl explained that J.Lo did this "to look sexy."

Being sexy is the latest fad for girls of all ages and with the current fashions available, their dreams can become a reality. Clothing designers work side by side with the entertainment industry. There is at least a $90 billion market targeting "tweens"—children between the ages of 8 and 12 who are in the in between stages of adolescence and teenagehood. It is this up-and-coming group who fuel pop culture. They listen to the music, worship the singers and crave their clothing. From Wal-Mart to the Limited Too, stores are fully aware of what their young consumers want and promote their merchandise accordingly.

Modest girls' clothing is hard to find among the racks of grown-up fashions like low-riding hip huggers, tight midriff-revealing shirts, high-heeled platforms and miniskirts. One of my co-workers said she had such a difficult time school shopping for her 13-year-old daughter that she ended up taking her to Academy for wind suits, free-flowing T-shirts and soccer shorts. Sporting stores will soon be the last option for frustrated parents, as more retailers prey on the tween market.

As a consequence of Spears's influence, parents are finding it more difficult to raise children, underscoring the initial claim in the argument.

However, my beef is not with these merchants. The clothing is harmless by itself. It would sit untouched and undesired if it weren't for Britney et al. flaunting revealing fashions in music videos, posters, magazine covers and award shows. As *FashionFollower.com* revealed: "Queen Britney single-handedly made the bare midriff a staple of 15-year-old wardrobes across the globe. Now that's something every mother should be proud of."

Pop culture seems to be in downward spiral, continually going from bad to worse. It's bad enough to have to endure countless images of exposed female bodies on every music channel, but it's so much worse to see those same "barely there" outfits on children. Hopefully, there will come a day when it's no longer trendy to be so overtly sexual and pop culture will replace Britney et al. with more respectable female icons.

My America

ANDREW SULLIVAN

Thursday, November 28, 2002
A THANKSGIVING POST: My old colleague, the legendary British journalist
and drunk Henry Fairlie, had a favourite story about his long, lascivious love
affair with America. He was walking down a suburban street one afternoon
in a suit and tie, passing familiar rows of detached middle-American
dwellings and lush, green Washington lawns. In the distance a small boy—
aged perhaps six or seven—was riding his bicycle towards him.

And in a few minutes, as their paths crossed on the pavement, the small
boy looked up at Henry and said, with no hesitation or particular affectation:
"Hi." As Henry told it, he was so taken aback by this unexpected outburst of
familiarity that he found it hard to say anything particularly coherent in
return. And by the time he did, the boy was already trundling past him into
the distance.

In that exchange, Henry used to reminisce, so much of America was
summed up. That distinctive form of American manners, for one thing: a
strong blend of careful politeness and easy informality. But beneath that,
something far more impressive. It never occurred to that little American boy
that he should be silent, or know his place, or defer to his elder. In America, a
six-year-old cyclist and a 55-year-old journalist were equals. The democratic
essence of America was present there on a quiet street on a lazy summer
afternoon.

Henry couldn't have imagined that exchange happening in England—or
Europe, for that matter. Perhaps now, as European—and especially British—
society has shed some of its more rigid hierarchies, it could. But what thrilled
him about that exchange is still a critical part of what makes America an
enduringly liberating place. And why so many of us who have come to live
here find, perhaps more than most native Americans, a reason to give thanks
this Thanksgiving.

Andrew Sullivan, an émigré from England, is the former editor of *The New Republic* and the
author of *Almost Normal* (1995) and *Love Undetectable* (1998). He has written for the *New York
Times Magazine* and many other publications such as *Time* and *Salon.com*. Sullivan maintains
one of the most read and often-cited Web logs at <andrewsullivan.com>.

"My America" was first published November 24, 1996, in the *Sunday Times of London*.

When I tuck into the turkey on Thursday, I'll have three things in particular in mind. First, the country's pathological obsession with the present. America is still a country where the past is anathema. Even when Americans are nostalgic, they are nostalgic for a myth of the future. What matters for Americans, in small ways and large, is never where you have come from — but where you are going, what you are doing now, or what you are about to become. In all the years I have lived in America — almost a decade and a half now — it never ceases to amaze me that almost nobody has ever demanded to know by what right I belong here. Almost nobody has asked what school I went to, what my family is like, or what my past contains. (In Britain I was asked those questions on a daily, almost hourly, basis.) Even when I took it on myself to be part of the American debate, nobody ever questioned my credentials for doing so. I don't think that could ever happen in a European context (when there's a gay American editor of *The Spectator*, let me know). If Europeans ever need to know why Ronald Reagan captured such a deep part of the American imagination, this is surely part of the answer. It was his reckless futurism (remember Star Wars and supply-side economics?) and his instinctive, personal generosity.

Second, I'm thankful for the American talent for contradiction. The country that sustained slavery for longer than any other civilised country is also the country that has perhaps struggled more honestly for the notion of racial equality than any other. The country that has a genuine public ethic of classlessness also has the most extreme economic inequality in the developed world. The country that is most obsessed with pressing the edge of modernity also has the oldest intact constitution in the world. The country that still contains a powerful religious right has also pushed the equality of homosexuals further than ever before in history. A country that cannot officially celebrate Christmas (it would erase the boundary between church and state) is also one of the most deeply religious nations on the planet. Americans have learnt how to reconcile the necessary contradictions not simply because their country is physically big enough to contain them, but because it is spiritually big enough to contain them. Americans have learnt how to reconcile the necessary contradictions of modern life with a verve and a serenity few others can muster. It is a deeply reassuring achievement.

Third, I'm thankful because America is, above all, a country of primary colours. Sometimes the pictures Americans paint are therefore not as subtle, or as elegant, or even as brilliant as masterpieces elsewhere. But they have a vigour and a simplicity that is often more viscerally alive. Other nations may have become bored with the Enlightenment, or comfortable in post-modern ennui. Americans find such postures irrelevant. Here the advertisements are cruel, the battles are stark and the sermons are terrifying. And here, more than anywhere else, the most vital of arguments still go on. Does God exist? Are the races equal? Can the genders get along? Americans believe that these debates can never get tired, and that their resolution still matters, because what happens in America still matters in the broader world. At its worst, this can bespeak a kind of arrogance and crudeness. But at its best, it reflects a resilient belief that the great questions can always be reinvented and that the answers are always relevant. In the end, I have come to appreciate this kind of naivety as a deeper form of sophistication. Even the subtlest of hues, after all, are merely primary colours mixed.

At the end of November each year this restless, contradictory and simple country finds a way to celebrate itself. The British, as befits a people at ease with themselves, do not have a national day. When the French do, their insecurity shows. Even America, on the Fourth of July, displays a slightly neurotic excess of patriotism. But on Thanksgiving, the Americans resolve the nationalist dilemma. They don't celebrate themselves, they celebrate their good fortune. And every November, as I reflect on a country that can make even an opinionated Englishman feel at home, I know exactly how they feel.

chapter eleven

Causal Arguments

Laid-off workers at a formerly prosperous technology firm have a hunch that the layoffs are related to mismanagement by their CEO. They quietly begin to track down possible causes of the layoffs, hoping to prove their hunch correct.

A local school board member notes that students at one high school consistently outscore all others in the district on standardized math tests. She decides to try to identify the cause(s) of these students' success.

Researchers in Marin County, California, discover that the occurrence of breast cancer cases is significantly higher than in any other urban area in California. They immediately begin work to investigate possible causes.

A large clothing manufacturer wants to increase its worldwide market share among teenage buyers of blue jeans. Its executives know that another company has been the overwhelming market leader for years—and they set out to learn exactly why.

Convinced that there is a strong and compelling causal link between secondhand smoke and lung cancer, the mayor of New York moves to institute a total ban of smoking, even in bars.

A state legislator notes that gasoline prices are consistently between twenty-five and fifty cents higher in one large city in the state than elsewhere. After some preliminary investigation, the legislator decides to bring a class action lawsuit on behalf of the people of this city, arguing that price fixing and insider deals are responsible for the price difference.

■ ■ ■

UNDERSTANDING CAUSAL ARGUMENTS

Arguments about causes and effects inform many everyday decisions and choices: You decide to swear off desserts since they inevitably lead to weight gain; because you failed last week's midterm you decide to form a study group, convinced that the new technique will bring up your test scores. Suppose you are explaining, in a petition for a grade change, why you were unable to submit the final assignment on time. You'd probably try to trace the causes of your failure to submit the assignment—the death of your grandmother followed by an attack of the flu followed by the theft of your car—in hopes that the committee reading the petition would see these causes as valid and change your grade. In identifying the causes of the situation, you are implicitly arguing that the effect—your failure to turn in the assignment on time—should be considered in a new light.

Like all arguments, those about causes can also be used to amuse or to poke fun. The drawing on page 207 takes a tongue-in-cheek look at the causal relationship between the cost and the quality of health care.

FIGURE 11.1   CAUSAL RELATIONSHIP EXPLAINED IN A CARTOON

*"And, in our continuing effort to minimize surgical costs, I'll be hitting
you over the head and tearing you open with my bare hands."*

Drawing by Danny Shanahan © 2003, The New Yorker Collection from Cartoonbank.com. All rights
reserved.

As this cartoon suggests, causal arguments exist in many forms and frequently appear as parts of other arguments (such as evaluations or proposals). It may help focus your work on causal arguments to separate
them into three major categories:

- arguments that state a cause and then examine its effect(s)
- arguments that state an effect and then trace the effect back to its
  cause(s)
- arguments that move through a series of links: A causes B, which leads
  to C and perhaps to D

Arguments that state a cause and then examine one or more of its effects

This type of argument might begin, for example, with a cause—say, putting women into combat—and then demonstrate the effects that such a

A childless couple in California placed advertisements in selected college newspapers offering $50,000—ten times the going rate—for eggs donated by a tall, athletic, intelligent student. See Gina Kolata's article discussing the possible social consequences of such advertisements.

·····································LINK TO P. 649

Norimitsu Onishi's article "Globalization of Beauty Makes Slimness Trendy" explores the reasons behind the shift in beauty standards in Nigeria.

·····································LINK TO P. 474

cause would have. In such an argument, you will be successful if you can show compellingly that the cause would indeed lead to the described effects. Take a look at the opening of an article exploring the causes of a slump in the sale of CDs; in this case, the cause does not lead to the expected effect.

> There is a lot of propaganda about MP3s being detrimental to the sales of music CDs. . . .
>
> As the popularity of MP3s continues to exponentially grow, it's been expected that sales of CDs will decline. Surprisingly, 1999 U.S. sales reports show an increase in music CD sales by 100 million units. To what or who does the RIAA [Recording Industry Association of America] credit such great success for 1999 sales?
>
> –StellaYu, "IWantMyMP3"

Arguments that begin with an effect and then trace the effect back to one or more causes

This type of argument might begin with a certain effect—for example, the fact that America's seventh-largest company, Enron, utterly collapsed in 2002—and then trace the effect or set of effects to the most likely causes—in this case, corporate greed, "cooking" the books, spectacular mismanagement, and the freefall in the value of Enron shares. Again, the special challenge of such arguments is to make the causal connection compelling to the audience. In 1962, scientist Rachel Carson seized the attention of millions with a causal argument about the effects of the overuse of chemical poisons in agricultural control programs. Here is an excerpt from the beginning of her book-length study of this subject; note how she begins with the *effects* before saying she will go on to explore the causes:

> [A] strange blight crept over the area and everything began to change. Some evil spell had settled on the community: mysterious maladies swept the flocks of chickens; the cattle and sheep sickened and died. Everywhere was a shadow of death. The farmers spoke of much illness among their families. . . . There had been several sudden and unexplained deaths, not only among adults but even among children, who would be stricken suddenly while at play and die within a few hours. . . .
>
> The roadsides, once so attractive, were now lined with browned and withered vegetation as though swept by fire. These, too, were silent, deserted by all living things. Even the streams were now lifeless. Anglers no longer visited them, for all the fish had died.
>
> In the gutters under the eaves and between the shingles of the roofs, a white granular powder still showed a few patches; some

weeks before it had fallen like snow upon the roofs and the lawns, the fields and streams.

No witchcraft, no enemy action had silenced the rebirth of new life in this stricken world. The people had done it themselves. . . .

What has already silenced the voices of spring in countless towns in America? This book is an attempt to explain.

–Rachel Carson, *Silent Spring*

Arguments that move through a series of links: Cause A leads to B, which leads to C and possibly to D

In an environmental science class, for example, you might decide to argue that a national law regulating smokestack emissions from utility plants is needed

1. because emissions from utility plants in the Midwest cause acid rain,

2. because acid rain causes the death of trees and other vegetation in eastern forests,

3. because powerful lobbyists have prevented midwestern states from passing strict laws to control emissions from these plants, and

4. as a result, acid rain will destroy most eastern forests by 2020.

In this case, the first link is that emissions cause acid rain; the second, that acid rain causes destruction in eastern forests; and the third, that states have not acted to break the cause-effect relationship established by the first two points. These links set the scene for the fourth link, which ties the previous points together to argue from effect: unless X, then Y.

At their most schematic, causal arguments may be diagrammed in relatively straightforward ways, as shown in Figure 11.2.

FIGURE 11.2   CAUSAL ARGUMENTS

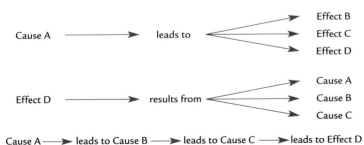

CHARACTERIZING CAUSAL ARGUMENTS

Causal arguments tend to share several characteristics.

They are often part of other arguments.

In his article urging changes in the rules and organization of college basketball, Thad Williamson argues about the consequences of commercialism in the game.

⋯⋯⋯⋯⋯⋯⋯⋯⋯⋯⋯⋯⋯⋯⋯**LINK TO P. 627**

Causal arguments often work to further other arguments, especially proposals, so you should remember that they can be useful in establishing the good reasons for arguments in general. For example, a proposal to limit the amount of time children spend playing video games would very likely draw on causal "good reasons" for support, ones that would attempt to establish that playing video games causes negative results—such as increased violent behavior, decreased attention spans, and so on.

They are almost always complex.

The complexity of most causal arguments makes establishing causes and effects extremely difficult. For example, scientists and politicians continue to disagree over the extent to which acid rain is actually responsible for the so-called dieback of many eastern forests. If you can show that X *definitely* causes Y, though, you will have a powerful argument at your disposal. That is why, for example, so much effort has gone into establishing a definite link between certain dietary habits and heart disease: providing the causal link amid the complex of factors that might be associated with heart disease would argue most forcefully for changing eating behavior in very significant ways.

They are often definition-based.

One reason causal arguments are so complex is that they often depend on extremely careful definitions. Recent figures from the U.S. Department of Education, for example, show that the number of high school dropouts is rising and that this rise has caused an increase in youth unemployment. But exactly how does the study define *dropout*? A closer look may suggest that some students (perhaps a lot) who drop out actually "drop back in" later and go on to complete high school. Further, how does the study define *employment*? Until you can provide explicit definitions that answer such questions, you should proceed cautiously with a causal argument like this one.

They usually yield probable rather than absolute conclusions.

Because causal relationships are almost always extremely complex, they seldom yield more than a high degree of probability. Scientists in particular are wary of making causal claims—that environmental factors cause infertility, for example, because it is highly unlikely that a condition as variable as infertility could be linked to any one cause. Even *after* an event, proving what caused it can be hard. No one would disagree that the Japanese bombing of Pearl Harbor took place on December 7, 1941, or that the United States entered World War II shortly thereafter. But what is the causal connection? Did the bombing "cause" the U.S. entry into the war? Even if you are convinced that the bombing was the most immediate cause, what of other related causes: the unstable and often hostile relationship between the U.S. and Japanese governments in the years leading up to the bombing; U.S. policies toward Japanese immigration; common U.S. stereotypes of "Oriental" peoples; U.S. reactions to the Japanese invasion of China; and so on? As another example, during the campus riots of the late 1960s, a special commission was charged with determining the "causes" of riots on a particular campus. After two years of work—and almost a thousand pages of evidence and reports—the commission was unable to pinpoint anything but a broad network of contributing causes and related conditions. Thus causal claims must be approached with care and supported with the strongest evidence available in order to demonstrate the highest probability that A caused B.

DEVELOPING CAUSAL ARGUMENTS

Formulating a Claim

Of course, you might decide to write a wildly exaggerated or parodic causal argument for humorous purposes. Dave Barry does precisely this in an article supposedly explaining the causes of El Niño and other weather effects: "So we see that the true cause of bad weather, contrary to what they have been claiming all these years, is TV weather forecasters, who have also single-handedly destroyed the ozone layer via overuse of hair spray."

Most of the causal reasoning you do, however, will probably take a more serious approach to subjects you, your family, and friends care about. To begin creating a strong causal claim, try listing some of the effects—events or phenomena—you would like to know the causes of. *Why do you tend to panic before meeting new people? What's responsible for the latest tuition hike? What has led to postings of "contamination" along your favorite creek?* Or try moving in the opposite direction, listing some events or causes you are interested in and then hypothesizing what kinds of effects they may produce. *What will happen if your academic major begins requiring a five-year program for a B.S.? What will be the effects of a total crackdown on peer-to-peer file sharing?*

When you find several possible causal relationships that interest you, try them out on friends and colleagues. Can they suggest ways to refocus or clarify what you want to do? Can they offer leads to finding information about your subject? If you have hypothesized various causes or effects, can they offer counterexamples or refutations?

Finally, map out a rough statement about the causal relationship you want to explore:

Read Michelle Cottle's article "Turning Boys into Girls" to see how she develops a claim about "how men's magazines are making guys as neurotic, insecure, and obsessive about their appearance as women."

⋯⋯⋯⋯⋯⋯⋯⋯⋯⋯⋯⋯⋯⋯⋯LINK TO P. 486

A causes (or is caused by) B for the following reasons:

1. _____

2. _____

3. _____

Developing the Argument

Once you have drafted a claim, you can explore the cause-effect relationship(s), drawing out the reasons, warrants, and evidence that can support the claim most effectively.

Claim	Losing seasons caused the football coach to lose his job.
Reason	The team lost more than half its games for three seasons in a row.
Warrant	Winning is the key to success for major-team college coaches.
Evidence	For the last ten years, coaches with more than two losing seasons in a row have lost their jobs.

Claim	Certain career patterns cause women to be paid less than men.
Reason	Women's career patterns differ from men's, and in spite of changes in the relative pay of other groups, women's pay still lags behind that of men.
Warrant	Successful careers are made during the period between ages twenty-five and thirty-five.
Evidence	Women often drop out of or reduce work during the decade between ages twenty-five and thirty-five in order to raise families.

In further developing a causal argument, you can draw on many of the strategies we have already touched on in this book. In the article from which the following passage is excerpted, for instance, Stephen King uses dozens of examples — from *The Texas Chainsaw Massacre*, *The Gory Ones*, and *Invasion of the Body Snatchers* to *Night of the Living Dead*, *Psycho*, *The Amityville Horror*, and *The Thing* — in explaining why people love horror movies:

> **The mythic horror movie, like the sick joke, has a dirty job to do. It deliberately appeals to all that is worst in us. It is morbidity unchained, our most base instincts let free, our nastiest fantasies realized . . . and it all happens, fittingly enough, in the dark. For those reasons, good liberals often shy away from horror films. For myself, I like to see the most aggressive of them—*Dawn of the Dead*, for instance— as lifting a trap door in the civilized forebrain and throwing a basket of raw meat to the hungry alligators swimming around in that subterranean river beneath.**
>
> **Why bother? Because it keeps them from getting out, man. It keeps them down there and me up here. It was Lennon and McCartney who said that all you need is love, and I would agree with that.**
>
> **As long as you keep the gators fed.**
> —Stephen King, "Why We Crave Horror Movies"

Another way to support a causal argument is through the use of analogies. In such an argument, the strength will lie in how closely you can relate the two phenomena being compared. In exploring why women consistently earn less pay than men even when they are performing the same jobs, Sarah Banda Purvis draws an analogy between working women and sports:

> **An analogy I use when describing my experiences as a female manager in corporate America is that I was allowed to sit on the bench but never given a chance to get on the field and play in the game.**
> —Sarah Banda Purvis, "What Do Working Women Want in the 21st Century?"

She goes on to trace the effects that constantly being relegated to the "bench" has on earning power.

Establishing causes for physical effects—like diseases—often calls for another means of support: testing hypotheses, or theories about possible causes. This kind of reasoning helped to determine the causes of recent school poisonings in Georgia, and some years ago it helped to solve a mystery disease that had struck some fifty people in Quebec City. Puzzled by cases all involving the same effects (nausea, shortness of breath, cough, stomach pain, weight loss, and a marked blue-gray coloration), doctors at first investigated the hypothesis that the cause was severe vitamin defi-

In his article arguing the merits of hospice care, Joe Loconte closes with this analogy: "hospice personnel could be to medical care what American GIs were to the Allied effort in Europe — the source of both its tactical and moral strength and, eventually, the foot soldiers for victory and reconciliation."

LINK TO P. 660

ciency. But too many cases in too short a time made this hypothesis unlikely, because vitamin deficiency does not ordinarily appear as a sudden epidemic. In addition, postmortem examinations of the twenty people who died revealed severe damage to the heart muscle and the liver, features that were inconsistent with the vitamin-deficiency hypothesis. The doctors therefore sought a clue to the mysterious disease in something the fifty victims were found to have shared: all fifty had been lovers of beer and had, in fact, drunk a particular brand of beer.

It seemed possible that the illness was somehow connected to the beer, brewed in Quebec City and Montreal. But Montreal had no incidence of the disease. The hypothesis, then, was further refined: perhaps the significant difference existed in the process of brewing. Eventually, this hypothesis was borne out. The Quebec brewery had added a cobalt compound to its product in order to enhance the beer's foaminess; the Montreal brewery had not. Furthermore, the compound had been added only a month before the first victims became ill.

In spite of the strength of this causal hypothesis, doctors in this case were still cautious, because the cobalt had not been present in sufficient quantities to kill a normal person. Yet twenty had died. After persistent study, the doctors decided that this fact must be related to the victims' drinking habits, which in some way reduced their resistance to the chemical. For those twenty people, a normally nonlethal dose of cobalt had been fatal.

The difficulties of such causal analysis were in the news a lot after the September 11, 2001, attacks on the Pentagon and World Trade Center. In the ensuing months, many sought to determine the causes of the crash of "the fourth plane," United flight #93, that went down in Pennsylvania. As the investigation unfolded, citizens saw investigators reject several hypotheses about the cause of the crash—it was not, for example, shot down by the U.S. military. When the flight recorder tape was finally played for family members some seven months after the crash, they came away convinced that the investigation had finally targeted the correct cause: the plane crashed into the Pennsylvania countryside as passengers fought to seize control of the plane from the hijackers. Even this information, however, cannot clarify completely the technical causes that led to the crash.

Causal arguments can also be supported by experimental evidence that is based less on strictly scientific investigation than on ethnographic observation—the study of the daily routines of ordinary people in a particular community. In an argument that attempts to explain why, when people meet head-on, some step aside and some do not, investigators Frank Willis, Joseph Gier, and David Smith observed "1,038 displacements involving 3,141 persons" at a Kansas City shopping mall. In results that

Deborah Tannen uses her own observation of gender differences in communication patterns to support her argument urging teachers to adopt new classroom strategies. She writes, "The classroom is a different environment for those who feel comfortable putting themselves forward in a group than it is for those who find the prospect of doing so chastening, or even terrifying."

LINK TO P. 730

surprised the investigators, "gallantry" seemed to play a significant role in causing people to step aside for one another—more so than other causes the investigators had anticipated (such as deferring to someone who is physically stronger or higher in status).

Yet another method of supporting a causal argument is through the use of one or more correlations. In such an argument you try to show that if A occurs, B is also likely to occur. You may be most familiar with correlations from statistical procedures that enable you to predict, within a degree of certainty, how likely it is that two elements or events will occur together. Recent advances in the human genome project, for example, have identified "clusters" of genes that, when found in correlation with one another, strongly suggest the occurrence of certain cancers. But correlation works in more informal ways as well. Kate Shindle, who was crowned Miss America 1998, objects strenuously to the correlation between beauty and brainlessness:

> I thought my work on the front lines of a life-and-death issue made it clear that there is more to the Miss America program than swimsuits and evening gowns. I quickly realized that wasn't the case. Though I was a dean's list student at Northwestern, suddenly people assumed I didn't have a brain. Administrators at one highly ranked university canceled an appearance, claiming that Miss America couldn't possibly have anything in common with their students. Another time, a representative of the group I had flown in to speak to picked me up at the airport, grabbed the heaviest of my three suitcases, and said, "Is this the one that holds all the makeup?" I didn't bother to explain that it held my files on AIDS research.
>
> –Kate Shindle, "Miss America: More Than a Beauty Queen?"

FIGURE 11.3 MISS AMERICA, KATE SHINDLE

Finally, you may want to consider using personal experience in support of a causal argument. Indeed, people's experiences generally lead them to seek out or to avoid various causes and effects. If you are consistently praised for your writing ability, chances are that you will look for opportunities to produce that pleasant effect. If three times in a row you get sick after eating shrimp, you will almost certainly identify the shellfish as the cause of your difficulties and stop eating it. Personal experience can also help build your credibility as a writer, gain the empathy of your listeners, and thus support your cause. Although one person's experiences cannot ordinarily be universalized, they can still argue eloquently for causal relationships. Leslie Marmon Silko uses personal experience to explain her shift from studying to become a lawyer to becoming a writer/photographer/activist, arguing that the best way to seek justice is not through the law but through the power of stories:

> When I was a sophomore in high school I decided law school was the place to seek justice. . . . I should have paid more attention to the lesson of the Laguna Pueblo land claims lawsuit from my childhood: The lawsuit was not settled until I was in law school. The U.S. Court of Indian Claims found in favor of the Pueblo of Laguna, but the Indian Claims Court never gives back land wrongfully taken; the court only pays tribes for the land. . . . The Laguna people wanted the land they cherished; instead, they got twenty-five cents for each of the six million acres stolen by the state. The lawsuit had lasted twenty years, so the lawyers' fees amounted to nearly $2 million.
>
> I completed three semesters in the American Indian Law School Fellowship Program before I realized that injustice is built into the Anglo-American legal system. . . . But I continued in law school until our criminal law class read an appeal to the U.S. Supreme Court to stop the execution of a retarded black man convicted of strangling a white librarian in Washington, D.C., in 1949. The majority on the Court refused to stop the execution, though it was clear that the man was so retarded that he had no comprehension of his crime. That case was the breaking point for me. I wanted nothing to do with such a barbaric legal system.
>
> My time in law school was not wasted: I had gained invaluable insights into the power structure of mainstream society, and I continue to follow developments in the law to calculate prevailing political winds. It seems to me there is no better way to uncover the deepest values of a culture than to observe the operation of that culture's system of justice.
>
> [But] I decided the only way to seek justice was through the power of stories.
> —Leslie Marmon Silko, *Yellow Woman and a Beauty of Spirit: Essays on Native American Life Today*

All these strategies—the use of examples, analogies, testing hypotheses, experimental evidence, correlations, and personal experience—can help you build good reasons in support of a causal argument. However, the success of the argument may ultimately depend on your ability to convince your readers that the reasons you offer are indeed good ones. In terms of causal arguments, that will mean distinguishing among immediate, necessary, and sufficient reasons. In the case of the mysterious illness in Quebec City, the immediate reasons for illness were the symptoms themselves: nausea, shortness of breath, and so on. But they were not the base or root causes of the disease. Drinking the particular beer in question served as a necessary reason: without the tainted beer, the illness would not have occurred. However, the researchers had to search much harder for the sufficient reason—the reason that will cause the effect (the illness) if it is present. In the case of the Quebec City beer, that reason turned out to be the addition of cobalt.

This example deals with the scientific investigation of a disease, but everyday causal analysis can draw on this distinction among reasons as well. What caused you, for instance, to pursue a college education? Immediate reasons might be that you needed to prepare for a career of some kind or that you had planned to do so for years. But what are the necessary reasons, the ones without which your pursuit of higher education could not occur? Adequate funds? Good test scores and academic record? The expectations of your family? You might even explore possible sufficient reasons, those that—if present—will guarantee the effect of your pursuing higher education. In such a case, you may be the only person with enough information to determine what the sufficient reasons might be.

KEY FEATURES OF CAUSAL ARGUMENTS

In drafting your own causal argument, keep in mind the following five elements:

- examination of each possible cause and effect
- description and explanation of the relationship among any links, especially in an argument based on a series of links in a causal chain
- evidence that your description and explanation are accurate and thorough

Myriam Marquez shares her analysis of the necessary and sufficient reasons why she and her family speak Spanish in public places.

LINK TO P. 751 ·································

- evidence to show that the causes and effects you have identified are highly probable and that they are backed by good reasons, usually presented in order of their strength and importance

- consideration of alternative causes and effects, and evidence that you have considered them carefully before rejecting them

Fully developing a causal argument will probably call for addressing each of these elements, though you can order them in several ways. You may want to open your essay with a dramatic description of the effect, for example, and then "flash back" to multiple causes. Or you might decide to open with a well-known phenomenon, identify it as a cause, and then trace its effects. In the same way, you might decide to lead off the body of the argument with your strongest, most compelling piece of evidence, or to hold that evidence for the culmination of your argument. In any case, you should make a careful organizational plan and get a response to that plan from your instructor, friends, and colleagues before proceeding to a full draft. When the draft is complete, you should again seek a response, testing out the strength of your causal argument on at least several readers.

Finding a Topic

Chances are that a little time spent brainstorming—either with friends or other students, or on paper—will turn up some good possibilities for causal arguments of several kinds, including those that grow out of your personal experience. *Just exactly what did lead to your much higher GPA last term?* Beyond your own personal concerns, you may find a good number of public issues that lend themselves to causal analysis and argument: *What factors have led to the near bankruptcy of the nation's major airlines? What will happen if the United States continues to refuse to sign the Kyoto Protocol aimed at reducing greenhouse emissions? What effects have been caused by the move to pay professional basketball players astronomical sums of money?* Finally, as you are brainstorming possibilities for a causal argument of your own, don't ignore important current campus issues: *What have been the effects of recent increases in tuition (or what factors caused the increases)? What are the likely outcomes of shifting the academic calendar from a quarter to a semester system? If, as some argue, there has been a significant increase of racism and homophobia on campus, what has caused that increase? What are its consequences?*

Researching Your Topic

Causal arguments will lead you to a number of different resources:

- current news media—especially magazines and newspapers (online or in print)
- online database
- scholarly journals
- books written on your subject (here you can do a keyword search, either in your library or online)
- Web sites, listservs, or newsgroups devoted to your subject

In addition, why not carry out some field research of your own? You could conduct interviews with appropriate authorities on your subject, for instance, or create a questionnaire aimed at getting a range of opinion on a particular aspect of your subject. The information you get from interviews or from analyzing responses to a questionnaire can provide strong evidence to back up the claim you are making.

Formulating a Claim

You may begin to formulate your claim by identifying the particular kind of causal argument you want to make—one moving from cause(s) to effect(s);

one moving from effect(s) to cause(s); or one involving a series of links, with Cause A leading to B, which then leads to C. (See pp. 207–209 for a review of these kinds of arguments.)

Your next move may be to explore your own relationship to your subject. What do you know about the subject and its causes and effects? On what basis do you agree with the claim? What significant reasons can you offer in support of it?

In short, you should end this process of exploration by formulating a brief claim or thesis about a particular causal relationship. It should include *a statement that says, in effect, A causes (or does not cause, or is caused by) B, and a summary of the reasons supporting this causal relationship.* Remember to make sure that your thesis is as specific as possible and that it is sufficiently controversial or interesting to hold your readers' interest.

Examples of Causal Claims

- Lax current gun laws are responsible, in large part, for an increase in gun-related violent crimes.

- Rising support for third-party political candidates in three key states and increasing disillusionment with the major parties are paving the way for moving beyond the two-party system.

- The proliferation of images in film, television, and computer-generated texts is bringing profound changes to literacy.

- The many extensions to the copyright terms have led to a serious imbalance between the necessary incentive to creators and the right of the public to information, closing off the public commons, doing away, in effect, with the fair use doctrine, and adding billions of dollars to the coffers of Disney and other huge entertainment conglomerates.

Preparing a Proposal

If your instructor asks you to prepare a proposal for your project, here's a simple format that may help.

State the thesis of your argument fully, perhaps using the Toulmin schema:

> Claim:
>
> Reason(s):
>
> Warrant(s):

Explain why this argument deserves attention. Why is it important for your readers to consider?

Specify those whom you hope to reach with this argument, and explain why this group of readers is an appropriate audience. What interest or investment do they have in the issue? Why will they (or should they) be concerned?

Briefly identify and explore the major challenges you expect to face in supporting your argument. Will demonstrating a clear causal link between A and B be particularly difficult? Will the data you need to support the claim be hard to obtain?

List the strategies you expect to use in researching your argument—will you be interviewing? Surveying opinion? Conducting library and online searches? Other?

List the major sources you will need to consult—and note whether they are readily available to you.

Briefly identify and explore the major counterarguments you might expect in response to your argument.

Consider what format and genre will work best for your argument: Will you be preparing a Web site? A press release? An editorial for the local newspaper? A report for an organization you belong to?

Thinking about Organization

Whatever genre or format you decide to use, your causal argument should address the following elements:

- a specific causal claim: *Devastating flash floods associated with El Niño were responsible for the dramatic loss of homes in central California in early 2003.*

- an explanation of the claim's significance or importance: *Claims for damage from flooding put some big insurance companies out of business; as a result, homeowners couldn't get coverage and many who lost their homes had to declare bankruptcy.*

- supporting evidence sufficient to support each cause or effect—or, in an argument based on a series of causal links, evidence to support the relationships among the links: *The amount of rain that fell in central California in early 2003 was 50 percent above normal, leading inexorably to rapidly rising rivers and creeks.*

- consideration of alternative causes and effects, and evidence that you understand these alternatives and have thought carefully about them

221

before rejecting them: *Although some say that excessive and sloppy logging and poor building codes were responsible for the loss of homes, the evidence supporting these alternative causes is not convincing.*

Getting and Giving Response

All arguments can benefit from the scrutiny of others. Your instructor may assign you to a peer group for the purpose of reading and responding to each other's drafts; if not, make the effort yourself to get some careful response. You can use the following questions to evaluate a draft. If you are evaluating someone else's draft, be sure to supply examples to illustrate your points. Specific comments are always more helpful than general observations.

The Claim

- What is most effective about the claim? What are its strengths?
- Is the claim sufficiently qualified?
- Is the claim specific enough to be clear? How could it be narrowed and focused more clearly?
- How strong is the relationship between the claim and the reasons given to support it? How could that relationship be made more explicit?
- Is it immediately evident why the claim is important? How could it be rephrased in a way that more forcefully and clearly suggests its significance?
- Does the claim reveal a causal connection? How could it be revised to make the causal links clearer?

Evidence for the Claim

- What is the strongest evidence offered for the claim? What, if any, evidence needs to be strengthened?
- Is enough evidence offered that these particular causes are responsible for the effect that has been identified, that these particular effects result from the identified cause, or that a series of causes and effects are linked? If not, what kind of additional evidence is needed? What kinds of sources might provide this evidence?
- How credible and persuasive will the sources likely be to potential readers? What other kinds of sources might be more credible and persuasive?

222

- Is the evidence in support of the claim simply announced, or is it analyzed in terms of its appropriateness and significance? Is a more detailed discussion necessary?

- Have all the major alternative causes and effects as well as objections to the claim been considered? What support is offered for rejecting these alternatives? Where is additional support needed?

Organization and Style

- How are the parts of the argument organized? Is this organization effective, or would some other structure work better?

- Will readers understand the relationships among the claims, supporting reasons, warrants, and evidence? If not, what could be done to make those connections clearer? Are more transitional words and phrases needed? Would headings or graphic devices help?

- Are the transitions or links from point to point, paragraph to paragraph, and sentence to sentence clear and effective? If not, how could they be improved?

- Is the style suited to the subject? Is it too formal? Too casual? Too technical? Too bland? How can it be improved?

- Which sentences seem particularly effective? Which ones seem weakest, and how could they be improved? Should some short sentences be combined, or should any long ones be separated into two or more sentences?

- How effective are the paragraphs? Do any seem too skimpy or too long, and how can they be improved?

- Which words or phrases seem particularly effective, vivid, and memorable? Do any seem dull, unclear, or inappropriate for the audience or the writer's purpose? Are definitions provided for terms that readers might not know?

Spelling, Punctuation, Mechanics, Documentation, Format

- What errors in spelling, punctuation, capitalization, and the like can you identify?

- Is an appropriate and consistent style of documentation used for parenthetical citations and the list of works cited or references? (See Chapter 22.)

- Does the paper or project follow an appropriate format? Is it appropriately designed and attractively presented? How can it be improved? If it is a Web site, do all the links work?

RESPOND•

1. The causes of some of the following events and phenomena are quite well known and frequently discussed. But do you understand them well enough yourself to spell out the causes to someone else? Working in a group, see how well (and in how much detail) you can explain each of the following events or phenomena. Which explanations are relatively clear-cut, and which seem more open to debate?

   rain

   the Burning Man festival

   the collapse of communism in 1989

   earthquakes

   the common cold

   the popularity of the Harry Potter films

   the itching caused by a mosquito bite

   the economic slump of 2002–2003

   a skid in your car on a slippery road

   the destruction of the space shuttle *Columbia*

   the rise in cases of autism

2. One of the fallacies of argument discussed in Chapter 19 is the *post hoc, ergo propter hoc* fallacy: "after this, therefore because of this." Causal arguments are particularly prone to this kind of fallacious reasoning, in which a writer asserts a causal relationship between two entirely unconnected events. After Elvis Presley's death, for instance, oil prices in the United States rose precipitously—but it would be a real stretch to argue that the King's passing caused gas prices to skyrocket.

   Because causal arguments can easily fall prey to this fallacy, you might find it useful to take absurd causal positions and see where they go—if only to learn how to avoid making such mistakes. As a class, have some fun creating an argument that goes from cause to effect—or from effect to cause—in a series of completely ridiculous steps (A leads to B leads to C leads to D). Start with one person stating a cause (such as someone sleeping late or missing a test) and move on one by one through the class, building effects on effects. (For example: *Because Jamie stepped on a crack in the sidewalk, he failed his physics exam.* Next person: *Because he failed his physics exam, he couldn't face any of his friends.* Next person: *Because he couldn't face any of his friends.* . . . In an exercise like this, the more absurd or silly the causal links, the better!)

3. In an article at the end of this chapter, Damien Cave conducts an interview with economist Stan Liebowitz, who has spent a great deal of time and effort trying to identify the causes of slumping CD sales and, more specifically, to answer the question, *Does MP3 file trading hurt the music industry?* Cave's article traces the changes in Liebowitz's answer to this question as he analyzes thirty years of record sales figures. Read this article carefully and then, working with another person in your class, decide how strong the causal evidence is for the conclusion Liebowitz puts forth.

TWO SAMPLE CAUSAL ARGUMENTS

What Makes a Serial Killer?

LA DONNA BEATY

The cause-effect relationship is raised in a question: What (the causes) makes a serial killer (the effect)?

Jeffrey Dahmer, John Wayne Gacy, Mark Allen Smith, Richard Chase, Ted Bundy—the list goes on and on. These five men alone have been responsible for at least ninety deaths, and many suspect that their victims may total twice that number. They are serial killers, the most feared and hated of criminals. What deep, hidden secret makes them lust for blood? What can possibly motivate a person to kill over and over again with no guilt, no remorse, no hint of human compassion? What makes a serial killer?

An important term (serial killer) is defined through examples.

Serial killings are not a new phenomenon. In 1798, for example, Micajah and Wiley Harpe traveled the backwoods of Kentucky and Tennessee in a violent, year-long killing spree that left at least twenty—and possibly as many as thirty-eight—men, women, and children dead. Their crimes were especially chilling as they seemed particularly to enjoy grabbing small children by the ankles and smashing their heads against trees (Holmes and DeBurger 28). In modern society, however, serial killings have grown to near epidemic proportions. Ann Rule, a respected author and expert on serial murders, stated in a seminar at the University of Louisville on serial murder that between 3,500 and 5,000 people become victims of serial murder each year in the United States alone (qtd. in Holmes and DeBurger 21). Many others estimate that there are close to 350 serial killers currently at large in our society (Holmes and DeBurger 22).

Authority is cited to emphasize the importance of the causal question.

La Donna Beaty wrote this essay while she was a student at Sinclair Community College in Dayton, Ohio. In the essay, she explores the complex web of possible causes—cultural, psychological, genetic, and others—that may help to produce a serial killer. The essay follows MLA style.

Fascination with murder and murderers is not new, but researchers in recent years have made great strides in determining the characteristics of criminals. Looking back, we can see how naive early experts were in their evaluations: in 1911, for example, Italian criminologist Cesare Lombrosco concluded that "murderers as a group [are] biologically degenerate [with] bloodshot eyes, aquiline noses, curly black hair, strong jaws, big ears, thin lips, and menacing grins" (qtd. in Lunde 84). Today, however, we don't expect killers to have fangs that drip human blood, and many realize that the boy-next-door may be doing more than woodworking in his basement. While there are no specific physical characteristics shared by all serial killers, they are almost always male and 92 percent are white. Most are between the ages of twenty-five and thirty-five and often physically attractive. While they may hold a job, many switch employment frequently as they become easily frustrated when advancement does not come as quickly as expected. They tend to believe that they are entitled to whatever they desire but feel that they should have to exert no effort to attain their goals (Samenow 88, 96). What could possibly turn attractive, ambitious human beings into cold-blooded monsters?

Evidence about general characteristics of serial killers is presented.

One popular theory suggests that many murderers are the product of our violent society. Our culture tends to approve of violence and find it acceptable, even preferable, in many circumstances (Holmes and DeBurger 27). According to research done in 1970, one out of every four men and one out of every six women believed that it was appropriate for a husband to hit his wife under certain conditions (Holmes and DeBurger 33). This emphasis on violence is especially prevalent in television programs. Violence occurs in 80 percent of all prime-time shows, while cartoons, presumably made for children, average eighteen violent acts per hour. It is estimated that by the age of eighteen, the average child will have viewed more than 16,000 television murders (Holmes and DeBurger 34). Some experts feel that children demonstrate increasingly aggressive behavior with each violent act they view (Lunde 15) and become so accustomed to violence that these acts

One possible cause is explored: violence in society.

Evidence, including statistics and authority, is offered to support the first cause.

seem normal (35). In fact, most serial killers do begin to show patterns of aggressive behavior at a young age. It is, therefore, possible that after viewing increasing amounts of violence, such children determine that this is acceptable behavior; when they are then punished for similar actions, they may become confused and angry and eventually lash out by committing horrible, violent acts.

A second possible cause is introduced: family context.

Another theory concentrates on the family atmosphere into which the serial killer is born. Most killers state that they experienced psychological abuse as children and never established good relationships with the male figures in their lives (Ressler, Burgess, and Douglas 19). As children, they were often rejected by their parents and received little nurturing (Lunde 94; Holmes and DeBurger

Evidence is offered in support of the second cause.

64–70). It has also been established that the families of serial killers often move repeatedly, never allowing the child to feel a sense of stability; in many cases, they are also forced to live outside the family home before reaching the age of eighteen (Ressler, Burgess, and Douglas 19–20). Our culture's tolerance for violence may overlap with such family dynamics: with 79 percent of the population believing that slapping a twelve-year-old is either necessary, normal, or good, it is no wonder that serial killers relate tales of physical abuse (Holmes and DeBurger 30; Ressler, Burgess, and Douglas 19–20) and view themselves as the "black sheep" of the family. They may even, perhaps unconsciously, assume this same role in society.

An alternative analysis of the evidence in support of the second cause is explored.

While the foregoing analysis portrays the serial killer as a lost, lonely, abused, little child, another theory, based on the same information, gives an entirely different view. In this analysis, the killer is indeed rejected by his family but only after being repeatedly defiant, sneaky, and threatening. As verbal lies and destructiveness increase, the parents give the child the distance he seems to want in order to maintain a small amount of domestic peace (Samenow 13). This interpretation suggests that the killer shapes his parents much more than his parents shape him. It also denies that the media can influence a child's mind and turn him into something that he doesn't already long to be. Since most children view similar amounts of violence, the argument goes, a responsible child filters what he sees and will not resort to criminal activity no matter how acceptable it seems to be (Samenow 15–18). In 1930, the noted psychologist Alfred Adler seemed to find this true of any criminal. As he put it, "With criminals it is different: they have a private logic, a private intelligence. They are suffering from a wrong outlook upon the world, a wrong estimate of their own importance and the importance of other people" (qtd. in Samenow 20).

Most people agree that Jeffrey Dahmer or Ted Bundy had to be "crazy" to commit horrendous multiple murders, and scientists have long maintained that serial killers are indeed mentally disturbed (Lunde 48). While the percentage of murders committed by mental hospital patients is much lower than that among the general population (35), it cannot be ignored that the rise in serial killings happened at almost the same time as the deinstitutionalization movement in the mental health care system during the 1960s (Markman and Bosco 266). While reform was greatly needed in the mental health care system, it has now become nearly impossible to hospitalize those with severe problems. In the United States, people have a constitutional right to remain mentally ill. Involuntary commitment can only be accomplished if the person is deemed dangerous to self, dangerous to others, or gravely disabled. However, in the words of Ronald Markman, "According to the way that the law is interpreted, if you can go to the mailbox to pick up your Social Security check, you're not gravely disabled even if you think you're living on Mars"; even if a patient is thought to be dangerous, he or she cannot be held longer than ninety days unless it can be proved that the patient actually committed dangerous acts while in the hospital (Markman and Bosco 267). Many of the most heinous criminals have had long histories of mental illness but could not be hospitalized due to these stringent requirements. Richard Chase, the notorious Vampire of Sacramento, believed that he needed blood in order to survive, and while in the care of a psychiatric hospital, he often killed birds and other small animals in order to quench this desire. When he was

A third possible cause is introduced: mental instability.

Evidence in support of the third cause, including a series of examples, is offered.

released, he went on to kill eight people, one of them an eighteen-month-old baby (Biondi and Hecox 206). Edmund Kemper was equally insane. At the age of fifteen, he killed both of his grandparents and spent five years in a psychiatric facility. Doctors determined that he was "cured" and released him into an unsuspecting society. He killed eight women, including his own mother (Lunde 53–56). In another case, the world was soon to be disturbed by a cataclysmic earthquake, and Herbert Mullin knew that he had been appointed by God to prevent the catastrophe. The fervor of his religious delusion resulted in a death toll of thirteen (Lunde 63–81). All of these men had been treated for their mental disorders, and all were released by doctors who did not have enough proof to hold them against their will.

A fourth possible cause is introduced: genetic makeup.

Recently, studies have given increasing consideration to the genetic makeup of serial killers. The connection between biology and behavior is strengthened by research in which scientists have been able to develop a violently aggressive strain of mice simply through selective inbreeding (Taylor 23). These studies have caused scientists to become increasingly interested in the limbic system of the brain, which houses the amygdala, an almond-shaped structure located in the front of the temporal lobe. It has long been known that surgically altering that portion of the brain, in an operation known as a lobotomy, is one way of controlling behavior. This surgery was used frequently in the 1960s but has since been discontinued as it also erases most of a person's personality. More recent developments, however, have shown that temporal lobe epilepsy causes electrical impulses to be discharged directly into the amygdala. When this electronic stimulation is re-created in the laboratory, it causes violent behavior in lab animals. Additionally, other forms of epilepsy do not cause abnormalities in behavior, except during seizure activity. Temporal lobe epilepsy is linked with a wide range of antisocial behavior, including anger, paranoia, and aggression. It is also interesting to note that this form of epilepsy produces extremely unusual brain waves. These waves have been found in only 10 to 15 percent of the general population, but over 79 percent of known serial killers test positive for these waves (Taylor 28–33).

Statistical evidence in support of the fourth cause is offered.

The look at biological factors that control human behavior is by no means limited to brain waves or other brain abnormalities. Much work is also being done with neurotransmitters, levels of testosterone, and patterns of trace minerals. While none of these studies is conclusive, they all show a high correlation between antisocial behavior and chemical interactions within the body (Taylor 63–69).

One of the most common traits that all researchers have noted among serial killers is heavy use of alcohol. Whether this correlation is brought about by external factors or whether alcohol is an actual stimulus that causes certain behavior is still unclear, but the idea deserves consideration. Lunde found that the majority of those who commit murder had been drinking beforehand and commonly had a urine alcohol level of between .20 and .29, nearly twice the legal level of intoxication (31–32). Additionally, 70 percent of the families that reared serial killers had verifiable records of alcohol abuse (Ressler, Burgess, and Douglas 17). Jeffrey Dahmer had been arrested in 1981 on charges of drunkenness and, before his release from prison on sexual assault charges, his father had written a heartbreaking letter which pleaded that Jeffrey be forced to undergo treatment for alcoholism, a plea that, if heeded, might have changed the course of future events (Davis 70, 103). Whether alcoholism is a learned behavior or an inherited predisposition is still hotly debated, but a 1979 report issued by Harvard Medical School stated that "[a]lcoholism in the biological parent appears to be a more reliable predictor of alcoholism in the children than any other environmental factor examined" (qtd. in Taylor 117). While alcohol was once thought to alleviate anxiety and depression, we now know that it can aggravate and intensify such moods (Taylor 110), which may lead to irrational feelings of powerlessness that are brought under control only when the killer proves he has the ultimate power to control life and death.

A fifth possible cause—heavy use of alcohol—is introduced and immediately qualified.

The complexity of causal relationships is emphasized: one cannot say with certainty what produces a particular serial killer.

The conclusion looks toward the future: the web of causes examined here suggests that much more work needs to be done to understand, predict, and ultimately control the behavior of potential serial killers.

"Man's inhumanity to man" began when Cain killed Abel, but this legacy has grown to frightening proportions, as evidenced by the vast number of books that line the shelves of modern bookstores—row after row of titles dealing with death, anger, and blood. We may never know what causes a serial killer to exact his revenge on an unsuspecting society. But we need to continue to probe the interior of the human brain to discover the delicate balance of chemicals that controls behavior. We need to be able to fix what goes wrong. We must also work harder to protect our children. Their cries must not go unheard. Their pain must not become so intense that it demands bloody revenge. As today becomes tomorrow, we must remember the words of Ted Bundy, one of the most ruthless serial killers of our time: "Most serial killers are people who kill for the pure pleasure of killing and cannot be rehabilitated. Some of the killers themselves would even say so" (qtd. in Holmes and DeBurger 150).

WORKS CITED

Biondi, Ray, and Walt Hecox. *The Dracula Killer*. New York: Simon, 1992.

Davis, Ron. *The Milwaukee Murders*. New York: St. Martin's, 1991.

Holmes, Ronald M., and James DeBurger. *Serial Murder*. Newbury Park, CA: Sage, 1988.

Lunde, Donald T. *Murder and Madness*. San Francisco: San Francisco Book, 1976.

Markman, Ronald, and Dominick Bosco. *Alone with the Devil*. New York: Doubleday, 1989.

Ressler, Robert K., Ann W. Burgess, and John E. Douglas. *Sexual Homicide—Patterns and Motives*. Lexington, MA: Heath, 1988.

Samenow, Stanton E. *Inside the Criminal Mind*. New York: Times, 1984.

Taylor, Lawrence. *Born to Crime*. Westport, CT: Greenwood, 1984.

File Sharing: Guilty as Charged?

DAMIEN CAVE

DOES MP3 FILE TRADING HURT THE MUSIC INDUSTRY?

It's a question that has caused heated debate ever since Napster exploded on the scene in 1999. And as sales of recorded music have declined over the past two years, it's a question that has taken on ever-greater importance—for the music business, Congress and music fans.

Up until recently, there has been little hard data to support anyone's claims that file trading is hurting—or helping—music sales. But at least one researcher, University of Texas (at Dallas) economist Stan Liebowitz, author of an upcoming book titled *Rethinking the Network Economy*, is digging hard for quantitative answers.

In May, Liebowitz published a paper suggesting that the record industry would soon be seriously harmed by MP3s. But in June, by the time Salon caught up with him, he was questioning his own conclusions after having examined the numbers and finding little solid proof that file sharing was hurting CD sales.

Two months later, he's changed his mind again. Sort of. In an insightful, yet-to-be published paper that analyzes 30 years of record sales figures, Liebowitz argues that MP3s are in fact having a significant negative effect on the CD market. He acknowledges that new data could once again lead to new conclusions, but for now, Liebowitz says, "I've moved somewhat closer to the record company position."

Salon called Liebowitz at his home in Dallas to discuss his findings.

When we last spoke, you said you had yet to find proof of harm from MP3s. What's changed?
The one big piece of evidence that I didn't have when we talked before was a half-year 2002 number [that appears to indicate a 9.8 percent decrease in album sales]. There has to be a caveat in here, which is that I don't know if this number is correct. It's a half-year number that I saw in *USA Today*, from SoundScan.

Damien Cave, a senior writer for Salon.com, has written numerous articles on technology. The selection reprinted here, from August 23, 2002, contains an interview with Stan Liebowitz, an economist at the University of Texas.

233

If it were the case that there was a 9.8 percent drop on albums, when you look at the historical record of the ups and downs of the CD industry, [that's] a bigger decline than we've seen in 30 years. It starts to look unusual.

How much bigger is the decline? Is it a significant drop or a slight depression?
I haven't figured out the percentage but it's definitely bigger than the other ones. Now, let me add another point. When we last spoke, we were talking about a 5 percent decline in sales and I said, "Look, if this is a recession then a 5 percent decline isn't so unusual." At that time, I had assumed that record sales moved with income; during a recession, you could expect fewer records to be sold. When I actually ran the numbers, with income as a variable, it had a very small impact. It was what is known as statistically significant but it was so small that you could ignore it. So in fact, you couldn't conclude that because we're having a recession, you might expect a 5 percent reduction in record sales. That's the other prop I was leaning on. . . . There's evidence that something different is going on.

But assuming SoundScan's figures are correct, your paper seems to hang on a matter of degree. If 2002 sales are down 9.8 percent, you argue, and if this continues, the decline will be the biggest in 30 years. But aren't there other possible reasons for the decline?
I mention that there are these supposed instances of doldrums in musical creativity and you read about them from time to time. But it's a hard thing, at the moment, to measure that.

But isn't it possible that the intersection of several other unprecedented factors wholly independent of MP3s could be causing the decline in sales?
That's right. It is certainly not conclusive, by any means, that there's real damage going on from MP3s. It could be that we're having a bit of doldrums in terms of taste; it could be that we're all using CDs now and nothing else, so since they're a little more durable than other formats that could be part of it. But it is at least beginning to look like there is damage being caused. But remember, the original story was that there's so much MP3 downloading going on so we should see a really big impact fairly easy. And now we're seeing a medium impact, which still could be explained by other things—but we can't discount the MP3 possibility.

If the record industry is somehow not able to stop the downloading, I think we'll know by 2003. We'll get the end of the 2002 year numbers when December's over. We'll see what actually happened. And I expect that by 2003, whatever's going to happen will have happened. This is a great experiment for people who are curious about issues like this. We'll eventually find out. So while it's premature to say this is the smoking gun that shows that harm is there, it is certainly more indicative of harm than what had been there with just the 2001 numbers.

In your paper you argue that MP3s will create a 20 percent decline in sales. How did you get this figure?
I may be going out on a limb in trying to do that but what I'm saying is, let's throw out the fact that cassettes are dying, because that seems to be happening on its own. If we remove that, and assume that half the computer owners have CD burners—a number that I've seen—you just double the decline that's already occurred. It should be less than that because the people who would be doing the most burning would be the ones who already have the burners. So that's where I come up with that number. That's not the death of the industry, but it's a severe decline.

Is this decline significant enough to justify new laws, like the Berman bill, which would give copyright owners the power to hack into people's computers to stop copying and trading?
In my own mind, I don't think a 20 percent decline warrants letting them override the other laws we have out there saying that you're not supposed to tamper with people's computers. That's my own view.

If [file-trading] was going to kill the record industry, you could understand why the record industry would be willing to go to any lengths to get [the Berman bill] passed. They also might be willing to do that for 20 percent if they're not paying the costs. But is society willing to impose a law like this on the public to protect the industry from a 20 percent decline?

If the industry wants to prosecute 18-year-old kids, they can make that decision. But I suspect I wouldn't be in favor of that if the government is going to be prosecuting 18-year-old kids. You don't want to, in my mind, create a situation in which we're saying that a large proportion of our population are criminals unless you think that there's some really strong reason to do that.

People can debate whether, say, criminalizing marijuana and making so many people violate the law is good or bad, but at least you have to understand what the costs and benefits are. And at least the people who are in favor of criminalizing it think it's a terrible, terrible thing. If you're going to do that [with file trading], you have to ask if in fact there's a terrible thing going on. Is a 20 percent decline enough of a problem to say that we should go after these kids? If the record industry wants to foot the bill, because they think the benefits are greater than the costs, fine. But I don't want my district attorney spending my money going after 18-year-old kids who are downloading if it's only going to cause a 20 percent decline in sales for the industry.

When we last spoke, you said that a key historical sign would come from whether the introduction of audiocassettes had a negative effect on music sales. Your analysis here argues that tapes had no effect on sales, and if anything, sales went up when cassettes were introduced. What makes you think MP3s will be different?
The net effect of tapes was positive. But it doesn't mean that it wouldn't have been more positive if people weren't making more copies. [What is clear is that] there's no evidence in the data that the tapes caused a decline.

MP3s wouldn't do the same thing. The reason cassettes led to growth was that before cassettes existed, you didn't have portable music. You couldn't play recorded music in your car, and you couldn't play it walking around, in a Walkman. It was the little cassette that basically allowed you to do that. To be technically correct, there were 8-track players prior to cassettes. But they didn't have quite the same penetration. My theory as to what went on is that [the rise in cassettes] coincides almost perfectly with the penetration rate of the portable, Walkman type of thing. So it opened up this whole new market, which overwhelmed any copying that went on.

You mention that price doesn't matter because album prices have tracked with inflation for the last 30 years: A 10-song recording today costs as much as it did in the '70s. This runs counter to the public perception that CDs are wildly overpriced, and I'm wondering if people think CDs are expensive because other musical components such as CD players have decreased in price, while CDs have not . . .
It's possible, but the technology in creating stereos is not necessarily related to the technology used to create CDs. If you take a look at the book *Entertainment Industry Economics*, the author goes through the cost of a CD, and in his older editions, he goes through the cost of an LP or a cassette. And the majority of the cost is not the production of the actual physical item. That may go down, but the majority of the costs are the other costs:

publicizing albums, finding talent. There's no reason to think that those are going down because they're not technology-based. The small part, technology, is 15 percent of the item and that may be going down, but it doesn't have much of an impact. It's really amazing how prices have tracked so closely with inflation. It's almost as if the industry just bumps up prices with the inflation rate.

You also point out in your paper that there's been no differentiation in price when it comes to music, which is radically different from most markets for other products, such as TVs, for example, which come in a variety of sizes and prices. Do you think the industry needs to abandon this business model? Could this be a solution to the problem of MP3s?

I don't know if that's necessary but one of the things that the entertainment industry has always been really good at is differentiating products. With movies, you have the theater, the tapes, the pay-per-view, the HBO, then the TV. To me, the interesting thing is that historically, the record industry hasn't done much differentiation. What you might have expected was, say, a CD that was half the price of current high-quality CDs that just has a lower sampling rate. With MP3s, for example, when you rip a CD, you have a choice about whether you want to have CD-quality or near-CD quality or FM-radio quality. When you're playing music on low-quality stereos, you wouldn't really hear the difference. So one of the things the industry could do with their downloads is have different prices. People with high-quality stereos aren't going to want to put the low-quality material on, and the people who have lower-quality stereos, with speakers that are incapable of producing the frequencies that let you hear the difference, then they'll buy the cheap ones. That would be a way to broaden the market and increase their revenues. In a way it's surprising that the industry hasn't done that. And as they are trying to figure out their models for online sales, that would be one way of doing it.

How willing do you think the industry is to make such changes?

That depends on the individuals involved. But the fact of the matter is that if they're too rigid, they'll get replaced by some start-up that's not. That much is certain. You can't be terribly inefficient, terribly rigid and hang on.

chapter twelve

Proposals

A student looking forward to a much-needed vacation emails three friends proposing that they pool their resources and rent a cottage at a nearby surfing beach.

A cartoonist works to develop a cartoon arguing that for-profit health care may well kill the (national) patient.

The members of a club for business majors begin to talk about their common need to create informative, appealing—and easily scannable—résumés. After much talk, three members suggest that the club develop a Web site that will guide members in building such résumés and provide links to other resources.

A project team at a large consulting engineering firm works for three months developing a proposal in response to an RFP (request for proposal) to convert a military facility to a community camp.

Members of a youth activist organization propose to start an after-school program for neighborhood kids, using the organization's meeting place and volunteering their time as tutors and mentors.

The undergraduate student organization at a large state university asks the administration for information about how long it takes to complete a degree in each academic major. After analyzing this information, the group recommends a reduction in the number of hours needed to graduate.

■ ■ ■

UNDERSTANDING AND CATEGORIZING PROPOSALS

How many proposals do you make or respond to every day? Chances are, more than a few: Your roommate suggests you both skip breakfast in order to get in an extra hour of exercise; you and a colleague decide to go out to dinner rather than work late once again; you call your best friend to propose checking out a new movie; you decide to approach your boss about implementing an idea you've just had. In each case, the proposal implies that some action should take place and implicitly suggests that there are good reasons why it should.

In their simplest form, proposal arguments look something like this:

A should do B because of C.

⌐A⌐ ⌐————————— B —————————⌐
We should see Eminem's *Eight Mile* tonight
⌐————————————— C —————————————⌐

because both the *New York Times* and *Rolling Stone* (reluctantly) gave it good reviews.

Because proposals come at us in so many ways, it's no surprise that they cover a dizzyingly wide range of possibilities, from very local and concrete practices (*A student should switch dorms immediately; A company should switch from one supplier of paper to another*) to very broad matters of policy (*The United States Congress should repeal the Homeland Security Act*). So it may help to think of proposal arguments as divided roughly into two kinds—those that focus on practices, and those that focus on policies. Here are several examples:

PROPOSALS ABOUT PRACTICES

- The city should use brighter lightbulbs in employee parking garages.
- The college should allow students to pay tuition on a month-by-month basis.
- College Bowl games should all be held during a two-day period.

PROPOSALS ABOUT POLICIES

- Congress should institute a national youth service plan.
- The college should adopt a policy guaranteeing a "living wage" to all campus workers.
- The state should repeal all English Only legislation.

CHARACTERIZING PROPOSALS

Proposals have three main characteristics:

- They call for action.
- They focus on the future.
- They center on the audience.

Proposals always call for some kind of action; they aim at getting something done. So while proposals may rely on analysis and careful reflection about ideas and information, these strategies all aim to urge the audience to decide what to do. This feature of proposals will almost always present a challenge, one put very well in the old saying, "You can lead a horse to water, but you can't make it drink." You can present a proposal as cogently and compellingly as possible—but most of the time you can't *make* the audience take the action you propose. Thus proposal arguments must stress the ethos of the writer: if your word and experience and judgment are all credible, the audience is more likely to carry out the action you propose.

In addition, proposal arguments focus on the future, which the actions proposed will affect. Aristotle referred to such arguments as *deliberative* and associated them with the work of government, which is most often concerned with what a society should do over the upcoming years or decades. This future orientation also presents special challenges, since few of us have crystal balls that predict the future. Proposal arguments must therefore concentrate on marshaling all available evidence to demonstrate that the proposed action is very likely to produce the effects it sets out to achieve.

Finally, proposal arguments are highly focused on audience and audience response, since the success of the argument often (if not always) depends on the degree to which the audience agrees to carry out the proposed action.

Let's say that as president of your church youth organization, you decide to propose that the group take on a community tutoring project. Your proposal aims at action: you want members to do volunteer tutoring in an after-school program at the local community center. Your proposal is also future-oriented: you believe that such a project would help teach your group's members about conditions in the inner city as well as help inner-city children in ways that could make them more successful in future schooling. And certainly your proposal is heavily audience-dependent, because only if you can convince members that such service is needed, that it is feasible and likely to achieve the desired effects, and that it will be beneficial to members and to the organization, is your proposal likely to be acted on positively.

In a humorous proposal argument called "Gloom, Gloom, Go Away," Walter Kirn focuses on action—he wants the United States to institute an "emergency extension of daylight saving time, whose ending a couple of weeks ago plunged a lot of folks I know into a funk they still haven't recovered from." Arguing that "desperate times call for desperate measures," Kirn points out that one such measure has traditionally been "to goose our biorhythms by monkeying with the clock." This tongue-in-cheek proposal is certainly action- and future-oriented. But it also appeals directly to its audience, assuming that "winter brings darkness that we don't need right now" and describing the uplifting benefits of "sunlit winter evenings."

In the advertisement on the following page, Americans for the Arts argues "there's not enough art in our schools." The argument targets its audience—parents—in several explicit ways.

Faye Girsh's article, "Should Physician-Assisted Suicide Be Legalized? Yes!" is a good example of a proposal aimed at action. As you read, consider who she targets as her intended audience.

LINK TO P. 654 ·······························

FIGURE **12.1**   THIS ADVERTISEMENT BY AMERICANS FOR THE ARTS MAKES A CLEAR PROPOSAL.

DEVELOPING PROPOSALS

How do you develop an effective proposal? Start by making a strong and clear claim; then go on to show that the proposal meets a need or solves a problem; present good reasons why adopting the proposal will effectively address the need or problem; and show that the proposal is feasible and should therefore be adopted.

Making a Strong and Clear Claim

Begin with a *claim* (what X or Y should do) followed by the *reason(s)* why X or Y should act and the *effects* of adopting the proposal:

Claim	Communities should encourage the development of charter schools
Reason	because they are not burdened by the bureaucracy associated with most public schooling, and
Effects	because instituting such schools will bring more effective educational progress to the community and offer a positive incentive to the public schools to improve their programs as well.

Having established a claim, you can explore its implications by drawing out the reasons, warrants, and evidence that can support it most effectively:

Claim	Congress should pass a bill legalizing the use of marijuana for medical purposes.
Reason	Medical marijuana is an effective pain reliever for millions suffering from cancer and AIDS.
Warrant	The relief of intractable chronic pain is desirable.
Evidence	Nine states have already approved the use of cannabis for medical purposes, and referendums are planned in many other states. Evidence gathered in large double-blind studies demonstrates that marijuana relieves pain associated with cancer and AIDS.

In this proposal argument the reason sets up the need for the proposal, whereas the warrant and evidence demonstrate that the proposal is just and could meet its objective.

Relating the Claim to a Need or Problem

To be effective, claims must be clearly related to a significant need or problem. Thus establishing that the need or problem exists is one of the most important tasks the writer of a proposal argument faces. For this reason, you should explore this part of any proposal you want to make very early on; if you can't establish a clear need for the proposal or show that it solves an important problem, you should probably work toward a revision or a new claim.

You'll often establish the need or problem at the beginning of your introduction—as a way of leading up to your claim. But in some cases you could put the need or problem right *after* your introduction as the major reason for adopting the proposal. In the preceding examples about charter schools and the use of medical marijuana, a writer might choose either strategy.

Regardless of the practical choices about organization, the task of establishing a need or problem calls on you to

- paint a picture of the need or problem in concrete and memorable ways
- show how the need or problem affects the audience for the argument as well as the larger society
- explain why the need or problem is significant

In an argument proposing that a state board of higher education institute courses that involve students in community service in all state colleges, for example, you might begin by painting a fairly negative picture of a "me first and only" society that is self-absorbed and concentrated only on instant gratification. After evoking such a scene, you might explore how this particular problem affects society in general and the state's colleges in particular: It results in hyper-competition that creates a kind of pressure-cooker atmosphere on campuses; it leaves many of society's most vulnerable members without resources or helping hands; it puts the responsibility of helping people solely in the hands of government, thereby adding to the size and cost of government and raising taxes for all; it deprives many of the satisfaction that helping others can bring, a satisfaction that should be a part of every student's education. Finally, you might demonstrate this problem's importance by relating it to the needs of those who would benefit from various kinds of volunteer service: child care, elder care, health care, community learning, arts and cultural projects—the list of areas affected could go on and on.

Look at how Craig R. Dean, a lawyer and executive director of the Equal Marriage Rights Fund, relates his claim—that the United States should

In "Hospice, Not Hemlock," Joe Loconte proposes the use of hospice treatment rather than physician-assisted suicide for the terminally ill. He opens his article by laying out a major problem: "Most people with terminal illnesses die in the sterile settings of hospitals or nursing homes, often in prolonged, uncontrolled pain."

·········LINK TO P. 660

legalize same-sex marriage—to a significant problem (and how he evokes, or renders, the problem):

> In November 1990, my lover, Patrick Gill, and I were denied a marriage license because we are gay. In a memorandum explaining the District's decision, the clerk of the court wrote that "the sections of the District of Columbia code governing marriage do not authorize marriage between persons of the same sex." By refusing to give us the same legal recognition that is given to heterosexual couples, the District has degraded our relationship as well as that of every other gay and lesbian couple.
>
> At one time, interracial couples were not allowed to marry. Gays and lesbians are still denied this basic civil right in the U.S.—and around the world. Can you imagine the outcry if any other minority group was denied the right to legally marry today?
>
> Marriage is more than a piece of paper. It gives societal recognition and legal protection to a relationship. It confers numerous benefits to spouses; in the District alone, there are more than 100 automatic marriage-based rights. In every state in the nation, married couples have the right to be on each other's health, disability, life insurance and pension plans. Married couples receive special tax exemptions, deductions and refunds. Spouses may automatically inherit property and have rights of survivorship that avoid inheritance tax. Though unmarried couples—both gay and heterosexual—are entitled to some of these rights, they are by no means guaranteed.
>
> For married couples, the spouse is legally the next of kin in case of death, medical emergency or mental incapacity. In stark contrast, the family is generally the next of kin for same-sex couples. In the shadow of AIDS, the denial of marriage rights can be even more ominous. . . .
>
> Some argue that gay marriage is too radical for society. We disagree. According to a 1989 study by the American Bar Association, eight to 10 million children are currently being reared in three million gay households. Therefore, approximately 6 percent of the U.S. population is made up of gay and lesbian families with children. Why should these families be denied the protection granted to other families?
>
> Allowing gay marriage would strengthen society by increasing tolerance. It is paradoxical that mainstream America perceives gays and lesbians as unable to maintain long-term relationships while at the same time denying them the very institutions that stabilize such relationships.
>
> –Craig R. Dean, "Legalize Gay Marriage"

Showing That the Proposal Addresses the Need or Problem

An important but tricky part of making a successful proposal lies in relating the claim to the need or problem it addresses. Everyone you know may agree that rising tuition costs at your college constitute a major problem. But will your spur-of-the-moment letter to the college newspaper proposing to reduce the size of the faculty and eliminate all campus bus services really address the problem effectively? Chances are, you would have a very hard time making this connection. On the other hand, proposing that the college establish a joint commission of students, administrators and faculty, and legislative leaders charged with studying the problem and proposing a series of alternatives for solving it would be much more likely to present a clear connection between the problem and the claim.

If you were working on the argument about charter schools, you'd need to show that establishing such schools could successfully tackle at least one of the problems associated with current public education. And in the passage from "Legalize Gay Marriage," the writer must show explicitly how carrying out the recommended action would directly affect the problems he has identified.

Showing That the Proposal Is Workable

To be effective, proposals must be workable: that is, the action proposed can be carried out in a reasonable way. Demonstrating "workability" calls on you to present more evidence—from similar cases, from personal experience, from observational data, from interview or survey data, from Internet research, or from any other sources that help show that what you propose can indeed be done. In addition, it will help your case if you can show that the proposal can be carried out with the resources available. If instead the proposal calls for personnel or funds far beyond reach or reason, your audience is unlikely to accept it. As you think about revising your proposal argument, you can test it against these criteria. In addition, you can try to think of proposals that others might say are better, more effective, or more workable than yours—and you can ask friends to help you think of such counterproposals. If your own proposal can stand up to counterproposals, it's likely a strong one.

Using Personal Experience

If your own experience demonstrates the need or problem your proposal aims to address, or backs up your claim, consider using it to develop your proposal (as Craig R. Dean does in the opening of his proposal to legalize gay marriage). Consider the following questions in deciding when to include your own experiences in making a proposal:

- Is your experience directly related to the need or problem you seek to address, or to your proposal about it?

Proposing changes in the U.S. customs policies vis-à-vis strip searches, Daria MonDesire uses her own experience as powerful evidence of problems in the current system, saying "There have, in my life, been two occasions when underwear was removed against my will. The first occurred at the hands of a rapist. The second time was at the hands of my government."

·······················LINK TO P. 525

- Will your experience be appropriate and speak convincingly to the audience? Will the audience immediately understand its significance, or will it require explanation?
- Does your personal experience fit logically with the other reasons you are using to support your claim?

KEY FEATURES OF PROPOSALS

In drafting a proposal, make sure you include:

- a claim that proposes a practice or policy to address a problem or need and that is oriented toward action, directed at the future, and appropriate to your audience
- statements that clearly relate the claim to the problem or need
- evidence that the proposal will effectively address the need or solve the problem, and that it is workable

Fully developing your proposal will call for addressing all these elements, though you may choose to order them in several different ways. As you organize your proposal, you may decide to open with an introductory paragraph that paints a dramatic picture of the problem you are addressing, and you may decide to conclude with a kind of flashback to this dramatic scene. Or you may choose to start right off with your claim and offer strong support for it before showing the ways in which your proposal addresses a need or solves a problem. In any case, organize your proposal carefully and get response to your organizational plan from your instructor and classmates.

Considering Design

Because proposals often address very specific audiences, they can take any number of forms: a letter or memo, a Web page, a feasibility report, a brochure, a prospectus. Each form has different design requirements; indeed, the design may add powerfully to—or detract significantly from—the effectiveness of the proposal. Even in a college essay written on a computer, the use of white space and margins, headings and subheadings, and variations in type (such as boldface or italics) can guide readers through the proposal and enhance its persuasiveness. So before you produce a final copy of any proposal, make a careful plan for its design. Then get response to the proposal in terms of its content and its design, asking friends, classmates, or instructors to read the proposal and give you their responses. Finally, revise to address all the concerns they raise.

Finding a Topic

Your everyday experience calls on you to make proposals all the time; for example, to spend the weekend snowboarding or doing some other much-loved sport, to change your academic major for some very important reasons, or to add to the family income by starting a small, home-based business. In addition, your community group work or your job may require you to make proposals—to a boss, a board of directors, the local school board, someone you want to impress—the list could go on and on. Of course, you also have many opportunities to make proposals to online groups—with email one click away, the whole world could be the audience for your proposal. In all these cases, you will be aiming to call for action: so why not make an informal list of proposals you'd like to explore in a number of different areas? Or do some freewriting on a subject of great interest to you and see if it leads to a proposal? Either method of exploration is likely to turn up several possibilities for a good proposal argument.

Researching Your Topic

Proposals often call for some research. Even a simple one like "Let's all paint the house this weekend" would raise questions that require some investigation: *Who has the time for the job? What sort of paint will be the best? How much will the job cost?* A proposal that your school board adopt block scheduling would call for careful research into evidence supporting the use of such a system. *Where has it been effective, and why?* And for proposals about social issues (for example, that information on the Internet be freely accessible to everyone, even youngsters), extensive research would be necessary to provide sufficient support. For many proposals, you can begin your research by consulting the following types of sources:

- newspapers, magazines, reviews, and journals (online and print)
- online databases
- government documents and reports
- Web sites and listservs or newsgroups
- books
- experts in the field, some of whom might be right on your campus

In addition, you might decide to carry out some field research: a survey of student opinion on Internet accessibility, for example, or interviews with people who are well informed about your subject.

248

Formulating a Claim

As you think about and explore your topic, begin formulating a claim about it. To do so, come up with a clear and complete thesis that makes a proposal and states the reasons why this proposal should be followed. To get started on formulating a claim, explore and respond to the following questions:

- What do I know about the proposal I am making?
- What reasons can I offer to support my proposal?
- What evidence do I have that implementing my proposal will lead to the results I want?

Examples of Proposal Claims

- Because Senator Dianne Feinstein is highly principled, is a proven leader, and has a powerful political story to tell, Democrats should consider nominating her as the first woman Presidential candidate.
- Hospitals, state and local security agencies, and even citizens should stockpile surgical masks that could help prevent the rapid spread of plague pneumonia.
- Congress should repeal the Copyright Extension Act, since it disrupts the balance between incentives for creators and the right of the public to information set forth in the U.S. Constitution.
- The Environmental Protection Agency must move immediately to regulate power-plant emissions of carbon dioxide, a leading cause of global warming.

Preparing a Proposal

If your instructor asks you to prepare a proposal for your project, here's a format that may help.

State the thesis of your proposal completely. If you are having trouble doing so, try outlining it in terms of the Toulmin system:

Claim:

Reason(s):

Warrant(s):

Explain why your proposal is important. What is at stake in taking, or not taking, the action you propose?

Identify and describe those readers you most hope to reach with your proposal. Why is this group of readers most appropriate for your proposal? What are their interests in the subject?

Briefly discuss the major difficulties you foresee in preparing your argument. Demonstrating that the action you propose is necessary? Demonstrating that it is workable? Moving the audience beyond agreement to action? Something else?

List the research you need to do. What kinds of sources do you expect to consult?

Note down the format or genre you expect to use: An academic essay? A formal report? A Web site?

Thinking about Organization

Proposals, which can take many different forms, generally include the following elements:

- a clear and strong proposal, including the reasons for taking the action proposed and the effects that taking this action will have: *Our neighborhood should establish a "Block Watch" program that will help reduce break-ins and vandalism, and involve our kids in building neighborhood pride.*

- a clear connection between the proposal and a significant need or problem: *Break-ins and vandalism have been on the rise in our neighborhood for the last three years.*

- a demonstration of ways in which the proposal addresses the need: *A Block Watch program establishes a rotating monitor system for the streets in a neighborhood and a voluntary plan to watch out for others' homes.*

- evidence that the proposal will achieve the desired outcome: *Block Watch programs in three other local areas have significantly reduced break-ins and vandalism.*

- consideration of alternative ways to achieve the desired outcome, and a discussion of why these are not preferable: *We could ask for additional police presence, but funding would be hard to get.*

- a demonstration that the proposal is workable and practical: *Because Block Watch is voluntary, our own determination and commitment are all we need to make it work.*

Getting and Giving Response

All arguments can benefit from the scrutiny of others. Your instructor may assign you to a peer group for the purpose of reading and responding to each other's drafts; if not, make the effort yourself to get some careful response. You can use the following questions to evaluate a draft. If you are evaluating someone else's draft, be sure to illustrate your points with examples. Specific comments are always more helpful than general observations.

The Claim

- Does the claim clearly call for action? Is the proposal as clear and specific as possible?
- Is the proposal too sweeping? Does it need to be qualified? If so, how?
- Does the proposal clearly address the problem it intends to solve? If not, how could the connection be strengthened?
- Is the claim likely to get the audience to act rather than just to agree? If not, how could it be revised to do so?

Evidence for the Claim

- Is enough evidence provided to get the audience to support the proposal? If not, what kind of additional evidence is needed? Does any of the evidence provided seem inappropriate or otherwise ineffective? Why?
- Is the evidence in support of the claim simply announced, or are its significance and appropriateness analyzed? Is a more detailed discussion needed?
- Are any objections readers might have to the claim or evidence adequately addressed?
- What kinds of sources are cited? How credible and persuasive will they be to readers? What other kinds of sources might be more credible and persuasive?
- Are all quotations introduced with appropriate signal phrases ("As Ehrenreich argues") and blended smoothly into the writer's sentences?
- Are all visuals titled and labeled appropriately? Have you introduced them and commented on their significance?

Organization and Style

- How are the parts of the argument organized? Is this organization effective, or would some other structure work better?
- Will readers understand the relationships among the claims, supporting reasons, warrants, and evidence? If not, what could be done to make those connections clearer? Are more transitional words and phrases needed? Would headings or graphic devices help?

- How have you used visual design elements to make your proposal more effective?

- Are the transitions or links from point to point, paragraph to paragraph, and sentence to sentence clear and effective? If not, how could they be improved?

- Is the style suited to the subject? Is it too formal? Too casual? Too technical? Too bland? How can it be improved?

- Which sentences seem particularly effective? Which ones seem weakest, and how could they be improved? Should some short sentences be combined, or should any long ones be separated into two or more sentences?

- How effective are the paragraphs? Do any seem too skimpy or too long? How can they be improved?

- Which words or phrases seem particularly effective, vivid, and memorable? Do any seem dull, vague, unclear, or inappropriate for the audience or the writer's purpose? Are definitions provided for technical or other terms that readers might not know?

Spelling, Punctuation, Mechanics, Documentation, Format

- What errors in spelling, punctuation, capitalization, and the like can you identify?

- Is an appropriate and consistent style of documentation used for parenthetical citations and the list of works cited or references? (See Chapter 22.)

- Does the paper or project follow an appropriate format? Is it appropriately designed and attractively presented? How could it be improved? If it is a Web site, do all the links work?

RESPOND.

1. For each problem and solution, make a list of readers' likely objections to the off-the-wall solution offered. Then propose a more defensible solution of your own and explain why you think it is more workable.

   Problem   Future bankruptcy of the Social Security system in the United States.

   Solution   Raise the age of retirement to eighty.

   Problem   Traffic gridlock in major cities.

   Solution   Allow only men to drive on Mondays, Wednesdays, and Fridays and only women on Tuesdays, Thursdays, and Saturdays. Everyone can drive on Sunday.

   Problem   Increasing rates of obesity in the general population.

   Solution   Ban the sale of all high-fat items in fast-food restaurants, including hamburgers, fries, and shakes.

   Problem   Increasing school violence.

   Solution   Authorize teachers and students to carry handguns.

   Problem   Excessive drinking on campus.

   Solution   Establish an 8:00 P.M. curfew on weekends.

2. We write proposal arguments to solve problems, to change the way things are. But problems are not always obvious; what troubles some people might be no big deal to others.

   To get an idea of the range of problems people face on your campus—some of which you may not even have thought of as problems—divide into groups and brainstorm about things that annoy you on and around campus, including everything from bad food in the cafeterias to 8:00 A.M. classes to long lines at the registrar's office. Ask each group to aim for at least twenty gripes. Then choose one problem and, as a group, discuss how you'd go about writing a proposal to deal with it. Remember that you will need to (a) make a strong and clear claim, (b) show that the proposal meets a clear need or solves a significant problem, (c) present good reasons why adopting the proposal will effectively address the need or problem, and (d) show that the proposal is workable and should be adopted.

3. In the essay "The Fat Tax" (see pages 259–61), Jonathan Rauch playfully proposes a tax on overweight folks as a way to decrease obesity and increase health. Using the Toulmin model discussed in Chapter 8, analyze the proposal's structure. What claim(s) does Rauch make, and what reasons does he give to support the claim? What are the warrants that connect the reasons to the claim? What evidence does he provide? Alternatively, make up a rough outline of Rauch's proposal and track the good reasons he presents in support of his claim.

Devastating Beauty

Title uses play on words to pique interest.

TEAL PFEIFER

Opening uses emotional appeals to get readers' attention and point toward a problem or need.

Background information on the problem is presented.

Collarbones, hipbones, cheekbones—so many bones. She looks at the camera with sunken eyes, smiling, acting beautiful. Her dress is Versace, or Gucci, or Dior, and it is revealing, revealing every bone and joint in her thin, thin body. She looks fragile and beautiful, as if I could snap her in two. I look at her and feel the soft cushion of flesh that surrounds my own joints, my own shoulders and hips that are broad, my own ribs surrounded by skin and muscle and fat. I am not nearly as fragile or graceful or thin. I look away and wonder what kind of self-discipline it takes to become beautiful like the model in my magazine.

By age seventeen a young woman has seen an average of 250,000 ads featuring a severely underweight woman whose body type is, for the most part, unattainable by any means, including extreme ones such as anorexia, bulimia, and drug use, according to Allison LaVoie. The media promote clothing, cigarettes, fragrances, and even food with images like these. In a culture that has become increasingly visual, the images put out for public consumption feature women that are a smaller size than ever before. In 1950, the White Rock Mineral Water girl was 5'4" tall and weighed 140 pounds; now she is 5'10" tall and weighs only 110 pounds, signifying the growing deviation between the weight of models and that of the normal female population (Pipher 184).

Teal Pfeifer wrote this essay during her sophomore year at Stanford University, where she has just declared an English major. Teal plans to complete her undergraduate education in a speedy three years and hopes to travel and write about diverse cultures, including the Native American ones she knows best.

This media phenomenon has had a major effect on the female population as a whole, both young and old. Five to ten million women in America today suffer from an eating disorder related to poor self-image, and yet advertisements continue to prey on insecurities fueled by a woman's desire to be thin. Current estimates reveal that eighty percent of women are dissatisfied with their appearance and forty-five percent of those are on a diet on any given day ("Statistics," *National Eating Disorders Association*). Yet even the most stringent dieting will generally fail to create the paper-thin body so valued in the media, and continuing efforts to do so can lead to serious psychological problems such as depression.

Causal relationship between ads and women's body image is considered.

While many young women express dissatisfaction with their bodies, they are not the only victims of the emaciated images so frequently presented to them. Young girls are equally affected by these images, if not more so. Eighty percent of girls under age ten have already been on a diet and expressed the desire to be thinner and more beautiful (*Slim Hopes*). Thus from a young age, beauty is equated to a specific size. The message girls get is an insidious one: In order to be your best self, you should wear size 0 or 1, yet these clothing sizes are not even available in the children's section of clothing stores. The pressure only grows more intense as girls grow up. According to Liz Dittrich, when eleven- to seventeen-year-old girls were asked to name their number one wish, they overwhelmingly said they wanted to be thinner; twenty-seven percent reported that the images of models exerted direct pressure on them to lose weight. Yet only twenty-nine percent of the girls who wanted to lose weight were medically overweight; the rest were a size that is healthy and should be considered desirable.

Evidence that the problem extends across age groups is provided.

Logical appeals are emphasized.

It is tragic to see so much of the American population obsessed with weight and reaching an ideal that is, for the most part, ultimately unattainable. Equally troubling is the role magazines play in feeding this obsession. When a researcher asked female students from Stanford University to flip through several magazines

The role magazines play in perpetuating the problem is established.

FIGURE 1. *YOUNG WOMAN READING MAGAZINE* (PERSONAL PHOTOGRAPH). THIS MAGAZINE'S COVER IMAGE EXEMPLIFIES THE SEXY, THIN STEREOTYPE.

containing images of glamorized, super-thin models, sixty-eight percent of the women felt significantly worse about themselves after viewing the magazine models (Dittrich). This same study showed that looking at models on a long-term basis leads to stress, depression, guilt, and lowered self-worth. As Naomi Wolfe points out in *The Beauty Myth*, thinking obsessively about fat and dieting has actually been shown to change thought patterns and brain chemistry.

How do we reject images that are so harmful to the women and young girls who view them (such as those appearing in magazines like the one in Figure 1)? Legislation regarding what can be printed and distributed is not an option because of First Amendment rights. Equally untenable is the idea of appealing to the industries that

Alternative proposals to address the problem are considered and rejected.

employ emaciated models. As long as the beauty and clothing industry are making a profit from the physically insecure women who view their ads, nothing will change.

What, however, might happen if those women stopped viewing such destructive images and buying the magazines that print them? A boycott is the most effective way to rid the print medium of emaciated models and eliminate the harmful effects they cause. If women stopped buying magazines that target them with such harmful advertising, magazines would be forced to change the selection of ads they print. Such a boycott would send a clear message that women reject the victimization that takes place every time a woman or young girl looks at a skeletally thin model and feels worse about herself. Consumers can ultimately control what is put on the market: If we don't buy, funding for such ads will dry up fast.

The proposal claim: a boycott would effectively solve the problem.

In the past, boycotts have proved effective in effecting change quickly. Rosa Parks, often identified as the mother of the modern-day civil rights movement, played a pivotal role in the Montgomery Bus Boycott in December 1955. In protest of the mistreatment of African Americans on the public transit system, people chose to walk instead of employ the buses. This act was successful not because of the status or influence of the people involved; rather, when seventy-five percent of the people who rode the bus chose to walk instead, the buses lost too much money and were forced to change their treatment of African Americans. The boycott put the people in charge of the public transit system in a new way.

Precedent/example in support of the claim is presented.

Between 1965 and 1973, Cesar Chavez also used boycotts successfully to change wage policies and working conditions for millions of Mexicans and Mexican Americans who were being exploited by growers of grapes and lettuce. In his boycott efforts, Chavez moved on two fronts, asking the workers to withhold their labor and, at the same time, asking consumers to refrain from purchasing table grapes (and later, lettuce) in order to show their support for the workers. In these instances, not only did the boycott force an industry to improve existing

Second precedent/ example in support of the claim is presented.

conditions, but it also created a profound awareness of pressing labor issues, often forming a bond between the workers and the community their labor was benefiting.

Severity of the problem is reiterated.

As a society, we have much to learn from boycotts of the past, and their lessons can help us confront contemporary social ills. As I have shown, body image and eating disorders are rising at an alarming rate among young girls and women in American society every year. This growing desire for an unrealistically thin body affects our minds and our spirits, especially when we are pummeled dozens of times a day with glamorized images of emaciated and unhealthy women. The resulting anorexia and bulimia that women suffer from are not only diseases that can be cured; they are also ones that can be prevented—if women will take a solid stand against such advertisements and the magazines that publish them. While we are not the publishers or advertisers who choose the pictures of starving women represented in magazines, we are the ones who decide whether or not their images will be consumed. This is where power lies—in the hands of those who hand over the dollars that support the glorification of unhealthy and unrealistic bodies. It is our choice to exert this power and to reject magazines that promote such images.

Appeals to emotion underscore the importance of the proposal.

Proposal is reiterated.

Works Cited

Dittrich, Liz. "About-Face Facts on the Media." *About Face.* 10 March 2003 <http://www.about-face.org/r/facts/ses.html>.

LaVoie, Allison. "Media Influence on Teens." *The Green Ladies.* 11 March 2003 <http://kidsnrg.simplenet.com/grit.dev/london/g2_jan12/green_ladies/media/>.

Pipher, Mary. *Reviving Ophelia.* New York: Ballantyne, 1994.

Slim Hopes. Dir. Sut Jhally. Prod. Jean Kilbourne. Videocassette. Media Education Foundation, 1995.

"Statistics." *National Eating Disorders Association.* 2002. 14 March 2003 <http://www.nationaleatingdisorders.org>.

Wolfe, Naomi. *The Beauty Myth.* New York: Harper, 2002.

Young woman reading magazine. Personal photograph by author. 14 March 2003.

The Fat Tax:
A Modest Proposal

JONATHAN RAUCH

In September, McDonald's announced plans to cook its fries in healthier oil. And not a moment too soon. Just a few days later the Centers for Disease Control and Prevention announced that in 2000 (the latest year for which final figures are available) the death rate in America, adjusted for the fact that the population is aging, reached an all-time low. Not only that, but life expectancy reached an all-time high, of about seventy-seven years. Obviously, those numbers can mean only one thing: America is in the grip of a gigantic public-health crisis. To wit—an obesity epidemic!

That America is marching fatward seems not to be in doubt. Obesity has risen substantially in recent years, to 31 percent of adults, according to the most recent data from the National Center for Health Statistics. Soft-drink cups are bigger, restaurant portions are larger, and health campaigns condemning fatty foods have persuaded people, wrongly, that they can eat twice as much bread as before, provided that they cut down on the butter. Also not in doubt is that other things being equal, being blubbery is not good. Still, one cannot help scratching one's head. If Americans are living longer, and if they are dying less (so to speak), and if, as the CDC reports, the proportion rating their own health as excellent or very good has remained at a solid 69 percent for the past five years, what exactly is the problem?

Call me oversensitive, but I think I detect a hint of snobbery in the national anti-fat drive. More than occasionally I read things like a recent article from the online *Bully Magazine*, which was headlined "AMERICA: LAND OF THE FAT, DRUNKEN SLOBS." The author, one Ken Wohlrob, writes, "We're quickly becoming a society of sloths who spend their free hours driving around in SUVs and staring at televisions or computer monitors. . . . [As] if we need more fat, bloated people in America." Do I sniff a trace of condescension here? In the September issue of *The Atlantic* a letter writer named Ken Weiss pointedly (and wrongly) mentioned that

Jonathan Rauch, a senior writer for *National Journal*, wrote this article for *The Atlantic*. Inspired by Jonathan Swift's "A Modest Proposal," another satirical proposal to amend society's ills, "The Fat Tax" presents evidence of an obesity epidemic and offers a solution.

"more than 50 percent of our population is obese" amid a list of ways in which America is inferior to Europe, beginning with our shorter vacations, continuing through our lack of a national health plan, and ending, inevitably, with our "polluting SUVs." It's not just that Americans are fat, apparently. It's that Americans are the kind of people who *would* be fat, in the kind of country that would encourage their piggishness.

What is to be done? The letters pages of magazines are often good places to preview the great bad ideas of tomorrow, and recently three letters in *The New Republic* offered a peek. The first, co-signed by the executive director of the Center for Science in the Public Interest and an academic nutritionist, said that the government should "slap small taxes on junk foods like soft drinks" to generate money for public-health campaigns. The next letter, from someone with the Center for the Advancement of Public Health, in Washington, D.C., said, "No one is suggesting the creation of a refrigerator police, but so long as the government is spending $360 billion per year at the federal level on health through Medicare, Medicaid, and the Children's Health Insurance Program, the government's interest in trying to prevent needless illness and death from obesity is kind of simple." The third letter came from a professor of public-interest law who wrote that he had helped to sue McDonald's for "failing to disclose the fat content of its French fries." He warned that more such suits could be on the way. "As with smoking," he wrote, "health advocates may increasingly be forced"—forced?—"to turn to the courts if legislatures continue to do little or nothing about the problem."

If obesity really is such a big crisis, I want to suggest a different approach, because the ones above seem deficient. For one thing, snack taxes that pay for public-health campaigns, and lawsuits against food companies, seem pretty likely to fatten the wallets of the people advocating them—public-health activists and lawyers—without necessarily making anyone any thinner. Besides, most people snack sensibly, so why should they pay to harangue lazy gluttons? And I know of no conclusive evidence that people are fat because food companies fail to disclose that fries and bacon cheeseburgers are fattening.

It seems to me that the only honest and effective way to confront this issue is to tax not fattening foods or fattening companies but fat people. It is they, after all, who drive up the government's health-care costs, so it is they who should pay. What I propose, then, is to tax people by the pound.

This needn't be very complicated. Fat-tax rates would be set by a National Avoirdupois Governing System (NAGS). To hit the worst offenders the hardest, the tax could be graduated. People would pay one per-pound rate above the "overweight" threshold, and a stiffer rate above the "obese" threshold. Fat people might not like this tax, but of course they could avoid it by becoming thinner.

In fact, I might go further. Carrots often work even better than sticks, so I propose a skinny subsidy to complement the fat tax. People who maintain trim, firm physiques should be rewarded for their public-spiritedness with large tax credits—funded, of course, by the fat tax.

My plan would address the nation's fat epidemic equitably and efficiently. It would make Americans put their money where their mouths are. And did I mention that I weigh 135 pounds?

chapter thirteen

Humorous Arguments

When the local city council passes an ordinance requiring bicyclists to wear helmets to protect against head injuries, a cyclist responds by writing a letter to the editor of the local newspaper suggesting other requirements the council might impose to protect citizens — including wearing earplugs in dance clubs, water wings in city pools, and blinders in City Hall.

A distinguished professor at a prestigious school dashes off a column for the campus paper on a controversial issue, perhaps spending a little less time than she should backing up her claims. The op-ed gets picked up by a Web logger who circulates it nationally and responses flood in — including one from a student who grades the paper like a freshman essay. The professor doesn't get an "A."

An undergraduate who thinks his school's new sexual harassment policy amounts to puritanism parodies it for the school humor magazine by describing in a short fictional drama what would happen if Romeo and Juliet strayed onto campus.

Tired of looking at the advertisements that cover every square inch of the campus sports arena walls, a student sends the college newspaper a satirical "news" article entitled "Sports Arena for Sale—to Advertisers!"

■ ■ ■

UNDERSTANDING HUMOR AS ARGUMENT

Breathes there a college student who doesn't read *The Onion* in its print or online versions? Sure, its humor can be sophomoric, yet that's just fine with many undergraduates. But it's not just four-letter words and bathroom jokes that make young people fans of *The Onion* today or that made their parents avid readers of *The National Lampoon* or even *Mad Magazine*. Nor has *Saturday Night Live* survived almost thirty years on TV because viewers (again, mainly young) want to hear Madonna sing "Fever" or watch the Rolling Stones creak through "Brown Sugar" one more time. No, we suspect that these productions—print and video—have attracted and held audiences for years because they use humor to argue passionately against all that is pompous, absurd, irritating, irrational, venal, hypocritical, and even evil in the adult world. *The Onion* (see Figure 13.1) describes itself as *satire*, and satires are, down deep, powerful assaults on the way things are by people who'd like to see some changes.

In particular, no one who read it is likely to forget the impact of *The Onion*'s post-9/11 issue, famously known as the "Holy F—king Sh-t" issue. Offensive? Sure—potentially. Yet the phrase rang true. It described what many Americans were feeling that dismal autumn but didn't dare admit, even to themselves. The headlines and stories in that issue of *The Onion* helped them put the cataclysmic events in an oddly human perspective: "God Angrily Clarifies 'Don't Kill' Rule"; "Hijackers Surprised to Find Themselves in Hell"; "Not Knowing What Else to Do, Woman Bakes American-Flag Cake"; and, perceptively, "A Shattered Nation Longs to Care About Stupid Bullsh-t Again." Clearly, humor has a point and a place even—perhaps especially—in the toughest of times. It's a powerful form of argument.

King Kaufman targets those with power and prestige in his article "Tiger's Burden." Consider how Kaufman's humor might be considered risky.

LINK TO P. 617

FIGURE 13.1 JUST ONE OF MANY SATIRICAL STORIES IN THE OCTOBER 3, 2001 ISSUE OF *THE ONION*

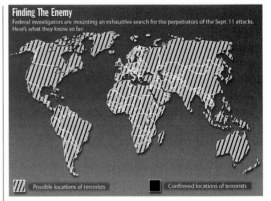

U.S. Vows To Defeat Whoever It Is We're At War With

WASHINGTON, DC—In a televised address to the American people Tuesday, a determined President Bush vowed that the U.S. would defeat "whoever exactly it is we're at war with here."

"America's enemy, be it Osama bin Laden, Saddam Hussein, the Taliban, a multinational coalition of terrorist organizations, any of a rogue's gallery of violent Islamic fringe groups, or an entirely different, non-Islamic aggressor we've never even heard of... be warned," Bush said during an 11-minute speech from the Oval Office. "The United States is preparing to strike, directly and decisively, against you, whoever you are, just as soon as we have a rough idea of your identity and a reasonably decent estimate as to where your base is located."

Added Bush: "That is, assuming you have a base."

Bush is acting with the full support of Congress, which on Sept. 14 authorized him to use any necessary force against the undetermined attackers. According to House Speaker Dennis Hastert (R-IL), the congressional move enables the president to declare war, "to the extent that war can

again, what if we declared war on Afghanistan and they didn't send anyone to fight us? It's plausible that we could

"Christ," McCain continued, "what if the terrorists' base of operation turns out to be Detroit? Would we declare war on the state

By its very nature, humor is risky. Playing fast and loose with good taste and sound reason, humorists turn what is comfortable and familiar inside out and hope readers get the joke. If they play it too safe, they lose their audiences; if they step over an unseen line, people groan or hiss or act offended. Humor, especially satire, is a knife's edge that had better cut deep or not at all.

To manage humor, you must understand people and the foibles of human nature. That's because humor often works best when it deals with ordinary life and current events. (You'd be surprised how many Americans get their daily news from the comic monologues of late-night comedians.) Timeliness is what makes comedians seem hip and smart: their sharp minds decide what many people will be chuckling and *thinking* about the next day. But for the same reason, a lot of humor doesn't have the shelf life of lettuce. And some humor doesn't easily cross canyons that divide ethnic groups, classes, or generations. Catholics laugh hardest at jokes about Catholic schools, and Jews doubtless understand Jewish mothers and princesses better than the goyim do.

Obviously, then, humor cannot be learned quickly or easily. But it is too powerful a tool to leave to comedians. For writers and speakers, humor can sharpen any rhetorical strategy, giving heightened presence to appeals to reason, emotion, character, or value.

Humor can simply make people pay attention or feel good—or make them want to buy stuff or do what others ask. That's the rationale behind many "soft sell" commercials, from classic VW pitches of a generation ago ("Think small") to more recent ads for products as different as insurance ("AFLAC!") and computers ("Dude, you're getting a Dell!"). Advertisers use humor to capture your interest and make you feel good about their products. Who focused on AFLAC insurance prior to the duck, Geico before the gecko, or Energizer pre-bunny?

Humor has a darker side, too; it can make people feel superior to its targets of ridicule. And most of us don't want to associate with people who seem ridiculous. Bullies and cliques in secondary school often use humor to torment their innocent victims, behavior that is really nasty. In the political arena, however, politicians may be fairer game, given their resources and ambitions. So when *Saturday Night Live* set out after both George W. Bush and Al Gore Jr. during the presidential campaign season of 2000, the parodies of these men rang true. Voters were left to choose between what was portrayed as a moronic mangler of the English language and a pompous, preening windbag. Does such humor have an effect on voting? Maybe.

Humor plays a large role, too, in arguments of character. If you want audiences to like you, make them laugh. It is no accident that all but the most serious speeches begin with a few jokes or stories. The humor puts listeners at ease and helps them identify with the speaker. In fact, a little self-deprecation can endear writers or speakers to the toughest audiences. You'll listen to people who are confident enough to make fun of themselves because they seem clever and yet aware of their own limitations. No one likes a stuffed shirt.

Humor also works because a funny remark usually contains, at its core, an element of truth:

Clothes make the man. Naked people have little or no influence in society.

–Samuel Clemens

Fame changes a lot of things, but it can't change a light bulb.
                                                    –Gilda Radner

Some humor may even involve looking at a subject a little too logically. Dave Barry, for example, analyzes precisely why Florida failed to solve the problems it had counting votes in the 2000 presidential election when it tried again in 2002 (Barry's full piece is reprinted at the end of this chapter):

> **THE PROBLEM: Voters had trouble understanding a balloting system that required them to punch holes in a piece of cardboard.**
>
> **SOLUTION A: Use an even simpler system.**
> **SOLUTION B: Use a more complicated system.**
>
> **Pretty much any life form with a central nervous system, including a reasonably bright squid, would choose Solution A. So naturally our election officials went with Solution B. Yes. Having seen that South Florida voters—people who have yet to figure out how an automobile turn signal works—were baffled by pieces of cardboard, our leaders decided to confront them with . . . computers! And we all know how easy it is to figure out unfamiliar computer systems! That's why the expression "As easy as figuring out an unfamiliar computer system" is so common.**
>   –Dave Barry, "How to Vote in One Easy Step: Use Chisel, Tablet"

Many forms of humor, especially satire and parody, get their power from just such twists of logic. When Jonathan Swift in the eighteenth century suggested in "A Modest Proposal" that Ireland's English rulers consider a diet of fricasseed Irish toddlers, he gambled on readers seeing the parallel between his outrageous proposal and the brutal policies of an oppressive English colonial government. The satire works precisely because it is perfectly logical, given the political facts of Swift's time—though some of his contemporaries missed the joke.

> **I profess, in the sincerity of my heart, that I have not the least personal interest in endeavoring to promote this necessary work, having no other motive but the public good of my country, by advancing our trade, providing for infants, relieving the poor, and giving some pleasure to the rich.**
>   –Jonathan Swift, "A Modest Proposal"

In our own era, columnist Molly Ivins ridicules opponents of gun control by seeming to agree with them and then adding a logical twist that makes her real point:

I think that's what we need: more people carrying weapons. I support the [concealed gun] legislation but I'd like to propose one small amendment. Everyone should be able to carry a concealed weapon. But everyone who carries a weapon should be required to wear one of those little beanies on their heads with a little propeller on it so the rest of us can see them coming.

– Molly Ivins

CHARACTERIZING KINDS OF HUMOR

It's possible to write whole books about comedy, exploring its many forms such as satire, parody, burlesque, travesty, pastiche, lampoon, caricature, farce, and more. Almost all types of humor involve some kind of argument because laughter can make people think, even while they are having a good time. As we've noted, not all such purposes are praiseworthy; schoolyard bullies and vicious editorial cartoonists may use their humor just to hurt or humiliate their targets. But laughter can also expose hypocrisy or break down barriers of prejudice and thereby help people see their worlds differently. When it is robust and honest, humor is a powerful rhetorical form.

Humor

Humor can contribute to almost any argument, but you have to know when to use it—especially in academic writing. You'll catch a reader's attention if you insert a little laughter to lighten the tone of a serious or dry piece. Here, for example, is the African American writer Zora Neale Hurston addressing the very real issue of discrimination, with a nod and a wink:

> Sometimes I feel discriminated against, but it does not make me angry. It merely astonishes me. How can any deny themselves the pleasure of my company? It's beyond me.
> –Zora Neale Hurston, "How It Feels to Be Colored Me"

You might use a whole sequence of comic examples and anecdotes to keep readers interested in a serious point. How might you, for example, make the rather academic point that nurture and socialization alone can't account for certain differences between girls and boys? Here's how Prudence Makintosh, mother of three sons, defends that claim:

> How can I explain why a little girl baby sits on a quilt in the park thoughtfully examining a blade of grass, while my baby William uproots grass by handfuls and eats it? Why does a mother of very

Ellen Goodman deals with the serious topics of eating disorders and school killings, yet she uses humor to hold readers' attention and goodwill. She opens her deadly serious argument by asking readers to "imagine a place [where] women greet one another at the market with open arms, loving smiles, and a cheerful exchange of ritual compliments: 'You look wonderful! You've put on weight.'"

LINK TO P. 477 ···

bright and active daughters confide that until she went camping with another family of boys, she feared that my sons had a hyperactivity problem? I am sure there are plenty of noisy, rowdy little girls, but I'm not just talking about rowdiness and noise. I'm talking about some sort of primal physicalness that causes the walls of my house to pulsate on rainy days. I'm talking about something inexplicable that makes my sons fall into a mad, scrambling, pull-your-ears-off-kick-your-teeth-in heap just before bedtime, when they're not even mad at each other. I mean something that causes them to climb the doorjamb with honey and peanut butter on their hands while giving me a synopsis of *Star Wars* that contains only five unintelligible words. . . . When Jack and Drew are not kicking a soccer ball or each other, they are kicking the chair legs, the cat, the baby's silver rattle, and inadvertently, Baby William himself, whom they have affectionately dubbed "Tough Eddy."

–Prudence Makintosh, "Masculine/Feminine"

In reading these words, you can just about feel the angst of a mother who thought she could raise her boys to be different. Most readers will chuckle at little William eating grass, the house pulsating, doorjambs sticky with peanut butter—and appreciate Makintosh's point, whether they agree with it or not. Her intention, however, is not so much to be funny as to give her opinion presence. And, of course, she exaggerates. But exaggeration is a basic technique of humor. We make a situation bigger than life so we can see it better.

Satire

Most of the humor college students write is either satire or parody, which is discussed in the next section. Type "college humor magazines" into the search engine Google and you will find Web sites that list dozens of journals such as the University of Michigan's *Gargoyle*, Penn State's *Phroth*, UC Berkeley's *The Heuristic Squelch*, and Ohio State's *The Shaft*. In these journals you will find humor of all kinds, some pretty raunchy, but much of it aimed at the oddities of college life ranging from unsympathetic administrations to crummy teachers and courses. There is lots of grousing, too, about women and men and campus parking. Much of this material is satire, a genre of writing that uses humor to unmask problems and then suggest (not always directly) how they might be fixed. The most famous piece of satire in English literature is probably Jonathan Swift's *Gulliver's Travels*, which pokes fun at all human shortcomings, targeting especially politics, religion, science, and sexuality. For page after page, Swift argues for change in human character and institutions. In a much different way, so do campus humor magazines.

You'll find social and political satire in television programs such as *The Simpsons* and *Saturday Night Live* and movies such as *This Is Spinal Tap, Dr. Strangelove,* and *Election.* Most editorial cartoons are also satiric when they highlight a problem in society that the cartoonist feels needs to be remedied.

Satire often involves a shift in perspective that asks readers to look at a situation in a new way. In *Gulliver's Travels,* for example, we see human society reduced in scale (in Lilliput), exaggerated in size (in Brobdingnang), even through the eyes of a superior race of horses (the Houyhnhnms). In the land of the giants, Gulliver notices that, up close, women aren't as beautiful as they once seemed to him:

> **Their skins appeared so coarse and uneven, so variously coloured, when I saw them near, with a mole here and there as broad as a trencher, and hairs hanging from it thicker than pack-threads, to say nothing further concerning the rest of their persons.**
> –Jonathan Swift, *Gulliver's Travels*

So much for human beauty. You'll note that there's nothing especially funny in Gulliver's remarks. That's because satire is sometimes more clever than funny, the point of some satire being to open readers' eyes rather than to make them laugh out loud.

The key to writing effective satire may be finding a humorous or novel angle on a subject and then following through. In other words, you say "What if?" and then employ a kind of mad logic, outlining in great detail all that follows from the question. For example, to satirize groups that believe homosexuals are using the nation's public schools to recruit children to their lifestyle, *The Onion* asks its readers to consider that the charge might be true. For paragraph after paragraph, the satirists let the idea unfold using all the logic and apparatus of a news story happily reporting on the campaign, complete with a graph. You can see from just a few paragraphs how satire of this kind works by making the implausible seem comically real (see Figure 13.2).

Parody

Like satire, parody also offers an argument. What distinguishes the two forms is that parody makes its case by taking something familiar—be

Note the way that King Kaufman uses satire in his piece "Tiger's Burden."

LINK TO P. 617

FIGURE 13.2   THE COMPLETE STORY APPEARS IN *THE ONION*, JULY 30, 1998.

VOLUME 33 ISSUE 26   AMERICA'S FINEST NEWS SOURCE™   30 JULY–5 AUGUST 1998

'98 Homosexual-Recruitment Drive Nearing Goal

SAN FRANCISCO—Spokespersons for the National Gay & Lesbian Recruitment Task Force announced Monday that more than 288,000 straights have been converted to homosexuality since Jan. 1, 1998, putting the group well on pace to reach its goal of 350,000 conversions by the end of the year.

"Thanks to the tireless efforts of our missionaries nationwide, in the first seven months of 1998, nearly 300,000 heterosexuals were ensnared in the Pink Triangle," said NGLRTF co-director Patricia Emmonds. "Clearly, the activist homosexual lobby is winning."

Emmonds credited much of the recruiting success to the gay lobby's infiltration of America's public schools, where programs promoting

phia's Lakeside Elementary School, one of thousands of public schools nationwide that actively promote the homosexual agenda. "I don't want to have a family or go to church."

"Straight people don't have any fun," said Teddy Nance, 11, after watching *Breeders Are Boring!*, an anti-heterosexual filmstrip, in his fifth-grade class at Crestwood Elementary School in Roanoke, VA. "Gay people get to do whatever they want."

In addition to school programs that target youths, the NGLRTF launched a $630 million advertising campaign this year in an effort to convert adults to homosexuality. The campaign, which features TV and radio spots, as well as print advertising in major national magazines, has

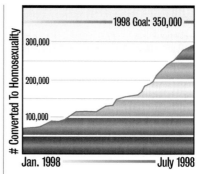

constantly had to worry about things like taking the kids to Little League practice, paying

"For all the progress we've made, America is still overwhelmingly heterosexual."

it songs, passages of prose, TV shows, poems, films, even people—and turning it into something new. The argument sparkles in the tension between the original work and its imitation. That's where the humor lies, too.

Needless to say, parodies work best when audiences make that connection. For instance, you wouldn't entirely appreciate the film *Galaxy Quest* unless you knew the *Star Trek* series, and you could probably name a dozen films that work the same way. A parody of the sitcom *Friends* will likely be pointless fifty years from now unless it has the staying power of *I Love Lucy*. Even today, allusions to President Gerald Ford's clumsiness make sense mostly to those who remember comedian Chevy Chase poking merciless fun at him. Younger people would prefer to laugh at Bill Clinton and George Bush.

Even if the half-life of parody is brief, the form is potent in its prime. Just a few years ago, when a men's movement danced briefly in the national consciousness, Joe Bob Briggs brought the fragile trend to its

FIGURE **13.3** THE COVER OF THIS COLLEGE HUMOR MAGAZINE MIGHT SEEM PUZZLING UNLESS YOU RECOGNIZE THAT IT PARODIES SUPERMARKET TABLOIDS.

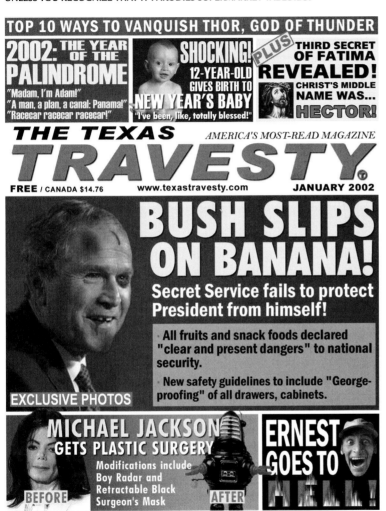

knees with a ruthless parody of Wild Man weekends, when boorish males finally got in touch with their inner selves:

> I'll never forget it. I sweated a lot. I cried. I sweated while I was crying. Of course, I was crying because they made me sweat so much. We had

> this one part of the weekend where we went into a giant sauna and
> turned it up to about, oh, 280, until everybody's skin turned the color
> of strawberry Jell-O and the veins of our heads started exploding, and
> it turned into this communal out-of-body male thing, where every-
> body was screaming, "I want out of my body!"
>
> –Joe Bob Briggs, "Get in Touch with Your Ancient Spear"

When a subject or work becomes the object of a successful parody, it's
never seen in quite the same way again.

DEVELOPING HUMOROUS ARGUMENTS

It's doubtful anyone can offer a formula for being funny; some would suggest that humor is a gift. But at least the comic perspective is a trait
widely distributed among the population. Most people can be funny, given
the right circumstances.

However, the stars may not always be aligned when you need them in
composing an argument. And just working hard may not help: laughter
arises from high-spirited, not labored, insights. Yet once you strike the
spark, a blaze usually follows.

Look for humor in obvious situations. Bill Cosby began a stellar career
as a humorist with a comedy album that posed the rather simple question: *Why Is There Air?* The late columnist and author Erma Bombeck, too,
endeared herself to millions of people by pointing out the humor in daily
routines.

Look for humor in incongruity or in "what if?" situations, and then
imagine the consequences. *What if men had monthlies? What if reading
caused flatulence? What if students hired special prosecutors to handle their grade
complaints? What if broccoli tasted like chocolate? What if politicians always told
the truth? What if the Pope wasn't Catholic?*

Don't look for humor in complicated ideas. You're more apt to find it in
simple premises, for instance, a question Dave Barry once asked: "How
come guys care so much about sports?" There are, of course, serious
answers to the question. But the humor practically bubbles up on its own
once you think about men and their games. You can write a piece of your
own just by listing details: *Monday Night Football, sports bars, beer commercials, sagging couches, fantasy camps, 50-inch plasma-screen TVs, Little League,
angry wives.* Push a little further, relate such items to personal insights
and experiences, and you are likely to discover some of the incongruities
and implausibilities at the heart of humor.

Let us stress detail. Abstract humor probably doesn't work for anyone except German philosophers and drunken graduate students. Look for humor in concrete and proper nouns, in people and places readers will recognize but not expect to find in your writing. Consider the technique Dave Barry uses in the following passage defending himself against those who might question his motives for attacking "sports guys":

> **And before you accuse me of being some kind of sherry-sipping ascot-wearing ballet-attending MacNeil-Lehrer-NewsHour-watching wussy, please note that I am a sports guy myself, having had a legendary athletic career consisting of nearly a third of the 1965 season on the track team at Pleasantville High School ("Where the Leaders of Tomorrow Are Leaving Wads of Gum on the Auditorium Seats of Today").**
> —Dave Barry, "A Look at Sports Nuts—And We Do Mean Nuts"

Remove the lively details from the passage, and this is what's left:

> **And before you accuse me of being some kind of wussy, please note that I am a sports guy myself, having had an athletic career on the track team at Pleasantville High School.**

Enough said?

KEY FEATURES OF HUMOROUS ARGUMENTS

Drafting humor and revising humor are yin-yang propositions—opposites that complement each other. Think Democrats and Republicans.

Creating humor is, by nature, a robust, excessive, and egotistical activity. It requires assertiveness, courage, and often a (temporary) suspension of good judgment and taste. Whereas drafting more material than necessary usually makes good sense for writers, you can afford to be downright prodigal with humor. Pile on the examples and illustrations. Take all the risks you can with language. Indulge in puns. Leap into innuendo. Be clever, but not childishly obscene. Push your vocabulary. Play with words and have fun.

Then, when you revise, do the opposite. Recall that Polonius in Shakespeare's *Hamlet* is right about one thing: "Brevity is the soul of wit." Once you have written a humorous passage, whether a tooting horn or a full symphonic parody, you must pare your language to the bone. Think: less is more. Cut, then cut again.

That's all there is to it.

Complaining about the proliferation of T-shirts bearing humorous insults, Steve Rushin takes the climate of "clever contempt" even further in order to argue against it. He suggests that "on our one-dollar bill George Washington ought to smirk like Mona Lisa. On the five, Lincoln's fingers could form a *W,* the international symbol for *whatever."*

LINK TO P. 737 ··

Finding a Topic

You may use humor in an argument to

- point out flaws in a policy, proposal, or argument
- suggest a policy of your own
- set people in a favorable frame of mind
- admit weaknesses or deflect criticism
- satirize or parody a position, point of view, or style

Opportunities to use humor in daily life are too numerous to list, but they are much rarer in academic and professional writing. You can find amusing topics everywhere if you think about the absurdities of your job, home life, or surrounding culture. Try to see things you take for granted from radically different perspectives. Or flip-flop the normal order of affairs: Make a small issue cosmic; chop a huge matter to fritters.

Researching Your Topic

You can't exactly research a whimsical argument, but humor does call for some attention to detail. Satires and parodies thrive on actual events, specific facts, telling allusions, or memorable images that can be located in sources or recorded in discussions and conversations. Timeliness is a factor, too; you need to know whom or what your readers will recognize and how they might respond. Seek inspiration for humor in these sources:

- popular magazines, especially weekly journals (for current events)
- TV, including commercials (especially for material about people)
- classic books, music, films, artwork (as inspiration for parodies)
- comedians (to observe how they make a subject funny)

Formulating a Claim

With humorous arguments, satires, and parodies, you won't so much develop a thesis as play upon a theme. But humor of the sort that can grow for several pages does need a focal point, a central claim that requires support and evidence—even if that support strains credulity. (In fact, it probably should.) Here are lines to kick-start a humorous argument:

- What if . . . ?
- What would happen if . . . ?
- Why is it that . . . ?

- How come . . . never happens to . . . ?
- When was the last time you tried to . . . ?
- Why is it that men/women . . . ?
- Can you believe that . . . ?

Preparing a Proposal

If your instructor asks you to prepare a proposal for a satire, parody, or other humorous argument, here's a format you might use (or parody!).

Explain the focus of your project.

Articulate the point of your humor. What is at stake? What do you hope to accomplish?

Specify any models you have for your project. Who or what are you trying to emulate? If you are writing a parody, what is your target or inspiration?

Explain whom you hope to reach by your humor and why this group of readers will be amused.

Briefly discuss the key challenges you anticipate: Defining a point? Finding comic ideas?

Identify the sources you expect to consult. What facts might you have to establish?

Determine the format you expect to use for your project. A conventional paper? A letter to the editor? A Web page?

Thinking about Organization

Humorous arguments can be structured exactly like more serious ones—with claims, supporting reasons, warrants, evidence, qualifiers, and rebuttals. In fact, humor has its own relentless logic. Once you set an argument going, you should press it home with the same vigor you apply in serious pieces.

If you write a parody, you need to be thoroughly familiar with the work on which it is based, particularly its organization and distinctive features. In parodying a song, for example, you've got to be sure listeners recognize familiar lines or choruses. In parodying a longer piece, boil it down to essential elements—the most familiar actions in the plot, the most distinctive characters, the best-known passages of dialogue—and then arrange those elements within a compact and rapidly moving design.

Getting and Giving Response

All arguments can benefit from the scrutiny of others. Your instructor may assign you to a peer group for the purpose of reading and responding to each other's drafts; if not, go out of your way to get some careful response. You can use the following questions to evaluate your own draft, to secure response to it from others, or to prepare a response to a colleague's work. If you are evaluating someone else's draft, be sure to supply examples to illustrate your points. Most writers respond better to specific comments than to general observations.

Focus

- Is the argument funny? Would another approach to the topic — even a serious one — be more effective?
- Does the humor make a clear argumentative point? Is its target clear?
- If the piece is a satire, does it suggest a better alternative to the present situation? If not, does it need to?

Logic, Organization, and Format

- Is there logic to the humor? If so, will readers appreciate it?
- Are the points in the argument clearly connected? Are additional or clearer transitions needed?
- Does the humor build toward a climax? If not, would saving the best laughs for last be more effective?
- Is the piece too long, making the humor seem belabored? If so, how might it be cut?
- Does the format of the piece contribute to the humor? Would it be funnier if it were formatted to look like a particular genre—an advertisement, an email message, a sports column, a greeting card? If you've used illustrations, do they enhance the humor? If there are no illustrations, would adding some help?

Style and Detail

- Is the humor too abstract? Does it need more details about specific people, events, and so on?
- If the piece is a parody, does it successfully imitate the features and language of whatever is being parodied?
- Are the sentences wordy or too complex for the type of humor being attempted?
- Are there any problems with spelling, grammar, punctuation, or mechanics?

RESPOND●

1. For each of the following items, list particular details that might contribute to a humorous look at the subject.

   zealous environmentalists

   clueless builders and developers

   aggressive drivers

   violent Hollywood films

   anti-war or hemp activists

   drivers of lumbering recreational vehicles

   Martha Stewart

   high school coaches

   college instructors

   malls and the people who visit them

2. Spend some time listening to a friend who you think is funny. What kind of humor does he or she use? What sorts of details crop up in it? Once you've put in a few days of careful listening, try to write down some of the jokes and stories just as your friend told them. Writing humor may be excruciating at first, but you might find it easier with practice.

   After you've written a few humorous selections, think about how well they translate from the spoken word to the written. What's different? Do they work better in one medium than in another? Show your written efforts to your funny friend and ask for comments. How would he or she revise your written efforts?

3. Using Internet search tools, find a transcript of a funny television or radio show. Read the transcript a few times, paying attention to the places where you laugh the most. Then analyze the humor, trying to understand what makes it funny. This chapter suggests several possible avenues for analysis, including normality, incongruity, simplicity, and details. How does the transcript reflect these principles? Or does it operate by a completely different set of principles? (Some of the best humor is funny because it breaks all the rules.)

Texas Nerds Celebrate "Geek Week"

TREVOR ROSEN

Geek Week obviously parodies the Greek weeks common on some campuses.

CAMPUS—Dorks, dweebs and gaywads from all areas of the UT community will come together this week for the first Annual Texas Geek Week, a celebration of hyper-intellectual fetishism and bad fashion sense representing the widely diverse population of lame-o's at the nation's largest University. "We really felt that the campus needed to hear more about the achievements of Texas Geeks," said Fred Sawser, physics sophomore and Texas Geek Week co-chair. "The great things that we do in the fields of role-playing/strategy games and as TAs in engineering classes go largely unheralded, but we'd really like to change all that." Sawser expressed optimism about Texas Geek Week's impact on the other more socially and sexually experienced members of the UT community. "I think that they'll really start to appreciate us—some of us might even get laid." Sawser then laughed through his nose several times in quick succession before characterizing such a possibility as being "freakin' awesome."

The humor is in the details here.

Among the events to be held on the West Mall are: a comparison of the relative merits of Lieutenant Uhura and Counselor Troi—of *Star Trek* and *Star Trek: The Next Generation*, respectively, an exhibit on the evolution of the Devorak keyboard, and an interactive rodent-powered robot named JoJo that makes cup after cup of rich, delicious, healthy chocolate Ovaltine.

"I've never seen anything like this," exclaimed wide-eyed super geek Winston Morris, taking off his electrical-

---

Trevor Rosen wrote this parody of Greek week activities while editor-in-chief of *The Texas Travesty*, the humor magazine at the University of Texas, Austin. In the essay, Rosen pokes fun at both nerds and Greeks, though the former bear the brunt of his humor. But at least nerds go on to be university presidents.

taped glasses in order to blow his nose on his caffeine molecule t-shirt. "This week just for us is great for Geek publicity. I mean, people have a really bad idea of who geeks are and what they stand for. They think that we're just all about school and D&D and Renaissance Fairs and getting drunk as a duck at our hard-core parties where we smoke out on grape vine and have wild cyber sex—but that's not all we are. Geeks have a rich cultural heritage that goes well beyond stuff like that. Most people think that Geeks are simple, but if anything, we're multifarious. Think hexadecimal, not binary."

The piece pokes fun, too, at campus events celebrating different cultures.

President Faulkner took a time-out from teaching his informal break-dancing class to weigh in with his opinion on Geek Week: "I'm very excited to see that students are taking an interest and reforming the stereotypes that surround geek culture. Where do you think that the people who make the money in this country come from? Look at me, I've got a Ph.D. in chemistry—but love of the covalent bonds didn't hurt me none, did it? I make the mad Benjamins runnin' this piece—probably more in a year than you'll see in a decade. Geek power!"

How to Vote in One Easy Step: Use Chisel, Tablet

DAVE BARRY

Friday, Sept. 13, 2002

The question you're asking yourself is: Does South Florida contain the highest concentration of morons in the entire world? Or just in the United States?

The reason you're asking this, of course, is South Florida's performance in Tuesday's election. This election was critical to our image, because of our performance in the 2000 presidential election—the one that ended up with the entire rest of the nation watching, impatiently, as clumps of sleep-deprived South Florida election officials squinted at cardboard ballots, trying to figure out what the hell the voters were thinking when they apparently voted for two presidents, or no presidents, or part of a president, or, in some cases, simply drooled on the ballot.

Before it was over, we had roughly 23 million lawyers down here—nearly a quarter of the nation's lawyer supply—filing briefs and torts and arguing in endless televised hearings, until finally the whole mess wound up in the U.S. Supreme Court, which declared George W. Bush the winner, but only because it would have been unconstitutional to apply the more logical remedy, which would be to kick Florida out of the union. We were a national joke. The phrase "Florida voter" became a standard comedy-routine synonym for "idiot."

And thus there was a lot of pressure on Florida, and particularly South Florida, to redeem itself in Tuesday's election. We knew that we could not afford to repeat the 2000 fiasco, and our election officials had more than a year and a half to develop, and test, a voting procedure that even we could not screw up.

So what did our election officials do? Let's examine the problem, and two possible solutions:

THE PROBLEM: Voters had trouble understanding a balloting system that required them to punch holes in a piece of cardboard.

SOLUTION A: Use an even simpler system.
SOLUTION B: Use a more complicated system.

Dave Barry is a syndicated columnist and the author of numerous books, including *Dave Barry's Complete Guide to Guys: A Fairly Short Book* (1995), *Dave Barry Is from Mars and Venus* (1997), and *Dave Barry Talks Back* (1991). Barry resides in Florida, so his comments on the 2002 election primaries in that state are especially pointed. As you'll see, his satire is also a proposal argument (see Chapter 12).

Pretty much any life form with a central nervous system, including a reasonably bright squid, would choose Solution A. So naturally our election officials went with Solution B. Yes. Having seen that South Florida voters—people who have yet to figure out how an automobile turn signal works—were baffled by pieces of cardboard, our leaders decided to confront them with . . . computers! And we all know how easy it is to figure out unfamiliar computer systems! That's why the expression "As easy as figuring out an unfamiliar computer system" is so common.

So Miami-Dade County spent $24.5 million on 7,200 computerized voting machines. Broward spent $17.2 million on 5,200 of the same machines. The particular model that we bought is called the "iVotronic."

> TIP FOR CONSUMERS: Never buy a product whose manufacturer does not understand the basic rules of capitalization.

But confronting voters with unfamiliar machines does not, by itself, ensure that your election will be a mess. No, to GUARANTEE failure, you need to take additional precautions, such as: (1) Not training poll workers adequately; (2) Providing confusing instructions; (3) Not having enough technical support; (4) Changing the voting-machine software at the last minute.

We managed to make all of these mistakes, and more, which is why today, days later, we are still not 100 percent certain which candidates won on Tuesday. I would not completely rule out Pat Buchanan.

And so once again, South Florida is making life easy for Leno and Letterman. What is the solution? How can we avoid being international laughingstocks in the next election?

My suggestion—call me crazy—is that we print the ballot on paper, with a box next to each candidate's name. We instruct the voters to put an "X" in their candidate's box. Then we have human beings count the "X"s, and the candidate with the most votes wins.

I realize this is a radical system, but I believe that it would be difficult for even South Floridians to screw it up.

We could get our elections over within a single day, like everybody else, and we would have more time to enjoy the pleasures of South Florida.

Such as scuba diving. On our new artificial reef.

Formed by 12,400 iVotronics.

PART 4

STYLISH argument

chapter fourteen

Figurative Language and Argument

Look at any magazine or Web site and you will see figurative language working on behalf of arguments. When the writer of a letter to the editor complains that "Donna Haraway's supposition that because we rely on cell phones and laptops we are cyborgs is [like] saying the Plains Indians were centaurs because they relied on horses," he is using an analogy to rebut (and perhaps ridicule) Haraway's claim. When another writer says that "the digital revolution is whipping through our lives like a Bengali typhoon," she is making an implicit argument about the speed and strength of the digital revolution. When still another writer calls Disney World a "smile factory," she begins a stinging critique of the way pleasure is "manufactured" there.

Just what is figurative language? Traditionally, the terms *figurative language* and *figures of speech* refer to language that differs from the ordinary—language that calls up, or "figures," something else. But in fact, all language could be said to call up something else. The word *table*, for example, is not itself a table; rather, it calls up a table in our imaginations. Thus, just as all language is by nature argumentative, so too is it all figurative. Far from being mere decoration or embellishment (something like icing on the cake of thought), figures of speech are indispensable to language use.

More specifically, figurative language brings two major strengths to arguments. First, it often aids understanding by likening something unknown to something known. For example, in arguing for the existence of DNA as they had identified and described it, scientists Watson and Crick used two familiar examples—a helix (spiral) and a zipper—to make their point. Today, arguments about new computer technologies are filled with similar uses of figurative language. Indeed, Microsoft's entire word-processing system depends on likening items to those in an office (as in Microsoft Office) to make them more understandable and familiar to users. Second, figurative language can be helpful in arguments because it is often extremely memorable. Someone arguing that slang should be used in formal writing turns to this memorable definition for support: "Slang is language that takes off its coat, spits on its hands, and gets to work." In a brief poem that carries a powerful argument, Langston Hughes (see Figure 14.1) uses figurative language to explore the consequences of unfulfilled dreams:

> **What happens to a dream deferred?**
> **Does it dry up**
> **Like a raisin in the sun?**
> **Or fester like a sore—**
> **And then run?**
> **Does it stink like rotten meat?**
> **Or crust and sugar over—**
> **Like a syrupy sweet?**
> **Maybe it just sags**
> **Like a heavy load.**
> **Or does it explode?**
>
> –Langston Hughes, "Harlem—A Dream Deferred"

FIGURE 14.1 WRITER LANGSTON HUGHES

In 1963, Martin Luther King Jr. used figurative language to make his argument for civil rights unmistakably clear as well as memorable:

> In a sense we have come to our nation's capital to cash a check. When the architects of our republic wrote the magnificent words of the Constitution and the Declaration of Independence, they were signing a promissory note to which every American was to fall heir. This note was a promise that all men would be guaranteed the unalienable rights of life, liberty, and the pursuit of happiness.
>
> It is obvious today that America has defaulted on this promissory note insofar as her citizens of color are concerned. Instead of honoring

> this sacred obligation, America has given the Negro people a bad check; a check which has come back marked "insufficient funds." But we refuse to believe that the bank of justice is bankrupt. We refuse to believe that there are insufficient funds in the great vaults of opportunity in this nation. So we have come to cash this check—a check that will give us upon demand the riches of freedom and the security of justice.
>
> –Martin Luther King Jr., "I Have a Dream"

The figures of the promissory note and the bad check are especially effective in this passage because they suggest financial exploitation, which fits perfectly with the overall theme of King's speech.

You may be surprised to learn that during the European Renaissance, schoolchildren sometimes learned and practiced using as many as 180 figures of speech. Such practice seems more than a little excessive today, especially because figures of speech come so naturally to native speakers of the English language; you hear of "chilling out," "taking flak," "nipping a plot in the bud," "getting our act together," "blowing your cover," "marching to a different drummer," "seeing red," "smelling a rat," "being on cloud nine," "throwing in the towel," "tightening our belts," "rolling in the aisles," "turning the screws"—you get the picture. In fact, you and your friends no doubt have favorite figures of speech, ones you use every day. Why not take a quick inventory during one day—just listen to everything that's said around you and take down any figurative language you hear.

We can't aim for a complete catalog of figures of speech here, much less for a thorough analysis of the power of figurative language. What we can offer, however, is a brief listing—with examples—of some of the most familiar kinds of figures, along with a reminder that they can be used to extremely good effect in the arguments you write.

Figures have traditionally been classified into two main types: *tropes*, which involve a change in the ordinary signification, or meaning, of a word or phrase; and *schemes*, which involve a special arrangement of words. Here are the most frequently used figures in each category, beginning with the familiar tropes of metaphor, simile, and analogy.

TROPES

Metaphor

One of the most pervasive uses of figurative language, metaphor offers an implied comparison between two things and thereby clarifies and enlivens many arguments. In the following passage, bell hooks uses the metaphor of the hope chest to enhance her argument that autobiography involves a special kind of treasure hunt:

> Conceptually, the autobiography was framed in the manner of a hope chest. I remembered my mother's hope chest, with its wonderful odor of cedar, and thought about her taking the most precious items and placing them there for safekeeping. Certain memories were for me a similar treasure. I wanted to place them somewhere for safekeeping. An autobiographical narrative seemed an appropriate place.
>
> –bell hooks, *Bone Black*

In another argument, a *New York Times* editorial, calling on the Augusta National Golf Club to admit women members, says, "If next year's gathering becomes a battlefield for women's rights, as seems likely, the Masters will be an embarrassment for the corporate crowd, for CBS and for the nation's top golfers." Here the writer uses the metaphor of a battlefield to describe a famous golf tournament and suggests how transforming the Augusta course into a scene of warfare will have negative consequences.

English language use is so filled with metaphors that these powerful, persuasive tools often zip by unnoticed, so be on the lookout for effective metaphors in everything you read. For example, when a reviewer of new software that promises complete filtering of advertisements on the World Wide Web refers to the product as "a weedwhacker for the Web," he is using a metaphor to advance an argument about the nature and function of that product.

Metaphors can work powerfully in an argument. Consider the metaphoric use of the verb *pump* in John Levesque's article about the poor image of fatherhood conveyed by many TV sitcoms: ". . . because we have a crisis in fatherhood today, we have to take seriously the kinds of images we pump into kids' homes." What underlying statement does this metaphor make?

LINK TO P. 506

Simile

A direct comparison between two things, simile is pervasive in written and spoken language. You may even have your own favorites: someone's hair is "plastered to him like white on rice," for instance, or, as one of our grandmothers used to say, "prices are high as a cat's back," or, as a special compliment, "you look as pretty as red shoes." Similes are also at work in many arguments, as you can see in this excerpt from a brief *Wired* magazine review of a new magazine for women:

> Women's magazines occupy a special niche in the cluttered infoscape of modern media. Ask any *Vogue* junkie: no girl-themed Web site or CNN segment on women's health can replace the guilty pleasure of slipping a glossy fashion rag into your shopping cart. Smooth as a pint of chocolate Häagen-Dazs, feckless as a thousand-dollar slip dress, women's magazines wrap culture, trends, health, and trash in a single, decadent package.

> But like the diet dessert recipes they print, these slick publications
> can leave a bad taste in your mouth.
>
> –Tiffany Lee Brown, "En Vogue"

Here three similes are in prominent display: "smooth as a pint of choco-late Häagen-Dazs" and "feckless as a thousand-dollar slip dress" in the third sentence, and "like the diet dessert recipes" in the fourth. Together, the similes add to the image the writer is trying to create of mass-market women's magazines as a mishmash of "trash" and "trends."

In another use of simile, Lerone Bennett Jr. argues that Chicago needs to return to the ideals of its founder, Jean Baptiste Point DuSable:

> [A]s Chicago turned the corner of the 200th-plus year since the Black
> Founding, it was as clear as the Sears Tower that the city cannot reach its
> full height or fulfill its destiny without a continuing confrontation with
> DuSable's dream and the fact that all Chicagoans—Black, White, Brown,
> African, Irish, Polish, Italian—are DuSable's children and debtors.
>
> –Lerone Bennett Jr.

Analogy

Caryn James uses an analogy that links the reality television show "Extreme Makeover" with sports competitions. She argues that with the show presented as "all a game," viewers lose sight of the permanence of plastic surgery.

·······················LINK TO P. 480

Analogies compare two different or dissimilar things for special effect, arguing that if two things are alike in one way they are probably alike in other ways as well. Often extended to several sentences, paragraphs, or even whole essays, analogies can help clarify and emphasize points of comparison. The Web in Motion site contains a list of "web analogies," including this one, contributed by Jill W:

> People who think they can build a stellar website because they bought
> a copy of *FrontPage* are probably the same people who would think
> that they can be a best-selling author after buying a pen.

And in an argument about the failures of the aircraft industry, another writer uses an analogy for potent contrast:

> If the aircraft industry had evolved as spectacularly as the computer
> industry over the past twenty-five years, a Boeing 767 would cost five
> hundred dollars today, and it would circle the globe in twenty minutes
> on five gallons of fuel.

Signifying

One distinctive trope found extensively in African American English is *sig-nifying*, in which a speaker cleverly and often humorously needles the lis-tener. In the following passage, two African American men (Grave Digger and Coffin Ed) signify on their white supervisor (Anderson), who ordered them to discover the originators of a riot:

"I take it you've discovered who started the riot," Anderson said.

"We knew who he was all along," Grave Digger said.

"It's just nothing we can do to him," Coffin Ed echoed.

"Why not, for God's sake?"

"He's dead," Coffin Ed said.

"Who?"

"Lincoln," Grave Digger said.

"He hadn't ought to have freed us if he didn't want to make provisions to feed us," Coffin Ed said.

"Anyone could have told him that."

–Chester Himes, *Hot Day, Hot Night*

Coffin Ed and Grave Digger demonstrate the major characteristics of effective signifying: indirection, ironic humor, fluid rhythm—and a surprising twist at the end. Rather than insulting Anderson directly by pointing out that he's asked a dumb question, they criticize the question indirectly by ultimately blaming a white man (and not just any white man, but one they're all supposed to revere). This twist leaves the supervisor speechless, teaching him something and giving Grave Digger and Coffin Ed the last word—and the last laugh.

You will find examples of signifying in the work of many African American writers. You may also hear signifying in NBA basketball, for it is an important element of trash talking; what Grave Digger and Coffin Ed do to Anderson, Allen Iverson regularly does to his opponents on the court.

Take a look at the example of signifying from a *Doonesbury* cartoon (see Figure 14.2). Note how Thor satirizes white attitudes about Black language, first by giving a mini-lecture in "standard" academic English and then underscoring his point (and putting down Mike) by reverting to "sho 'nuff."

Other Tropes

Several other tropes deserve special mention.

Hyperbole is the use of overstatement for special effect, a kind of pyrotechnics in prose. The tabloid papers whose headlines scream at shoppers in the grocery checkout line probably qualify as the all-time champions of hyperbole (journalist Tom Wolfe once wrote a satirical review of a *National Enquirer* writers' convention that he titled "Keeps His Mom-in-Law in Chains Meets Kills Son and Feeds Corpse to Pigs"). Everyone has seen these overstated arguments and, perhaps, marveled at the way they seem to sell.

FIGURE 14.2 *DOONESBURY* CARTOON

Hyperbole is also the trademark of more serious writers. In a column arguing that men's magazines fuel the same kind of neurotic anxieties about appearance that have plagued women for so long, Michelle Cottle uses hyperbole and humor to make her point:

> What self-respecting '90s woman could embrace a publication that runs such enlightened articles as "Turn Your Good Girl Bad" and "How to Wake Up Next to a One-Night Stand"? Or maybe you'll smile and wink knowingly: What red-blooded hetero chick wouldn't love all those glossy photo spreads of buff young beefcake in various states of undress, ripped abs and glutes flexed so tightly you could bounce a check on them? Either way you've got the wrong idea. My affection for *Men's Health* is driven by pure gender politics. . . . With page after page of bulging biceps and Gillette jaws, robust hairlines and silken skin, *Men's Health* is peddling a standard of male beauty as unforgiving and unrealistic as the female version sold by those dewy-eyed pre-teen waifs draped across covers of *Glamour* and *Elle*.
>
> –Michelle Cottle, "Turning Boys into Girls"

As you can well imagine, hyperbole of this sort can easily backfire, so it pays to use it sparingly and for an audience whose reactions you believe you can effectively predict. American journalist H. L. Mencken ignored this advice in 1921 when he used hyperbole to savage the literary style of President Warren Harding—and note that in doing so he says that he is offering a "small tribute," making the irony even more notable:

> I rise to pay my small tribute to Dr. Harding. Setting aside a college professor or two and half a dozen dipsomaniacal newspaper reporters, he takes the first place in my Valhalla of literati. That is to say, he writes the worst English that I have ever encountered. It reminds me of a string of wet sponges; it reminds me of tattered washing on the line; it reminds me of stale bean-soup, of college yells, of dogs barking idiotically through endless nights. It is so bad that a sort of grandeur creeps into it. It drags itself out of the dark abysm (I was about to write abcess!) of pish, and crawls insanely up the topmost pinnacle of posh. It is rumble and bumble. It is flap and doodle. It is balder and dash.
>
> —H. L. Mencken, *The Evening Sun*

Understatement, on the other hand, requires a quiet, muted message to make its point effectively. In her memoir, Rosa Parks—a civil rights activist who made history in 1955 by refusing to give up her bus seat to a white passenger—uses understatement so often that it might be said to be characteristic of her writing, a mark of her ethos. She refers to Martin Luther King Jr. simply as "a true leader," to Malcolm X as a person of "strong conviction," and to her own lifelong efforts as simply a small way of "carrying on."

As the examples from Rosa Parks suggest, quiet understatement can be particularly effective in arguments. When Watson and Crick published their first article on the structure of DNA, they felt that they had done nothing less than discover the secret of life. (Imagine what the *National Enquirer* headlines might have been for this story!) Yet in an atmosphere of extreme scientific competitiveness they chose to close their article with a vast understatement, using it purposely to gain emphasis: "It has not escaped our notice," they wrote, "that the specific pairing we have postulated immediately suggests a possible copying mechanism for the genetic material." Forty-some years later, considering the profound developments that have taken place in genetics, including the cloning of animals, the power of this understatement resonates even more strongly.

Rhetorical questions don't really require answers. Rather, they are used to help assert or deny something about an argument. Most of us use rhetorical questions frequently; think, for instance, of the times you have said "Who cares?" or "Why me?" or "How should I know?"—rhetorical questions all. Rhetorical questions also show up in written arguments. In a review of a book-length argument about the use and misuse of power in

Margaret Curtis opposes the suit brought by the family of Martin Luther King Jr. to copyright his "I Have a Dream" speech, noting that many elements of his speech were drawn from the Bible. She asks the following rhetorical question: "How can the speech be divided into which part was his invention and which was not?"

LINK TO P. 696 ·····

the Disney dynasty, the reviewer uses a series of rhetorical questions to sketch in part of the book's argument:

> If you have ever visited one of the Disney theme parks, though, you have likely wondered at the labor—both seen and unseen—necessary to maintain these fanciful environments. How and when are the grounds tended so painstakingly? How are the signs of high traffic erased from public facilities? What keeps employees so poised, meticulously groomed, and endlessly cheerful?
>
> –Linda S. Watts, review of *Inside the Mouse*

And here is Debra Saunders, opening an argument for the legalization of medical marijuana, with a rhetorical question: "If the federal government were right that medical marijuana has no medicinal value, why have so many doctors risked their practices by recommending its use for patients with cancer or AIDS?"

Antonomasia is probably most familiar to you from the sports pages: "His Airness" still means Michael Jordan; "The Great One," Wayne Gretzky; "The Sultan of Swat," Babe Ruth; "The Swiss Miss," Martina Hingis. And "The Answer" is Allen Iverson. Such shorthand substitutions of a descrip-

FIGURE 14.3 ALLEN "THE ANSWER" IVERSON

tive word or phrase for a proper name can pack arguments into just one phrase. What does calling Jordan "His Airness" argue about him?

Irony, the use of words to convey a meaning in tension with or opposite to their literal meanings, also works powerfully in arguments. One of the most famous sustained uses of irony in literature occurs in Shakespeare's *Julius Caesar*, as Mark Antony punctuates his condemnation of Brutus with the repeated ironic phrase "But Brutus is an honourable man." You may be a reader of *The Onion*, noted for its ironic treatment of politics. Another journal, the online *Ironic Times*, devotes itself to irony. Take a look at one front page:

FIGURE 14.4 FRONT PAGE OF THE *IRONIC TIMES*

Ironic Times

NO. 115   *"Expect the Ironic"*   NOV 25 - DEC 1, 2002

Nov 18   . . . In first act, Ridge orders all copies of '1984' destrc   Dec 2

WHY WE LIKE THANKSGIVING

34% Opportunity to put on a few pounds.

28% Excitement of traveling during the busiest travel days of the year.

21% Chance to see relatives we would not otherwise choose to see.

10% Chance to eat foods we would not otherwise choose to eat.

7% Animal slaughter.

WORLD NEWS

▸ **New Book Says U.S. Bought Warlords' Loyalty in Afghanistan**
Gave them $70 million in Enron stock options.

U. S. NEWS

▸ **White House Prepares for "Unthinkable" Worst-Case Scenario**
Emergency contingency disaster plan in place should Iraq comply with UN inspectors.

▸ **Homeland Security Bill Passes**
Watch what you say.

▸ **White House Tightens Dirty Air Rules**
Coal-firing plants ordered to pollute more or face fines.

REMINDER
Rome didn't fall in a day.

▸ **New York City Mulls Putting Homeless on Cruise Ships**
Would sleep on deck, outside passengers' cabins.

▸ **Eight Cubans Fly Into Key West, Seek Asylum**
Want to live here, open Haitian restaurant.

BUSINESS

▸ **Air of Optimism Pervades Wall Street**

SCHEMES

Schemes, figures that depend on word order, can add quite a bit of syntactic "zing" to arguments. Here we present the ones you are likely to see most often.

Parallelism uses grammatically similar words, phrases, or clauses for special effect:

> The Wild Man process involves five basic phases: Sweating, Yelling, Crying, Drum-Beating, and Ripping Your Shirt off Even If It's Expensive.
>
> > –Joe Bob Briggs, "Get in Touch with Your Ancient Spear"

> Infertility is not a modern problem, but it has created a modern industry.
>
> > –Jessica Cohen, "Grade A: The Market for a Yale Woman's Eggs"

> The laws of our land are said to be "by the people, of the people, and for the people."

Antithesis is the use of parallel structures to mark contrast or opposition:

> That's one small step for a man, one giant leap for mankind.
>
> > –Neil Armstrong

> Marriage has many pains, but celibacy has no pleasures.
>
> > –Samuel Johnson

> Those who kill people are called murderers; those who kill animals, sportsmen.

Inverted word order, in which the parts of a sentence or clause are not in the usual subject-verb-object order, can help make arguments particularly memorable:

> Into this grey lake plopped the thought, I know this man, don't I?
>
> > –Doris Lessing

> Hard to see, the dark side is.
>
> > –Yoda

> Good looking he was not; wealthy he was not; but brilliant—he was.

As with anything else, however, too much of such a figure can quickly become, well, too much.

Anaphora, or effective repetition, can act like a drumbeat in an argument, bringing the point home. In an argument about the future of Chicago, Lerone Bennett Jr. uses repetition to link Chicago to innovation and creativity:

> [Chicago]'s the place where organized Black history was born, where gospel music was born, where jazz and the blues were reborn, where the Beatles and the Rolling Stones went up to the mountaintop to get the new musical commandments from Chuck Berry and the rock'n'roll apostles.
>
> –Lerone Bennett Jr., "Blacks in Chicago"

And speaking of the Rolling Stones, here is Dave Barry using repetition in his comments on their 2002 tour:

> Recently I attended a Rolling Stones concert. This is something I do every two decades. I saw the Stones in the 1960s, and then again in the 1980s. I plan to see them next in the 2020s, then the 2040s, then the 2060s, at their 100th anniversary concert.
>
> –Dave Barry, "OK, What Will Stones Do for 100th Anniversary?"

Reversed structures for special effect have been used widely in political argumentation since President John F. Kennedy's inaugural address in 1961 charged citizens, "Ask not what your country can do for you; ask what you can do for your country." Like the other figures we have listed here, this one can help make arguments memorable:

> The Democrats won't get elected unless things get worse, and things won't get worse until the Democrats get elected.
>
> –Jeanne Kirkpatrick

> Your manuscript is both good and original. But the part that is good is not original, and the part that is original is not good.
>
> –Samuel Johnson

> When the going gets tough, the tough get going.

DANGERS OF UNDULY SLANTED LANGUAGE

Although all arguments depend on figurative language to some degree, if the words used call attention to themselves as "stacking the deck" in unfair ways, they will not be particularly helpful in achieving the goals of the argument. In preparing your own arguments, you will want to pay special attention to the connotations of the words you choose—those associations that words and phrases always carry with them. The choices

CULTURAL CONTEXTS FOR ARGUMENT

Style is always affected by language, culture, and rhetorical tradition. What constitutes effective style, therefore, varies broadly across cultures and depends on the rhetorical situation—purpose, audience, and so on. There is at least one important style question to consider when arguing across cultures: what level of formality is most appropriate? In the United States a fairly informal style is often acceptable, even appreciated. Many cultures, however, tend to value more formality. If you are in doubt, therefore, it is probably wise to err on the side of formality, especially in communicating with elders or with those in authority.

- Take care to use proper titles as appropriate—*Ms., Mr., Dr.,* and so on.

- Do not use first names unless invited to do so.

- Steer clear of slang. Especially when you're communicating with members of other cultures, slang may not be understood—or it may be seen as disrespectful.

Beyond formality, stylistic preferences vary widely. When arguing across cultures, the most important stylistic issue might be clarity, especially when you're communicating with people whose native languages are different from your own. In such situations, analogies and similes almost always aid in understanding. Likening something unknown to something familiar can help make your argument forceful—and understandable.

you make will always depend on the purpose you have in mind and those to whom you wish to speak. Should you choose *skinny* or *slender* in describing someone? Should you label a group *left-wing agitators, student demonstrators*—or *supporters of human rights?*

The lesson for writers of arguments is a simple one that can be devilishly hard to follow: know your audience and be respectful of them, even as you argue strenuously to make your case.

RESPOND

1. Identify the types of figurative language used in the following advertising slogans—metaphor, simile, analogy, hyperbole, understatement, rhetorical question, antonomasia, irony, parallelism, antithesis, inverted word order, anaphora, or reversed structure.

"Good to the last drop." (Maxwell House coffee)

"It's the real thing." (Coca-Cola)

"Melts in your mouth, not in your hands." (M&M's)

"Be all that you can be." (U.S. Army)

"Got Milk?" (America's Milk Processors)

"Breakfast of champions." (Wheaties)

"Double your pleasure; double your fun." (Doublemint gum)

"Let your fingers do the walking." (the Yellow Pages)

"Think small." (Volkswagen)

"Like a Rock." (Chevy Trailblazer)

"Real bonding, real popcorn, real butter, real good times." (Pop-Secret Popcorn)

2. We mentioned in this chapter that during the Renaissance, students would memorize and practice more than a hundred figures of speech. As part of their lessons, these students would be asked to write whole paragraphs using each of the figures *in order*, in what might be called "connected discourse": The paragraph makes sense, and each sentence builds on the one that precedes it. Use the following list of figures to write a paragraph of connected discourse on a topic of your choice. Each sentence should use a different figure, starting with simile and ending with antonomasia.

simile

irony

parallelism

analogy

antithesis

hyperbole

inverted word order

understatement

anaphora

rhetorical question

reversed structure

antonomasia

Now rewrite the paragraph, still on the same topic but using the list of figures in *reverse order*. The first sentence should use antonomasia and the last should use simile.

3. Some public speakers are well known for their use of tropes and schemes. (Jesse Jackson comes to mind, as does George W. Bush, who employs folksy sayings to achieve a certain effect.) Using the Internet, find the text of a recent speech by a speaker who uses figures liberally. Pick a paragraph that seems particularly rich in figures and rewrite it, eliminating every trace of figurative language. Then read the two paragraphs—the original and your revised version—aloud to your class. With the class's help, try to imagine rhetorical situations in which the figure-free version would be most appropriate.

 Now find some prose that seems dry and pretty much non-figurative. (A technical manual, instructions for operating appliances, or a legal document might serve.) Rewrite a part of the piece in the most figurative language you can muster. Then try to list rhetorical situations in which this newly figured language might be most appropriate.

chapter fifteen

Visual Arguments

You know you shouldn't buy camping gear just because you see it advertised on TV. But what's the harm in imagining yourself on that Arizona mesa with the sun setting, the camp stove open, the tent up and ready? That could be you reminiscing about the rugged trek that got you there, just like the tanned campers in the ad. Now what's that brand name again, and what's its URL?

A student government committee is meeting to talk about campus safety. One member has prepared a series of graphs showing the steady increase in the number of on-campus attacks over the last five years, along with several photographs that bring these crimes vividly to life.

It turns out that the governor and now presidential candidate who claims to be against taxes actually raised taxes in his home state—according to his opponent, who is running thirty-second TV spots to make that point. The ads feature a plainly dressed woman who sure looks credible; she's got to be a real person, not an actor, and she says he raised taxes. She wouldn't lie—would she?

You've never heard of the trading firm. But the letter, printed on thick bond with smart color graphics, is impressive—and hey, the company CEO is offering you $75 just to open an online account. The $75 check is right at the top of the letter, and it looks real enough. The company's Web site seems quite professional—quick-loading and easy to navigate. Somebody's on the ball. Perhaps you should sign up?

A shiny black coupe passes you effortlessly on a steep slope along a curving mountain interstate. It's moving too fast for you to read the nameplate, but on the trunk lid you see a three-pointed star. Hmmmm . . . Maybe after you graduate from law school and your student loans are paid off . . .

FIGURE 15.1 A VISUAL ARGUMENT ON WHEELS

THE POWER OF VISUAL ARGUMENTS

We don't need to be reminded that visual images have clout. Just think for a moment of where you were on September 11, 2001, and what you remember of the events of that day: almost everyone we know still reports being able to see the hijacked planes slamming into the World Trade Towers as though that image were forever etched in some inner eye.

What other potent images are engraved in your memory? Even in mundane moments, not memorable in the way an event like 9/11 is, visual images still surround us, from T-shirts to billboards to computer screens. It seems everyone is trying to get our attention, and they are doing it with images as well as words. In fact, several recently published books argue that images today pack more punch than words. As technology makes it easier for people to create and transmit images, those images are more compelling than ever, brought to us via DVD and HDTV on our computers, on our walls, in our pockets, even in our cars.

FIGURE 15.2 LEONARD SHLAIN'S BOOK EXAMINES THE GROWING INFLUENCE OF IMAGES.

But let's put this in perspective. Visual arguments weren't invented by Bill Gates, and they've always had power. The pharaohs of Egypt lined the Nile with statues of themselves to assert their authority, and Roman emperors stamped their portraits on coins for the same reason. Some thirty thousand years ago people in the south of France created magnificent cave paintings, suggesting that people have indeed always used images to celebrate and to communicate.

FIGURE 15.3 CEILING OF THE LASCAUX CAVES

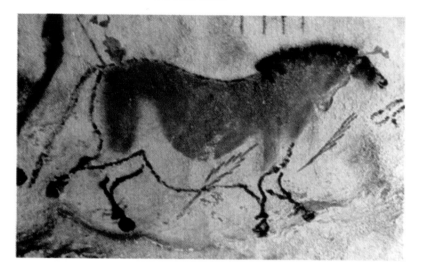

In our own era, two events marked turning points in the growing power of media images. The first occurred in 1960, when presidential candidates John F. Kennedy and Richard M. Nixon met in a nationally televised debate. Kennedy, robust and confident in a dark suit, faced a pale and haggard Nixon barely recovered from an illness. Kennedy looked cool and "presidential"; Nixon did not. Many viewers believe that the contrasting images Kennedy and Nixon presented on that evening radically changed the direction of the 1960 election campaign, leading to Kennedy's narrow victory. For better or worse, the debate also established television as the chief medium for political communication in the United States.

The second event is more recent—the introduction in the early 1980s of personal computers with graphic interfaces. These machines, which

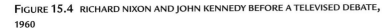

FIGURE 15.4 RICHARD NIXON AND JOHN KENNEDY BEFORE A TELEVISED DEBATE, 1960

initially seemed strange and toylike, operated with icons and pictures rather than through arcane commands. Subtly at first, and then with the smack of a tsunami, graphic computers (the only kind we use now) moved people away from an age of print into an era of electronic, image-saturated communications.

So that's where we are in the opening decade of a new millennium. People today are adjusting rapidly to a world of seamless, multichannel communications. The prophet of this time is Marshall McLuhan, the guru of *Wired* magazine who proclaimed some forty years ago that "the medium is the massage," with the play on words (*message/massage*) definitely intentional. Certainly images "massage" us all the time, and anyone reading and writing today has to be prepared to deal with arguments that shuffle more than words.

SHAPING THE MESSAGE

Images make arguments of their own. A photograph, for example, isn't a faithful representation of reality; it's reality shaped by the photographer's point of view. You can see photographic and video arguments at work everywhere, but perhaps particularly so during political campaigns. Staff photographers work to place candidates in settings that will show them in the best possible light—shirtsleeves rolled up, surrounded by smiling children and red-white-and-blue bunting—whereas their opponents look for opportunities to present them in a bad light. Closer to home, you may well have chosen photographs that showed you at your best to include in your college applications.

One of the most often reprinted photographs appearing in the wake of the September 11, 2001, terrorist attacks was shot by Thomas Franklin and shows three firefighters struggling to hoist the American flag as dust settles all around them. This photo, and others like Bridget Besaw Gorman's shown in Figure 15.5, immediately brought another famous photo to the minds of many Americans: Joe Rosenthal's photo of U.S. Marines raising the flag on Iwo Jima in 1945 (see Figure 15.6).

FIGURE 15.5 BRIDGET BESAW GORMAN'S 2001 PHOTO

Figure 15.6 Joe Rosenthal's 1945 photo

Take a look at the two photos and consider how they are composed—
what attracts your attention, how your eyes move over the image, what
immediate impression they create. What do you read in these images—
heroism, endurance, character, conviction, hope? Gorman's and Rosenthal's skill as photographers enables viewers to take a lot of meaning from
these images; they are ones viewers come back to again and again.

Even if those who produce images shape the messages those images
convey, those of us who "read" them are by no means passive. Human
vision is selective: to some extent, we actively shape what we see. Much of
what we see is laden with cultural meanings, too, and we must have
"learned" to see things in certain ways. Consider the Statue of Liberty wel-
coming immigrants to America's shores—and then imagine her instead
as Bellona, the goddess of war, guarding New York Harbor with a blazing
torch. For a moment, at least, she'd be a different statue.

FIGURE 15.7 STATUE OF LIBERTY

Of course, we don't always see things the same way, which is one reason eyewitnesses to the same event often report it differently. Or why even instant replays don't always solve disputed calls on football fields.

The visual images that surround us today—and that argue forcefully for our attention and often for our time and money—are constructed to invite, perhaps even coerce, us into seeing them in just one way. But each of us has our own powers of vision, our own frames of reference that influence how we see. So visual arguments might best be described as a give-and-take, a dialogue, or even a tussle.

ACHIEVING VISUAL LITERACY

Why take images so seriously? Because they matter. Images change lives and shape behavior. When advertisements for sneakers are powerful enough to lead some kids to kill for the coveted footwear, when five- and ten-second images and sound bites are deciding factors in presidential elections, when the image of Joe Camel is credibly accused of enticing youngsters to smoke, or when a cultural icon like Oprah Winfrey can sell more books in one TV show than a hundred writers might do—it's high time to start paying careful attention to visual elements of argument.

How text is presented affects how it is read—whether it is set in fancy type, plain type, or handwritten; whether it has illustrations or not; whether it looks serious, fanciful, scholarly, or commercial. Figure 15.8 shows information about a peer-tutoring service presented visually in three different ways—as an email message, as a flyer with a table, and as a flyer with a visual (this is how it actually exists). Look at the three different versions of this text and consider in each case how the presentation affects how you perceive the information. Does the photograph and play on the movie *The Usual Suspects*, for example, make you more or less likely to use this tutoring service? The point, of course, is that as you read any text, you need to consider its presentation—a crucial element in any written argument.

ANALYZING VISUAL ELEMENTS OF ARGUMENTS

We've probably said enough to suggest that analyzing the visual elements of argument is a challenge, one that's even greater as we encounter multimedia appeals as well, especially on the Web. Here are some questions that can help you recognize—and analyze—visual and multimedia arguments:

Consider the photo of Calista Flockhart that illustrates Ellen Goodman's article about changing notions of body image in Fiji. What does this photo contribute to Goodman's argument and to its persuasiveness?

LINK TO P. 478 ·······································

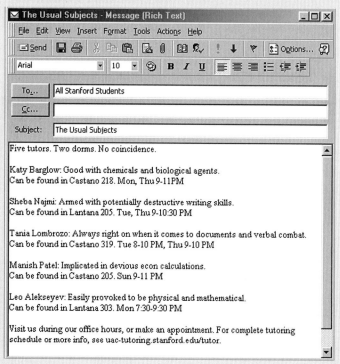

a

THE USUAL SUBJECTS

Five tutors. Two dorms. No coincidence.

Katy Barglow	*Sheba Najmi*	*Tania Lombrozo*	*Manish Patel*	*Leo Alekseyev*
Good with chemicals and biological agents.	Armed with potentially destructive writing skills.	Always right on when it comes to documents and verbal combat.	Implicated in devious econ calculations.	Easily provoked to be physical and mathematical.
Can be found in: Castano 218 Mon, Thu 9–11 PM	Can be found in: Lantana 205 Tue, Thu 9–10:30 PM	Can be found in: Castano 319 Tue 8–10 PM Thu 9–10 PM	Can be found in: Castano 205 Sun 9–11 PM	Can be found in: Lantana 303 Mon 7:30–9:30 PM

Visit us during our office hours, or make an appointment. For complete tutoring schedule or more info, see uac-tutoring.stanford.edu/tutor.

b

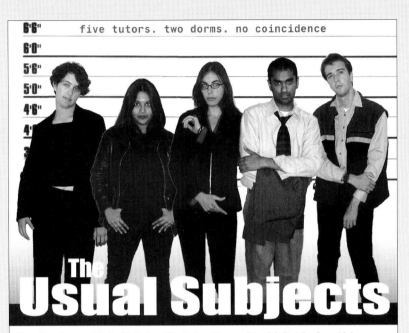

five tutors. two dorms. no coincidence

The Usual Subjects

Katy Barglow	Sheba Najmi	Tania Lombrozo	Manish Patel	Leo Alekseyev
Good with chemicals and biological agents.	Armed with potentially destructive writing skills.	Always right on when it comes to documents and verbal combat.	Implicated in devious econ calculations.	Easily provoked to be physical and mathematical.
Can be found in:	*Can be found in:*	*Can be found in:*	*Can be found in:*	*Can be found in:*
Castano 218	Lantana 205	Castano 319	Castano 205	Lantana 303
Mon, Thu	*Tue, Thu*	*Tue* 8 – 10 PM	*Sun* 9 – 11 PM	*Mon*
9 – 11 PM	9 – 10:30 PM	*Thu* 9 – 10 PM		7:30 – 9:30 PM

Visit us during our office hours, or make an appointment.
For complete tutoring schedule or more info, see

uac-tutoring.stanford.edu/tutor

c

ABOUT THE CREATORS/AUTHORS

- Who created this visual text?
- What can you find out about this person(s), and what other work they have done?
- What does the creator's attitude seem to be toward the visual image?
- What do the creators intend its effects to be?

ABOUT THE MEDIUM

- Which media are used for this visual text? Images only? Words and images? Sound, video, graphs, charts?
- What effect does the choice of medium have on the message of the visual text? How would the message be altered if different media were used?
- What is the role of words that may accompany the visual text? How do they clarify or reinforce (or blur or contradict) the message?

ABOUT VIEWERS/READERS

- What does the visual text assume about its viewers—and about what they know and agree with?
- What overall impression does the visual text create in you?
- Does the visual evoke positive—or negative—feelings about individuals, scenes, or ideas?

ABOUT CONTENT AND PURPOSE

- What argumentative purpose does the visual text convey? What is it designed to convey?
- What cultural values or ideals does the visual evoke or suggest? The good life? Love and harmony? Sex appeal? Youth? Adventure? Economic power or dominance? Freedom? Does the visual reinforce these values or question them? What does the visual do to strengthen the argument?
- What emotions does the visual evoke? Which ones do you think it intends to evoke? Desire? Envy? Empathy? Shame or guilt? Pride? Nostalgia? Something else?

ABOUT DESIGN

- How is the visual text composed? What is your eye drawn to first? Why?
- What is in the foreground? In the background? What is in or out of focus? What is moving? What is placed high, and what is placed low?

What is to the left, in the center, and to the right? What effect do these placements have on the message?

- Is any particular information (such as a name, face, or scene) high-lighted or stressed in some way to attract your attention?

- How are light and color used? What effect(s) are they intended to have on you? What about video? Sound?

- What details are included or emphasized? What details are omitted or deemphasized? To what effect? Is anything downplayed, ambiguous, confusing, distracting, or obviously omitted? To what ends?

- What, if anything, is surprising about the design of the visual text? What do you think is the purpose of that surprise?

- Is anything in the visual repeated, intensified, or exaggerated? Is anything presented as "supernormal" or idealistic? What effects are intended by these strategies, and what effects do they have on you as a viewer? How do they clarify or reinforce (or blur or contradict) the message?

- How are you directed to move within the argument? Are you encouraged to read further? Click on a link? Scroll down? Fill out a form? Provide your email address? Place an order?

Take a look at the home page of United Colors of Benetton, a company that sells sportswear, handbags, shoes, and more. You might expect a company that sells eighty million items of clothing and accessories annually to feature garments on its home page or to make a pitch to sell you something. And you would find many of those items if you probed the Benetton site more deeply. But on the company's main page (see Figure 15.9) you see the torso of a man, his right arm ending not in a hand but in a prosthetic device attached to a spoon and what looks like a makeshift knife. To the left of this arresting image is the simple heading Food for Life. Clicking on that area takes you to a second page that announces "Food for Life: United Colors of Benetton and World Food Programme Communication Campaign 2003." This campaign is presented on the World Food Programme's Web site, as well (see Figure 15.10). Taken together, these pages make a powerful argument that we should all be concerned about world hunger—and take action to address it.

Even this brief investigation of the Benetton site reveals that this manufacturer of clothing and accessories promotes its wares through an involvement in social activism. So its images challenge viewers to join in— or at least to consider doing so. What effect do these pages have on you?

FIGURE 15.9   UNITED COLORS OF BENETTON HOME PAGE

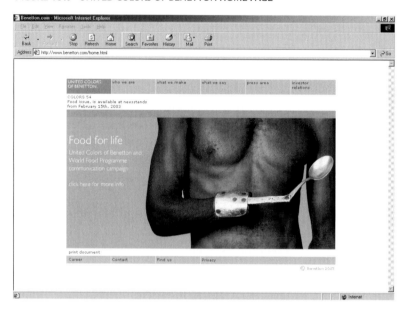

FIGURE 15.10   WORLD FOOD PROGRAMME HOME PAGE

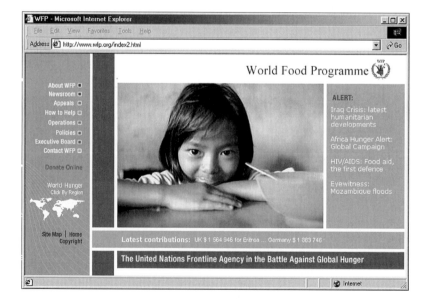

USING VISUALS IN YOUR OWN ARGUMENTS

You too can, and perhaps must, use visuals in your writing. Many college classes now call for projects to be posted on the Web, which almost always involves the use of images. Many courses also require students to make multimedia presentations using software such as PowerPoint, or even good, old-fashioned overhead projectors with transparencies.

Here we sketch out some basic principles of visual rhetoric. To help you appreciate the argumentative character of visual texts, we examine them under some of the same categories we use for written and oral arguments earlier in this book (Chapters 4, 6, and 7), though in a different order. You may be surprised by some of the similarities you will see in visual and verbal arguments.

Visual Arguments Based on Character

What does character have to do with visual argument? Consider two argumentative essays submitted to an instructor. One is scrawled in thick pencil on pages ripped from a spiral notebook, little curls of paper still dangling from the left margin. The other is neatly typed on bond paper and in a form the professor likely regards as "professional." Is there much doubt about which argument will (at least initially) get the more sympathetic reading? You might object that appearances shouldn't count for so much, and you would have a point. The argument scratched in pencil could be the stronger piece, but it faces an uphill battle because its author has sent the wrong signals. Visually, the writer seems to be saying, "I don't much care about this message or the people to whom I am sending it."

There may be times when you want to send exactly such a signal to an audience. Some TV advertisements aimed at young people are deliberately designed to antagonize older audiences with their blaring soundtracks, MTV-style quick cuts, and in-your-face style. The point is that the visual rhetoric of any piece you create ought to be a deliberate choice, not an accident. Also keep control of your own visual image. In most cases, when you present an argument, you want to appear authoritative and credible.

Look for images that reinforce your authority and credibility.

For a brochure about your new small business, for instance, you would need to consider images that prove your company has the resources to do its job. Consumers might feel reassured seeing pictures that show you have an actual office, up-to-date equipment, and a competent staff. Similarly, for a Web site about a company or organization you represent, you would consider including its logo or emblem. Such emblems have authority and weight. That's why university Web sites so often include the seal of the institution somewhere on the home page, or why the president of the United States always travels with a presidential seal to hang upon the speaker's podium. The emblem or logo, like the hood ornament on a car, can convey a wealth of cultural and historical implications.

FIGURE 15.11 THREE IMAGES: THE U.S. PRESIDENTIAL SEAL, THE MCDONALD'S LOGO, AND THE BMW ORNAMENT

Consider how design reflects your character.

Almost every design element sends signals about character and ethos, so be sure you think carefully about them. For example, the type fonts you select for a document can mark you as warm and inviting or efficient and contemporary. The warm and readable fonts often belong to a family called *serif*. The serifs are those little flourishes at the ends of their strokes that make the fonts seem handcrafted and artful:

> warm and readable (Bookman Old Style)

> warm and readable (Times New Roman)

> **warm and readable (Bookman)**

Cleaner, modern fonts go without those little flourishes and are called *sans serif*. These fonts are cooler and simpler — and, some argue, more readable on a computer screen (depending on screen resolution):

> efficient and contemporary (Helvetica)

> **efficient and contemporary (Arial Black)**

> efficient and contemporary (Arial)

You may also be able to use decorative fonts. These are appropriate for special uses, but not for extended texts:

decorative and special uses (Zapf Chancery)

decorative and special uses (Goundy Handtooled BT)

Other typographic elements shape your ethos as well. The size of type, for one, can make a difference. You'll seem to be shouting if your headings or text is boldfaced and too large. Tiny type might make you seem evasive:

Lose weight! Pay nothing!*

*Excludes the costs of enrollment and required meal purchases. Minimum contract: 12 months.

Similarly, your choice of color—especially for backgrounds—can make a statement about your taste, personality, and common sense. For instance, you'll make a bad impression with a Web page whose background colors or patterns make reading difficult. If you want to be noticed, you might use bright colors—the same sort that would make an impression in clothing or cars. But more subtle shades might be a better choice in most situations.

Don't ignore the impact of illustrations and photographs. Because they reveal what you visualize, images can send powerful signals about your preferences, sensitivities, and inclusiveness—and it's not always easy. Conference planners designing a program, for example, wanted to make sure to include pictures that represent the members who will be attending; as a result, they double-checked to make sure that they didn't show only women in their photos, or only men, or only members of one race or ethnic group.

Even your choice of medium says something important about you. If you decide to make an appeal on a Web site, you send signals about your technical skills and contemporary orientation as well as about your personality. Take a look at the Web site of undergraduate student Dennis Tyler (see Figure 15.12). What can you deduce about Tyler from this page—his personality, his values, and so on?

A presentation that relies on an overhead projector gives a different impression from one presented on an LCD projector with software—or one presented with a poster and handouts. If you are reporting on a children's story you're writing, the most effective medium of presentation might be old-fashioned cardboard and paper made into an oversized book and illustrated by hand.

FIGURE 15.12 DENNIS TYLER'S WEB SITE

Follow required design conventions.

Many kinds of writing have required design conventions. When that's the case, follow them to the letter. It's no accident that lab reports for science courses are sober and unembellished. Visually, they reinforce the serious character of scientific work. The same is true of a college research paper. You might resent the tediousness of placing page numbers in the right place or aligning long quotations just so, but these visual details help convey your competence. So whether you are composing a term paper, résumé, screenplay, or Web site, look for authoritative models and follow them. Here is Dennis Tyler's résumé. Note that its look is serious: The type is clear and easy to read; the black on white is simple and no-nonsense; the headings call attention to Tyler's accomplishments.

FIGURE **15.13**   DENNIS TYLER'S RÉSUMÉ

DENNIS TYLER JR.

CURRENT ADDRESS
P.O. Box 12345
Stanford, CA 94309
Phone: (650) 498-4731
Email: dtyler@yahoo.com

PERMANENT ADDRESS
506 Chanelle Court
Baton Rouge, LA 70128
Phone: (504) 246-9847

| CAREER OBJECTIVE | Position on editorial staff of a major newspaper |

EDUCATION

| 9/98–6/02 | **Stanford University**, Stanford, CA
B.A., ENGLISH AND AMERICAN STUDIES, June 2002 |
| 9/00–12/00 | **Morehouse College**, Atlanta, GA
STANFORD STUDY EXCHANGE PROGRAM |

EXPERIENCE

6/01–9/01	**Business Scholar Intern**, Finance, AOL Time Warner, New York, NY Responsible for analyzing data for strategic marketing plans. Researched the mergers and acquisitions of companies to which Time Inc. sells advertising space.
1/00–6/01	**Editor-in-Chief**, *Enigma* (a literary journal), Stanford University, CA Oversaw the entire process of Enigma. Edited numerous creative works: short stories, poems, essays, and interviews. Selected appropriate material for the journal. Responsible for designing cover and publicity to the greater community.
8/00–12/00	**Community Development Intern**, University Center Development Corporation (UCDC), Atlanta, GA Facilitated workshops and meetings on the importance of home buying and neighborhood preservation. Created UCDC brochure and assisted in the publication of the center's newsletter.
6/00–8/00	**News Editor**, *Stanford Daily,* Stanford University, CA Responsible for editing stories and creating story ideas for the newspaper. Assisted with the layout for the newspaper and designs for the cover.

SKILLS AND HONORS

- Computer Skills: MS Word, Excel, PageMaker, Microsoft Publisher; Internet research
- Language: Proficient in Spanish
- Trained in making presentations, conducting research, acting, and singing
- Mellon Fellow, Gates Millennium Scholar, Public Service Scholar, National Collegiate Scholar
- Black Community Service Arts Award. 2001–2002

| REFERENCES | Available upon request |

Visual Arguments Based on Facts and Reason

We tend to associate facts and reason with verbal arguments, but here too visual elements play an essential role. Indeed, it is hard to imagine a compelling presentation these days that doesn't rely, to some degree, on visual elements to enhance or even make the argument.

Many readers and listeners now expect ideas to be represented graphically. Not long ago, media critics ridiculed the colorful charts and graphs in newspapers like *USA Today*. Today, comparable features appear in even the most traditional publications because they work. They convey information efficiently.

Organize information visually.

A design works well when readers can look at an item and understand what it does. A brilliant, much-copied example of such an intuitive design is a seat adjuster invented many years ago by Mercedes-Benz. It is shaped like a tiny seat. Push any element of the control, and the real seat moves the same way—back and forth, up and down. No instructions are necessary.

Good visual design can work the same way in an argument, conveying information without elaborate instructions. Titles, headings, subheadings, pull quotes, running heads, boxes, and so on are some common visual signals. When you present parallel headings in a similar type font, size, and color, you make it clear that the information under these headings is in some way related. So in a conventional term paper, you should use headings and subheadings to group information that is connected or parallel. Similarly, on a Web site, you might create two or three types of headings for groups of related information.

Use headings when they will help guide your readers through the document you are presenting. For more complex and longer pieces, you may choose to use both headings and subheadings.

You should also make comparable inferences about the way text should be arranged on a page: look for relationships among items that should look alike. In this book, for example, bulleted lists are used to offer specific guidelines while boxes mark sections on "Cultural Contexts for Argument." You might use a list or a box to set off information that should be treated differently from the rest of the presentation, or you might visually mark it in other ways—by shading, color, or typography.

An item presented in large type or under a larger headline should be more important than one that gets less visual attention. Place illustrations carefully: what you position front and center will appear more

FIGURE **15.14** THE SERVICE EMPLOYEES INTERNATIONAL UNION'S WEB SITE USES VARIOUS HEADINGS TO GROUP DIFFERENT KINDS OF INFORMATION.

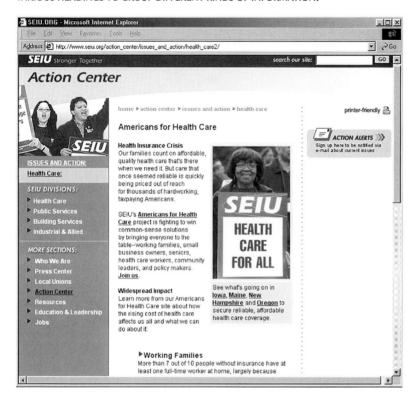

important than items in less conspicuous places. On a Web site, key headings should usually lead to subsequent pages on the site.

Needless to say, you take a risk if you violate the expectations of your audience or if you present a visual text without coherent signals. Particularly for Web-based materials that may be accessible to people around the world, you can't make many assumptions about what will count as "coherent" across cultures. So you need to think about the roadmap you are giving viewers whenever you present them with a visual text. Remember that design principles evolve and change from medium to medium. A printed text or an overhead slide, for example, ordinarily works best when its elements are easy to read, simply organized, and surrounded by restful white space. But some types of Web pages seem to thrive on visual clutter, attracting and holding audiences' attention through the variety of information they can pack onto a relatively limited screen. Check out the way the opening screens of most search engines assault a viewer with enticements. Yet look closely, and you may find the logic in these designs.

One group that regularly analyzes Web sites, the Stanford Persuasive Technology Lab, recently concluded that Google News may soon become the most credible Web site of all. Here are just a few of the Lab's points about what makes Google News credible: It's easy to navigate; it provides a diversity of viewpoints; it has a reputation for outstanding performance in other areas; it has no broken links, typos, and so on; it provides clear information about the site; it has an easy-to-understand structure; it discloses information about the organization; and it has no ads. Take a look at Google News yourself: do you agree that it is a fairly credible site?

FIGURE 15.15   GOOGLE NEWS SITE

Use visuals to convey information efficiently.

Words are immensely powerful and capable of enormous precision and subtlety. But the simple fact is that some information is conveyed more efficiently by charts, graphs, drawings, maps, or photos than by words. When making an argument, especially to a large group, consider what information should be delivered in nonverbal form.

A *pie chart* is an effective way of comparing a part to the whole. You might use a pie chart to illustrate the ethnic composition of your school, the percentage of taxes paid by people at different income levels, or the consumption of energy by different nations. Pie charts depict such information memorably, as Figure 15.16 shows:

FIGURE 15.16 HISPANIC POPULATION, BY TYPE OF ORIGIN, 1996 (IN PERCENT)

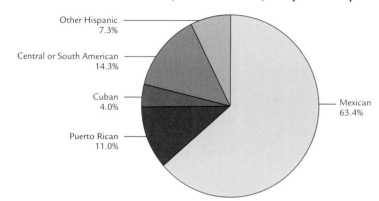

Source: U.S. Census Bureau, Current Population Survey. "The Hispanic Population." *1997 Population Profile of the United States.* Ed. John M. Reed. Washington: U.S. Department of Commerce, September 1998.

A *graph* is an efficient device for comparing items over time or according to other variables. You could use a graph to trace the rise and fall of test scores over several decades, or to show college enrollment for men and women, as in Figure 15.17.

Diagrams or drawings are useful for drawing attention to details. You can use drawings to illustrate complex physical processes or designs of all sorts. After the attack on the World Trade Center, for example, engineers used drawings and diagrams to help citizens understand precisely what led to the total collapse of the buildings.

You can use *maps* to illustrate location and spatial relationships — something as simple as the distribution of office space in your student union or as complex as the topography of Utah. Such information would probably be far more difficult to explain using words alone.

FIGURE 15.17 COLLEGE ENROLLMENT FOR MEN AND WOMEN BY AGE, 1998 (IN MILLIONS)

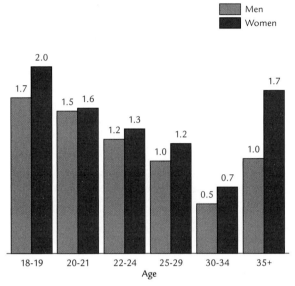

Source: U.S. Census Bureau, Current Population Survey, October 1998. "Scholars of All Ages: School Enrollment, 1998." *1998 Population Profile of the United States.* Washington: U.S. Department of Commerce, March 2001.

Follow professional guidelines for presenting visuals.

Charts, graphs, tables, and illustrations play such an important role in many fields that professional groups have come up with specific guidelines for labeling and formatting these items. You need to become familiar with those conventions as you advance in a field. A guide such as the *Publication Manual of the American Psychological Association* (5th edition) or the *MLA Style Manual and Guide to Scholarly Publishing* (6th edition) describes these rules in detail.

Remember to check for copyrighted material.

You also must be careful to respect copyright rules when you use visual items created by someone else. It is relatively easy these days to download visual texts of all kinds from the Web. Some of these items—such as clip art or government documents—may be in the public domain, meaning that you are free to use them without requesting permission or paying a royalty. But other visual texts may require permission, especially if you intend to publish your work or use the item commercially. And remember: anything you place on a Web site is considered "published." (See Chapter 20 for more on intellectual property.)

Visual Arguments That Appeal to Emotion

To some extent, we tend to be suspicious of arguments supported by visual and multimedia elements because they can seem to manipulate our senses. And many advertisements, political documentaries, rallies, marches, and even church services do in fact use visuals to trigger our emotions. Who has not teared up at a funeral when members of a veteran's family are presented with the American flag, with a bugler blowing taps in the distance? Who doesn't remember being moved emotionally by a powerful film performance accompanied by a heart-wrenching musical score? But you might also have seen or heard about *Triumph of the Will*, a Nazi propaganda film from the 1930s that powerfully depicts Hitler as the benign savior of the German people, a hero of Wagnerian dimensions. It is a chilling reminder of how images can be manipulated and abused.

Yet you cannot flip through a magazine without being cajoled or seduced by images of all kinds—most of them designed in some way to attract your eye and attention. Not all such seductions are illicit, nor should you avoid using them when emotions can support the legitimate claims you hope to advance. What is the effect of the image presented in Figure 15.18?

FIGURE 15.18 SOMALI CHILD, 1992

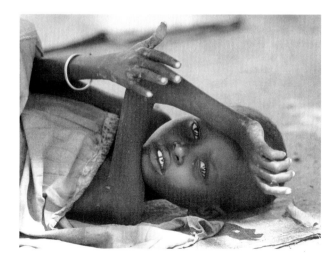

Appreciate the emotional power of images.

Images can bring a text or presentation to life. Sometimes the images have power in and of themselves to persuade. This was the case with images in the 1960s that showed civil rights demonstrators being assaulted by police dogs and water hoses, and with horrifying images in 2001 of dead Afghani children, which led many people to contribute to relief for Afghanistan.

Images you select for a presentation may be equally effective if the visual text works well with other components of the argument. Indeed, a given image might support many different kinds of arguments. Take, for example, the famous *Apollo 8* photograph of our planet as a big blue mar-

FIGURE **15.19** EARTH SHINING OVER THE MOON

ble hanging above the horizon of the moon. You might use this image to introduce an argument about the need for additional investment in the space program. Or it might become part of an argument about the need to preserve our frail natural environment, or part of an argument against nationalism: *from space, we are one world*. You could, of course, make any of these claims without the image. But the photograph—like most images—might touch members of your audience more powerfully than words alone could.

Appreciate the emotional power of color.

Consider the color red. It attracts hummingbirds—and cops. It excites the human eye in ways that other colors don't. You can make a powerful statement with a red dress or a red car—or red shoes. In short, red evokes emotions. But so do black, green, pink, and even brown. That we respond to color is part of our biological and cultural makeup. So it makes sense to consider carefully what colors are compatible with the kind of argument you are making. You might find that the best choice is black on a white background.

In most situations, you can be guided in your selection of colors by your own good taste (guys—check your ties), by designs you admire, or by the advice of friends or helpful professionals. Some design and presentation software will even help you choose colors by offering you dependable "default" shades or by offering an array of preexisting designs and compatible colors—for example, of presentation slides.

The colors you choose for a design should follow certain common-sense principles. If you are using background colors on a poster, Web site, or slide, the contrast between words and background should be vivid enough to make reading easy. For example, white letters on a yellow background will likely prove illegible. Any bright background color should be avoided for a long document. Indeed, reading seems easiest with dark letters against a light or white background. Avoid complex patterns, even though they might look interesting and be easy to create. Quite often, they interfere with other, more important elements of your presentation.

As you use visuals in your college projects, test them on prospective readers. That's what professionals do because they appreciate how delicate the choices about visual and multimedia texts can be. These responses will help you analyze your own arguments as well as improve your success with them.

RESPOND•

1. The December 2002 issue of the *Atlantic Monthly* included the following poem, along with the photograph that may have inspired it, shown in Figure 15.20. Look carefully at the image and then read the poem several times, at least once aloud. Working with another person in your class, discuss how the words of the poem and the image interact with one another. What difference would it make if the image had not accompanied this text? Write a brief report of your findings, and bring it to class for discussion.

The Launching Chains of The Great Eastern (By Robert Howlett, 1857)

JOHN SPAULDING

A waterfall of black chains
looms behind the man in the stovepipe hat.
Cigar. Wrinkled clothes. This is
Isambard Kingdom Brunel.
Who could not stop working. Slept
and ate at the shipyard.
The largest ship in the world.
Driven to outdo himself.
Fashioned from iron plate and
powered by three separate means.
Able to sail to Ceylon and back
without refueling. Fated
to lay the Atlantic cable, the India cable.
Untouched in size for forty years.
The Great Leviathan. The Little Giant,
Isambard Kingdom Brunel.
Builder of tunnels, ships, railroads, bridges.
Engineer and Genius of England.
He should have built churches, you know.
Everything he prayed for came true.

FIGURE **15.20** THIS PHOTOGRAPH OF ISAMBARD KINGDOM BRUNEL WAS TAKEN BY ROBERT HOWLETT AND IS INCLUDED IN THE NATIONAL PORTRAIT GALLERY'S COLLECTION IN LONDON.

2. Find an advertisement with both verbal and visual elements. Analyze the ad's visual argument by answering some of the questions on pp. 312–13, taking care to "reread" its visual elements just as carefully as you would its words. After you've answered each question as thoroughly as possible, switch ads with a classmate and analyze the new argument in the same way. Then compare your own and your classmate's responses to the two advertisements. If they are different—and there is every reason to expect they will be—how do you account for the differences? What is the effect of audience on the argument's reception? What are the differences between your own active reading and your classmate's?

3. If you have used the World Wide Web, you have no doubt noticed the relationships between visual design and textual material. In the best Web pages, the elements work together rather than simply competing for space. In fact, even if you have not used the Web, you still know a great deal about graphic design: newspapers, magazines, and your own college papers make use of design principles to create effective texts.

Find three or four Web or magazine pages that you think exemplify good visual design—and then find just as many that do not. When you've picked the good and bad designs, draw a rough sketch of their physical layout. Where are the graphics? Where is the text? What are the relative size and relationship of text blocks to graphics? How is color used? Can you discern common principles among the pages, or does each good page work well in its own way? Write a brief explanation of what you find, focusing on the way the visual arguments influence audiences.

4. If you have access to the Internet, go to the Pulitzer Prize Archives at <pulitzer.org>. Pick a year to review, and then study the images of the winners in three categories: editorial cartooning, spot news photography, and feature photography. (Click on "Works" to see the images.) From among the images you review, choose one you believe makes a strong argument. Then, in a paragraph, describe that image and the argument it makes.

5. Choose one chapter of this textbook, and then spend some time looking at its design and use of visual images. Note the use of white space and margins as well as color, font and type size—and all images. How effective do you find the design of this chapter? What recommendations would you make for improving the design?

chapter sixteen

Arguments in Electronic Environments

A student who has just loaded a new Web browser goes looking for online sources to develop a research assignment about a contemporary political issue. Looking for newsgroups, she notices that the default service on the browser offers many discussion groups sponsored by a big software company. But many of the groups she ordinarily consults don't seem to be available. She contemplates writing her research paper on the way commercial interests can shape and limit political discussion on the Web.

You send email to a friend questioning the integrity of your state's high school competency examinations. You mention irregularities you yourself have witnessed in testing procedures. A week later, you find passages from your original email circulating in a listserv. The remarks aren't attributed to you, but they sure are stirring up a ruckus.

A group of students on your campus have tried to disrupt a lecture by a controversial writer, shouting questions and insults throughout her talk until she finally walks off stage. The incident is reported in your campus newspaper—which includes an electronic version. You send a link to the online story to your favorite Web logger, who posts it. The attempt to suppress free speech on your campus becomes a national issue, putting pressure on your school's administration to take action against those who disrupted the lecture.

One of the news-talk channels is exploring the issue of genetically engineered foods. Unfortunately, the experts being interviewed have to squeeze in their opinions among interruptions from two aggressive hosts, questions from generally hostile callers, and commercials for Viagra. Meanwhile, the hosts are urging viewers to participate in an online poll on the subject posted on the network's Web site. The results, they admit, are unscientific.

You've been discussing gender roles on a MOO with a woman who calls herself Taurean. She sure seems to have your number, almost anticipating the arguments you make. Even though you find her positions untenable, you admire her intuition and perception. Then you discover that Taurean is really your roommate Julio! He says he has enjoyed playing with your mind.

■ ■ ■

Within the last decade or so, computers have created new environments where ideas can be examined, discussed, and debated in shapes many might never have imagined—some custom-fitted to the give-and-take of argument. Serious thinkers and determined advertisers alike are still learning how (and when) to use these new media, which users can tap into through a growing array of increasingly integrated devices. Cell phones and wireless PDAs can now download images, email, and even Internet services, while powerful laptop computers can crunch huge image files fed to them by mega-pixel digital cameras. Is there a special rhetoric of argument for such environments, a way of making effective and honest claims in this brave new world where each of us controls such powerful tools? Clearly there is, but it remains a work in progress, evolving gradually as people learn to cross boundaries among written, aural, and visual texts.

It's an exciting time for extending the reach of the human mind. What follows are some observations and speculations about the play of argument online, including Web logs and Web pages, email and discussion groups, and synchronous communications.

WEB LOGS

Web logs have recently exploded into public consciousness, though they have evolved from Internet-based magazines such as <Slate.com>, news services such as <drudgereport.com>, and the give-and-take of listservs and news groups. A Web log—or blog, for short—is an interactive Web site maintained by an individual who updates it frequently, often daily, posting items and links related to the theme of the site. Bloggers frequently link to information on other Web logs, creating an active community of writers and readers, able in some cases to reach remarkably large audiences in a short time.

There are at least a half-million Web logs on the Web now, covering every subject and interest you could imagine. Some blogs are highly personal, specialized, and even eccentric. But the most influential and interesting as examples of argument tend to be political sites such as <andrewsullivan.com>, <InstaPundit.com>, and <talkingpointsmemo.com> visited by hundreds of thousands of readers a day. These and many similar blogs provide forums for the political opinions of their hosts; the daily, even hourly, postings are like long-running national bull sessions—at varying levels of quality—keeping the more prestigious traditional media on their toes. Some of the bloggers, for example, enjoy pointing out errors or biases in the *New York Times* or *Washington Post* or national TV networks. But the bloggers also create news on their own, focusing on local issues or small stories ignored by the mainstream press—at least until the drumbeat of attention from the Web forces a topic into wider circulation. In fact, it is the bloggers' sense of community that is one of their most appealing features. Almost every site includes links to pages of other favorite Web loggers. Visit any site and you are well on your way to finding many more. Or you could go to a blog directory such as <GlobeofBlogs.com>, <Portal.Eatonweb.com>, or the Pepys Project at < pepys.akacooties.com>.

FIGURE 16.1 PATRICK RUFFINI OFFERS A CONSERVATIVE POINT OF VIEW ON HIS WEB LOG AT <PATRICKRUFFINI.COM>.

By their nature, blogs favor compressed forms of argument—paragraphs rather than extended essays, although bloggers like Andrew Sullivan (often cited in this book) and Virginia Postrel at <dynamist.com> will link to their articles published elsewhere. Bloggers pay attention, too, to facts and information, linking frequently to data or online archives to support or refute claims. Pity politicians these days who switch their positions to serve new ends, hoping the general public won't notice. If their earlier words are on record, a blogger will find them and send the awkward quotations scurrying around the "blogosphere"—the informal net-

FIGURE **16.2** JERLYNN MERRITT RUNS TALKLEFT, A BLOG ABOUT CRIME THAT
ANNOUNCES OPENLY THAT IT IS "NOT A NEUTRAL SITE." IT IS AT <TALKLEFT.COM>.

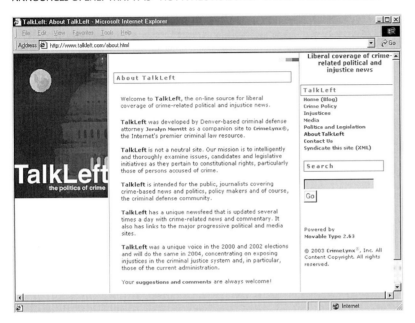

work of active Web loggers. Bloggers are fond, too, of what InstaPundit
author Glenn Reynolds calls a "fisking": an almost line-by-line, often sarcastic or humorous, refutation of an argument considered inaccurate or
rhetorically suspect. You can learn a lot about argument from these close
analyses, recognizing always that the blogger is almost certainly grinding
an axe. But that's one of the defining features of Web logs: they are usually upfront about their distinctive points of view.

Here's Australian blogger Tim Blair <timblair.blogspot.com> fisking the
opening paragraphs of a book on 9/11, one that Blair obviously finds pretentious and shallow. Following a blogger convention, the lines Blair is cri-
tiquing are indented and italicized. On the Web site, the underlined words
link to other pages.

> DR. JOHN CARROLL is a reader in sociology at Melbourne's La Trobe
> University. That is to say, he is paid to educate young adults.

This bland statement of fact may mean nothing to you now, but let's
see how you feel after we've finished examining the highlights from

chapter one of Carroll's <u>awesomely pretentious and imbecilic new book</u>, Terror: A Meditation on the Meaning of September 11 . . .

> *The highjacked planes were flown through the bright early-morning American east-coast sky. This is the hour of Apollo, the sun god, who presided over ancient Delphi. His oracle dwelt high on the side of the sacred mountain, with two mottos carved over its portal. Two sayings watched over the foundation of our civilization, in exhortation and warning: "Know Thyself!" and "Nothing Too Much!"*

Not to mention "Nothing Over 99 Cents!" and "Si habla Espanol!"

> *Ignorantly and flagrantly, the modern West has violated both.*

As will shortly be revealed, <u>Carroll</u> follows a combination of both: "Know Nothing!"

> *We all know the story—about the events of September 11 and their aftermath. We all share the shock, surreal image of the second plane slicing through the World Trade Center tower like . . .*

All together now . . .

> *. . . a knife through butter. We will take to our graves the slow-motion horror of watching, many of us as it happened, the tallest skyscrapers in the world crumpling, one after the other . . .*

The World Trade Center towers weren't even the <u>tallest skyscrapers in the United States</u>.

> *. . . each no more substantial than a child's house of cards. Nothing was left of where 50,000 people had once worked but dust and smoke, numb pain for those trapped inside, and speechless awe at the power that had done this.*

Nothing was left? Then how come it took eight months to clear all that nothing away? Lazy teamsters!

> *These, however, are surface facts. The heart of the matter lies deep beneath. This is a story that is hard to read, essential to read.*

He's got that half right.

> *Our culture has developed the shrug of the shoulders into a cosy reflex while we pour another drink, switch on the amusement parade, and wait for the house prices and stock market to rise.*

"Honey, I'm home! Get me a Scotch and switch on the amusement parade!"

> *Will this culture be able to relearn how to take itself seriously?*

<u>Carroll</u> isn't making it very easy.

Will anyone again choose to work in a skyscraper?

Beats me. I guess you could ask all the people worldwide who work in them every day.

Which insurance company will cover a landmark tower?

Er . . . the ones that *do?*

Indeed, were the twin 110-storey towers to be rebuilt they would stand like pyramids, colossal empty tombs, in memoriam to a lost civilization.

I'm no architect, but I'm pretty sure that rebuilt towers would stand like *towers.* Pyramids are lots more pointy and triangly. Here's a picture.

And if the age of the skyscraper is over, so is that of New York. Nothing big is safe anymore. Icarus never flew twice.

Icarus's problem was that he flew too close to the sun. New York's problem was that scum flew too close to it. Slight difference.

Web logs, of course, are not edited, nor do they subscribe to any journalistic standards except those enforced by the bloggers themselves. You should read blogs at least as critically as anything else you encounter on the Web. But you can learn a great deal about argument by participating in these sites either as a reader or as a blogger yourself. In fact, you can find just about everything you need to know about setting up your own Web log (at modest cost) at <blogspot.com/>.

WEB SITES

The Web supports many traditional components of argument, but it complicates them too. For example, a Web site for a political or special interest group might include many conventional claims supported with evidence and good reasons. But instead of merely summarizing the evidence and providing a source citation as you might in a conventional paper, a Web author might furnish links to the primary evidence itself—to statistics borrowed directly from a government Web site or to online documents at a university library. Indeed, the links within a Web page can be a version of documentation, leading to the very material the original author examined, full and complete.

A site might also provide links to other sites dealing with the same issue, connect readers to discussion groups about it, or even support chatrooms where anyone can offer an opinion in real time. And, of course, a Web site can incorporate visual and aural elements of all sorts into its argument, not as embellishments but as persuasive devices. For this reason, writers today need to learn new techniques of document design if they expect to communicate in this complex medium.

When crafting a Web site designed to present an argument of your own, you will want not only to take full advantage of the electronic medium but also to meet its distinctive challenges. Your pages need to be graphically interesting to persuade readers to enter your site and to encourage them to read your lengthier arguments (see Chapter 15). If you just post a traditional argument, thick with prose paragraphs that have to be scrolled endlessly, readers might ignore it. Check out the way online periodicals — whether newspapers or magazines — arrange their articles

FIGURE 16.3   THE ASPCA SITE OFFERS PLENTY OF LINKS AND VISUALS TO HELP ARGUE ITS CASE.

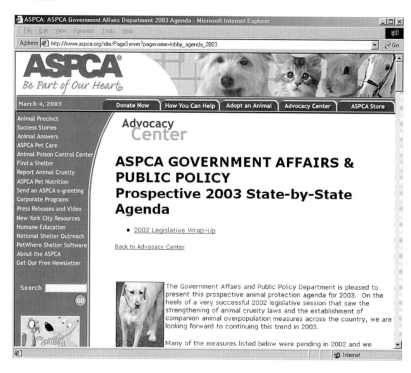

to make them Web readable, or examine the design of other sites you find especially effective in presenting an argument.

Because the Web encourages browsing and surfing, you also need to consider how to cluster ideas so that they retain their appeal. In a traditional print argument, though you can't prevent readers from skipping around and looking ahead, you can largely control the direction they take through your material, from claim to warrant to evidence. On a Web page, however, readers usually want to choose their own paths. Inevitably that means they will play a larger role in constructing your argument. You lose

FIGURE 16.4 THE WEB SITE FOR FIRE CLUSTERS IDEAS EFFECTIVELY AND PROVIDES LINKS TO ADDITIONAL NEWS SOURCES.

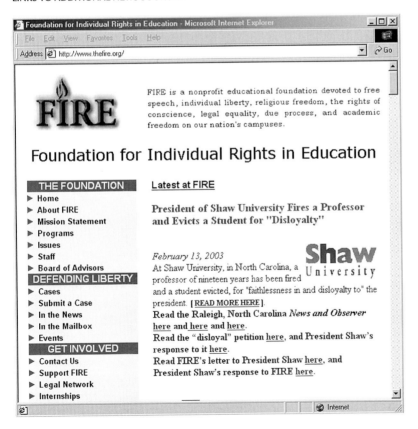

an element of control, but your argument gains a new dimension, particularly if you provide links that help readers understand how you came to your conclusions. Sometimes that may mean including links to sites that don't necessarily support your views. But you enhance your credibility by recognizing a full range of ideas, hoping that, on their own, readers will reach the same conclusions you have reached.

EMAIL AND DISCUSSION GROUPS

Email, Usenet groups, and listservs all transmit electronic messages via the Internet from person to person. Sometimes the messages go from one individual to another; in other cases, they are distributed to groups or to anyone with Internet access. As you'll see, this rapid communication has changed more than the speed by which individuals can share ideas.

Email

Ed Madden's piece was written originally as an email message to many of his friends and colleagues in response to the many questions and comments he heard after Ellen DeGeneres came out on her TV show.

······················· LINK TO P. 794

Everyone does email today. Of course, an email message can be a private communication to one person or a message distributed among groups, large and small, creating communities linked by information. Unlike regular ("snail") mail, email makes back-and-forth discussions easy and quick: people can speak their minds, survey opinion, or set agendas for face-to-face meetings. And they can meet at all hours, since electronic messages arrive whenever a server routes them. Increasingly, email communication is going wireless, available via cell phone, PDA, or other mobile devices.

An email message has a character of its own, halfway between the formality of a letter and the intimacy of a telephone call. It can feel less pushy than a phone call, yet at the same time be more insistent—the person too shy to say something in person or on the phone may speak up boldly in email. Like a letter, email preserves a written record of all thoughts and comments, which can be an advantage in many situations. Yet because it is less formal than a business letter, many readers tend to ignore or forgive slips in email (misspellings, irregular punctuation and capitalization) that might disturb them in another type of message.

Arguments in email operate by some relatively new conventions. First, they tend to be "dialogic," with a rapid back-and-forth of voices in conversation. When you send an email, you can usually anticipate a quick reply. Second, the very speed of response in email invites answers that may be less carefully considered than those sent by snail mail. Third, because email can be easily forwarded, your arguments may travel well beyond your intended audience, a factor to consider before clicking on "send."

Much advice about email is obvious once you've used it for a while. For one thing, although email messages can be quite long, most people won't read an argument that asks them to scroll through page after page of single-spaced print. You'll make a stronger impression with a concise claim, one that fits on a single screen if possible. And when replying to an email message, send back just enough of the original posting so that your reader knows what you are responding to; this will set your claim within its context.

Remember, too, that your email messages need to be verbally powerful. You can highlight your ideas by skipping lines between paragraphs to open some white space, bulleting key ideas or short lists, drawing lines, and using boldface and italic type as appropriate. In general, don't use all capital letters, LIKE THIS, for emphasis. The online equivalent of shouting, it will alienate many readers—as will using all lowercase letters, which makes text harder to read. You can attach photographs and other images to email messages, but don't clog your readers' mailboxes with five million–pixel jpegs.

Your email signature, known as a .sig file, can influence readers, too. Automatically attached to the bottom of every email you send (unless you switch this function off), your .sig file might include your address, phone numbers, fax numbers, and professional credentials. You can use the signature as a way to reinforce your credibility by explaining who you are and what you do. Here is an example:

Celia Garcia

Executive Secretary

Students for Responsive Government

University of Texas at San Antonio

Usenet Newsgroups and Listservs

Usenet is an electronic network that provides access to thousands of newsgroups, which are interactive discussion forums grouped by subject and open to anyone with email access to the network. Listservs also use the Internet to bring together people with common interests, but they are more focused: you have to subscribe to a particular listserv to receive its messages. In both newsgroups and listservs, messages consist of email-like postings that can be linked to form threads exploring particular subjects.

Newsgroups and listservs would seem to be great places for productive arguments—where knowledgeable people worldwide can exchange their ideas. Unfortunately, not all group discussions live up to this potential. Some people in these groups don't behave like good citizens: they forget the importance of their own character in making an argument (see Chapter 6). The result has been a dumbing down of many discussions, especially in newsgroups with the less-regulated "alt." designation. And because postings are so easy in either type of forum, even more responsible groups can be spammed with pointless messages, unwanted advertisements, and worse.

Nevertheless, newsgroups and listservs can be stimulating places for interchanges, particularly where the subject matter is specialized enough to attract informed and interested participants. Before posting, you owe it to the group to learn something about it, either by reading some messages already posted in a newsgroup or by subscribing to a listserv and lurking for enough time to gain a feel for the way issues are introduced, discussed, and debated. If a group offers a file of frequently asked questions (known as FAQs), read what it has to say about the group's rules of discourse and print it out for later reference.

When you decide to join in a conversation, be sure your posting contains enough information to make a smooth transition between the message to which you are responding and your own contribution to the group. If you have little to contribute, don't bother posting. A comment such as "I agree" wastes the time of everyone in the group who bothers to download your item—as some of the members may tell you in none-too-polite terms. In fact, if you are new to the Internet, you may be surprised at the temper of some online conversation participants. You can get flamed—bombarded with email—for asking a question that has already been asked and answered repeatedly by other members, for veering too far from the topic of discussion, or just for sending a message someone doesn't like. Flaming is unfortunate, but it is also a reality of newsgroups and listservs.

As sources for academic work, listservs are probably more reliable than newsgroups, though both forums can help you grasp the range of opinion on an issue. In fact, the range expressed in some groups may be startling. You'll likely discover much information too, including the names of reputable authorities, the titles of useful books and articles, and guidance to other groups or Web sites concerned with related topics. But don't quote facts, figures, statistics, or specific claims from newsgroups or listservs

FIGURE 16.5 TO LOCATE AND SEARCH NEWSGROUPS, YOU CAN CLICK ON THE "GROUPS" BUTTON AT <GOOGLE.COM>.

unless you cross-check them with more conventional sources, such as library reference material. Remember, too, that you can usually query individual members of a group by going "off list" to find out more information. In effect you have an email exchange with one person rather than with the whole group.

REAL-TIME COMMUNICATION: IRCS AND MOOS

Newsgroups and listservs operate like email, with a delay between the time a message is typed and the time it is received. The senders and receivers of email messages need not even be at their computers at the same time; in fact, the mailbox metaphor common to email systems assumes they are not. Now imagine an electronic conversation in which multiple participants are all online at the same time, although in different places, all receiving messages almost instantaneously as others are typing them—just like a conference call, except that the communication is in words that appear on computer screens. That's the basic shape of Internet relay chat (IRC) and MUD object-oriented (MOO) environments, examples of synchronous communication—communication in real time—on the Internet.

IRCs

IRCs are chatrooms that allow for relatively straightforward online conversations among people gathered together electronically to discuss particular subjects or topics. Typically, IRCs involve people in different and distant locations, but some schools provide local IRC networks to encourage students to participate in online class discussions. Once a topic is established, members of the IRC group begin typing in their comments and responding to one another.

As you might guess, an IRC environment can create a conversational free-for-all as opinions come rolling in. Their sequence can feel frustratingly random, especially to outsiders reading a transcript of such exchanges. After all, by the time a participant responds to a particular message, a dozen more may have appeared on the screen. In such an environment it is difficult to build or sustain complex arguments, especially because the rapid pace of the conversation favors witty or sharp remarks. A chatroom working at its best keeps writers on their toes. Indeed, it can be a form of dialogic freewriting, with writers pouring out their thoughts and watching as they receive almost instantaneous feedback. Since participants can be spread all over the world, IRCs also can support diverse conversations. So IRCs might work well as tools of invention for other, more conventional forms of argument. A good exercise is to print out an IRC transcript and highlight its best comments or exchanges for future reference.

MOOs

MOOs resemble IRCs in that participants communicate online in real time. But MOOs, unlike IRCs, have a spatial dimension: participants enter an imaginary place, take on assumed characters, and follow specified routines.

Arguments in MOOs can involve powerful stretches of the imagination because a participant can be anyone he or she wants to be. Thus the environment encourages writers to create an ethos self-consciously and to experience what it is like to be someone else—rich rather than poor, powerful rather than powerless, female rather than male. Imaginary situations are crafted, too, making participants unusually sensitive to the contexts in which their words and ideas exist. Indeed, MOOs reflect the power of words to shape one's reality. As such, they raise interesting and powerful questions about the nature of the world "outside."

Not everyone takes MOOs seriously. There's a learning curve for those entering such environments, and to some they remain games—hardly worth serious attention. But game or not, MOOs are an environment for argument that is out there, open for anyone willing to experiment with something new.

KEY POINTS TO REMEMBER IN ARGUING ELECTRONICALLY

EMAIL

- Keep your remarks short and pertinent.
- Think twice before replying immediately to an argumentative message. Don't lose your cool.
- Remember that email is easily forwarded. Your actual audience may prove to be much larger than you initially intended.

NEWSGROUPS, LISTSERVS, IRCS, AND MOOS

- Get a feel for groups before posting to them.
- Post concise messages directly related to the interests of the group.
- Consider whether your posting should go to everyone on the list. Would an individual email message be more appropriate?
- Resist the temptation to flame or be impolite, especially when an argument heats up.

WEB SITES AND WEB LOGS

- Plan your site carefully. Use your home page to direct readers to more detailed information within the site.
- Think of design in terms of pages. When you can, chunk a claim to fit within a single page. If your argument is highly readable, readers won't mind some scrolling, but don't expect them to advance through more than four or five screens' worth of material.
- Shape pages according to their purpose. A page of useful links will differ in arrangement from a page of prose argument.
- When your argument requires a lot of text, break it up with concise, helpful headings and white space.

- At the bottom of the home page, include your name, your contact information, and the date you created or last updated the site. This information will help other readers cite your work or reach you one-on-one to continue a discussion.

GRAPHICS

- Use graphics purposefully to support an argument. Images should make points you can't convey as effectively in prose.

- Keep graphics to a minimum. It takes time to download pages heavy in graphics—time readers might not have.

- Avoid images that pulse, rotate, or blink. Such glitz will likely distract readers from your argument.

- Graphics taken from the Web may be copyrighted items. Be sure to request permission from and to credit the source for any materials you import into your own pages. See Chapter 20, pages 408–409.

LINKS

- Use links to guide readers to evidence that explains your ideas.

- Be sure your links are diverse. You'll gain credibility by acknowledging alternative views.

- Be sure readers can understand from the context what the links you create will do or where they will lead.

RESPOND ●

1. Begin with a single political Web log that is regularly updated, and read it for several days to gain a sense of its focus and methods (a good directory to these is <GlobeofBlogs.com>). Also note how it often leads you to other blogs and sites. Does it ever take you to sites that provide significantly different perspectives? Does it encourage you to participate in the discussions?

2. Take a copy of an argumentative paper you've written for any class—it should be longer than two pages—and literally cut it up into separate paragraphs. Shuffle the stack of paragraphs so that they are completely reordered. Then read the paragraphs in their new order, from top to bottom. How is the argument affected? Is your claim still clear? Is your evidence powerful?

   Now imagine that those paragraphs were separate pages on a Web site that readers could browse through in any order. Would the site's argument be effective? If not, how could you rearrange the argument so that readers could move among its sections without being confused? Try to make an arrangement that could translate well to the Web's hypertextual environment. You might need to create headings that point readers in appropriate directions, or you might need to write transitions that help readers make decisions about what to read next.

3. Newcomers to a newsgroup or listserv normally lurk for a while, reading postings and getting to know the people who participate in the group, before entering the conversation themselves. Over the next several days, pick a group that interests you—there are thousands to choose from—and read as many of its postings as you can. For some groups, this might entail a tremendous amount of work, so limit your reading to those threads (topics within a group) that interest you.

   When you have a sense of the direction of the group, pick a single thread and follow the postings on that topic. Read all the postings that you can, making special note of quoting techniques—how writers refer to previous postings—and other interplay among writers. On the basis of the small evidence that you have (the group may have existed for several years), try to reconstruct the "conversation" on this thread that went on before you arrived. Who were the most frequent writers? What did they claim? How did others respond to those claims? What is the current state of the conversation? Are people in general agreement or disagreement?

4. FAQs can tell a careful reader a lot about a particular newsgroup or listserv and its contributors. Find the FAQs of three different groups and read them carefully. What suppositions about audience are inherent in these texts? Write an audience analysis of each FAQ, based on the kinds of questions and answers you see there, their tone, and their length. Who are the FAQs' intended readers? What kinds of rules about argument does each FAQ offer?

5. Find several Web sites that make explicit argumentative claims, and evaluate them on the basis of a set of criteria you develop. What constitutes a good Web-based argument? What are the characteristics of effective Web rhetoric? Do these sites exhibit those characteristics? How does the nonlinear nature of the site affect your reading or its persuasiveness? If your instructor requests, make a presentation to the class, showing printouts of the site (or directing the class to look at it if you are in a networked classroom) and explaining why the Web-based arguments are effective or ineffective.

chapter seventeen

Spoken Arguments

In the wake of a devastating hurricane, local ministers search for just the right words to offer comfort and inspire hope in their congregations.

At a campus rally, student leaders call for the administration to provide a living wage for campus workers.

A customer looking for a good buy on a new car settles in for some tough negotiations with the salesperson and manager.

At the half, the team is down by ten. In the locker room, the captain calls on all her persuasive powers to rebuild morale and help seize the momentum.

For a course in psychology, a student gives a multimedia presentation on the work of neuroscientist Constance Pert.

During their wedding, a couple exchanges the special vows they have worked together to create.

■ ■ ■

As these examples suggest, people are called on every day to present spoken arguments of one kind or another. Successful speakers point to several crucial elements in that success:

- They have thorough knowledge of their subjects;

- They pay very careful attention to the values, ideas, and needs of their listeners;

- They use structures and styles that make their spoken arguments easy to follow;

- They keep in mind the interactive nature of spoken arguments (live audiences can argue back!);

- They realize that most oral presentations involve visuals of some sort, and they plan accordingly for the use of presentation software, illustrations, and so on;

- They practice, practice—and then practice some more.

SPOKEN ARGUMENTS IN DISCUSSIONS

Perhaps the most common context for spoken argument takes place in ordinary discussions, whether you're trying to persuade your parents that you need a new computer for your college work, to explore the meaning of a poem in class, or to make a decision about a new company health plan. In such everyday contexts, many people automatically choose the tone of voice, kind of evidence, and length of speaking time to suit the situation. You can improve your own performance in such contexts by observing closely other speakers you find effective and by joining in on conversations whenever you possibly can: the more you participate in lively discussions, the more comfortable you will be doing so. To make sure your in-class comments count, follow these tips:

- Be well prepared so that your comments will be relevant to the class;

- Listen with a purpose, jotting down important points;

- Ask a key question—or offer a brief analysis or summary of the points that have already been made, to make sure you and other students (and the instructor) are "on the same page";

- Respond to questions or comments by others in specific rather than vague terms;

- Offer a brief analysis of an issue or text that invites others to join in and build on your comments.

Speaking up in class is viewed as inappropriate or even rude in some cultures. In the United States, however, doing so is expected and encouraged. Some instructors even assign credit for such class participation.

FORMAL PRESENTATIONS

You have probably already been asked to make a formal presentation in some of your classes or on the job. In such cases, you need to consider the full context carefully. Note how much time you have to prepare and how long the presentation should be. You want to use the allotted time effectively, while not infringing on the time of others. Consider also what visual aids, handouts, or other materials might help make the presentation successful. Will you have an overhead projector? Can you use PowerPoint or other presentation software? A statistical pie chart may carry a lot of weight in one argument whereas photographs will make your point better in another. (See Chapter 15.)

Think about whether you are to make the presentation alone or as part of a group—and plan and practice accordingly. Especially with a group, turn-taking will need to be worked out carefully. Check out where your presentation will take place—in a classroom with fixed chairs? A lecture or assembly hall? An informal sitting area? Will you have a lectern? An overhead projector? Will you sit or stand? Remain in one place or move around? What will the lighting be, and can you adjust it? Finally, note any criteria for evaluation: how will your spoken argument be assessed?

Whenever you make a formal presentation, you need to consider several key elements:

Purpose

- Determine your major argumentative purpose. Is it to inform? Convince or persuade? Explore? Make a decision? Entertain? Something else?

Audience

- Who is your audience? What will be the mix of age groups, men and women, and so on: think carefully about what they will know about your topic and what opinions they are likely to hold. If your audience is an academic one, your instructor may be one important member, in addition to other class members. Can you count on the audience being interested in your topic? If not, how can you capture their interest and attention?

President George W. Bush's speech was delivered to Congress and the American people only nine days after September 11, 2001. How does he make his tone appropriate to the occasion?

LINK TO P. 836

Stance

- Consider your own stance toward your topic and audience. Are you an expert? Novice? Fairly well informed? Interested observer? Peer?

Support

- Make sure that you have plenty of support—examples, facts, anecdotes, statistics, testimony of authorities—for your argument.

Structure

- Structure your presentation to make it easy to follow, and remember to take special care to plan an introduction that gets the audience's attention and a conclusion that makes your argument memorable. You'll find more help with structure on page 353.

ARGUMENTS TO BE HEARD

Even if you work from a printed text in delivering a presentation, that text must be written to be *heard* rather than read. Such a text—whether in the form of an overhead list, note cards, or a fully written-out text—should

feature a strong introduction and conclusion, a clear organization with helpful signposts and structures, straightforward syntax, and concrete diction.

Introductions and Conclusions

Like readers, listeners tend to remember beginnings and endings most
readily. Work hard, therefore, to make these elements of your spoken
argument especially memorable. Consider including a provocative or puzzling statement, opinion, or question; a memorable anecdote; a powerful
quotation; or a vivid visual image. If you can refer to the interests or experiences of your listeners in the introduction or conclusion, do so.

Look at the introduction in Toni Morrison's acceptance speech to the
Nobel Academy when she won the Nobel Prize for Literature:

> "Once upon a time there was an old woman. Blind but wise." Or was it
> an old man? A guru, perhaps. Or a griot soothing restless children. I have
> heard this story, or one exactly like it, in the lore of several cultures.
>
> "Once upon a time there was an old woman. Blind. Wise."
>
> – Toni Morrison

Here Morrison uses a storytelling strategy, calling on the traditional "Once
upon a time" to signal to her audience that she is doing so. Note also the use

FIGURE 17.1 TONI MORRISON ACCEPTING THE NOBEL PRIZE FOR LITERATURE IN 1993

of repetition and questioning. These strategies raise interest and anticipation in her audience: how will she use this story in accepting the Nobel Prize?

Structures and Signposts

For a spoken argument, you want your organizational structure to be crystal clear. Offer an overview of your main points toward the beginning of your presentation, and make sure that you have a clearly delineated beginning, middle, and end to the presentation. Throughout, remember to pause between major points and to use helpful "signposts" to mark your movement from one topic to the next. Such signposts act as explicit transitions in your spoken argument and thus should be clear and concrete: *The second crisis point in the breakup of the Soviet Union occurred hard on the heels of the first*, rather than *The breakup of the Soviet Union came to another crisis*. In addition to such explicit transitions as *next, on the contrary*, or *finally*, you can offer signposts to your listeners by repeating key words and ideas as well as by carefully introducing each new idea with concrete topic sentences.

Diction and Syntax

Avoid long, complicated sentences, and use straightforward syntax (subject-verb-object, for instance, rather than an inversion of that order) as much as possible. Remember, too, that listeners can hold onto concrete verbs and nouns more easily than they can grasp a steady stream of abstractions. So when you need to deal with abstract ideas, try to illustrate them with concrete examples.

Take a look at the following paragraph from an essay that student Ben McCorkle wrote on the Simpsons, first as he wrote it for his essay and then for an oral presentation:

Written Version

The Simpson family has occasionally been described as a "nuclear" family, which obviously has a double meaning: first, the family consists of two parents and three children, and, second, Homer works at a nuclear power plant with very relaxed safety codes. The overused label *dysfunctional*, when applied to the Simpsons, suddenly takes on new meaning. Every episode seems to include a scene in which son Bart is being choked by his father, the baby is being neglected, or Homer is sitting in a drunken stupor transfixed by the television screen. The comedy in these scenes comes from the exaggeration of

Radio reports are edited very tightly; they need to maintain the integrity of the story while moving seamlessly and clearly between different speakers. Madeleine Brand and Bob Edwards' piece "Schoolchildren Debating What It Means to Be a Patriot" includes the voices of fifteen different people. How do they transition between speakers? How do they produce a coherent argument?

LINK TO P. 828

commonplace household events (although some talk shows and news programs would have us believe that these exaggerations are not confined to the madcap world of cartoons).

—Ben McCorkle, "The Simpsons: A Mirror of Society"

Spoken Version (with a visual illustration)

What does it mean to describe the Simpsons as a *nuclear* family? Clearly, a double meaning is at work. First, the Simpsons fit the dictionary meaning—a family unit consisting of two parents and some children. The second meaning, however, packs more of a punch. You see, Homer works at a nuclear power plant [pause here] with *very* relaxed safety codes!

Still another overused family label describes the Simpsons. Did everyone guess I was going to say *dysfunctional*? And like "nuclear," when it comes to the Simpsons, "dysfunctional" takes on a whole new meaning.

Remember the scene when Bart is being choked by his father?

How about the many times the baby is being neglected?

Or the classic view—Homer sitting in a stupor transfixed by the TV screen!

My point here is that the comedy in these scenes often comes from double meanings—and from a lot of exaggeration of everyday household events.

FIGURE 17.2 HOMER SIMPSON IN A TYPICAL POSE

Note that the revised paragraph presents the same information, but this time it is written to be heard. See how the revision uses helpful signposts, some repetition, a list, italicized words to prompt the speaker to give special emphasis, and simple syntax to help make it easy to listen to.

ARGUMENTS TO BE REMEMBERED

You can probably think of spoken arguments that still stick in your memory—a song like Bruce Springsteen's "Born in the USA," for instance. Such arguments are memorable in part because they call on the power of figures of speech and other devices of language. In addition, careful repetition can make spoken arguments memorable, especially when linked with parallelism and climactic order. (See Chapter 14 for more on using figurative language to make arguments more vivid and memorable.)

FIGURE 17.3   BRUCE SPRINGSTEEN

Repetition, Parallelism, and Climactic Order

Whether they are used alone or in combination, repetition, parallelism, and climactic order are especially appropriate for spoken arguments that sound a call to arms or that seek passionate engagement from the audience. Perhaps no person in the twentieth century used them more effectively than Martin Luther King Jr., whose sermons and speeches helped to spearhead the civil rights movement. Standing on the steps of the Lincoln Memorial in Washington, D.C., on August 28, 1963, with hundreds of thousands of marchers before him, King called on the nation to make good on the promissory note represented by the Emancipation Proclamation.

FIGURE 17.4 MARTIN LUTHER KING JR., SPEAKING AT THE LINCOLN MEMORIAL

Look at the way King uses repetition, parallelism, and climactic order in the following paragraph to invoke a nation to action (emphasis added):

> It is obvious today that America has defaulted on this promissory note insofar as her citizens of color are concerned. Instead of honoring this sacred obligation, America has given the Negro people a bad check which has come back marked "insufficient funds." But *we refuse* to believe that the bank of justice is bankrupt. *We refuse* to believe that there are insufficient funds in the great vaults of opportunity of this nation. So *we have come* to cash this check—a check that will give us upon demand the riches of freedom and the security of justice. *We have also come* to this hallowed spot to remind America of the fierce urgency of now. This is *no time* to engage in the luxury of cooling off or to take the tranquilizing drug of gradualism. *Now is the time* to rise from the dark and desolate valley of segregation to the sunlit path of racial justice. *Now is the time* to open the doors of opportunity to all of God's children. *Now is the time* to lift our nation from the quicksands of racial injustice to the solid rock of brotherhood.
>
> –Martin Luther King Jr., "I Have a Dream"

The italicized words highlight the way King uses repetition to drum home his theme. But along with that repetition, King sets up a powerful set of parallel verb phrases, calling on all "to rise" from the "dark and desolate valley of segregation" to the "sunlit path of racial justice" and "to open the doors of opportunity" for all. The final verb phrase ("to lift") leads to a strong climax, as King moves from what each individual should do to what the entire nation should do: "to lift our nation from the quicksands of racial injustice to the solid rock of brotherhood." These stylistic choices, together with the vivid image of the "bad check," help to make King's speech powerful, persuasive—and memorable.

Thank goodness you don't have to be as highly skilled as Dr. King to take advantage of the power of repetition and parallelism: simply repeating a key word in your argument can help impress it on your audience, as can arranging parts of sentences or items in a list in parallel order.

Examine how, in this one short paragraph, President George W. Bush uses repetition, parallelism, and climactic order to effectively rally his audience: "This is not, however, just America's fight. And what is at stake is not just America's freedom. This is the world's fight. This is civilization's fight. This is the fight of all who believe in progress and pluralism, tolerance and freedom."

LINK TO P. 841

THE ROLE OF VISUALS AND MULTIMEDIA

Visuals often play an important part in spoken arguments, and they should be prepared with great care. Don't think of them as add-ons but rather as a major means of getting across your message and supporting the claims you are making. In this regard, a visual—like a picture—can be worth a thousand words, helping your audience see examples or illustrations or other data that make your argument compelling. Test the effectiveness of your visuals on classmates, friends, or family members, asking them to judge whether the visuals help advance your argument.

Whatever visuals you use—charts, graphs, photographs, summary statements, sample quotations, lists—must be large enough to be readily seen by your audience. If you use slides or overhead projections, be sure that the information on each frame is simple, clear, and easy to read and process. In order for audience members to read information on a transparency, this means using 36 point type for major headings; 24 point for subheadings; and at least 18 point for all other text. For slides, use 24 point for major headings; 18 point for subheadings; and at least 14 point for other text.

The same rule for clarity and simplicity holds true for posters, flip charts, or a chalkboard. And remember not to turn your back on your audience while you refer to any of these visuals. Finally, if you prepare supplementary materials for your audience—bibliographies or other handouts—distribute these at the moment the audience will need them or at the end of the presentation so that they will not distract the audience from your spoken argument.

If you plan to use PowerPoint or other presentation software, take care with the colors you choose for background and for text and illustrations. Light text on a dark background is particularly hard to read, so as a general rule you'll be better off to use white or light cream-colored backgrounds. If you've seen many PowerPoint presentations, you are sure to have seen some really bad ones: the speaker just stands up and reads off what is on each slide. Nothing can be more deadly boring than that. So in your own use of PowerPoint or other presentation slides, make sure that they provide an overview of what you are talking about, but do not repeat word for word what you are saying.

For a talk about how best to make an effective oral presentation, one writer used the PowerPoint slides shown in Figure 17.5. Note how easy these slides are to read. The first one introduces the topic simply and clearly. Subsequent slides provide an overview of major points and an easy-to-read graph, clearly labeled. All are uncluttered and simple.

The best way to test the effectiveness of all your visuals is to try them out on friends, classmates, or roommates. If they don't get the meaning of the visuals right away, revise and try again.

Finally, remember that visuals can help you be sure your presentation is accessible: some members of your audience may not be able to see your

FIGURE 17.5 SLIDES FROM A POWERPOINT PRESENTATION

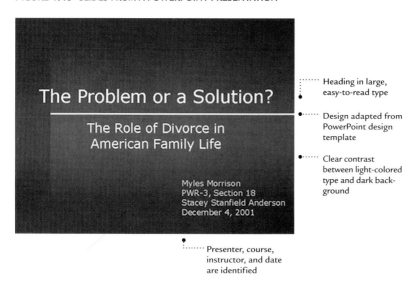

Heading in large, easy-to-read type

Design adapted from PowerPoint design template

Clear contrast between light-colored type and dark background

Presenter, course, instructor, and date are identified

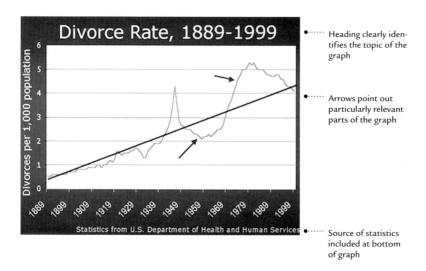

Heading clearly identifies the topic of the graph

Arrows point out particularly relevant parts of the graph

Source of statistics included at bottom of graph

Dark background and light type are easy to read onscreen in a well-lit room

Bulleted points announce presentation's topics and subtopics

Bulleted points kept brief

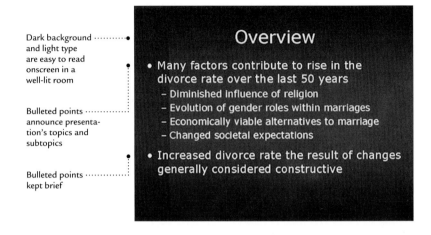

presentation or may have trouble hearing it. Here are a few key rules to remember:

- Don't rely on color or graphics alone to get across information: use words along with them.
- Consider providing a written overview of your presentation, or put the text on an overhead projector—for those who learn better by reading *and* listening.
- If you use video, label sounds that won't be audible to some audience members. (Be sure your equipment is caption capable.)

THE IMPORTANCE OF DELIVERY

When a famous orator in ancient times was asked to rank the most important parts of effective rhetoric, he said, "Delivery, delivery, delivery." Indeed, most effective spoken arguments are performances that call on you to pay very careful attention to the persuasive effects your clothing, body language, voice, and so on will have on the audience. Many practiced speakers say that they learned to improve the performance of spoken arguments through extensive practice. To make this advice work for you, get together a draft of your presentation, including all visuals, enough in advance to allow for several run-throughs. Some speakers audiotape or videotape these rehearsals and then revise the argument and the performance based on a study of the tapes. Others practice in front of a mirror, watching every movement with a critical eye. Still others practice in front of friends. Any of these techniques can work; the main thing is to practice.

One point of all that practice is to make sure you can be heard clearly. Especially if you are at all soft-spoken, you will need to concentrate on projecting your voice. Or you may need to practice lowering the pitch or speaking more slowly or enunciating each word more clearly. Tone of voice can dispose audiences for—or against—speakers. Those who sound sarcastic, for instance, usually win few friends. For most spoken arguments, you want to develop a tone that conveys interest and commitment to your position as well as respect for your audience.

The way you dress, the way you move, as well as the sound of your voice make arguments of their own that can either add to or detract from the main one you are trying to make. How to dress for an effective presentation, of course, depends on what is appropriate for your topic, audience, and setting, but most experienced speakers like to wear clothes that are simple and comfortable and that allow for easy movement—but that are not overly casual: "dressing up" a little indicates that you take pride in your appearance, that you have confidence in your argument, and that you respect your audience.

Most speakers make a stronger impression standing than sitting. Stand with your hands resting lightly on the lectern or at your side (don't fidget with anything) and with both feet solidly on the floor—and move about a little, even if you are using a lectern. Moving a bit may also help you make good eye contact with members of your audience. According to several studies, making eye contact is especially important for spoken arguments, since audiences perceive those who look at them directly to be more honest, friendly, and informed than others who do not.

Last but not at all least: time your presentation carefully to make sure you will stay within the allotted time. If you are working from a written text, a good rule of thumb is to allow roughly two and a half minutes for every double-spaced $8\frac{1}{2} \times 11$-inch page of text (or one and a half minutes for every 5×7-inch card). The only way to make sure of your time, however, is to set a clock and time the presentation precisely. Preparing so that you will not intrude on the time allotted to other speakers not only signals your respect for their presentations but will also help you relax and gain self-confidence; and when your audience senses your self-confidence, they will become increasingly receptive to your message.

Choose a few paragraphs from Amy Tan's speech in Chapter 27 or President Bush's in Chapter 28, and try delivering them the way you think it might have been done originally. What do you notice about the ways you modify your voice and manner of speaking?

LINK TO PP. 712 AND 836

Some Helpful Presentation Strategies

In spite of your best preparation, you may feel some anxiety before your presentation. (According to one Gallup poll, Americans often identify public speaking as a major fear, scarier than attacks from outer space!) Experienced speakers say they have strategies for dealing with anxiety—and even that a little anxiety (and accompanying adrenaline) can act to a speaker's advantage.

The most effective strategy seems to be knowing your topic and material through and through. Confidence in your own knowledge goes a long way toward making you a confident speaker. In addition to being well prepared, you may wish to try some of the following strategies:

- Visualize your presentation. Go over the scene of the presentation in your mind, and think it through completely.

- Get some rest before the presentation, and avoid consuming excessive amounts of caffeine.

- Concentrate on relaxing. Consider doing some deep-breathing exercises right before you begin.

- Pause before you begin, concentrating on your opening lines.

- Remember to interact with the audience whenever possible; doing so will often help you relax and even have some fun.

Finally, remember to allow time for audience members to respond and ask questions. Try to keep your answers brief so that others may get in on the conversation. And at the very end of your presentation, thank your audience for attending so generously to your arguments.

RESPOND

1. Take a brief passage—three or four paragraphs—from an essay you've recently written. Then, following the guidelines in this chapter, rewrite the passage to be *heard*. Finally, make a list of every change you made.

2. Look in the TV listings for a speech or oral presentation you'd like to hear. Check out C-SPAN or Sunday morning news shows such as *Meet the Press*. Watch and listen to the presentation, making notes of the strategies the speaker uses to good effect—signpost language, repetition, figurative language, and so on.

3. Attend a lecture or presentation on your campus and observe the speaker's delivery very carefully. Note what strategies the speaker uses to capture and hold your attention (or not). What signpost language and other guides to listening can you detect? How well are any visuals integrated into the presentation? What aspects of the speaker's tone, dress, eye contact, and movement affect your understanding and appreciation (or lack of it)? What is most memorable about the presentation and why? Finally, write up an analysis of this presentation's effectiveness.

PART 5

CONVENTIONS OF argument

chapter eighteen

What Counts as Evidence

A downtown office worker who can never find a space in the company lot to park her motorcycle decides to argue for a designated motorcycle parking area. In building her argument, she conducts a survey to find out exactly how many employees drive cars to work and how many ride motorcycles.

A business consultant wants to identify characteristics of effective teamwork so that he can convince his partners to adopt these characteristics as part of their training program. To begin gathering evidence for this argument, the consultant decides to conduct on-site observations of three effective teams, followed by in-depth interviews with each member.

For an argument aimed at showing that occupations are still often unconsciously thought of as either masculine or feminine, a student decides to carry out an experiment: she will ask fifty people chosen at random to draw pictures of a doctor, a police officer, a nurse, a CEO, a lawyer, and a secretary—and see which are depicted as men, which as women. The results of this experiment will become evidence for (or against) the argument.

Trying to convince her younger brother to invest in a PC laptop, a college student mentions her three years of personal experience using a similar computer for her college coursework.

In arguing that virtual reality technology may lead people to ignore or disregard the most serious of "real" world problems, a student writer provides evidence for this claim in part by citing sixteen library sources that review and critique cyberspace and virtual reality.

■ ■ ■

EVIDENCE AND THE RHETORICAL SITUATION

As the examples above demonstrate, people use all kinds of evidence in making and supporting claims. But this evidence doesn't exist in a vacuum; instead, it becomes part of the larger context of the argument and its rhetorical situation: when, where, and to whom it is made. Remembering the rhetorical situation that evidence becomes a part of leads to an important point regarding argumentative evidence: It may be persuasive in one time and place but not in another; it may convince one kind of audience but not another; it may work with one genre of discourse but not another.

To be most persuasive, then, evidence should match the time and place in which you make your argument. For example, arguing that a military leader should employ a certain tactic because that very tactic worked effectively for George Washington is likely to fail if Washington's use of the tactic is the only evidence provided. After all, a military tactic that was effective in 1776 is more than likely an *ineffective* one today. In the same way, a writer may achieve excellent results by using her own experience as well as an extensive survey of local leaders and teenagers as evidence to support a proposal for a new teen center in her small-town community—but she may have far less success in arguing for the same thing in a distant, large inner-city area.

Careful writers also need to consider the disciplinary context in which they plan to use evidence, since some disciplines privilege certain kinds of evidence and others do not. Observable, quantifiable data may constitute the best evidence in, say, experimental psychology, but the same kind of data may be less appropriate—or impossible to come by—in a historical study. As you become more familiar with a particular discipline or area of study, you will gain a sense of just what it takes to prove a point or support a claim in that field. The following questions will help you begin understanding the rhetorical situation of a particular discipline:

- How do other writers in the field use precedence—examples of actions or decisions that are very similar—and authority as evidence? What or who counts as an authority in this field? How are the credentials of authorities established?

- What kinds of data seem to be preferred as evidence? How are such data gathered and presented?

- How are statistics or other numerical information used and presented as evidence? Are tables, charts, or graphs commonly used? How much weight do they carry?

- How are definitions, causal analyses, evaluations, analogies, and examples used as evidence?

- How does the field use firsthand and secondhand sources as evidence?

- How is personal experience used as evidence?

- How are quotations used as part of evidence?

- How are images used as part of evidence, and how closely are they related to the verbal parts of the argument being presented?

As these questions suggest, evidence may not always travel well from one field to another. As you consider the kinds of evidence surveyed in the rest of this chapter, consider in which contexts or rhetorical situations each kind of evidence would be most (or least) effective.

FIRSTHAND EVIDENCE AND RESEARCH

Firsthand evidence comes from research you have carried out or been closely involved with, and much of this kind of research requires you to collect and examine data. Here we will discuss the kinds of firsthand research most commonly conducted by student writers.

Observations

"What," you may wonder, "could be any easier than observing something?" You just choose a subject, look at it closely, and record what you see and hear. If observing were so easy, eyewitnesses would all provide reliable accounts. Yet experience shows that several people who have observed the same phenomenon generally offer different, sometimes even contradictory, evidence on the basis of those observations. Trained observers say that getting down a faithful record of an observation requires intense concentration and mental agility.

Before you begin an observation, then, decide exactly what you want to find out and anticipate what you are likely to see. Do you want to observe an action repeated by many people (such as pedestrians crossing a street, in relation to an argument for putting in a new stoplight), a sequence of actions (such as the stages involved in student registration, which you want to argue is far too complicated), or the interactions of a group (such as meetings of the campus Young Republicans, which you want to see adhere to strict parliamentary procedures)? Once you have a clear sense of what you will observe and what questions you wish to answer through the observation, use the following guidelines to achieve the best results:

- Make sure the observation relates directly to your claim.

- Brainstorm about what you are looking for, but don't be rigidly bound to your expectations.

- Develop an appropriate system for collecting data. Consider using a split notebook or page: On one side, record the minute details of your observations directly; on the other, record your thoughts or impressions.

- Be aware that the way you record data will affect the outcome, if only in respect to what you decide to include in your observational notes and what you leave out.

- Record the precise date, time, and place of the observation.

In the following excerpt, Pico Iyer uses information drawn from minute and prolonged observation in an argument about what the Los Angeles International Airport (LAX) symbolizes about America:

LAX is, in fact, a surprisingly shabby and hollowed-out kind of place, certainly not adorned with the amenities one might expect of the world's strongest and richest power. When you come out into the Arrivals area in the International Terminal, you will find exactly one tiny snack bar, which serves nine items; of them, five are identified as Cheese Dog, Chili Dog, Chili Cheese Dog, Nachos with Cheese, and Chili Cheese Nachos. There is a large panel on the wall offering rental-car services and hotels, and the newly deplaned American dreamer can choose between the Cadillac Hotel, the Banana Bungalow . . . and the Backpacker's Paradise.

–Pico Iyer, "Where Worlds Collide"

FIGURE 18.1 LOS ANGELES INTERNATIONAL AIRPORT

Interviews

Some evidence is best obtained through direct interviews. If you can talk with an expert—in person, on the phone, or online—you might get information you could not have obtained through any other type of research. In addition to getting expert opinion, you might ask for firsthand accounts, biographical information, or suggestions of other places to look or other people to consult. The following guidelines will help you conduct effective interviews:

- Determine the exact purpose of the interview, and be sure it is directly related to your claim.

- Set up the interview well in advance. Specify how long it will take, and if you wish to tape-record the session, ask permission to do so.

- Prepare a written list of both factual and open-ended questions. (Brainstorming with friends can help you come up with good questions.) Leave plenty of space for notes after each question. If the interview proceeds in a direction that you had not expected but that seems promising, don't feel you have to cover every one of your questions.

- Record the subject's full name and title, as well as the date, time, and place of the interview.

- Be sure to thank those you interview, either in person or with a follow-up letter or email message.

In arguing that the Gay Games offer a truly inclusive alternative—rather than a parallel—to the Olympics, Caroline Symons uses data drawn from extensive interviews with organizers and participants in the Gay Games:

> Out of twenty-four in-depth interviews I conducted with gay men involved in the Gay Games as organizers, over half indicated that they had sufficiently alienating experiences with sport during childhood and adolescence to be put off participating until the advent of gay sports organizations and events. . . . Gay men in particular have found a safe and welcoming environment to engage in sport through the emergence of gay sports organizations and the Gay Games.
>
> –Caroline Symons, "Not the Gay Olympic Games"

FIGURE **18.2** THE GAY GAMES WEB SITE

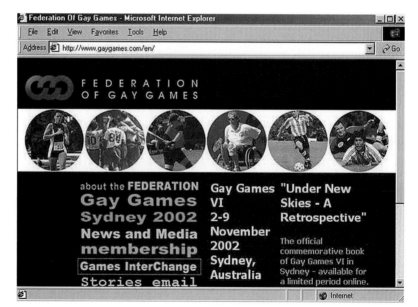

Surveys and Questionnaires

Surveys usually require the use of questionnaires. On any questionnaire, the questions should be clear, easy to understand, and designed so that respondents' answers can be analyzed easily. Questions that ask respondents to say "yes" or "no" or to rank items on a scale (1 to 5, for example, or "most helpful" to "least helpful") are particularly easy to tabulate. Here are some guidelines to help you prepare for and carry out a survey:

- Write out your purpose in conducting the survey, and make sure its results will be directly related to your claim.

- Brainstorm potential questions to include in the survey, and ask how each relates to your purpose and claim.

- Figure out how many people you want to contact, what the demographics of your sample should be (men in their twenties, or an equal number of men and women?), and how you plan to reach these people.

- Draft questions, making sure that each calls for a short, specific answer.

- Think about possible ways respondents could misunderstand you or your questions, and revise with these points in mind.

- Test the questions on several people, and revise those questions that are ambiguous, hard to answer, or too time-consuming to answer.

- If your questionnaire is to be sent by mail or email or posted on the Web, draft a cover letter explaining your purpose and giving a clear deadline. For mail, provide an addressed, stamped return envelope.

- On the final draft of the questionnaire, leave plenty of space for answers.

- Proofread the final draft carefully; typos will make a bad impression on those whose help you are seeking.

- Finally, you will need to tabulate the responses to your survey. Because tabulation can take time and effort, limit the number of questions you ask (people often resent being asked to answer more than about twenty questions, especially online). After you have done your tabulations, set out your findings in a clear, easily readable fashion, using a chart or spreadsheet if possible.

In an argument about whether the government should label genetically modified foods, analyst Gary Langer draws on data from a recent ABC News Poll asking Americans what they thought about such food:

Nearly everyone—93 percent—says the federal government should require labels on food saying whether it's been genetically modified, or "bio-engineered" (this poll used both phrases). Such near-unanimity in public opinion is rare.

Fifty-seven percent also say they'd be less likely to buy foods labeled as genetically modified. That puts the food industry in a quandary: By meeting consumer demand for labeling, it would be steering business away from its genetically modified products.

—Gary Langer, "Behind the Label: Many Skeptical of Genetically Modified Foods"

Experiments

Some arguments may be supported by evidence gathered through experiments. In the sciences, experimental data are highly valued—if the experiment is conducted in a rigorously controlled situation. For other kinds of writing, "looser" and more informal experiments can be acceptable, especially if they are intended to provide only part of the support for an argument. If you want to argue that the recipes in *Gourmand* magazine are impossibly tedious to follow and take far more time than the average person wishes to spend, you might ask five or six people to conduct a little experiment with you: following two recipes apiece from a recent issue, and recording and timing every step. The evidence you gather from this informal experiment could provide some concrete support—by way of specific examples—for your contention. But such experiments should be taken with a grain of salt; they may not be effective with certain audiences, and if they can easily be attacked as skewed or sloppily done ("The people you asked to make these recipes couldn't cook their way out of paper bags!"), then they may do more harm than good.

In an essay about computer hackers and the threats they pose to various individuals and systems, Winn Schwartau reports on an experiment performed by a former hacker he knows. One afternoon in Newport Beach, Jesse [the former hacker] carried out an experiment aimed at showing how easy it was to rob a bank. The experiment Schwartau describes makes his claim about bank security more believable.

Jesse took his audience to a trash bin behind Pacific Bell, the Southern California Baby Bell service provider. Dumpster diving proved to be an effective means of social engineering because within minutes, an internal telephone company employee list was dredged out of the garbage. On it, predictably, were handwritten notes with computer passwords.

In the neighborhood was a bank, which shall go nameless. After some more dumpster diving, financial and personal profiles of wealthy bank customers surfaced. That was all Jesse said he needed to commit the crime.

At a nearby phone booth, Jesse used a portable computer with an acoustic modem to dial into the telephone company's computer. Jesse knew a lot about the telephone company's computers, so he made a few changes. He gave the pay phone a new number, that of one of the wealthy clients about whom he now knew almost everything. He also turned off the victim's phone with that same number. Jesse then called the bank and identified himself as Mr. Rich, an alias.

"How can we help you, Mr. Rich?"

"I would like to transfer $100,000 to this bank account number."

"I will need certain information."

"Of course."

"What is your balance?"

"About _____," he supplied the number accurately.

"What is your address?"

Jesse gave the address.

"Are you at home, Mr. Rich?"

"Yes."

"We'll need to call you back for positive identification."

"I understand. Thank you for providing such good security."

In less than a minute the phone rang.

"Hello, Rich here."

The money was transferred, then transferred back to Mr. Rich's account again, to the surprise and embarrassment of the bank. The money was returned and the point was made.

–Winn Schwartau, "Hackers: The First Information Warriors"

Personal Experience

Personal experience can serve as powerful evidence when it is appropriate to the subject, to your purpose, and to the audience. Remember that if it is your *only* evidence, however, personal experience probably will not be sufficient to carry the argument. Nevertheless, it can be especially effective for drawing listeners or readers into an argument, as Gloria Naylor demonstrates early in an argument about language and racism:

I remember the first time I heard the word "nigger." In my third-grade class, our math tests were being passed down the rows, and as I handed the papers to a little boy in back of me, I remarked that once again he had received a much lower mark than I did. He snatched his test from me and spit out that word. Had he called me a nymphoma-niac or a necrophiliac, I couldn't have been more puzzled. I didn't know what a nigger was, but I knew that whatever it meant, it was something he shouldn't have called me. This was verified when I raised my hand, and in a loud voice repeated what he had said and watched the teacher scold him for using a "bad" word. I was later to go home and ask the inevitable question that every black parent must face—"Mommy, what does 'nigger' mean?"

–Gloria Naylor, "Mommy, What Does 'Nigger' Mean?"

CULTURAL CONTEXTS FOR ARGUMENT

Personal experience counts in making academic arguments in some but not all cultures. Showing that you have personal experience with a topic can carry strong persuasive appeal with many English-speaking audi-ences, however, so it will probably be a useful way to argue a point in the United States. As with all evidence used to make a point, evidence based on your own experience must be pertinent to the topic, understandable to the audience, and clearly related to your purpose and claim.

SECONDHAND EVIDENCE AND RESEARCH

Secondhand evidence comes from sources beyond yourself—books, arti-cles, films, online documents, and so on.

Library Sources

Your college library has not only a great number of print materials (books, periodicals, reference works) but also computer terminals that provide access to electronic catalogs and indexes as well as to other libraries' cata-logs via the Internet. Although this book isn't designed to give a complete overview of library resources, we can offer some important distinctions and pose a few key questions that can help you use the library most efficiently.

TWO IMPORTANT DISTINCTIONS

- Remember the distinction between the library databases and the Internet/Web. Your library computers hold important resources that are either not available on the Web at all or are not easily accessible to you except through the library's own system. The most important of these resources is the library's own catalog of its holdings (mostly books), but college libraries also pay to subscribe to a large number of scholarly databases—guides to journal and magazine articles, the Lexis/Nexis database of news stories and legal cases, and compilations of statistics, for example—that you can use for free. You'll be wise, then, to begin research using the electronic sources available to you through your college library before turning to the Web.

- Remember the distinction between subject headings and keywords. The library catalog and databases usually index contents by author, by title, by publication date, and by subject headings—a standardized set of words and phrases used to classify the subject matter of books and articles. When you do a subject search of the catalog, then, you are searching only one part of the electronic record of the library's books, and you will need to use the exact wording of the *Library of Congress Subject Headings* (LCSH) classifications. Searches using keywords, on the other hand, make use of the computer's ability to look for any term in any field of the electronic record. Keyword searching is less restrictive, but it requires you to think carefully about your search terms in order to get good results. In addition, you need to learn to use the techniques for combining keywords with the words *and*, *or*, and *not* and with parentheses and quotation marks to limit (or expand) your search.

SOME QUESTIONS FOR BEGINNING RESEARCH

- What kinds of sources do you need to consult? Check your assignment to see whether you are required to consult different kinds of sources. If you will use print sources, find out whether they are readily available in your library or whether you must make special arrangements (such as an interlibrary loan) to use them. If you need to locate nonprint sources, find out where those are kept and whether you need special permission to examine them.

- How current do your sources need to be? If you must investigate the very latest findings about, say, a new treatment for Alzheimer's, you will probably want to check periodicals, medical journals, or the Web. If you want broader, more detailed coverage and background information, you may need to depend more on books. If your argument deals with a specific time period, you may need to examine newspapers, magazines, or books written during that period.

- How many sources should you consult? Expect to look over many more sources than you will end up using. The best guideline is to make sure you have enough sources to support your claim.

- Do you know your way around the library? If not, ask a librarian for help in locating the following resources in the library: general and specialized encyclopedias; biographical resources; almanacs, yearbooks, and atlases; book and periodical indexes; specialized indexes and abstracts; the circulation computer or library catalog; special collections; audio, video, and art collections; the interlibrary loan office.

- Do you know how to conduct subject heading searches about your topic? Consult the *Library of Congress Subject Headings* (LCSH) for a list of standard subject headings related to your topic. This reference work, available in print and online, is a helpful starting point because it lists the subject headings used in most library catalogs and indexes.

Online Sources

Many important resources for argument are now available in databases, either online or on CD-ROM. But the Internet has no overall index such as the *Library of Congress Subject Headings*—at least not yet. Like library catalogs and databases, however, the Internet and Web offer two basic ways to search for sources related to your argument: one using subject categories and one using keywords. A subject directory organized by categories allows you to choose a broad category like "Entertainment" or "Science" and then click on increasingly narrow categories like "Movies" or "Astronomy" and then "Thrillers" or "The Solar System" until you reach a point where you are given a list of Web sites or the opportunity to do a keyword search. With the second kind of Internet search option, a search engine, you start right off with a keyword search. Because the Internet contains vastly more material than even the largest library catalog or database, searching it with a search engine requires even more thought and care in the choice and combination of keywords. For an argument about the fate of the hero in contemporary films, for example, you might find that *film* and *hero* produce far too many possible matches, or "hits." You might further narrow the search by adding a third keyword, say, *American* or *current*.

In doing such searches, you will need to observe the search logic for a particular database. Using *and* between keywords (*movies and heroes*) usually indicates that both terms must appear in a file for it to be called up. Using *or* between keywords usually instructs the computer to locate every file in which either one word or the other shows up, whereas using *not* tells the computer to exclude files containing a particular word from the search results (*movies not heroes*).

Software programs called browsers enable you to navigate the contents of the Web and to move from one Web site to another. Today, most browsers—such as Netscape Navigator, Safari, and Microsoft Explorer—are graphics browsers that display both text and visual images.

Web-based search engines can be used to carry out keyword searches or view a list of contents available in a series of directories. Here are a few of the most popular search engines:

Search Tools

AltaVista <*altavista.digital.com*> lets you search the entire Web using either a single keyword or multiple keywords.

Excite <*excite.com*> allows you to do keyword and subject directory searches.

Google <*google.com*> is a popular search tool that is a favorite of many students. Allows subject directory and keyword searches.

HotBot <*hotbot.com*> lets you search for individual words or phrases, names, or URLs in millions of Web sites and narrow the search to specific dates, media, and other criteria. Allows keyword and subject directory searches.

Lycos <*lycos.com*> allows you to search a huge catalog of Web sites and includes multimedia documents. Allows keyword and subject directory searches.

Magellan <*magellan.com*> allows you to search the entire Web or Web sites that have been evaluated for the quality of their content and organization. Allows keyword and subject directory searches.

WebCrawler <*webcrawler.com*> lets you search millions of Web sites with an easy-to-use procedure that is especially helpful for those new to keyword searching. Also allows for subject directory searches.

Yahoo! <*yahoo.com*> allows you either to search directories of sites related to particular subjects (such as entertainment or education) or to enter keywords that Yahoo! gives to a search engine (Google), which sends back the results.

USING EVIDENCE EFFECTIVELY

You may gather an impressive amount of evidence on your topic—from firsthand interviews, from careful observations, and from intensive library and online research. But until that evidence is woven into the fabric of your own argument, it is just a pile of data. Using your evidence effectively calls for turning data into information that will be persuasive to your intended audience.

Considering Audiences

The ethos you bring to an argument is crucial to your success in connecting with your audience. Of course, you want to present yourself as reliable and credible, but you also need to think carefully about the way your evidence relates to your audience. Is it appropriate to this particular group of readers or listeners? Does it speak to them in ways they will understand and respond to? Does it acknowledge and appeal to where they are "coming from"? It's hard to give any definite advice for making sure that your evidence is appropriate to the audience. But in general, timeliness is important to audiences: the more up-to-date your evidence, the better. In addition, evidence that is representative is usually more persuasive than evidence that is extreme or unusual. For example, in arguing for a campuswide escort service after 10 P.M., a writer who cites numbers of students frightened, threatened, or attacked on their way across campus after dark and numbers of calls for help from campus phone boxes will be in a stronger position than one who cites only an attack that occurred four years ago.

Building a Critical Mass

Throughout this chapter we have stressed the need to discover as much evidence as possible in support of your claim. If you can find only one or two pieces of evidence, only one or two reasons to back up your contention, then you may be on weak ground. Although there is no magic number, no definite way of saying how much is "enough" evidence, you should build toward a critical mass, with a number of pieces of evidence all pulling in the direction of your claim. Especially if your evidence relies heavily on personal experience or on one major example, you should stretch your search for additional sources and good reasons to back up your claim.

Compare the intended and invoked audiences of two texts by the Veterans Against The Iraq War. While the first text is a letter written to assess the support of veterans, the second text is the organization's statement of purpose that was presented to the White House and Congress. How do the writers adjust their use of evidence when they shift audiences?

·······················LINK TO P. 867

CULTURAL CONTEXTS FOR ARGUMENT

How do you decide what evidence will best support your claims? The answer depends, in large part, on how you define evidence. Differing notions of what counts as evidence can lead to arguments that go nowhere fast.

Many examples of such failed arguments occurred during the 2003 war with Iraq. Even before the war began, members of the United Nations were less than satisfied with the evidence that Iraq represented a clear and present danger. What was completely persuasive to the U.S. government—pictures of convoys that could be moving around chemical weapons, for example—was not at all persuasive to others; they did not count as adequate evidence. Journalists are often called on to interview those whose view of what constitutes effective evidence differs markedly from their own. When Italian journalist Oriana Fallaci interviewed the Ayatollah Khomeini in 1971, for example, she argued in a way that is common in North American and Western European cultures: she presented what she considered adequate assertions backed up with facts ("Iran denies freedom to people. . . . Many people have been put in prison and even executed, just for speaking out in opposition"). In response, Khomeini relied on very different kinds of evidence: analogies ("Just as a finger with gangrene should be cut off so that it will not destroy the whole body, so should people who corrupt others be pulled out like weeds so they will not infect the whole field") and, above all, the authority of the Qur'an. Partly because of these differing beliefs about what counts as evidence, the interview ended unsuccessfully.

People in the United States tend to give great weight to factual evidence, but as this example shows, the same is not true in some other parts of the world. In arguing across cultures, you need to think carefully about how you are accustomed to using evidence—and to pay attention to what counts as evidence to members of other cultures.

- Do you rely on facts? Examples? Firsthand experience?
- Do you include testimony from experts? Which experts are valued most (and why)?
- Do you cite religious or philosophical texts? Proverbs or everyday wisdom?
- Do you use analogies as evidence? How much do they count?

Once you determine what counts as evidence in your own arguments, ask these same questions about the use of evidence by members of other cultures.

Arranging Evidence

You can begin to devise a plan for arranging your evidence effectively by producing a rough outline or diagram of your argument, a series of hand-written or computer note cards that can be grouped into categories, or anything else that makes the major points of the argument very clear. Then review your evidence, deciding which pieces support which points in the argument. In general, try to position your strongest pieces of evidence in key places—near the beginning of paragraphs, at the end of the introduction, or where you build toward a powerful conclusion. In addition, try to achieve a balance between, on the one hand, your own argument and your own words, and on the other hand, the sources you use or quote in support of the argument. The sources of evidence are important props in the structure, but they should not overpower the structure (your argument) itself.

RESPOND ●

1. What counts as evidence depends in large part on the rhetorical situation. One audience might find personal testimony compelling in a given case, whereas another might require data that only experimental studies can provide.

   Imagine that you want to argue for a national educational campaign for ending spousal and partner abuse, composed of television ads to air before and during the Super Bowl—and you want the National Football League to pay for those ads. Make a list of reasons and evidence to support your claim, aimed at NFL executives. What kind of evidence would be most compelling to that group? How would you rethink your use of evidence if you were writing for the newsletter of a local women's shelter? This is not an exercise in pulling the wool over anyone's eyes; your goal is simply to anticipate the kind of evidence that different audiences would find persuasive given the same case.

2. Finding, evaluating, and arranging evidence in an argument is often a *discovery* process: sometimes you're concerned not only with digging up support for an already established claim but also with creating and revising tentative claims. Surveys and interviews can help you figure out what to argue, as well as provide evidence for a claim.

   Interview a classmate with the goal of writing a brief proposal argument about his or her career goals. The claim should be *My classmate should be doing X five years from now.* Limit yourself to ten questions; write them ahead of time and do not deviate from them. Record the results of the interview (written notes are fine—you don't need a tape recorder).

Then interview another classmate, with the same goal in mind. Ask the same first question, but this time let the answer dictate the rest of the questions. You still get only ten questions.

Which interview gave you more information? Which one helped you learn more about your classmate's goals? Which one better helped you develop claims about his or her future?

3. Imagine that you're trying to decide whether to take a class with a particular professor, but you don't know if he or she is a good teacher. You might already have an opinion, based on some vaguely defined criteria and dormitory gossip, but you're not sure if that evidence is reliable. You decide to observe a class to inform your decision.

Visit a class in which you are not a student, and make notes on your observations following the guidelines in this chapter (p. 370). You probably only need a single day's visit to get a sense of the note-taking process, though you would, of course, need much more time to write a thorough evaluation of the professor.

Write a short evaluation of the professor's teaching abilities on the basis of your observations. Then write an analysis of your evaluation. Is it honest? Fair? What other kinds of evidence might you need if you wanted to make an informed decision about the class and the teacher?

chapter nineteen

Fallacies of Argument

"That villainous abominable misleader of youth . . . that old white-bearded Satan."

"But if I don't get an 'A' in this class, I won't get into medical school."

"Ask not what your country can do for you; ask what you can do for your country."

"Make love, not war."

"All my friends have AOL. I'm the only one who can't get instant messages!"

■ ■ ■

Certain types of argumentative moves are so controversial they have been traditionally classified as *fallacies*, a term we use in this chapter. But you might find it more interesting to think of them as *flashpoints* or *hotspots*

384

because they instantly raise questions about the ethics of argument—that is, whether a particular strategy of argument is fair, accurate, or principled. Fallacies are arguments supposedly flawed by their very nature or structure; as such, you should avoid them in your own writing and challenge them in arguments you hear or read. That said, it's important to appreciate that one person's fallacy may well be another person's stroke of genius.

Consider, for example, the fallacy termed *ad hominem* argument—"to the man." It describes a strategy of attacking the character of people you disagree with rather than the substance of their arguments: *So you think Eminem is a homophobic racist? Well, you're just a thumb-sucking, white-bread elitist.* Everyone has blurted out such insults at some time in their lives.

But there are also situations when someone's character is central to an argument. If that weren't so, appeals based on character would be pointless. The problem arises in deciding when such arguments are legitimate and when they are flashpoints. You are much more likely to think of attacks on people you admire as *ad hominem* slurs, but personal attacks on those you disagree with as reasonable criticisms. Obviously, debates about character can become quite ugly and polarizing. Consider Anita Hill and Clarence Thomas, Eminem and Moby, Pete Rose and major league baseball. (For more on arguments based on character, see Chapter 6.)

FIGURE 19.1   MOBY PERFORMING

It might be wise to think of fallacies not in terms of errors you can detect and expose in someone else's work, but as strategies that hurt everyone (including the person using them) because they make productive argument more difficult. Fallacies muck up the frank but civil conversations people should be able to have—regardless of their differences.

To help you understand flashpoints of argument, we've classified them according to three rhetorical appeals discussed in earlier chapters: emotional arguments, arguments based on character, and logical arguments. (See Chapters 4, 6, and 7.)

FLASHPOINTS OF EMOTIONAL ARGUMENT

Many people deride emotional arguments as "womanish" and, therefore, weak and suspect. But such views are not only close-minded and sexist; they're flat-out wrong. Emotional arguments can be both powerful and suitable in many circumstances, and most writers use them frequently. However, writers who pull on their readers' heartstrings too often can violate the good faith on which legitimate argument depends. Readers won't trust a writer who can't make a point without frightening someone or provoking tears or stirring up hatred.

Scare Tactics

Corrupters of children, the New Testament warns, would be better off dropped into the sea with millstones around their necks. Would that politicians, advertisers, and public figures who peddle their ideas by scaring people and exaggerating possible dangers well beyond their statistical likelihood face similarly stern warnings. Yet scare tactics are remarkably common in everything ranging from ads for life insurance to threats of audits by the Internal Revenue Service. Such ploys work because it is usually easier to imagine something terrible happening than to appreciate its statistical rarity. That may be why so many people fear flying more than driving. Auto accidents occur much more frequently, but they don't have the same impact on our imaginations as do air disasters.

Scare tactics can also be used to stampede legitimate fears into panic or prejudice. People who genuinely fear losing their jobs can be persuaded, easily enough, to mistrust all immigrants as people who might work for less money; people living on fixed incomes can be convinced that even minor modifications of entitlement programs represent dire threats to their standard of living. Such tactics have the effect of closing off thinking because people who are scared seldom act rationally.

Even well-intended fear campaigns—like those directed against drugs or HIV infection—can misfire if their warnings prove too shrill. When health professionals originally overestimated the rate at which AIDS would occur within the heterosexual population in the United States, many people became suspicious of the establishment's warnings and so grew careless about their own sexual behavior, thereby greatly increasing their risk of exposure to infection.

Either-Or Choices

A way to simplify arguments and give them power is to reduce the options for action to only two choices. The preferred option might be drawn in the warmest light, whereas the alternative is cast as an ominous shadow. That's the nature of the choices President George W. Bush offered to the United Nations in its dealings with Iraq in the fall of 2002:

> **Events can turn in one of two ways: If we fail to act in the face of danger, the people of Iraq will continue to live in brutal submission. The regime will have new power to bully and dominate and conquer its neighbors, condemning the Middle East to more years of bloodshed and fear. . . . If we meet our responsibilities, if we overcome this danger, we can arrive at a very different future. The people of Iraq can shake off their captivity.**
> —George W. Bush, September 12, 2002

Sometimes neither of the alternatives is pleasant: that's the nature of many "ultimatums." For instance, the allies in World War II offered the Axis powers only two choices as the conflict drew to a close: either continued war and destruction, or unconditional surrender. No third option was available.

Either-or arguments can be well-intentioned strategies to get something accomplished. Parents use them all the time; they will tell children either to eat their broccoli or they won't get dessert. Such arguments become fallacious when they reduce a complicated issue to excessively simple terms or when they are designed to obscure legitimate alternatives.

For instance, to suggest that Social Security must be privatized or the system will go broke may have rhetorical power, but the choice is too simple. The financial problems of Social Security can be fixed in any number of ways, including privatization. But to defend privatization, falsely, as the *only* possible course of action is to risk losing the support of people who know better.

But then *either-or* arguments—like most scare tactics—are often purposefully designed to seduce those who don't know much about a subject. That's another reason the tactic violates principles of civil discourse. Argument should enlighten people, making them more knowledgeable and more capable of acting intelligently and independently. Very often, we don't have to choose one side over the other. Listen to Bill Clinton make exactly that point in defending the environmental record of his administration [emphasis added]:

> **From our inner cities to our pristine wild lands, we have worked hard to ensure that every American has a clean and healthy environment. We've rid hundreds of neighborhoods of toxic waste dumps, and taken the most dramatic steps in a generation to clean the air we breathe. We have made record investments in science and technology to protect future generations from the threat of global warming. We've worked to protect and restore our most glorious natural resources, from the Florida Everglades to California's redwoods to Yellowstone. *And we have, I hope, finally put to rest the false choice between the economy and the environment, for we have the strongest economy perhaps in our history, with a cleaner environment.***
>
> —Bill Clinton, January 11, 2000

Slippery Slope

The slippery slope flashpoint is well named, describing an argument that casts today's tiny misstep as tomorrow's avalanche. Of course, not all arguments aimed at preventing dire consequences are slippery slope fallacies: the parent who corrects a child for misbehavior now is acting sensibly to prevent more serious problems as the child grows older. And like the homeowner who repairs a loose shingle to prevent an entire roof from rotting, businesses and institutions that worry about little problems often prevent bigger ones. The city of New York learned an important lesson in the 1990s about controlling crime by applying what had become known as "the broken window theory": after former mayor Rudolph Giuliani directed police to crack down on petty crimes that make urban life especially unpleasant, major crimes declined as well.

A slippery slope argument becomes a flashpoint when a writer exaggerates the future consequences of an action, usually to frighten readers. As such, slippery slope arguments are also scare tactics. But people encounter them so often that they come to seem almost reasonable. For instance, defenders of free speech often regard even mild attempts to regulate behavior as constitutional matters: for example, a school board's request that a school pupil cut his ponytail becomes a direct assault on the child's First Amendment rights, litigated through the courts. Similarly, opponents of gun control warn that any legislation regulating firearms is just a first step toward the government knocking down citizens' doors and seizing weapons.

Ideas and actions do have consequences, but they aren't always as dire as writers fond of slippery slope tactics would have you believe.

Sentimental Appeals

Sentimental appeals are arguments that use emotions excessively to distract readers from facts. Quite often, such appeals are highly personal and individual—focusing attention on heart-warming or heart-wrenching situations that make readers feel guilty if they challenge an idea, policy, or proposal. Emotions become an impediment to civil discourse when they keep people from thinking clearly.

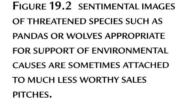

GIVE THEM
SHELTER FROM
THE STORM.

1 800 CALL WWF
www.worldwildlife.org/ad

Man's abuse of Earth's natural resources has created a storm that many animals and their habitats
have difficulty weathering. Help World Wildlife Fund protect them by ordering a free Action Kit
Together we can help leave our children a living planet.

WWF

FIGURE 19.2 SENTIMENTAL IMAGES OF THREATENED SPECIES SUCH AS PANDAS OR WOLVES APPROPRIATE FOR SUPPORT OF ENVIRONMENTAL CAUSES ARE SOMETIMES ATTACHED TO MUCH LESS WORTHY SALES PITCHES.

Yet sentimental appeals are a major vehicle of television news, where it is customary to convey ideas through personal tales that tug at viewers' heartstrings. For example, a camera might document the day-to-day life of a single mother on welfare whose on-screen generosity, kindness, and tears come to represent the spirit of an entire welfare clientele under attack by callous legislators; or the welfare recipient might be shown driving a new pickup and illegally trading food stamps for money while a lower-middle-class family struggles to meet its grocery budget. In either case, the conclusion the reporter wants you to reach is supported by powerful images that evoke emotions in support of that conclusion. But though the individual stories presented may be genuinely moving, they seldom give a complete picture of a complex social or economic issue.

Bandwagon Appeals

Bandwagon appeals are arguments that urge people to follow the same path everyone else is taking. Curiously, many American parents seem

FIGURE 19.3 JIMMY MARGULIES, EDITORIAL CARTOONIST FOR *THE RECORD*, BLAMES TV CABLE CHANNELS FOR BANDWAGON APPROACHES TO THE NEWS.

endowed with the ability to refute bandwagon appeals. When their kids whine that *Everyone else is going camping overnight without chaperones*, the parents reply instinctively, *And if everyone else jumps off a cliff (or a railroad bridge, or the Empire State Building), you will too?* The children stomp and groan—and then try a different line of argument.

Unfortunately, not all bandwagon approaches are so transparent. Though Americans like to imagine themselves as rugged individualists, they're easily seduced by ideas endorsed by the mass media and popular culture. Such trends are often little more than harmless fashion statements. At other times, however, Americans become obsessed by issues that politicians or the media select for their attention—such as the seemingly endless coverage of Gary Condit in 2001 and Elián Gonzalez the year before. In recent decades, bandwagon issues have included the war on drugs, the nuclear freeze movement, health care reform, AIDS prevention, gun control, drunk driving, tax reform, welfare reform, teen smoking, campaign finance reform, and post 9/11 antiwar movements.

In the atmosphere of obsession, there is a feeling that everyone must be concerned by this issue-of-the-day, and something—*anything*—must be done! More often than not, enough people jump on the bandwagon to achieve a measure of reform. And when changes occur because people have become sufficiently informed to exercise good judgment, then one can speak of "achieving consensus," a rational goal for civil argument.

But sometimes bandwagons run out of control, as they did in the 1950s when some careers were destroyed by "witch hunts" for suspected communists during the McCarthy era and in the late 1980s when concerns over child abuse mushroomed into indiscriminate prosecutions of parents and child care workers. In a democratic society, the bandwagon appeal is among the most potentially serious and permanently damaging flashpoints of argument.

FLASHPOINTS OF ETHICAL ARGUMENT

Not surprisingly, readers give their closest attention to authors whom they respect or trust. So, writers usually want to present themselves as honest, well informed, likable, or sympathetic in some way. But *trust me* is a scary warrant. Not all the devices writers use to gain the attention and confidence of readers are admirable. (For more on appeals of character, see Chapter 6.)

Appeals to False Authority

One of the effective strategies a writer can use to support an idea is to draw on the authority of widely respected people, institutions, and texts. In fact, many academic research papers are essentially exercises in finding and reflecting on the work of reputable authorities. Writers usually introduce these authorities into their arguments through direct quotations, citations (such as footnotes), or allusions. (See Chapter 21 for more on assessing the reliability of sources.)

False authority occurs chiefly when writers offer themselves, or other authorities they cite, as sufficient warrant for believing a claim:

Claim	X is true because I say so.
Warrant	What I say must be true.
Claim	X is true because Y says so.
Warrant	What Y says must be true.

Rarely will you see authority asserted quite so baldly as in these formulas, because few readers would accept a claim stated in either of these ways. Nonetheless, claims of authority drive many persuasive campaigns. American pundits and politicians are fond of citing the U.S. Constitution or Bill of Rights as ultimate authorities, a reasonable practice when the documents are interpreted respectfully. However, as often as not, the constitutional rights claimed aren't in the texts themselves or don't mean what the speakers think they do. And most constitutional matters are quite debatable—as centuries of court records could prove.

Likewise, communities of believers often base their religious beliefs on books or traditions that claim great authority. However, the power of these texts is usually somewhat limited outside that group and, hence, less capable of persuading others solely on the grounds of their authority alone—though arguments of faith often have power on other grounds.

Institutions can be cited as authorities too. Certainly, serious attention should be paid to claims supported by authorities one respects or recognizes—the White House, the FBI, the FDA, the National Science Foundation, the *New York Times*, the *Wall Street Journal,* and so on. But one ought not to accept facts or information simply because they have the imprimatur of such offices and agencies. To quote a Russian proverb made famous by Ronald Reagan, "Trust, but verify."

Dogmatism

A writer who attempts to persuade by asserting or assuming that a particular position is the only one conceivably acceptable within a community is trying to enforce dogmatism. Indeed, dogmatism is a flashpoint of character because the tactic undermines the trust that must exist between those who would make and those who would receive arguments. In effect, people who speak or write dogmatically imply that there are no arguments to be made: the truth is self-evident to those who know better. You can usually be sure you are listening to a dogmatic opinion when someone begins a sentence or phrase with *No rational person would disagree that . . .* or *It is clear to anyone who has thought about it that . . .*

Of course, there are some arguments beyond the pale of civil discourse—positions and claims so outrageous or absurd that they are unworthy of serious attention. For example, attacks on the historical reality of the Holocaust fall into this category. But relatively few subjects in a free society ought to be off the table from the start—certainly none that can be defended with facts, testimony, and good reasons. In general, therefore, when someone suggests that merely raising an issue for debate is somehow "politically incorrect"—whether racist or sexist, unpatriotic or sacrilegious, or insensitive or offensive in some other way—you should be suspicious. It is likely you are dealing with someone more interested in repressing ideas than exploring them.

Moral Equivalence

A fallacy of argument perhaps more common today than a decade ago is moral equivalence—that is, suggesting that serious wrongdoings don't differ in kind from minor offenses. A warning sign that this fallacy is likely to come into play is the retort of the politician or bureaucrat accused of wrongdoing: *But everyone else does it too!* Richard Nixon insisted that the crimes that led to his resignation did not differ from the activities of previous presidents; Bill Clinton made similar claims about the fund-raising and other scandals of his administration. Regardless of the validity of these particular defenses, there is a point at which comparisons become absurd. For example, many readers thought that Joan Jacobs Brumberg and Jacquelyn Jackson reached such a point when they suggested in an article in the *Boston Globe* that American women might not be much better off than women in Afghanistan living under Taliban rule:

> **The war on terrorism has certainly raised our awareness of the ways in which women's bodies are controlled by a repressive regime in a faraway land, but what about the constraints on women's bodies here at home, right here in America? . . . Whether it's the dark, sad eyes of a woman in purdah or the anxious darkly circled eyes of a girl with anorexia nervosa, the woman trapped inside needs to be liberated**

from cultural confines in whatever form they take. The burka and the bikini represent opposite ends of the political spectrum but each can exert a noose-like grip on the psyche and physical health of girls and women.
–Joan Jacobs Brumberg and Jacquelyn Jackson, "The Burka and the Bikini"

Moral equivalence can work both ways. You've probably seen arguments in which relatively innocuous activities are raised to the level of major crimes. Some would say that the national campaign against smoking falls into this category—a common and legally sanctioned behavior now given the social stigma of serious drug abuse. And if smoking is almost criminal, should one not be equally concerned with people who use and abuse chocolate—a sweet and fatty food responsible for a host of health problems? You see how easy it is to make an equivalence argument. Yet suggesting that all behaviors of a particular kind—in this case, abuses of substances—are equally wrong (whether they involve cigarettes, alcohol, drugs, or fatty foods) blurs the distinctions people need to make in weighing claims.

Ad Hominem Arguments

Ad hominem (from the Latin for "to the man") arguments are attacks directed at the character of a person rather than at the claims he or she makes. The theory is simple: Destroy the credibility of your opponents, and either you destroy their ability to present reasonable appeals or you distract from the successful arguments they may be offering. Here, for example, is social critic Christopher Hitchens questioning whether former secretary of state Henry Kissinger should be appointed to head an important government commission in 2002: "But can Congress and the media be expected to swallow the appointment of a proven coverup artist, a discredited historian, a busted liar, and a man who is wanted in many jurisdictions for the vilest of offenses?" Not much doubt where Hitchens stands. Critics of Rush Limbaugh's conservative politics rarely fail to note his weight (even after he has lost most of it); critics of Bill Clinton's policies just as reliably still mention his womanizing.

In such cases, *ad hominem* tactics turn arguments into ham-fisted, two-sided affairs with good guys and bad guys. Civil argument resists this destructive nastiness, though the temptation to use such tactics persists even (some would say, especially) in colleges and universities.

Of course, character does matter in argument. People expect the proponent of peace to be civil, the advocate of ecology to respect the environment, the champion of justice to be fair even in private dealings. But it is fallacious to attack an idea by uncovering the foibles of its advocates or attacking their motives, backgrounds, or unchangeable traits.

FLASHPOINTS OF LOGICAL ARGUMENT

You'll encounter a flashpoint in any argument when the claims, warrants, and/or evidence in it are invalid, insufficient, or disconnected. In the abstract, such problems seem easy enough to spot; in practice, they can be camouflaged by a skillful use of words or images. Indeed, logical fallacies pose a challenge to civil argument because they often seem quite reasonable and natural, especially when they appeal to people's self-interests. Whole industries (such as phone-in psychic networks) depend on one or more of the logical fallacies for their existence; political campaigns, too, rely on them to prop up that current staple of democratic interchange — the fifteen-second TV spot.

Hasty Generalization

Among logical fallacies, only faulty causality might be able to challenge hasty generalization for the crown of most prevalent. A hasty generalization is an inference drawn from insufficient evidence: *Because my Honda broke down, all Hondas must be junk.* It also forms the basis for most stereotypes about people or institutions: because a few people in a large group are observed to act in a certain way, one infers that all members of that group will behave similarly. The resulting conclusions are usually sweeping claims of little merit: *Women are bad drivers; men are boors; Scots are stingy; Italians are romantic; English teachers are nit-picking; scientists are nerds.* You could, no doubt, expand this roster of stereotypes by the hundreds.

To draw valid inferences, you must always have sufficient evidence: a random sample of a population, a selection large enough to represent fully the subjects of your study, an objective methodology for sampling the population or evidence, and so on (see Chapter 18). And you must qualify your claims appropriately. After all, people do need generalizations to help make reasonable decisions in life; such claims can be offered legitimately if placed in context and tagged with appropriate qualifiers: *some, a few, many, most, occasionally, rarely, possibly, in some cases, under certain circumstances, in my experience.*

You should be especially alert to the fallacy of hasty generalization when you read reports and studies of any kind, especially case studies based on carefully selected populations. Be alert for the fallacy, too, in the interpretation of poll numbers. Everything from the number of people selected to the time the poll was taken to the exact wording of the questions may affect its outcome.

Faulty Causality

In Latin, the fallacy of faulty causality is described by the expression *post hoc, ergo propter hoc*, which translates word-for-word as "after this, therefore because of this." Odd as the translation may sound, it accurately describes what faulty causality is—the fallacious assumption that because one event or action follows another, the first necessarily causes the second.

Some actions, of course, do produce reactions. Step on the brake pedal in your car, and you move hydraulic fluid that pushes calipers against disks to create friction that stops the vehicle. Or, if you happen to be chair of the Federal Reserve Board, you raise interest rates to increase the cost of borrowing to slow the growth of the economy in order to curb inflation—you hope. Causal relationships of this kind are reasonably convincing because one can provide evidence of relationships between the events sufficient to convince most people that an initial action did, indeed, cause others.

But as even the Federal Reserve example suggests, causality can be difficult to control when economic, political, or social relationships are involved. That's why suspiciously simple or politically convenient causal claims should always be subject to scrutiny.

Begging the Question

There's probably not a teacher in the country who hasn't heard the following argument from a student: *You can't give me a "C" in this course; I'm an "A" student.* The accused felon's version of the same argument goes this way: *I can't be guilty of embezzlement; I'm an honest person.* In both cases, the problem with the claim is that it is made on grounds that cannot be accepted as true because those grounds are in doubt. How can the student claim to be an "A" student when she just earned a "C"? How can the accused felon defend himself on the grounds of honesty when that honesty is now suspect? Setting such arguments in Toulmin terms helps to expose the fallacy:

Claim + *Reason*	You can't give me a "C" in this course because I'm an "A" student.
Warrant	An "A" student is someone who can't receive "C"s.
Claim + *Reason*	I can't be guilty of embezzlement because I'm an honest person.
Warrant	An honest person cannot be guilty of embezzlement.

With the warrants stated, you can see why begging the question—that is, assuming as true the very claim that is disputed—is a form of circular argument, divorced from reality. If you assume that an "A" student can't receive "C"s, then the first argument stands. But no one is an "A" student *by definition*; that standing has to be earned by performance in individual courses. Otherwise, there would be no point for a student who once earned an "A" to be taking additional courses; "A" students can only get "A"s, right?

Likewise, even though someone with a record of honesty is unlikely to embezzle, a claim of honesty is not an adequate defense against specific charges. An honest person won't embezzle, but merely claiming to be honest does not make one so. (For more on Toulmin argument, see Chapter 8.)

Equivocation

Both the finest definition and the most famous literary examples of equivocation come from Shakespeare's tragedy *Macbeth*. In the drama three witches, representing the fates, make prophecies that favor the ambitious Macbeth but that prove disastrous when understood more fully. He is told, for example, that he has nothing to fear from his enemies "till Birnam wood / Do come to Dunsinane" (*Mac.* V.v.44–45); but these woods do move when enemy soldiers cut down branches from the forest of Birnam for camouflage and march on Macbeth's fortress. Catching on to the game, Macbeth starts "[t]o doubt the equivocation of the fiend / That *lies like truth*" (V.v.43–44, emphasis added). An equivocation, then, is an argument that gives a lie an honest appearance; it is a half-truth.

Equivocations are usually juvenile tricks of language. Consider the plagiarist who copies a paper word-for-word from a source and then declares—honestly, she thinks—that "I wrote the entire paper myself," meaning that she physically copied the piece on her own. But the plagiarist is using "wrote" equivocally—that is, in a limited sense, knowing that most people would understand "writing" as something more than the mere copying of words. Certainly the most famous equivocation of the last decade was Bill Clinton's "I never had sex with that woman" claim, but many public figures are fond of parsing their words carefully so that no certain meaning emerges.

Non Sequitur

A *non sequitur* is an argument in which claims, reasons, or warrants fail to connect logically; one point does not follow from another. As with other fallacies, children are notably adept at framing *non sequiturs*. Consider this familiar form: *You don't love me or you'd buy me that bicycle!* It might be more evident to harassed parents that no connection exists between love and Huffys if they were to consider the implied warrant:

Claim	**You must not love me**
Reason	**. . . because you haven't bought me that bicycle.**
Warrant	**Buying bicycles for children is essential to loving them.**

A five-year-old might endorse that warrant, but no responsible adult would because love does not depend on buying things, at least not a particular bicycle. Activities more logically related to love might include feeding and clothing children, taking care of them when they are sick, providing shelter and education, and so on.

In effect, *non sequiturs* occur when writers omit a step in an otherwise logical chain of reasoning, assuming that readers agree with what may be a highly contestable claim. For example, it is a *non sequitur* simply to argue that the comparatively poor performance of American students on international mathematics examinations means the country should spend more money on math education. Such a conclusion might be justified if a correlation were known or found to exist between mathematical ability and money spent on education. But the students' performance might be poor for reasons other than education funding, so a writer should first establish the nature of the problem before offering a solution.

Faulty Analogy

Comparisons give ideas greater presence or help clarify concepts. Consider all the comparisons packed into this reference to Jack Kennedy from a tribute to Jacqueline Kennedy by Stanley Crouch:

The Kennedys had spark and Jack had grown into a handsome man, a male swan rising out of the Billy the Kid version of an Irish duckling he had been when he was a young senator.

–Stanley Crouch, "Blues for Jackie"

When comparisons are extended, they become analogies—ways of understanding unfamiliar ideas by comparing them with something that is already known. Some argue that it is through comparisons, metaphors, and analogies that people come to understand the universe. But useful as such comparisons are, they may prove quite false either on their own or when pushed too far or taken too seriously. At this point they become faulty analogies, inaccurate or inconsequential comparisons between objects or concepts. For instance, to think of a human mind as a garden has charm: Gardens thrive only if carefully planted, weeded, watered, pruned, and harvested; so too the mind must be cultivated, if it is to bear fruit. But gardens also thrive when spread with aged manure. Need we follow the analogy down that path? Probably not.

RESPOND●

1. Following is a list of political slogans or phrases that may be examples of logical fallacies. Discuss each item to determine what you may know about the slogan and then decide which, if any, fallacy might be used to describe it.

   "It's the economy, stupid." (sign on the wall at Bill Clinton's campaign headquarters)

   "Nixon's the one." (campaign slogan)

   "Remember the Alamo."

   "Make love, not war." (antiwar slogan during the Vietnam War)

   "A chicken in every pot."

   "No taxation without representation."

   "No Payne, your gain." (aimed at an opponent named Payne)

   "Loose lips sink ships."

   "Guns don't kill, people do." (NRA slogan)

   "If you can't stand the heat, get out of the kitchen."

2. We don't want you to argue fallaciously, but it's fun and good practice to frame argumentative fallacies in your own language. Pick an argumentative topic—maybe even one that you've used for a paper in this class—and write a few paragraphs making nothing but fallacious

arguments in each sentence. Try to include all the fallacies of emotional, ethical, and logical argument that are discussed in this chapter. It will be a challenge, since some of the fallacies are difficult to recognize, much less produce. Then revise the paragraphs, removing all traces of fallacious reasoning, rewriting for clarity, and improving the quality of the argument. This may be an even greater challenge — sometimes fallacies are hard to fix.

3. Choose a paper you've written for this or another class, and analyze it carefully for signs of fallacious reasoning. Once you've tried analyzing your own prose, find an editorial, a syndicated column, and a political speech and look for the fallacies in them. Which fallacies are most common in the four arguments? How do you account for their prevalence? Which are the least common? How do you account for their absence? What seems to be the role of audience in determining what is a fallacy and what is not? Did you find what seem to be fallacies other than the kinds discussed in this chapter?

4. Arguments on the Web are no more likely to contain fallacies than are arguments in any other text, but the fallacies can take on different forms. The hypertextual nature of Web arguments and the ease of including visuals along with text make certain fallacies more likely to occur there. Find a Web site sponsored by an organization, business, government entity, or other group (such as the sites of the Democratic and Republican National Committees), and analyze the site for fallacious reasoning. Among other considerations, look at the relationship between text and graphics, and between individual pages and the pages that surround or are linked to them. How does the technique of separating information into discrete pages affect the argument? Then send an email message to the site's creators, explaining what you found and proposing ways the arguments in the site could be improved.

5. Political Web logs such as andrewsullivan.com and InstaPundit.com typically provide quick responses to daily events and detailed critiques of material in other media sites, including national newspapers. Study one active political Web log for a few days to determine whether and how the blogger critiques the material he links to in his or her site. Does the blogger point to flashpoints and fallacies in arguments? Summarize your findings in an oral report to your class on that particular Web log.

chapter twenty

Intellectual Property, Academic Integrity, and Avoiding Plagiarism

On a college campus, a student receives a warning: she has been detected using peer-to-peer music file sharing software. Has she been practicing fair use, or is she guilty of copyright infringement?

A student writing an essay about Title IX's effect on college athletic programs finds some powerful supporting evidence for her argument on a Web site. Can she use this information without gaining permission?

Day care centers around the country receive letters arguing that they will be liable to lawsuit if they use representations of Disney characters without explicit permission or show Disney films "outside the home."

In California, one large vintner sues another, claiming that the second "stole" the idea of a wine label from the first, although a judge later finds that even though the labels were similar, the second was not "copied" from the first.

Musicians argue against other musicians, saying that the popular use of "sampling" in songs amounts to a form of musical "plagiarism."

In cyberspace, the development of digital "watermarks" and other forms of tracking systems have made it possible to trace not only documents printed out but those read online as well; as a result, some lawyers argue that public access to information is being limited in ways that are unconstitutional.

■ ■ ■

In prior ages of agriculture and industrialization, products that could provide a livelihood were likely to be concrete things: crops, tools, machines. But in an age of information such as the current one, ideas (intellectual property) are arguably society's most important products. Hence the growing importance of—and growing controversies surrounding—what counts as "property" in an information age.

Perhaps the framers of the Constitution foresaw such a shift in the bases of the nation's economy. At any rate, they articulated in the Constitution a delicate balance between the public's need for information and the incentives necessary to encourage people to produce work—both material and intellectual. Thus the Constitution empowers Congress "[t]o promote the progress of Science and useful Arts, by securing for limited Times to Authors and Inventors the exclusive Right to their respective Writings and Discoveries" (Article 1, Section 8, Clause 8). This passage allows for limited protection (copyright) of the expression of ideas ("Writings and Discoveries"), and through the years that time limit has been extended to up to lifetime plus seventy-five years (and it may be extended yet again to lifetime plus one hundred years).

Why is this historical information important to student writers? First, because writers need to know that ideas themselves cannot be copyrighted—only the expression of those ideas. Second, this information explains why some works fall out of copyright and are available for students to use without paying a fee (as you have to do for copyright-protected material in a coursepack, for instance). Third, this information is crucial to the current debates over who owns online materials—

A cluster of arguments in Chapter 26 considers the matter of who owns words and ideas, presenting several different arguments about intellectual property. Charles Mann writes about the future of intellectual property in general, and four other pieces consider who should have the rights to use Martin Luther King Jr.'s "I Have a Dream" speech.

LINK TO P. 675

FIGURE 20.1 AS A UNIT WITHIN THE LIBRARY OF CONGRESS, THE U.S. COPYRIGHT
OFFICE WORKS TO UPHOLD CONSTITUTIONAL COPYRIGHT LAWS.

United States Copyright Office

materials that may never take any form of concrete expression. The
debate will certainly be raging during and after the publication of this
book—and the way in which it is resolved will have many direct effects
on students and teachers. For up-to-date information about copyright law,
see the Digital Future Coalition site at <dfc.org> or the U.S. Copyright site
at <lcweb.loc.gov/copyright/>.

Although you may not have thought much about it, all of your work in
college represents a growing bank of intellectual property, and this
includes all the writing you do online and off. In fact, such original work is
automatically copyrighted, even if it lacks the © symbol. As a result, you
should be careful with your passwords and with discs you carry around
with you. Whatever method you use for storing your work should be
secure; only *you* should be able to give someone access to that work. In
addition, remember that any email you send or any posting you make to a
listserv or online forum is public. If you don't want your thoughts and
ideas repeated (or forwarded), keep them offline. In turn, remember that

you should not use material from email, discussion groups, or other online forums without asking the writer for permission to do so.

CREDITING SOURCES IN ARGUMENTS

Acknowledging your sources and giving full credit is especially important in argumentative writing because doing so helps establish your ethos as a writer. In the first place, saying "thank you" to those who have been of help to you reflects gratitude and openness, qualities that audiences generally respond to very well. Second, acknowledging your sources demonstrates that you have "done your homework," that you know the conversation surrounding your topic and are familiar with what others have thought and said about it, and that you want to help readers find other contributions to the conversation and perhaps join it themselves. Finally, acknowledging sources reminds you to think very critically about your own stance in your argument and about how well you have used your sources. Are they timely and reliable? Have you used them in a biased or overly selective way? Have you used them accurately, double-checking all quotations and paraphrases? Thinking through these questions will improve your overall argument.

CITING SOURCES AND RECOGNIZING PLAGIARISM

In some ways, it is completely true that there is "nothing new under the sun." Indeed, whatever you think or write or say draws on everything you have ever heard or read or experienced. Trying to recall every influence or source of information you have drawn on, even in one day, would take so long that you would have little time left in which to say anything at all. Luckily, people are seldom if ever called on to list every single influence or source of their ideas and writings.

Certainly, recognizing and avoiding plagiarism is a good deal easier and more practical than that. And avoiding plagiarism is very important, for in Western culture *the use of someone else's words or ideas without acknowledgment and as your own is an act of academic dishonesty that can bring devastating results.* Moreover, as we noted above, taking care to cite your sources works to your advantage in an academic setting: it builds your credibility, showing that you have done your homework as a researcher.

FIGURE 20.2 *DOONESBURY* CARTOON ON INTELLECTUAL PROPERTY

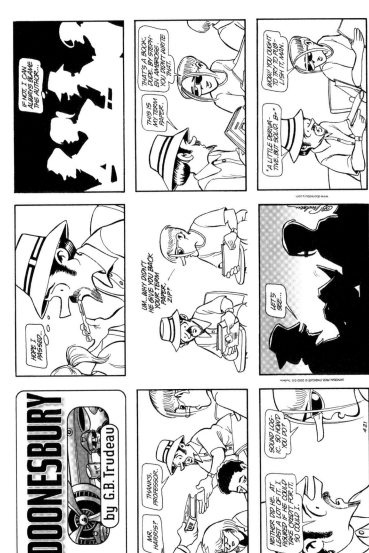

INACCURATE OR INCOMPLETE CITATION OF SOURCES

If you use a paraphrase that is too close to the original wording or sentence structure, if you leave out the parenthetical reference for a quotation (even if you include the quotation marks themselves), or if you don't indicate clearly the source of an idea you obviously didn't come up with on your own, you may be accused of plagiarism — even if that was not your intent. This kind of inaccurate or incomplete citation of sources often results either from carelessness or from not trying to learn how to use citations accurately and fully. Still, because the costs of even unintentional plagiarism can be severe, it's important to understand how it can happen and how you can guard against it.

In a January 2002 article published in *Time* magazine, historian Doris Kearns Goodwin (see Figure 20.3) explains how someone else's writing wound up in her book. The book in question, nine hundred pages long and with thirty-five hundred footnotes, took Goodwin ten years to write. During these ten years, she says, she took most of her notes by hand, organized the notes into boxes, and — once the draft was complete — went back to all her sources to check that all the material from them was correctly cited. "Somehow in this process," Goodwin goes on to say, "a few books were not fully rechecked," and so she omitted some necessary quotation marks in material she didn't acknowledge. Reflecting back on this experience, Goodwin says that discovering such carelessness in her own work was very troubling — so troubling that in the storm of criticism that ensued over the discovery of these failures to cite properly, she resigned from her position as a member of the Pulitzer Prize Committee.

FIGURE 20.3 DORIS KEARNS GOODWIN

CULTURAL CONTEXTS FOR ARGUMENT

Not all cultures accept Western notions of plagiarism, which rest on a belief that language can be owned by writers. Indeed, in many countries, and in some communities within the United States, using the words of others is considered a sign of deep respect and an indication of knowledge—and attribution is not expected or required. In writing arguments in the United States, however, you should credit all materials but those that are common knowledge, that are available in a wide variety of sources, or that are your own findings from field research.

ACKNOWLEDGING YOUR USE OF SOURCES

The safest way to avoid charges of plagiarism is to acknowledge as many of your sources as possible, with the following three exceptions:

- *common knowledge*, a specific piece of information most readers will know (that Bill Clinton won the 1996 presidential election, for instance)
- *facts available from a wide variety of sources* (that the Japanese bombing of Pearl Harbor occurred on December 7, 1941, for example)
- *your own findings from field research* (observations, interviews, experiments, or surveys you have conducted), which should simply be announced as your own

For all other source material you should give credit as fully as possible, placing quotation marks around any quoted material, citing your sources according to the documentation style you are using, and including them in a list of references or works cited. Material to be credited includes all of the following:

- *direct quotations*
- *facts not widely known or arguable statements*
- *judgments, opinions, and claims made by others*
- *images, statistics, charts, tables, graphs, or other illustrations* from any source
- *collaboration, the help provided by friends, colleagues, instructors, supervisors, or others*

(See Chapters 21 and 22 for more on using and documenting sources.)

Giving full credit to your sources needn't be awkward or interfere with the flow of your writing. Check out the way William Bennett smoothly weaves fully credited quotes into his article about patriotism.

LINK TO P. 854

USING COPYRIGHTED INTERNET SOURCES

If you've done any surfing on the Net, you already know that it opens the doors to worldwide collaborations, as you can contact individuals and groups around the globe and have access to whole libraries of information. As a result, writing (most especially, online writing) seems increasingly to be made up of a huge patchwork of materials that you alone or you and many others weave together. (For a fascinating discussion of just how complicated charges and countercharges of plagiarism can be on the Internet, see <ombuds.org/narrative1.html>, where you can read a description of a mediation involving a Web site that included summaries of other people's work.) But when you use information gathered from Internet sources in your own work, it is subject to the same rules that govern information gathered from other types of sources.

Thus, whether or not the material includes a copyright notice or symbol ("© 2004 by John J. Ruszkiewicz and Andrea A. Lunsford," for example), it is more than likely copyrighted—and you may need to request permission to use part or all of it. Although they are currently in danger, "fair use" laws still allow writers to quote brief passages from published works without permission from the copyright holder if the use is for educational or personal, noncommercial reasons and full credit is given to the source. For personal communication such as email or for listserv postings, however, you should ask permission of the writer before you include any of his or her material in your own argument. For graphics, photos, or other images you wish to reproduce in your text, you should also request permission from the creator or owner (except when you are using them in work only turned in to an instructor, which is "fair use"). And if you are going to disseminate your work beyond your classroom—especially by publishing it online—you must ask permission for any material you borrow from an Internet source.

Here are some examples of student requests for permission:

To: litman@mindspring.com
CC: lunsford.2@stanford.edu
Subject: Request for permission

Dear Professor Litman:

I am writing to request permission to quote from your essay "Copyright, Owners' Rights and Users' Privileges on the Internet: Implied Licences, Caching, Linking, Fair Use, and Sign-on Licences." I want to quote some of your work as part of an essay I am writing for my composition class at Stanford University to explain the complex debates over ownership on the Internet and to argue that students in my class should be participating in these debates. I will give full credit to you and will cite the URL where I first found your work: <msen.com/~litman/dayton/htm>.

Thank you very much for considering my request.

Raul Sanchez <sanchez.32@stanford.edu>

To: fridanet@aol.com
CC: lunsford.2@stanford.edu
Subject: Request for permission

Dear Kimberley Masters:

I am a student at Stanford University writing to request your permission to download and use a photograph of Frida Kahlo in a three-piece suit <fridanet/suit.htm#top> as an illustration in a project about Kahlo that I and two other students are working on in our composition class. In the report on our project, we will cite <members.aol.com/fridanet/kahlo.htm> as the URL, unless you wish for us to use a different source.

Thank you very much for considering our request.

Jennifer Fox <fox.360@stanford.edu>

ACKNOWLEDGING COLLABORATION

We have already noted the importance of acknowledging the inspirations and ideas you derive from talking with others. Such help counts as one form of collaboration, and you may also be involved in more formal kinds of collaborative work—preparing for a group presentation to a class, for example, or writing a group report. Writers generally acknowledge all participants in collaborative projects at the beginning of the presentation, report, or essay—in print texts, often in a footnote or brief prefatory note. The sixth edition of the *MLA Handbook for Writers of Research Papers* (2003) calls attention to the growing importance of collaborative work and gives the following advice on how to deal with issues of assigning fair credit all around:

Joint participation in research and writing is common and, in fact, encouraged in many courses and in many professions. It does not constitute plagiarism provided that credit is given for all contributions. One way to give credit, if roles were clearly demarcated or were unequal, is to state exactly who did what. Another way, especially if roles and contributions were merged and shared, is to acknowledge all concerned equally. Ask your instructor for advice if you are not certain how to acknowledge collaboration.

RESPOND.

1. Not everyone agrees with the concept of intellectual material as property, as something to be protected. Lately the slogan "information wants to be free" has been showing up in popular magazines and on the Internet, often along with a call to readers to take action against forms of protection such as data encryption and further extension of copyright.

   Using a Web search engine, look for pages where the phrase "free information" appears. Find several sites that make arguments in favor of free information, and analyze them in terms of their rhetorical appeals. What claims do the authors make? How do they appeal to their audience? What is the site's ethos, and how is it created? Once you have read some arguments in favor of free information, return to this chapter's arguments about intellectual property. Which do you find more persuasive? Why?

2. Although this text is principally concerned with ideas and their written expression, there are other forms of protection available for intellectual property. Scientific and technological developments are protectable under patent law, which differs in some significant ways from copyright law.

   Find the standards for protection under U.S. copyright law and U.S. patent law. You might begin by visiting the U.S. copyright Web site at <lcweb.loc.gov/copyright/>. Then, imagine that you are the president of a small, high-tech corporation and are trying to inform your employees of the legal protections available to them and their work. Write a paragraph or two explaining the differences between copyright and patent and suggesting a policy that balances employees' rights to intellectual property with the business's needs to develop new products.

3. Define plagiarism in your own terms, making your definition as clear and explicit as possible. Then compare your definition with those of two or three other classmates and write a brief report on the similarities and differences you noted in the definitions.

4. Spend fifteen or twenty minutes jotting down your ideas about intellectual property and plagiarism. Where do you stand, for example, on the issue of music file sharing? On downloading movies free of charge? Do you think these forms of intellectual property should be protected under copyright law? How do you define your own intellectual property, and in what ways and under what conditions are you willing to share it? Finally, come up with your own definition of "academic integrity."

chapter twenty-one

Evaluating and Using Sources

EVALUATING SOURCES

As many examples in this text have shown, the quality of an argument often depends on the quality of the sources used to support or prove it. As a result, careful evaluation and assessment of all your sources is important, including those you gather in libraries or from other print sources, in online searches, or in field research you conduct yourself.

Print Sources

Since you want the information you glean from sources to be reliable and persuasive, it pays to evaluate thoroughly each potential source. The following principles can help you in conducting such an evaluation for print sources:

- *Relevance.* Begin by asking what a particular source will add to your argument and how closely related to your argumentative claim it is. For a book, the table of contents and the index may help you decide. For an article, check to see if there is an abstract that summarizes the contents. And if you can't think of a good reason for using the source, set it aside; you can almost certainly find something better.

- *Credentials of the author.* You may find the author's credentials set forth in an article, book, or Web site, so be sure to look for a description of the author. Is the author an expert on the topic? To find out, you can also go to the Internet to gather information: Just open a search tool such as InfoSeek or AltaVista, and type in the name of the person you are looking for. Still another way to learn about the credibility of an author is to search Google Groups for postings that mention the author or to check the Citation Index to find out how others refer to this author. And if you see your source cited by other sources you are using, look at how they cite it and what they say about it that could provide clues to the author's credibility.

- *Stance of the author.* What is the author's stance on the issue(s) involved, and how does this stance influence the information in the source? Does the author's stance support or challenge your own views?

- *Credentials of the publisher or sponsor.* If your source is from a newspaper, is it a major one (such as the *San Francisco Chronicle* or the *New York Times*) that is known for integrity in reporting, or is it a tabloid? Is it a

FIGURE 21.1   NOTE THE DIFFERENCES BETWEEN THE *PEOPLE* MAGAZINE COVER AND THAT OF A LITERARY JOURNAL.

popular magazine like *People* or a journal sponsored by a professional group, such as the *Journal of the American Medical Association?* If your source is a book, is the publisher one you recognize or can find described on its own Web site?

- *Stance of the publisher or sponsor.* Sometimes the rhetorical stance of a source will be absolutely obvious: A Web site titled "Save the Spotted Owl" strongly suggests that the sponsor will take a pro-environmental stance, whereas the Web site for the Republican National Committee will certainly take a conservative stance. But other times, you need to read carefully between the lines to identify particular stances, so you can see how the stance affects the message the source presents. Start by asking what the source's goals are: what does the sponsoring group want to make happen?

- *Currency.* Check the date of publication of any book or article as well as the date of posting or updating on a Web source. (And remember that the publication dates of Internet sites can often be hard to pin down; most reliable will be those that are updated regularly.) Recent sources are often more useful than older ones, particularly in the sciences. However, in some fields such as history or literature, the most authoritative works can be the older ones.

- *Level of specialization.* General sources can be helpful as you begin your research, but later in the project you may need the authority or currency of more specialized sources. On the other hand, keep in mind that extremely specialized works on your topic may be too difficult for your audience to understand easily.

- *Audience.* Was the source written for a general readership? For specialists? For advocates or opponents?

- *Length.* Is the source long enough to provide adequate detail in support of your claim?

- *Availability.* Do you have access to the source? If it is not readily accessible, your time might be better spent looking elsewhere.

- *Omissions.* What is missing or omitted from the source? Might such exclusions affect whether or how you can use the source as evidence?

Electronic Sources

You will probably find working on the Internet and the World Wide Web both exciting and frustrating, for even though these tools have great potential, they still hold loads of suspect information. As a result, careful researchers look for corroboration before accepting evidence they find online, especially if it comes from a site whose sponsor's identity is less than clear. In such an environment, you must be the judge of how accurate and trustworthy particular electronic sources are. In making these judgments you should rely on the same kind of careful thinking you would use to assess any source. In addition, you may find some of the following questions helpful in evaluating online sources:

- Who has posted the document or message or created the site? An individual? An interest group? A company? A government agency? Does the URL offer any clues? Note especially the final suffix in a domain name: .com (commercial); .org (nonprofit organization); .edu (educational institution); .gov (government agency); .mil (military); .net (network)—or the geographical domains that indicate country of origin, as in .ca (Canada) or .ar (Argentina). The home page or first page of a site should tell you something about the sponsorship of the source, letting you know who can be held accountable for its information. (You may need to click on an "About Us" button.) Finally, links may help you learn how credible and useful the source is. Click on some of them to see if they lead to legitimate and helpful sites.

- What can you determine about the credibility of the author or sponsor? Can the information in the document or site be verified in other sources? How accurate and complete is it?

- Who can be held accountable for the information in the document or site? How well and thoroughly does it credit its own sources?

- How current is the document or site? Be especially cautious of undated materials. Most reliable will be those that are updated regularly.

- How effectively is the document or site designed? How "friendly" is it? Are its links, if any, helpful? What effects do design, visuals, and/or sound have on the message? (See Chapters 15 and 16.)

- What perspectives are represented? If only one perspective is represented, how can you balance or expand this point of view?

At a recent conference, the Stanford Persuasive Technology Lab argued that Google News may soon be the "most credible Web site of them all." The Lab listed twenty-five reasons in support of this conclusion, from the timeliness of the information, to the lack of a single viewpoint or ideology, to the ad-free policy. The next time you log on to Google News, ask yourself what other features of this site help build its credibility.

Field Research

If you have conducted experiments, surveys, interviews, observations, or any other field research in developing and supporting an argument, make sure to review your own results with a critical eye. The following questions can help you evaluate your own field research:

- Have you rechecked all data and all conclusions to make sure they are accurate and warranted?

- Have you identified the exact time, place, and participants in all field research?

- Have you made clear what part you played in the research and how, if at all, your role could have influenced the results or findings?

- If your research involved other people, have you gotten their permission to use their words or other material in your argument? Have you asked whether you could use their names or whether the names should be kept confidential?

USING SOURCES

As you locate, examine, and evaluate sources in support of an argument, remember to keep a careful record of where you have found them. For print sources, you may want to keep a working bibliography on your computer—or a list in a notebook you can carry with you. In any case, make sure you take down the *name of the author*; the *title* of the book or periodical and article, if any; the *publisher* and *city of publication*; the *date of publication*; relevant *volume, issue,* and exact *page numbers*; and any other information you may later need in preparing a works-cited or references list. In addition, for a book, note where you found it—the section of the library, for example, along with the call number for the book.

For electronic sources, you should also keep a careful record of the information you will need in your works-cited or references list—particularly the *name of the database or online source*, the full *electronic address (URL)*, and several potentially important dates: (1) the *date the document was first produced*; (2) the *date the document was published on the Web*—this may be a version number or a revision date; and (3) the *date you accessed the document*. The simplest way to ensure that you have this information is to get a printout of the source, highlighting source information and writing down any other pertinent information.

Signal Words and Introductions

Because your sources are crucial to the success of your arguments, you need to introduce them carefully to your readers. Doing so usually calls for beginning a sentence in which you are going to use a source with a signal phrase of some kind: *According to noted child psychiatrist Robert Coles, children develop complex ethical systems at extremely young ages.* In this sentence, the signal phrase tells readers that you are about to draw on the work of a person named Robert Coles and that this person is a "noted child psychiatrist." Now look at an example that uses a quotation from a source in more than one sentence:

> In *Job Shift*, consultant William Bridges worries about "dejobbing and about what a future shaped by it is going to be like." Even more worrisome, Bridges argues, is the possibility that "the sense of craft and of professional vocation . . . will break down under the need to earn a fee" (228).

The signal verbs "worries" and "argues" add a sense of urgency to the message Bridges offers and suggest that the writer either agrees with—or is neutral about—Bridges's points. Other signal verbs have a more negative slant, indicating that the point being introduced in the quotation is open to debate and that others (including the writer) might disagree with it. If the writer of the passage above had said, for instance, that Bridges "unreasonably contends" or that he "fantasizes," these signal verbs would carry quite different connotations from those associated with "argues." In some cases, a signal verb may require more complex phrasing to get the writer's full meaning across:

> Bridges recognizes the dangers of changes in work yet refuses to be overcome by them: "The real issue is not how to stop the change but how to provide the necessary knowledge and skills to equip people to operate successfully in this New World" (229).

As these examples illustrate, the signal verb is important because it allows you to characterize the author's or source's viewpoint or perspective as well as your own—so choose these verbs with care. Other frequently used signal verbs include *acknowledges, advises, agrees, allows, asserts, believes, charges, claims, concludes, concurs, confirms, criticizes, declares, disagrees, discusses, disputes, emphasizes, expresses, interprets, lists, objects, observes, offers, opposes, remarks, replies, reports, responds, reveals, states, suggests, thinks,* and *writes.*

Quotations

For supporting argumentative claims, you will want to quote—that is, to reproduce an author's precise words—in at least three kinds of situations: when the wording is so memorable or expresses a point so well that you cannot improve it or shorten it without weakening it; when the author is a respected authority whose opinion supports your own ideas particularly well; and when an author challenges or disagrees profoundly with others in the field.

Direct quotations can be effective in capturing your readers' attention—for example, through quoting a memorable phrase in your introduction or quoting an eyewitness account in arresting detail. In an argument, quotations from respected authorities can help build your ethos as someone who has sought out experts in the field. Finally, carefully chosen quotations can broaden the appeal of your argument by drawing on emotion as well as logic, appealing to the reader's mind and heart. A student writing on the ethical issues of bullfighting, for example, might introduce an argument that bullfighting is not a sport by quoting Ernest Hemingway's comment that "the formal bull-fight is a tragedy, not a sport, and the bull is certain to be killed," and might accompany the quotation with an image such as the one below:

FIGURE 21.2 BULLFIGHT

The following guidelines can help you make sure that you quote accurately:

- If the quotation extends over more than one page in the original source, note the placement of page breaks in case you decide to use only part of the quotation in your argument.

- Label the quotation with a note that tells you where and/or how you think you will use it.

- Make sure you have all the information necessary to create an in-text citation as well as an item in your works-cited or references list.

- When you use a quotation in your argument, make sure you have introduced the author(s) of the quotation and that you follow the quotation with some commentary of your own that points out the significance of the quotation.

- Copy quotations carefully, being sure that punctuation, capitalization, and spelling are exactly as they are in the original.

- Enclose the quotation in quotation marks; don't rely on your memory to distinguish your own words from those of your source. If in doubt, recheck all quotations for accuracy.

- Use square brackets if you introduce words of your own into the quotation or make changes to it. (*"And [more] brain research isn't going to define further the matter of 'mind.'"*)

- Use ellipsis marks if you omit material. (*"And brain research isn't going to define . . . the matter of 'mind.'"*)

- If you're quoting a short passage (four lines or less, MLA style; forty words or less, APA style), it should be worked into your text, enclosed by quotation marks. Longer quotations should be set off from the regular text. Begin such a quotation on a new line, indenting every line one inch or ten spaces (MLA) or five to seven spaces (APA). Set-off quotations do not need to be enclosed in quotation marks.

CULTURAL CONTEXTS FOR ARGUMENT

Although some language communities and cultures expect audiences to recognize the sources of important documents and texts, thereby eliminating the need to cite them directly, conventions for writing in North America call for careful attribution of any quoted, paraphrased, or summarized material. When in doubt, explicitly identify your sources.

Paraphrases

Paraphrases involve putting an author's material (including major and minor points, usually in the order they are presented in the original) into *your own words and sentence structures*. Here are some guidelines that can help you paraphrase accurately:

- When you use a paraphrase in your argument, make sure that you identify the source of the paraphrase and that you comment on its significance.
- Make sure you have all the information necessary to create an in-text citation as well as an item in your works-cited or references list. For online sources without page numbers, record the paragraph, screen, or other section number(s) if indicated.
- If you are paraphrasing material that extends over more than one page in the original source, note the placement of page breaks in case you decide to use only part of the paraphrase in your argument.
- Label the paraphrase with a note suggesting where and/or how you intend to use it in your argument.
- Include all main points and any important details from the original source, in the same order in which the author presents them.
- Leave out your own comments, elaborations, or reactions.
- State the meaning in your own words and sentence structures. If you want to include especially memorable or powerful language from the original source, enclose it in quotation marks.
- Recheck to make sure that the words and sentence structures are your own and that they express the author's meaning accurately.

Summaries

A summary is a significantly shortened version of a passage—or even a whole chapter of a work—that captures the main ideas *in your own words*. Unlike a paraphrase, a summary uses just enough information to record the points you want to emphasize. Summaries can be extremely valuable in supporting arguments. Here are some guidelines to help you prepare accurate and helpful summaries:

- When you use a summary in an argument, be sure to identify the source of the summary and add your own comments about why the material in the summary is significant for the argument you are making.

- Make sure you have all the information necessary to create an in-text citation as well as an item in your works-cited or references list. For online sources without page numbers, record the paragraph, screen, or other section number(s) if available.
- If you are summarizing material that extends over more than one page, indicate page breaks in case you decide to use only part of the summary in your argument.
- Label the summary with a note that suggests where and/or how you intend to use it in your argument.
- Include just enough information to recount the main points you want to cite. A summary is usually much shorter than the original.
- Use your own words. If you include any language from the original, enclose it in quotation marks.
- Recheck to make sure that you have captured the author's meaning accurately and that the wording is entirely your own.

Visuals

If a picture is worth a thousand words, then using pictures calls for caution: one picture might overwhelm or undermine the message you are trying to send in your argument. On the other hand, as you've seen in Chapter 15, visuals can have a powerful impact on audiences and can help bring them to understand or accept your arguments. In choosing visuals to include in your argument, make sure that each one makes a strong contribution to your message and that each is appropriate and fair to your subject or topic and your audience.

When you use a visual in your written arguments, treat them as you would any other sources you integrate into your text. Like quotations, paraphrases, and summaries, visuals need to be introduced and commented on in some way. In addition, label (as figures or as tables) and number (Figure 1, Figure 2, and so on) all visuals, provide a caption that includes source information and describes the visual, and cite the source in your bibliography or list of works cited. Keep in mind that even if you create a visual (such as a bar graph) by using information from a source (the results, say, of a Gallup Poll), you must cite the source. If you use a photograph you took yourself, cite it as a personal photograph.

Here is a visual that accompanied the introduction to an argument about bankruptcy that appeared on the front page of the December 15, 2002, *New York Times* Business section. Note that the source of the visual is

FIGURE 21.3 A LAWYER WITH A BINDER OF PAPERWORK INVOLVING THE US AIRWAYS BANKRUPTCY FILING. COMPANIES CAN LOSE CONSIDERABLE VALUE DURING THE CHAPTER 11 PROCESS. (SOURCE: BLOOMBERG NEWS)

listed (Bloomberg News) and that the caption indicates in what way the visual is related to the argument (in this case, the visual depicts bankruptcy papers). If you were going to use this as the first visual in an essay of your own, you would need to include the source, describe the image in relationship to your topic, and head it *Figure 1*. As long as you are using this image in a print text only, you are allowed fair use of it. If you intend to post your argument on the Web, however, or otherwise publish it, you would need to request permission from the copyright owner (see Chapter 20, page 408).

RESPOND●

1. Select one of the essays at the end of Chapters 9 to 13. Then write a brief summary of the essay that includes both direct quotations and paraphrases. Be careful to attribute the ideas properly, even when you paraphrase, and to use signal phrases to introduce quotations.

Trade summaries with a partner, and compare the passages you selected to quote and paraphrase, and the signal phrases you used to introduce them. How do your choices create an ethos for the original author that differs from the one your partner has created? How do the signal phrases shape a reader's sense of the author's position? Which summary best represents the author's argument? Why?

2. Return to the Internet sites you found in exercise 1 of Chapter 20 that discuss free information. Using the criteria in this chapter for evaluating electronic sources, judge each of those sites. Select three that you think are most trustworthy, and write a paragraph summarizing their arguments and recommending them to an audience unfamiliar with the debate.

3. Choose a Web site that you visit frequently. Then, using the guidelines discussed in this chapter, spend some time evaluating its credibility. You might begin by comparing it with Google News or another site that has a reputation for being extremely reliable.

chapter twenty-two

Documenting Sources

What does documenting sources have to do with argument? First, the sources themselves form part of the argument, showing that a writer has done some homework, knows what others have said about the topic, and understands how to use these sources as support for a claim. The list of works cited or references makes an argument, saying, perhaps, "Look at how thoroughly this essay has been researched" or "Note how up-to-date I am!" Even the style of documentation makes an argument, though in a very subtle way. You will note in the instructions that follow, for example, that for a print source the Modern Language Association (MLA) style for a list of works cited requires putting the date of publication at or near the end of an entry, whereas the American Psychological Association (APA) style for a list of references involves putting the date near the beginning. (An exercise at the end of this chapter asks you to consider what argument this difference represents.) And when a documentation style calls for listing only the first author followed by "et al." in citing works by multiple authors, it is subtly arguing that only the first author really matters—or at least that acknowledging the others is less important than keeping citations brief. Pay attention to the fine points of documentation and documentation style, always asking what these elements add (or do not add) to your arguments.

MLA STYLE

Documentation styles vary from discipline to discipline, with different formats favored in the social sciences and the natural sciences, for example. Widely used in the humanities, the MLA style is fully described in the *MLA Handbook for Writers of Research Papers* (6th edition, 2003). In this discussion, we provide guidelines drawn from the *MLA Handbook* for in-text citations, notes, and entries in the list of works cited.

FIGURE 22.1 THE *MLA HANDBOOK FOR WRITERS OF RESEARCH PAPERS*

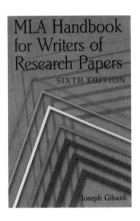

In-Text Citations

MLA style calls for in-text citations in the body of an argument to document sources of quotations, paraphrases, summaries, and so on. For in-text citations, use a signal phrase to introduce the material, often with the author's name (*As LaDoris Cordell explains . . .*). Keep an in-text citation short, but include enough information for readers to locate the source in the list of works cited. Place the parenthetical citation as near to the relevant material as possible without disrupting the flow of the sentence, as in the following examples.

The essay by La Donna Beaty uses MLA style.

LINK TO P. 226 ·

1. *Author Named in a Signal Phrase*

Ordinarily, use the author's name in a signal phrase—to introduce the material—and cite the page number(s) in parentheses.

> Loomba argues that Caliban's "political colour" is black, given his stage representations, which have varied from animalistic to a kind of missing link (143).

2. Author Named in Parentheses

When you don't mention the author in a signal phrase, include the author's last name before the page number(s) in the parentheses.

> Renaissance visions of "other" worlds, particularly in plays and travel narratives, often accentuated the differences of the Other even when striking similarities to the English existed (Bartels 434).

3. Two or Three Authors

Use all authors' last names.

> Gortner, Hebrun, and Nicolson maintain that "opinion leaders" influence other people in an organization because they are respected, not because they hold high positions (175).

4. Four or More Authors

The MLA allows you to use all authors' last names, or to use only the first author's name with *et al.* (in regular type, not underlined or italicized). Although either format is acceptable when applied consistently throughout a paper, in an argument it may be better to name all authors who contributed to the work.

> Similarly, as Goldberger, Tarule, Clinchy, and Belenky note, their new book builds on their collaborative experiences (xii).

5. Organization as Author

Give the full name of a corporate author if it is brief or a shortened form if it is long.

> In fact, one of the leading foundations in the field of higher education supports the recent proposals for community-run public schools (Carnegie Corporation 45).

6. Unknown Author

Use the full title of the work if it is brief or a shortened form if it is long.

> "Hype," by one analysis, is "an artificially engendered atmosphere of hysteria" ("Today's Marketplace" 51).

7. Author of Two or More Works

When you use two or more works by the same author, include the title of the work or shortened version of it in the citation.

> Gardner presents readers with their own silliness through his description of a "pointless, ridiculous monster, crouched in the shadows, stinking of dead men, murdered children, and martyred cows" (Grendel 2).

8. Authors with the Same Last Name

When you use works by two or more authors with the same last name, include each author's first initial in the in-text citation.

> Father Divine's teachings focused on eternal life, salvation, and socio-economic progress (R. Washington 17).

9. Multivolume Work

Note the volume number first and then the page number(s), with a colon and one space between them.

> Aristotle's "On Plants" is now available in a new translation, edited by Barnes (2: 1252).

10. Literary Work

Because literary works are often available in many different editions, you need to include enough information for readers to locate the passage in any edition. For a prose work such as a novel or play, first cite the page number from the edition you used, followed by a semicolon; then indicate the part or chapter number (114; ch. 3) or act or scene in a play (42; sc. 2). For verse plays, omit the page number and give instead the act, scene, and line numbers, separated by periods.

> Before he takes his own life, Othello says he is "one that loved not wisely but too well" (5.2.348).

For a poem, cite the stanza and line numbers. If the poem has only line numbers, use the word line(s) in the first reference (lines 33–34).

> On dying, Whitman speculates "All that goes onward and outward, nothing collapses, / And to die is different from what any one supposed, and luckier" (6.129-30).

For a verse play, give only the act, scene, and line numbers, separated by periods.

> As Macbeth begins, the witches greet Banquo as "Lesser than Macbeth, and greater" (1.3.65).

11. Works in an Anthology

For an essay, short story, or other short work within an anthology, use the name of the author of the work, not the editor of the anthology; but use the page number(s) from the anthology.

> In the end, if the black artist accepts any duties at all, that duty is to express the beauty of blackness (Hughes 1271).

12. Sacred Text

To cite a sacred text, such as the Qur'an or the Bible, give the title of the edition you used, the book, and the chapter and verse (or their equivalent), separated by a period. In your text, spell out the names of books. In a parenthetical reference, use an abbreviation for books with names of five or more letters (*Gen.* for *Genesis*).

> He ignored the admonition "Pride goes before destruction, and a haughty spirit before a fall" (New Oxford Annotated Bible, Prov. 16.18).

13. Indirect Source

Use the abbreviation *qtd. in* to indicate that what you are quoting or paraphrasing is quoted (as part of a conversation, interview, letter, or excerpt) in the source you are using.

> As Catherine Belsey states, "to speak is to have access to the language which defines, delimits and locates power" (qtd. in Bartels 453).

14. Two or More Sources in the Same Citation

Separate the information for each source with a semicolon.

> Adefunmi was able to patch up the subsequent holes left in worship by substituting various Yoruba, Dahomean, or Fon customs made available to him through research (Brandon 115-17; Hunt 27).

15. Entire Work or One-Page Article

Include the citation in the text without any page numbers or parentheses.

> The relationship between revolutionary innocence and the preservation of an oppressive post-revolutionary regime is one theme Milan Kundera explores in <u>The Book of Laughter and Forgetting</u>.

16. *Work without Page Numbers*

If the work is not paginated but has another kind of numbered section, such as parts or paragraphs, include the name and number(s) of the section(s) you are citing. (For paragraphs, use the abbreviation *par.* or *pars.*; for section, use *sec.*; for part, use *pt.*)

> Zora Neale Hurston is one of the great anthropologists of the twentieth century, according to Kip Hinton (par. 2).

17. *Electronic or Nonprint Source*

Give enough information in a signal phrase or parenthetical citation for readers to locate the source in the list of works cited. Usually give the author or title under which you list the source.

> In his film version of <u>Hamlet</u>, Zefferelli highlights the sexual tension between the prince and his mother.

> Describing children's language acquisition, Pinker explains that "what's innate about language is just a way of paying attention to parental speech" (Johnson, sec. 1).

Explanatory and Bibliographic Notes

The MLA recommends using explanatory notes for information or commentary that does not readily fit into your text but is needed for clarification, further explanation, or justification. In addition, the MLA allows bibliographic notes for citing several sources for one point and for offering thanks to, information about, or evaluation of a source. Use superscript numbers in your text at the end of a sentence to refer readers to the notes, which usually appear as endnotes (with the heading *Notes*) on a separate page before the list of works cited. Indent the first line of each note five spaces, and double-space all entries.

Text with Superscript Indicating a Note

> Stewart emphasizes the existence of social contacts in Hawthorne's life so that the audience will accept a different Hawthorne, one more attuned to modern times than the figure in Woodberry.[3]

Note

> ³ Woodberry does, however, show that Hawthorne was often unsociable. He emphasizes the seclusion of Hawthorne's mother, who separated herself from her family after the death of her husband, often even taking meals alone (28). Woodberry seems to imply that Mrs. Hawthorne's isolation rubbed off onto her son.

List of Works Cited

A list of works cited is an alphabetical listing of the sources you cite in your essay. The list appears on a separate page at the end of your argument, after any notes, with the heading *Works Cited* centered an inch from the top of the page; do not underline or italicize it or enclose it in quotation marks. Double-space between the heading and the first entry, and double-space the entire list. (If you are asked to list everything you have read as background—not just the sources you cite—call the list *Works Consulted*.)

The first line of each entry should align on the left; subsequent lines indent one-half inch or five spaces. See page 442 for a sample Works Cited page.

Books

The basic information for a book includes three elements, each followed by a period:

- the author's name, last name first
- the title and subtitle, underlined
- and the publication information, including the city, a shortened form of the publisher's name, and the date.

For a book with multiple authors, only the first author's name is inverted.

1. One Author

Castle, Terry. <u>Boss Ladies, Watch Out: Essays on Women, Sex, and Writing</u>. New York: Routledge, 2002.

2. Two or More Authors

Appleby, Joyce, Lynn Hunt, and Margaret Jacob. <u>Telling the Truth about History</u>. New York: Norton, 1994.

3. *Organization as Author*

> American Horticultural Society. The Fully Illustrated Plant-by-Plant Manual of Practical Techniques. New York: American Horticultural Society and DK Publishing, 1999.

4. *Unknown Author*

> National Geographic Atlas of the World. New York: National Geographic, 1999.

5. *Two or More Books by the Same Author*

List the works alphabetically by title.

> Lorde, Audre. A Burst of Light. Ithaca: Firebrand, 1988.
>
> ---. Sister Outsider. Trumansburg: Crossing, 1984.

6. *Editor*

> Rorty, Amelie Oksenberg, ed. Essays on Aristotle's Poetics. Princeton: Princeton UP, 1992.

7. *Author and Editor*

> Shakespeare, William. The Tempest. Ed. Frank Kermode. London: Routledge, 1994.

8. *Selection in an Anthology or Chapter in an Edited Book*

> Brown, Paul. "'This thing of darkness I acknowledge mine': The Tempest and the Discourse of Colonialism." Political Shakespeare: Essays in Cultural Materialism. Ed. Jonathan Dillimore and Alan Sinfield. Ithaca: Cornell UP, 1985. 48-71.

9. *Two or More Works from the Same Anthology*

> Gates, Henry Louis, Jr., and Nellie McKay, eds. The Norton Anthology of African American Literature. New York: Norton, 1997.
>
> Neal, Larry. "The Black Arts Movement." Gates and McKay 1960-72.
>
> Karenga, Maulana. "Black Art: Mute Matter Given Force and Function." Gates and McKay 1973-77.

10. Translation

Zamora, Martha. Frida Kahlo: The Brush of Anguish. Trans. Marilyn Sode Smith. San Francisco: Chronicle, 1990.

11. Edition Other than the First

Lunsford, Andrea, John Ruszkiewicz, and Keith Walters. Everything's an Argument. 3rd ed. New York: Bedford/St.Martin's, 2004.

12. One Volume of a Multivolume Work

Byron, Lord George. Byron's Letters and Journals. Ed. Leslie A. Marchand. Vol. 2. London: J. Murray, 1973-1982.

13. Two or More Volumes of a Multivolume Work

Byron, Lord George. Byron's Letters and Journals. Ed. Leslie A. Marchand. 12 vols. London: J. Murray, 1973-1982.

14. Preface, Foreword, Introduction, or Afterword

Hymes, Dell. Foreword. Beyond Ebonics: Linguistic Pride and Racial Prejudice. By John Baugh. New York: Oxford, 2000. vii-viii.

15. Article in a Reference Work

West, William W. "Memory." Encyclopedia of Rhetoric. Ed. Thomas O. Sloane. New York: Oxford, 2001. 482-93.

"Hero." Merriam-Webster's Collegiate Dictionary. 10th ed. 1996.

16. Book That Is Part of a Series

Moss, Beverly J. A Community Text Arises. Language and Social Processes Ser. 8. Cresskill: Hampton, 2003.

17. Republication

Scott, Walter. Kenilworth. 1821. New York: Dodd, 1996.

18. Government Document

United States. Cong. House Committee on the Judiciary. Impeachment of the President. 40th Cong., 1st sess. H. Rept. 7. Washington: GPO, 1867.

19. Pamphlet

An Answer to the President's Message to the Fiftieth Congress. Philadelphia: Manufacturer's Club of Philadelphia, 1887.

20. Published Proceedings of a Conference

Edwards, Ron, ed. Proceedings of the Third National Folklore Conference. Canberra, Austral.: Australian Folk Trust, 1988.

21. Title within a Title

Tauernier-Courbin, Jacqueline. Ernest Hemingway's A Moveable Feast: The Making of a Myth. Boston: Northeastern UP, 1991.

Periodicals

The basic entry for a periodical includes the following three elements, separated by periods:

- the author's name, last name first
- the article title, in quotation marks
- and the publication information, including the periodical title (underlined), the volume and issue numbers (if any), the date of publication, and the page number(s).

For works with multiple authors, only the first author's name is inverted. Note, too, that the period following the article title goes inside the closing quotation mark.

22. Article in a Journal Paginated by Volume

Anderson, Virginia. "'The Perfect Enemy': Clinton, the Contradictions of Capitalism, and Slaying the Sin Within." Rhetoric Review 21 (2002): 384-400.

23. Article in a Journal Paginated by Issue

Radavich, David. "Man among Men: David Mamet's Homosocial Order." American Drama 1.1 (1991): 46-66.

24. Article in a Monthly Magazine

Wallraff, Barbara. "Word Count." The Atlantic Nov. 2002: 144-45.

25. Article in a Weekly Magazine

Dorfman, Andrea. "A Tree Hugger's Delight." Time 14 Oct. 2002: 58-59.

26. Article in a Newspaper

Friend, Tim. "Scientists Map the Mouse Genome." USA Today 2 Dec. 2002: A1.

27. Editorial or Letter to Editor

Danto, Arthur. "'Elitism' and the N.E.A." Editorial. The Nation 17 Nov. 1997: 6-7.

Judson, Judith. Letter. Washington Post 12 Mar. 2003: A20.

28. Unsigned Article

"Court Rejects the Sale of Medical Marijuana." New York Times 26 Feb. 1998, late ed.: A21.

29. Review

Partner, Peter. "The Dangers of Divinity." Rev. of The Shape of the Holy: Early Islamic Jerusalem, by Oleg Grabar. New York Review of Books 5 Feb. 1998: 27-28.

Electronic Sources

Most of the following models are based on the MLA's guidelines for citing electronic sources in the *MLA Handbook* (6th edition, 2003), as well as on up-to-date information available at <mla.org/>.

The MLA requires that URLs be enclosed in angle brackets. Also, if a URL will not all fit on one line, it should be broken only after a slash. If a particular URL is extremely complicated, you can instead give the URL for the site's search page, if it exists, or for the site's home page.

The basic MLA entry for most electronic sources should include the following elements:

- name of the author, editor, or compiler
- title of the work, document, or posting
- information for print publication, if any
- information for electronic publication

- date of access
- URL in angle brackets

30. *CD-ROM, Diskette, or Magnetic Tape, Single Issue*

> McPherson, James M., ed. <u>The American Heritage New History of the Civil War</u>. CD-ROM. New York: Viking, 1996.

31. *Periodically Revised CD-ROM*

Include the author's name; publication information for the print version of the text (including its title and date of publication); the title of the database; the medium (CD-ROM); the name of the company producing it; and the electronic publication date (month and year, if possible).

> Heyman, Steven. "The Dangerously Exciting Client." <u>Psychotherapy Patient</u> 9.1 (1994): 37-46. <u>PsycLIT</u>. CD-ROM. SilverPlatter. Nov. 1996.

32. *Multidisc CD-ROM*

> <u>The 1998 Grolier Multimedia Encyclopedia</u>. CD-ROM. 2 discs. Danbury: Grolier Interactive, 1999.

33. *Document from a Web Site*

When possible, include the author's name; title of the document; print publication information; electronic publication information; date of access; and the URL.

> "A History of Women's Writing." <u>The Orlando Project: An Integrated History of Women's Writing in the British Isles</u>. 2000. U of Alberta. 14 Mar. 2003 <http://www.ualberta.ca/ORLANDO/>.

34. *Entire Web Site*

Include the name of the person or group who created the site, if relevant; the title of the site (underlined) or (if there is no title) a description such as *Home page*; the electronic publication date or last update, if available; the name of any institution or organization associated with the site; the date of access; and the URL.

> Bowman, Laurel. <u>Classical Myth: The Ancient Source</u>. Dept. of Greek and Roman Studies, U of Victoria. 7 Mar. 2000 <http://web.uvic.ca/grs/bowman/myth>.

Mitten, Lisa. The Mascot Issue. 8 Apr. 2002. American Indian Library
Assn. 12 Sept. 2002 <http://www.nativeculture.com/lisamitten/
mascots.html>.

35. Course, Department, or Personal Web Site

Include the Web site's author; name of the site; description of site (such
as *Course home page, Dept. home page,* or *Home page*); dates for the course;
date of publication or last update; name of academic department, if relevant; date of access; and the URL.

Lunsford, Andrea A. "Memory and Media." Course home page. Sept.-
Dec. 2002. Dept. of English, Stanford U. 13 Mar. 2003 <http://
www.stanford.edu/class/english12sc>.

Lunsford, Andrea A. Home page. 15 Mar. 2003 <http://www.stanford.edu/
~lunsfor1/>.

36. Online Book

Begin with the name of the author—or, if only an editor, a compiler, or a
translator is identified, the name of that person followed by *ed., comp.,* or
trans. Then give the title and the name of any editor, compiler, or translator
not listed earlier, preceded by *Ed., Comp.,* or *Trans.* If the online version of
the text has not been published before, give the date of electronic publication and the name of any sponsoring institution or organization. Then give
any publication information (city, publisher, and/or year) for the original
print version that is given in the source; the date of access; and the URL.

Riis, Jacob A. How the Other Half Lives: Studies among the Tenements
of New York. Ed. David Phillips. New York: Scribner's, 1890. 26
Mar. 1998 <http://www.cis.yale.edu/amstud/Inforev/riis/title.html>.

For a poem, essay, or other short work within an online book, include its
title after the author's name. Give the URL of the short work, not of the
book, if they differ.

Dickinson, Emily. "The Grass." Poems: Emily Dickinson. Boston: Roberts
Brothers, 1891. Humanities Text Initiative American Verse Collection. Ed. Nancy Kushigian. 1995. U of Michigan. 9 Oct. 1997
<http://www.planet.net/pkrisxle/emily/poemsOnline.html>.

37. Article in an Online Periodical

Follow the formats for citing articles in print periodicals, but adapt them
as necessary to the online medium. Include the page numbers of the arti-

cle or the total number of pages, paragraphs, parts, or other numbered sections, if any; the date of access; and the URL.

> Johnson, Eric. "The 10,000-Word Question: Using Images on the World-Wide Web." Kairos 4.1 (1999). 20 Mar. 2003 <http://english.ttu.edu/kairos/4.1/>.

> Walsh, Joan. "The Ugly Truth about Republican Racial Politics." Salon 15 Dec. 2002. 3 Jan. 2003 <http://www.salon.com/politics/feature/2002/12/14/race/index_np.html>.

38. *Posting to a Discussion Group*

Begin with the author's name, the title of the posting, the description *Online posting*, and the date of the posting. For a listserv posting, give the name of the listserv, the date of access, and either the URL of the listserv or (preferably) the URL of an archival version of the posting. If a URL is unavailable, give the email address of the list moderator. For a newsgroup posting, end with the date of access and the name of the newsgroup, in angle brackets.

> "Web Publishing and Censorship." Online posting. 2 Feb. 1997. ACW: Alliance for Computers and Writing Discussion List. 10 Oct. 1997 <http://english.ttu.edu/acw-1/archive.htm>.

> Martin, Jerry. "The IRA & Sinn Fein." Online posting. 31 Mar. 1998. 31 Mar. 1998 <news:soc.culture.irish>.

39. *Work from an Online Subscription Service*

For a work from an online service to which your library subscribes, list the information about the work, followed by the name of the service, the library, the date of access, and the URL.

> "Breaking the Dieting Habit: Drug Therapy for Eating Disorders." Pschyology Today Mar 1995: 12+. Electric Lib. Green Lib., Stanford, CA. 30 Nov. 2002 <http://www.elibrary.com/>.

If you are citing an article from a subscription service to which you subscribe (such as AOL), use the following model:

> Weeks, W. William. "Beyond the Ark." Nature Conservancy. Mar.-Apr. 1999. America Online. 30 Nov. 2002. Keyword: Ecology.

40. Email Message

Include the writer's name, the subject line, the description *Email to the author* or *Email to [the recipient's name]*, and the date of the message.

Moller, Marilyn. "Seeing _Crowns_." Email to Beverly Moss. 3 Jan. 2003.

41. Synchronous Communication (MOO, MUD, or IRC)

Include the name of any specific speaker(s) you are citing; a description of the event; its date; the name of the forum; the date of access; and the URL of the posting (with the prefix *telnet:*) or (preferably) of an archival version.

Patuto, Jeremy, Simon Fennel, and James Goss. The Mytilene debate. 9 May 1996. MiamiMOO. 28 Mar. 1998 <http://moo.cas.muohio.edu>.

42. Online Interview, Work of Art, or Film

Follow the general guidelines for the print version of the source, but also include information on the electronic medium, such as publication information for a CD-ROM or the date of electronic publication, the date of access, and the URL for a Web site.

McGray, Douglas. Interview with Andrew Marshall. Wired. Feb. 2003. 17 Mar. 2003 <http://www.wired.com/wired/archive/11.02/marshall.html>.

Aleni, Guilio. K'un-yu t'u-shu. ca. 1620. Vatican, Rome. 28 Mar. 1998 <http://www.ncsa.uiuc.edu/SDG/Experimental/vatican.exhibit/exhibit/full-images/i-rome-to-china/china02.gif>.

Harry Potter and the Chamber of Secrets. Dir. Chris Columbus. 16 Dec. 2002 <http://movies.go.com/movies/H/harrypotterandthechamberofsecrets_2002/>.

43. FTP (File Transfer Protocol), Telnet, or Gopher Site

Substitute *FTP*, *telnet*, or *gopher* for *http* at the beginning of the URL.

Korn, Peter. "How Much Does Breast Cancer Really Cost?" Self Oct. 1994. 5 May 1997 <gopher://nysernet.org:70/00/BCTC/Sources/SELF/94/how-much>.

Other Sources

44. *Unpublished Dissertation*

Fishman, Jenn. "'The Active Republic of Literature': Performance and Literary Culture in Britain, 1656-1790." Diss. Stanford U, 2003.

45. *Published Dissertation*

Baum, Bernard. Decentralization of Authority in a Bureaucracy. Diss. U of Chicago. Englewood Cliffs: Prentice-Hall, 1961.

46. *Article from a Microform*

Sharpe, Lora. "A Quilter's Tribute." Boston Globe 25 Mar. 1989: 13. Newsbank: Social Relations 12 (1989): fiche 6, grids B4-6.

47. *Personal and Published Interview*

Royster, Jacqueline Jones. Personal interview. 2 Feb. 2003.

Schorr, Daniel. Interview. Weekend Edition. Natl. Public Radio. KQED, San Francisco. 23 Dec. 2002.

48. *Letter*

Jacobs, Harriet. "Letter to Amy Post." 4 Apr. 1853. Incidents in the Life of a Slave Girl. Ed. Jean Fagan Yellin. Cambridge: Harvard UP, 1987. 234-35.

49. *Film*

The Lord of the Rings: The Two Towers. Dir. Peter Jackson. Perf. Elijah Wood, Ian McKellan. New Line Cinema, 2002.

50. *Television or Radio Program*

Box Office Bombshell: Marilyn Monroe. Nar. Peter Graves. Writ. Andy Thomas, Jeff Schefel, and Kevin Burns. Dir. Bill Harris. A&E Biography. Arts and Entertainment Network. 23 Oct. 2002.

51. *Sound Recording*

Fugees. "Ready or Not." The Score. Sony, 1996.

52. *Work of Art or Photograph*

Kahlo, Frida. Self-Portrait with Cropped Hair. 1940. Museum of Modern Art, New York.

53. *Lecture or Speech*

Condoleezza Rice. Baccalaureate Address. Stanford University. 18 June 2002.

54. *Performance*

Freak. By John Leguizamo. Dir. David Bar Katz. Cort Theater, New York. 7 Mar. 1998.

55. *Map or Chart*

The Political and Physical World. Map. Washington: Natl. Geographic, 1975.

56. *Cartoon*

Brodner, Steve. Cartoon. Nation 31 Mar. 2003: 2.

57. *Advertisement*

Chevy Avalanche. Advertisement. Time 14 Oct. 2002: 104.

On page 441, note the formatting of the first page of a sample essay written in MLA style. On page 442, you will find a sample Works Cited page written for this same student essay.

SAMPLE FIRST PAGE FOR AN ESSAY IN MLA STYLE

Lesk 1

Emily Lesk
Professor Arraéz
Electric Rhetoric
November 15, 2002

Red, White, and Everywhere

America, I have a confession to make: I don't drink Coke. But don't call me a hypocrite just because I am still the proud owner of a bright red shirt that advertises it. Just call me an American.

Even before setting foot in Israel three years ago, I knew exactly where I could find one. The tiny T-shirt shop in the central block of Jerusalem's Ben Yehuda Street did offer other designs, but the one with a bright white "Drink Coca-Cola Classic" written in Hebrew cursive across the chest was what drew in most of the dollar-carrying tourists. While waiting almost twenty minutes for my shirt (depicted in Fig. 1), I watched nearly every customer ahead of me ask for "the Coke shirt, todah rabah [thank you very much]."

At the time, I never thought it strange that I wanted one, too. After having absorbed sixteen years of Coca-Cola propaganda through everything from NBC's Saturday morning cartoon lineup to the concession stand at Camden Yards (the Baltimore Orioles' ballpark), I associated the shirt with singing

Fig. 1. Hebrew Coca-Cola T-shirt. Personal photograph. Despite my dislike for the beverage, I bought this Coca-Cola T-shirt in Israel.

SAMPLE LIST OF WORKS CITED FOR AN ESSAY IN MLA STYLE

Lesk 7

Works Cited

Coca-Cola Santa pin. Personal photograph by author.
9 Nov. 2002.

"The Fabulous Fifties." Beverage Industry 87:6
(1996) 16. 2 Nov. 2002 <http://memory.loc/
gov.ammem/ccmphtml/indshst.html>.

"Haddon Sundblom." Coca-Cola and Christmas 1999. 2
Nov. 2002 <http://www.coca-cola.com.ar/
Coca-colaweb/paginas_ingles/christmas.html>.

Hebrew Coca-Cola T-shirt. Personal photograph by
author. 8 Nov. 2002.

Ikuta, Yasutoshi, ed. '50s American Magazine Ads.
Tokyo: Graphic-Sha, 1987.

Library of Congress. Motion Picture, Broadcasting
and Recorded Sound Division. 5 Nov. 2002
<http://memory.loc.gov/ammem/ccmphtml/
index.html>.

Pendergrast, Mark. For God, Country, and Coca-Cola:
The Unauthorized History of the Great American
Soft Drink and the Company That Makes It. New
York: Macmillan, 1993.

APA STYLE

The *Publication Manual of the American Psychological Association* (5th edition, 2001) provides comprehensive advice to student and professional writers in the social sciences. Here we draw on the *Publication Manual*'s guidelines to provide an overview of APA style for in-text citations, content notes, and entries in the list of references.

In-Text Citations

APA style calls for in-text citations in the body of an argument to document sources of quotations, paraphrases, summaries, and so on. These in-text citations correspond to full bibliographic entries in the list of references at the end of the text.

1. Author Named in a Signal Phrase

Generally, use the author's name in a signal phrase to introduce the cited material, and place the date, in parentheses, immediately after the author's name. For a quotation, the page number, preceded by *p.*, appears in parentheses after the quotation. For electronic texts or other works without page numbers, paragraph numbers may be used instead, preceded by the ¶ symbol or the abbreviation *para.* For a long, set-off quotation, position the page reference in parentheses two spaces after the punctuation at the end of the quotation.

> According to Brandon (1993), Adefunmi opposed all forms of racism and believed that black nationalism should not be a destructive force.

> As Toobin (2002) demonstrates, Joseph Lieberman unintentionally aided the Republican cause during most of 2002, playing into the hands of the administration and becoming increasingly unwilling "to question the President's motives, because he doesn't like visceral politics" (p. 43).

2. Author Named in Parentheses

When you do not mention the author in a signal phrase, give the name and the date, separated by a comma, in parentheses at the end of the cited material.

> *The Sopranos* has achieved a much wider viewing audience than ever expected, spawning a cookbook and several serious scholarly studies (Franklin, 2002).

FIGURE **22.2** PUBLICATION MANUAL OF THE AMERICAN PSYCHOLOGICAL ASSOCIATION

3. Two Authors

Use both names in all citations. Use *and* in a signal phrase, but use an ampersand (&) in parentheses.

> Associated with purity and wisdom, Obatala is the creator of human beings, whom he is said to have formed out of clay (Edwards & Mason, 1985).

4. Three to Five Authors

List all the authors' names for the first reference. In subsequent references, use just the first author's name followed by *et al.* (in regular type, not underlined or italicized).

> Lenhoff, Wang, Greenberg, and Bellugi (1997) cite tests that indicate that segments of the left brain hemisphere are not affected by Williams syndrome whereas the right hemisphere is significantly affected.

> Shackelford drew on the study by Lenhoff et al. (1997).

5. Six or More Authors

Use only the first author's name and *et al.* (in regular type, not underlined or italicized) in every citation, including the first.

> As Flower et al. (2003) demonstrate, reading and writing involve both cognitive and social processes.

6. Organization as Author

If the name of an organization or a corporation is long, spell it out the first time, followed by an abbreviation in brackets. In later citations, use the abbreviation only.

> **First Citation**. (Federal Bureau of Investigation [FBI], 2002)

> **Subsequent Citations**. (FBI, 2002)

7. Unknown Author

Use the title or its first few words in a signal phrase or in parentheses (in the example below, a book's title is italicized).

> The school profiles for the county substantiate this trend (*Guide to secondary schools*, 2003).

8. *Authors with the Same Last Name*

If your list of references includes works by different authors with the same last name, include the authors' initials in each citation.

G. Jones (1998) conducted the groundbreaking study of retroviruses.

9. *Two or More Sources in the Same Citation*

List sources by the same author chronologically by publication year. List sources by different authors in alphabetical order by the authors' last names, separated by semicolons.

While traditional forms of argument are warlike and agonistic, alternative models do exist (Foss & Foss, 1997; Makau, 1999).

10. *Specific Parts of a Source*

Use abbreviations (*chap.*, *p.*, and so on) in a parenthetical citation to name the part of a work you are citing.

Pinker (2003, chap. 6) argued that his research yielded the opposite results.

11. *Electronic World Wide Web Document*

To cite a source found on the Web, use the author's name and date as you would for a print source, then indicate the chapter or figure of the document, as appropriate. If the source's publication date is unknown, use *n.d.* (no date). To document a quotation, include paragraph numbers if page numbers are unavailable.

Werbach argued convincingly that "Despite the best efforts of legislators, lawyers, and computer programmers, spam has won. Spam is killing email" (2002, p. 1).

12. *Email and Other Personal Communication*

Cite any personal letters, email messages, electronic postings, telephone conversations, or personal interviews by giving the person's initial(s) and last name, the identification *personal communication*, and the date.

E. Ashdown (personal communication, March 9, 2003) supported these claims.

Content Notes

The APA recommends using content notes for material that will expand or supplement your argument but otherwise would interrupt the text. Indicate such notes in your text by inserting superscript numerals. Type the notes themselves on a separate page headed *Footnotes*, centered at the top of the page. Double-space all entries. Indent the first line of each note five to seven spaces, and begin subsequent lines at the left margin.

Text with Superscript Indicating a Note

Data related to children's preferences in books were instrumental in designing the questionnaire.[1]

Note

[1] Rudine Sims Bishop and members of the Reading Readiness Research Group provided helpful data.

List of References

The alphabetical list of sources cited in your text is called *References*. (If your instructor asks you to list everything you have read as background—not just the sources you cite—call the list *Bibliography*.) The list of references appears on a separate page or pages at the end of your paper, with the heading *References*, not underlined or italicized, or in quotation marks, centered one inch from the top of the page. Double-space after the heading and begin your first entry. Double-space the entire list.

For print sources, APA style specifies the treatment and placement of four basic elements—author, publication date, title, and publication information. Each element is followed by a period.

- Author: list *all* authors with last name first, and use only initials for first and middle names. Separate the names of multiple authors with commas, and use an ampersand (&) before the last author's name.
- Publication date: enclose the publication date in parentheses. Use only the year for books and journals; use the year, a comma, and the month or month and day for magazines. Do not abbreviate the month.
- Title: italicize titles and subtitles of books and periodicals. Do not enclose titles of articles in quotation marks. For books and articles, cap-

italize only the first word of the title and subtitle and any proper nouns or proper adjectives. Capitalize all major words in a periodical title.

- Publication information: for a book, list the city of publication (and the country or postal abbreviation for the state if the city is unfamiliar) and the publisher's name, dropping *Inc.*, *Co.*, or *Publishers*. For a periodical, follow the periodical title with a comma, the volume number (italicized), the issue number (if provided) in parentheses and followed by a comma, and the inclusive page numbers of the article. For newspaper articles and for articles or chapters in books, include the abbreviation *p.* ("page") or *pp.* ("pages").

The following APA-style examples appear double-spaced and in a "hanging indent" format, in which the first line aligns on the left and the subsequent lines indent one-half inch or five spaces.

Books

1. One Author

Rheingold, H. (2002). *Smart mobs: The next social revolution*. Cambridge, MA: Perseus.

2. Two or More Authors

Steininger, M., Newell, J. D., & Garcia, L. (1984). *Ethical issues in psychology*. Homewood, IL: Dow Jones-Irwin.

3. Organization as Author

Use the word *Author* as the publisher when the organization is both the author and the publisher.

Linguistics Society of America. (2002). *Guidelines for using sign language interpreters*. Washington, DC: Author.

4. Unknown Author

National Geographic atlas of the world. (1999). Washington, DC: National Geographic Society.

5. Book Prepared by an Editor

Hardy, H. H. (Ed.). (1998). *The proper study of mankind*. New York: Farrar, Straus.

6. Selection in a Book with an Editor

Villanueva, V. (1999). An introduction to social scientific discussions on class. In A. Shepard, J. McMillan, & G. Tate (Eds.), *Coming to Class: Pedagogy and the social class of teachers* (pp. 262-77). Portsmouth, NH: Heinemann.

7. Translation

Perez-Reverte, A. (2002). *The nautical chart* (M. S. Peaden, Trans.). New York: Harvest. (Original work published 2000)

8. Edition Other than the First

Wrightsman, L. (1998). *Psychology and the legal system* (3rd ed.). Newbury Park, CA: Sage.

9. One Volume of a Multivolume Work

Will, J. S. (1921). *Protestantism in France* (Vol. 2). Toronto: University of Toronto Press.

10. Article in a Reference Work

Chernow, B., & Vattasi, G. (Eds.). (1993). Psychomimetic drug. In *The Columbia encyclopedia* (5th ed., p. 2238). New York: Columbia University Press.

If no author is listed, begin with the title.

11. Republication

Sharp, C. (1978). *History of Hartlepool.* Hartlepool, UK: Hartlepool Borough Council. (Original work published 1816)

12. Government Document

U.S. Bureau of the Census. (2001). *Survey of women-owned business enterprises.* Washington, DC: U.S. Government Printing Office.

13. Two or More Works by the Same Author

List the works in chronological order of publication. Repeat the author's name in each entry.

Rose, M. (1984). *Writer's block: The cognitive dimension.* Carbondale, IL: Southern Illinois University Press.

Rose, M. (1995). *Possible lives: The promise of public education in America.* Boston: Houghton Mifflin.

Periodicals

14. *Article in a Journal Paginated by Volume*

Kirsch, G. E. (2002). Toward an engaged rhetoric of professional practice. *Journal of Advanced Composition, 22,* 414-423.

15. *Article in a Journal Paginated by Issue*

Carr, S. (2002). The circulation of Blair's *Lectures. Rhetoric Society Quarterly, 32*(4), 75-104.

16. *Article in a Monthly Magazine*

Dallek, R. (2002, December). The medical ordeals of JFK. *The Atlantic Monthly,* 49-64.

17. *Article in a Newspaper*

Nagourney, A. (2002, December 16). Gore rules out running in '04. *The New York Times,* pp. A1, A8.

18. *Editorial or Letter to the Editor*

Sonnenklar, M. (2002, January). Gaza revisited [Letter to the editor]. *Harper's,* 4.

19. *Unsigned Article*

Guidelines issued on assisted suicide. (1998, March 4). *The New York Times,* p. A15.

20. *Review*

Richardson, S. (1998, February). [Review of the book *The Secret Family*]. *Discover,* 88.

21. *Published Interview*

Shor, I. (1997). [Interview with A. Greenbaum]. *Writing on the Edge, 8*(2), 7-20.

22. *Two or More Works by the Same Author in the Same Year*

List two or more works by the same author published in the same year alphabetically, and place lowercase letters (*a*, *b*, etc.) after the dates.

> Murray, F. B. (1983a). Equilibration as cognitive conflict. *Developmental Review, 3*, 54-61.

> Murray, F. B. (1983b). Learning and development through social interaction. In L. Liben (Ed.), *Piaget and the foundations of knowledge* (pp. 176-201). Hillsdale, NJ: Erlbaum.

Electronic Sources

The following models are based on the APA's updated guidelines for citing electronic sources posted at the APA Web site <apa.org> as well as in the APA *Publication Manual* (5th edition).

The basic APA entry for most electronic sources should include the following elements:

- name of the author, editor, or compiler
- date of electronic publication or most recent update
- title of the work, document, or posting
- publication information, including the title, volume or issue number, and page numbers
- a retrieval statement that includes date of access, followed by a comma
- URL, with no angle brackets and no closing punctuation

23. *World Wide Web Site*

To cite a whole site, give the address in a parenthetical reference. To cite a document from a Web site, include information as you would for a print document, followed by a note on its retrieval.

> American Psychological Association. (2000). DotComSense: Common-sense ways to protect your privacy and assess online mental health information. Retrieved January 25, 2002, from http://helping.apa.org/dotcomsense/

> Mullins, B. (1995). Introduction to Robert Hass. Readings in contemporary poetry at Dia Center for the Arts. Retrieved April 24, 1999, from http://www.diacenter.org/prg/poetry/95-96/intrhass.html

24. Article from an Online Periodical

If the article also appears in a print journal, you don't need a retrieval statement; instead, include the label *[Electronic version]* after the article title. However, if the online article is a revision of the print document (if the format differs or page numbers are not indicated), include the date of access and URL.

> Steedman, M., & Jones, G. P. (2000). Information structure and the syntax-phonology interface [Electronic version]. *Linguistic Inquiry, 31*, 649-689.

> Palmer, K. S. (2000, September 12). In academia, males under a micro-scope. *The Washington Post.* Retrieved October 23, 2002, from http://www.washingtonpost.com

25. Article or Abstract from a Database (Online or on CD-ROM)

> Hayhoe, G. (2001). The long and winding road: Technology's future. *Technical Communication, 48*(2), 133-145. Retrieved September 22, 2002, from ProQuest database.

> McCall, R. B. (1998). Science and the press: Like oil and water? *American Psychologist, 43*(2), 87-94. Abstract retrieved August 23, 2002, from PsycINFO database (1988-18263-001).

> Pryor, T., & Wiederman, M. W. (1998). Personality features and expressed concerns of adolescents with eating disorders. *Adolescence, 33,* 291-301. Retrieved November 26, 2002, from Electric Library database.

26. Software or Computer Program

> McAfee Office 2000. (Version 2.0) [Computer software]. (1999). Santa Clara, CA: Network Associates.

27. Online Government Document

Cite an online government document as you would a printed government work, adding the date of access and the URL. If you don't find a date, use *n.d.*

> Finn, J. D. (1998, April). *Class size and students at risk: What is known? What is next?* Retrieved September 25, 2002, from United States Department of Education Web site http://www.ed.gov/pubs/ClassSize/title.html

28. FTP, Telnet, or Gopher Site

After the retrieval statement, give the address (substituting *ftp, telnet,* or *gopher* for *http* at the beginning of the URL) or the path followed to access information, with slashes to indicate menu selections.

> Korn, P. (1994, October). How much does breast cancer really cost? *Self.* Retrieved May 5, 2002, from gopher://nysernet.org:70/00/BCIC/ Sources/SELF/94/how-much

29. Posting to a Discussion Group

List an online posting in the references list only if you are able to retrieve the message from a mailing list's archive. Provide the author's name; the date of posting, in parentheses; and the subject line from the posting. Include any information that further identifies the message in square brackets. For a listserv message, end with the retrieval statement, including the name of the list and the URL of the archived message.

> Troike, R. C. (2001, June 21). Buttercups and primroses [Msg 8]. Message posted to the American Dialect Society's ADS-L electronic mailing list, archived at http://listserv.linguistlist.org/archives/ ads-1.html

30. Newsgroup Posting

Include the author's name, the date and subject line of the posting, the access date, and the name of the newsgroup.

> Wittenberg, E. (2001, July 11). Gender and the Internet [Msg 4]. Message posted to news://comp.edu.composition

31. Email Message or Synchronous Communication

Because the APA stresses that any sources cited in your list of references must be retrievable by your readers, you should not include entries for email messages or synchronous communications (MOOs, MUDs); instead, cite these sources in your text as forms of *personal communication* (see p. 445). And remember that you should not quote from other people's email without asking their permission to do so.

Other Sources

32. *Technical or Research Reports and Working Papers*

Wilson, K. S. (1986). *Palenque: An interactive multimedia optical disc prototype for children* (Working Paper No. 2). New York: Center for Children and Technology, Bank Street College of Education.

33. *Unpublished Paper Presented at a Meeting or Symposium*

Welch, K. (2002, March). *Electric rhetoric and screen literacy.* Paper presented at the meeting of the Conference on College Composition and Communication, Chicago.

34. *Unpublished Dissertation*

Barnett, T. (1997). *Communities in conflict: Composition, racial discourse, and the 60s revolution.* Unpublished doctoral dissertation, Ohio State University, Columbus.

35. *Poster Session*

Mensching, G. (2002, May). *A simple, effective one-shot for disinterested students.* Poster session presented at the National LOEX Library Instruction Conference, Ann Arbor, MI.

36. *Film, Video, or DVD*

Jackson, P. (Director). (2002). *The Lord of the Rings: The Two Towers.* [Film]. Los Angeles: New Line Cinema.

37. *Television Program, Single Episode*

Imperioli, M. (Writer), & Buscemi, S. (Director). (2002, October 20). Everybody hurts [Television series episode]. In D. Chase (Executive Producer), *The Sopranos.* New York: Home Box Office.

38. *Sound Recording*

Begin with the writer's name, followed by the date of copyright. Give the recording date at the end of the entry (in parentheses, after the period) if it is different from the copyright date.

Ivey, A., Jr., & Sall, R. (1995). Rollin' with my homies [Recorded by Coolio]. On *Clueless* soundtrack [CD]. Hollywood, CA: Capitol Records.

RESPOND

1. The MLA and APA styles differ in several important ways, both for in-text citations and for lists of sources. You've probably noticed a few: The APA lowercases most words in titles and lists the publication date right after the author's name, whereas the MLA capitalizes most words and puts the publication date at the end of the works-cited entry. More interesting than the details, though, is the reasoning behind the differences. Placing the publication date near the front of a citation, for instance, reveals a special concern for that information in the APA style. Similarly, the MLA's decision to capitalize titles is not arbitrary: that style is preferred in the humanities for a reason.

   Find as many consistent differences between the MLA and APA styles as you can. Then, for each difference, try to discover the reasons these groups organize or present information in that way. The MLA and APA style manuals themselves may be of help. You might also begin by determining which academic disciplines subscribe to the APA style and which to the MLA.

2. Working with another person in your class, look for examples of the following sources: an article in a journal, a book, a film, a song, and a TV show. Then make a bibliography entry for each one, using either MLA or APA style.

arguments

chapter twenty-three

Mirror, Mirror . . . Images and the Media

If you look in the mirror of media in America, what images do you see? Your own? Those of people who look or act like you in some way? Are the people you see like those you encounter in your daily life? Do the media serve as a mirror? Should they? How do some get to be the "fairest of them all" while others remain invisible — or are typecast in roles they contend are far from reality? Should these matters concern us? Do they affect us? How? These are the questions the readings in this chapter challenge you to consider.

The readings in the first cluster examine a favorite American obsession — our bodies — and how the body is represented in popular culture. As the arguments demonstrate, media representations of the "perfect body" no longer concern only American women. The availability of U.S. TV programs around the world seems to be changing how women in distant lands see themselves. And from a very different perspective, men in this and other countries increasingly feel pressured to strive for a perfect body — or at least one that is more nearly perfect than the one they're currently inhabiting. In other words, questions of images and the media ultimately matter to each of us.

The second cluster considers stereotypes in media and popular culture. Many argue that the media representations of various groups — ethnic groups, social classes, people of certain faiths, Americans from certain regions, even dads — are not accurate and, hence, not fair. These texts remind us that although such representations — stereotypes, really — may often go unnoticed, they are not without consequence.

If you see your image in the mirror of the media when you gaze at it, you probably have to work hard to stay there. Should you not see your image reflected in the media at all or should the image you see there bear little resemblance to who you are, what might the consequences be? After studying the arguments presented here, you'll likely agree that far more is at stake than an old ditty from a children's fairy tale.

www.
For additional readings on **Images and the Media**, visit bedfordstmartins.com /everythingsanargument.

If the media become the mirror that reflects the fairest of us all, what sorts of bodies appear there, what sorts don't, and what might the consequences of this situation be? This cluster of readings asks you to consider the question **who's the fairest of them all?** for and about yourself.

The cluster of readings opens with a cartoon of a baby studying its reflection in a mirror. Carey Goldberg's *New York Times* news story "'People of Size' Gather to Promote Fat Acceptance" and W. Charisse Goodman's essay "One Picture Is Worth a Thousand Diets" document the struggle of Americans who are overweight, especially women, to combat what they label prejudice against fat people. Focusing on America's obsession with slender women, Norimitsu Onishi's "Globalization of Beauty Makes Slimness Trendy" documents how Nigerian notions of beauty with respect to women's bodies are changing. Similarly, Ellen Goodman's syndicated column "The Culture of Thin Bites Fiji" uses a psychologist's study of how U.S. television is changing the view that Fijian girls have of themselves and their bodies as the basis for claiming that little girls in Fiji learn to hate and harm themselves as a result of the unrealistic notions of beauty promoted by the media—television in particular. Finally, Caryn James offers a review of a reality TV show involving plastic surgery in which she raises uncomfortable questions about Americans' relationships with their bodies.

And it's not only women who find themselves under pressure because of the fair bodies represented in the media. Men of all ages are hitting the gym in record numbers, and as several texts make clear, they're also visiting the plastic surgeon. Reflecting on the men in their lives and the possibility that they might resort to plastic surgery, Angela Neustatter and Louisa Young take opposing sides in answering the question "Should they, or shouldn't they?" In her essay "Turning Boys into Girls," Michelle Cottle, a self-acknowledged feminist, declares that magazines like *Men's Health*, which feed men's newly found obsessions with their bodies, are the greatest thing since spandex because they've forced men to worry about their bodies the way women have long had to. Finally, "Selling Men's Underwear across the Decades" challenges you to examine three advertisements from the last fifty years—two from magazines and one from a billboard—and then to draw conclusions about how these ads reflect changing attitudes toward the male body and its representation in the media even as they've helped create new attitudes toward body image.

Look in the mirror. Are you pleased with what you see? Look in the media. Do you see bodies like yours? Should you be more worried if you do, or if you don't?

◄ This cartoon, by artist P. Byrnes, appeared in a March 2000 issue of the New Yorker. As you study it, consider the argument we're making by using this cartoon to open the cluster about body image and the media.

RESPOND.

1. Is the baby in this cartoon male or female? Why do you think so?

2. What is the "it" of "It begins"?

3. Why is this cartoon humorous? What knowledge about American culture does it assume?

▼ This New York Times *news article reports on the 1999 annual conven-tion of the National Association to Advance Fat Acceptance (NAAFA), which met in Framingham, Massachusetts. As you read, note the arguments made by NAAFA members about why they should be accepted as they are.*

"People of Size" Gather to Promote Fat Acceptance
Group Celebrates Idea of Liberation

CAREY GOLDBERG

FRAMINGHAM, Mass., July 28 — The caramel lollipops at registration; the black thong bikini that Marilyn Wann, a proud 270 pounds, wore at the pool party; the very pool party itself, for people who are usually pool pariahs: All these were political statements of defiance here at the convention of the National Association to Advance Fat Acceptance, as political as the T-shirts that read, "Fat!So?"

Most of the year the association lobbies on behalf of fat people ("fat" is the preferred adjective, members said, a simple description they want to reclaim; "overweight" and especially "morbidly obese" are despised). With about 4,000 members, the association helps fat people cope in a society that hates their girth; it fights the diet industry, pointing out its overwhelming long-term failure rate, and it combats discrimination.

But once a year, it takes the added step of bringing together hundreds of members — nearly 500 this year — to create a place where "people of size" are just people, where everyone has a story of an airplane-seat nightmare or gibes in a job interview, and where no one suggests a new diet.

"This particular one week a year when, in one particular hotel, everyone who's larger than average looks normal, is like a Brigadoon," Ms. Wann, a writer from San Francisco, said, referring to the Scottish village that comes to life for a day every 100 years. "It's odd to be in a place where you look like everyone else."

Odd, and for many, deeply affecting and energizing. In an orientation session for first-time convention-goers, several spoke about "coming out of the closet" as fat people, strange as that may seem when their size has always been visible to everybody. What they meant, they said, was the moment when they simply accepted their size and the likelihood that it would never change, and wanted others to do the same.

"Finally, after being tormented about being fat from the time I was a baby, I've decided I'm going to embrace it," said Barbara Lehmann, a social worker from Orono, Me., who estimated that she had gained and lost thousands of pounds in her lifetime.

Looking around the circle of more than 20 members, mainly women, Ms. Lehmann commented, in a sort of wonderment, "This is the first time I've been in a room where I'm not the fattest person or close to it, and it's — it's — what am I trying to say?"

"Liberating?" suggested Frances White, the group leader.

The association has been pursuing such fat liberation — officially, it is known as the "size acceptance movement" — for 30 years now, with mixed success. Commenting on the current climate, Bettye Travis, the group's president, said there was good fat-acceptance news and bad: the popularity of Camryn Manheim, the television actress, is good; the portrayal of a gluttonous, disgusting character in the latest Austin Powers film is bad.

Others say it still rankles that Oprah Winfrey, with all her accomplishments, has described losing weight as her greatest achievement.

More people are getting skeptical about diets, Ms. Travis said, but new diet drugs with dangerous side effects

462

Participants at the convention of the National Association to Advance Fat Acceptance. Notice their use of figurative language.

keep sweeping the country, and the medical establishment sometimes seems to be sending the message that "it's better to die than be fat."

The association's policy is to take the emphasis off dieting, which often does more harm than good, and put it on health, encouraging people to eat well, exercise and take care of them-selves, and let their bodies settle into their natural weight—and then to work on getting comfortable as a person who takes up substantial space.

A strong current of pain ran through the convention—the accu-mulated wounds of rejection and ostracism, mean jokes, and cruel re-marks that accrue to members of what Ms. Travis called "one of the last marginal groups that are still targeted, that it's still 'O.K.' to make fun of." There were stories about chairs that broke, about rude doctors, about ugly plus-sized clothes and the difficulties of buying a car with enough room or fitting into a hospital wheelchair, about people who assumed that fat meant ugly and lazy and dumb.

But there was also a strong current of humor and defiance, a celebration of snappy comebacks. Recently, in San Francisco, Ms. Travis said, a health club had a billboard advertisement showing an alien from space and saying, "When they come, they will eat the fat ones first." So some of the association's members did aerobics in front of the fitness club in protest.

The association is planning a sim- 15 ilar rally outside the Fanueil Hall Marketplace in Boston this Saturday, titled "Every Body—Good Body."

Last year the association staged a "million pound march" in Santa Monica, Calif. And in the San Francisco area, a fat women's swimming group calls itself "Making Waves."

The fat-acceptance cause has made some political progress. Although Michigan is the only state that includes a ban on size discrimination in its civil rights law, passed in the 1970s, Santa Monica has a similar city ordinance, and one is pending in San Francisco.

In Massachusetts, such a law has been proposed twice before but has never made it to the floor of the Legislature. Another effort is now under way, and convention organizers said today that the state's Governor, Paul Cellucci, had sent over a proclamation declaring that this would be "Size Acceptance Week" in Massachusetts.

In the past, said State Representative Byron Rushing, who has sponsored the size-discrimination bills, legislators have always sent them on for further study. "What they are studying," Mr. Rushing said, "is whether their constituents will elect them again if they vote for this."

Jody Abrams, an association 20 member who testified on behalf of Mr. Rushing's bill, said that legislators, like others who still believe in dieting, "haven't accepted that there are just going to be fat people in the world." And that, he added, is "a hard thing to come up against."

Association members say they pin many of their hopes on influencing the younger generation's attitudes toward fat people, and are setting up a special fat speakers' bureau to send members around to talk at schools.

Ultimately, said Ms. Wann, who has talked to students herself and has written a book called "Fat!So?" (Ten Speed Press, 1998), "the thing we have to do is, like drag queens, make it funky to be a rebel."

"I'm sorry, but Madonna has nothing on me as a rebel," Ms. Wann added. "Madonna in a thong, me in a thong—which one is more challenging to the status quo?"

Arguments are often difficult to categorize; one single article may contain a causal argument, a definition argument, an evaluation argument, and/or a proposal argument. Does Goldberg's article contain any features of a proposal argument? See Chapter 12 to read about the features of a proposal.

···· LINK TO P. 240

RESPOND•

1. The goal of the National Association to Advance Fat Acceptance (NAAFA) is to do exactly that: to convince the public to accept fat people as they are. What sorts of arguments (such as arguments of the heart or arguments based on character, facts and reason, or values) are put forth to support this position? How do members of the organization use humor as part of their arguments?

2. In some ways, Goldberg's argument is similar to Ellen Goodman's argument (p. 477) about women's obsession with thinness being physically and psychologically unhealthy. However, the two authors make their points in very different ways. Compare this article with the article by Goodman in terms of the kinds of arguments put forth. (Obviously, answering question 1 gets you partway to an answer.)

3. How does the photograph accompanying this article influence your response to it? To the goals of NAAFA? Had the photograph not been included, do you imagine your response to the article would have been different? Why or why not?

4. **Write an essay** in response to the question posed by NAAFA member Marilyn Wann in the closing lines of the article: Who is the greater threat to the status quo in this society, Madonna in a thong bathing suit, or Wann, who weighs 270 pounds, in a thong bathing suit? How does each question the status quo? Who is the more rebellious? Why?

► As the title of W. Charisse Goodman's 1995 book, The Invisible Woman: Confronting Weight Prejudice in America, implies, her thesis is that American society tolerates and even encourages prejudice against people, especially women, who are not thin. The chapter excerpted here, "One Picture Is Worth a Thousand Diets," focuses on the ways in which the media render invisible or treat with disdain women whom Goodman refers to as "large."

One Picture Is Worth a Thousand Diets

W. CHARISSE GOODMAN

> Loyalty to petrified opinions never yet broke a chain or freed a human soul in *this* world—and never *will*.
> —Mark Twain

In our consumption-addled culture, the mass media encourage us to absorb as many goods as possible far beyond the saturation point. We are urged to buy things we don't really need and luxuries we may not be able to afford. Not only is more better, but we are advised that it will make us sexier or more successful. But this rule has one notable exception: if a woman is perceived as having consumed too much food, she finds she has committed a social crime. By projecting the image of gluttony onto the large woman exclusively, our society can deny and rationalize its colossal overindulgence in the cult of conspicuous consumption. Greed, after all, is hardly restricted to a preoccupation with food. Movies, television, magazines, newspapers, and preachifying self-help books all reinforce and amplify the ignorant stereotypes about fat people that America holds so close and dear; taken together, they constitute a framework of "petrified opinions" which few dare to question.

A survey of merely eleven mainstream magazines, including *Vogue, Redbook, Time, McCall's,* even *Audubon* and *Modern Maturity,* turned up an astounding 645 pictures of thin women as opposed to 11 of heavy women. Scrutinizing the local newspapers over a period of several weeks left me with a body count of 221 thin women as opposed to nine large women; newspaper advertising inserts added another 288 pictures of individual thin women and approximately a dozen heavy women (most of whom were pictured in a single store flyer for large-size clothing). An examination of almost 160 commercials—after that point, it was either stop or incinerate the TV set—contributed 120 ads featuring thin women exclusively, 27 ads depicting heavy males, mostly in a normal or positive light, and all of 12 heavy women, half of whom, interestingly, were either African-American, older, or both. Of ads including fat women, one offered an evil old cartoon witch, another pictured two big women dressed as opera-singer Valkyrie types, and a third depicted *Alice in Wonderland*'s mean-tempered Red Queen. A . . . series of commercials for Snapple soft drinks featured a fairly heavy woman who read complimentary letters from consumers of the product; however, in most of the commercials this woman is visible only from the shoulders up, while the rest of her body is hidden by a very high counter. Ultimately, the burden of proof in this respect was no more than a counting exercise.

After drowning in an ocean of slender female figures everywhere I looked, it was easy to see how women are persuaded that thinness equals happiness and fulfillment. The women of the media are not only overwhelmingly small but also smiling, self-satisfied, exciting, dynamic, romantically involved, and generally having a splendid time. This is sheer marketing fantasy—and yet, as a society, we buy it, we eat it up, we swallow it whole and ask for more.

Television and Movies

The most obvious pattern in television and movies, other than the predominant absence of large women, reflects the unsurprising fact that heavy men, although they suffer from the same general type of discrimination as heavy women, are not as severely censured for being large. Size in a man is often considered either a sign of physical power or a matter of no consequence. In a scene from the movie *Diner,* a large man eats plate after plate of sandwiches in a diner, apparently trying to set a personal record. The main characters, all male, are watching him in awe and cheering him on; no cracks are made about his size or his appetite. It is utterly impossible to imagine a big woman playing the same scene.

In even a cursory review of mass media presentations, one finds 5 many more large men than women. Take, for example, actors John Goodman, the late John Candy (whose death has been attributed not purely to his weight but also to a rapid and substantial weight loss), *Cheers'* George Wendt, Bob Hoskins, the late John Belushi (dead of an overdose of drugs, not food), the late comic Sam Kinison (car accident, not clogged arteries), French actor Gerard Depardieu, and British comic Robbie Coltrane, to name a few. All these men have played characters who, although heavy, are nonetheless portrayed as lovable and appealing enough to attract thin, conventionally attractive women.

John Candy

Can anyone imagine a female version of *Cheers'* Norm—a lazy, work-phobic, beer-guzzling woman who assiduously avoids home and husband—being hailed as funny, let alone "beloved," as one news article put it?

Of course, we're all well acquainted with that popular movie plot involving the sweet but physically unexceptional male who yearns after the beautiful, thin heroine and eventually, by means of his irresistible personality, wins his true love (*Minnie and Moskowitz* comes immediately to mind). The male-dominated film industry never misses an opportunity to remind us that men should always be loved for themselves. But what about women?

When Hollywood was casting for the 1991 film *Frankie and Johnnie*, a story about an ordinary-looking woman who falls in love with a plain-looking man, Kathy Bates, an Oscar-winning actress who portrayed Frankie on the stage and who just happens to be large, was passed over for the film role. The part went instead to Michelle Pfeiffer, a thin, conventionally glamorous blonde who obviously wanted to prove that she could play a character role. This is typical. If the heavy woman has any consistent role in commercial American films, it is as the peripheral, asexual mother or "buddy," and rarely, if ever, the central, romantic character. Message to all large women: You're not sexy. The only beautiful woman is a thin woman.

Bates herself pointed out in a 1991 interview that when she read for a part in the Sylvester Stallone movie *Paradise Alley*, the character breakdown showed that "after every single female character's name was the adjective 'beautiful,' even if the character was age 82." When Bates questioned the casting director about this, he replied, "Well if you want to make your own female version of *Marty* [a movie about a lonely, aging, unattractive man], be my guest" (Finke, 1991).

Of the approximately 70 movies I randomly surveyed—mostly mainstream commercial American films—only 17 had any large female characters at all in the script, most of whom represented the standard domineering mother figure, the comically unattractive woman, the whore figure, and Bates as her *Misery* psychopath character. Only six of these 17 films presented a big woman as a positive figure, and of these six, only three—*Daddy's Dyin'—Who's Got the Will?* and John Waters' *Hairspray* and *Crybaby*—featured fat women as romantic figures and central characters.

Television shows are not much better, although they occasionally 10 make an effort. Ricki Lake, who has since lost weight, was featured in the defunct series *China Beach*; Delta Burke once co-starred in *Designing Women* and had her own series; and Roseanne's show has long resided among the Top 10 in the Nielsen ratings. Although these women are encouraging examples of talent overcoming prejudice, they are too few and far between. At best, TV shows typically treat large female characters as special cases whose weight is always a matter of comment, rather than integrating women of all sizes and shapes into their programs as a matter of course.

On *L.A. Law*, heavy actress Conchata Ferrell played a new character who was dumped from the program after a relatively short tenure. Her role, that of a tough attorney, was variously described in reviews and on the show as "loud, brash and overbearing," "tubby," "aggressive," "bullying, overpowering," and "a real cash cow." At one point in the series, Ferrell's character marries a handsome, slender man amidst tittering speculation by the firm's slender female attorneys as to the groom's ulterior motive. Naturally, it turns out that he is a foreigner who has married the fat attorney solely to gain citizenship.

The Personals: "No Fat Women, Please"

Although it's true the personals are not strictly part of the media establishment, they do constitute a public forum and mass-communication network, and they illustrate in a very raw fashion the reflection of media imagery in the desires of men.

The patterns of the personals reflect the usual stale stereotypes and sexism of weight prejudice. Out of 324 ads by men seeking women in which the men specified body size, 312 requested, or rather demanded, a thin body type, employing [no less than 17] synonyms for "thin." Men have a most creative vocabulary when it comes to describing a woman's body. Indeed, to judge by the phrasing of the ads, "slender" and "attractive" are one word, not two, in the same fashion as "fat" and "ugly."

It is most interesting that male admirers of big women are commonly portrayed as little boys looking for a mother figure; yet here, one finds men who appear to be looking for a very small, dependent, childwoman/daughter figure and status symbol. Could it be that they have

WM 46, 5'8" non-smoker looking for woman of my dreams: You are kind, helpful, caring, fun-loving, funny, polite, and smart. You like Sci-fi, comedy, travel, and cats. You're reasonably close to being height/weight proportionate.

NATIVE TEXAN NEW to town interested in SF between 24-34, slim or athletic, attractive, and intelligent. Must love to have fun and be positive about life. Non-smoker, light drinker.

A TALL, THIN woman. Yeah! That's what I want. 5'8" to 6'2", fun, pretty, seeking long-term relationship. I'm 6', muscular, grey and green, 40s, intelligent, V.I.P. businesses. Country life, boating, camping to limousine trips, dinners, tours.

TALL, FIT, HANDSOME, intelligent, emotionally stable, financially secure, laid back professional SWM, mid-40s, looking to fall in love with pretty, fit, SW/HF, 32-45, with varied interests. ☎ 1301

Surveys of newspaper classified ads or TV commercials can be rich sources of evidence for many kinds of arguments that deal with current cultural or social issues. See Chapter 18 for suggestions about other types of firsthand evidence.

································LINK TO P. 369

their own peculiar incest fantasies? Might one go even further and speculate that the preference for women with androgynous or boyish figures represents a closeted homosexuality in some men, or an unconscious fear of and hostility toward the more powerful femininity of the large woman?

In any case, the overall impression of the personals is that men still care more about a woman's body and looks than her qualities as a human being. An S/B/M (single black male) summed it up perfectly when he wrote, in search of a woman who "weighs no more than 140. Be any race, be yourself, be beautiful." Or else? 15

Newspapers

The problem with mainstream newspaper journalism is twofold: first, its hearty participation in the national pastime of describing fat people in contemptuous terms; and second, that it purports to be an objective, unbiased observer and reporter of news and culture. But when entertainment journalists describe a large actress as "a blimp on the way to full zeppelin status" (Miller, 1992) or a bone-thin actress as "deliciously gorgeous," the reader can make a pretty good guess as to their personal views as well as their degree of impartiality.

One of the best—or worst—examples of journalistic weight prejudice was the local sports columnist reporting from the 1992 Barcelona Olympics on the Spanish beaches, and his disparaging remarks about local older women possessed of the sheer tasteless gall to walk on said beaches in "nothing but" their swimsuits. This same columnist also deplored women who dared to sunbathe undraped on a topless beach—not because they were naked, but because they lacked the flawless breasts and figures that appeal so to the male eye (Nevius, 1992).

Even in newspaper articles that have nothing to do with diet and weight, women are frequently described in terms of their approximate or specific weight and appearance. Phrases like "tall sexy . . . type," "the mountain of blond hair she balances on 102 pounds," "slender beauty," and "California girl beauty" appear in one article alone about female stand-up comics which includes, interestingly, a graphic description of a man helping himself to generous portions of a buffet while the women sit and drink only water (Kahn, 1991). One newspaper item about singer Ann Peebles refers to her as "the 99-pound vocalist" (Selvin, 1992); another article briefly profiling four blues musicians describes the one woman in the group as "5-foot-3 and 105 pounds" but makes no mention of any of the three men's physical attributes (Orr, 1992).

[M]ost newspaper items omit such detailed descriptions of men's sizes and body parts. One interview of director Robert Altman describes him in terms of his age and hair color, and compares him to a "bemused, slightly grumpy, extremely shrewd owl," but makes no mention of his weight, although the full-body shot accompanying the article reveals a clearly heavyset man (Guthmann, 1992).

As for print advertisements, they lack the dynamics of television 20 ads, and consequently they can come on quite strong in their promotion of thinness as the ultimate aphrodisiac. One diet product ad out of *TV Guide* depicts a thin woman in a leotard examining her hips. Superimposed upon the picture are the words "We'll help you turn on more than your metabolism." Next to the picture, the ad begins, "You're not only dieting for yourself. That's why it's so important to lose those extra pounds. . . ." Another item in a different issue of this magazine hawks an exercise machine, and while the words describing the health benefits are in rather small print, the impossibly slender and leggy female model in the ad is quite noticeable, as are the words, "Hurry! Get that NordicTrack figure you always wanted." Then there are the ubiquitous exercise club advertisements featuring women who are dressed, shaped, and posed more like centerfolds than athletes or average people.

The mass media do not really reflect an idealized reality, as its gurus would like us to think. From the movie studios and directors, to the ad executives and the TV producers and the novelists, rock stars, and music video producers, the media masters have constructed a universe of "petrified opinions" where the only valuable woman is a thin woman, while big women function primarily as shrewish, silly, asexual mommy figures or cheap jokes. Not only is this one-dimensional viewpoint warped and oppressive, it is crashingly dull, redundant, and predictable. Taken as a whole, this so-called creative product conspires to turn impressionable young women into insecure nervous wrecks trying to compete with image upon image of the same tiny-waisted, big-breasted dream girl.

If art really is a reflection of life, and the mass media in turn are a businesslike imitation of art, then when Americans struggle and strive to shape their lives in media's image, they are living life twice removed. The constricted vision of the world fabricated by Hollywood and Madison Avenue compresses the individual and her hopes, needs, and dreams into narrow channels, reducing life to a hopeless pursuit of false perfection in imitation of people who exist primarily for the illusions they can project.

"Be any race, be yourself, but be beautiful." Or else.

WORKS CITED

Finke, N. "Actress Is Weighed Down by Hollywood Attitudes." *San Francisco Chronicle,* February 17, 1991, Sunday Datebook: 33–34.

Guthmann, E. "Altman's 'Player' for the 90's." *San Francisco Chronicle,* April 23, 1992: E2.

Kahn, A. "The Women of the Night." *San Francisco Chronicle,* June 17, 1991: D3.

Miller, R. "Don't Expect Any Good, Clean Fun from 'Maid.' " *San Jose Mercury News,* January 13, 1992: 10B.

Nevius, C.W. "Life's a Beach—Just Barely." *San Francisco Chronicle,* July 28, 1992: E5.

Orr, J. "Twelve Bars and a Turnaround." *San Jose Mercury News,* July 19, 1992, West Magazine: 18.

Selvin, J. "Ann Peebles Redeems Her Rain Check." *San Francisco Chronicle,* April 16, 1992, Sunday Datebook: 51.

RESPOND ●

1. Goodman contends that "[m]ovies, television, magazines, newspapers, and preachifying self-help books all reinforce and amplify the ignorant stereotypes about fat people that America holds so close and dear; taken together, they constitute a framework of 'petrified opinions' which few dare to question" (paragraph 1). What sorts of evidence does she use to support this claim? How is Goodman's evidence similar to the evidence used by Carey Goldberg in "'People of Size' Gather to Promote Fat Acceptance" (p. 462)?

2. Examine how Goodman uses quotations as evidence, especially the opening quote about "petrified opinions" from Mark Twain and the one from the personals section of a newspaper ("Be any race, be yourself, but be beautiful") in paragraphs 15 and 23. In what ways do quotations help structure the argument?

3. Personal ads are especially interesting as arguments because of their brevity. Examine some personal ads in a local newspaper, surveying systematically the images that emerge of the ideal male or female partner. What images emerge as the ideals for each group? To what extent are these ideals the ones that occur most frequently in television, movies, and magazines? Are you concerned about the gap between the ideal and the reality of everyday life? Why or why not?

4. Goodman challenges readers to scrutinize the world, looking to see how large women are or are not represented. Part of the persuasiveness of her argument for many readers, especially for readers who are not large women, likely comes from the volume of evidence she offers. Take the Goodman challenge: choose three familiar magazines or television shows, and survey them as systematically as possible. (For magazines, for example, you will want to distinguish between photographs in advertisements and those in articles.) **Write an essay** arguing for a particular position with regard to the representation of large women in the media.

▼ As this New York Times *article by Norimitsu Onishi from October 2002 reminds us, notions of beauty are not universal but culture specific. Further, they change over time, sometimes quite quickly. This article links the changes in the case of Nigeria to the spread of international beauty contests and competitions for models who will be perceived as attractive according to Western standards. Likely, these events reflect larger trends in globalization.*

Some readers may recall that the Miss World pageant was to have been held in Nigeria late in November 2002, each year's pageant being held in the home country of the previous year's winner. However, riots in Kaduna, Nigeria, led pageant organizers to move the contest to London. The riots, which resulted in over two hundred deaths, were sparked by a comment made by a local Christian journalist that offended local Muslims, who had already been protesting their country's hosting of the event on religious grounds—clear evidence that things like beauty pageants are far from universally accepted. (For more information on the November riots, their causes, and their consequences, use a search engine to locate the following article: Somini Sengupta, "Piety and Politics Sunder a Riot-Torn Nigerian City," New York Times, February 21, 2003.)

Globalization of Beauty Makes Slimness Trendy

NORIMITSU ONISHI

LAGOS, Nigeria—With no success, Nigeria had been sending contestants to the Miss World pageant for years. Winners of the Most Beautiful Girl in Nigeria went year after year to the Miss World competition, and year after year the beauty queens performed remarkably poorly.

Guy Murray-Bruce, the executive director of Silverbird Productions, which runs the Most Beautiful Girl contest, said he had almost resigned himself to the fact that black African women had little chance of winning an international competition in a world dominated by Western beauty ideals.

Then in 2000 he carried out a drastic change of strategy in picking the Most Beautiful Girl and Nigeria's next international representative.

"The judges had always looked for a local queen, someone they considered a beautiful African woman," Mr. Murray-Bruce, 38, said. "So I told the judges not to look for a local queen, but someone to represent us internationally."

The new strategy's success was 5 immediate. The Most Beautiful Girl of 2001, Agbani Darego, went on to clinch the Miss World title in Sun City, South Africa, last October. She became the first African winner in the contest's 51-year history.

Her victory stunned Nigerians, whose country had earned a worldwide reputation for corruption and fraud. Now, all of a sudden, Nigeria was No. 1 in beautiful women. Ms. Darego, who was 18 at the time, instantly became a national heroine.

But soon pride gave way to puzzlement. In a culture where Coca-Cola-bottle voluptuousness is celebrated and ample backsides and bosoms are considered ideals of female beauty, the new Miss World shared none of those attributes. She was 6 feet tall, stately and so, so skinny. She was, some said uncharitably, a white girl in black skin.

The perverse reality was that most Nigerians, especially those over 40, did not find the new Miss World particularly beautiful.

The story does not end there, though. In the year since her victory,

Nigerian aesthetics are under pressure from the West.

a social transformation has begun to take hold across this nation, Africa's most populous.

The change is an example of the 10 power of Western culture on a conti-

474

nent caught between tradition and modernity. Older Nigerians' views of beauty have not changed. But among young, fashionable Nigerians, voluptuousness is out and thin is in.

"After Agbani won, girls look up to me and ask me how to get slim," said Linda Ikeji, 22, an English major at the University of Lagos.

"Before, fat girls were the rave of the moment," said Ms. Ikeji, who is 5 feet 8, weighs 130 pounds and now finds work as a part-time model. "Some fat girls thought they had an advantage over me. But Agbani changed everything."

Here in Lagos, the commercial capital, the thin "It" girls are now called lepa, using a Yoruba word that means thin but that was not applied to people before. The lepa girl has had a popular song written about her, called simply "Lepa." Nigeria's booming film industry has capitalized on the trend by producing a movie, "Lepa Shandi"; the title means a girl as slim as a 20-naira bill.

To anyone who has traveled across the continent, especially in West and Central Africa, the cultural shift is striking. In the United States slimness may be an ideal, but many ethnic groups in this region hold festivals celebrating big women. In Niger many women take livestock feed or vitamins to bulk up.

Among the Calabari people in southeastern Nigeria, fat has traditionally held a cherished place. Before their weddings, brides are sent to fattening farms, where their caretakers feed them huge amounts of food and massage them into rounder shapes. After weeks inside the fattening farms, the big brides are finally let out and paraded in the village square.

Ms. Darego, the same Miss World who has helped change young Nigerians' perception of beauty, belongs to the Calabari ethnic group — and thus may seem particularly unattractive to her own people.

Ms. Darego as Miss World 2001.

"If she was in a crowd of other African women, I wouldn't regard her as a beautiful woman," said Ken Calebs-Olumese, who does not belong to that ethnic group but, as the owner of the exclusive Coliseum nightclub here, knows beautiful women.

"The average African woman is robust, has big hips, a lot of bust," he said. "That's what she offers in terms of beauty. It's in our culture." Mr. Calebs-Olumese, who is 56, drew a blank at the mention of lepa. Still, he acknowledged that he was "speaking from my generation's perspective."

While the transformation in youthful tastes was linked to the Miss World victory, it started, some said, with an earlier event.

In 1998, M-Net, the South African network seen across Africa on satellite television, opened a search for the "Face of Africa." The winner was promised a three-year, $150,000 modeling contract with the Elite agency in New York.

Not surprisingly, M-Net, which shows mostly American movies and TV shows, chose a skinny, 6-foot-2 teenager from Lagos, Oluchi Onweagba, who was not considered particularly pretty here but became a hit on the runways.

"That was the start," said Frank Osodi, 36, a fashion designer whose studio in the Surulere district in Lagos was a hive for models and beauty queens one recent morning. "Before, if you were thin, people thought you were sick, like an AIDS patient. Now if you have a skinny member in your family, you don't have to be ashamed."

Indeed, parents are now urging their daughters to take part in beauty pageants. In the past, the Most Beau-

---

Onishi uses ethnographic observation to support her causal argument. See Chapter 11 for examples of other ways to make an effective causal argument.

LINK TO P. 205 ··

tiful Girl competition drew just enough contestants to hold a pageant, Mr. Murray-Bruce said. For the 2001 contest there were only 40; this year there were 400.

No one is predicting whether the youthful preference for thinness represents a fad or a lasting cultural change. But Maureen and Mary-Jane Mekowulu, slim 18-year-old twins who are students at the University of Nsukka in southeastern Nigeria and were visiting their parents here, said they would continue to exercise every morning and abstain from eating after 6 p.m.

"Because of Agbani, people have 25 realized that slim is beautiful," Maureen said of the Miss World.

And the Most Beautiful Girl of 2002 would reinforce that impression, said the contest's producer, Mr. Murray-Bruce. "She's even skinnier than Agbani," he said.

RESPOND ●

1. Although news articles generally have a single topic, they are complex in structure, often incorporating examples and quotations — testimonies of various sorts — to contribute to their overall claim. What is the major argument made by this news article? What sorts of specific evidence does Onishi use to support his claim? (Recall that Chapter 18 details the many kinds of evidence writers use.)

2. Onishi claims that the change in definitions of female beauty in Nigeria is a distinction between "tradition and modernity" (paragraph 10) but then contrasts the views of "older Nigerians" with those of "young fashionable Nigerians." To what extent are the change and the conflict it has engendered limited to a conflict between old and young? Does Onishi provide evidence that the change is likewise about matters such as social class, education, and urbanity?

3. This news article by Norimitsu Onishi about changing notions of beauty in Nigeria and Ellen Goodman's article about beauty and Fijian girls (p. 477) treat similar topics, although for different purposes. How would you characterize each writer's purpose (Chapter 1)? How are these different purposes reflected in the stance the writers take toward their subjects?

4. The article contrasts traditional Nigerian ideas of beauty and practices such as the fattening of brides-to-be with the notions of beauty represented by the 2001 Miss World. What sorts of conflicting ideals of beauty exist within our own culture? **Write an essay** in which you characterize and define these conflicting ideals for women or for men. As you begin thinking about these issues, you'll likely realize that there are differences in the ideals of beauty held by groups from different regions, classes, and ethnic backgrounds. Thus you may wish to treat the ideals for beauty held by a single group so that you can do a thorough job.

▼ *Ellen Goodman, an award-winning columnist, writes regularly for the* Boston Globe, *where this article first appeared in May 1999, a few days after many newspapers had featured a news story about the effects of watching American TV on adolescent Fijian girls' self-image. Goodman's column generally appears on the op-ed (opinion-editorial) pages of newspapers across the country. As you read, consider how she uses a discussion of a scientific study and the evidence it cites to make a claim about what she sees as a larger social problem. Keep in mind that Goodman is writing shortly after the shootings at Columbine High School in Colorado, where two male students killed and wounded a number of other students and teachers.*

The Culture of Thin Bites Fiji

ELLEN GOODMAN

First of all, imagine a place women greet one another at the market with open arms, loving smiles, and a cheerful exchange of ritual compliments:

"You look wonderful! You've put on weight!"

Does that sound like dialogue from Fat Fantasyland? Or a skit from fat-is-a-feminist-issue satire? Well, this Western fantasy was a South Pacific fact of life. In Fiji, before 1995, big was beautiful and bigger was more beautiful — and people really did flatter one another with exclamations about weight gain.

In this island paradise, food was not only love, it was a cultural imperative. Eating and overeating were rites of mutual hospitality. Everyone worried about losing weight — but not the way we do. "Going thin" was considered to be a sign of some social problem, a worrisome indication

the person wasn't getting enough to eat.

The Fijians were, to be sure, a bit 5 obsessed with food; they prescribed herbs to stimulate the appetite. They were a reverse image of our culture. And that turns out to be the point.

Something happened in 1995. A Western mirror was shoved into the face of the Fijians. Television came to the island. Suddenly, the girls of rural coastal villages were watching the girls of "Melrose Place" and "Beverly Hills 90210," not to mention "Seinfeld" and "E.R."

Within 38 months, the number of teenagers at risk for eating disorders more than doubled to 29 percent. The number of high school girls who vomited for weight control went up five times to 15 percent. Worse yet, 74 percent of the Fiji teens in the study said they felt "too big or fat" at least some of the time and 62 percent said they had dieted in the past month.

This before-and-after television portrait of a body image takeover was drawn by Anne Becker, an anthropologist and psychiatrist who directs research at the Harvard Eating Disorders Center. She presented her research at the American Psychiatric Association last week with all the usual caveats. No, you cannot prove a direct causal link between television and eating disorders. Heather Locklear doesn't cause anorexia. Nor does Tori Spelling cause bulimia.

Fiji is not just a Fat Paradise Lost. It's an economy in transition from subsistence agriculture to tourism and its entry into the global economy has threatened many old values.

Nevertheless, you don't get a 10 much better lab experiment than this. In just 38 months, and with only one channel, a television-free culture that defined a fat person as robust has become a television culture that sees robust as, well, repulsive.

All that and these islanders didn't even get "Ally McBeal."

"Going thin" is no longer a social disease but the perceived requirement for getting a good job, nice clothes, and fancy cars. As Becker says carefully, "The acute and constant bombardment of certain images in the media are apparently quite influential in how teens experience their bodies."

Speaking of Fiji teenagers in a way that sounds all too familiar, she adds, "We have a set of vulnerable teens consuming television. There's a huge disparity between what they see on television and what they look like themselves — that goes not only to clothing, hairstyles, and skin color, but size of bodies."

In short, the sum of Western culture, the big success story of our entertainment industry, is our ability to export insecurity: We can make

Calista Flockhart

any woman anywhere feel perfectly rotten about her shape. At this rate,

we owe the islanders at least one year of the ample lawyer Camryn Manheim in "The Practice" for free.

I'm not surprised by research 15 showing that eating disorders are a cultural byproduct. We've watched the female image shrink down to Calista Flockhart at the same time we've seen eating problems grow. But Hollywood hasn't been exactly eager to acknowledge the connection between image and illness.

Over the past few weeks since the Columbine High massacre, we've broken through some denial about violence as a teaching tool. It's pretty clear that boys are literally learning how to hate and harm others.

Maybe we ought to worry a little more about what girls learn: To hate and harm themselves.

Chapter 11 notes that causal arguments are often included as part of other arguments. Goodman's article reports on Anne Becker's research to support a larger argument.

LINK TO P. 210

RESPOND •

1. What is Goodman's argument? How does she build it around Becker's study while not limiting herself to that evidence alone? (Consider, especially, paragraphs 15–17.)

2. What cultural knowledge does Goodman assume her *Boston Globe* audience to have? How does she use allusions to American TV programs to build her argument? Note, for example, that she sometimes uses such allusions as conversational asides — "All that and these islanders didn't even get 'Ally McBeal,'" and "At this rate, we owe the islanders at least one year of the ample lawyer Camryn Manheim in 'The Practice' for free" — to establish her ethos. In what other ways do allusions to TV programs contribute to Goodman's argument?

3. At least by implication, if not in fact, Goodman makes a causal argument about the entertainment industry, women's body image, and the consequences of such an image. What sort of causal argument (Chapter 11) does she set up? How effective do you find it? Why?

4. Many professors would find Goodman's conversational style inappropriate for most academic writing assignments. Choose several paragraphs of the text that contain information appropriate for an argumentative academic paper. Then **write a few well-developed paragraphs** on the topic. (Paragraphs 4–8 could be revised in this way, though you would put the information contained in these five paragraphs into only two or three longer paragraphs. Newspaper articles often feature shorter paragraphs, even paragraphs of a single sentence, that are generally inappropriate in academic writing.)

▼ *In this article from the December 11, 2002,* New York Times, *Caryn James uses her review of a television show as an occasion to reflect on what we learn about ourselves from examining critically the extremes to which television networks will go to attract viewers. In other words, she's asking what the television in front of us reflects about us as viewers. As you read, notice how James uses specific details and allusions to popular culture to support her claims.*

It's All in the Mix:
A Plastic Surgery Reality Show

CARYN JAMES

When Greta Van Susteren unveiled her new face earlier this year—setting off a blizzard of magazine covers and interviews about the eye-lift she had on her way from CNN to the Fox News Channel—it became a cultural turning point. She was supposed to be a brainy television anchor, not some glamour puss whose job depended on her looks. If *she* decided to revamp her eyes, maybe cosmetic surgery was no longer the preserve of the idle rich and obsessives like Michael Jackson and Joan Rivers, their noses growing ever narrower, the corners of their eyes reaching for the stars. Maybe taking a scalpel to your face was for everyone.

"Extreme Makeover," the reality show that transforms average people through plastic surgery—mutilation as entertainment—was probably inevitable after that. The producers received thousands of applications, and chose three people whose make-overs will be charted on tonight's ABC special.

As a reality show it's a flop, with bad casting and the tackiness of a cheap syndicated series. Every one of its cynical calculations misses, from the title that evokes a sports competition to the way the contest winners are notified: messengers turn up on their doorsteps in scenes that resemble commercials for the Publishers Clearing House sweepstakes. It is easy to see why ABC moved the show out of its original slot, during the November sweeps period, and replaced it with a repeat of Barbara Walters's highly rated interview with the Osbournes.

As a cultural barometer, though, "Extreme Makeover" is fascinating. It displays both the voyeuristic excess of reality shows and the cultural ideal of creating a purely artificial personality (everyone gets to go Hollywood). "This is the last night that I'm going to look like me," Stacey says happily the day before her surgery, revealing more than she probably knew. The hint of self-loathing and lack of an essential self seem both ordinary and chilling.

We're not talking about Elephant Man disfigurement here. The people transformed were average Middle Americans with bumps on their noses. Stephanie is a 24-year-old single mother, who could never have afforded to have her nose fixed. Stacey is a 31-year-old health care worker with a weak chin as well as a bad nose, not to mention a sister who was always prettier. Luke, 29, is a personal trainer and the most sympathetic. He recently lost 125 pounds, and the change left him with huge rolls of skin around his stomach that could never be exercised away.

The show asks us to live vicariously through these everyday people, but we never warm up to them, partly because they go way beyond "Off with her nose!" Stephanie also gets breast implants and liposuction on her stomach and thighs. Luke gets a new

"Extreme Makeover" participant

nose to go with his flatter stomach. Stacey gets a new nose, a new chin, a new body. We all fantasize about changing something, but these Frankenstein dreams seem spooky.

So does the sense that it's all a game. The sports metaphor extends to the Extreme Team that does the makeovers, a group that includes a dentist who promotes his new method of tooth whitening and the hairstylist José Eber, known from his info-

mercials. You might fear for the so-called winners, putting themselves in the hands of such shameless self-promoters, but everything turns out all right.

The show minimizes the blood and pain of surgery, although in one post-op scene a groggy Stephanie has her head covered in bandages and sounds as if she has been hit by a truck. But soon little bandages on their noses are the only traces left,

James employs various types of figurative language — simile, metaphor, hyperbole, and others. Check out Chapter 14 to see how many of the writing techniques described there you can find in James's article.

LINK TO P. 285 ··································

and six weeks later three new selves are revealed. Those final scenes were deleted from the review tape, as if that might generate any interest.

The dream of sudden glamour may be universal, but most make-overs are like the ever-popular segments on "Oprah" that involve nothing more permanent than new hair, clothes and makeup. The radical permanence of its transformations is what puts "Extreme Makeover" in a smarmier category than other reality games, with their winking promises of altered lives, like the sort-of engagements of "The Bachelor." Even eating reindeer testicles, as contestants did this week on NBC's holiday edition of "Fear Factor," seems like a harmless lapse of taste next to a surgically rebuilt body.

Meanwhile, Ms. Van Susteren's face has, as she predicted, become less distorted and stretched out than it looked right after surgery. But she doesn't look like her old self, either. She is a daily reminder of a change that "Extreme Makeover" takes to a creepy low: how television is shifting our idea of what cosmetic revisions seem normal. 10

RESPOND●

1. Reviews are, by definition, evaluative. James contends that "Extreme Makeover" is a "flop" as a case of reality television, but she finds it an excellent "cultural barometer." How does she structure and support her evaluative argument? (You may find the "Guide to Writing an Evaluation," Chapter 10, pp. 190–194, helpful in responding to this question.)

2. What does James mean when she makes claims like "The hint of self-loathing and lack of an essential self seem both ordinary and chilling" (paragraph 4) and "We all fantasize about changing something [about our body], but these Frankenstein dreams seem spooky" (paragraph 6)? How do such claims, which conclude their respective paragraphs, contribute to the author's argument? Why are such generalizations useful as the concluding sentences of paragraphs?

3. In this television review, James has used "Extreme Makeover" as the basis for an analysis of the way media functions in our society. Choose another contemporary television program or series, and perform a similar analysis. In other words, **write an essay** in which you describe and evaluate what television reflects about American society. (A good way to gather evidence for your claims is to watch a TV program with a group of friends, making notes about their comments and responses to the show. Ask permission before taking notes or taping!)

In the two articles that follow, Angela Neustatter and Louisa Young debate whether or not men should avail themselves of cosmetic surgery. The two articles appeared together in the Guardian, a London newspaper, in 1997. As you read, examine the writers' arguments critically and consider how you'd respond to them.

Men Seeking Cosmetic Surgery:
Two Women Give Their Views

Why Shouldn't the Epidermally Challenged Get Help?

ANGELA NEUSTATTER

I have caught him in the mirror more than once, smoothing out a wrinkle here, contorting his lower jaw muscles, a copy of Eva Fraser's facial exercises taken furtively from the bookshelf. Then there was the day some Liv Tyleresque young thing, working with him on a film set in lights that would have made even Samuel Beckett look like a baby's bum, murmured that he looked not a day over 32. (He's not by a long stretch.) He paraded around like a demented peacock for days.

I am indulgent about all this, not being entirely free of human frailty myself. But if Olly° announced that he was planning a face-lift, how would I feel? Rather as I might if Sylvester Stallone turned out to be a woman—flabbergasted. It seems so far from anything I can imagine in my practical, child-of-the-sixties old man. But, who knows, he may be pondering on the Albert Camus thought: "After a certain age, every man is responsible for his own face" and wondering if the man in the street is muttering that he ought to do the decent thing and tighten up.

I've spent years pointing out the differences between men and women, but I think we are

Men Should Have Better Things to Do

LOUISA YOUNG

There are those who like to see the mighty fallen, to see their enemy humiliated. There are those who consider men the mighty, and the enemy. These people are delighted with the apparent growing trend of men having cosmetic surgery.

Me, I hate cosmetic surgery. I differentiate here between cosmetic and reconstructive: we all know that the world can be cruel to those it considers abnormal-looking, and for those who face that cruelty, it is a miracle when they can show themselves, "normalised," to this nasty world. But when it is only the person her or himself who thinks she/he looks abnormal, and only thinks it because she/he doesn't look like Pamela Anderson or Brad Pitt, perhaps the only treatment needed is between the ears.

And when it is a case of just wanting to look prettier—oh God, just mass-mail them Oxfam° leaflets, tell them how long a starving child could survive on the calorific value of their liposucted fat, and ask them if there really isn't anything better they can think of to do with the money.

Women have had the excuse of pressure to be pretty—yeah, yeah. Men apparently are now get-

remarkably similar when it comes to fears about ageing and how we are judged. Show me a middle-aged woman or man who hasn't looked at their face at some time and mourned, as Gypsy Rose Lee ° did: "I have everything I had 20 years ago—except now it's all lower."

Then there would be the matter of where it left me. It's not that I'd fear him running off with a chick scarcely out of her gym slip, but he'd be taking a decision about his appearance that would probably exclude me. When he's planning a haircut, I can dissuade him from a Liam crop; I can lead him to water and get him to swim as a way of toning up the tummy muscles; and he listens to my views on clothes. But I suspect if he were choosing cosmetic surgery, he'd schmooze with the surgeon

ting the same pressure. So do we crow with delight that they are being reduced to our level? Or do we wonder at their sanity—haven't they noticed what succumbing to that pressure has done to women? Do we just quietly remind them that behind the whole thing is that age-old evil, money? Reaching some kind of saturation point in the profitability of pulchritude-paranoia among women, profit-makers have simply turned to the next market—men. And men seem to be falling for it.

Surgery hurts. It takes time to get over it. It is 5 dangerous. Unless there is something that really needs fixing, why face it? Of course everybody has their own standard of what constitutes unbearable or improvable in their own appearance, but when there is so much profit being made by the

---

Neustatter's readers probably don't already know "Olly" by name, but we have a good sense of their intimate domestic relationship. Neustatter pulls us right in to her domestic

familiarity; see Chapter 3 to learn more about other ways of establishing bonds with your readers.

························LINK TO P. 58

Gypsy Rose Lee: stage name of Rose Louise Hovick (1914–1970), who danced in the Ziegfeld Follies and later became known as America's greatest strip-tease performer. The Broadway musical *Gypsy* is based on her life.

Oxfam: British-based privately funded organization founded in 1942 to provide disaster relief and development assistance. This is an illustration from an Oxfam leaflet.

and seek guidance there. Would he ask me which bits to get bobbed and tautened? I doubt it and he might choose the wrong style.

Yet I couldn't and wouldn't condemn it or him 5 because no way do I want to join the band of puritans who deify their wrinkles and castigate, for their failure to age naturally, anyone who so much as has a collagen implant, because puritanism is a far nastier vice than narcissism. I share the view that the Tony Curtis look, with skin so stretched, is ugly and probably the desperate effort of someone who still wants to be a young man, but I've seen plenty of people use cosmetic surgery for a discreet lift rather as they might use car maintenance, to keep the equipment in good nick for as long as possible. And what is wrong with that? There is no divine justice in the different ways we age, so why shouldn't the epidermally challenged get a bit of help?

But of course the key question is: would I still fancy him? I don't think I'd go off him if he had a face-lift, but it would help if he emerged looking like Antonio Banderas.

very people who advise on whether or not the process is desirable or necessary, how can you know?

People often have cosmetic surgery because they think it will make them more attractive. Speaking as one who thinks men look better for looking the worse for . . . wear, I can't help thinking that men should have better things to do than this. So, of course, should women; our only excuse is the centuries of exaggerated value put on female beauty, and the fact that it has warped our minds. Men have no such excuse. They should know better.

RESPOND •

1. Neustatter and Young take opposing views on the same issue. Make a brief list of the arguments each writer makes—both for her position and against the opposing position. Putting aside your own feelings on the issue, which writer do you think presents the stronger argument? Why?

2. Neustatter contends that "puritanism is a far nastier vice than narcissism" (paragraph 5). **Write an essay** in which you defend or refute this claim.

3. "Should They? Shouldn't They?" Now it's your turn to **write an essay** (of about seven hundred words) in which you argue why men should or should not see cosmetic surgery as an answer to at least some of their woes.

▼ *In this excerpt from a 1998 issue of the* Washington Monthly, *Michelle Cottle uses humor to argue that popular men's magazines such as* Men's Health *encourage men to be obsessive about their appearance—in the way that women have long been expected to. The passage reprinted here is from the opening third of the article; later sections examine the sorts of advice offered by* Men's Health *on everything from exercise regimes to low-calorie snacks and the extent to which such advice is designed primarily to "move merchandise"—in fact, very expensive merchandise for a growing niche market.*

Turning Boys into Girls

How Men's Magazines Are Making Guys as Neurotic, Insecure, and Obsessive about Their Appearance as Women

MICHELLE COTTLE

I love *Men's Health* magazine. There. I'm out of the closet, and I'm not ashamed. Sure, I know what some of you are thinking: What self-respecting '90s woman could embrace a publication that runs such enlightened articles as "Turn Your Good Girl Bad" and "How to Wake Up Next to a One-Night Stand"? Or maybe you'll smile and wink knowingly: What red-blooded hetero chick *wouldn't* love all those glossy photo spreads of buff young beefcake in various states of undress, rippled abs and glutes flexed so tightly you could bounce a check on them? Either way you've got the wrong idea. My affection for *Men's Health* is driven by pure gender politics—by the realization that this magazine, and a handful of others like it, are leveling the playing field in a way that *Ms.* can only dream of. With page after page of bulging biceps and Gillette jaws, robust hairlines and silken skin, *Men's Health* is peddling a standard of male beauty as unforgiving and unrealistic as the female version sold by those dewy-eyed pre-teen waifs draped across the covers of *Glamour* and *Elle*. And with a variety of helpful features on "Foods That Fight Fat," "Banish Your Potbelly," and "Save Your Hair (Before it's Too Late)," *Men's Health* is well on its way to making the male species as insane, insecure, and irrational about physical appearance as any *Cosmo* girl.

Don't you see, ladies? We've been going about this equality business all wrong. Instead of battling to get society fixated on something besides our breast size, we should have been fighting spandex with spandex. Bra burning was a nice gesture, but the greater justice is in convincing our male counterparts that the key to their happiness lies in a pair of made-for-him Super Shaper Briefs with the optional "fly front endowment pad" (as advertised in *Men's Journal*, $29.95 plus shipping and handling). Make the men as neurotic about the circumference of their waists and the whiteness of their smiles as the women, and at least the burden of vanity and self-loathing will be shared by all.

This is precisely what lads' mags like *Men's Health* are accomplishing. The rugged John Wayne days when men scrubbed their faces with deodorant soap and viewed gray hair and wrinkles as a badge of honor are fading. Last year, international market analyst Euromonitor placed the U.S. men's toiletries market—hair color, skin moisturizer, tooth whiteners, etc.—at $3.5 billion. According to a survey

conducted by DYG researchers for *Men's Health* in November 1996, approximately 20 percent of American men get manicures or pedicures, 18 percent use skin treatments such as masks or mud packs, and 10 percent enjoy professional facials. That same month, *Psychology Today* reported that a poll by Roper Starch Worldwide showed that "6 percent of men nationwide actually use such traditionally female products as bronzers and foundation to create the illusion of a youthful appearance."

What men are putting *on* their bodies, however, is nothing compared to what they're doing *to* their bodies: While in the 1980s only an estimated one in 10 plastic surgery patients were men, as of 1996, that ratio had shrunk to one in five. The American Academy of Cosmetic Surgery estimates that nationwide more than 690,000 men had cosmetic procedures performed in '96, the most recent year for which figures are available. And we're not just talking "hair restoration" here, though such procedures do command the lion's share of the male market. We're also seeing an increasing number of men shelling out mucho dinero for face peels, liposuction, collagen injections, eyelid lifts, chin tucks, and, of course, the real man's answer to breast implants: penile enlargements (now available to increase both length and diameter).

Granted, *Men's Health* and its journalistic cousins (*Men's Journal, Details, GQ,* etc.) cannot take all the credit for this breakthrough in gender parity. The fashion and glamour industries have perfected the art of creating consumer "needs," and with the women's market pretty much saturated, men have become the obvious target for the purveyors of everything from lip balm to lycra. Meanwhile, advances in medical science have made cosmetic surgery a quicker, cleaner option for busy executives (just as the tight fiscal leash of managed care is driving more and more doctors toward this cash-based specialty). Don't have several weeks to recover from a full-blown facelift? No prob-

5

lem. For a few hundred bucks you can get a microdermabrasion face peel on your lunch hour.

Then there are the underlying social factors. With women growing ever more financially independent, aspiring suitors are discovering that they must bring more to the table than a well-endowed wallet if they expect to win (and keep) the fair maiden. Nor should we overlook the increased market power of the gay population — in general a more image-conscious lot than straight guys. But perhaps most significant is the ongoing, ungraceful descent into middle age by legions of narcissistic baby boomers. Gone are the days when the elder statesmen of this demographic bulge could see themselves in the relatively youthful faces of those insipid yuppies on "Thirtysomething." Increasingly, boomers are finding they have more in common with the *parents* of today's TV, movie, and sports stars. Everywhere they turn some upstart Gen Xer is flaunting his youthful vitality, threatening boomer dominance on both the social and professional fronts. (Don't think even Hollywood didn't shudder when the Oscar for best original screenplay this year went to a couple of guys barely old enough to shave.) With whippersnappers looking to steal everything from their jobs to their women, postpubescent men have at long last discovered the terror of losing their springtime radiance.

Whatever combo of factors is feeding the frenzy of male vanity, magazines such as *Men's Health* provide the ideal meeting place for men's insecurities and marketers' greed. Like its more established female counterparts, *Men's Health* is an affordable, efficient delivery vehicle for the message that physical imperfection, age, and an underdeveloped fashion sense are potentially crippling disabilities. And as with women's mags, this cycle of insanity is self-perpetuating: The more men obsess about growing old or unattractive, the more marketers will exploit and expand that fear; the more marketers bombard men with messages about the need to be beautiful, the more they will obsess. Younger and younger men will be sucked into the vortex of self-doubt. Since 1990, *Men's Health* has seen its paid circulation rise from 250,000 to more than 1.5 million; the magazine estimates that half of its 5.3 million readers are under age 35 and 46 percent are married. And while most major magazines have suffered sluggish growth or even a decline in circulation in recent years, during the first half of 1997, *Men's Health* saw its paid circulation increase 14 percent over its '96 figures. (Likewise, its smaller, more outdoorsy relative, Wenner Media's *Men's Journal*, enjoyed an even bigger jump of 26.5 percent.) At this rate, one day soon, that farcical TV commercial featuring men hanging out in bars, whining about having inherited their mothers' thighs will be a reality. Now *that's* progress. ■

RESPOND●

1. What does Cottle mean when she claims that her "affection for *Men's Health* is driven by pure gender politics"? How well does she explain and support this claim? Do you find her argument persuasive? Why or why not?

2. Evaluate Cottle's use of humorous argument. Cite examples of humor from the text that you find especially effective or ineffective, and explain why you find them so. Would her argument be more or less effective if she had adopted a serious rather than a humorous tone? Why do you think Cottle uses humor in this piece? What goals does she hope to achieve by doing so?

3. Cottle's humorous argument is written for a specific audience: readers of the *Washington Monthly*. What other readers do you think she invokes? (See Chapter 3 on invoked readers.) Might some readers find her humor offensive? Who might they be, and on what grounds might they be less than amused? Why would Cottle risk alienating some of her readers with humor?

4. In paragraph 7, Cottle claims that "magazines such as *Men's Health* provide the ideal meeting place for men's insecurities and marketers' greed." How effectively does she support this claim? What consequences does she foresee for the situation she describes? Do you agree with her claim? Why or why not?

5. **Write a response** to Cottle. Imagine that you are an assistant editor of *Men's Health* and that your boss—who is steaming because he's just read Cottle's article—has given you the task of responding to her in a letter to the editor of the *Washington Monthly*. Your aim is to make the magazine look good while taking issue with Cottle's criticisms. The letter should be about five hundred words in length. Before you start writing it, you may want to examine a copy of *Men's Health*—the more you know about the magazine, the better your defense of it is likely to be.

Cottle knows she's walking into a minefield of stereotypes about her topic and establishes her credentials in the opening paragraph by referring to—and dismissing—each stereotype. Read about other ways to establish credibility in Chapter 3.

LINK TO P. 56 ·······························

Selling Men's Underwear across the Decades

Several readings in this cluster contend that the high heel is now on the other foot: Men are being held to standards of "beauty" or physical appearance that formerly applied only to women. One way of testing such a claim is to examine the images of men used in advertising a product designed for them, such as underwear. Analyze the three

Figured rayon pajamas, A-D, about $10. • Rayon shorts, 30-44, about $1.75

Stop! Look! Such skillful tailoring...such slick designs

He's trying to engineer you into giving him Textron Menswear. He likes the special Textron tailoring—fuller seams, roomier armholes, longer trousers in the pajamas. He likes the "boxer" shorts with the famous "parachute" seat for extra comfort...the soft, non-restraining elastic at the waist. Finest Textron pajamas in rayon from about $7 to $10...shorts at about $1.75. At leading stores throughout the country. TEXTRON, INC., Textron Building, 401 Fifth Avenue, New York 16, N.Y.

Rayon satin striped pajamas, A-D, about $7
Rayon striped shorts, 30-44, about $1.75

TEXTRON
REG. U. S. PAT. OFF.

LINGERIE • BLOUSES • HOSTESS COATS • HOME FASHIONS • MENSWEAR

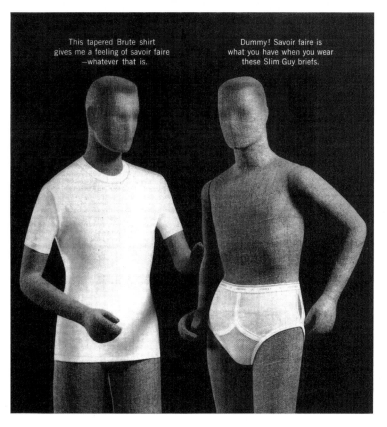

This tapered Brute shirt gives me a feeling of savoir faire —whatever that is.

Dummy! Savoir faire is what you have when you wear these Slim Guy briefs.

Look alive in new *Life*® underwear by Jockey®

You're really living. You're going places. You're doing things. You're always on the move. Jockey Menswear's new Life underwear is for *you*. Get with *Life*®!

The Life tapered Brute shirt has all the same quality features as the classic Jockey T-shirt, except it's tapered to fit a guy without a paunch. Has a slightly higher neck, too.

Life Slim Guy briefs give you famous

Jockey MENSWEAR

JOCKEY MENSWEAR, KENOSHA, WISCONSIN
A DIVISION OF COOPER'S, INC.

Jockey support plus mesh pouch ventilation, low-cut waistband, vented sides, high-cut leg openings.

If you agree that underwear doesn't have to be dull, stop at your favorite men's store. Ask to see the entire Life line—briefs, boxers and five styles of T-shirts. (Styles illustrated —$1.50.) They're all designed for young men who enjoy life.

1. If we take these advertisements to be representative, how has the representation of the male body changed over the past five decades? Some commentators see the changes as evidence of a new "eroticization of the male body." What do they mean? Do you agree that such a process is occurring? Why or why not?

2. Collect ten other advertisements for female underwear or a product such as cologne from across the decades. You might choose a single magazine and take your advertisement from the same monthly issue in each year. What do changes in the advertisements tell you about the representation of the "ideal female"? How do the ads reflect larger shifts in societal attitudes toward what it means to be female?

3. **Write an essay** evaluating the evidence you gathered for question 2 and using your findings to argue for a specific point. Your essay should include examples of the ads, an explanation of how you chose them, and an evaluation of what you think they mean. You'll likely want to include copies of at least some of the ads in your paper and comment on them.

If you check a dictionary, you'll find that the term *stereotype* originally referred to a plate for printing cast in metal from a mold of a page of set type. English borrowed the term from French, but its parts are ultimately of Greek origin, *stereo*, meaning "solid" or "three-dimensional," and *type*, meaning "model." By extension, a stereotype has come to mean a widely held conception of a group that is fixed and allows for little individuality among the group's members. Ironic, isn't it, that a term that originally referred to a three-dimensional printing plate has come to refer to one-dimensional representations of groups?

This cluster of readings focuses on issues of stereotypes, specifically **stereotypes in media and pop culture.** These readings consider what many would argue are unsavory stereotypes of many groups. In "Fu Manchu on Naboo," John Leo examines stereotyping of African Americans, Asians, Middle Easterners, Republicans, and Catholics in a single film from the late 1990s — *The Phantom Menace*. James Sterngold writes about the movie *Smoke Signals*, the first feature-length film written, directed, and acted by Native Americans, in his *New York Times* article, "Able to Laugh at Their People, Not Just Cry for Them," and the efforts of Native Americans to question stereotypes about who they are. In "The Exaggeration of Despair," Sherman Alexie, author of the book that became the basis of *Smoke Signals*, writes a poem to argue with a member of his tribe about whether Alexie's representations of Indian life in one of his novels were exaggerated and, hence, stereotypical. John Levesque examines a 1999 study of fifteen television series that include fathers as characters; the results, he suggests, are not encouraging. Writing in the Business Section of the *New York Times*, David Carr examines the extent to which the covers of women's popular magazines in the United States reflect the racial and ethnic diversity of the country—or even the magazines' readership.

These arguments ask us to think hard about how various groups are represented in media and pop culture. They remind us that media and pop culture representations of various groups quickly become the topic of debate, whether or not you belong to the group in question. They also challenge us to consider how such representations become stereotypes and how those stereotypes ultimately influence us all. Originally, stereotypes were part of the printer's trade, enabling a printer to disseminate information quickly and relatively cheaply. No less a part of popular culture today, stereotypes of a different sort still disseminate information. You'll have to evaluate that information's worth.

▼ In this July 1999 essay from the "On Society" column in U.S. News & World Report, *a weekly newsmagazine that generally takes a conservative stance, John Leo criticizes the* Star Wars *movie,* Episode I: The Phantom Menace. *As you read, pay special attention to the structure of Leo's argument: specifically, how does he support his claim that the film perpetuates stereotypes of certain groups?*

See "Giving an Argument Style" in Chapter 2 for examples of other opening paragraphs that grab readers' attention by breaking their expectations.

LINK TO P. 40·······················

Fu Manchu on Naboo

JOHN LEO

Everyone's a victim these days, so America's touchiness industry is dedicated to seeing group slights everywhere. But sometimes even touchy people are right. Complaints about the new *Star Wars* movie, for instance, are valid. *Episode I: The Phantom Menace* is packed with awful stereotypes.

Consider the evil Neimoidians. They are stock Asian villains out of black-and-white B movies of the 1930s and 1940s, complete with Hollywood oriental accents, sinister speech patterns, and a space-age version of stock Fu Manchu clothing. Watto, the fat, greedy junk dealer with wings, is a conventional, crooked Middle Eastern merchant. This is a generic antisemitic image, Jewish if you want him to be, or Arab if you don't.

Law Prof. Patricia Williams says Watto looks strikingly like an anti-Jewish caricature published in Vienna at the turn of the century—round bellied, big nosed, with spindly arms, wings sprouting from his shoulders, and a scroll that says, "Anything for money." Perhaps Watto isn't supposed to be Jewish. Some people thought he sounded Italian. But by presenting the character as an unprincipled, hook-nosed merchant (and a slave owner, to boot), the movie is at least playing around with traditional antisemitic imagery. It shouldn't.

> **"A stereotype on this level is more than an insult. It is a teaching instrument."**

496

The loudest criticism has been directed at Jar Jar Binks, the annoying, computer-generated amphibian who looks like a cross between a frog and a camel and acts, as one critic put it, like a cross between Butterfly McQueen's Prissy° and Stepin Fetchit.° His voice, the work of a black actor, is a sort of slurred, pidgin Caribbean English, much of it impossible to understand. "Me berry, berry scayyud," says Jar Jar, in one of his modestly successful attempts at English. For some reason, he keeps saying "yousa" and "meesa," instead of "you" and "me." He is the first character in the four *Star Wars* movies to mess up Galactic Basic (the English language) on a regular basis.

RACIST CARICATURE

Fractured English is one of the key traits of a racist 5 caricature in America, from all the 19th-century characters named Snowball down to Amos 'n' Andy.° Whether endearing or pathetic, this trouble with language is supposed to demonstrate the intellectual inferiority of blacks. Childlike confusion is another familiar way of stereotyping blacks, and Jar Jar shows that trait too. He steps in alien-creature doo-doo, gets his tongue caught in a racing engine, and panics during the big battle scene. He is, in fact, a standard-issue, caricatured black who becomes hopelessly flustered when called upon to function in a white man's world.

A stereotype on this level is more than an insult. It is a teaching instrument and a powerful, nonverbal argument saying that racial equality is a hopeless cause. If blacks talk and act like this movie says they do, how can they possibly expect equal treatment?

What is going on in this movie? George Lucas, director of the *Star Wars* movies, says media talk about stereotypes is creating "a controversy out of nothing." But many visual cues support the charge that stereotypes are indeed built into the film. Jar Jar

Jar Jar Binks

Butterfly McQueen: the actress (1911–1995) who played Prissy, Scarlett O'Hara's young slave in *Gone with the Wind.* She is best remembered for the scene in which she tells O'Hara "Lawsy, Miss Scarlett — Lawsy, we's got ter have a doctah! Ah doan know nothin' 'bout birthin' babies!" Like many African American actors of the period, she refused to be filmed eating chicken or watermelon. Why might these actors have refused such a thing?

has head flaps drawn to look like dreadlocks. The ruler of his tribe, Boss Nass, wears what looks to be an African robe and African headdress. A Neimoidian senator named Lott (Trent Lott?), representing the evil viceroy Nute Gunray (Newt Gingrich?) wears a version of a Catholic bishop's mitre and a Catholic priest's stole over a dark robe. This can't be an accident. It duplicates, almost exactly, the appearance of a real bishop. It's a small reference but an unmistakable one. So Catholics, along with Asians and Republicans, are at least vaguely associated with Neimoidian treachery.

Lucas is a visually sophisticated and careful moviemaker. In a TV interview, he said that he researched imagery of Satan in every known culture before deciding on how the evil warrior Darth Maul should look in the film (tattooed, with horns). A *Star Wars* book, *The Visual Dictionary,* that came out with the movie describes in detail almost every image used in the film. So it's hard to believe that all the stereotyped imagery just happened.

One of the keys to Lucas's success is that his movies are made up of brilliantly re-imagined scenes from earlier films (World War II aerial dogfights, cowboys and Indians, swashbuckling sword fights, a *Ben-Hur* chariot race, etc.). After three very inventive *Star Wars* movies, the not-so-inventive fourth seems to have fallen back on some tired Hollywood ethnic themes he mostly avoided in the first three.

So *The Phantom Menace* offers us revived versions 10 of some famous stereotypes. Jar Jar Binks as the dithery Prissy; Watto, a devious, child-owning wheeler-dealer, as the new Fagin; the two reptilian Neimoidian leaders as the inscrutably evil Fu Manchu° and Dr. No. What's next — an interplanetary version of the Frito Bandito? The *Star Wars* films deserve better than this. Let's put all these characters to sleep and start over in the next movie. ∎

Stepin Fetchit: the professional name of Theodore Monroe Andrew Perry (1902–1985), who was the first African American movie star. He first worked in stage revues and vaudeville shows for African American audiences and later became an international star in Hollywood films that cast him in roles where he played a lackey or provided comic relief. Much criticized for these roles, he in many ways paved the way for later generations of African Americans in Hollywood. The name, a play on the phrase "step and fetch it," has come to represent "slow-witted, shuffling servility," as Eric Lott puts it.

Fu Manchu *as played by Boris Karloff in the 1932 movie* The Mask of Fu Manchu.

Amos 'n' Andy: originally a radio show in which White actors took the roles of two African American men from the South who had moved to Chicago. The program began in 1926 and went on to become the most popular U.S. radio show. By 1951, when it became a television series, the actors were Black, but many Americans believe the program contributed to creating derogatory stereotypes of African Americans in the national consciousness for years to come.

RESPOND ●

1. What kinds of evidence does Leo use in structuring his argument? How, specifically, does he use facts about earlier portrayals of various groups? (Why, for example, does he allude to Butterfly McQueen's Prissy, Stepin Fetchit, Snowball, and Amos 'n' Andy? How many of these characters do you recognize? Even if you recognize none of them, what can you imagine them to be like?) How does Leo use testimony? (What might his motivation be in citing law professor Patricia Williams when talking about an anti-Jewish caricature? How does he use testimony from Lucas, the filmmaker?)

2. Leo begins his argument by agreeing with the general criticism of those Americans who sometimes cast themselves as victims. He then immediately admits that some groups are justified in their complaints if *The Phantom Menace* is taken as evidence. Why is Leo's opening statement an appropriate way to begin his essay, particularly given the stance that *U.S. News & World Report* generally takes on issues?

3. Leo lets Lucas speak for himself. How does Leo use Lucas's own words and the existence of the *Star Wars Visual Dictionary* as evidence against Lucas's claim that "media talk about stereotypes is creating 'a controversy out of nothing'"?

4. Leo argues that the way movie characters speak is an important part of racist caricature; one imagines that Leo would be willing to extend his claim to cases of sexism and, likely, classism. **Write an essay** disagreeing with Leo's contention, presenting evidence why such portrayals do not reinforce racist (or sexist or classist or other) stereotypes—or supporting his claim, using evidence from familiar movies or television programs to back up your arguments.

▼ *James Sterngold's article originally appeared in the "Arts and Leisure" section of the New York Times in 1998 at about the time that Smoke Signals was released around the United States. In addition to providing background about the movie, which, as he notes, is the first film written, directed, and acted by Native Americans, the article raises many issues about the representation of American Indians in the media in general.*

Able to Laugh at Their People, Not Just Cry for Them

JAMES STERNGOLD

SLIAMMON INDIAN RESERVE, British Columbia—One morning recently, Evan Adams, a 31-year-old American Indian actor, was telling stories in the small living room of his parents' home on this beautiful, heavily wooded stretch of the Canadian coast. Surrounded by his mother, three sisters and a brother, he explained in his singsong voice how he had terrified some of the participants in a first-aid course he had taken by reacting with passionate alarm toward a doll that was supposedly choking and its inflatable mother.

He was telling the story as a testament to his acting ability, but his normally soft-spoken sister Maureen slyly deflated the boast by asking, "Was it acting or were you excited about that blow-up doll?"

This gentle gibe brought gales of laughter from Mr. Adams's family, and it was just one episode in a day of wordplay among a group of people clearly comfortable communicating through sometimes bawdy humor and irony. That, of course, would be unremarkable in such a close-knit family except for the fact that Indians have

LOOKING AT THEMSELVES *Adam Beach, right, and Evan Adams in "Smoke Signals," the first feature-length movie written, directed and acted by American Indians*

500

generally been depicted in popular culture, and especially in movies, as earnest and stoic, sometimes pathetic and at times bloodthirsty, but rarely wry.

Indians have also been pictured as living in poor, if not squalid conditions. And in fact Mr. Adams, a Coast Salish Indian, said that he had eaten so much salmon as a child growing up in a subsistence economy based on fishing that he took to calling it "Indian bologna." But the economic poverty has often been interpreted as cultural impoverishment—as an implication that Indian culture lacks a playful or a cerebral dimension.

That is one reason the new movie 5 in which Mr. Adams is a co-star, "Smoke Signals," which opens Friday, is so distinctive. It's funny and complex, as well as poignant, casting a new light on the Indian sensibility.

"Smoke Signals," based on a book of short stories by Sherman Alexie titled "The Lone Ranger and Tonto Fistfight in Heaven," is the first feature-length movie written, directed and acted by American Indians. But the film, which won two awards at the Sundance festival in January and has been acclaimed by critics, is something more too: it is a step by a new generation of Indian artists toward finding an idiom for exploring their individual and cultural identities without resorting to self-pity, political correctness or Hollywood clichés.

The tone of "Smoke Signals," which documents the unexpected ways two young men living on the Coeur d'Alene reservation in Idaho come to terms with absent fathers,

is brash and self-confident in its self-examination. In one scene, for instance, Thomas Builds-the-Fire (Mr. Adams) notes as he watches a western, "The only thing more pathetic than Indians on TV is Indians watching Indians on TV."

This movie, which was directed by the 28-year-old Chris Eyre, is the

> # "In 'Smoke Signals,' young American Indians make brash use of stereotypes, both to mock them and embrace them."

work not just of a group of creative people with full hearts but of aggressive achievers determined to stake their claim to high ground on the American cultural map. The best known of them is Mr. Alexie. A 31-year-old novelist and poet who grew up on the Spokane reservation in Washington, he was a producer of "Smoke Signals" and wrote its screenplay and is also producing a movie adapted from his recent novel "Indian Killer." He said in an interview that one of his primary goals was to take away from so-called white experts the responsibility for describing contemporary Indian culture. His aim, he said, is not to avoid criticism of Indian society but to make sure that it is Indians doing the criticizing and interpreting.

Mr. Adams, an athletic-looking man with a broad smile, a long ponytail and wire-framed glasses, is also a good example of restless ambition— but with a twist. He has acted in four full-length features; he will appear in

"Indian Killer," and he is completing a script for a movie in which he will also act later this year, with Loretta Todd, a Cree from Northern Alberta, directing.

But beyond all that, Mr. Adams— 10 whose grandparents and several aunts died of tuberculosis—will begin medical school at the University of Calgary this fall, to fulfill a goal of bringing something back to his reservation, a hamlet of 650 people about 100 miles north of Vancouver amid mountains, towering cedars and rich blue waters.

The people involved in "Smoke Signals" are not, in short, willing to passively accept conventional images of Indian life.

"Smoke Signals" is a slow-moving, often wistful drama that turns into a road movie as Thomas, a confident nerd who maintains his people's storytelling tradition in an offbeat manner, accompanies the angry, self-conscious Victor Joseph (Adam Beach) on a journey to Arizona. But the story is enlivened by a self-deprecating sense of humor, one of the most enduring Indian cultural characteristics, particularly on the reservations, the filmmakers say.

"Smoke Signals" is clearly a product of a post-Wounded Knee generation. The filmmakers paid tribute to the American Indian Movement, saying that those angry demonstrators of the 1970's had helped establish a contemporary tradition of Indian pride that made a movie like "Smoke Signals" possible. But the film has a far different sensibility. The characters are angry, but they're also silly, loving, careless, vulnerable, witty and persistent. They play basketball. They laugh at their squalor. At one point the only way they can go forward is by driving a car backward. They mock Indian stereotypes, and they embrace them. In fact, they are much like the group of people who made the film.

Mr. Eyre, a graduate of the film school at New York University, is a Cheyenne-Arapaho who was adopted as a baby and brought up by a white family in Oregon. He has spent the last few years tracking down his biological parents and embracing his Indian heritage. "Smoke Signals," the first feature he has directed, was integral to that process. "In this movie, we're all searching for home to different degrees," he said.

was 8; she was eight months pregnant at the time. His father drowned two months later. "Living with that loss and not understanding it, you kind of feel you're not in the right place," said Mr. Beach, an avid hockey player and rock musician. "I'm kind of looking for the right place in this movie."

Mr. Beach also described the making of "Smoke Signals" as a means by which he could confront his own anger about the loss of his parents. "It was the first time in my life I was able to get that out of myself," said Mr. Beach in describing the filming of the tearful closing sequence of the movie. "I remember I was crying on Chris's shoulder and saying, 'It still hurts.' And he'd say, 'Well, you have to go do it again.'"

And then there is Mr. Adams, who has been almost frenetic in his efforts both to investigate his culture through writing and acting and to serve his people as a doctor. His parallel career paths reflect a tension that runs through the lives of many Indians, he

an actor's career when he can do movies that are life changing or magical," he said. "That's not enough for me. I need to do something that really helps my people all the time."

Mr. Adams's father, Les, the captain of a tugboat, said he had long contemplated these issues. As he sat bobbing on his boat, he explained that he knew many years ago that Evan was capable of extraordinary accomplishments. And he said that he had sternly instructed his son to focus his ambition on the world beyond the reservation. But, he admitted, Evan made it clear early on that he had his own ideas about heritage and creativity. As a teenager, for example, Evan learned and performed traditional dances that had been little seen for years. Les Adams recalled bringing a friend, the chief of a nearby tribe, to one of Evan's performances and being struck to see his friend cry at one point.

"He said he had not seen those 20 dances since he was a boy and that he never expected to see them again in his life," said Mr. Adams. "He was impressed that these young people wanted to bring them back."

Evan Adams did go away to a private high school when he was 14 and then to McGill University in Montreal. His father said he was crushed when Evan announced that he was leaving McGill after a year, to pursue acting.

The younger Mr. Adams said that part of his struggle over the years had come from his mixed feelings about living in a dominantly white society. "My family had a very high status on the reservation," he said, whose father

---

" 'We're all searching for home to different degrees,' the director says."

Mr. Beach, a 25-year-old Ojibway 15 from north of Winnipeg, bluntly described how much of his own personal history was reflected in that of his character, Victor, who is haunted by the absence of a parent. He said the defining element of his early life was the death of his mother, who was killed by a drunken driver when he

said: whether to concentrate on articulating a distinct cultural vision to the world outside the reservations or to focus on their own people. Mr. Adams is still undecided on which path will win out in his case, but he seems to be leaning in one direction.

"I do love acting and I'm working at it, but there are only a few times in

was the elected chief of his tribe for a number of years. "I was low status in the town. It was a constant source of irritation and humiliation."

Ultimately, Mr. Adams enrolled at the University of British Columbia in Vancouver and completed his premed studies, while continuing to write and act, doing everything from Shake-speare to a play he wrote, "Snapshots," about how two Indian families deal with illness and death.

He described his swings from one world to the other while showing a reporter an extraordinary collection of totem poles, masks and other ceremonial objects preserved in the glass and concrete Museum of Anthropology on the University of British Columbia campus. He insisted that he was trying to find a way of revering the past while shaping a new kind of future that was true to both the Indian spirit and the modern spirit.

"The Indian way," he concluded, 25 "is being adaptable and flexible."

RESPOND ●

1. One resource any writer has in constructing arguments is to appeal to readers' emotions, feelings, or values (including cultural values). How does Sterngold appeal to his readers' emotions? Which emotions in particular does he appeal to? Where do you see evidence of these appeals?

2. How does Sterngold's discussion of media representations of Native Americans compare with John Leo's discussion of media representations of African Americans and other groups in his essay "Fu Manchu on Naboo" (p. 496)? How do the different purposes—writing a news article versus writing a column that takes a strong stance on an issue— influence the ways in which each author makes his main point?

3. Watch the movie *Smoke Signals*. Pay particular attention to the ways in which the movie and those in it "mock Indian stereotypes . . . and . . . embrace them" (paragraph 13). List any events or situations in the movie that call into question stereotypes about Native Americans you have seen in other media. In what ways is the Sterngold article useful background for seeing the film? If you had been in Sterngold's place, writing an article about the film *before* it appeared, what would you have told potential viewers? How would your comments differ from his? Why?

4. The Native Americans cited in this article raise several complex issues about representations of groups. One is the issue of authority: who has the right and the responsibility to represent a group? **Write an essay** discussing the advantages of representations crafted by insiders and by outsiders. One way to complete this assignment is to focus on a specific group of which you are—or are not—a member, using it as an example.

Sterngold's interviews with Evan Adams, Chris Eyre, and Adam Beach provide nearly all of the information and evidence in this article. See the guidelines in Chapter 18 to help you plan and conduct your own interviews.

LINK TO P. 371 ·······························

Sherman Alexie is the writer whose book of short stories, The Lone Ranger and Tonto Fistfight in Heaven *(1993), became the basis for the film* Smoke Signals. *He wrote "The Exaggeration of Despair" as a response to a review of* Reservation Blues, *a novel he published in 1995. The reviewer, who belonged to the same tribe, argued that Alexie had been too negative in his portrayal of the reservation and of Indians generally. To voice disagreement with the review, Alexie chose to compose a poem "using negative language and imagery to create a chant-like quality," noting "Obviously, my poem cannot completely reproduce the despair and loss in the Indian world. For that matter, I could never write a poem that completely replicated the level of joy and magic in our lives. My poems are an attempt to capture moments, not whole lives or complete worlds." The poem was first published in* Urbanus, *a poetry magazine from San Francisco.*

THE EXAGGERATION OF DESPAIR

SHERMAN ALEXIE

I open the door

(this Indian girl writes that her brother tried to hang himself
with a belt just two weeks after her other brother did hang himself

and this Indian man tells us that, back in boarding school, five priests
took him into a back room and raped him repeatedly

and this homeless Indian woman begs for quarters, and when I ask
her about the tribe, she says she's horny and bends over in front of me

and this Indian brother dies in a car wreck on the same road
as his older brother, his youngest brother, and the middle brother

and this homeless Indian man is the uncle of an Indian man
who writes for a large metropolitan newspaper, and so I know them both

and this Indian child cries when he sits to eat at our table
because he had never known his family to sit at the same table

and this Indian poet shivers beneath the freeway
and begs for enough quarters to buy a pencil and paper

and this fancydancer passes out at the powwow
and wakes up naked, with no memory of the evening, all of his regalia gone

and this is my sister, who waits years for an eagle, receives it
and stores it with our cousins, who then tell her it has disappeared

and this is my father, whose own father died on Okinawa, shot
by a Japanese soldier who must have looked so much like him

and this is my father, whose mother died of tuberculosis
not long after he was born, and so my father must hear coughing ghosts

and this is my grandmother who saw, before the white men came,
three ravens with white necks, and knew our God was going to change)

and invite the wind inside.

RESPOND●

1. This poem uses a common literary technique, providing a list or catalog of situations, events, individuals, and so on. What is the power of a
   catalog as argument? What particular themes recur in this particular
   catalog? How do they support the poet's argument?

2. The first and last lines of the poem describe two events. What is the
   relationship between these events and the catalog, which is enclosed
   in parentheses? How is the title part of the poem's argument? What
   does it mean?

3. In what ways can poetry be an argument? In what ways is this particular poem an argument? What claim(s) do you think the poet is making? What evidence does the poet give for his claim(s)? Who are the
   poet's audiences? How do you know?

4. In James Sterngold's article, "Able to Laugh at Their People, Not Just
   Cry for Them," Alexie is noted as having said he seeks not to avoid
   criticism of Native American society but to ensure that Native Americans are speaking for themselves. In what ways is this poem an illustration of Alexie achieving his aim? How is criticism by an insider
   similar to—and different from—criticism by an outsider? You may
   wish to compare and contrast Alexie's poem with John Leo's critique
   of *The Phantom Menace* in "Fu Manchu on Naboo" (p. 496).

5. **Write an essay** describing and evaluating Alexie's argument. How
   does the poem's structure contribute to its success or failure as an
   argument?

The style of repetition that Alexie
uses in his poem is known as
anaphora. Read more about
anaphora and other structural
schemes in Chapter 14.

LINK TO P. 296

▼ *In this article originally published in the entertainment section of the Seattle Post-Intelligencer in early June 1999, John Levesque reports on a 1999 study of the ways in which fathers are represented in television situation comedies. As you read, consider how the photograph from 7th Heaven and the chart on the next page contribute to Levesque's argument.*

Sitcom Dads Rarely Know Best, Study of TV Laments

JOHN LEVESQUE

Only nine shopping days till Father's Day, so let's decide once and for all. Who's the better sitcom dad: Ray Romano or Homer Simpson?

No contest, right? I mean, Ray Romano has never been arrested for trying to murder his boss, never been charged with sexual harassment for pulling a Gummi Venus de Milo off a baby-sitter's tush, and never been an unwitting accomplice in a terrorist takeover of the East Coast.

Homer Simpson has been there, done that. Many times over.

But with every precinct reporting, the tabulations indicate there's not much to choose between Romano and Simpson on the fatherhood scale. So says the National Fatherhood Initiative in Gaithersburg, Md., which looked at 15 television series on five networks last fall and decided that — surprise! — father rarely knows best.

While comedian Ray Romano, 5 who plays himself on "Everybody Loves Raymond," does better than the bumbling patriarch of "The Simpsons" in areas of parental competence and guidance, Homer Simpson cleans Romano's clock when it comes to family involvement and engagement.

Stephen Collins as Eric Camden on "7th Heaven" was one of two dads who got perfect scores in the study of fathers on sitcoms.

Simpson even has an edge in placing the role of father at the top of his priority list.

On a scale of 0 to 25, Romano and Simpson both tallied scores of 16 in NFI's "Fatherhood & TV" report, barely staying out of the "negative portrayal" range (see chart on page 507).

The fact that we're even comparing a live-action character with a cartoon figure seems a little goofy, but it was NFI that lumped them together, not I.

Founded in 1994, NFI is a non-profit, non-partisan organization

(www.fatherhood.org) that "encourages and supports family and father-friendly policies (and) develops national public education campaigns to highlight the importance of fathers in the lives of their children."

Wade Horn, a psychologist/columnist who is NFI's president, intends to revisit the dads-on-TV report each year to see if there's any improvement at the networks, particularly in the area of comedies. Of the 15 shows studied by NFI, 12 are sitcoms and only three — "Smart Guy," "Two of a Kind" and "Mad About You" — were seen as portraying fatherhood positively. Ironically, none of the three will be back next season.

Two dramas, "Promised Land" 10 and "7th Heaven," got perfect scores, but the overall conclusion is that the typical portrayal of fathers on network television "is one of incompetence."

The report focused only on shows where a father was a recurring character, where the relationship between the father and his children was a defining feature, and where the father's children were 18 or younger.

Thus, dramas like "Profiler," "ER," "NYPD Blue" and "Law & Order," where parenthood is a secondary or occasional story element, weren't evaluated. Nor was the comedy "Frasier," in which a richly drawn father-son relationship involves adults.

Horn says these shows will be examined in future reports, as will UPN, which was left out of this year's study because NFI didn't consider it to be on a par with the other networks.

It is not Horn's aim to have every father on TV be the never-flustered type played by Robert Young on "Father Knows Best" in the '50s and '60s. But he *would* like to see more than four shows—out of the 100-plus airing on the networks during a season—give dads a fair shake.

"I wouldn't make this argument in 1962," Horn said. "But because we 15 have a crisis in fatherhood today, we have to take seriously the kinds of images we pump into kids' homes."

Horn asks that the networks look at their schedules and ask themselves: "When one out of three kids is not likely to have a father in the home, are we doing enough, are we fulfilling our public responsibility to ensure that there are at least some positive images of fatherhood coming into our households?"

By the way, Horn is a fan of "The Simpsons." He thinks it's clever and funny, but he also knows his two daughters have no illusions that Homer Simpson is your typical dad.

"They can watch the Homer Simpsons and laugh it off, and they know that's not what real fatherhood is about because they have a contrasting model. But what about the one-third who go to sleep without a father? How easy is it for them to separate the entertainment image from reality?"

And as for those who would dismiss the NFI study as just another attempt by a special-interest group to angle for some attention, Horn seeks to distance himself from other studies, such as a recent one suggesting that federal employees are also treated shabbily in TV shows.

"I'm not suggesting every father 20 should be portrayed as a superhero," he said. "But . . . it's not the same as negative stereotypes of government workers. We as a society can survive without government workers, but we cannot survive without fathers."

Fatherhood Portrayals on Network TV

Network/Show	Involvement	Engagement	Guidance	Competence	Priority	Total
WB/7th Heaven	5	5	5	5	5	25
CBS/Promised Land	5	5	5	5	5	25
WB/Smart Guy	5	4	5	5	5	24
ABC/Two of a Kind	4.5	4.5	5	4	5	23
ABC/The Hughleys	4.75	3.75	3.75	2.75	4	19
NBC/Mad About You	4	4.3	3.7	2.3	4	18.3
Fox/Holding the Baby	3	3.5	3	3.5	4.5	17.5
Fox/King of the Hill	4.3	4	3	2	3.67	17
ABC/Home Improvement	4.25	4.5	2.5	2	3.5	16.75
CBS/Everybody Loves Raymond	3.67	2.67	3	3.67	3	16
Fox/The Simpsons	4.5	4	2	2	3.5	16
WB/Dawson's Creek	3	3	2.5	4	2.5	15
Fox/That '70s Show	2.5	1.5	1.5	4	2.5	12
ABC/Brother's Keeper	2.3	2.67	1.67	2.3	2	11
CBS/The Nanny	1	1	1.67	2.3	1.67	7.67

Scoring—*20 or more points:* positive fatherhood portrayal; *16 to 19 points:* mixed fatherhood portrayal; *15 or fewer points:* negative fatherhood portrayal.

Source: National Fatherhood Initiative

RESPOND •

1. Even though the primary function of Levesque's article is to report information about the National Fatherhood Initiative's (NFI) study of how fathers are portrayed on network TV, you might argue that by reporting the study and framing it as he does, Levesque is making an argument himself. How would you characterize his argument? (Hint: What is Levesque's stance toward the study he reports on? How do you know?)

2. Consider the chart that is part of the article. Does the chart make an argument? Why or why not? In what ways might you interpret the information given in the chart? Draw some generalizations about how fathers are represented on network television based on the information given in the chart.

3. Evaluate the categories—involvement, engagement, guidance, competence, priority, and total—used in the chart and the study. Do these seem to you to be the most relevant or appropriate categories to use in evaluating portrayals of fatherhood? Why or why not? Would you suggest others? Which ones? Why?

4. How does Levesque's argument about the portrayals of fatherhood reported in this article compare with the arguments made by John Leo (p. 496), James Sterngold (p. 500), and Sherman Alexie (p. 504) about the representation of various other groups? Which of these arguments do you find most convincing? Least convincing? Why?

5. If a writer argues that we should be concerned about the portrayals of fathers on network television, would it be inconsistent for that writer to contend that representations of ethnic minorities in movies or television are unimportant? Could another writer convincingly argue that we should be concerned about the representation of ethnic minorities while not paying attention to TV's portrayal of fathers? Why or why not? **Write an essay** in which you take a stance on media portrayals of various groups and their significance (or insignificance) for us all.

▼ *This news article from the Business Section of the* New York Times *in fall 2003 uses many kinds of evidence to examine a situation that many Americans find troubling, namely, the difference between the demographics of the country's population at large and the characteristics of people who end up on the covers of magazines. In so doing, David Carr raises important questions about representation: Who or what do magazine covers represent? Why don't the people on magazine covers look like the population at large? As you read, pay special attention to the kinds of evidence Carr uses, particularly the ways he incorporates statistics and charts based on statistics.*

On Covers of Many Magazines, a Full Racial Palette Is Still Rare

DAVID CARR

Halle Berry, in her role as the sexy superspy Jinx in "Die Another Day," helps James Bond save the world from certain doom. But Ms. Berry may be performing an even more improbable feat as the cover model of the December issue of Cosmopolitan magazine.

Ms. Berry became only the fifth black to appear on the cover of Cosmopolitan since the magazine began using cover photographs in 1964, and she is the first since Naomi Campbell in 1990. Ms. Berry is evidently one of a tiny cadre of nonwhite celebrities who are deemed to have enough crossover appeal to appear on the cover of mass consumer magazines.

There are signs that the freeze-out may be beginning to thaw, as the continuing explosion of hip-hop has pushed many black artists into prominence, and as teenagers' magazines that are less anxious about race are bringing more diversity. But in many broad-circulation magazines, the unspoken but routinely observed practice of not using nonwhite cover subjects—for fear they will depress newsstand sales—remains largely in effect.

A survey of 471 covers from 31 magazines published in 2002—an array of men's and women's magazines, entertainment publications and teenagers' magazines—conducted two weeks ago by The New York Times found that about one in five depicted minority members. Five years ago, according to the survey, which examined all the covers of those 31 magazines back through 1998, the figure was only 12.7 percent. And fashion magazines have more than doubled their use of nonwhite cover subjects.

But in a country with a nonwhite population of almost 30 percent, the incremental progress leaves some people unimpressed.

"The magazine industry has been slow and reluctant to embrace the change in our culture," said Roy S. Johnson, editorial director of Vanguarde Media and editor in chief of Savoy, a magazine aimed at black men. "The change is broad and profound, and in many ways is now the mainstream."

The absence of cover-model diversity could reflect the industry's racial homogeneity. Four years ago, the trade publication Mediaweek found that only 6.1 percent of the magazine industry's professional staff was nonwhite.

"We do not see ourselves in magazines," said Diane Weathers, editor in chief of Essence, a monthly magazine for black women. "Considering what the country we live in looks like today, I think it's appalling."

The women's category has seen the most profound changes, largely as a result of O, the Oprah Magazine, whose cover repeatedly hosts Oprah Winfrey and has a large white readership.

Carr could have asked almost anybody for his or her opinion, but each of the interviewees here contributes a specific kind of credibility to the piece. Adapt the criteria given in Chapter 21 for evaluating print sources to the task of evaluating Carr's choice of interview subjects with respect to their credentials and relevance.

LINK TO P. 412 ·······································

509

Both Cosmo and O are published by Hearst magazines. As a newsstand giant, selling two million copies a month, Cosmo uses a near scientific blend of sex and Middle American beauty on its covers—a formula that does not seem to include black women. O magazine, in contrast, transcends race with a new, spiritually based female empowerment.

Publishing is a conservative industry, one that has been known to define risk as using a cover model with dark hair instead of blond. But a wave of Latina superstars like Jennifer Lopez, along with genre-breaking athletes like Tiger Woods and the Williams sisters, have redefined what a celebrity looks like. And the audience is changing as well. In the last five years, the nonwhite audience for magazines has increased to 17 percent from 15 percent, according to Mediamark Research Inc.

Yet, even as black and Hispanic women slowly make their way onto the covers of magazines of various genres, black males still find themselves mainly confined to a ghetto of music and sports magazines.

"When it comes to magazine covers, my client, who is one of the busiest guys in Hollywood, can't get arrested," said an agent for an A-list Hollywood actor who declined to give her name or the name of her client for fear of making a bad situation even worse. "Magazines are in trouble and they are fearful of offending their audience of Middle Americans," she said. "But those same people are buying tickets to his movies."

Daniel Peres, editor of Details, a men's magazine owned by Fairchild Publications, said there was pressure [10] to stick with outdated conventions because newsstands now display so many more titles competing for the consumer's attention.

Magazines aimed at teenagers use far more nonwhite cover subjects.

"Everyone is terrified of a mis-[15] step," he said. "While most people in the business would prefer it go unspoken because they are horrified at being perceived as racist, it is a well-known legend that blacks, especially black males, do not help generate newsstand sales."

Christina Kelly, now editor in chief of YM, a teenagers' magazine owned by Gruner & Jahr USA, recalls a struggle with the circulation people when she worked as an editor in 1993 at the now-closed Sassy magazine.

"We wanted to put Mecca from the band Digable Planets on the cover because she was huge at the time and gorgeous," she recalled. "The circulation guys hated the idea, but we just went ahead and did it. The magazine was bagged with a separate beauty booklet, which was usually placed in the back, but this time, it was bagged in front. It just happened to have a picture of a blond, blue-eyed woman on it."

Today, magazines like Teen People and YM feature cover subjects of a variety of hues. In the last year, YM has had covers that included nonwhite artists like Ashanti and Enrique Iglesias. And in August, Teen People chose Usher, a black R&B singer, as its No. 1 "hot guy" and featured him on the cover.

"Race is a much more fluid concept among teens," said Barbara O'Dair, managing editor of Teen People.

Magazines for teenagers, because [20] of their reliance on the heavily integrated music industry, use 25 percent nonwhite subjects on their covers. If white teenagers are crossing over to embrace minority artists, many artists are meeting them halfway in terms of style.

Fashion, previously a very segregated world, has become transracial, with young white women adopting street fashion while black artists wear long, flowing tresses. Certain totems of beauty—blond hair, among other things—can now be seamlessly situated on almost anyone regardless of race. The singers Shakira, Beyoncé Knowles, and Christina Aguilera, all nonwhite, have at times worn blond hair that is indiscernible from that of Britney Spears.

"There is virtually no stigma attached to black celebrities changing their hair as there has been in the past," said Leon E. Wynter, author of "American Skin: Pop Culture, Big Business, and the End of White America" (Crown Publishers, 2002). "The hair thing is completely over."

And race itself has become more complicated and less definable, said Mr. Wynter. He suggests that many of the Latin superstars like Jennifer Lopez are often seen not as minorities by young white teenagers, but as a different kind of white person. Very few of the breakout artists featured on covers are dark skinned.

The growing acceptance of non-white cover subjects is not restricted to teenaged girls. Men's magazines, for example, are not as racially monolithic as they once were. GQ, which has a nonwhite readership of 18 percent, has always had more diverse images by featuring minority athletes and actors.

But a newer generation of men's 25 magazines seem to find ethnicity sexy. In the last year, 5 of the 12 women featured on the cover of Maxim, the spectacularly successful young men's magazine owned by Dennis Publishing USA, were other than white.

"It doesn't stem from any political motivation," said Keith Blanchard, editor in chief of Maxim. His readers, mostly white young men, "are listening to Shakira and Beyoncé. They are cheering for Lucy Liu kicking butt in 'Charlie's Angels.' And I think there is a certain attraction to exotic women."

But there are those who would argue that equal opportunity objectification of women does not represent progress. "What is attractive is socially constructed," said Robin D. G. Kelley, a professor of history at New York University who has written extensively about race and black culture. "I think that race still matters, and many times what is happening is that these poly-racial figures are used to fulfill fantasies. It's the Jezebel phenomenon."

As for the December Cosmopolitan, Kate White, the magazine's editor in chief, said Ms. Berry was on her cover simply because she meets all the criteria of a typical Cosmo girl. "She is beautiful, powerful, success-

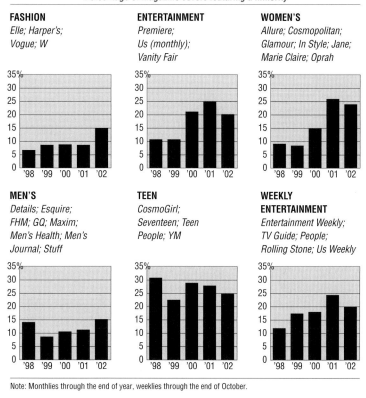

Cover Census

According to the United States Census Bureau, almost 30 percent of America's population belongs to minority groups. Over the last five years, however, the images on the covers of mass-market consumer magazines featured members of a minority less than 25 percent of the time in most categories.

Percentage of magazine covers featuring a minority

FASHION
Elle; Harper's; Vogue; W

ENTERTAINMENT
Premiere; Us (monthly); Vanity Fair

WOMEN'S
Allure; Cosmopolitan; Glamour; In Style; Jane; Marie Claire; Oprah

MEN'S
Details; Esquire; FHM; GQ; Maxim; Men's Health; Men's Journal; Stuff

TEEN
CosmoGirl; Seventeen; Teen People; YM

WEEKLY ENTERTAINMENT
Entertainment Weekly; TV Guide; People; Rolling Stone; Us Weekly

Note: Monthlies through the end of year, weeklies through the end of October.

ful, and she can open a movie," Ms. White said, suggesting that Ms. Berry has the kind of wattage that can draw people into a movie, or to buy a magazine. Ms. White said the absence of nonwhite women on the cover of Cosmo reflected the celebrities that Hollywood produces, not the magazine's preferences.

Still, when the magazine uses a model instead of a celebrity, it almost invariably chooses a white person. "We choose models who have already started to gain critical mass, regardless of hair or eye color," said a Hearst spokeswoman in response. "We want the reader to have a sense of having seen them before."

It probably helps, in terms of both newsstand and advertising, that Ms. Berry's face is everywhere now that she has been selected as a spokeswoman for the cosmetics company Revlon. There are important business, as well as cultural reasons, why after so many years that black, at least in some magazines, may be beautiful.

"Part of what is going on is that the beauty industry woke up and realized there was a big market there," said Roberta Myers, editor in chief of Elle, a women's fashion magazine that is uncommonly diverse in cover selections. "The old assumptions that there was only one kind of beauty, the typical blond, blue-eyed Christie Brinkley type, are gone."

While editors sweat over the consequences of diversifying their cover mix, they may fall behind a coming generation of young consumers who have decided that race is much less important than how hot a given celebrity's latest record or film is.

"The list of who is acceptable or hot is slowly expanding," said Mr. Wynter. "In the current generation, there is an underlying urge, an aspiration, to assert one's common humanity. You can't see it in the magazines that are on the shelves now, but it is coming to the fore."

RESPOND •

1. What argument is being made in Carr's article? Does it surprise you in any way? Does it matter that the article appeared in the business section of the newspaper rather than, say, on the front page or in the lifestyle section? Why or why not? How might the argument have been framed differently if it had been written for a different section of the newspaper? Why?

2. What sorts of arguments does Carr use to support his thesis? Certainly consider the kinds of evidence discussed in Chapter 18, but do not limit yourself to these sorts of support. For example, how does Carr use figurative language (e.g., "a ghetto of music and sports and magazines," paragraph 12) to advance his argument?

3. How do we evaluate Carr's discussion of Black males continuing to end up on the covers of sports and music magazines and of the growing number of "exotic" women who appear on the covers of magazines designed for primarily young White men? Do these facts serve as evidence of "progress"? In what sense? Might they be interpreted in other ways?

4. Obviously, magazine covers play a critical role in influencing buyers, especially "impulse" buyers who do not subscribe but purchase the magazine at a newsstand. Thus some might claim that magazine publishers are merely responding to the whims of their buyers. Others will claim that publishers have a hand in creating consumer preferences. **Write an essay** in which you evaluate the situation described by Carr; you may wish to offer a proposal of some sort about this situation, especially if you see it as a problem. An example of a proposal based on an evaluation of a similar situation is found in Teal Pheifer's essay on page 254. Note that your own approach might very well differ considerably from Pheifer's.

chapter twenty-four

What's Public?
What's Private?

What do supermarket discount cards, mail-order catalogs, and many Web sites have in common? For starters, they collect information about you and what you like every time you make a purchase, place an order, or visit a Web site. What becomes of that information? Does it go to some central repository where computers hum away, combining billions of discrete bits of information into profiles of you and everyone else? Should it? Who might control those computers? Does it matter? Should you care if someone else knows about your purchases? How about your medical records or financial transactions? Or your old love letters? Each of these cases raises questions about what is public and what is private in American society today.

While Americans claim to cherish privacy, each of us defines it in a slightly different way, especially in specific situations. Legal experts don't always agree either. One famous definition from an influential 1890 article in the *Harvard Law Review* by Samuel D. Warren and Louis D. Brandeis claims that privacy is "the right to be let alone." A quite different perspective can be found in the work of Alan F. Westin, whose 1967 book *Privacy and Freedom* characterizes privacy as the right of individuals to determine when and how much information about them is made available to others. The readings in this chapter challenge you to consider how you define privacy and why.

The chapter opens with a group of arguments that raise questions about the nature of privacy in a range of situations—Internet marketing, pornographic images on office computers, strip searches of Americans returning home from abroad, and a mother's epilepsy. Then comes a cluster of texts entitled Privacy and Civil Liberties after September 11, which focuses on how the events on that day have led to public debate about privacy in an age when nation-states seem no longer able to protect their borders. Each text challenges you to consider where you would draw the line between public and private.

www.
For additional readings on
What's Public? What's Private?
visit bedfordstmartins.com
/everythingsanargument.

▼ The following two articles appeared during the summer of 1999 on the editorial page of the Daily Texan, the student newspaper of the University of Texas at Austin. Russ Cobb, a graduate student in Spanish, and Roahn Wynar, a graduate student in physics, argue about whether the sophisticated marketing devices made possible by high technology and the Internet are helpful or harmful to consumers. As you read, consider the tone of each piece, the relationship that each author is trying to establish with his audience, and the kinds of appeals each author uses.

Point/Counterpoint:
They Know
What You're Buying

Point: Internet Target Marketing Threatens Consumer Privacy

Counterpoint: Paranoid Privacy Hawks Don't Realize How Good They've Got It

RUSS COBB

"78704—It's more than just a ZIP code, it's a way of life" a popular Austin bumper sticker proclaims. In the Information Age, numbers have become just as important markers of identity as the traditional demographics determined by income bracket, ethnicity and race. In the booming industry of Internet marketing, a seemingly unimportant postal code has become the means by which marketing specialists "target" and then "tailor" information to the unsuspecting consumer.

While super-hip Austinites may lay claim to a different "way of life" according to an arbitrary assignment by the post office, advertisers are realizing the true potential [of] a seemingly neutral code, investing millions of dollars into profiling consumers online. Ever bought a set of guitar strings from Mars, a TV antennae from Radio Shack, or a bike tube from Sears and wondered why you were

ROAHN WYNAR

The Internet is a target for college-of-liberal-arts-type demagogues who lately complain about invasive marketing practices. The claim is nebulous, but goes something like this: anytime you make a business transaction online, your demographic information is collected and exploited. Your privacy is invaded and there's nothing you can do about it.

For example, you sign up for an online newspaper, which is usually a free service. The newspaper collects a great deal of your personal information not only during sign-up, but also as you select articles and this information is used to route appropriate advertising your way, often while you browse. There is no doubt that this data can be stored and sold to direct mail and telephone marketing companies. In fact whenever you do business online you are broadcasting a piece of your personality.

Critics of this information gathering technique are making the absurd claim that some online com-

asked for your ZIP code? Whether you like it or not, you are slowly becoming part of [a] picture which is being painted by multinational marketing corporations to be sold to online advertisers.

ZIP codes have become all Internet users' de facto racial, ethnic and class identity indicators to a multimillion dollar advertising industry. By requesting your ZIP code in all online transactions, advertisers are allowed to construct a general profile of your interests. Likewise, the more your online activity is monitored by marketing experts, the more specific your profile becomes. You are then gently guided through the Internet Leviathan° by the people who know what's best for you—twenty-something techies with six figure salaries.

Internet technology works in mysterious ways . . .

To use an ostensibly "free" service like the *New York Times Online,* for example, you must first register according to your gender, income bracket and ZIP code. This information is then given to a marketing firm which specializes in "tailoring" information for everyone on the Internet, making sure you know your virtual place in virtual reality.

While the *Times* may boast that it publishes "all the news that's fit to print," the advertisers who fund this free service will eventually be able to "tailor" it—in other words censor it—to give you only the news you want.

Want to be updated on the latest stock prices and sports scores without having to sift through all that garbage about refugees and welfare reform? It will be done, and best of all, free of charge. Even now, the cynical intellectual can be kindly guided from the *New York Times* Book Review straight to the

panies are evil because they're observant and have good memories.

A specific case is Amazon.com. When you browse for a book online a helpful message displays, "Other people who bought this book also bought. . . ." Don't even try to argue that this is not a handy resource. Of course they also know the names, credit card numbers and browsing habits of every one of their customers.

It's easy to picture some social studies major somewhere, waxing nostalgic at their electric typewriter, wondering how they can make a name for themselves by inventing an unforeseen cultural consequence of Internet commerce.

Warnings about target marketing [have] become their—dare I say it?—zeitgeist. One can almost predict the title of the essay— *"Internet marketing and the contextualization of American self-identity: a critique of the new technocratic psychology—and its subtext of economic voyeurism."*

Target marketing is neither evil nor new. Marketing companies don't want to waste time advertising rosary beads to Mormons, as much as Mormons don't want to be bothered by such ads. What a wonderful day it will be when during the Superbowl I get to see commercials for photomultiplier tubes, diode lasers, computer games and violent action movies while our anti-progress Internet critics get to watch ads for kerosene lanterns, horse-drawn buggies, bows and arrows and the latest play at the amphitheatre.

Then there are those who claim this is an invasion of privacy. Here's a good point to consider: nobody gives a damn about you. Nobody cares if you buy hockey equipment online or spend 15 hours a day at hardcore.com. Privacy freaks are mild conspiracy theorists who think someone is watching them. Get over it. It is not the responsibility of online businesses to place their customers into therapy for paranoia.

Leviathan: in Jewish mythology, a primordial sea monster, sometimes multiheaded.

Barnes & Noble home page to purchase the latest scathing indictment of capitalism.

Lest you assume that the people behind Internet profiling are involved in some sort of altruistic endeavor for the sake of your pursuit of knowledge, it is important to recognize that the same practice is used in tailoring pornography and violence. In fact, Web sites like the *Times* have nothing to do with your profile; there are larger corporations such as doubleclick.com which buy that information you unwittingly provided as a guest the first time you visited the site.

The executives at one billion dollar-plus Internet "solutions" companies like doubleclick.com would have us believe there is a benevolent, democratic force behind the "tailoring" of online news information services. After all, it is their multi-million dollar investments in the traditional news media that keeps news on the Internet free-of-charge.

So what's wrong with this picture? 10

The "tailoring" of news by means of sly demographic profiling, i.e. ZIP codes, amounts to free market censorship. Corporate consolidation by marketing companies such as doubleclick.com, which just bought out its largest competitor, will never restrict, per se, what you can and cannot see on the Internet. They will, however, lull you into conformity with what they have found to obviously be in your best interest.

The survival of a democratic society requires an open forum for ideas which run contrary to conventional wisdom and across ZIP codes.

An opinion expressed this week in the *New York Times Magazine* was that quality of online news reporting will diminish as news sites focus on target marketing and abandon sections that don't produce many hits. Why report about Bosnia when the Yankees get a hundred times as many hits? There is no indication yet that this is happening, and the possibility that it will is empty speculation. There will always be a market for all sectors of news coverage and further specialization is good for consumers.

Will people ever stop inventing new reasons to 10 oppose technological advancement? It should be obvious by now that any notion of human progress is completely dependent on techno-nerds inventing better gizmos, and yet some people remain suspicious.

If I were in charge, Internet commerce would be run in such a way that every customer had their own special number. This number would connect to a database that has bucketloads of personal information ranging from clothing, food and travel tastes, to lifestyle habits, education, religion, legal histories, and credit ratings. You wouldn't be allowed to buy and sell on the Internet without this number. Soon all commerce will be done by computer and therefore everyone must have the number. No number, no food. Then, the fun part. After I implement the plan, I wait until the first 665 numbers have been issued, then I get mine!

Well, there's a reason to worry that is as logical as any I've heard.

Cobb invokes a powerful value for U.S. readers—the survival of a democratic society. See Chapter 5 for more information about making arguments based on values.

LINK TO P. 78

RESPOND ●

1. Summarize the position each writer takes on the question of Internet marketing and consumer privacy. To what extent do Cobb and Wynar directly address each other's arguments or evidence? What is each writer's attitude toward the other? Toward the audience? Cite evidence from the texts to support your answers.

2. Does either author engage in fallacious argumentation? How do you know? Cite examples. (You may want to review Chapter 19 on fallacies of argument.)

3. Which essay presents the better arguments based on fact and reason? Why? Which essay presents the better arguments based on values? Why? How and how effectively does each writer use humor?

4. **Write an essay** evaluating the relative effectiveness of Cobb's and Wynar's arguments. In the essay, you will need to state which writer's arguments you find superior and why. If your only reason for preferring one essay over the other is that the author's opinion matches yours, you will likely want to discuss the sorts of arguments necessary to persuade you that the other position is the more defensible one.

Divinity and Pornography

DENNIS PRAGER

Last fall, after serving thirteen years as the dean of the Harvard University Divinity School, Ronald F. Thiemann resigned. The reason has just been made public.

Harvard president Neil L. Rudenstine asked for the resignation. According to Joe Wrinn, a university spokesman, the Harvard president was told that Dean Thiemann had pornographic images on his computer. The dean had apparently asked computer technicians to supply him with a bigger computer hard drive, and the technicians, transferring files, found the images.

All parties to the issue note that none of the images were of minors. There is not the slightest suggestion that the dean ever acted improperly toward a female, whether student or employee. Indeed there is not the slightest suggestion that he ever did anything improper at all. This Harvard University dean was told to give up his position because of what he looked at, not what he did.

We have entered an era that is beyond what George Orwell imagined in *Nineteen Eighty-Four:* a time wherein the fantasy life of citizens is monitored by authorities.

Those who defend Harvard's position argue as follows: 5

(1) Thiemann was the dean of the divinity school, from whom different behavior is expected than from the dean of any other school. Had he been the dean of, let us say, the business school, he would not have been asked to resign.

(2) Any man who consumes pornography is a misogynist or, at the very least, regards women as less than human (as sexual objects) and is unworthy of a position of moral or other authority.

(3) The computer with the pornographic images was owned by Harvard University and therefore should not have been used for private purposes.

There are a number of problems with the first argument. One is that it misrepresents the task of the contemporary school of divinity. Unlike seminaries, which seek to inculcate a religion in their students,

◀ *This essay by theologian and talk-show host Dennis Prager appeared in July 1999 in the* Weekly Standard, *a magazine that describes itself as "a weekly journal of conservative opinion." Prager criticizes the decision by the Harvard University Divinity School to ask for the resignation of its dean, Ronald Thiemann, after pornographic images of women were found on his office computer. Although the right to privacy and its meaning is a major focus of this essay, Prager simultaneously constructs another argument about what he terms "heterophobia," "the fear and loathing of male heterosexuals." As you read this essay, consider how the evidence Prager chooses relates to each of his arguments.*

divinity schools teach their students *about* religion, just as schools of business teach about business and schools of education teach about education. Indeed, there are students and faculty at schools of divinity who believe in no religion or are even atheists.

It is true that Dean Thiemann is an ordained Lutheran minister, but that is only of concern to the Lutheran church. If it wishes to defrock a minister who has viewed pornography, that is its business and its prerogative. Religions are free to make any rules they want for their clergy. However, to the best of the public's knowledge, the Lutheran church has taken no steps toward punishing Pastor Thiemann, let alone removing him.

Harvard University clearly deems the private viewing of pornography more worthy of punishment than does the Lutheran church. I have long argued that contemporary liberalism serves for many of its adherents as a secular fundamentalist religion, and here is an example of that.

If Thiemann had been dean of another of its schools, would Harvard have ignored his pictures? Not likely. The Harvard feminists who protested against Dean Thiemann after they learned about the pornography—and who intimidate most universities' administrators—would have protested just as strongly against any other dean. The protesters' argument was not that Thiemann was the dean of a religious institution (which he was not), but that he engaged in a form of misogyny by consuming pornography. No politically correct college—which unfortunately means almost no college—has a president who will say the truth: that it is none of our business what legal pictures a man looks at in private, and that there is no correlation between viewing pornography and woman-hating. A university president who admitted that would be out of office before he could say "Catharine MacKinnon."°

This brings us to the second and most important argument—that men who use pornography demean women, or regard them as second-class beings, or simply harbor some conscious or unconscious hatred of them.

Those who make this argument either know very little about men's sexuality or are afraid of male heterosexuality (which is understandable—it can be frightening) and therefore demonize it. The plain fact of life is that normal and honorable heterosexual men enjoy looking at

Catharine MacKinnon: an American feminist and legal scholar (1946–) whose work has focused on pornography and sexual harassment. In the 1980s, MacKinnon came to public attention when she argued that pornography legitimizes the abuse and exploitation of women in society and thus constitutes a kind of sex discrimination. Thus, in her opinion, pornography is illegal.

partially clad and naked women. I feel a bit silly having to write in a publication read by college graduates what my unschooled grand-mother knew. But the denial of unpleasant realities is one of the features of the highly educated at the end of the twentieth century.

Enjoying looking at pictures of naked women no more means a het-   15 erosexual man loathes women or wants them demeaned than looking at pictures of naked men means a homosexual man loathes men or wants them demeaned. In fact, it means absolutely nothing.

The Harvard affair is an example of heterophobia, the fear and loathing of male heterosexuality—a far more accepted condition among modern elites than homophobia. After all, if the dean had been a homosexual man who had pictures of naked men on his computer, the chances that Harvard would have asked him to resign his position are next to nothing. And if it had asked him to resign, charges of homo-phobia would have engulfed the university.

As it happens, the minister of Harvard University—the person who embodies whatever commitment Harvard has to religion—is a gay man. Presumably, Harvard neither has asked nor cares if the minister is chaste. Presumably, it is of no concern to Harvard University whether the minister it has chosen to embody its concept of the holy has sexual relations with another man, other men, or men and women. But Harvard cannot tolerate a dean who is married, who is the father of two children, who, to the best of Harvard's knowledge, is faithful to his wife, yet who, in private, looks at pictures of naked women! Such lunacy can only be explained by ideological fervor. And the ideology in question is heterophobia.

As for the third argument, that the computer was owned by Har-vard—one wonders if those who offer this argument actually believe it or merely use it because they somehow know that having a dean resign because workmen found pictures of naked women on his com-puter is neither moral nor American. Harvard law professor Alan Der-showitz, who should be commended for his lonely defense of Dean Thiemann, has effectively refuted this argument. What if, Dershowitz asked, the dean had been a philatelist who had downloaded images of postage stamps—would anyone ask for his resignation because he kept these images on a Harvard-owned computer? Of course not. So, let's drop the pretense. At Harvard and in much of contemporary

Why does Prager include the information that the Harvard University minister is gay? Is that fact relevant to his argument? Does it qualify as a non sequitur? Check out Chapter 19 on logical fallacies, to help you answer that question.

LINK TO P. 398 ·······························

America, male heterosexuality is on notice not to rear its ugly head. (As for Prof. Dershowitz, I wonder when he will acknowledge that the greatest threats to liberty in America come from the left side of the political spectrum and from academia.)

Even if the three arguments had any merit, they would still pale in comparison to the deprivation of privacy in this case.

Why is abortion private and the viewing of pornography not?   20

Right to privacy—do these words ring a bell? The U.S. Supreme Court invoked this right in order to allow every woman the right to destroy a human fetus for any reason. I suspect that the president of Harvard and certainly all the feminists who protested Dean Thiemann's looking at pornography are pro-choice on abortion, on the grounds that society must protect a woman's right to privacy.

But do we not have a major contradiction here? On the one hand, these people declare the destroying of another being, a human fetus, an entirely private act that society has no right to judge, let alone restrict by legislation. On the other hand, they deny that what a man does in his most private world of sexual fantasy, by himself, to no one other than himself, is not private and that Harvard has every right to judge it and punish it.

How can we explain such a contradiction? Only by heterophobia—a hostility to heterosexual male sexuality.

And what is the reaction to this unprecedented violation of an entirely private area of a man's life? According to the *Los Angeles Times,* Thiemann's "colleagues at the school, known for its liberal philosophy, maintained a silence over the affair."

Why are Harvard's faculty members so quiet? Because at American 25 universities today there is no contest between feminist political correctness and a man's right to privacy. For a Harvard professor to come out in defense of Dean Thiemann's right to keep his fantasy life private would mean offending the feminist heterophobia that rules academia.

There is another fascinating contradiction here. I suspect that some of those who vociferously criticized Dean Thiemann were also among the most vocal defenders of President Clinton. They argued that society should allow the president of the United States to do whatever he wants sexually so long as it does not implicate his public duties. But how then can they criticize a college dean for his fantasy life? If looking at pictures of naked females alone in one's office fatally compromises a man's ability to be a university dean, why doesn't acting out sexual fantasies in the Oval Office with a real female compromise a man's ability to be president of the United States?

Too bad the dean resigned. I wouldn't have. I would have insisted on a public hearing. The only party in this matter deserving of humiliation is the party that did the humiliating—Harvard.

Fear and loathing of heterosexual male nature is a major problem in American life. That is why first-grade boys are kicked out of school for giving girls kisses on the cheek. The war on boys' natures also explains the desire to drug so many boys to calm them down. America is the first society ever to attempt to remake men's nature in the image of women's. Both men and women will suffer for it.

RESPOND ●

1. Prager considers Thiemann's firing to be an example of "hetero-phobia." Do you agree with his assessment? Why or why not?

2. How would you describe Prager's treatment of opposing views? Is it fair or unfair? Does he provide sufficient information about them? To what degree? How does his discussion of opposing positions support his own? (Try to imagine his argument with the treatment of opposing views removed.)

3. In paragraph 15, Prager draws an analogy between heterosexual men looking at pictures of naked women and homosexual men looking at pictures of naked men in order to argue that men who look at pictures of naked women do not loathe or demean women in general. Do you think this analogy is a good one? Is it limited in any way? Why or why not?

4. Prager boldly claims in paragraph 11 that contemporary liberalism is for many a "secular fundamentalist religion." What does Prager mean by this provocative claim? (What do you think Prager's opinion of fundamentalism is? How do you know?) **Write an essay** in which you argue for or against his position and the effectiveness of his argumentation.

5. In paragraph 20 Prager asks, "Why is abortion private and the viewing of pornography not?" In the following two paragraphs, he sets up another extended metaphor, specifically an analogy that juxtaposes abortion and pornography on the one hand, and the nature of privacy and publicness (or perhaps public acceptability) on the other. **Write an essay** evaluating the appropriateness of this analogy. Be sure to pay special attention to Prager's word choice as he characterizes abortion.

▼ *"Stripped of More than My Clothes" appeared in April 1999 in USA Today, a mainstream national newspaper that is often distributed free to airline passengers and guests at hotel chains. Daria MonDesire, a freelance writer based in Vermont, writes of the grave indignity she suffered upon returning to the United States after a trip abroad when she was strip-searched by U.S. Customs agents. Had she written in an irate tone and demanded reparations, few readers would have been surprised. MonDesire, however, uses a completely different rhetorical strategy. As you read, think about how her choice of style influences your response to her argument.*

Stripped of More than My Clothes

DARIA MONDESIRE

The most comforting part of a trip abroad used to be the part that brought me home.

There were only so many Yucatan pyramids to descend dizzily or Moorish castles to sigh over before not-to-be-denied nesting instincts kicked in and I missed the chaotic confusion of home. Souvenir mugs would get packed away, wet bathing suits tossed into carry-ons and unmailed postcards readied for repentant hand delivery.

Once aloft, I'd settle into a window seat, savor being above the clouds and think about the noisy welcome that awaited me.

Then came the day I found myself in a gray, windowless room in San Juan's airport politely being strip-searched by U.S. Customs agents.

There have, in my life, been two occasions when underwear was removed against my will. The first occurred at the hands of a rapist. The second time was at the hands of my government.

The agents told me they'd picked me out because I was dressed in bulky clothes: a backless sundress, a light cotton shirt and sandals. They told me that if they'd failed to stop me, their boss would have wanted to know why. They told me, after they'd made me remove my underwear and prove to their satisfaction the sanitary pad was there for its intended purpose, that I should consider working undercover as a drug agent.

Then they let me go.

Drugs have taken a numbing toll on this country. Lives have been lost, minds wasted. Heroin and cocaine should not be allowed to flow onto our shores unchallenged and unabated. Yet there's something chilling about a federal policy where law-abiding American citizens are forced to disrobe, detained without counsel, subjected to intrusive body cavity searches and at times held for as long as it takes laxatives to empty their stomachs.

Last year, 50,892 international airline passengers went through the rigors of some type of body search courtesy of the U.S. Customs Service—most of them "pat-downs" that fall short of the service's definition of a strip-search. One would surmise, given the professionalism of U.S. Customs officers, that drugs and maybe a mango or two would turn up on at least half the passengers subjected to such scrutiny.

Guess again. According to the Customs Service, 96% of them were found to be carrying nothing more than memories of a Caribbean honeymoon, gaudy sombreros destined to collect dust on a family room wall or mildewed laundry in need of a washer. Even three out of four of the 2,797 travelers subjected to partial or full strip searches, X-ray exams or cavity searches turned out not to be carrying drugs or contraband.

Those strip-searched were everyday people going about their everyday lives, until a federal agent labeled them with two loaded words: "potential courier." Had a municipal police department or a state police force attempted to do what U.S. Customs zealously did, constitutional safeguards against unreasonable search and seizure would bring the attempts to a screeching halt.

I can't say with absolute certainty why I, the one African-American on my flight, also was the one passenger on my flight singled out for that search several years ago. The official Customs line is that it focuses on high-risk flights from high-risk countries. Perhaps Grenada is famous for more than nutmeg and American intervention. Perhaps I should have taken care of those unpaid parking tickets. Perhaps I was a victim of a vast, right-wing conspiracy. It's all so wearying to think that, in addition to everything else being black in America entails, it may signal prima facie° grounds for agents of my government to strip me.

This much is clear: Minorities bear the brunt of the examinations. Of the total number of airline passengers who were searched in some manner in 1998 and on whom Customs kept race-identifying statistics, two-thirds were black, Latino or Asian.

---

prima facie: a Latin phrase that means "on first view" or "before additional examination."

MonDesire uses a rhetorical strategy when she defers the description of her proposal until the end of her article. You may wish to use a different strategy in your writing; see Chapter 12 for suggestions on ways of constructing a proposal argument.

LINK TO P. 238

Customs officials, noting that three times as many whites as blacks were strip-searched, say they don't discriminate against blacks.

This official position, however, does not include the opinion of Cathy Harris, a Customs inspector in Atlanta who has filed complaints alleging discrimination against black travelers. Nor is it supported by about four dozen black women who launched a class-action lawsuit in Chicago against the Customs Service alleging they were targeted for strip-searches because of their race. According to their attorney, Edward M. Fox, they include a 15-year-old searched while traveling with her white mother and aunt, who were not searched, a mentally retarded woman and a travel agent who has been repeatedly searched. Fox says he's now heard from more than 90 women from across the country.

The low number of body searches leading to drug seizures, the lawsuits and the complaints have convinced the Customs Service that things are not going swimmingly. A new commissioner, Raymond W. Kelly, has a consultant examining the agency's policies. Customs officers are taking classes

in cultural diversity. Some targeted passengers are being given the option of having machines scan their bodies.

Here's my proposal. Let's level the probing field and make it, indeed, a war against drugs.

Strip-search everyone who travels out of the country.

Strip-search Martha Stewart the second she steps off the Concorde. Strip-search Al Gore, members of Congress, all nine Supreme Court justices and every last one of the Daughters of the American Revolution. Strip-search Barbara Walters, Ivana Trump and ditto for The Donald. Strip search the Toujours Provence tourists, the Tuscany villa vacationers and the Hollywood-St. Barts brigade. Strip-search everyone who heretofore labored under the privileged assumption they could return to this country with some shred of dignity.

And then let the chips fall where they may.

15

20

RESPOND ●

1. MonDesire's proposal that all U.S. citizens returning home after a trip abroad be strip-searched is made for rhetorical effect; she knows (and so do we) that no such policy would ever be seriously considered. However, accept for a moment her proposal and analyze its logic. What are its strengths and weaknesses? What evidence can you provide for your position?

2. MonDesire incorporates statistics into her argument as part of the evidence for her claims. Sometimes she uses exact numbers (50,892; 2,797; 96 percent), and sometimes she uses prose figures (three out of four; two-thirds). Can you see any logic to her choices?

3. MonDesire offers one solution to what she sees as a major problem caused by U.S. Customs policy. Later in this chapter, you will find an essay by Mona Charen, "We Should Relinquish Some Liberty in Exchange for Security" (p. 540). Charen would likely offer a very different proposal to problems like the one described by MonDesire. How would she propose responding to the overzealousness and inequities in the U.S. Customs' treatment of returning citizens? Which solution do you think would be the better one—MonDesire's or Charen's—and why?

4. How does the woodcut-style illustration accompanying this article contribute to its force? What visual symbols does Marcy E. Mullins, the artist, use to establish the power and authority of the Customs agents? The vulnerability of the woman, whom we take to be MonDesire?

5. Research the practices of U.S. Customs with regard to drug searches, the agency's rate of success, and the controversies surrounding these practices. **Write a letter** to U.S. Customs commissioners either proposing changes in the policy on searching returning citizens or urging the commissioners to maintain the current system. Provide solid evidence for your argument, and establish yourself as knowledgeable about this subject.

▶ Patricia Hampl, Regents Professor at the University of Minnesota, is an award-winning poet and memoirist. This excerpt from "Other People's Secrets" raises profound questions about privacy: Do we have a right to tell some family secrets, or should they remain classified information? In this essay, Hampl recounts her changing understanding of a disagreement she had with her mother about the opening poem in her first published book of poems, **Woman before an Aquarium** (1978). Following the essay, we reprint the poem, "Mother-Daughter Dance," which acknowledges Hampl's mother's epilepsy. The first stanza recounts a fight the narrator has had with another adult, likely a male partner or lover, which forces her to remember her mother's epilepsy and her own struggles with her mother. The speaker simultaneously becomes herself as a child— watching her father try to help her mother—and her mother—someone victimized by epilepsy and her husband. At the same time, she is the daughter fighting to become independent from her mother and the partner in a relationship where she, the poet, cannot speak.

Other People's Secrets

PATRICIA HAMPL

When I was thirty-two, my first book was accepted for publication, a collection of poems. My mother was ecstatic. She wrote in her calendar for that June day—practically crowing—"First Book Accepted!!" as if she were signing a contract of her own, one which committed her to overseeing an imaginary multiple-book deal she had negotiated with the future on my behalf. She asked to see the manuscript out of sheer delight and pride. My first reader.

And here began my career of betrayal. The opening poem in the manuscript, called "Mother-Daughter Dance," was agreeably imagistic, the predictable struggle of the suffocated daughter and the protean mother padded with nicely opaque figurative language. No problem. Only at the end, rising to a crescendo of impacted meaning, had the poem, seemingly of its own volition, reached out of its complacent obscurity to filch a plain and serviceable fact—my mother's epilepsy. There it was, the grand mal seizure as the finishing touch, a personal fact that morphed into a symbol, opening the poem, I knew, wide, wide, wide.

"You cannot publish that poem," she said on the telephone, not, for once, my stage mother egging me on. The voice of the betrayed, I heard for the first time, is not sad. It is coldly outraged.

"Why not?" I said with brazen innocence.

Just who did I think I was?   5

A writer, of course. We get to do this—tell secrets and get away with it. It's called, in book reviews and graduate seminars, courage. *She displays remarkable courage in exploring the family's. . . . the book is sustained by his exemplary courage in revealing. . . .*

I am trying now to remember if I cared about her feelings at all. I know I did not approve of the secrecy in which for years she had wrapped the dark jewel of her condition. I did not feel she *deserved* to be so upset about something that should be seen in purely practical terms. I hated—feared, really—the freight she loaded on the idea of epilepsy, her belief that she would lose her job if anyone "found out," her baleful stories of people having to cross the border into Iowa to get married because "not so long ago" Minnesota refused to issue marriage licenses to epileptics. The idea of Iowa being "across the border" was itself absurd.

She had always said she was a feminist before there was feminism, but where was that buoyant *Our Bodies, Ourselves* ° spirit? Vanished. When it came to epilepsy, something darkly medieval had bewitched her, making it impossible to appeal to her usually wry common sense. I rebelled against her shivery horror of seizures, although her own had been successfully controlled by medication for years. It was all, as I told her, no big deal. Couldn't she see that?

Stony silence.

She was outraged by my betrayal. I was furious at her theatrical 10 secrecy. Would you feel this way, I asked sensibly, if you had diabetes?

"This isn't diabetes," she said darkly, the rich unction of her shame refusing my hygienic approach.

Even as we faced off, I felt obscurely how thin my reasonableness was. The gravitas of her disgrace infuriated me partly because it had such natural force. I was a reed easily snapped in the fierce gale of her shame. I sensed obliquely that her loyalty to her secret bespoke a firmer grasp of the world than my poems could imagine. But poetry was everything! That I knew. Her ferocious secrecy made me feel foolish, a lightweight, but for no reason I could articulate. Perhaps I had, as yet, no secret of my own to guard, no humiliation against which I measured myself and the cruelly dispassionate world with its casual, intrusive gaze.

I tried, of course, to make *her* feel foolish. It was ridiculous, I said, to think anyone would fire her for a medical condition—especially her employer, a progressive liberal-arts college where she worked in the library. "You don't know people," she said, her dignified mistrust subtly trumping my credulous open-air policy.

This was tougher than I had expected. I changed tactics. Nobody even reads poetry, I assured her shamelessly. You have nothing to worry about.

She dismissed this pandering. "You have no right," she said simply. 15

It is pointless to claim your First Amendment rights with your mother. My arguments proved to be no argument at all, and she was impervious to any blandishment.

Our Bodies, Ourselves: best-selling reference book, first commercially published in 1973 by the Boston Women's Health Book Collective, a grass-roots collective that became an important non-profit organization devoted to women's health issues. Frustrated over an inability to get adequate and accurate information about matters of health and sexuality from the medical establishment, overwhelmingly male dominated at the time, the collective began compiling information to educate women about their bodies. The book has been translated or adapted into nineteen languages. In its most recent edition, it is entitled *Our Bodies, Ourselves for the New Century.* For additional information on the Collective and the book, go to <ourbodiesourselves.org>.

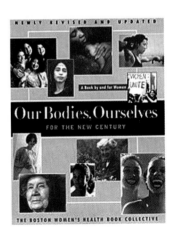

Our Bodies, Ourselves

It seems particularly appropriate that Hampl would use her personal experience as the evidence in an argument about the privacy of personal experience. Check out what Chapter 18 has to say about using personal experience in your writing.

LINK TO P. 375

Then, when things looked lost, I was visited by a strange inspiration.

I simply reversed field. I told her that if she wanted, I would cut the poem from the book. I paused, let this magnanimous gesture sink in. "You think it over," I said. "I'll do whatever you want. But Mother . . ."

"What?" she asked, wary, full of misgivings as well she might have been.

"One thing," I said, the soul of an aluminum-siding salesman rising 20 within me, "I just want you to know—before you make your decision— it really is the best poem in the book." Click.

This was not, after all, an inspiration. It was a gamble. And although it was largely unconscious, still, there was calculation to it. She loved to play the horses. And I was my mother's daughter; instinctively I put my money on a winner. The next morning she called and told me I could publish the poem. "It's a good poem," she said, echoing my own self-promoting point. Her voice was rinsed of outrage, a little weary but without resentment.

Describe it as I saw it then: she had read the poem, and like God in His heaven, she saw that it was good. I didn't pause to think she was doing me a favor, that she might be making a terrible sacrifice. This was good for her, I told myself with the satisfied righteousness of a nurse entering a terrified patient's room armed with long needles and body restraints. The wicked witch of secrecy had been vanquished. I hadn't simply won (although that was delicious). I had liberated my mother, unlocked her from the prison of the dank secret where she had been cruelly chained for so long.

I felt heroic in a low-grade literary sort of way. I understood that poetry—my poem!—had performed this liberating deed. My mother had been unable to speak. I had spoken for her. It had been hard for both of us. But this was the whole point of literature, its deepest good, this voicing of the unspoken, the forbidden. And look at the prize we won with our struggle—for doesn't the truth, as John, the beloved apostle promised, set you free? . . .

What memory "sees," it must regard through the image-making faculty of mind. The parallel lines of memory and imagination cross finally, and collide in narrative. The casualty is the dead body of privacy lying smashed on the track.

MOTHER-DAUGHTER DANCE

PATRICIA HAMPL

Because it is late
because we fought today
because it was hot
and heat is an excuse
to be alone,
I sit in this chair stuffed
with old sun, leftover heat.

Our fight. The subject as always was history.
You made me look over my shoulder.
Mother was back there, speaking
to us in epilepsy, that language
she learned on her own,
the one we encouraged her to use
at the dinner table.
In my mind, I fell down, writhing,
trying to make history repeat itself,
burning with translations of guilt
for the men in the family.
Father forced a yellow pencil
between Mother's teeth, like a rose:
you die if you swallow your tongue.

All afternoon you yelled at me
as I slithered nearer to her.
We were doing the mother-daughter sweat dance,
salt dance, sexy Spanish rose dance.
You were yelling from the English language,
that fringed island I swim toward at night.
"The pencil," you were screaming in your language,
"Take the pencil from her mouth.
Write it down,
write your message down."

We expect poetry to use figurative language of the types described in Chapter 14. Which tropes does Hampl use in her poem? See descriptions of the different types of figurative language in Chapter 14 to help you figure out your answer.

LINK TO P. 288

RESPOND ●

1. What does Hampl mean when she claims, in the closing lines of the essay, that "The parallel lines of memory and imagination cross finally, and collide in narrative. The casualty is the dead body of privacy lying smashed on the track?" (By "narrative," Hampl simply means the stories people tell about themselves and their experiences, whether published essays like this one or the stories that are told in everyday conversation.)

2. We should not be surprised that as a poet, Hampl uses figurative language (Chapter 14) strategically and effectively when writing an essay. Particularly noteworthy is her word choice, especially her use of verbs and adjectives, which often creates clear and powerful images. Find at least five examples of Hampl's effective word choice, and be prepared to explain why you find them so.

3. In an era much accustomed to television shows on which Jerry Springer and other hosts encourage guests to tell all, and to published discussions of scandals involving child sexual abuse, Hampl's essay and concern may seem a bit old-fashioned. Do you find them so? Why or why not? How sympathetic are you to the stance of Hampl's mother? To Hampl's changing understanding of her own behavior and that of her mother? Why?

4. Do you have a right to make public (even to your closest friends) the secrets of your family members? Should there be privacy about family matters? Why or why not? Under what circumstances? And what might the limits of such privacy be? **Write a proposal essay** in which you define and justify the limits of privacy within families. It is quite possible to write such an essay without referring to specific incidents from your own past. Whether or not you choose to do so will have consequences for the ethos you create (see Chapter 12).

This cluster of arguments focuses on **privacy and civil liberties after September 11,** the national debate about whether and how our government should or should not limit privacy in America in the name of national security. Declan McCullagh's essay, "Why Liberty Suffers in Wartime," seeks to put the question in a historical context by examining our government's response to this challenge during previous times of war. Mona Charen, a syndicated columnist, contends that the need for security is worth the sacrifice of some civil liberties, whereas an editorial from the *Minneapolis Daily* offers a different perspective on the topic. Matthew Brzezinksi's "The Homeland Security State: How Far Should We Go?" challenges us to think in terms of the specific changes we're willing to accept or reject as the country seeks security in a world that seems permanently changed in important ways. Essays by Alan Dershowitz and Ira Berkow investigate in detail two of the proposed changes Brzezinski mentions: national identity cards and racial or ethnic profiling. Jose Hernandez's personal essay reminds readers that despite the best efforts of any state to control its borders, where there is a will to penetrate them, there is likely a way, especially in a country as ethnically diverse as the United States.

Research on privacy in this country over the twenty-five or so years prior to the events of September 11 showed that about a quarter of Americans were vigilant about their privacy, nearly a quarter seemed to be indifferent to the issue, and the remaining 55 percent—whom retired Columbia University professor Alan Westin labels "privacy pragmatists"—were interested in knowing how they might benefit from permitting information about themselves to be gathered. How would you characterize yourself? What information about you should the government have access to, and what information should remain private? What price are you willing to pay for security—or the illusion of security? Has your opinion about these matters changed since September 11? As you read, give some thought in particular to the ways in which our evolving response to the events of that day continue to redefine the terms—and the stakes—of debates about privacy.

Why Liberty Suffers in Wartime

DECLAN MCCULLAGH

WASHINGTON—Anyone worried about the fate of civil liberties during the U.S. government's growing war on terrorism might want to consider this Latin maxim: Inter arma silent leges. It means, "In time of war the laws are silent," and it encapsulates the supremacy of security over liberty that typically accompanies national emergencies.

Consider this: During all of America's major wars—the Civil War, World War I and World War II—the government restricted Americans' civil liberties in the name of quelling dissent, silencing criticism of political decisions and preserving national security.

It's far too soon to predict what additional powers the government will assume after the catastrophic attacks on the World Trade Center and the Pentagon. To their credit, many politicians have already stressed that sacrificing liberty for security, even temporarily, is an unacceptable trade. "We will not violate people's basic rights as we make this nation more secure," said House Majority Leader Dick Armey (R-Texas). Sen. Max Baucus (D-Montana) said: "This does not mean that we can allow terrorists to alter the fundamental openness of U.S. society or the government's respect for civil liberties. If we do so, they will have won."

These statements come as Congress is deliberating a sweeping set of proposals from the Bush administration that would increase wiretapping of phones and the Internet, boost police authority to detain suspected terrorists, and rewrite immigration laws. In response, a coalition of over 100 groups from across the political spectrum asked Congress to tread carefully in this area last week.

Yet history has shown that during moments of national crisis, real or perceived, politicians have been quick to seize new authority, and courts have been impotent or reluctant to interfere. 5

In July 1798, Congress enacted the Alien and Sedition Acts, ostensibly to respond to the possible threat posed by the French Revolution, but also in an attempt to punish Thomas Jefferson's Republican party. The laws made it a crime to "write, print, utter or publish" any "false,

◀ *In this essay posted in late September 2001 on* Wired News, *Declan McCullagh surveys American history for evidence that "In time of war the laws are silent" even as he mentions the birth of groups like In Defense of Freedom <indefenseoffreedom.org> that sprang up shortly after the tragedy of September 11, vowing to ensure that liberties did not disappear during the war on terrorism. As you read, note McCullagh's choice of historical events to include, and ask yourself whether or not you believe he is able to support his claim adequately.*

Use the criteria given in Chapter 18 to determine whether you think McCullagh chose appropriate evidence and used it effectively.

LINK TO P. 367 ·····························

scandalous and malicious writing or writings against the government of the United States, or either house of the Congress of the United States or the president of the United States."

That enraged Kentucky and Virginia. Kentucky's legislature approved a statement saying, "This commonwealth does upon the most deliberate reconsideration declare, that the said alien and sedition laws, are in their opinion, palpable violations of the Constitution." (An earlier draft, relying on libertarian principles, went so far as to say such laws were "void and of no force.")

During the Civil War, President Lincoln interfered with freedom of speech and of the press and ordered that suspected political criminals be tried before military tribunals. Much as President Bush now is concerned with protecting airplane safety, Lincoln wanted to preserve the railroads: Rebels were destroying railroad bridges near Baltimore in 1861.

Probably Lincoln's most controversial act was suspending the writ of habeas corpus, a safeguard of liberty that dates back to English common law and England's Habeas Corpus Act of 1671. A vital check on the government's power, habeas corpus says that authorities must bring a person they arrest before a judge who orders it. The U.S. Constitution says: "The privilege of the writ of habeas corpus shall not be suspended, unless when in cases of rebellion or invasion the public safety may require it." But Lincoln suspended habeas corpus without waiting for Congress to authorize it.

Lincoln's decision led to a showdown between the military and 10 United States Chief Justice Roger Taney. After the U.S. Army arrested John Merryman on charges of destroying railroad bridges and imprisoned him in Fort McHenry, Merryman's lawyer drew up a habeas corpus petition that Taney quickly signed. When the Army refused to bring Merryman before the high court, Taney said the U.S. marshals had the authority to haul Army General George Cadwalader into the courtroom on contempt charges—but Taney would not order it since the marshals would likely be outgunned. Instead, Taney protested and called on Lincoln "to perform his constitutional duty to enforce the laws" and the "process of this court."

This was a controversial decision: *The New York Times* described Taney's decision the next day as one that "can only be regarded as at once officious and improper."

Soon after declaring war on Germany and its allies in 1917, Congress banned using the U.S. mail for sending any material urging "treason, insurrection or forcible resistance to any law." It punished offenders with a fine of up to $5,000 and a five-year prison term, and the government used this new authority to ban magazines such as *The Nation* from the mail. President Wilson asked Congress to go even further: His draft of the Espionage Act included a $10,000 fine and 10 years imprisonment for anyone publishing information that could be useful to the enemy. The House of Representatives narrowly defeated it by a vote of 184-144.

Even without Wilson's proposals, the Espionage Act gave birth to a famous civil liberties case: U.S. v. Charles Schenck. The Supreme Court unanimously upheld his conviction for printing leaflets that urged Americans to resist the draft. The justices ruled: "When a nation is at war, many things that might be said in time of peace are such a hindrance to its effort that their utterance will not be endured so long as men fight and that no court could regard them as protected by any constitutional right."

While there were no trials before military tribunals, the Justice Department unsuccessfully asked Congress to enact a law—punishable by death—that would have authorized such trials for anyone "interfering with the war effort."

Civil liberties groups recently have repeatedly offered reminders of 15 the internment of Japanese immigrants and their children in walled camps in the aftermath of Pearl Harbor. In Executive Order 9066, President Roosevelt authorized the military to remove Japanese-Americans from America's west coast, home to many military bases and manufacturing plants—and viewed at the time as vulnerable to Japanese attack. In a remarkable silence, the American Civil Liberties Union did not object to the internment camps until years later.

A collection of challenges to the internment camps found their way to the U.S. Supreme Court. In a brief supporting the camps, the states of Washington, Oregon and California noted that Japanese submarines had attacked oil platforms at Santa Barbara, California, the town of Brookings, Oregon, and a gun installation at Astoria, Oregon. On June 7, 1942, the brief said, the Japanese had invaded North America by occupying some Aleutian islands.

In its response, drafted by Chief Justice Harlan Stone in 1943, the

World War II Japanese internment camp

court ducked the constitutionality of internment camps, ruling only on a related curfew requirement. The justices upheld the action: "Whatever views we may entertain regarding the loyalty to this country of the citizens of Japanese ancestry, we cannot reject as unfounded the judgment of the military authorities and of Congress that there were disloyal members of that population."

Some of America's most respected legal thinkers, while saying that the government went too far in World War II, say that some erosion of freedom in wartime is necessary. "There is no reason to think that future wartime presidents will act differently from Lincoln, Wilson or Roosevelt, or that future justices of the Supreme Court will decide questions differently from their predecessors," William Rehnquist, chief justice of the United States, wrote in a book published in 1998. "It is neither desirable nor it is remotely likely that civil liberty will occupy as favored a position in wartime as it does in peacetime," Rehnquist wrote in *All the Laws But One*.

The 100-plus groups whose representatives gathered at the National Press Club on Thusday aren't quite so certain. In a statement posted on a new website, In Defense of Freedom, they say: "We need to ensure that actions by our government uphold the principles of a democratic society, accountable government and international law, and that all decisions are taken in a manner consistent with the Constitution."

RESPOND•

1. McCullagh's article is based largely on historical evidence. What is his thesis? What is his perspective on the question of civil liberties in time of war? What evidence can you cite for your response?

2. If you are unfamiliar with the historical incidents that McCullagh cites, investigate one or more of them using the Internet. Be prepared to share with your classmates the information you find. In particular, be ready to explain whether and why you believe McCullagh did or did not represent the incident fairly and accurately.

3. How has your thinking about the topic of civil liberties changed since the events of September 11? Why? Near the end of his essay, McCullagh quotes Chief Justice of the U.S. Supreme Court William Rehnquist, who in a 1998 book claims that "It is neither desirable nor is it remotely likely that civil liberty will occupy as favored a position in wartime as it does in peacetime" (paragraph 18). **Write an essay** in which you argue for or against Rehnquist's claim. Regardless of your position, you will need to present a proposal addressing the extent to which civil liberties should or should not occupy a favored position during wartime. The Internet might prove useful in helping you find recent discussions of particular debates about civil liberties in American society. Analyzing your own response to the Web site for In Defense of Freedom will likely help you clarify your thinking on this subject, as will studying the other readings in this cluster.

▼ *In this editorial from November 2002, columnist Mona Charen argues that Americans should be willing to relinquish some of the liberties they may take for granted—not only as a response to the events of September 11 but also as a corrective to "decades of liberal 'reforms,'" which she contends were excessive. As you read, pay attention to the language she uses in characterizing those she labels "liberals" and those she contrasts as "others" who "see the world differently," as well as the way in which she sets up a single dichotomy of possible perspectives on this topic.*

We Should Relinquish Some Liberty in Exchange for Security

MONA CHAREN

It will be interesting to see how the debate over civil liberties and the war on terror plays out now that the electorate has given President George W. Bush such a vote of confidence. Since Sept. 11, the left has pitched fits about military commissions, alleged attorney-client privilege infringements, telephone taps, surveillance of suspected terrorists, fingerprinting and photographing of some foreign visitors, and particularly round-ups of visa violators. Each of these measures has been met with loud objections from liberals who are convinced that the Bush administration is on the verge of creating a police state.

Others see the world differently. Instead of an out-of-control government behemoth spying on you and me in complete disregard for civil liberties, they see our domestic and foreign intelligence services as toothless watchdogs, powerless to detect or stop terrorism after decades of liberal "reforms."

No one, least of all a conservative concerned about government power, should take civil liberties protection lightly. But the liberal reforms of the past generation have gone way beyond protecting the privacy

Osama bin Laden

rights of American citizens — they've protected the ability of international terrorists to function in this country virtually unimpeded. Everyone now knows that FBI agent Colleen Rowley pleaded with her superiors for permission to inspect the computer of Zacharias Moussaoui, only to be told that she lacked "probable cause." If investigors had searched that laptop, they would have found the name and phone number of one of the ringleaders of the Sept. 11 plot.

This bit of recent history is raised to imply that the FBI screwed up in August 2001. Yet when the suggestion is made that perhaps the "probable cause" standard be brought down a notch, say to "reasonable suspicion," the civil-liberties types go ballistic. When the Justice Department interviewed several thousand men from Arab nations, The New York Times decried the "vast roundup" and the American Civil Liberties Union shrilled that this "dragnet approach . . . is likely to magnify concerns of racial and ethnic profiling." In fact, as Professor Robert Turner of the University of Virginia Law School relates, interviewees were treated politely and asked, among other things, whether they had encountered any acts of bigotry.

Before Sept. 11, and thanks to a process of emasculation stretching back to the Church committee hearings of the 1970s, the FBI and CIA were forbidden to share information. Even within the FBI, thanks to "the wall" inaugurated under Attorney General Janet Reno, a counter-terrorism agent examining a terror cell in Buffalo could not walk down the hall and chat with a criminal investigator who was looking into money laundering by the same people. The FBI was forbidden to conduct general Internet searches, or to visit public places open to all.

Seventy-five percent of the American people told the Gallup organization that the Bush administration has not gone too far in restricting civil liberties. Fifty percent thought they'd gone far enough, but 25 percent thought they should have been tougher. Only 11 percent thought the administration had gone too far.

What liberals are urging is that suspected terrorists, here or abroad, be accorded the full panoply of rights we give to ordinary criminal defendants. But this judicializes war. President Bill Clinton adhered to this model and accordingly turned down an opportunity to capture Osama bin Laden because he feared we might not have proper evidence for a criminal indictment.

But the war powers of the presidency, long respected by the courts, permit special action in the case of war. Even before Sept. 11, bin Laden had declared war on the United States and was clearly ineligible for a criminal trial. He was morally and legally an enemy combatant. Similarly, though, President Bush has not taken any action since Sept. 11 that was not also approved overwhelmingly by the Congress.

5 But the key point is this: If we err on the side of civil liberties instead of on the side of security, hundreds of thousands or millions of Americans could die. If we err on the side of security, many people will be inconvenienced and a few individuals may be wrongly imprisoned for some time. In which direction would you lean? ■

Who is Charen writing for in this article? How does she establish rapport with her readers? See Chapter 3 to learn techniques for connecting with your readers.

LINK TO P. 56 ·································

RESPOND●

1. For Charen, the question of civil liberties can be reduced to a simple dichotomy—a pair of options—which she formulates as the "key point" in the closing paragraph of this editorial (paragraph 9). Do you agree with her formulation? What are the advantages of such a dichotomy, especially in a newspaper editorial? What are the disadvantages of such a position? If forced to choose one of the two options she formulates, which would you choose? Why? If forced to reformulate the situation in a dichotomous way, what would your dichotomy look like? If you had to reframe the "key point" in a way that is not a dichotomy—that is, in a way that assumes more than two options—how would you reframe it?

2. In paragraph 7, Charen contends that "accord[ing] the full panoply of rights we give to ordinary criminal defendants . . . judicializes war." What does she mean by this claim? What sorts of rights, if any, do you believe "ordinary criminal defendants" should be accorded? Why? Why must we consider the rights of criminals and those alleged to have committed crimes when we explore the question of civil liberties? How did the events of September 11, in particular, complicate our discussions of the civil liberties of criminals and alleged criminals?

3. Evaluate Charen's use of language with respect to how she characterizes liberals and others. Do you find it unduly slanted (Chapter 14)? Why or why not? How does her word choice relate to her intended and invoked readers (Chapter 3)? How does it affect the likelihood that she will be persuasive to readers who do not already agree with her? Why?

4. Based on your response to question 1, **write an essay** in which you evaluate Charen's formulation of the "key point" in debates about civil liberties in the United States after September 11. In other words, relying on the discussion of evaluative arguments in Chapter 10, evaluate Charen's understanding of the question of civil liberties at this time. If you find her formulation an appropriate one, you will need to state the criteria you used in arriving at that conclusion. If you are unhappy with her formulation of the "key point," you may wish to propose a reformulation of the question; that is, you might offer a different way of stating what the "key point" is with regard to civil liberties. (See Chapter 12 on proposal arguments.)

▼ *In this unsigned editorial from August 2002, the staff of the* Minnesota Daily *take a decidedly different stance from the one taken by Charen in the previous selection ("We Should Relinquish Some Liberty in Exchange for Security"). It is important to note that they formulate the question of civil liberties from a different perspective than Charen does. As you read, think about how their approach to the question of civil liberties differs from Charen's.*

Privacy, Civil Rights Infringements Multiply after Sept. 11

STAFF, *MINNESOTA DAILY*

The increasingly omnipresent Big Brother was scolded Friday by its lawful mother, the federal court system, for overstepping its constitutional right in the war on terrorism. U.S. District Court Judge Gladys Kessler ruled the Justice Department, led by Attorney General John Ashcroft, had not proven the need to withhold the names of the more than 1,000 people rounded up by the government following the terrorist attacks of Sept. 11. She gave the government 15 days to release the names.

In her decision, Kessler wrote, "The first priority of the judicial branch must be to ensure that our government always operates within the statutory and constitutional constraints, which distinguish a democracy from a dictatorship." And it is this democratic concept supported by law and grounded in the ideals of Americans that will help stave off the enigmatic Big Brother from coalescing into a juggernaut of invasive control.

But this ruling, although a victory for civil liberties and good reason to collectively release our breath, should not be seen as the end-all to the recent infringements on American freedom perpetrated by our own government as a result of Sept. 11.

Some of the most critical battles over civil liberties are now being waged in the courts and on Capitol Hill. For instance, the George W. Bush administration recently proposed Operation Terrorist Information and Prevention System [TIPS]. The program plans to recruit 1 million volunteers to act as spies and informants against their neighbors. TIPS, if enacted by Congress, would enlist the work of cable installers, utility workers, letter carriers and others who have some access to Americans' private lives. They would report what they deemed abnormal behavior to the government, which could then be acted upon. If that doesn't sound Orwellian, then you haven't read "1984."

Making matters worse is other legislation—both enacted and pending—that, coupled with things such as TIPS, could give the government odious control and invasive insight into our lives. Take for instance the Patriot Act, perhaps the most far-reaching of such laws. Under this law the government can, among other things, put recording devices into places of religious sanctity such as the confessional booth or the neighborhood mosque. Also, there is a provision in the proposed Andean Trade Bill that would give the U.S. Customs Service virtual immu-

Film still from Orwell's 1984, *with Big Brother in the background.*

nity from lawsuits related to racial and religious profiling.

The sacrifice of civil liberties goes on. A personal computer located in the confines of your home has no legal right of privacy if it is connected to the Internet. The government contends that since people do not always know what they are downloading, or if they are being hacked, they should not have a reasonable sense of privacy on their computers. Therefore, computers are not protected by the Fifth Amendment. Any e-mail, document or other piece of information stored on computers connected to the Internet can be used by the government.

Yet many Americans still blindly believe: "If I'm not doing anything wrong, then why should I worry?" They should worry because the government has the power to determine what is right and what is wrong. But what is right today can be made wrong tomorrow. That means that the dossier the government created on a citizen could be the evidence against that person if the law changes.

So while Friday's ruling is a sign the encroachment of the government on the individual rights and freedoms of American citizens is finding oppositional force within the legal system, it is still important that all Americans vigilantly defend their rights. Many current college students grew up with the Saturday morning slogan of G.I. Joe, "Knowing is half the battle," which is true. But the other half is standing steadfast upon that knowledge, turning wisdom into action. Otherwise we might have to redefine what it means to be an American. ∎

RESPOND •

1. What is the editorial staff of the *Minnesota Daily* arguing for? What are they arguing against? How does their formulation of the problem compare with Charen's?

2. Evaluate this editorial's use of language with respect to how it characterizes those who would support its stance and those who would not. Do you find it unduly slanted (Chapter 14)? Why or why not? How does the editorial's word choice relate to its intended and invoked readers (Chapter 3)? How does it affect the likelihood that the editorial will be persuasive to readers who do not already agree with the stance it takes? Why?

3. In what ways is this editorial an argument about privacy? How do the writers link the questions of privacy and civil liberties? How effective and convincing do you find the links they claim to exist? Why?

4. **Write a letter to the editor** of an imaginary newspaper that published the editorial by Charen or this editorial. In your letter, you may agree or disagree with the stance taken by one of the authors. If you agree, you will likely need to elaborate on the point in some novel way (for example, discuss its relevance to the current political situation) or offer additional support for the correctness of its viewpoint. If, on the other hand, you disagree with the perspective taken, you will need to explain why and perhaps offer a contrasting opinion. Most newspapers ask that letters to the editor be limited to 250 words, so you'll need to make every word count.

The editorial staff of the *Minnesota Daily* assumes that their readers are familiar with Orwell's *1984* and G.I. Joe. Check out Chapter 7 to see more about how writers use cultural assumptions to further their arguments.

LINK TO P. 114 ·······································

▼ *In this excerpt from a feature article in a February 2002 issue of the* New York Times Magazine, *Matthew Brzezinski describes what life in America could become if we, as a nation, agree to take advantage of available technology to maximize the likelihood of safety for our citizens. The power of his exploratory argument comes (1) from his use of specific details as he imagines what daily life would be like for Americans as they went to work, attended sporting events, or traveled by air, and (2) from the comparison he draws between the United States and Israel, where a high level of security has long been perceived as a matter of survival for individual citizens and the state. As you read, prepare yourself to answer the question with which the article ends: "What are you willing to pay or put up with to stay safe?"*

The Homeland Security State:
How Far Should We Go?

Creating genuine homeland security would cost trillions of dollars and completely change the way we go about our lives.
Is this where you want to live?

MATTHEW BRZEZINSKI

Until recently, the United States and countries like Israel occupied opposite ends of the security spectrum: one a confident and carefree superpower, seemingly untouchable, the other a tiny garrison state, surrounded by fortifications and barbed wire, fighting for its survival. But the security gap between the U.S. and places like Israel is narrowing. Subways, sewers, shopping centers, food processing and water systems are all now seen as easy prey for terrorists.

Is Brzezinski's purpose here to inform? To explore? To convince? Something else? See Chapter 1 to decide.

······················· LINK TO P. 6

There is no clear consensus yet on how to go about protecting ourselves. The federal government recently concluded a 16-month risk assessment, and last month, the new Department of Homeland Security was officially born, with an annual budget of $36 billion. Big money has already been allocated to shore up certain perceived weaknesses, including the $5.8 billion spent hiring, training and equipping federal airport screeners and the $3 billion allocated for "bioterrorism preparedness." All that has been well publicized. Other measures, like sophisticated radiation sensors and surveillance systems, have been installed in some cities with less fanfare. Meanwhile, the F.B.I. is carrying out labor-intensive tasks that would have seemed a ludicrous waste of time 18 months ago, like assem-

bling dossiers on people who take scuba-diving courses.

This marks only the very beginning. A national conversation is starting about what kind of country we want to live in and what balance we will tolerate between public safety and private freedom. The decisions won't come all at once, and we may be changing our minds a lot, depending on whether there are more attacks here, what our government tells us and what we believe. Two weeks ago, Congress decided to sharply curtail the activities of the Total Information Awareness [T.I.A.] program, a Pentagon project led by Rear Adm. John Poindexter and invested with power to electronically sift through the private affairs of American citizens. For the time being, it was felt that the threat of having the government look

> **"As long as you worry too much about making false arrests and don't start taking greater risks,"** says a 15-year Shin Bet veteran, **"you are never going to beat terrorism."**

Surveillance cameras stand guard

over our credit-card statements and medical records was more dangerous than its promised benefits.

Congress didn't completely shut the door on the T.I.A., though. Agents can still look into the lives of foreigners, and its functions could be expanded at any time. We could, for instance, reach the point where we demand the installation of systems, like the one along the Israeli coastline, to maim or kill intruders in certain sensitive areas before they have a chance to explain who they are or why they're there. We may come to think nothing of American citizens who act suspiciously being held with-

out bail or denied legal representation for indeterminate periods or tried in courts whose proceedings are under seal. At shopping malls and restaurants, we may prefer to encounter heavily armed guards and be subjected to routine searches at the door. We may be willing to give up the freedom and ease of movement that has defined American life, if we come to believe our safety depends upon it.

For the better part of a generation 5 now, Americans have gone to great lengths to protect their homes — living in gated communities, wiring their property with sophisticated alarms, arming themselves with

deadly weapons. Now imagine this kind of intensity turned outward, into the public realm. As a culture, our tolerance for fear is low, and our capacity to do something about it is unrivaled. We could have the highest degree of public safety the world has ever seen. But what would that country look like, and what will it be like to live in it? Perhaps something like this.

ELECTRONIC FRISKING EVERY DAY ON YOUR COMMUTE

As a homebound commuter entering Washington's Foggy Bottom subway station swipes his fare card through the turnstile reader, a computer in the bowels of the mass transit authority takes note. A suspicious pattern of movements has triggered the computer's curiosity.

The giveaway is a microchip in the new digital fare cards, derived from the electronic ID cards many of us already use to enter our workplaces. It could be in use throughout the U.S. within a couple of years. If embedded with the user's driver's license or national ID number, it would allow transportation authorities to keep tabs on who rides the subway, and on when and where they get on and off.

The commuter steps through the turnstile and is scanned by the radiation portal. These would be a natural extension of the hand-held detectors that the police have started using in the New York subways. A cancer patient was actually strip-searched in a New York subway station in 2002 after residue from radiation treatments tripped the meters. But this doesn't happen to our fictitious commuter. The meters barely flicker, registering less than one on a scale of one to nine, the equivalent of a few microroentgens an hour, nowhere near the 3,800 readout that triggers evacuation sirens.

Imagine a battery of video cameras following the commuter's progress to the platform, where he reads a newspaper, standing next to an old utility room that contains gas masks. Cops in New York already have them as part of their standard-issue gear, and a fully secure subway system would need them for everybody, just as every ferryboat must have a life preserver for every passenger. Sensors, which are already used in parts of the New York subway system, would test the air around him for the presence of chemical agents like sarin and mustard gases.

The commuter finishes reading his newspaper, but there is no place to throw it away because all trash cans have been removed, as they were in London when the I.R.A. used them to plant bombs. Cameras show the commuter boarding one of the subway cars, which have been reconfigured to drop oxygen masks from the ceiling in the event of a chemical attack, much like jetliners during decompression. The added security measures have probably pushed fares up throughout the country, maybe as much as 40 percent in some places.

The commuter—now the surveillance subject—gets off at the next stop. As he rides the escalator up, a camera positioned overhead zooms in for a close-up of him. This image, which will be used to confirm his identity, travels through fiber-optic cables to the Joint Operations Command Center at police headquarters. There, a computer scans his facial features, breaks them down into three-dimensional plots and compares them with a databank of criminal mug shots, people on watch lists and anyone who has ever posed for a government-issue ID. The facial-recognition program was originally developed at M.I.T. Used before 9/11 mainly by casinos to ferret out known cardsharps, the system has been tried by airport and law enforcement authorities and costs $75,000 to $100,000 per tower, as the camera stations are called.

"It can be used at A.T.M.'s, car-rental agencies, D.M.V. offices, border crossings," says an executive of Viisage Technology, maker of the Face-Finder recognition system. "These are the sorts of facilities the 19 hijackers used."

Almost instantly, the software verifies the subject's identity and forwards the information to federal authorities. What they do with it depends on the powers of the Total Information Awareness program or whatever its successors will be known as. But let's say that Congress has granted the government authority to note certain suspicious patterns, like when someone buys an airline ticket with cash and leaves the return date open. And let's say the commuter did just that—his credit cards were maxed out, so he had no choice. And he didn't fill in a return date because he wasn't sure when his next consulting assignment was going to start, and he thought he might be able to extend his vacation a few days.

On top of that, let's say he was also indiscreet in an e-mail message, making a crude joke to a client about a recent airline crash. Software programs that scan for suspect words are not new. Corporations have long used them to automatically block employee e-mail containing, for instance, multiple references to sex. The National Security Agency's global spy satellites and supercomputers have for years taken the search capability to the next level, processing the content of up to two million calls and e-mail messages per hour around the world.

Turning the snooping technology on Americans would not be difficult, if political circumstances made it seem necessary. Right now, there would be fierce resistance to this, but the debate could swing radically to the other side if the government showed that intercepting e-mail could deter terrorists from communicating with one another. Already, says Barry Steinhardt, director of the A.C.L.U. program on technology and liberty, authorities have been demanding records from Internet providers and public libraries about what books people are taking out and what Web sites they're looking at.

Once the commuter is on the government's radar screen, it would be hard for him to get off — as anyone who has ever found themselves on a mailing or telemarketers' list can attest. It will be like when you refinance a mortgage — suddenly every financial institution in America sends you a preapproved platinum card. Once a computer detects a pattern, hidden or overt, your identity in the digital world is fixed.

Technicians manning the Command Center probably wouldn't know why the subject is on a surveillance list, or whether he should even be on it in the first place. That would be classified, as most aspects of the government's counterterrorist calculations are.

Nonetheless, they begin to monitor his movements. Cameras on K Street pick him up as he exits the subway station and hails a waiting taxi.

The cab's license plate number, as a matter of routine procedure, is run through another software program — first used in Peru in the 1990's to detect vehicles that have been stolen or registered to terrorist sympathizers, and most recently introduced in central London to nab motorists who have not paid peak-hour traffic tariffs. Technicians get another positive reading; the cabdriver is also on a watch list. He is a Pakistani immigrant and has traveled back and forth to Karachi twice in the last six months, once when his father died, the other to attend his brother's wedding. These trips seem harmless, but the trackers are trained not to make these sorts of distinctions.

So what they see is the possible beginning of a terrorist conspiracy — one slightly suspicious character has just crossed paths with another slightly suspicious character, and that makes them seriously suspicious. At this moment, the case is forwarded to the new National Counterintelligence Service [N.C.S.], which will pay very close attention to whatever both men do next.

The N.C.S. does not exist yet, but its creation is advocated by the likes of Lt. Gen. William Odom, a former head of the National Security Agency. Whether modeled after Britain's MI5, a domestic spy agency, or Israel's much more proactive and unrestricted Shin Bet, the N.C.S. would most likely require a budget similar to the F.B.I.'s $4.2 billion and nearly as much personnel as the bureau's 11,400-strong special agent force, mostly for surveillance duties.

N.C.S. surveillance agents dispatched to tail the two subjects in the taxi would have little difficulty following their quarry through Georgetown, up Wisconsin Avenue and into Woodley Park. One tool at their disposal could be a nationwide vehicle tracking system, adapted from the technology used by Singapore's Land Transport Authority to regulate traffic and parking. The system works on the same principle as the E-ZPass toll-road technology, in which scanners at tollbooths read signals from transponders installed on the windshields of passing vehicles to pay tolls automatically. In a future application, electronic readers installed throughout major American metropolitan centers could pinpoint the location of just about any vehicle equipped with mandatory transponders. (American motorists would most likely each have to pay an extra $90 fee, similar to what Singapore charges.)

When the commuter arrives home, N.C.S. agents arrange to put his house under 24-hour aerial surveillance. The same thing happens to the cabdriver when he arrives home. The technology, discreet and effective, is already deployed in Washington. Modified UH-60A Blackhawk helicopters, the kind U.S. Customs uses to intercept drug runners, now patrol the skies over the capital to enforce no-fly zones. The Pentagon deployed its ultrasophisticated RC-7 reconnaissance planes during the sniper siege last fall. The surveillance craft, which have proved their worth along the DMZ in North Korea and against cocaine barons in Colombia, come loaded with long-range night-vision and infrared sensors that permit operators to detect movement and snap photos of virtually anyone's backyard from as far as 20 miles away.

A GOVERNMENT THAT KNOWS WHEN YOU'VE BEEN BAD OR GOOD

In the here and now, an aerial photo of my backyard is on file at the Joint Operations Command Center in Washington, which, unlike the N.C.S., already exists. The center looks like NASA, starting with the biometric palm-print scanners on its reinforced doors.

The center has not singled me out for any special surveillance. My neighbors' houses are all pictured, too, as are still shots and even three-dimensional images of just about every building, landmark and lot in central D.C.

The technology isn't revolutionary. How many times a day is the average American already on camera? There's one in the corner deli where I get my morning coffee and bagel. Another one at the A.T.M. ouside. Yet another one films traffic on Connecticut Avenue when I drive my wife to work. The lobby of her office building has several. So that's at least four, and it's only 9 a.m.

There are few legal restraints governing video surveillance. It is perfectly legal for the government to track anyone, anywhere, using cameras except for inside his own home, where a warrant is needed to use thermal imaging that can see all the way into the basement. Backyards or rooftops, however, are fair game.

There is a growing network of video cameras positioned throughout the capital that feed into the Joint Operations Command Center, otherwise known as the JOCC, which has been operational since 9/11. The experimental facility is shared by several government agencies, including the Metropolitan Police Department, the F.B.I., the Secret Service, the State Department and the Defense Intelligence Agency. Agents from different law enforcement bodies man the JOCC's 36 computer terminals, which are arrayed in long rows beneath wall-size projection screens, like the Houston space center. The wall screens simultaneously display live feeds, digital simulations, city maps with the locations of recently released felons and gory crime scene footage.

"From here we can tap into schools, subways, landmarks and main streets," says Chief Charles Ramsey of the D.C. Police, with evident pride. Theoretically, with a few clicks of the mouse the system could also link up with thousands of closed-circuit cameras in shopping malls, department stores and office build-

ings, and is programmed to handle live feeds from up to six helicopters simultaneously. Ramsey is careful to add that, for now, the majority of the cameras are off-line most of the time,

---

To those uneasy with the notion of blanket national surveillance, Chief Charles Ramsey of the D.C. Police says: "We can't pretend we live in the 19th century. We have to take advantage of technology."

---

and that the police aren't using them to look into elevators or to spy on individuals.

But they could if they wanted to. I ask for a demonstration of the system's capabilities. A technician punches in a few keystrokes. An aerial photo of the city shot earlier from a surveillance plane flashes on one of the big screens. "Can you zoom in on Dupont Circle?" I ask. The screen flickers, and the thoroughfare's round fountain comes into view. "Go up Connecticut Avenue." The outline of the Hilton Hotel where President Reagan was shot materializes. "Up a few more blocks, and toward Rock Creek Park," I instruct. "There, can you get any closer?" The image blurs and focuses, and I can suddenly see the air-conditioning unit on my roof, my garden furniture and the cypress hedge I recently planted in my yard.

The fact that government officials can, from a remote location, snoop into the backyards of most Washingtonians opens up a whole new level of information they can find out about us almost effortlessly. They could keep track of when you come and go from your house, discovering in the process that you work a second job or that you are carrying on an extramarital affair. Under normal circumstances, there's not much they could do with this information. And for the time being, that is the way most Americans want it. But this is the kind of issue that will come up over the next few years. How many extra tools will we be willing to grant to the police and federal authorities? How much will we allow our notions of privacy to narrow?

Because if domestic intelligence agents were able to find out secret details of people's lives, they could get the cooperation of crucial witnesses who might otherwise be inclined to keep quiet. There is more than a whiff of McCarthyism to all this, but perhaps we will be afraid enough to endure it.

THE MALL GUARD WHO CARRIES A MACHINE GUN

Imagine a wintry scene: snowdrifts and dirty slush and a long line of people muffled against the cold. This is a line to get into the mall, and it is moving frustratingly slowly. What's the holdup? There is no new blockbuster movie opening that day, or any of those "everything must go" clearance sales that might justify standing outside freezing for 20 minutes. Customers are simply waiting to clear security.

Shopping in an environment of total terrorist preparedness promises to be a vastly different experience from anything ever imagined in America. But for millions of people who live in terror-prone places like Israel or the Philippines, tight security at shopping malls has long been a fact of life. "I was shocked when I first came to the States and could go into any shopping plaza without going through security," says Aviv Tene, a 33-year-old Haifa attorney. "It seemed so strange, and risky."

It took me just under eight minutes to clear the security checkpoint outside the Dizengoff Center in downtown Tel Aviv. But that was on a rainy weekday morning before the food courts and multiplex theater had opened.

The future shopping experience 35 will start at the parking-lot entrance. Booths manned by guards will control access to and from lots to prevent terrorists from emulating the Washington sniper and using parking lots as shooting galleries. Cars entering underground garages will have their trunks searched for explosives, as is the practice in Manila. It has also become common outside New York City hotels. This will guard against car or truck bombs of the type that blew up beneath the World Trade Center in 1993.

No one will be able to drive closer than a hundred yards to mall entrances. Concrete Jersey barriers will stop anyone from crashing a vehicle into the buildings — a favored terrorist tactic for American targets overseas — or into the crowds of customers lining up. Screening will follow the Israeli model: metal barricades will funnel shoppers through checkpoints at all doors. They will be frisked, and both they and their bags will be searched and run through metal detectors. Security would be tightest in winter, says a former senior F.B.I. agent, because AK-47's and grenade belts are easily concealed beneath heavy coats.

What won't be concealed, of course, are the weapons carried by the police at the mall. Major shopping areas will not be patrolled by the docile, paid-by-the-hour guards to whom we're accustomed, but — like airports and New York City tourist attractions — by uniformed cops and soldiers with rifles.

What will it be like to encounter such firearms on a regular basis? I lived for years in Moscow, and after a short time, I rarely noticed the guns. In fact, I tended to feel more uncomfortable when armed guards were *not* around; Israelis traveling in the United States occasionally say the same thing. But despite the powerful presence of guns in popular culture, few Americans have had much contact with the kind of heavy weapons that are now becoming a common sight on city streets. Such prominent displays are meant to convey the notion that the government is doing something to ward off terrorists, but they can have the reverse effect too, of constantly reminding us of imminent danger.

Even more mundane procedures might have the same effect — for example, being asked to produce a national identification card every time you go into a store, much the same way clubgoers have to prove they are of age. The idea of a national identity card, once widely viewed as un-American, is gaining ground in Washington, where some are advocating standardizing driver's licenses throughout the country as a first step in that direction. Though perhaps reminiscent of Big Brother, these cards are not uncommon in the rest of the world, even in Western Europe. In Singapore, the police frequently ask people to produce their papers; it becomes so routine that people cease being bothered by it. How long would it take Americans to become similarly inured?

The new ID's, which are advo- 40 cated by computer industry leaders like Larry Ellison of Oracle, could resemble the digital smart cards that Chinese authorities plan to introduce in Hong Kong by the end of the year. These contain computer chips with room to store biographical, financial and medical histories, and tamper-proof algorithms of the cardholder's thumbprint that can be verified by hand-held optical readers. Based on the $394 million Hong Kong has budgeted for smart cards for its 6.8 million residents, a similar program in the U.S. could run as high as $16 billion.

Among other things, a national identity card program would make it much harder for people without proper ID to move around and therefore much easier for police and domestic-intelligence agents to track them down. And once found, such people might discover they don't quite have the rights they thought

they had. Even now, for instance, U.S. citizens can be declared "enemy combatants" and be detained without counsel. Within a few years, America's counterterrorist agencies could have the kind of sweeping powers of arrest and interrogation that have developed in places like Israel, the Philippines and even France, where the constant threat of terrorism enabled governments to do virtually whatever it takes to prevent terrorism. "As long as you worry too much about making false arrests and don't start taking greater risks," says Offer Einav, a 15-year Shin Bet veteran who now runs a security consulting firm, "you are never going to beat terrorism."

In years past, the U.S. has had to rely on other governments to take these risks. For example, the mastermind of the 1993 W.T.C. bombing, Ramzi Yousef, was caught only after Philippine investigators used what official intelligence documents delicately refer to as "tactical interrogation" to elicit a confession from an accomplice arrested in Manila. In U.S. court testimony, the accomplice, Abdul Hakim Murad, later testified that he was beaten to within an inch of his life.

In Israel, it is touted that 90 percent of suicide bombers are caught before they get near their targets, a record achieved partly because the Shin Bet can do almost anything it deems necessary to save lives. "They do things we would not be comfortable with in this country," says former Assistant F.B.I. Director Steve Pomerantz, who, along with a grow-

ing number of U.S. officials, has traveled to Israel recently for antiterror training seminars.

But the U.S. is moving in the Israeli direction. The U.S.A. Patriot Act, rushed into law six weeks after 9/11, has given government agencies wide latitude to invoke the Foreign Intelligence Surveillance Act [FISA] and get around judicial restraints on search, seizure and surveillance of American citizens. FISA, originally intended to hunt international spies, permits the authorities to wiretap virtually at will and break into people's homes to plant bugs or copy documents. Last year, surveillance requests by the federal government under FISA outnumbered for the first time in U.S. history all of those under domestic law.

New legislative proposals by the 45 Justice Department now seek to take the Patriot Act's antiterror powers several steps further, including the right to strip terror suspects of their U.S. citizenship. Under the new bill — titled the Domestic Security Enhancement Act of 2003 — the government would not be required to disclose the identity of anyone detained in connection with a terror investigation, and the names of those arrested, be they Americans or foreign nationals, would be exempt from the Freedom of Information Act, according to the Center for Public Integrity, a rights group in Washington, which has obtained a draft of the bill. An American citizen suspected of being part of a terrorist conspiracy could be held by investigators without anyone being notified. He could simply disappear.

THE FACE-TO-FACE INTERROGATION ON YOUR VACATION

Some aspects of life would, in superficial ways, seem easier, depending on who you are and what sort of specialized ID you carry. Boarding an international flight, for example, might not require a passport for frequent fliers. At Schiphol Airport in Amsterdam, "trusted" travelers — those who have submitted to background checks — are issued a smart card encoded with the pattern of their iris. When they want to pass through security, a scanner checks their eyes and verifies their identities, and they are off. The whole process takes 20 seconds, according to Dutch officials. At Ben-Gurion in Israel, the same basic function is carried out by electronic palm readers.

"We start building dossiers the moment someone buys a ticket," says Einav, the Shin Bet veteran who also once served as head of El Al security. "We have quite a bit of information on our frequent fliers. So we know they are not a security risk."

The technology frees up security personnel to focus their efforts on everybody else, who, on my recent trip to Jerusalem, included me. As a holder of a Canadian passport (a favorite of forgers) that has visa stamps from a number of high-risk countries ending in "stan," I was subjected to a 40-minute interrogation. My clothes and belongings were swabbed for explosives residue. Taken to a separate room, I was questioned about every detail of my stay in Israel, often twice to make certain my story stayed consistent. Whom did you meet? Where did you meet? What was the address? Do you have the business cards of the people you met? Can we see them? What did you discuss? Can we see your notes? Do you have any maps with you? Did you take any photographs while you were in Israel? Are you sure? Did you rent a car? Where did you drive to? Do you have a copy of your hotel bill? Why do you have a visa to Pakistan? Why do you live in Washington? Can we see your D.C. driver's license? Where did you live before Washington? Why did you live in Moscow? Are you always this nervous?

A Russian speaker was produced to verify that I spoke the language. By the time I was finally cleared, I almost missed my flight. "Sorry for the delay," apologized the young security officer. "Don't take it personally."

El Al is a tiny airline that has a fleet of just 30 planes and flies to a small handful of destinations. It is also heavily subsidized by the government. This is what has made El Al and Ben-Gurion safe from terrorists for more than 30 years.

Getting the American airline system up to this level would require a great deal more than reinforced cockpit doors and the armed air marshals now aboard domestic and international flights. It would require changing everything, including the cost and frequency of flights. Nothing could be simpler, right now, than flying from New York to Pittsburgh — every day, there are at least a dozen direct flights available from the city's three airports and countless more connecting flights. Bought a week or two in advance, these tickets can be as cheap as $150 round-trip.

Making U.S. airlines as security-conscious as El Al would put the U.S. back where the rest of the world is — maybe a flight or two a day from New York to Pittsburgh, at much higher costs, and no assurance whatsoever you can get on the plane you want. Flights would take longer, and landings might be a little more interesting, because pilots would have to stay away from densely populated areas, where a plane downed by a shoulder-launched Stinger missile could do terrible damage.

EVERY DAY IS SUPER BOWL SUNDAY

But you probably won't be thinking about any of that when you go out to dinner or to the movies or to a ball game. By then, it could all be second nature. The restaurant attendant will go through your purse and wave a metal-detector wand over your jacket, as they do in Tel Aviv. The valet parker will pop open your trunk and look through it before dropping your car off at an underground garage, just as in Manila.

If you take the family to a Dodgers game, you'll be able to tell your kids how, back in the day, they used to have blimps and small planes trailing ad banners over stadiums. The flight restrictions, started at Super Bowl XXXVII in 2002, would not permit any planes within seven miles of any significant sporting events. Fans would have to park at least five miles from the stadium and board shuttle buses to gates. Spectators would be funneled through airport-style metal detectors and watched over by a network of 50 cameras installed throughout the stadium. Air quality would be monitored for pathogens by the type of portable detectors brought in by the Army at last year's Olympics.

Even people with no interest in sports who live in high-rises near stadiums would know whenever game day came round. "Tall buildings near stadiums are also a risk," says Col. Mena Bacharach, a former Israeli secret-service agent who is one of the lead security consultants for the 2004 Summer Olympics in Athens. "They would have to be swept for snipers or R.P.G.'s." *R.P.G.'s?* Those are rocket-propelled grenades, another term that could become an American colloquialism.

It's still too early to tell what all this would mean to ticket prices, but, in a sign of the changing times, the security allocation alone for last month's Super Bowl was $9 million — the equivalent of $134 for every one of the 67,000 fans in attendance.

Of course, public awareness programs could help to significantly cut down counterterror costs. In Israel, televised public service announcements similar to antidrug commercials in the U.S. warn viewers to be on the lookout for signs of suspicious activity. The messages are even taught to schoolchildren, along with other important survival tips, like how to assemble gas masks. "I was out with my 7-year-old granddaughter the other day," recalls Joel Feldschuh, a former Israeli brigadier general and president of El Al. "And

she sees a bag on the street and starts shouting: 'Granddaddy, granddaddy, look. Quickly call a policeman. It could be left by terrorists.'"

WHAT IS YOUR SECURITY WORTH TO YOU?

It is commonly held that a country as big and confident in its freedoms as the United States could never fully protect itself against terrorists. The means available to them are too vast, the potentially deadly targets too plentiful. And there is a strong conviction in many quarters that there is a limit to which Americans will let their daily patterns be disturbed for security precautions. Discussing the possibility that we might all need to be equipped with our own gas masks, as Israelis are, Sergeant McClaskey of Baltimore assured me it would never happen. "If it ever reaches the point where we all need gas masks," McClaskey said, shaking his head with disgust, "then we have lost the war on terror because we are living in fear."

What does it really mean, however, to "lose the war on terror"? It's as ephemeral a concept as "winning the war on terror." In what sense will it ever be possible to declare an end of any kind?

One thing that makes the decisions of how to protect ourselves so difficult is that the terrorism we face is fundamentally different from what other governments have faced in the past. The Israelis live in tight quarters with an enemy they know well and can readily lay their eyes on. Terror attacks on European countries have always come from colonies or nearby

provinces that have generally had specific grievances and demands. Americans don't know exactly who our enemies are or where they are coming from. Two of the recent thwarted terrorists, Richard Reid and Zacarias Moussaoui, were in fact Europeans.

The United States also lacks the national identity that binds Israel and most European countries and helps make the psychic wounds of terrorism heal faster. In Israel, hours after a bombing, the streets are crowded again — people are determined to keep going. Immediately after 9/11, that's how many Americans felt, too, but it's not at all clear how long this kind of spirit will endure.

Nor is it clear how we will absorb the cost. An adviser to President Bush estimates that as much as $100 billion will have to be spent annually on domestic security over the next 10 years, if you factor in all the overtime accrued by police departments every time there is a heightened alert. There are many who believe, as General Odom does, that the money is "insignificant." "At the height of the cold war we used to spend 7.2 percent of G.D.P. on defense and intelligence," he says. "We spend less than half that now."

Outside of defense and some of the entitlement programs, however, domestic security will dwarf every other kind of federal spending: education, roads, subsidized housing, environmental protection. More than that, the decisions we make about how to protect ourselves — the measures we demand, the ones we resist — will take over our political discourse and define our ideas about government in the years to come.

One significant argument against the creation of an American security state, a United States that resembles Israel, is that even there, in a society rigorously organized around security, the safety of its citizens is far from guaranteed. But what keeps Israelis going about their daily lives — and what might help Americans do the same despite the fear of violence here — is the conspicuousness of the response and the minor sacrifices that have to be made every day. The more often we have to have our bags searched, the better we might feel. Sitting in the kind of traffic jam that would have normally frayed our nerves might seem almost comforting if it's because all the cars in front of us are being checked for bombs. We may demand more daily inconveniences, more routine abrogations of our rights. These decisions are not only going to change how we go about our days; they're also going to change our notion of what it means to be an American. How far do we want to go?

"Security is a balancing act," says 65 Einav, the former El Al security chief. "And there are always trade-offs. Give me the resources, and I can guarantee your safety. The question is, What are you willing to pay or put up with to stay safe?"

RESPOND.

1. What sort of emotional response do you have to Brzezinski's argument, and specifically the question posed in its closing lines? What sort of rational response do you have to it? To what extent do the two responses match up? In what ways are they different? Why?

2. In what ways is Brzezinski's text an argument based on values (Chapter 5)? One based on emotions (Chapter 4)? One based on facts and reason (Chapter 7)? How does Brzezinski combine these kinds of arguments in the section entitled "The Face-to-Face Interrogation on Your Vacation" (paragraphs 46–52)? In another section of your choosing?

3. In the opening paragraphs of this excerpt, Brzezinski discusses the beginning of a new conversation in the United States about "what balance we will tolerate between public safety and private freedom" (paragraph 3). How does this formulation of our current situation compare and contrast with those offered by McCullagh's essay "Why Liberty Suffers in Wartime" (p. 535), Charen's editorial "We Should Relinquish Some Liberty in Exchange for Security" (p. 540), and the *Minnesota Daily* staff editorial "Privacy, Civil Rights Infringements Multiply after Sept. 11" (p. 543)?

4. **Write an essay** in which you respond to the question posed by Offer Einav, the former El Al security chief, in Brzezinski's closing paragraph. In other words, what is the proper balance, for you, between public safety and private freedom? As this article demonstrates, the potential costs are many — and of many kinds. As earlier readings in this cluster remind us, in responding to this question one must consider not only oneself but also others: criminals, alleged criminals, and people one knows and loves whose behaviors might, under certain circumstances, come to be considered criminal.

Why Fear National ID Cards?

ALAN M. DERSHOWITZ

At many bridges and tunnels across the country, drivers avoid long delays at the toll booths with an unobtrusive device that fits on a car's dashboard. Instead of fumbling for change, they drive right through; the device sends a radio signal that records their passage. They are billed later. It's a trade-off between privacy and convenience: the toll-takers know more about you — when you entered and left Manhattan, for instance — but you save time and money.

An optional identity card could be used in a similar way, offering a similar kind of tradeoff: a little less anonymity for a lot more security. Anyone who had the card could be allowed to pass through airports or building security more expeditiously, and anyone who opted out could be examined much more closely.

As a civil libertarian, I am instinctively skeptical of such tradeoffs. But I support a national identity card with a chip that can match the holder's fingerprint. It could be an effective tool for preventing terrorism, reducing the need for other law-enforcement mechanisms — especially racial and ethnic profiling — that pose even greater dangers to civil liberties.

Are E-ZPass lanes just like national ID cards?

I can hear the objections: What about the specter of Big Brother? What about fears of identity cards leading to more intrusive measures? (The National Rifle Association, for example, worries that a government that registered people might also decide to register guns.) What about fears that such cards would lead to increased deportation of illegal immigrants?

First, we already require photo ID's for many activities, including flying, driving, drinking and check-cashing. And fingerprints differ from photographs only in that they are harder to fake. The vast majority of Americans routinely carry photo ID's in their wallets and pocketbooks. These ID's are issued by state motor vehicle bureaus and other public and private entities. A national card would be uniform and difficult to forge or alter. It would reduce the likelihood that someone could, intentionally or not, get lost in the cracks of multiple bureaucracies.

The fear of an intrusive government can be addressed by setting criteria for any official who demands to see the card. Even without a national card, people are always being asked to show identification. The existence of a national card need not change the rules about when ID can properly be demanded. It is true that the card would facilitate the deportation of illegal immigrants. But President Bush has proposed giving legal status to many of the illegal immigrants now in this country. And legal immigrants would actually benefit from a national ID card that could demonstrate their status to government officials.

Finally, there is the question of the right to anonymity. I don't believe we can afford to recognize such a right in this age of terrorism. No such right is hinted at in the Constitution. And though the Supreme Court has identified a right to privacy, privacy and anonymity are not the same. American tax-payers, voters and drivers long ago gave up any right of anonymity without loss of our right to engage in lawful conduct within zones of privacy. Rights are a function of experience, and our recent experiences teach that it is far too easy to be anonymous — even to create a false identity — in this large and decentralized country. A national ID card would not prevent all threats of terrorism, but it would make it more difficult for potential terrorists to hide in open view, as many of the Sept. 11 hijackers apparently managed to do.

A national ID card could actually enhance civil liberties by reducing the need for racial and ethnic stereotyping. There would be no excuse for hassling someone merely because he belongs to a particular racial or ethnic group if he presented a card that matched his print and that permitted his name to be checked instantly against the kind of computerized criminal-history retrieval systems that are already in use. (If there is too much personal information in the system, or if the information is being used improperly, that is a separate issue. The only information the card need contain is name, address, photo and print.)

From a civil liberties perspective, I prefer a system that takes a little bit of freedom from all to one that takes a great deal of freedom and dignity from the few — especially since those few are usually from a racially or ethnically disfavored group. A national ID card would be much more effective in preventing terrorism than profiling millions of men simply because of their appearance.   ■

In what ways is Dershowitz's argument a perfect example of a proposal argument as outlined in Chapter 12?

LINK TO P. 238 ⋯⋯⋯⋯⋯⋯⋯⋯⋯⋯⋯⋯⋯⋯⋯⋯⋯⋯⋯⋯⋯⋯⋯⋯⋯⋯⋯⋯

RESPOND •

1. In this article, what specifically does Dershowitz propose with respect to national ID cards? In what concrete ways does he qualify his proposal for a national ID card? (Chapter 8 on Toulmin argumentation discusses the need to qualify claims.)

2. What differences might Dershowitz's reputation as a supporter of liberal causes, including civil rights, make to readers? In other words, how does the author use arguments based on character in this essay (Chapter 6)?

3. Dershowitz, as a law professor, is used to anticipating possible rebuttals to his arguments and refuting them in advance. Cite several examples where he does so. In paragraph 7, he distinguishes between a right to anonymity and a right to privacy. How does he illustrate this distinction? How does he use this distinction to his advantage?

4. **Write an essay** in which you explain why you would or would not choose to participate in the national ID card program Dershowitz describes. (What would be the advantages and disadvantages of doing so? For whom? How does his proposal compare with the national ID cards discussed by Brzezinski?) In writing the essay, you will have to evaluate Dershowitz's proposal in some way; you may also need to critique its possible consequences (a causal argument) or propose an alternative program.

▼ *In this feature article from the sports pages of the* New York Times *in February 2002, Ira Berkow focuses on the experiences of All-American rower Aquil Abdullah, an African American with a Muslim name. In so doing, Berkow raises questions about a decidedly post–September 11 phenomenon: profiling of people, especially males, with Muslim names. (Long before September 11, African Americans and Latinos had complained of racial profiling, being pulled over for DWB—Driving While Black or Driving While Brown. After September 11, the nature of profiling and debates about it grew considerably.) As you read, note the ways in which Berkow is able to use Abdullah's experiences to demonstrate the complexity of profiling for those who endure it.*

Rower with Muslim Name Is an All-American Suspect

IRA BERKOW

They weren't going to let Aquil Abdullah on the plane at Newark International Airport, at least not right away.

"We need you to step to the side," he was told by a reservations clerk for his prospective flight to Seattle. "I have to call a police officer."

"What's the problem?" asked Abdullah, a 29-year-old member of the United States national rowing team and the single sculls winner in the 2002 United States national rowing championships. The incident at the airport happened a few weeks ago, on the morning of Jan. 31, and Abdullah had a good idea what the problem was. A similar incident happened to him a few months earlier.

Abdullah was on a no-fly list. "What this means," Andrew Kurpat, a police officer with the Port Authority in Newark, explained yesterday, "is that anyone with a common Muslim name has to be checked out, to see if it's an alias, to see if he's on a terrorist list."

So the Port Authority officers checked through their files, contacted the F.B.I. and the immigration authorities, and then came back to Abdullah. He was no terrorist. By this time, his flight had departed.

"I can understand the concern," Abdullah said recently with a graceful, disarming demeanor and an easy smile. "It's legitimate, of course, and some of my friends are angrier about the name profiling than I am, but I do wish the authorities could be quicker about the check."

Abdullah had arisen at 3:30 a.m. in his apartment in Princeton, N.J., the town in which the national rowing team trains, to get to the airport two hours before his flight. He didn't get the next flight until 6 in the evening, didn't arrive in Seattle until 1:30 in the morning. "It took me almost 24 hours to get from Princeton to Newark to Seattle," he said. "Someone joked that I could have made it faster by rowing."

There are a few things that set 5 Abdullah apart from someone with another common Muslim name like Muhammad or Hussein. One is that he is the only African-American man to win either a national single sculls rowing championship or a race at the prestigious Henley Royal Regatta in England. He was a silver medalist in the 1999 Pan-American Games, and in the 2000 United States Olympic trials he was just 33-hundredths of a second away from making the Olympic team. (Anita DeFrantz and

How is Berkow's article an argument based on values? What shared values does he focus on? See Chapter 5 for more examples of arguments based on values.

LINK TO P. 78 ·······

Aquil Abdullah at rowing practice

Pat Spratlen Etem, both women, are the only other African-Americans to have made the national rowing team.)

Another difference is that Abdullah was not even his name at birth. He was born in Washington with the name Aquilibn Michael X. Shumate. When his father, Michael Shumate, converted to Islam when Aquil was 6, he changed his and his son's last name to Abdullah.

Aquil, who grew to be 6 feet, 185 10 pounds, was a high-school football star (a wide receiver at Woodrow Wilson), won a rowing scholarship to George Washington University (after rowing for Wilson High in his senior year) and earned a degree in physics.

"I can understand his being detained at an airport once," said Mike Teti, head coach of the national rowing team, "but when it happens again, that's unfortunate. Here's a guy representing his country in athletics and he's as American as you can get. A second time, they should know who he is."

As for his rowing ambitions, Abdullah's not making the Olympic team in 2000 remains a spur. He recalls the last day of the single sculling competition, Monday morning, June 12, on the Cooper River in Camden, N.J. Midway through the race, Abdullah slipped ahead, but with 750 meters to go in the 2,000-meter course, Abdullah and Don Smith were dead even, plunging their oars at about 31 strokes a minute. Smith pulled four feet ahead and won the Olympic spot with a time of 6:50.18, to Abdullah's 6:50.51. (Smith finished eighth at Sydney.)

Abdullah was heartbroken about his loss, but a friend put it into perspective for him. "What do we win when we don't win?" he asked.

Abdullah now seems able to answer it to his satisfaction, as he did in "Perfect Balance," a book he wrote with Chris Ingraham in 2001. It is a small philosophical book on a young man's thoughtful journey to self-understanding. "Growing as people is the most important victory we can ever achieve in our lives," he writes. "Because each person is the only one accountable for his actions, each person is also the only one responsible for his success or failure."

Abdullah's goals include not only 15 trying to improve personal traits — greater consistency, dependability and determination, greater family values — but also to win in the world championships in Milan in August and make the Olympic team in 2004.

"Aquil is a multidimensional, multitalented guy," Teti said, "and he has been pulled in different directions. He'd be out until 3 in the morning playing saxophone in his band in nightclubs. He also works freelance as a computer programmer. I told him: 'Aquil, you have to put all your eggs in one basket if you're going to reach your goals in rowing.' I think he has, now."

Meanwhile, the chance that Abdullah will again be checked and

Understanding the need for doing checks but still not happy about it.

double-checked before a flight is likely. "I oscillate between feeling great, that the government is taking such measures to protect the citizens of the United States — I know that there is a price to pay for this protection," he said, "but then I get feelings of indignation that I'm being singled out. I mean, I have obligations, too. I don't want to miss my flights. And I'm concerned as to what comes next, what infringements on our personal freedoms."

And if he were on an airplane with someone with Arab characteristics, how would he feel? "I would raise an eyebrow and get a good look at who he was, and check out what he was doing," he said. "But I know I'd feel a sense of shame, too, because I know the feeling of being followed by a detective in a department store because of assumptions he made because I was black. The issue is terribly conflicting for me."

Finally, Abdullah was asked the name of the mosque he attends. "I'm not a member of any mosque," he said. "I'm Catholic, actually."

RESPOND●

1. How does Berkow use the experiences of Abdullah (whose family name, by the way, means "Servant of God") to problematize profiling for Abdullah? As a general practice of society at this time? Why is the case of Abdullah an especially effective one to use in discussing profiling? (Chapter 18 on "What Counts as Evidence" should give you some ideas about how to respond to this question.) How do you think Mona Charen ("We Should Relinquish Some Liberty in Exchange for Security") and Alan Dershowitz ("Why Fear National ID Cards?") would respond to this article? Why?

2. Would Berkow's article or its impact be different in any way if Abdullah had not been African American? Why or why not? Nobel Prize–winning novelist Toni Morrison has claimed that our culture often uses African Americans and their lives in a particularly moralizing way; in other words, we, as a society, use their stories to examine what is good or bad about our society at large. What might Morrison see in this article? In Daria MonDesire's "Stripped of More than My Clothes" earlier in this chapter (p. 525)? In King Kaufman's "Tiger's Burden" in the following chapter (p. 617)? In Gordon Marino's "Me? Apologize for Slavery?" (p. 806) in Chapter 28, "Beliefs and Stances"?

3. **Write an essay** in which you evaluate ethnic profiling with respect to national security issues and civil liberties. As noted in question 2, in addition to this reading, this book also includes the account of Daria MonDesire, which focuses on ethnic or racial profiling pre–September 11. Further, in "The Homeland Security State" (p. 546) Matthew Brzezinski recounts his experiences when flying El Al, the Israeli national airline, where profiling of a different sort occurred. If you argue for some system of profiling, you will also need to address how or why specific groups should have to endure profiling. If you argue against it on the basis of civil liberties, you will need to anticipate and respond to potential rebuttals from those who favor security over civil liberties.

Another System to Subvert

JOSE HERNANDEZ

The attacks on civil liberties—INS roundups, Homeland Security laws, increased surveillance—have a lot of Americans worried about their rights being taken away, but my family and I dealt with not having rights long before 9/11.

Call me Jose Hernandez. It's not my real name.

As an immigrant from Mexico who has been undocumented until recently, I am used to not having my rights respected here. The fact is that my family and I had to survive without rights for quite some time, so giving some more for "security" really doesn't bother us the way it would folks used to having their rights on paper.

I remember what it feels like to be thought of as the threat to American security. And I can feel for Arab-Americans who are now getting looked at with suspicion everywhere they go. We all fall into the same boat. In my mind, the policies aren't all that different from the 1990s. The INS just changed their target from Mexicans crossing the border at Tijuana to anyone who looks like an Arab getting off the plane.

My family came from Mexico when I was 11 years old. In California 5 we led discreet lives and rarely went out. My life as an undocumented immigrant meant that I grew up with added challenges and frustrations other kids didn't have to deal with. I did not have the freedoms of feeling comfortable in public or getting a driver's license or bank account. Getting a job was nearly impossible.

When I had to go to the free clinic for vaccine shots, I had to memorize my fake Social Security number. Even when we would get food from the church, I made it a point to never contradict the information my mom gave.

These new INS roundups of men from certain countries strike a powerful chord in me. I remember when my mom and I pushed a grocery cart from our apartment complex to a local strip mall. At the time, my mother was still really young, and I was dressed like a city boy. We were buying food at a taco-burger place when I felt the tight grip of my mother's hand. When I looked outside, people who were running were

◀ Jose Hernandez is a pseudonym for a 23-year-old writer for Silicon Valley De-Bug, a Pacific News Service project involving young writers and workers in the Silicon Valley. In this autobiographical essay about his experience as an undocumented immigrant from Mexico, Hernandez adds to the complexity of the challenge the nation faces in balancing concerns with privacy and civil liberty, on the one hand, and matters of security and safety, on the other. As you read, consider how Hernandez's point of view on these issues compares with those of other writers in this cluster and why.

Who are Hernandez's intended readers? Who are his invoked readers? His real readers? See Chapter 3 for more on how writers address audiences.

LINK TO P. 53

563

falling all over the place. Officers in mint-green suits were rounding everyone up like cattle. It was an INS raid.

When I saw an officer approach my mother, fear ran through my body. I tried to keep my cool, and apparently so did my mom. The officer looked at us for a quick minute, said hello to my mom, and she said the word she knew very well: "Hi." He left us alone.

We learned that looking American can save you from deportation.

Still, if the government or public has made you an enemy, you live 10 constantly with paranoia. Every time a cop got next to me, I thought I would be pulled over, taken in, and eventually deported. I got a ticket once, and I was terrified in traffic court. For everyone else, all they had to worry about was traffic school, but for me, a misdemeanor could have meant a ticket out of the country. Luckily, the judge didn't do a deep search on my background, and I just got fined.

When I was 18, I saw the light. I came across a connection at the Department of Motor Vehicles. It cost me about $2,000, but it got me a license. From then on, I adapted and learned to live in survival mode. I developed a unique way to not be noticed or stand out. I dodged anything that had to do with cops, and with the right cash, I purchased anything that the law required an American to have.

The Homeland Security folks may think that limiting peoples' civil liberties will smoke out the immigrants who are underground, but the truth is that many of us are used to getting around the tactics. If you have street smarts, you can make your own rights and buy your freedoms. What my family and I learned over the years is that even if the government sets up ways to restrict your freedoms, you can almost always find a way to beat the system.

Illegal alien? Undocumented worker? Neither term is neutral in the argument it makes. See Chapter 14 on the dangers of unduly slanted language.

LINK TO P. 297

Illegal aliens seen through an x-ray of a truck

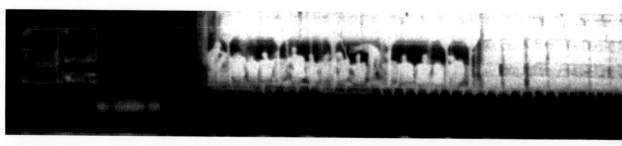

RESPOND.

1. How do you respond to Hernandez's essay? In what ways does or might his recounting of his experiences work to gain the sympathy of readers? In what ways does or might his recounting of them work to alienate readers? In what ways does the existence of what are officially termed *illegal aliens* complicate the nation's efforts to balance concerns with privacy and civil liberty, on the one hand, and matters of security and safety, on the other?

2. Hernandez contends that "even if the government sets up ways to restrict your freedoms, you can almost always find a way to beat the system" (paragraph 12). Do you agree? Do you believe it is possible to "make your own rights" and "buy your freedoms"? Why or why not? To the extent that Hernandez is correct, is the validity of his claims something to make Americans proud or ashamed? Why? What sorts of limits might there be to Hernandez's claim? How do these limits intersect with questions of civil liberties? Of national security?

3. The version of Hernandez's article that appears in this textbook has, in fact, been lightly edited to bring it more in line with the expectations that readers and teachers of argument textbooks have of the texts they contain. Compare the version of the text that appears here with the original version, which can be found at <alternet.org/story.html?StoryID=15117>. Which version do you prefer? The more sanitized, corrected version that appears here, or the original version? Why? Which do you believe is more powerful? More convincing? Why? Has editing Hernandez's text tampered with his voice? Why or why not? Which groups of readers might prefer the version that appears here? Which groups might prefer the original? Why?

4. **Write a dialogue** between Hernandez and Dershowitz ("Why Fear National ID Cards?" p. 556), Hernandez and Brzezinski ("The Homeland Security State," p. 546), or Hernandez and Charen ("We Should Relinquish Some Liberty in Exchange for Security," p. 540) about the nature and limits of security for the United States post–September 11. (You may want to involve Hernandez and two others in the conversation.) As you'll soon realize, writing a dialogue that can function as an argument is quite complex. Before writing, you will have to plan which positions each speaker might support and which specific issues will be raised as well as how the participants will interact. The argument may be agonistic or Rogerian, exploratory or proposal oriented (see Chapter 1).

chapter twenty-five

Time Off, Time Out

Athletics is likely Americans'—especially American males'—main diversion. Even bars and restaurants that don't advertise themselves as "sports bars" often have televisions tuned to sporting events, in some sense claiming these public spaces as male spaces. The arguments in this chapter dare us to admit the obvious: like it or not, athletics cannot help but become an arena in which larger social issues play themselves out. For example, college athletics isn't just about having a good time for the spectators or the players. Each year, several outstanding college basketball players have to decide whether to gamble their collegiate eligibility against the possibility of being a first-round NBA draft pick. It is a choice that often comes down to dollars and common sense, though it also means leaving college without a degree.

College athletics also raises questions about gender equity: depending on one's perspective, Title IX is necessary or discriminatory. More broadly, arguments about how much spent on college football is too much, or whether winning at all costs trumps issues such as giving athletes a serious education, remind us that when we talk about athletics we're really talking about larger issues, often in reductionist ways.

This chapter comprises two clusters of readings. The first, "Still Grappling with the Implications of Title IX," examines what Title IX has and has not achieved with regard to gender equity in college sports since its passage in 1972 by considering current debates about the law as well as its most contested repercussion, the reduction of athletic programs for men at some colleges. It also examines certain Title IX victories as well as areas where the progress for women seems much too limited. The readings in the second cluster, "Is Sports Just a Proxy for Politics?" scrutinize several cases in which sports seems to be about little more than politics. Four of the readings deal with fights about membership for women in the Augusta National Golf Club, home to the Masters Tournament: gender discrimination (again?) or freedom of association? One reading explains how the integration of golf clubs has worked against African American caddies, telling what some may find to be a surprising story about Augusta National. The two final articles address ways in which the athletic tail seems to be wagging the academic dog at many schools.

www.
For additional readings on
Time Off, Time Out, visit
bedfordstmartins.com
/everythingsanargument.

The arguments in this cluster ask you to consider critically the state of affairs brought about by a simple and seemingly clear federal policy enacted in 1972 known as Title IX. The policy states, "No person in the United States shall, on the basis of sex, be excluded from participation in, be denied benefits of, or be subjected to discrimination under any education program or activity receiving Federal assistance" and then goes on to list a number of exceptions. College athletes and sports fans are **still grappling with the implications of Title IX.** Over thirty years later, we continue to argue about the rules, their nature and extent, and even the goals of the game. In fact, the controversy has continued to heat up since 1996, when changes to the law required that colleges and universities make public the participation rates of female and male students and the funding allotted to sports for each sex. Subsequent guidelines have given rise to more debate. Things got even more heated when the Bush administration suggested changes in the implementation of the guidelines.

The cluster begins with a selection from the Women's Sports Foundation's Web page. "Title IX Facts Everyone Should Know" presents the now-common "fact sheet" found on many Web sites in which information is presented about a specific issue: here, Title IX. Jessica Gavora's "Time's Up for Title IX Sports" offers a very different reading of the "facts," even using some of the same data found in the selection from the Women's Sports Foundation. Ruth Conniff seeks to defend Title IX, protecting it from the likes of Gavora. As you'll see, part of the argument is about who supports Title IX: radical feminists or soccer dads? Conniff's very positive view of Title IX is followed by two perspectives on the increasingly common practice of reducing the number of men's sports teams in order to comply with Title IX guidelines instead of, say, cutting back on expenditures for sports like football and men's basketball. Welch Suggs, in "Colleges Consider Fairness of Cutting Men's Teams to Comply with Title IX," and Peter Monaghan, in "Dropping Men's Teams to Comply with Title IX," weigh in on this practice. Both articles are from the *Chronicle of Higher Education*, a weekly newspaper reporting on items of interest to college and university administrators and professors. As should be clear, the *Chronicle*'s sports page is less about who's winning and losing than about issues of all kinds affecting college athletics. Leslie Heywood's essay, "Despite the Positive Rhetoric about Women's Sports, Female Athletes Face a Culture of Sexual Harassment," argues that sexual harassment is still all too common an experience for female athletes in the United States regardless of the promises of Title IX. Indeed, Title IX and its enforcement raise many issues about the meaning and nature of fairness, the rights and responsibilities of government to engage in what some consider social engineering, the remedying of past injustice, and how best to balance these competing priorities. Whatever we think about the implications of Title IX, one thing is clear: the final score isn't in.

▼ *The Women's Sports Foundation, <womenssportsfoundation.org>, was founded in 1974 by Billie Jean King, a pro tennis legend. According to its home page, the organization is "dedicated to ensuring equal access to participation and leadership opportunities for all girls and women in sports and fitness."*

This selection, posted June 20, 2002, presents the Foundation's perspective on Title IX. Featuring bulleted lists of evidence, it argues for why Title IX is beneficial and necessary. (Such "fact sheets" or "talking points" are a common genre of argument on Web sites and in promotional literature about organizations and causes.) As you read, consider critically the evidence presented. As you'll see later in this cluster, another author will use some of the same data to argue against Title IX.

Title IX Facts Everyone Should Know

WOMEN'S SPORTS FOUNDATION

Title IX is arguably one of the most important pieces of legislation passed in the 20th century. Now, women and girls can also enjoy the benefits of sport at nearly the same level as men. Read on to find out more about the extent of Title IX's impact.

BENEFITS OF TITLE IX

Title IX of the Education Amendments of 1972 prohibits discrimination on the basis of sex in educational programs and activities at educational institutions that receive federal funds. It is an omnibus education law affecting all curricular and extracurricular offerings, from medicine, law and science to drama, dance and athletics.

No law has meant more to women in sport than Title IX. With regard to collegiate educational opportunities for females, leveling the playing field has meant $372 million a year in college athletic scholarship funding and varsity sport opportunities for over 150,000 women. At the high school level, Title IX has provided the chance to play varsity sports for millions of high school girls. One of every 2.5 high school girls now participates in high school varsity sports (compared to 1 in 27 in 1972). This law has had a profound impact.

Even more important than college athletic scholarships and varsity athletic participation, which affect a relatively small number of talented female athletes, are the health benefits of physical education. Title IX applies to general physical education as well as intramural and recreational sports activities. These physical activity programs motivate even more girls and women to lead active lifestyles that produce significant health benefits:

- 80% of all people with osteoporosis (brittle bones) are female and one of every two women over the age of 60 has osteoporosis. Adequate calcium intake and weight-bearing exercise, especially in a female's

Who might be the target audience of this fact sheet? How can you tell? See Chapter 3 to learn techniques for connecting with your readers.

LINK TO P. 51

high school and college years, is crucial in the prevention of osteoporosis, a $15 billion/year health problem (Teegarden, Proulx, et al., 1996, Medicine and Science in Sports and Exercise, 1996; vol. 28, pp. 105–113).

- Girls who participate in as little as four hours of exercise per week may reduce their lifelong risk of breast cancer (a disease that will affect one out of every eight women) by up to 60% (Journal of the National Cancer Institute, 1994).

- Girls and women who participate in sports have higher levels of confidence, stronger self-images and lower levels of depression. Sports is an investment in the psychological health of women (Miller Lite Report, 1985; Melpomene Institute, 1995; Colton & Gore, Risk, Resiliency, and Resistance: Current Research on Adolescent Girls, Ms. Foundation, 1991).

- High school girls who participate in sport are less likely to experience an unintended pregnancy, more likely to graduate from high school and get better grades and less likely to engage in an array of health-risk behaviors (The Women's Sports Foundation Report: Sport and Teen Pregnancy, May 1998; Women's Sports Foundation, 1989, The Women's Sports Foundation Report: Health Behavior and the Teen Athlete, 2000).

FEW SCHOOLS IN COMPLIANCE

Title IX supporters will continue to ask for more aggressive enforcement because an estimated 80% of all schools and colleges are still not close to being in compliance with Title IX after 30 years.

- While over 50% of our college populations are female, female athletes still receive approximately 36% of all sports operating expenditures, 42% of all college athletic scholarship money, 42% of all athletic participation opportunities, and 32% of all

college athlete recruitment spending (1999–00 NCAA Gender-Equity Report and NCAA Participation Statistics, 2002).

- While more female athletes are getting a college education because of the award of $372,476,500 in athletic scholarships each year, male athletes receive 36 percent ($133 million) more than that amount (1999–00 NCAA Gender-Equity Report, Women's Sports Foundation calculation).

- Since Title IX was adopted 30 years ago, the Office for Civil Rights (OCR) has not found one educational institution out of compliance with the athletics regulations and has not initiated proceedings to remove federal funds at one school or college. Instead, the OCR negotiates settlements which are often less than the law requires and further extends the time institutions are given to comply with federal law.

- Cedric Dempsey, the Executive Director of the National Collegiate Athletic Association, assessed the status of gender equity in college sports in October 1999 as follows: "Improvements are being made, but being made much too slowly . . . we must continue to add programs for women and dedicate more resources to women's programs on our campuses at a faster rate."

PUBLIC SUPPORT OF TITLE IX

The public understands the important women's health and wellness issues represented by Title IX. We also know that the public fully supports Title IX and opposes unnecessary efforts to protect men's sports as evidenced by a 2000 Wall Street Journal/NBC News Poll:

> "Title Nine is a federal law that prohibits high schools and colleges that receive federal funds from discriminating on the basis of gender. Title Nine is most commonly invoked to ensure equal opportuni-

ties for girls and women in high school and college athletics. Do you approve or disapprove of Title Nine as it is described here?"

Yes, approve of Title IX: 79%

No, do not approve of Title IX: 14%

Do not know enough about it: 4%

Not sure: 3%

"To comply with Title Nine, many schools and universities have had to cut back on resources for men's athletic programs and invest more in women's athletic programs to make the programs more equal. Do you approve or disapprove of cutting back on men's athletics to ensure equivalent athletic opportunities for women?"

Yes, approve of cuts: 76%

No, do not approve of cuts: 19%

Not sure: 5%

(2000 Wall Street Journal/NBC poll of 2,000 adults; margin of error of 2.2 percentage points; on the second question, 79% of women, 73% of men, 70% of Republicans, and 79% of Democrats all stated, categorically, that they approved of cutting resources for men's sports to finance women's.)

MEN'S SPORTS DO NOT NEED PROTECTION

During his election campaign, President Bush indicated he would support amending Title IX to change the law's proportionality provision. A public information campaign has erroneously communicated that this provision is hurting men's sports opportunities. In fact, Title IX reform was a plank on the Republican presidential election platform.

The facts simply do not support the contention that Title IX's proportionality provision is responsible for the elimination of men's sports. Men's sports participation and funding has continued to grow. Men's sports participation is at the highest level ever. If some sports have been dropped, other more popular sports have been added. Decisions to drop men's non-revenue sports are institutional decisions related to choosing to place more resources into revenue-producing men's sports rather than women's sports. That same institution could choose to keep all men's sports by lowering expenditures on the men's sports with the largest operating budgets. But institutions are not doing this.

THE FACTS

- In the past four years, for every new dollar going into athletics at the Division I and Division II level, male sports receive 58 cents while female sports receive 42 cents (1999–00 NCAA Gender-Equity Report).

- NCAA participation opportunities for male and female athletes have grown to record levels. Between 1981–82 and 2000–01, NCAA female sports participation has increased from 74,239 to 150,916 and NCAA male sports participation has increased from 169,800 to 208,966 (NCAA Participation Statistics, 2002).

- More and more male and female athletes are getting a college education because of athletic scholarships, with more than $372,000,000 in athletic scholarships being awarded to female athletes each year while male athletes receive 36 percent ($133 million) more than that amount (1999–00 NCAA Gender-Equity Report, Women's Sports Foundation calculation).

- There will never be enough participation opportunities at the high school or college level to fully meet the interests of all boys or girls. These opportunities are limited by what schools can afford. For example, there are approximately 209,000 men and 151,000 women participating on college varsity teams in the NCAA. These opportunities will never fully accommodate the needs of over 5 million boys and girls participating in high school athletics. The fairest way to parcel out limited resources and participation opportunities is to have athletic opportunities match up to general student enrollment.

- The data shows that lost opportunities for some men whose sports have been dropped have resulted in new opportunities for men in other sports. For instance, between 1981–82 and 1998–99, 1,022 men's gymnastics, 2,648 men's wrestling, 683 women's gymnastics and 229 women's field hockey participation opportunities were lost. During that same period, men's football, soccer and lacrosse opportunities increased by 7,199, 1,932 and 2,000, respectively, as did numerous women's sports (GAO Report, Intercollegiate Athletics, 2001). There are natural shifts of funding and interest in men's and women's sports that occur and sports participation is affected by changes in NCAA institutional membership. It is inaccurate to blame these shifts on Title IX. Similarly, a 1997 study of individual institutions revealed that programs commonly added and dropped men's and women's sports between 1978 and 1996 with men's and women's sports programs showing a net gain (Women's Sports Foundation, 1997).

- NCAA average squad size data for male athletes in 1981–82 and 2000–01 has remained constant (within one participant) and more sports show an increase in average squad size than show decreases (NCAA Participation Statistics, 2002).

- Dollars in men's sports do not have to be reallocated to further support football in order to "maintain revenue production." It's a myth that football makes the money that funds other sports. Football brings in more money than other sports but spends more than it makes. Approximately 65 football programs of the 1,200 universities in this country make more than they spend.

- Conferences, leagues and the NCAA have not been willing to legislate expenditure limitations, lower scholarship limits, or even require fewer games if that's what it takes to have sufficient resources to make sure that male non-revenue-producing sport participants as well as females get the chance to play.

WOMEN'S SPORTS FOUNDATION POSITION

- The Women's Sports Foundation does not support reducing opportunities for male or female athletes to play sports. The purpose of laws prohibiting discrimination is to bring the disadvantaged population up to the level of the advantaged population, not to treat male athletes in minor sports like female athletes who weren't given a chance to play.

- The key to affording current men's sport opportunities while expanding opportunities for female athletes is to stop the men's revenue sports arms race. Schools should not be cutting men's non-revenue-producing teams like swimming, wrestling and gymnastics when they are spending money on putting football teams in hotels the night before home football games and spending excessively on similar items in one or two sports.

- College presidents must take the responsibility to reduce athletic program spending and stop the arms race. In addition, athletic conferences, leagues and governance organizations like the NCAA have not been willing to legislate expenditure limitations, lower scholarship limits, even require fewer games if that's what it takes to make sure that male non-revenue-producing sport participants as well as females get the chance to play.

- The financial solution to affording Title IX compliance without cutting men's sports opportunities is for every sport to receive a smaller portion of the athletic budget, each sport tightening its belt so that everyone can continue to play.

RESPOND•

1. What sorts of arguments does the Women's Sports Foundation offer for Title IX? What benefits does it see accruing from the legislation? What is the Foundation arguing against? Why? How would you summarize the overall argument of this selection and its main points?

2. Using the discussion of what counts as evidence in Chapter 18, describe the support the Foundation offers for its position. What are the advantages and disadvantages of relying exclusively on the sorts of evidence, presented as bulleted talking points, used in arguments like this one?

3. Why, in your opinion, does the Foundation place such an emphasis on the health benefits to women of physical activity? (As you will see, generally in debates about Title IX, potential benefits for women of physical activity do not become part of the argument.)

4. At least several causal arguments are being made here. What are they? What is or are the causes? Their effects? Figure 11.2 (p. 209) illustrates three kinds of causal arguments. How would you characterize each of the causal arguments you have listed?

5. Using the information provided in this selection, **write the following short texts** of the sort that you might use in a longer research paper on Title IX:

   a. a one-paragraph summary of the benefits of Title IX as represented by the Women's Sports Foundation,

   b. a one-paragraph summary of the Foundation's interpretation of the 2000 poll on Title IX,

   c. a one-paragraph summary of the Foundation's position on why Title IX should not be changed, and

   d. a two-to-three paragraph summary and critical evaluation of the Foundation's position on why Title IX should not be changed.

   Note that a through c ask you to summarize whereas d asks you to evaluate and include your own opinion of the arguments the Foundation makes.

Time's Up for Title IX Sports

JESSICA GAVORA

◀ *This essay, which appeared in the June 2002 issue of* The American Spectator, *is an excerpt from* Tilting the Playing Field: Schools, Sports, Sex, and Title IX *(Encounter, 2002) by Jessica Gavora. She is the chief speechwriter for Attorney General John Ashcroft. As you read the essay, pay special attention to the ways in which Gavora seeks to discredit not only Title IX but also its supporters. In particular, note her discussion of the 2000 poll about Title IX that was mentioned in the previous selection, "Title IX Facts Everyone Should Know."*

In the spring of 2001 an ad sponsored by the Independent Women's Forum appeared in UCLA's Daily Bruin, offering to expose "the 10 most common feminist myths." Myth number nine—"Gender is a social construction"—was answered thus:

> While environment and socialization do play a significant role in human life, a growing body of research in neuroscience, endocrinology and psychology over the past 40 years suggests there is a biological basis for many sex differences in aptitudes and preferences. Of course, this doesn't mean that women should be prevented from pursuing their goals in any field they choose; what it does suggest is that we should not expect parity in all fields.

The ad's impact on the UCLA campus was immediate and explosive. Rallies were organized. The university women's center demanded that the Daily Bruin "retract" the ad. When the paper's editor defended it as an exercise in free speech, Christie Scott, head of the campus feminist "Clothesline Project," dismissed this rationale as "somewhat cowardly."

"Somewhat cowardly" is the wrong term to apply to the editors of the Daily Bruin, but the right term for most participants in the discussion of women's role in American life today. Few topics involve more disinformation and shaving of the truth on the one side and political cowardice on the other. Christina Hoff Sommers—the author of the UCLA ad—Judith Kleinfeld, author, and psychiatrist Sally Satel and others have done an excellent job of uncovering the disinformation and false statistics used by women's advocates to advance their agenda. But they are virtually alone. For far too long, a wittingly or unwittingly gullible media has treated even the most outrageous claims of feminists as fact. The effect has been to give artificial life support to the myth that girls and women are an oppressed minority, clinging weakly to their rights only with the assistance of the full weight and authority of government.

Nowhere is the reality gap wider than in women's sports. Congress did a seemingly simple and laudable thing when it passed Title IX of the Educational Amendments in 1972: "No person in the U.S. shall, on

What values does Gavora assume that you share with her? How do you know? Chapter 3 discusses how writers establish credibility by highlighting shared values.

LINK TO P. 56 ·······················

the basis of sex, be excluded from participation in, or denied the benefits of, or be subjected to discrimination under any educational program or activity receiving federal aid." But as applied to organized sports, Title IX has been interpreted and twisted and bent outside the institutions of our electoral democracy, conforming at last to the shape of unintended consequences: A law designed to end discrimination against women is now causing discrimination against men.

And yet Title IX is remarkably entrenched. Before the new Bush   5 administration even had the chance to appoint a secretary of education, the powerful Women's Sports Foundation fired a shot across the White House bow, vowing to fight "any change that weakens this law and results in unequal treatment of female athletes." And the WSF is just the vanguard of an army of seasoned veterans of the gender wars who stand ready and eager to defend the territory they've gained under Title IX.

To make sure that a risk-averse new Republican president doesn't make the mistake of thinking he can take on the Title IX lobby with impunity, these gender warriors point to the results of a 2000 NBC News/Wall Street Journal poll that seems to show widespread public support for Title IX quotas:

Q: Title IX is a federal law that prohibits high schools and colleges that receive federal funds from discriminating on the basis of gender. Title IX is most commonly invoked to ensure equal opportunities for girls and women in high school and college athletics. Do you approve or disapprove of Title IX as it is described here?

Yes, approve of Title IX: 79%

No, do not approve of Title IX: 14%

Do not know enough about it: 4%

Not sure: 3%

But the issue under Title IX isn't the fair and equal division of resources between men and women; it's an attempt to dictate how men and women should behave. Female athletes have more teams to choose from in colleges and universities today than male athletes. They receive more athletic scholarship aid per capita than male athletes. The battle for "gender equity" is not a battle for resources; if it were, women's groups would have declared victory some time ago. The struggle is about power and ideals.

CIVIL WRONGS

Q: Do you support eliminating men's opportunities to create a 50/50 gender balance in school sports programs?

This is not how the pollsters who conducted the survey for NBC 10 News and The Wall Street Journal asked the question. Journalists— even ink-stained veterans—routinely describe compliance with Title IX in terms of the equal sharing of resources between men and women in athletics. The result is that it is rare for a citizen who picks up a newspaper or turns on the television to see coverage of the law that is not glowingly positive. And it is a rare politician or government official who will tell the truth about the law's enforcement today. The first step toward re-leveling the playing field between the sexes in our schools, then, is simply beginning to tell the truth about Title IX.

The reality is that the federal government has enforced a quota standard in Title IX athletics for much of the past decade. This enforcement has been opportunistic; not every school has fallen under scrutiny from the Justice Department's Office for Civil Rights and been forced to cut men's teams, add women's teams or do both to achieve "proportionality." But schools don't need to experience a federal investigation or a lawsuit to know that their athletic departments are not under their control. They've read the "policy interpretations"; they've seen how OCR has treated schools like the University of Wisconsin and Boston University; and they've seen how the courts have ruled on the Brown and Cal State Bakersfield cases. American education has received the message loud and clear.

It is a measure of the power of liberal women's rights activists in academia today that universities are unable—or unwilling—to complain as the federal government micromanages more and more of their affairs in the name of "gender equity." When so-called "women's issues" are on the line, defenders of institutional autonomy like Brown's Vartan Gregorian are distressingly rare. Even among students whose lives are most affected by Title IX quotas, there is little questioning of the need or the rationale for federally mandated gender equity. "Nobody questions the underlying assumptions of Title IX, that male and female students will be equally interested in organized sports and that a lack of proportional numbers must indicate something is 'wrong,'" says Robert Geary, professor of English at James Madison University. "Universities are supposed to be places of inquiry, but some subjects appear closed to scrutiny—too sensitive."

Title IX quotas have never been the subject of debate. They were created outside the electoral process by unelected officials working hand in hand with special interest groups. The first step toward ending gender quotas, then, is to demand the truth from those who insist they don't exist.

Here's the reality. In June 1999 the OCR's Northeast regional office sent a letter to the athletic director and administrators of Central Connecticut State University, warning that they must add 20 female athletes to their sports roster to comply with the federal law. CCSU had already brought the percentage of its athletes who are female from 29 to 49 by dropping men's wrestling and adding women's lacrosse. But females made up 51 percent of the students at CCSU, so OCR insisted that twenty more female athletes were needed—the so-called "proportionality" principal.

Then there's the University of Wisconsin at Madison, which 15 received a similar letter in the fall of 2000. Having labored for a decade to attract women to programs, UWM had achieved near-perfect parity in the spring of that year: 429 athletes on campus were men and 425 were women. Not good enough, said Algis Tamosiunas, director of OCR compliance in Chicago. Because females now constituted a majority of students on the Madison campus (53.1 percent), the school would have to add another 25 women.

Letters like these are routinely sent to schools struggling to stay on the right side of the federal authorities. OCR officials such as the Clinton administration's Norma Cantu are being dishonest when they insist that because the regulations don't "require" sex quotas, those who administer the regulations don't work relentlessly to make quotas happen. Proportionality is the threshold test for Title IX compliance in federal regulation. It is the standard adopted by the courts and the only guarantee that a school will not be exposed to a federal investigation or a lawsuit. It is the standard for compliance with Title IX today. To say otherwise is to lie, plain and simple.

GET SMART

The good news is that there are storm clouds gathering on Title IX's horizon.

The past decade of gender-based quota expansion in women's sports has also been a time of relative prosperity for colleges and universities. In some cases, this has meant that schools struggling to meet the gender quota in athletics could do so in relatively painless ways, by adding women's sports and/or limiting men's participation by cutting walk-ons. As long as the funds were there, providing the scholarships and building or upgrading facilities for new women's teams were relatively easy.

A slowing economy combined with escalating expenses in athletic programs, however, threatens to change this. Budgets for women's sports are rising faster than those for men's sports, as is spending on scholarships for women. Another financial strain is accommodating the growing desire among athletic directors and fans alike that teams be competitive on the national level. Less and less are sports treated as another part of a well-rounded educational experience; increasingly teams must justify their existence by winning. This compulsion is helping to fuel an "arms race" in spending, not just on big-time football and basketball programs, but on women's teams and men's "nonrevenue" sports as well. According to the Chronicle of Higher Education, "nonrevenue" teams in NCAA Division I cost roughly $220,000 on average in 1999–2000. And at big-time football schools, where more money is available, women's teams and men's nonrevenue squads can cost up to half a million dollars apiece.

These exploding costs have already triggered a fresh round of 20 budget cuts. And because women's sports can't be touched, the sacrifice is borne by men's teams. Iowa State University, the University of Kansas and the University of Nebraska have all recently begun major cuts to their men's athletic programs. The bad news for Title IX quota advocates is that rising budget pressures may finally give schools a real incentive to go to court, to argue that women's programs should be fair game as well.

A school that invites a lawsuit by cutting a women's team or refusing to create a new team to meet the gender quota might very well decide to fight back in court rather than be forced to incur costs it can't afford. Alternately, male athletes whose positions are eliminated might decide to take a cue from Duane Naquin, a Boston College senior who was denied entry on the basis of his sex to a class in feminist ethics taught by theology professor Mary Daly; Naquin sued to win his right to coeducation. As that case showed, if there is one thing university administrators fear more than accusations of gender insensitivity, it's lawsuits. In the Daly case and others to come, public interest law firms like the Center for Individual Rights have been effective in reversing the course of sex discrimination in our schools.

Although Title IX preferences have yet to be struck down in a federal district court—and thus be made a prime target for Supreme Court review—creative legal challenges in the right circuits could yield results for fairness and gender-blind policies. "I have no doubt that the Supreme Court will take the case if and when there is a split in the circuit courts," says Maureen Mahoney, who argued Brown University's case to the Supreme Court. Women's advocates have been careful so far to push for Title IX quotas in liberal district courts that are likely to agree with their version of equity. But according to Mahoney and others, bringing the right challenge in the more conservative Fourth Circuit (which covers Maryland, South Carolina, North Carolina, Virginia and West Virginia) or the Fifth Circuit (including Texas, Louisiana and Mississippi) could bring a judgment that restores the original intent of the law.

The rising cost of fielding intercollegiate athletic teams is also contributing to a reexamination of how sports fit within the mission of the university. All recruited athletes, male or female, receive a preference from college admissions committees. But preferences for female athletes—and arguments for female quotas within athletic programs—are often justified on grounds above and beyond the contribution these women make to sports teams. Make women athletes, we are told, and you make better women. With some justification, women's groups argue that girls who play sports are associated with such positive traits as higher graduation rates, less drug use, higher self-esteem and lower levels of teenage pregnancy.

In *The Game of Life: College Sports and Educational Values*, James Shulman of the Andrew W. Mellon Foundation and former Princeton University president William Bowen examine what kind of students are currently being admitted to schools under athletic preferences. Using the same database that provided the intellectual fodder for Bowen's earlier defense of race-based affirmative action—data on 90,000 students who attended 30 selective colleges and universities in the 1950s, 1970s and 1990s—the authors claim that of all the recipients of affirmative action in colleges and universities today, female athletes are the most preferred. At a representative school in 1999, Shulman and

Bowen found that a female who is a member of a minority had a 20 percent admissions advantage, the daughter of an alumnus had a 24 percent advantage, a male athlete had a 48 percent advantage and a female athlete had a 53 percent advantage. That is, a female athlete had a 53 percent better chance of being admitted than a nonathlete with the same SAT score.

And what are schools gaining from this admissions preference? The 25 *Game of Life* sets out purposefully to shoot down the various "myths" of intercollegiate athletics, chief among them, in Shulman and Bowen's view, that athletics builds character. Shulman and Bowen argue that athletes today are less academically prepared, less concerned with scholarship and more financially directed than their fellow students. But what is most interesting about their analysis is their finding that these traits are increasing, among female athletes as well as male. And whereas female athletes were once at least as academically qualified as other female students, they now lag behind. Another benefit frequently cited to justify preferences for female athletes under Title IX is racial and ethnic diversity. But Shulman and Bowen found that Title IX produced gains mainly for white girls, not minorities.

The trend in women's athletics, particularly in the most competitive, high-profile sports, is away from the ideal often claimed by Title IX quota ideologues. Instead of representing the female ideal at the start of the twenty-first century—tough, smart, confident and empowered—female athletes are beginning to resemble the dimwitted, half-civilized male athletes of the feminist stereotype. And in such a situation, the rationale that women's preferences under Title IX are justified because they create better students and better citizens becomes hard to sustain.

LESS IS LESS

As I write this, the University of Kansas has eliminated its men's swimming and tennis teams, citing financial pressures and federal gender equity requirements. Bucknell University has announced it will drop wrestling and men's crew as varsity sports, eliminating 44 men's positions in order to reach male-female proportionality. Seton Hall, Capital University in Columbus, Ohio, and the University of St. Thomas have all dropped their wrestling teams. Iowa State has eliminated baseball and

men's swimming. The University of Nebraska has also axed men's swimming and diving, leaving only four of the schools in the Big 12 conference still participating in the sport. The Big 12 is now questioning whether it will continue to stage a men's swimming and diving championship or do away with it altogether, a move that will almost certainly result in the remaining schools eliminating their men's programs.

This denial of opportunity for men is occurring because a group of people with a narrow agenda has worked hard and successfully behind the scenes to make it happen. Driven by the desire to overcome real discrimination against girls and women, activists like Donna Lopiano and Norma Cantu and groups like the Women's Sports Foundation, the National Women's Law Center and the American Association of University Women set out to create preferences for girls and women. They sought out and co-opted friendly government officials. They initiated a shrewd legal strategy when friendly government officials were unavailable. Partly through government fiat, partly through a shared ideology, they built a phalanx of promoters and defenders of "gender equity" on college campuses and in high schools and grade schools across the country. They wooed their allies and cowed their enemies in Congress and insisted that both parrot their message. They conducted a highly effective and sophisticated media campaign. They helped draft regulations and interpretations of regulations and interpretations of interpretations of regulations. At each stage in the legal and bureaucratic evolution of Title IX, they out-thought, out-worked and out-cared the people whose opportunities were being destroyed. The edifice of discrimination these activists built is a testament to their commitment.

In the end, of course, it is up to those charged with enforcing our laws to apply Title IX honestly and forthrightly. This is not, needless to say, a politically painless proposition. After some significant rollback of race-based preferences in the 1990s, elected officials and even conservative activists seem to have lost their appetite for battling identity politics. To stand on principle, many seem to believe, is to risk appearing "mean-spirited" in an age when compassion is the opiate of the electorate.

Writing about the "conundrum of quotas" in The Wall Street Journal [30] in the opening months of the Bush administration, Shelby Steele noted that conservatives have a hard time not appearing mean when they stand on principle on the issue of race because they lack moral authority. "Were conservatives of the last generation fastidious about principles when segregation prevailed as a breach of every known democratic principle, including merit?" wrote Steele.

The equation of race preferences with Title IX sex preferences is not perfect. As we have seen, there are real, innate differences between the sexes, of the kind that cannot be shown to exist between people of different races. Even so, Steele's point can easily be applied to conservatives on the issue of sex today. Conservatives of the last generation certainly did not lead the charge for women's rights—properly understood to be the same rights before the law that men historically have enjoyed. It was liberals, of course, who took the battle for women's rights forward. Eventually they corrupted it into a separatist movement in which women's interests are portrayed to be at odds with those of men. Nonetheless, before feminism took that destructive turn, conservatives did not champion the cause of equality for women, and more often than not they resisted it.

Can we now credibly argue that the principle of gender-blindness be upheld in the laws meant to guarantee it? Liberalism has been suborned on the issue of sex quotas. Can a conservative administration challenge quotas for girls and women without appearing "mean" and losing the thin margin of centrist voters who put it in office—voters who would most likely oppose gender preferences if they knew they existed but who nonetheless distrust conservatives on issues involving women? This is a conundrum of sex quotas every bit as difficult as Shelby Steele's conundrum of race quotas.

The way out of this conundrum is the same as it was in the 1920s, when women struggled for the right to vote, and the same as it was in the 1950s, when blacks encountered segregationists at the schoolhouse door. The way out is to defend the principle of nondiscrimination, even when it is hard. Especially when it is hard.

And liberal feminist groups will make it hard to stand on this principle; they will challenge the moral authority of those who seek to restore the original intent of the law. But the principle of nondiscrimination that is embodied in the original intent of Title IX has stood the test of time. It has allowed girls and women to rise from uncomfortable interlopers to become the dominant force in American education. Conservatives can gain new moral authority by insisting on standing by this principle and resisting a distortion of the law that discriminates against a new group of victims and demeans the very achievements of the girls and women it purports to protect.

Re-leveling the playing field in American education will not be easy. 35 But those who go into this battle have at their side two often underrated assets: First, it's the law. And second, it's the right thing to do.

RESPOND ●

1. Whereas the previous reading promised the "facts" about Title IX, this selection promises "to tell the truth about Title IX." What, in Gavora's eyes, is the truth? What specific arguments does she make against Title IX? How does she use the 2000 poll cited in the earlier reading in order to contribute to her argument?

2. What sorts of evidence does Gavora use in constructing her argument? (Chapter 18 will help you here.) Unlike the previous reading, which offers an argument in the form of information and facts, Gavora's argument is explicitly combative. Who are the readers that her text invokes (Chapter 3)? What values does she assume they have? How do these values compare and contrast with those of the readers invoked by the previous selection?

3. What is Gavora's attitude toward feminism? How do you know? How does this attitude manifest itself in this essay? What does she concede about the role that conservatives have traditionally taken toward women's rights (paragraph 31 and following)? Does this concession strengthen or weaken her argument? Why?

4. The authors of the previous selection and Gavora would no doubt all claim to be supporters of nondiscrimination. What would each mean by the term? **Write an essay** in which you evaluate the definitions of nondiscrimination that each position on Title IX represents. Your goal should not be to write an essay in which you claim that one definition is correct and the other incorrect; rather, you should strive to show why one definition is superior to the other, a more complex kind of argument to construct because it assumes that you understand the strengths and weaknesses of each definition. Although your own values will influence the conclusion you reach, you may wish to make these values explicit, or you may wish to use them implicitly without making the values themselves an issue.

▼ *This article appeared in the March 24, 2003, issue of* The Nation, *a weekly magazine of political analysis and commentary that reflects a liberal point of view. Ruth Conniff is Washington editor of* The Progressive. *Conniff's writing style is rich in descriptive detail. As you read, notice how her word choice enhances her argument.*

Title IX: Political Football

RUTH CONNIFF

Girls in ponytails and soccer jerseys packed the front of a room at the National Press Club in Washington, DC. They elbowed each other and giggled as kids from across the nation spoke lovingly of basketball, pole vaulting and field hockey, and in support of Title IX — the 1972 law that has become synonymous with the rise of women's sports. Since Title IX went into effect thirty-one years ago, girls' athletic participation has skyrocketed. The number of girls playing varsity sports has gone up from one in twenty-seven in 1972 to almost one in two today.

Despite all the good feeling Title IX has engendered among girls and their parents, the law is currently under attack. The National Wrestling Coaches Association filed a lawsuit against the Education Department claiming that Title IX is decimating men's college sports, forcing colleges to cut hundreds of wrestling programs — along with gymnastics, diving and other teams — in order to meet "quotas" for female athletes. The aggrieved jocks have found an ally in President Bush, who formed the Commission on Opportunity in Athletics last June to re-examine the law.

The high school girls descended on Washington for their press conference–cum–pep rally just as the commission convened its final meeting at the Hotel Washington. Outside the hotel, the Feminist Majority and the conservative Independent Women's Forum held dueling press conferences. Inside the grand ballroom, a wrestling coach wearing a "No Quotas" button cruised the perimeter, handing out literature calling on the commission to "reject the gender politics of the special interest groups."

That would be groups like the Women's Sports Foundation — which helps girls seek equal funding and facilities for their teams — and Dads and Daughters, whose executive director, Joe Kelly, emceed the high school girls' event.

Title IX, said Kelly, "is one of the best things that ever happened to fathers." 5

"Sports is a natural comfort zone for men, and Title IX makes it a bridge to our daughters," he said. He told the story of a friend, Dave, who coached his son and daughter in basketball, and was appalled by the inferior facilities provided to his daughter's team.

"Dads get angry when daughters play on old fields or gyms that are in disrepair," Kelly said. And that's what Title IX was designed to fix. "Guys like Dave are not radical feminists. They simply know sports are good for girls. They also know sports are good for boys. Don't tell me you're going to treat my daughter differently than my son."

High school girls still get about 1.1 million fewer opportunities than boys to play sports, according to the National Coalition for Women and Girls in Education. But Bush's commission finished its work by making a series of recommendations to weaken Title IX. Instead of making girls' sports proportional to the number of female students enrolled, the commission recommended that schools aim for approximately 50/50 boy-girl representation. Schools that don't reach parity would be allowed to use interest surveys to show that girls are getting as much opportunity as they desire. According to the Women's Sports Foun-

> **"Sports is a natural comfort zone for men, and Title IX makes it a bridge to our daughters."**
> **–Joe Kelly, of Dads and Daughters**

dation, the changes could result in the loss of 300,000 participation opportunities and $100 million in scholarships for female athletes.

The deck was stacked at the commission from the beginning. High school athletes and coaches who support Title IX didn't get to testify. Title IX opponents like wrestlers' groups and the Independent Women's Forum had disproportionate input. The commission's two strongest Title IX advocates, Julie Foudy, captain of the US National Women's Soccer Team, and Olympic gold medalist Donna de Varona, were treated to eye-rolling by fellow commissioners

and outright hostility by wrestlers' groups. In late February, the two refused to sign the final report, charging that the commission failed to acknowledge continuing discrimination against female athletes.

Still, despite the battle-of-the-sexes tone in DC, 10 some sincere anguish is driving the backlash against Title IX.

Doug Klein coaches high school wrestling at the Ida Crown Jewish Academy in Chicago. "I had such a good time when I walked on the team at William and Mary," he recalls. Today his old college team has been cut, and other teams no longer take walk-ons (as opposed to recruits) because, he says, they have to keep their rosters small in order to comply with Title IX gender-equity rules. His star wrestler recently visited Lehigh and Cornell, and couldn't even get a coach to talk to him.

"Boys who aren't superstars—nobody is interested in them. And that's really unfair," Klein says. "Somebody made the point on one of these [wrestling] websites: 'I'm 5'5", 120 pounds, what sport am I going to do?' There are not many opportunities in sports for little boys and little men."

That may be the most painfully honest comment ever made by an opponent of Title IX. Instead of focusing on the big men's sports that suck up all the resources in college athletics, a lot of little guys who are getting crushed blame women. Klein, too, blames Title IX for "gutting wrestling"—though he concedes that Title IX may not be the main problem.

"When you read the wrestling magazines, they're reluctant to point the finger at football," Klein says. "But football is the 800-pound gorilla." Indeed, major teams award up to eighty-five scholarships a year and field rosters of 100 or more players, while top football coaches can earn more than $2 million a year. Schools could easily comply with Title IX by making small cuts in these big-budget programs, instead of cutting men's roster spots. Title IX advocates calculate that just by dropping scholarship spots for football bench-warmers — cutting back from the eighty-five players now allowed by the NCAA to the fifty-three used by the NFL, for example — and by dropping a few of the most ridiculous perks, such as hotel-room stays on home-game nights, schools could add back all those smaller programs they've been eliminating.

There is a myth that spending huge amounts of money on football makes sense because the game will bring in even more. The reality is that in the race to field a winning team, jack up alumni giving and secure lucrative TV contracts, even big-time football schools are losing money. Take the University of Wisconsin. UW lost $286,700 on its Rose Bowl appearance in 1998. Until schools get off the football treadmill, athletic program budgets will feel the squeeze, with or without Title IX.

Donna Shalala, President Clinton's Secretary of Health and Human Services, is one of the nation's biggest boosters of Title IX — and of big-budget football. As UW chancellor, Shalala brought the university's football program into the big time. She hired coach Barry Alvarez and built a giant new sports facility the same year she presided over the elimination of UW's baseball, men's and women's gymnastics, and men's and women's fencing teams. Now president of another football powerhouse, the University of Miami, Shalala is an unabashed proponent of Title IX: "It's had a huge impact on providing opportunities for women's sports." Yet she is also an unabashed proponent of big-time football.

Shalala says it was a budget crisis, not Title IX, that forced the cuts at Wisconsin. "We cannot use Title IX as an excuse for our lack of disciplined management and our financial problems," she says. She argues that it's possible to pay for minor sports and be a football power: "People have to restrain their costs, and they

have to be honest about what football costs, and go out and raise more money."

Shalala uses the populist language of Title IX, saying, "The whole point is to provide opportunities for men and women." But in practice, building an athletic department around big-time football has resulted in schools — including UW — killing sports programs that once provided opportunities for regular students. It has also meant that college sports, more and more, are not about promoting amateur participation, sportsmanship or character but rather about raising a school's profile and getting a piece of the sports entertainment action. "This is not," says Shalala, "intramural sports." While Title IX has protected many women from these trends, no structures are in place to save minor men's teams from the football monster.

Talking to university administrators about athletic department budgets is like talking to the Democrats about campaign finance reform. Everyone is in favor of more "opportunity" and "participation," but when it comes to reining in football spending, no one wants to cash out first.

According to Cheryl Marra, senior associate director of sports administration at UW, "We don't spend any more here than anywhere else. But who's gonna give first?" UW has to offer its football players chartered jets and posh facilities, says Marra; otherwise, "Ohio and Michigan will say to recruits, 'You know, at Wisconsin they don't treat you right.'" The only way out, according to Marra, is for the NCAA to crack down on excessive football spending. Then no school would be placed at a disadvantage.

The wrestlers' attack on Title IX is based on a gamble: that if the government relaxes Title IX rules, athletic departments will shift money back to their teams. But that's hardly a sure thing. Athletic directors are no more interested in minor men's sports now than they used to be in women's sports.

Responding to the complaints of downsized wrestlers, Marra says, dismissively, "Why can't they accept that people don't want to play the same sports they did 100 years ago?"

Ironically, Title IX's very success is being used as an argument for its dismantlement. As with affirmative action, the law's opponents argue that the job is done — women have reached equality and no longer need special attention. This argument resonates with girls of the post–Title IX generation, who feel pangs of guilt when Title IX is blamed for the elimination of minor men's sports. "I'm in favor of Title IX, but not for cutting guys' sports," says Kym Hubing, a sprinter at Wisconsin.

Indeed, many students now take women's athletics for granted. Male and female athletes hang out together and support each other. This is one of the most profound, positive effects of Title IX. "You're friends. You're equals," says Greta Bauer, a UW hurdler. "When you walk into a party, the guys will see you and punch you in the arm and say, 'Hey, how are you doing?' The other girls will look at you like, 'How did you get inside the circle?'"

Being "inside the circle" means that women in Division I sports are envied just like the men. There is an aura of exclusivity about hanging out in the expensive sports facilities, studying in the athletes' study hall, living in jock housing. Like breaking into any formerly segregated club, being part of the sports scene on campus means gaining privilege.

If the Education Department heeds the Commission on Opportunity in Athletics, the march toward equality will stall. High schools and colleges across the nation will stop counting heads and start taking interest surveys. That may sound fair to young athletes like Hubing. But when Title IX started, most girls couldn't imagine themselves as serious athletes. An interest survey at that time would have determined that only a few real tomboys deserved a chance to play. It was the opportunities offered under the law that created such a radical change in the culture. Women now make up 42 percent of college athletes — maybe not equality, but an enormous leap, thanks to the law. Interest surveys would freeze that progress where it is today. 25

And this would be a loss not only to girl athletes but to the culture of sports as a whole. Title IX has become one of the last bastions of amateur sports. While there are no limits on the amount of money a school can shift from other men's programs to football, Title IX insists they keep open athletic opportunities for women. Women's sports — often praised for their "purity," for the sheer joy of the athletes and for the fact that players get decent grades — have kept alive the ideal of the scholar-athlete.

But maybe not for long.

Consider how Conniff uses arguments from the heart to reach her audience. See Chapter 4 for more uses of emotional appeals.

LINK TO P. 65

RESPOND•

1. What arguments is Conniff putting forth about Title IX? What argument, in particular, is she making in the concluding section of her essay (paragraphs 22–27)? How well do you think she supports her claims? Why?

2. Conniff chooses carefully the sources she cites, especially with regard to quotations likely based on interviews. (See Chapter 18 for additional information on kinds of evidence such as interviews.) In paragraph 5, for example, she quotes Joe Kelly, a father, as claiming that Title IX "is one of the best things that ever happened to fathers." Later, she quotes Kelly as saying that he and other members of Dads and Daughters "are not radical feminists" (paragraph 7). Later, in paragraph 16, she quotes Donna Shalala, "one of the nation's biggest boosters of Title IX—and of big-budget football." Why are such details and characterizations important in the argument Conniff is constructing? In countering arguments put forth by authors like Jessica Gavora in the previous selection?

3. Notice the ways that Conniff's word choice supports her argument. Look back at the text to find several instances of effective word choice, including figurative language, and state why you think they are effective. (For additional information on figurative language, see Chapter 14.) How does word choice contribute to Conniff's ethos as an author? As an authority?

4. **Write a dialogue** between Ruth Conniff and Jessica Gavora about Title IX. You'll likely be most successful if you choose two or three major topics for them to discuss and keep the discussion focused on this text and the previous one. (For example, you may want to use your answer to question 2 above to help you think about relationships between the two texts in this way.)

▼ *Welch Suggs is a sportswriter for the* Chronicle of Higher Education, *a weekly paper covering issues of concern to college and university faculty and administrators. This article, which appeared in February 1999, discusses a then-pending court case involving the wrestling program at California State University at Bakersfield. (A preliminary injunction was later issued, prohibiting the university from cutting the team or any individual wrestlers.)*

Colleges Consider Fairness of Cutting Men's Teams to Comply with Title IX

Advocacy Groups, Colleges, and Lawyers Differ on Who Should Pay to Achieve Gender Equity

WELCH SUGGS

College coaches cut unskilled and unfit players from their teams every day. Almost everyone — except perhaps for the cut players — would say that's fair.

But what happens when a university cuts an entire team of male players to make room for women? Is that fair?

The question arises as athletics departments try to create an equitable situation for female athletes while preserving revenue streams from football and men's basketball. Making the number of female athletes proportional to the number of enrolled female students is one way that universities can comply with Title IX of the Education Amendments of 1972, the law that bars discrimination at institutions that receive federal aid.

Last week, the Board of Trustees at Miami University in Ohio delayed for two months a decision on whether to drop men's golf, tennis, soccer, and wrestling, moves that it is considering for financial as well as gender-equity reasons. Also last week, a federal judge in Illinois dismissed a suit that had been brought by former male soccer players and wrestlers at Illinois State University after it dropped their teams to meet gender-equity goals. And later this year, wrestlers at California State University at Bakersfield will go to court to argue that the university's decision to drop their sport to meet proportionality goals violates their rights under Title IX.

Activists, athletics directors, and government officials all take different sides on the issue. A coalition of conservative groups contends that it's unfair to both men and women to cut men's sports for gender-equity reasons. Men are more likely to be interested in playing sports than women, they say, and depriving men of opportunities just to meet proportionality guidelines is, on its face, discriminatory. Activists for women's sports say

athletics administrators are making bad decisions on how to spend money.

Government officials who enforce Title IX say that the rights of women to participate in college sports outweigh the rights of individual men to participate in particular sports. And administrators say their hands are tied by financial constraints. Many of them say they can't afford to add women's sports.

"I think almost everybody in higher education believes the goal of Title IX is worthy," says James C. Garland, Miami's president. "The controversy is whether the end justifies the means, and that's the battleground where this is being fought."

GRAPPLING WITH THE FUTURE

At center stage in this debate is Stephen Neal, a senior wrestler at Bakersfield. The defending national collegiate champion in the heavyweight division, Mr. Neal clearly prefers physical battles to legal ones.

"I'd rather talk about what I'm going to do out there," Mr. Neal says, gesturing to a wrestling mat during a meet at American University, "than what's going on with the suit."

Mr. Neal, who is undefeated this season and ranked No. 1 in the National Collegiate Athletic Association, has a great deal invested in the team's lawsuit. Besides being the lead plaintiff in the case, he hopes to coach wrestling after graduation. As more and more universities cut wrestling to meet proportionality standards, his chances of finding a college job dwindle.

He also has seen a number of friends and roommates lose direction after being cut from Bakersfield's team. In 1995, before it decided to abolish the team altogether, the university ordered the team to reduce its roster from 37 to 27, according to the wrestlers' suit.

"Sometimes in wrestling, it takes a couple of years for guys to develop," Mr. Neal says. "But they're the ones who come into their junior and senior years and get really good. And those are the guys who were cut."

At Bakersfield, the impetus to achieve proportionality is even greater than at most universities. The Cal State system is operating under a five-year-old consent agreement with the California chapter of the National Organization for Women. The agreement, reached after Cal-NOW (as it is known) filed a lawsuit, requires the 20 institutions in the system that have athletics programs to bring their proportion of female athletes within 10 percentage points of the proportion of undergraduate female students by the 1998–99 academic year. The requirement in the settlement is not quite as strict as Title IX, which requires

> "Almost everybody in higher education believes the goal of Title IX is worthy. The controversy is whether the end justifies the means, and that's the battleground."

universities to have proportionality within five percentage points, a condition known as "substantial proportionality." But unlike Title IX, the California consent agreement offers no other ways to achieve compliance.

"They've made some really tough decisions," says Linda C. Joplin, chairwoman of Cal-NOW's athletics equity committee. "I think it's unfortunate . . . but from what I've seen, there are too many administrators who continue to pay for things like hotels for football than to pay for women in minor sports. It's a matter of priorities."

Citing the lawsuit, Bakersfield athletics officials declined to comment for this story.

Other lawsuits that have challenged gender-equity decisions by universities have not been very successful. This month, for example, a federal court in Illinois dismissed a 1995 lawsuit against Illinois State University that had been brought by former soccer players and wrestlers whose sports were dropped to bring the university into compliance with Title IX.

The court cited its own 1993 decision in *Kelley v. Board of Trustees of the University of Illinois,* a case in which male swimmers sued the university for dropping their sport. "Under Title IX, the university could cut men's programs without violating the statute because men's interests and abilities are presumptively met when substantial proportionality exists," the decision states.

That presumption goes straight to the question of fairness. Why should courts and administrators presume that men's interests in competing in college sports are being met simply by providing them with opportunities proportional to their enrollment at a university? Curt A. Levey, a lawyer for the Center for Individual Rights, a non-profit law group that is representing the Bakersfield wrestling team, says that athletics is the only area in education in which quotas are permitted.

Should a university's nursing school, he wonders, be forced to enroll men in numbers proportional

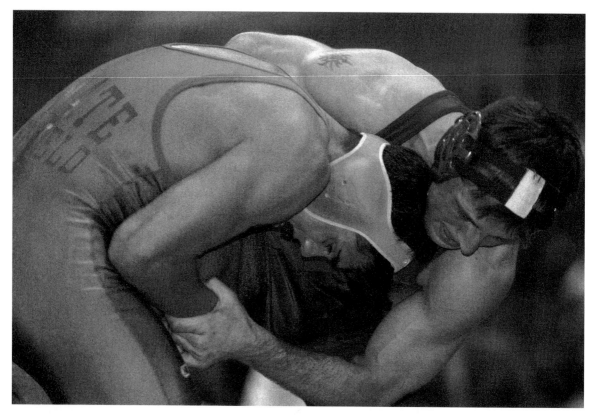

Stephen Neal (top) is the lead plaintiff in a suit seeking to block California State U at Bakersfield from eliminating its wrestling team.

to their overall enrollment at the university?

Sports programs are different, responds Mary Frances O'Shea, who oversees Title IX compliance in athletics for the U.S. Department of Education's Office for Civil Rights.

"Athletic programs are the only programs wherein schools can establish [teams] set aside for men and women," Ms. O'Shea says. "You can't have Algebra I-A for boys and Algebra I-B for girls, but in athletics, because of the nature of the program, you can." As such, rules must be in place to insure that men and women are treated equitably in athletics programs, Ms. O'Shea says.

Donna A. Lopiano, executive director of the Women's Sports Foundation, says the "easiest solution is to double your resources and give the women the same opportunities as the men." But there's only one problem: "How many schools can double revenues?"

Hard Choices

None can. At Miami, trustees will decide April 16 whether to cut soccer, golf, tennis, and wrestling.

Miami's sports program is huge, with 22 varsity teams, but its revenue sources are limited. And even with 11 women's teams, the university is not close to meeting proportionality standards. Women make up 55 per cent of Miami's undergraduate student body but only 45 per cent of campus athletes. To meet "substantial proportionality" mandates, at least 50 per cent of athletes should be women. Based on the number of 1997–98 participants in the threatened sports, dropping them would make the number of men and women playing on Redhawks teams roughly equal.

"We do not have the budget, at present, to fund 22 sports adequately," Mr. Mike Maturi of Miami University Athletics says. "Not only do we not have the budget for 22 sports, but we can't meet gender equity."

EQUITY BY OTHER MEANS

Officials from the Office for Civil Rights insist that institutions like Miami have options besides proportionality.

"The beauty of Title IX is that it recognizes the fact . . . that there might not be proportionally as many people in one group who are interested in athletics as in another group," says Ms. O'Shea.

Universities have two other ways to comply with the law. Institutions can demonstrate a continuing history of expanding opportunities for women to play sports. Alternatively, a university can demonstrate that it is fully and effectively meeting the identified needs, abilities, and interests of women on the campus.

Those options aren't available to Bakersfield, though, because of the Cal-NOW consent decree. And Mr. Garland, Miami's president, says the other goals aren't financially feasible for a university like his. "We've tried to comply with federal law by the continuing practice of adding women's teams," he says. "But any school can only do that for so long, because any time you add a sport, you add additional expenses."

Still more women at Miami have proposed adding additional sports, which proves that their interests are not being met. But Miami can't afford to add additional sports. That leaves participation, Mr. Garland says.

In cases like Bakersfield's, Ms. O'Shea doesn't think men who sue will have much of a case. "Title IX does not grant individuals the opportunity to participate in a particular sport," she says. "It doesn't look to individuals as such; it looks to the overall program."

That doesn't sit well with Kimberly Schuld, the manager of special projects for the Independent Women's Forum. It smacks of a government-sponsored quota, she says.

Despite Ms. O'Shea's thoughts, Mr. Neal and the other Bakersfield wrestlers may have some cause for optimism. A federal court in California has issued a restraining order preventing the university from forcing the team to cut wrestlers, and it has denied the university's motions to dismiss the case.

Everyone seems to agree that it is wrong for universities to cut men's teams. The question remains, however, whether providing equitable opportunities for women is right enough to supersede that wrong.

Although Suggs is writing about the present, his article could be interpreted as an argument about the future. See more about such arguments in Chapter 1.

LINK TO P. 14

RESPOND •

1. Suggs interviews people who take different positions on the controversy, but does he take a position himself—implicitly or explicitly? Give evidence for your answer.

2. In several places Suggs asserts a broad generalization about public opinion among "almost everyone": "Almost everyone—except perhaps for the cut players—would say that's fair. . . . Everyone seems to agree that it is wrong for universities to cut men's teams. . . . 'I think almost everybody in higher education believes the goal of Title IX is worthy'" (paragraphs 1, 34, and 7). (This last sentence is a quotation Suggs uses.) What is implied about those who disagree with "everyone"? What effect would the use of the qualifiers "everybody" or "almost everybody" have on an audience of people who disagree with Suggs's generalizations?

3. Can you find fallacies in Suggs's reasoning at any point? For example, does he imply that because Stephen Neal may not be able to find a job coaching wrestling at the university level, Neal deserves sympathy and perhaps legal redress? Do you think Suggs would be equally sympathetic to Latin or anthropology majors who can't find jobs? Find two or three fallacies in the text; for each one, tell what type of fallacy it is and why you think so. (You may want to review Chapter 19, "Fallacies of Argument.")

4. In "Bad As They Wanna Be" (p. 627), Thad Williamson claims that "[a] sad rite of passage for most college athletes is the existential realization that they will never make it to the pros," and he quotes former Florida State football player Sheray Gaffney as saying, "What was astonishing was the number of scars that [the program] left on athletes. . . . It was painful to see athletes crying in distress because they see their dreams slowly fading away" (paragraph 15). Does Gaffney's statement affect how you respond to Suggs's description of the emotional distress of the Bakersfield wrestlers who get cut from the team? Why or why not? Should it? How do you predict Williamson and Gaffney would respond to Suggs?

5. Suggs compares the gender imbalance in athletics programs with that in nursing programs, asking whether schools should be forced to admit men to nursing programs "in numbers proportional to their overall enrollment at the university." Do you think this question is genuine, or is it posed for rhetorical effect? Do you think nursing and athletics programs should strive for such gender balance? Why or why not? **Write an essay** explaining your position.

▼ *This article appeared in December 1998 in the* Chronicle of Higher Education, *a weekly paper covering issues of concern to college and university faculty and administrators. Although Peter Monaghan can safely assume that his audience is familiar with Title IX,* NCAA *regulations, Division I, and other terms related to college sports, he spends time defining some terms for his readers. As you read, pay attention to where Monaghan defines familiar terms and how the definitions support his argument.*

Dropping Men's Teams to Comply with Title IX

PETER MONAGHAN

In colleges' long, slow march toward gender equity in their athletics programs, nothing is more certain to generate heat than dropping men's teams to free up money for women's teams.

Yet that is the tactic that many institutions have employed—Providence College, the latest among them.

Providence quickly was met by protests when, in October, it said it would drop three men's programs as part of a four-year plan to comply with federal gender-equity law. The law in question, Title IX of the Education Amendments of 1972, forbids institutions that receive federal funds from discriminating on the basis of sex.

For many years, supporters of men's teams that have been dropped have claimed that such decisions demonstrate the ravages wrought by Title IX.

In one typical outburst, a sports columnist in Providence, R.I., had this to say about the college's recent cuts: "How crazy is it that, in order to create athletic opportunities for women, Providence College has had to take athletic opportunities away from men?"

He added: "Eliminating sports was never the intent of Title IX. But it has been the result."

The facts don't necessarily back up that argument, says Janet M. Justus, director of education outreach at the National Collegiate Athletic Association. "Cuts get the attention, but study might show that most schools have not cut programs to meet Title IX. Most have added programs."

A 1997 report by the Women's Sports Foundation showed that from 1978 to 1996, 853 men's programs in Division I had been dropped, and 927 added. Women certainly did gain: In the same period, 1,658 women's programs were added.

National data show that the number of men's teams has not shrunk, but some campuses, like Providence, have made cuts—usually with great reluctance, and significant pain.

Title IX requires colleges with sports teams to offer programs for men and women that are roughly proportional to their representation in the student body. If 50 per cent of a college's students are women, about 50 per cent of its athletes should be, too. And if 50 per cent of a college's athletes are women, they should get about half of the institution's athletics-scholarship budget as well, according to the U.S. Educational Department's guidelines for carrying out the law.

In fulfilling the obligations of Title IX, Providence has one edge over many other institutions: It has no football team. Colleges typically must sponsor more teams for women to offset the large number of players on a football squad.

Still, Providence's compliance with Title IX was complicated by its demographics. Its student body is 57 per cent female and 43 per cent male.

A survey last spring by *The Chronicle* showed that 52 per cent of Providence's athletes were men, and that male athletes got 54 per cent of the college's athletics-scholarship money (*The Chronicle*, April 3). Like many colleges in the survey, Providence's numbers indicated that it was in violation of Title IX.

Because government enforcement of Title IX compliance has been lackadaisical, colleges have typically made changes in their sports programs in response to lawsuits, or threats of lawsuits.

Providence officials say their 15 changes were motivated by another factor: an impending peer review as part of the N.C.A.A.'s certification process.

Starting in 1993, the association began a process in which colleges in Division I, its top competitive level, undergo periodic reviews of their compliance with a variety of rules, such as those on recruiting, as well as their fiscal and academic soundness.

In the first round of certification reviews, institutions had to have a program in place to advance their progress toward gender equity. By 1999, they must prove that they actually have made progress.

Almost 300 of the 307 Division I institutions have been inspected over the last five years, and all but one have been certified. Twenty-nine were certified with conditions, such as that they improve their gender-equity plans. N.C.A.A. officials say they don't know how many colleges stumbled over that requirement, but some did.

As their review approached, Providence officials knew they had a gender-equity problem. How to fix it was less clear.

They knew they needed to change 20 the proportions of male and female athletes. They also had to come up with enough money to add scholarships for women, either by starting new teams or by giving more grants for existing women's teams.

John M. Marinatto, the college's assistant vice-president for athletics, says Providence officials knew that adding to the number of women's

teams — a costly proposition — was not a viable option.

"It became apparent to us that we could not add funding to athletics, and that reallocation was our only path," he says.

Providence did weigh other options, such as withdrawing from the Big East Conference — to try to find a stable but less expensive competitive level. It rejected that step, even though some of its teams have struggled to compete in the league.

The university's president, the Rev. Philip A. Smith, says, "The decision to drop any of our sports teams was very difficult but very necessary, given the college's limited financial resources and our desire to continue

competitive, and their contribution to keeping total sports participation as high as possible, a factor in drawing students.

In October, officials announced that Providence would drop baseball, golf, and men's tennis at the end of this academic year, a decision that will affect 57 male athletes who have been sharing the equivalent of just under 11 athletics grants. Those scholarships will be redistributed to members of existing women's teams in field hockey, ice hockey, soccer, or softball. But the male athletes aren't being entirely cut off. They will be free to remain at Providence until after their fourth year of enrollment, at the same level of financial support.

Officials knew they had a gender-equity problem. How to fix it was less clear.

---

offering student-athletes the opportunity to participate at the highest level of varsity athletic competition without compromising academic priorities."

Once Providence decided that it 25 had no option but to drop men's teams, that still left tough decisions about which ones to cut.

Mr. Marinatto says that the only programs not considered for cuts were men's and women's basketball — teams that a college must field to remain in Division I. Everything else was on the table, he says.

Providence assessed its existing sports based on their financial viability, the likelihood of their staying

The changes will leave the college with 19 sports, eight for men and 11 for women. But within four years, the most important goal will have been attained: Providence's gender breakdown in sports, and its spending on athletics scholarships for women and men, will be in proportion to the female-male ratio of its student body.

Facts like those have not assuaged 30 supporters of the men's programs that will be dropped. Nor have they consoled the male athletes on those teams.

The day Providence administrators announced their plans, they called a meeting of the affected athletes. The officials describe the meeting as emotional. Players were tearful and angry.

A few days later, 200 students rallied on the campus to show support for the athletes. Much of the support came from female athletes; the women's volleyball team, for instance, wore baseball jerseys in warm-ups for a match soon after the decision was announced.

Officials met with the captains of all sports programs to explain their quandary. Mr. Marinatto says they told the captains what they later told members of support groups for the three men's sports, who had no warning that their teams were at risk and rushed to the campus for answers. Says Mr. Marinatto: "We told them we were happy to revisit it, but we don't think there's something out there. We believe we've covered every base."

Supporters and coaches are still trying to come up with creative alternatives to dropping the teams.

Says Charlie Hickey, a baseball 35 coach at Providence for eight years: "I don't believe that, from an alumni standpoint, there is an acceptance of this decision. There is a tremendous outpouring of support. Most of it is anger. They were never contacted or asked if they could be of help or service."

He remains hopeful that his program will be spared, but not optimistic. "Not only would we have to generate revenues to support the baseball program, but we'd also have to raise additional money for women, to still be in compliance" with Title IX, he says. Supporters of the 77-year-old baseball program have been told that the $300,000 needed each year to keep baseball alive would be only 43 per cent of the total they must raise.

He and other supporters are trying to convince the college that cutting the programs would hurt Providence financially. The college is having trouble attracting male students, and almost all of his players are paying part or full tuition fees.

Realistically, he says, he knows that most of his players will now leave the college. All 16 freshman and sophomore students on his roster as of last summer have said they'll transfer elsewhere.

RESPOND ●

1. What is Monaghan's position on Title IX compliance? How sure are you? How do you know?

2. Even though newspaper and magazine authors rarely write their own titles, those titles become part of the argument because the title is the first thing readers see and the thing that often attracts readers to read the article. In light of Welch Suggs's admission in the previous article (p. 590) — that many schools are cutting smaller men's teams to help support football programs — how accurate or fair is the title of Monaghan's article?

3. Read Ruth Conniff's article on "Title IX: Political Football" (p. 585). Consider how Conniff's and Monaghan's word choices create very different pictures of the effects of Title IX. Choose one passage in each article and change the language to create a more neutral impression, making as few changes as possible. Describe what you did and explain why.

4. **Write a letter** to the president of Providence College, supporting his decision or urging him to take a different course of action (be specific about your suggestion). Give reasons and evidence for your position.

Monaghan knows that many university administrators and policy makers are a large part of his audience. How did he choose his evidence with those readers in mind? Check out the section on considering audiences in Chapter 18.

LINK TO P. 380

▼ *Leslie Heywood teaches English and cultural studies at the State University of New York at Binghamton. This article appeared in a January 1999 issue of the* Chronicle of Higher Education, *a weekly paper covering issues of concern to college and university administrators and faculty. In it she raises difficult questions about women's sports that have received little attention. The* Chronicle *published only one letter—a critical one—in response to Heywood's article. As you read, think about whether—and how—the issues she raises have been addressed at your school.*

Despite the Positive Rhetoric about Women's Sports, Female Athletes Face a Culture of Sexual Harassment

LESLIE HEYWOOD

Last October, Nike and the Partnership for Women's Health at Columbia University announced Helping Girls Become Strong Women, an alliance formed in response to an on-line survey conducted by *Seventeen* and *Ladies' Home Journal*. That survey found that 50 per cent of the 1,100 girls polled reported feeling depressed at least once a week; 29 per cent felt somewhat or very uncomfortable with their bodies; and close to 50 per cent were unhappy with their appearances.

The alliance stresses sports as a major solution to those problems. It echoes a landmark study written under the auspices of the President's Council on Physical Fitness and Sports, which also emphasized the benefits of sports for girls and women. That report cited, for example, the way sports disprove gender stereotypes about female weakness and incompetency, and the ways in which

they foster better physical and mental health, self-esteem, and skills such as leadership and cooperation.

Certainly, sports can help with some of the problems faced by young girls and women. And female participation in sports has greatly increased in the years since the 1972 passage of Title IX of the Education Amendments, which barred schools and colleges receiving federal funds from discriminating against women. High-school girls' participation in sports grew from 300,000 in 1972 to 2.25 million in 1995, and today, one in three women in college participates in competitive sports.

But there is another, less-discussed side to the story. A discrepancy exists between the increasing equality and respect for female athletes on the one hand, and, on the other, behavior within the athletics culture that shows profound disrespect for female competitors.

For example, old assumptions that women who excel at sports are really more like men (and must, therefore, be lesbians, because they're not conventionally feminine) are rearticulated in the kind of "lesbian baiting" of female coaches and athletes that happens on many campuses.

In her book *Coming on Strong* (Free Press, 1994) the women's-sports historian Susan K. Cahn discusses the recent rumor circulated among coaches that an anonymous list had been mailed to prospective high-school recruits identifying programs as lesbian or straight. "Oddly," Cahn writes, "concerns about lesbianism in sports may even have increased, in inverse relationship to the greater acceptance of women's sports in general." Such concern shows a profound disrespect, because it assumes that good athletes are not "real women," and that lesbianism is something to fear, which undermines the fundamental dignity and worth of all female athletes and fosters a homophobia that may discourage women from participating in sports.

Other denigrating coaching practices—although they are officially discouraged—include mandatory weigh-ins and criticizing athletes about their weight. Many coaches are inordinately preoccupied with what their female athletes eat, and subject them to public ridicule about their diets and bodies. One group of athletes, from an athletically successful university in the South, told me about a coach who dubbed one of his athletes "Janie Snax" because he thought she was overweight (she weighed 125 at 5 feet 8 inches tall), and had the male athletes make fun of her every time she tried to eat anything. I have heard similar tales on many campuses.

Such practices, though disturbing, may stem from assumptions about women's "natures" that are widely accepted. In a recent issue of the *Nation*, in "The Joy of Women's Sports," Ruth Conniff applauds Anson Dorrance, who has coached the women's soccer team at the University of North Carolina at Chapel Hill to 15 national championships, for being responsive to women athletes by making changes in his coaching style. Conniff quotes Dorrance as saying, "You basically have to drive men, but you can lead women. . . . I think women bring something incredibly positive to athletics. They are wonderfully coachable and so appreciative of anything you give them."

Two weeks after the *Nation* article appeared, *The Chronicle* and other news media reported a sexual-harassment lawsuit filed by two of Dorrance's former players, Debbie Keller (now a player on the national women's soccer team) and Melissa Jennings. They charge that he "intentionally and systematically subjected his players to inappropriate conduct and unwelcome harassment and thereby created a hostile environment at U.N.C." The suit alleges that Dorrance made uninvited sexual advances, monitored players' whereabouts outside of practice, and sent them harassing e-mail messages.

The idea that women are "wonderfully coachable and so appreciative" has a sinister ring in light of these

5

10

Heywood claims that sexual exploitation of female athletes jeopardizes some of the benefits of sports for women. Would you agree that her article could be considered a qualitative evaluation argument? Check out Chapter 10.

LINK TO P. 174···

charges (which Dorrance has denied), and highlights some questionable assumptions underlying the positive rhetoric about women in sports. Gender-based assumptions like Dorrance's, such as the idea that women are more "coachable"—that is, open and manipulable—and that they are "appreciative" of whatever attentions the coach chooses to give them, may lead to unethical behavior such as that cited in the charges against Dorrance.

Yet the issue of coaches' behavior toward female athletes—what is acceptable and what is not—has been swept aside, and reports of the lawsuit against Dorrance have had no effect on recruiting for the U.N.C. women's soccer team. One of the nation's top soccer recruits, in a recent article in *College Soccer Weekly,* said that the allegations weren't "an issue"; that the lawsuit, in her opinion, "doesn't exist."

That kind of dismissal is a common response when a female athlete comes forward with charges of sexual harassment. As is the case at U.N.C., teams often rally around the coach and ostracize the accuser, creating an environment in which most women are afraid to speak out. In the November 14 issue of *USA Today,* Dorrance noted that there was a "silver lining" to the lawsuit in that it "unified the team very quickly." High-profile cases such as this one, in which the news media seem to stress support for the coach rather than for the athlete, communicate to other athletes that if they speak out, they will be brushed aside and disbelieved.

In fact, sexual harassment and abuse of female athletes are part of the reality of women's sports. The executive director of the Women's Sports Foundation, Donna Lopiano, has written on the foundation's site on the World-Wide Web: "Sexual harassment or even sexual assault is a significant problem in school and open amateur sport settings across the country that often goes unreported."

Michelle Hite, an athlete who competed in track in the mid-'90s at a major Division I university, told me that "one of the reasons I gave up my athletics scholarship was because of the sexual harassment that I felt was as much a part of my athletics routine as practice was." Hite and her teammates cite coaches' preoccupations with their bodies and weight, inappropriate comments about their bodies and their sexuality (and policing of that sexuality, such as forbidding athletes to have romantic relationships), direct sexual come-ons from members of the coaching staff, and romantic relationships between coaches and athletes—which were destructive and disruptive to the athletes involved and to the team as a whole.

It wasn't until recently, however, that romantic relationships between coaches and athletes were seen as a problem. When Mariah Burton Nelson wrote *The Stronger Women Get, the More Men Love Football* (Harcourt Brace, 1994), she found that harassment was a part of everyday reality in sports culture. "Some of the 'best' male coaches in the country have seduced a succession of female athletes," she writes. "Like their counterparts in medicine, education, psychotherapy, and the priesthood, coaches are rarely caught or punished."

In a crucial first step, most athletics organizations have drawn a hard line against such behavior. In his 1994 article "Ethics in Coaching: It's Time to Do the Right Thing" in *Olympic Coach* magazine, William V. Nielsens, of the U.S. Olympic Committee, wrote: "One of the most pressing issues today that needs to be addressed concerning coaching ethics is sexual abuse and harassment." The Women's Sports Foundation and WomenSport International have developed extensive anti-harassment and training guidelines for

15

> **"Creating a climate that fosters open discussion about sexual harassment is crucial, so that athletes feel authorized and safe in speaking out."**

coaches. In Canada, various sports organizations have joined to create the Harassment and Abuse in Sport Collective.

Athletics departments also claim to be sensitive to these issues, but it remains unclear how much action they have taken beyond paying lip service to the problem. Some more-progressive campuses have established preventive measures, such as educational training for coaches and athletes. The University of Arizona, for instance, has implemented an extensive education and support system, which includes seminars prepared for coaches by affirmative-action officers. The seminars specifically deal with the multifaceted nature of sexual harassment, and include case studies and "real-life scenarios" to clarify what exactly constitutes harassment. Freshman orientation for athletes covers "social issues" like harassment, unethical coach/athlete relationships, and eating disorders. This is supplemented by orientation for parents that lets them know about potential problems that may develop in their daughters' athletics careers, and the resources that are available to these young women.

There are several problems, though, with such prevention and treatment strategies at even the most-progressive campuses. The first is that almost all such education programs are initiated by affirmative-action officers, rather than originating in the athletics departments themselves. The Women's Sports Foundation recommends that athletics departments have

their own policies and programs, because there is so much more personal contact and interaction in the world of athletics than in ordinary teacher-student relationships.

Furthermore, typical seminars given by affirmative-action offices involve outsiders coming in to lecture individuals who are caught up in an athletics culture that doesn't always take such education seriously. In fact, a conflict exists between athletics, which values winning at all costs, and "sensitivity training," which many athletes see either as distracting or as not applying to them.

It is hard to convince coaches and athletes that the problems of female athletes are real and significant: After all, what does the self-esteem of a few girls matter when we've got to go out and win the big game? The women themselves, who may feel that achieving success and respect is bound up with gaining the approval of coaches, view the people who come to talk about harassment as an intrusion or distraction from the larger goal of athletics success.

Many sports administrators also assume that the athlete herself will report any abuses to the proper authorities. But many women rightly believe that doing so would bring about reprisals, such as being ostracized by their teammates and coaches, and being given less playing time.

The problems are complicated, tied up as they are with assumptions inherent in the athletics culture itself. If we really want to create an environment that is supportive to all athletes, we need to change traditional cultural assumptions about which athletes and which sports are most valuable. As continual debates about Title IX reveal, despite the widespread acceptance of female athletes, in many universities male athletes are still seen as "the real thing," the more-valued players. Over all, universities trivialize issues such as harassment,

because allegations are perceived as detracting from "business as usual"—that is, producing winning men's teams.

According to the Women's Sports Foundation, every sports organization, from university athletics departments to youth leagues, should have and implement its own code of ethics and conduct for coaches. Creating a climate that fosters open discussion about sexual harassment also is crucial, so that athletes feel authorized and safe in speaking out.

Often, athletes believe that they will be accused of consenting to sexual relations with coaches, or of making up incidents of harassment. Many athletes also feel ashamed to talk about sexual issues publicly. But harassment is an issue of power, not of sex, and college and university policies need to make that distinction clear.

Parents and athletes also should look for schools and colleges with education programs that inform coaches clearly about what kinds of behavior won't be tolerated, and that

inform athletes of their rights and the recourse available to them if they should encounter harassment. If parents and athletes show a preference for institutions with such programs, others will follow suit. But the programs need to go beyond lip service and show real support for women who file complaints, by showing zero tolerance for harassment and not—as has historically been the case—immediately leaping to the coaches' defense.

Sports are great for women. Some of my best experiences have been, and continue to be, in competitive sports. But for sports to really improve self-esteem and provide character building, camaraderie, and learning, greater attention needs to be paid to coaching, the assumptions that coaches sometimes make about female athletes, and how much control coaches should have over female athletes' lives. If we want women to truly benefit from participation in sports, we need to find ways to prevent their exploitation.

RESPOND●

1. What solutions does Heywood recommend for eliminating the sexual abuse and harassment of female athletes by coaches? Do you think her proposal is viable? Why or why not?

2. The first two paragraphs of Heywood's article do not directly address the main topic. What is Heywood doing in these paragraphs? Why does she open the article in this way? How well does the strategy work?

3. Writing to an audience of educators and policy-making officials of sports organizations such as the NCAA, Heywood uses a combination of personal and statistical evidence to construct her argument. How might she have changed her article for an audience of parents? Of athletes? How might she alter her appeal in a speech to a coaches' conference?

4. Heywood's article uses all four types of argument described in Chapters 4–7 of this book. Choose the type you think is most prominent in her article and **write an essay** analyzing the rhetorical techniques Heywood uses to construct that type of argument. Give examples from her text, and tell why you think her use of this type of argument is (or is not) effective.

You've surely seen word association tests. The examiner gives you a word, and you shout out all the words you can think of in one minute that relate to it. Take the word "sports," for example, and start shouting. What comes out? *Game? Stadium? Team? Fun? Bar? TV?* How many words would you come up with before you said *politics?* Likely a lot. The readings in this cluster will try to persuade you that perhaps *politics* (or maybe *money*) is the first word you should come up with. In one way or another, they all pose a simple question: **Is sports just a proxy for politics?** Is it ever possible simply to enjoy the game? These readings argue that it's not and that in one way or another, sports is necessarily about bigger political issues in this and other societies.

The first four readings in the cluster examine a debate that began in 2002 and may well continue as you read this page: membership for women in the Augusta National Golf Club, where the prestigious and lucrative Masters Tournament is held. The cluster opens with somewhat cryptic "statements of belief" from the Women's Sports Foundation about gender discrimination. The Foundation's discussion of the background to the statements and the statements themselves merit careful scrutiny, reminding us that questions about what does or does not happen in Augusta must, by nature, be complex. Deroy Murdock, writing for the *National Review*, claims that the fight about Augusta isn't about discrimination but about "Double Standards"; for him, the real issue is freedom of association, something those who call for a boycott of Augusta will, to his way of thinking, never understand. Deborah Rhode, a law professor at Stanford University, argues that because of the importance of golf as a networking opportunity for professional women, it should be "Tee Time for Equality" at Augusta and everywhere else. Salon.com writer King Kaufman wants to know why Tiger Woods is supposed to support every politically correct (P.C.) protest just because the media label him African American. His essay raises broader questions about the treatment of minority athletes by and in the media. Siobhan Benet, a freelance writer, discusses the Augusta National Golf Club but tells a quite different sort of tale, one about how the integration of golf clubs has nearly put African American caddies out of business. Thad Williamson mourns the changes in college basketball, using his beloved Tar Heels as a case study in what he thinks is wrong with collegiate athletics. In an excerpt from a longer article that made the cover of the weekly *New York Times Magazine* in spring 2003, Michael Sokolove examines college football as a money-making enterprise. His case study unfolds at the University of South Florida, which is investing its future—and a whole lot of money—on college football. His title, "Football Is a Sucker's Game," says it all, at least from his perspective.

▼ *The Women's Sports Foundation, <womenssportsfoundation.org>, was founded in 1974 by Billie Jean King, a pro tennis legend. According to its home page, the organization is "dedicated to ensuring equal access to participation and leadership opportunities for all girls and women in sports and fitness."*

This selection, posted September 18, 2002, explains the Foundation's stance on what was a hot issue at the time—the fact that the Augusta National Golf Club, home to the Masters Tournament, had at no time in its history had a female member. This selection and the three that follow present a range of opinions on the Augusta National controversy, demonstrating clearly that arguments involving sports are quite often arguments about larger social and political issues in American society. Whether or not the controversy in Augusta has been resolved at the time you read these texts, the principles and commitments that sparked the controversy in the first place will still be very vital.

You will see that this selection is complex: while providing the Foundation's view of relevant background information on the controversy, the selection closes with the formal statements adopted by the Foundation's Board of Trustees on "private clubs hosting sports events." As you read, work hard to understand the specific analysis of the relevant issues offered by the Foundation.

In this text, the Women's Sports Foundation is reporting its formal or official position on private clubs that host sports events. The position takes the form of a proposal argument. See Chapter 12 to learn more about the structure of proposal arguments.

························· LINK TO P. 238

National Council of Women's Organizations: a nonpartisan association of over 100 groups working for change on issues of importance to women, including education, health care, and equal opportunity.

Women at Augusta National Golf Club

The Women's Sports Foundation Supports Admission of Women to Augusta National Golf Club

WOMEN'S SPORTS FOUNDATION

Augusta National Golf Club, an exclusive men's club which hosts the prestigious Masters Tournament, has not had one female member in its history. The Women's Sports Foundation announced its support for a change in policy at the club.

The National Council of Women's Organizations°, of which the Foundation is a member, recently wrote Augusta National and requested that they admit a woman to the 300-member club. It urged the club to admit women before next year's Masters Tournament in April.

"While we fully support the right of 'private' clubs to self-determination, as soon as that club engages in staging public events and public commerce, they are no longer a private entity and the privileges of 'privacy' should therefore cease," said Donna Lopiano, Executive Director, Women's Sports Foundation. "Augusta benefits from incredible exposure by hosting the Masters Tournament and becomes a place of public accommodation when it charges for tickets, accepts rights fees from television networks and sponsorship fees from corporations. The media coverage of the event, in which the finest golfers in the world partici-pate, brings valuable exposure to the club. The price of such benefits should be non-discrimination. Similarly, since the LPGA° and the PGA° have policies against playing their sanctioned events at clubs which practice race or gender discrimination, it would be assumed that LPGA and PGA players would not par-ticipate in a tournament hosted by a club that does discriminate—as a matter of principle."

LPGA: the Ladies Professional Golf Association. Founded in 1950, the nonprofit organization hosts golf tournaments, golf education programs, and charity fundraisers.

PGA: the Professional Golfer's Association. Founded in 1916, the PGA is the largest sports organization in the world.

William Johnson, the chair of the Augusta National Golf Club, responded angrily to the suggestion that the club consider admitting women. "There may well come a day when women will be invited to join our membership," he said. "But that timetable will be ours, and not at the point of a bayonet."

The Augusta National Golf Club maintains that it has no restrictions based on race, gender, religion or national origin. However, the club has fewer than 10 African-American members and no women. Women are able to play at the club as guests of members.   5

In June, the Foundation's Board of Trustees approved a formal position on the matter of private clubs hosting sports events:

> Whereas the Women's Sports Foundation has adopted the following statements of belief:
>
> • Sports for males and females should embrace positive values and respect for others;
>
> • Equal opportunity, treatment and benefits in sports paticipation, sports leadership and sports-related careers should be assured;

- Sports and sports-related careers should include people of every age, color, gender, national origin, physical disability, race, religion and sexual orientation; and

Whereas, the Women's Sports Foundation is strongly opposed to discrimination on the basis of age, color, gender, national origin, physical disability, race, religion and sexual orientation in sport;

Therefore Be It Resolved that the Women's Sports Foundation go on record as calling for athletes, professionals in sports-related careers, sports organizations, spectators and sponsors of sports events to adopt strong non-discrimination positions with regard to the sanctioning of or participation in events or programs sponsored or hosted by organizations or facilities whose policies, practices or actions discriminate on the basis of age, color, gender, national origin, physical disability, race, religion or sexual orientation in sport.

Further Be It Resolved that athletes, professionals in sports-related careers and members of the general public who are members of sports organizations and clubs that have policies, practices, activities or have demonstrated decision-making which exclude individuals or groups from participating in that organization or club on the basis of age, color, gender, national origin, physical disability, race, religion or sexual orientation in sport, immediately call for a formal review and revision of such policies and practices.

RESPOND•

1. What, specifically, is the Women's Sports Foundation proposing in its "statements of belief"? Why? What would the consequences of such a proposal be if it is actually carried out? Why, in your opinion, do the "statements of belief" not mention the Augusta National Golf Club? Is not mentioning Augusta National a strength or a weakness? Why?

2. Perhaps you have noticed that formal resolutions, a subcategory of proposal argument, generally take the form "Whereas A, B, C . . ., Therefore, Be It Resolved that X, Y, Z." In what ways do the "statements of belief" work with the earlier part of the selection, which provides background information, to create a complete proposal argument? How effective a proposal do you believe the selection, as a whole, is? Why? (Check out Chapter 12, especially "Key Features of Proposals," p. 247, to answer this question.)

3. What's the argument about, from the Foundation's perspective? In other words, what particular values are in conflict in this situation, as the Foundation understands it? A distinction that may prove useful to you in answering this question is the one represented by a familiar pair of Latin phrases: *de jure*, which means "by law," and *de facto*, which means "by deed or action," that is, the way things, in fact, are. How might supporters of the Foundation's position use this pair of phrases to characterize the situation at Augusta National?

4. Like texts on many Web pages posted by organizations, the primary purpose of this selection is to state the organization's position on an issue that its creators perceive as relevant to the group's mission. As noted above, the selection seeks to achieve this goal by providing background information and presenting the Foundation's formal proposal in the form of "statements of belief." **Write an essay** in which you evaluate the effectiveness of this selection. In addition to the goals stated here, you will likely want to consider the potential audiences and the alternatives the organization might have had. (It could have produced a rant or a formal statement that focused purely on the situation in Augusta, but it did not. In other words, you'll want to consider why the Foundation didn't choose other alternatives, whether or not you write about any of them.) Chapter 10 on evaluative arguments may help you with this assignment.

▶ In this essay for the
National Review Online, *the
Web site maintained by the
conservative digest* National
Review, *Deroy Murdock provides a perspective on the
Augusta National controversy
that is very different from the
one offered in the previous
selection by the Women's
Sports Foundation. Murdock
is a columnist for the Scripps
Howard News Service, which
syndicates his column "This
Opinion Just In . . .," and a
senior fellow at the Atlas Economic Research Foundation.
This essay was posted on
November 21, 2002. As you
read, pay special attention to
Murdock's tone and his use of
humor to create it.*

Women's College Coalition: an
organization comprised of
all-women's colleges in the
United States and Canada.
Founded in 1972.

Use the criteria given in Chapter
18 to determine whether you
think Murdock chose appropriate
evidence and used it effectively.

LINK TO P. 367

Double Standards

Women who want Augusta National to admit women have some hypocrisy issues.

DEROY MURDOCK

Feminists who demand that Augusta National Golf Club admit women should think twice. If they succeed, men may try to gain entry to places now open only to females.

Located outside a small town in Georgia, Augusta National has been excoriated for its males-only membership policy. After the National Council of Women's Organizations planned to target sponsors of Augusta's 2003 Masters championship, the club preemptively asked several companies to withdraw their support for the golf classic.

"Any entity that holds itself out as publicly as they do ought to be open to men and women alike," NCWO chair Martha Burk tells me. "It does not reflect well on the club and its tournament, which is the crown jewel of golf, to be identified with discrimination."

Augusta, in turn, released a poll on November 13 that shows Americans disagree with Burk. Among 800 Americans surveyed between October 30 and November 4 by WomanTrend, a division of the polling company, 74 percent agreed that "Augusta National has the right to have members of one gender only." Asked whether the club was correct not to cave under Burk's pressure, 72 percent of males concurred, while 73 percent of women agreed. (The poll's margin of error is +/– 3.5 percent.)

"These are extraordinarily high numbers, especially when you consider how aggressive the campaign against the club has been," said WomanTrend president Kellyanne Conway. "What's also striking is how few women support Ms. Burk's demands."

It would be easier to take Burk seriously if she directed some of her wrath at other discriminatory establishments. Though far less controversial, there are venues where men are forbidden. If women penetrate Augusta, how will they bar males from all-female institutions?

Start with the 68 member-campuses of the Women's College Coalition.° Such schools as Barnard, Mount Holyoke and Smith offer top drawer, liberal arts instruction. Men need not apply.

With 296 chapters in America, Canada, Mexico and England, the Junior League's° active, dedicated associates perform community service projects. Its website explains that they also "share ideas and build networks for information exchange" when they gather. There are some 193,000 Junior League members—not one of them male. Women even have their own golf course, albeit abroad. Since its 1924 launch, the Ladies Golf Club of Toronto has had only female members. As *Sports Illustrated*'s Rick Reilly discovered, men may play there, but only when invited by members. Women sneered at Reilly, who was stunned by the separate but unequal amenities for male guests: a poorly appointed locker room and a gravel-covered parking lot behind the clubhouse. "This joint makes Augusta seem like the ACLU," Reilly wrote in SI's September 16 edition.

Junior League: founded in 1901 and dedicated to establishing groups of women who will work for change in their communities and in the world. Focusing on leadership and volunteerism, the Junior League has affected policy in such areas as domestic violence, health care, and literacy.

Martha Burk addresses a rally in Augusta, Georgia

Jim Crow: originally a caricature of a Black person performed in 1830s minstrel shows, played by a white man in blackface. The term came to refer to all the laws designed to enforce segregation by designating Blacks as inferior to whites, from the 1850s to the 1960s.

The vital principle here is freedom of association. As the First Amendment states, "Congress shall make no law . . . abridging . . . the right of the people peaceably to assemble." These words reflect the right of Americans to associate privately with whomever we wish, and not with others, for whatever reason.

There is no such freedom in the public sector. Since Americans are equal before the law, government schools, for instance, cannot discriminate on the basis of sex (although some exceptions apply in cases of military education). Public golf courses may not bar women (or men) from their fairways. If the CIA implemented a "men only" hiring policy, it would be sued at once, and rightly so.

Those who do not understand this distinction may wind up reducing everyone's liberties.

For example, gay rights activists have pressured the Boy Scouts to hire gay scoutmasters despite the group's ban on homosexual leaders. But if the Boy Scouts must employ those who clash with their teachings, must New Jersey's Mountain Meadow summer camp do likewise? Mountain Meadow is a place where gay parents can take their kids for outdoor recreation. Should it be forced to hire heterosexual camp counselors who might frown at Tommy's two daddies?

What about Jim Crow?° Southern states and cities imposed laws that required the segregation of private facilities. Thankfully, the civil-rights movement got those regulations killed.

But what if a private group opens its doors only to blacks (or only to whites)? It should be legally free to do so. Should it be ridiculed or even boycotted? Americans are free to do those things, too. But the First Amendment's free-association clause ultimately protects the right of private groups to define themselves as narrowly as they like.

Freedom of association keeps every organization from resembling every other. While public institutions should accept all classes of citizens (including GIs — gay and straight — who clutch their weapons and not other soldiers), private outfits and facilities should remain free to craft their membership rosters as they desire. That includes Spelman College° and the Daughters of the American Revolution.° Until feminists welcome men into all-female establishments, they should embrace freedom of association. Otherwise, they may learn the hard way that what's good for the gander is good for the goose, too.

RESPOND●

1. As Murdock sees it, what is at stake in Augusta? Why? Can his argument be read as supporting the membership policies of the Augusta National Golf Club? What, specifically, is he supporting? Why?

2. How would you describe Murdock's tone in this selection? It is quite different from the tone of the selection from the Women's Sports Foundation Web site. Why? How might audience differences, for example, influence the tone used in each?

3. What sorts of humor does Murdock use in this selection? How effective do you find it? Why? (Chapter 13 discusses humorous arguments.)

4. **Write a letter** addressed to the chair of the Augusta National Golf Club praising or criticizing its policies or practices regarding membership and women in the past—and perhaps in the present. Your letter will almost certainly include aspects of evaluative arguments; depending on your stance, it may also be a proposal argument.

Spelman College: a private, liberal arts, historically Black college for women located in Atlanta, Georgia.

Daughters of the American Revolution: an all-women's organization founded in 1890, dedicated to promoting patriotism and liberty through education and preserving the history of the founding of American independence.

▼ *"Tee Time for Equality" first appeared in the* National Law Journal, *the leading legal weekly in the United States, in October 2002. Its author, Deborah Rhode, is the Ernest W. McFarland Professor of Law at Stanford University, a specialist in matters of gender law and public policy, the author of numerous books, and a columnist for the* National Law Journal. *As you read this selection, note the ways in which Rhode qualifies her claims and the kinds of evidence she uses to support them.*

Tee Time for Equality

DEBORAH RHODE

For many women lawyers, golf is only partly about golf. It is also about status, networks and exclusion. Golf has long been a source of inequality for women — often to the indifference of men. The extent of insensitivity was brought home this summer when Tiger Woods was asked to comment on the exclusion of women from Augusta National Golf Club, the site of the prestigious Masters tournament. According to Woods, Augusta's members, including many top executives from Fortune 500 companies, are "entitled to set up their own rules the way they want them."

It seems unlikely that Woods would have made a similar statement a decade ago, when he would have been excluded from many clubs like Augusta because of the color of his skin. His response, and those of other defenders of club policies, speaks volumes about this nation's different tolerance for racism and sexism.

"It's just the way it is" no longer flies as an excuse to bar golfers of color. In 1990, a famous flap ensued when the Professional Golfer's Association's annual championship was scheduled for Shoal Creek, an Alabama country club that discriminated against blacks. After civil rights groups threatened to picket the tournament and to boycott its sponsors, some sponsors withdrew more than $2 million in advertising revenues.

Within weeks, Shoal Creek accepted its first black member, and within months, the nation's four major golf organizations adopted anti-discrimination policies. These policies prohibit the organizations from holding a tournament at a course that excludes individuals based on race, sex or national origin.

Augusta, which independently administers the 5 Masters, is not bound by these policies, and none of its corporate sponsors pulled their support after learning of its gender bias. Even Hewlett-Packard (one of the corporate sponsors), whose female CEO would be barred from membership, was "unavailable for comment" when contacted by the *New York Times.* A request by the National Council of Women's Organizations that Augusta admit a woman before next year's tournament provoked defiance by its chairman, William Johnson: "We will not be bullied, threatened or intimidated. . . . We do not intend to become a trophy in the [council's] display case."

WHY IT MATTERS

Should women care? To many women's rights activists, discrimination by private golf clubs is not high on the agenda compared to, say, domestic violence or the feminization of poverty. For many individuals who care about social equality, the goal should be trying to do in — not get in — these bastions of male privilege.

Yet gender bias on the golf course should not be omitted from the feminist wish list. Such discrimination has public consequences; it keeps professional women out of the informal networks where business and mentoring relationships are forged. According to the National Golf Foundation, about two-thirds of male executives now play golf. For women lawyers, lack of access to these potential clients is a significant problem. In an increasingly competitive practice climate, a broad client base is often crucial to professional power, status and economic reward.

Although few clubs now exclude women entirely, many discriminate in tee times and membership privileges like access to the "men's grill." Even public courses, which legally are barred from discrimination, often get away with it. In her research for *The Unplayable Lie*, a book about women and golf, Marcia Chambers documented countless instances of female players being refused tee times during peak hours, only to find that male colleagues calling later had no difficulty gaining access.

Despite these indignities, many professional women who are short on time, interest or innate athletic ability are nonetheless learning to play golf. More than 1 million women begin each year, according to Suzanne Woo's recent book, *On Course for Business: Women and Golf.* So it is all the more irritating when these women still are not invited, or entitled, to join their male colleagues' game.

As long as golf is a source of both economic and 10 symbolic inequality, it should be a focus of professional concern and social reform. Strategies include pickets, boycotts and enforcement or enactment of statutes withholding tax or liquor-license privileges from clubs that discriminate. Some women have also brought successful lawsuits under public-accommodations laws that prohibit discrimination by private clubs that offer services or facilities to non-members.

Few golf courses still retain the sign, legendary until five years ago, at the Royal St. George's Club in Britain: "Women and dogs prohibited." But women are not yet equal partners in this sport and until that changes, they will not be truly equal colleagues in the professional world outside it.

Chapter 8 explains how to do a Toulmin analysis of an argument, identifying such elements as enthymemes, warrants, or backing. What is Rhode's enthymeme? What would be the warrant for that enthymeme? Refer to Chapter 8 for help in answering the question.

LINK TO P. 121

RESPOND

1. What argument does Rhode make regarding Augusta? What sorts of appeals does she use? What sorts of evidence does she cite? Why might she expect these appeals and evidence to be effective with her audience of fellow attorneys? How persuasive do you find her argument?

2. Although Rhode admits that women's rights activists have far more pressing concerns than membership in institutions like the Augusta National Golf Club, she does not minimize the importance of such

membership for women. Why is anticipating and acknowledging such potential criticism important to the argument Rhode is constructing?

3. How would you characterize the parts of Rhode's argument? Which parts of it are definitional? Evaluative? Causal? Proposal? How do the parts work together?

4. The Augusta controversy can be seen as a conflict between "freedom of association," as Murdock puts it, and "discrimination by private golf clubs," as Rhode puts it. As both Murdock and Rhode make clear, much is at stake, directly and indirectly, in how this conflict is dealt with. **Write an essay** in which you seek to define the issues at stake for each side and the consequences, indirect and direct, for each side. In other words, what will be the consequences for freedom of association if private golf clubs can no longer engage in behaviors that thinkers like Rhode would label discriminatory? In contrast, what will be the consequences for the goal of an equitable society if women, or other groups, must continue to endure behaviors that thinkers like Rhode would label discriminatory? Note that the assignment does not ask you to offer an evaluation or make a proposal. Rather, it requires that you focus in detail on questions of definition in all their complexity.

Tiger's Burden

Must Tiger Woods support every p.c. protest, no matter how trivial, just because he's benefited from the "struggles" of others?

KING KAUFMAN

The *New York Times* says Tiger Woods should boycott the Masters Tournament to protest Augusta National Golf Club's policy of excluding women from membership. Jesse Jackson agrees.

I've been boycotting the Masters since 1964, but do I get any love for it?

The *Times* suggested in an editorial last week that Woods and CBS, which has televised the Masters since 1956, stay away from the event, thus sending a message to Augusta National that discrimination will not be tolerated. The Tiffany Network° said, in effect, "Right. Thanks for sharing. We'll see you in April." The *Times*, as has been noted gleefully elsewhere, didn't say anything about skipping the Masters itself. Evidently, "a tournament without Mr. Woods would send a powerful message that discrimination isn't good for the golfing business," but a tournament without the Great Gray Lady° wouldn't.

Woods, who can become the first man to win three straight Masters, also declined to carry water on this one. "I think there should be women members," he said, "but it's not up to me. I don't have voting rights, I'm just an honorary member."

That's not good enough for Jackson, who is threatening to organize protests at   5
the tournament. "He's much too intelligent and too much a beneficiary of our struggles to be neutral," he said of Woods. "His point of view does matter."

It's an interesting question: What do we expect from Tiger Woods?

It's actually a lot of questions: What are his obligations? Why do we expect more from black superstar athletes than from white ones? Black? The mixed-race Woods famously labeled himself "Cablinasian.°" But the old one-drop rule° is still alive and kicking when it comes to identifying public figures. When was the last time you heard Woods referred to as anything other than black?

◀ *King Kaufman is a senior writer for Salon.com, which was founded in 1995 and remains among the Web's most popular online magazines. In "Tiger's Burden," which was posted in November 2002, he belittles the behavior of both Martha Burk and William "Hootie" Johnson, focusing instead on a very different issue raised during the debates about the Augusta National Golf Club—namely, the expectations with which minority superstar athletes are saddled by society at large. As you read, enjoy Kaufman's equal-opportunity humor (nearly everyone takes a beating) and consider how he uses it to influence his readers and make his point.*

Tiffany Network: a nickname for television network CBS, dating from the 1940s through 1970s when it was consistently ranked number one in daytime, prime time, and evening news.

Great Gray Lady: a nickname for the *New York Times* dating back over 150 years. The title refers to the paper's reputation as a no-nonsense medium for journalism that was, until recently, printed solely in black, white, and shades of gray.

617

Cablinasian: Tiger Woods' term for his racial identity, a mixture of Caucasian, Black, Indian, and Asian.

one-drop rule: a law stating that anyone with at least "one drop" of African blood in their ancestry would be considered Black. Often invoked during the 1800s and early 1900s, it was frequently used to enforce segregation and discrimination.

Michael Jordan has long been criticized for his apolitical persona, while white contemporaries like Joe Montana and Wayne Gretzky never were. Why is Woods, as the beneficiary of others' struggles, required to fall in line with every political and social protest that touches golf when all we expect of white golfers is that they apologize in a timely manner for their racist jokes about fried chicken and collard greens? What player on the PGA Tour hasn't benefited from someone's struggles?

Blacks in sports get held up to the standard of Muhammad Ali° and Arthur Ashe,° politically active men of conscience who happened to be great athletes. Woods hasn't lived up to their standards. Then again, neither has anybody else.

Ali is a hero of mine, and I'd love to see Woods follow in his footsteps, even   10
though I rarely waste a thought on Woods or the game he plays. It's just that I'd
love to see anyone follow in Ali's footsteps. But I'm not holding my breath.

Woods has gotten a pass for his blandness from some quarters because of his
age. He's only 22, the thinking went, give him time. But he's almost 27 now, old
enough to have settled on some values and opinions, picked an issue or two to
speak out on if he was going to. Maybe he is going to, but I'm not holding my
breath for that either.

As the *New York Times* correctly noted, Woods is the most powerful golfer in
the world, because he's the best by such a wide margin. His absence from an
event turns it into a minor-league affair. A Tiger Woods boycott is, in the golf
world, a nuclear bomb. If he is ever going to start wielding his political power,
it's hard to argue that the Augusta National controversy is the place to start.

The Masters tempest began when Martha Burk, head of the National Council of
Women's Organizations, called this summer for Augusta National, a private
club, to admit female members, and the club's chairman, Hootie Johnson,
eventually responded by saying there was no chance a woman would be invited
before the April tournament, and that Augusta National would change its membership policy on its own terms, if ever.

I have a theory that you never would have heard a word of this if the club chairman weren't named Hootie, but never mind that. Political scientists, psycholo-
gists and others who study the human condition have a word for this kind of
public whizzing match: "dumb."

Reasonable people can fall on either side of the question of whether Augusta   15
National should be forced to admit women, but a reasonable person would find
himself with strange bedfellows no matter what side he takes, forgive the
gender-specific language.

Burk has a point in her argument that the Masters is such a public event that
regardless of Augusta National's private status, it ought not exclude entire
classes of people. It looks bad, sets a bad example, gives off a bad vibe. It
forces ordinary fans to tacitly approve of a policy that looks uncomfortably like
garden-variety discrimination if all they want to do is enjoy a favorite sporting
event. If this argument has no merit, then why did Augusta National finally begin
admitting black members in 1990?

Muhammad Ali: three-time heavyweight boxing champion (1942–),
became known for his defiant
stance against the United States
government. Citing his status as a
conscientious objector because of
his membership in the Nation of
Islam, Ali refused induction into
the military during the Vietnam
War draft.

Arthur Ashe: a prominent, award-
winning tennis player (1943 –
1993), made history in 1969,
when he challenged the tennis
world to expel South Africa from
its organizations because of the
racist Apartheid government. In
the 1980s and 1990s, became a
spokesperson for HIV/AIDS after
receiving the virus through a
blood transfusion.

Kaufman's tone is far too informal for (nearly) all academic writing. Which specific features make it so? See Chapter 3 for an example of a case where a writer misjudged his readers' expectations.

······································LINK TO P. 55

Barbershop: controversial movie, number one in the box office after its release in 2002. It chronicles a working-class Black barbershop on the south side of Chicago. Jesse Jackson's complaints responded to comments made in the film by Eddie, played by Cedric the Entertainer. Eddie discusses Martin Luther King's alleged promiscuity and says that Rosa Parks, famous for refusing to sit at the back of a desegregated bus, wasn't special, "just tired." Jackson demanded an apology, which the producers gave. Jackson further demanded that these scenes be deleted from any video or DVD release of the film, opening up a heated discussion about censorship.

On the other hand, it's hard to imagine that the chairwoman of something called the National Council of Women's Organizations doesn't have anything more important to get all het up about. Reproductive and contraceptive rights, family leave, equal pay, domestic violence, punitive welfare reform: There's no shortage of issues a little more vital to the interests of women than whether or not, say, two female Fortune 500 CEOs get to join a golf club in Georgia that escapes the notice of the vast majority of us 361 days out of the year.

Burk's campaign reeks of pointless grandstanding and p.c. weenieness. It's sort of like when People for the Ethical Treatment of Animals stages one of its occasional dumb protests, like the one a few years ago when it called for the Green Bay Packers to change their name because of its connection to the meatpacking industry, and thus "animal bloodshed." PETA pulls that sort of thing, and off in a lab somewhere, a rabbit that's been blinded by repeated blasts of hairspray in the eyes says, "Thanks. Thanks a lot." And even if you agree with the PETA folks that animals ought to be treated nicely, you find yourself wanting to strangle a squirrel just to spite them.

But if you believe that private clubs ought to be able to let whomever they want in and keep whomever they want out, you want to say to Hootie & Co., "Hootie, you're right. Now invite a woman into the club, you chucklehead. You're going to do it sooner or later anyway, and in the meantime you're dragging the club and the tournament through the muck because you sound like a Neanderthal."

Given Johnson's exemplary record on women's issues in the business world,   20 it's clear that this isn't a fight between feminists and their enemies, it's a fight between feminists and 2-year-olds. Johnson, who recently invited the University of South Carolina women's golf team to play Augusta National as his guest, isn't arguing against women's rights. He's screaming, "You are not the boss of me!" What a dolt.

It doesn't help when Jesse Jackson chimes in, because, much as I hate to say it, he's become a sort of poster boy for dumb protests, his campaign against the movie "Barbershop"° being a recent example. Jackson made a good point about the *Times*' call for a Woods boycott—"I don't remember them saying to Ben Hogan and Jack Nicklaus to boycott the Masters because blacks are not playing"—but he's become a self-parody, seemingly injecting himself into every controversy that comes down the pike, and thus lessening the impact of what he has to say.

If Tiger Woods is going to use his power, he'd be unwise to squander it on such a minor issue, one that affects so few people, that elicits the same kind of eye-rolling that meets most of Jackson's pronouncements these days. "Forget about a few distaff° executives getting into Augusta," he might say, "let's talk about the Bush administration's attacks on Title IX."

I think Woods should say something like that. I think the same thing about Phil Mickelson° and Brett Favre° and Mario Lemieux° (an excellent golfer, by the way). Why aren't we talking about them?

distaff: the staff used to hold wool from which the thread is drawn when spinning by hand. The word is used as a symbol of the holder of the distaff, hence a woman or women.

Phil Mickelson: one of golf's top players (1970–), recently gaining two PGA Tour wins in addition to being one of the highest paid golfers.

Brett Favre: quarterback for the Green Bay Packers (1969–). Favre is the NFL's only three-time MVP, and holds a host of records for passing and winning.

Mario Lemieux: one of the greatest ice hockey players in the history of the National Hockey League (1965–). He has won two Stanley Cups, six scoring titles, three MVP awards, and is among the all-time top ten for goals, assists, and points scored.

RESPOND •

1. What is Kaufman's argument in this essay? How does he use a controversy about alleged sex discrimination by a private golf club to discuss the way American society makes expectations of minority athletes? What do you imagine his attitude about the Augusta National Golf Club to be? How does Kaufman use the case of Tiger Woods as a way of making his own opinion known about Title IX?

2. How would you characterize Kaufman's voice and style? How does he use figurative language and humor to make his point, and make it memorably? (Chapters 13 and 14 will help you answer this question.)

3. What sort of ethos does Kaufman create? How does he establish his credibility as an authority on the subject he is writing about? As Chapter 3 notes, writers have several means to use in establishing credibility. Which, specifically, does Kaufman use?

4. **Write an essay** in which you define and evaluate the expectations American society should have of its superstar athletes with respect to the public stances they take or their private lives. You may wish to offer a proposal about what we can or should expect of them, and why. (In preparing your argument, you may find it useful to think about how the situation of athletes compares and contrasts with that of other well-known individuals. Research in early 2002, for example, showed that the public claimed to be little influenced by recording stars and media stars who took strong stances on controversial political issues such as our government's policy toward Iraq. In contrast, many of former president Clinton's most vociferous critics focused on his affair with Monica Lewinsky as irrefutable evidence that he was unfit to lead the country.)

▶ *Siobhan Benet, a freelance writer living in New York City, also serves as content manager for Women's Enews, a nonprofit, independent news service devoted to covering issues of relevance to women. In this essay, Benet deals not with issues of gender but with those of race, golf, and, interestingly, the Augusta National Golf Club; the piece originally appeared in September 2002 in Black Enterprise, a magazine targeted at African American businesspeople, entrepreneurs, and policy makers. As you read, note the ways in which Benet has written with the magazine's target audience in mind.*

Where We Once Roamed

SIOBHAN BENET

Pete McDaniel says it best: "Like the unknown soldiers, many African Americans who contributed to the growth of the game [of golf] in this country lie buried in history's tomb."

John Shippen, who played in the U.S. Open at Shinnecock in 1895, was a member of the work crew that built the famous Shinnecock Hills Golf Club in New York. He would later become a caddie and an assistant at the club. Robert "Hard Rock" Robinson's reputation as Pinehurst's most knowledgeable caddie is legendary in North Carolina. And Joseph Bartholomew was one of the country's first golf course architects. He designed the New Orleans public course originally named Pontchartrain Park, which was later renamed for him. These are all black men who have influenced the sport in some way and who have been all but forgotten. They were also caddies, a service industry that has helped the country's most famous golfers. Once, caddies were all young black men. Today, you would be lucky to find one. Not even Tiger Woods uses a black caddie. In fact, these men, along with others too numerous to mention in this article, would have remained forgotten if not for the efforts of sports journalist Pete McDaniel, author of *Uneven Lies: The Heroic Story of African-Americans in Golf* (The American Golfer Inc., $50).

Did you know the first patent for a wooden golf tee was held by a black man? In 1899, the U.S. Patent Office granted it to Dr. George F. Grant, a successful dentist residing in Boston at the time. McDaniel has unearthed the rich history of our participation in the game, including the disappearance of the black caddie. According to McDaniel, Shippen was one of many African Americans to work in various service positions at golf clubs around the country, a position that included the responsibility of being a caddie to the members of the club. At a time when job opportunities for blacks at these private clubs were limited, caddying and having other service-providing responsibilities were highly respected positions.

"It was a viable alternative to long hours in the tobacco fields or tannery," says McDaniel.

How is Benet's article an argument based on values? What shared values does she focus on? See Chapter 5 for more examples of arguments based on values.

LINK TO P. 78

622

Pro golfer Ted Rhodes

According to John Merchant, a former board member of the United   5
States Golf Association, "caddying offered African Americans the
opportunity to make money, do healthy, hard, outdoor work, and
enable these [young men] to learn the game. Golf offered an excellent
opportunity for [these men] to become players."

"Each caddie had to go through certain training, and that was how
you were ranked," adds McDaniel, who caddied as a young adult. "It paid

to be experienced and it also paid to be in good with the caddie supervisor. Caddying taught me a really strong work ethic and gave me a sense of independence. And it also began my life's long love affair with golf."

Back in the day, a good caddie was extremely valued. He knew his game and was very instrumental in the success or failure of a golfer participating in a tournament. These men, the majority of whom were teenagers, arrived on the course before sunup and typically carried two golf bags for 54 holes, or until the end of the day. In the 1920s and 1930s, caddies might work all day for $1—minimum wage standards at the time. By the 1950s, the wages went up. A caddie could receive $2 for a single loop around the course or about 50 cents an hour, and $3 to carry two bags of golf equipment. Today, caddies can earn hundreds of thousands of dollars if working for the right golfer.

But the advent of the golf cart in the 1960s heralded the end of an era for caddies. As the civil rights movement gained momentum and jobs in a variety of industries opened up, young African American teenagers and adults found higher-paying jobs in factories, manufacturing companies, offices, and in many other positions that were traditionally off limits to us. By the early 1970s, many caddie programs at these clubs were all but eliminated. However, the end of blacks dominating the caddie industry seemed to have come in 1983 when the Augusta National Golf Course stopped requiring its Masters participants to use club caddies, who were always black. As a result, players were given the option to select their own caddies, and these new caddies were overwhelmingly white.

"This marked the end of seeing black caddies on television," explains McDaniel. "It was the only time black caddies were treated well and recognized for their role in the sport."

[Four years ago], only one out of the top 50 golf players (Hal Sutton) 10 employed an African American caddie (Freddie Burns). Pete McDaniel breaks it down to dollars and cents. "Last year, there were 55 millionaires on the [PGA] tour, and caddies make 10% of a player's earnings and a bonus if the golfer wins the tournament. Fifty-four white caddies made $100,000; only one black caddie made this amount."

Private clubs have also witnessed a drastic decline in the number of black caddies. McDaniel partially attributes this to the ills of modern society: street life.

Golfer Lee Elder and caddy

There are still a few African American caddies, most of them middle-aged or older men, who work in mostly Southern clubs. But the professional numbers continue to dwindle. Today, most caddies are white high school or college students, and many more are players themselves. As a result of bypassing the opportunity to caddy, aspiring African American golfers are missing out on the opportunity of a life-

Lee Elder: in 1975, became the first black golfer to play in the Masters Tournament. Elder (1934–) also played in South Africa's first integrated tournament in 1972.

Charlie Sifford: in 1967, became the first black golfer to win a PGA event. Sifford (1922–) won the PGA Seniors Championship in 1975 and published his autobiography *Just Let Me Play* in 1992.

Ted Rhodes: the first African-American professional golfer, Rhodes (1913–1969) filed a civil rights suit against the PGA Tour to challenge their "Caucasian-only" clause in 1948.

Bill Spiller: considered one of the most militant black golfers, Spiller (1913–1988) joined Ted Rhodes in the lawsuit against the PGA's "Causasian-only" clause, and frequently asserted his anger about the racism of the golfing associations in the United States.

time: to network and improve their game as golfers by watching and assisting other, more established, players. According to McDaniel, many country club caddies may have peered through the fence hole but few had the courage or sense of adventure or sheer desperation to explore greener pastures. And while black caddies are virtually extinct on tours, they are not extinct in many country clubs. Our presence in the sport, though drastically lessened, will remain if only through the presence of Tiger Woods. McDaniel hopes that in a generation, those players coming up in the ranks of junior golf will take the place of legends like Lee Elder,° Charlie Sifford,° Ted Rhodes,° and Bill Spiller°— all of whom were introduced to the game of golf as caddies.

RESPOND ●

1. How much of the information Benet discusses is new for you? Is it surprising? Should it be? Why or why not?

2. Benet's text represents a common genre of article for popular magazines. Even though the article is not a book review, its major focus is a book, which is used as a way of informing readers about the book's existence, topic, and argument and, no doubt, encouraging them to consider purchasing the book. How does Benet write about Pete McDaniel's book for *Black Enterprise*'s target audience?

3. How does Benet's discussion of McDaniel's book remind us of the many ways in which sports itself became an arena where other social issues are played out and even argued about? What have been the specific consequences of this situation for African Americans? For caddies? For African American caddies? How can we historicize these situations? In other words, how did African American males come to be caddies at Augusta National and other golf clubs? How did changing social attitudes result in fewer economic opportunities for those who had caddied, even as new opportunities were opening up to African Americans more broadly?

4. Using this selection as a model, **write an essay** for the audience of a specific magazine or Web site you regularly visit about a book you've recently read. Your goal is not to write a book report but to use the essay as an opportunity to inform the readers of the magazine or Web site about the book and issues it addresses.

Bad As They Wanna Be

Loving the Game Is Harder As Colleges Sell Out Themselves, the Fans, the Athletes

THAD WILLIAMSON

Growing up in an American college town gives one a better than average chance of being infected with progressive politics, a certain intellectual curiosity and a love for intercollegiate athletics. Growing up in Chapel Hill, North Carolina, makes one susceptible to catching a strong dose of all three.

Such is the case with this writer, who grew up believing that Dean Smith, the legendary coach of the University of North Carolina Tar Heels basketball team (who retired recently after thirty-six years), embodied virtue and goodness as surely as Jesse Helms represented hate and ignorance. A passion for college basketball is *the* tie that binds in "The Triangle," where UNC, North Carolina State and Duke University all play. And if you live in this area, the team you root for inevitably becomes part of your identity. Duke is alternately denounced and adored as the South's answer to the Ivy League; UNC boasts of being the region's premier public university; North Carolina State, a school historically focused on agriculture and engineering, enjoys a large in-state following as the populist alternative to its liberal arts neighbors.

For decades young Tar Heels fans grew up aware of Dean Smith's unapologetic liberalism: a much-celebrated (albeit modest) role in integrating Chapel Hill in the late fifties and early sixties, opposition to the Vietnam War, support of a nuclear freeze and opposition to the death penalty. Smith's political bent and reputation for treating players like extended family made it possible to imagine that by rooting for UNC, you somehow showed support for doing the right thing.

No one held to that belief more than myself. From age 12 I watched Michael Jordan and others from a courtside perch as an operator of UNC's old manual scoreboard. Now, a decade after leaving Chapel Hill, I remain a devoted follower of Atlantic Coast Conference basketball. Writing a triweekly, inseason column for *InsideCarolina* (northcarolina .com), an independent magazine and Web site devoted to UNC sports,

◀ *Thad Williamson is an author of books and articles on theology, economic and social policy, and sports. This article was originally published in an August 1998 issue of* The Nation, *a magazine of social and political analysis that takes a liberal viewpoint. Williamson issues a call to action in this proposal argument. As you read, notice how he works to build his credibility and engender his readers' trust before he suggests that they take action on his proposal.*

Arguments based on character, such as Williamson's here, can be very effective. See more examples of effective arguments based on character in Chapter 6.

LINK TO P. 88 ···

I fancy myself in the rare (but not entirely unknown) position of left-wing sportswriter. Like a Latin American soccer commentator, I strive to keep the game in perspective but still feel elation when the Tar Heels win and supreme dejection when they lose in the Final Four.

For the thoughtful fan of college sports, however, it's getting harder   5
to check your critical intelligence at the door and simply enjoy the game. The appeal of college athletics has long rested on their "amateur" status, the notion that the kids play mostly for the love of the game, without the pressures and influences that suffuse professional sports. These days, however, it's increasingly clear that big-time college athletics — in particular, men's basketball and football — are as wrapped in commercial values as the pros, and the system is rapidly spinning out of control.

In college arenas the best seats are now routinely reserved not for students and die-hard fans but for big-money boosters and private donors to the universities. The arenas themselves are being turned into prime advertising venues: Georgia Tech's revamped Alexander Memorial Coliseum, for example, goes so far as to place the McDonald's trademark "M" on the floor. Meanwhile, the NCAA's lucrative television contracts — an eight-year, $1.7 billion deal with CBS for broadcast rights to the Men's Division I basketball tournament and similar deals in football — are changing the fabric of the game, as top competition is slotted for prime-time viewing hours and games are steadily lengthened by TV timeouts.

Even the school I cover, North Carolina, which to this day bans all corporate advertising inside arenas, has largely succumbed to the trend. In the eighties UNC used some $34 million in private funds to build a 21,500-seat basketball arena, in the process setting a precedent of entitlement for major boosters. Not only did they win rights to the best seats in the arena, they are also allowed to pass on those seats to their progeny. More recently, university officials convinced the state highway board to authorize $1.2 million for a special road to allow top-dollar Tar Heels donors a convenient exit from home games.

There's more. Last summer the university signed a five-year, $11 million contract to use Nike-provided gear in all practices (for all sports) and to wear the familiar swoosh. No faculty members or students were directly involved in the negotiations, and no serious questions were raised about Nike's notorious labor practices abroad.

Subsequently, concerned UNC students and faculty generated considerable public debate about the deal, but UNC plans to remain on the take.

Indeed, shoe companies like Adidas and Nike are now prime players in the college game. Most major Division I football and basketball coaches receive lucrative payments from the companies in exchange for outfitting their teams with the appropriate logo—and in some cases, such as the University of California, Berkeley, for encouraging their players to buy additional Nike gear. The sneaker sellers also operate most of the major summer camps for elite high school athletes, where schoolboy stars show their wares to college coaches (many of whom are themselves on Nike's or Reebok's payroll) in hopes of landing a top-flight scholarship. While the hottest prospects are showered with expenses-paid travel and free athletic gear, the companies develop relationships with future stars that might culminate in endorsement contracts. In his fine book *The Last Shot,* Darcy Frey likened the atmosphere at Nike's annual high school summer camp to a meatmarket, where the mostly black kids are herded around like cattle while the overwhelmingly white coaches and corporate sponsors look on.

Nowhere are the priorities of the new corporate order of college sports 10 clearer than in the treatment of athletes—though you'd never know it from the popular image of those athletes as coddled superstars. In *He Got Game,* Spike Lee depicts the campus as a pleasure dome for young men treated to unlimited cars, women and material perks for four blissfully hedonistic years.

The truth is often far less alluring. "It's not as glamorous as people think," cautions Sheray Gaffney, a former reserve fullback for the football powerhouse Florida State Seminoles. "If you're in the program, it's not glamorous at all."

One reason for this is the so-called grant-in-aid system that characterizes all athletic scholarships in the NCAA. Originally established in 1956, grant-in-aid was intended to level the playing field by providing a fixed set of benefits to college athletes. Schools were allowed to offer scholarships of one to four years and were bound to honor them even if the athlete quit the team altogether. In 1973, however, the NCAA abruptly shifted course and mandated that the grants be limited to a

one-year, annually renewable grant. The purpose of this change was to enable schools—in actuality, coaches—to keep tabs on each player's performance from year to year, and to cut off the scholarships of those whom the coach considered dispensable.

"Colleges changed the rule so they could run off the athletes who weren't good enough," explains Walter Byers, who oversaw the growth of college athletics while serving as NCAA executive director from 1951 to 1987. Back in the fifties Byers coined the term "student-athlete," a romantic idea that the NCAA continues to use in its promotional literature. These days, he is one of the NCAA's leading critics. "Once the colleges gave coaches the power to control those grants," he says, "that was a perversion that permanently changed the way things were done. It used to be that at least athletes could get an education if they couldn't play for the team."

Indeed, under the new system athletes do as the coaches say or risk being kicked out. Coach Rick Majerus of Utah, whose team reached the NCAA basketball finals this year, recently "released" Jordie McTavish saying he just wasn't good enough. A year ago, Coach Bobby Cremins of Georgia Tech asked freshman point guard Kevin Morris to leave for the same reason. More often than direct dismissals, coaches pressure players to leave on their own. Indiana's Bobby Knight, seeking to clean house after a disappointing 1996–97 season, drove starting point guard Neil Reed out of town with one year of eligibility remaining. Reed left, but not before accusing Knight of physical and emotional abuse.

Given the pressures to stay in the good graces of coaches—players know that missing even one session in the weight room risks incurring the coach's wrath—it's no wonder that graduation rates for Division I football and basketball players in the NCAA hover at roughly 50 percent, a figure that exaggerates the amount of learning that actually takes place. Instead of promoting a balance between sports and academics, the system forces athletes to pour every ounce of energy into the game, with little recognition that the vast majority of players are in a vocational dead end. A sad rite of passage for most college athletes is the existential realization that they will never make it to the pros. "What was astonishing was the number of scars that [the program] left on athletes that came to the surface behind closed doors," recalls Gaffney. "It was painful to see athletes crying in distress because they see their dreams slowly fading away. All of a sudden at age 20, 21, they are required to make a complete transition."

True, college sports still represent a way out for poor or working-class athletes. Some, with the help of coaches like Dean Smith, find jobs in coaching, pro leagues overseas or business. Others succeed in getting an education. But the inequities are glaring. While generating an enormous revenue stream for their universities through ticket sales, merchandising, advertising and TV deals, athletes are forbidden from sharing in any of the gains. "When these commercial activities came along," notes Byers, "the overseers and supervisors made sure that the benefits went to them, not the athletes." College coaches routinely earn six-figure salaries, sign endorsement deals with corporations and jump from school to school for more lucrative contracts. The athletes, meanwhile, are the focus of scandal and media outrage if they so much as accept money for an extra trip home. Under the grant-in-aid rule, athletes may not use their talent or name recognition to earn money while in school except under tightly defined conditions.

In Byers's view, the "gobs of money" now flowing to the universities make a return to the amateur ideal impossible. What is possible, he believes, is scrapping the current grant-in-aid system, which leads not only to the rampant exploitation of athletes but, he argues, violates antitrust laws because colleges essentially operate as a cartel, setting a national limit on what a whole class of students can earn. He would require athletes to apply for financial aid like any other student but would remove all restrictions on how they could earn money while in college.

Rick Telander, a *Sports Illustrated* writer and author of *The Hundred Yard Lie*, an exposé of college football, proposes a more radical solution: namely, severing big-time college football programs from the schools that lend them their name. In Telander's view, an NFL-subsidized "age-group professional league" could be established in which universities would own and operate teams, using university facilities and traditional school colors. Players need not be students but would earn a year of tuition for each year played, redeemable at any time, during or after their playing careers. College basketball would also benefit from the creation of an NBA-backed age-group league. Such leagues could offer gifted players with no interest in academics a credible alternative to college, and a second chance to earn an education should their professional dreams fade.

Of course, given the entrenched institutional support for the status quo, none of this can happen without a sustained demand from the public, including students, coaches not yet corrupted, and athletes themselves. In the meantime, students and faculty can make their voices heard by continuing—and expanding—their campaigns challenging the corporate sponsorship of university athletic departments. Over the past year campus activists at Duke and other universities have successfully pushed administrators to adopt rules requiring that all campus sweatshirts and athletic gear be produced in compliance with labor and human rights standards. These same activists should insist that corporate advertising be banned from all arenas; that universities cap athletic budgets for football and basketball and put an end to the "arms race" for bigger facilities and more amenities; and that the influence of big-money donors be limited so that students and fans can continue to attend athletic events at reasonable prices. Activists might also find unexpected common ground with coaches and fans concerned about how the integrity of the game has been subordinated to television, or how corporations are colonizing and poisoning the high school recruiting scene.

Speaking for myself, probably only death will cure my love affair 20 with North Carolina basketball, and no doubt there are millions of people who feel the same way about their own teams. But loving the game need not mean having a romantic view of how college sports are organized. College sports are far too visible an arena in American society to be simply thrown to the wolves. Ultimately, the only productive route forward is to insist that those who love the game also fight to change it.

RESPOND●

1. What evidence does Williamson provide to support his contention that "the [college athletics] system is rapidly spinning out of control"? What kinds of appeals does he use? Arguments from the heart? Arguments of character? Other kinds? (See Chapters 4–7.)

2. Why does Williamson give us so much detailed information about North Carolina coach Dean Smith's political beliefs? Does that information contribute to the argument? How? Why? If not, why not?

3. Williamson's article ends with a strong call to action, yet there is no hint of such an appeal in the title or opening paragraphs of the article. Why do you think Williamson chose this rhetorical strategy?

4. Do you agree with Williamson's suggestion (in paragraph 16) that collegiate sports are "a way out" for poor and working-class students? Do you think that assertion is more (or less) true today than it was in the past? What evidence would you want to present to support or refute Williamson's claim?

5. Walter Byers, NCAA executive director from 1951 to 1987, has proposed removing all restrictions on how student-athletes can earn money while in college. Imagine that your school is considering adopting Byers's proposal. **Write a letter** to your college administrators supporting or rejecting Byers's plan. Provide detailed evidence for your position.

▼ *In this excerpt Michael Sokolove, a contributing writer for the* New York Times Magazine, *where this article originally appeared, offers an evaluative argument about college football, using the University of South Florida as a case study. His thesis is clear from the title: (college) football is a sucker's game. Yet students, alums, and donors love it. As you read, pay special attention to the many kinds of evidence Sokolove uses in weaving together his argument and the ways in which he uses them to support different parts of his overall argument. Sokolove's article appeared in 2002.*

Football Is a Sucker's Game

MICHAEL SOKOLOVE

Football is the S.U.V. of the college campus: aggressively big, resource-guzzling, lots and lots of fun and potentially destructive of everything around it. Big-time teams award 85 scholarships and, with walk-ons, field rosters of 100 or more players. (National Football League teams make do with half that.) At the highest level, universities wage what has been called an "athletic arms race" to see who can build the most lavish facilities to attract the highest-quality players. Dollars are directed from general funds and wrestled from donors, and what does not go into cherry-wood lockers, plush carpets and million-dollar weight rooms ends up in the pockets of coaches, the most exalted of whom now make upward of $2 million a year.

The current college sports landscape is meaner than ever, more overtly commercial, more winner-take-all. And just as in the rest of the economy, the gap between rich and poor is widening. College sports now consists of a class of super-behemoths — perhaps a dozen or so athletic departments with budgets of $40 million and up — and a much larger group of schools that face the choice of spending themselves into oblivion or being embarrassed on the field. (Which may happen in any case.) It is common for lesser college football teams to play at places like Tennessee or Michigan, where average attendance exceeds 100,000, in return for "guarantees" from the

> **The University of Michigan, which averages more than 110,000 fans for football games, lost an estimated $7 million on athletics between 1998 and 2000.**

host school of as much as $500,000. They are paid, in other words, to take a beating.

Any thought of becoming one of the giants and sharing in the real money is in most cases a fantasy. Universities new to Division I-A football (in addition to the University of South Florida, the University of Connecticut and the University of Buffalo have just stepped up to the big time) know that the first level of competition is financial. It is a dangerous game. "The mantra of the need to 'spend money to make money' can be used to justify a great deal of spending, without leading an institution to any destination other than a deeper financial hole," write James Shulman and William Bowen in "The Game of Life: College Sports and Educational Values," their 2001 examination of the finances of college athletics.

The current college bowl season began last week and ends Jan. 3 with the national championship game, the Fiesta Bowl. This year, the cartel of teams belonging to the Bowl Championship Series — members of the six most prominent conferences plus independent Notre Dame, a total of 63 teams — will split a guaranteed payoff of at least $120 million from the Fiesta, Orange, Sugar and Rose Bowls. Teams outside the B.C.S. are eligible to play in such low-wattage affairs as the Humanitarian Bowl, the Motor City Bowl and the Continental Tire Bowl. For the privilege, they will almost certainly lose money, because the bowl payouts will not even cover travel and other expenses.

"We are receiving letters and calls from conferences that want in," Mike Tranghese, coordinator of the five-year-old B.C.S., told me. "And we have formed a presidential oversight panel to form an answer." But letting more members in would mean splitting up the money more ways. I asked Tranghese if I was missing something in assuming the B.C.S. had no incentive to cut more schools in. "If you were missing something, I would let you know," he said. "The B.C.S. consists of the major teams as determined by the marketplace. Any other system is socialism. And if we're going to have socialism, then why don't we share our endowments?"

One reason B.C.S. members do not want to share is that college sports have become so immensely expensive that even some of the biggest of the big lose money. The University of Michigan, which averages more than 110,000 fans for home football games, lost an estimated $7 million on athletics over the course of two seasons, between 1998 and 2000. Ohio State had athletic revenues of $73 million in 1999–2000 and "barely managed to break even," according to the book "Unpaid Professionals: Commercialism and Conflict in Big-Time College Sports," by Andrew Zimbalist, a Smith College economics professor. A state audit revealed that the University of Wisconsin lost $286,700 on its Rose Bowl appearance in 1998 because it took a small army, a traveling party of 832, to Pasadena.

The endemic criminal and ethical scandals of college sports are connected by a straight line to the money. Teams that do not win do not excite their boosters, fill up stadiums, appear on national TV or get into postseason play, thereby endangering the revenue stream that supports the immense infrastructure. It is the desperation for cash, every bit as much as the pursuit of victory, that causes university athletic departments to overlook all kinds of rule-breaking until it splatters out into the open.

One day this fall I opened my morning sports page and, in glancing at the college football briefs, took note that it was a particularly bad day for the Big Ten. The headlines were: "Spartan Tailback Dismissed"; "Iowa Player Arrested"; "Wisconsin Back Stabbed." The Michigan State Spartans dismissed two co-captains within 10 days: the starting quarterback, who checked into rehab for a substance-abuse problem, as well as the tailback, who was accused of drunken driving and eluding arrest by dragging a police officer with his car. The next day, the head coach, Bobby Williams, with his team's record at 3-6, was fired — and sent off with a $550,000 buyout.

At tiny Gardner-Webb University in Boiling Springs, N.C. — a Baptist institution in its first season of Division I basketball — the university president resigned in the fall after acknowledging that he ordered a change in the calculation of a star basketball player's grade-point average. At Florida State University, quarterback Adrian McPherson was suspended days before his arrest for supposedly stealing a blank check, then expressed shock at the discipline meted out by the normally lenient head coach, Bobby Bowden. (When a star player was accused of theft a few years back, Bowden said, "I'm praying for a misdemeanor.") The University of Alabama at Birmingham, which started football just over a decade ago, is playing this season under a cloud. The trustees of the Alabama higher-education system have given the university two years to reverse a $7.6 million budget deficit or face being shut down. In addition, pending civil suits charge that a 15-year-old girl who enrolled at U.A.B. was sexually assaulted, repeatedly, by a large number of football and basketball players, as well as by the person who performed as the school's mascot, a dragon.

The list goes on. Ohio State's thrilling 14-9 victory 10 over Michigan on Nov. 23 occasioned a full-scale riot by inebriated Buckeye fans who burned cars, looted businesses and caused tens of thousands of dollars in damage before 250 police officers finally restored order at 5 A.M. These sorts of things have become the background music of college sports.

"Schools get on a treadmill, and there's no getting off."

Being a striving team trying to keep up in a big-time conference can be a particular kind of debacle. Rutgers University, in this regard, is Exhibit A. It belongs to the Big East, a B.C.S. football conference that also boasts powerful basketball programs. Rutgers can't compete in either sport. Its cellar-dwelling teams draw poor crowds, and the athletic department ran a deficit of about $13 million last year.

A dissident group, the Rutgers 1,000, has waged a passionate campaign to get Rutgers to leave the Big East and to de-emphasize athletics. This has led, indirectly, to yet an entirely new way of throwing money away on sports. The administration tried to block publication of a Rutgers 1,000 advertisement in an alumni magazine. Not only did Rutgers lose the ensuing court battle, but it also spent $375,000 fighting it, including court-ordered reimbursement of legal fees to the A.C.L.U., which took up the case of the Rutgers 1,000 as a free-speech issue.

"Schools get on a treadmill, and there's no getting off," says James Shulman, an author of "The Game of Life." "They have to stay on; they have too much invested." The former Princeton basketball coach Pete Carill once said of the big-time programs: "If you want to get into the rat race, you've got to be a rat."

Another way to look at big-time college sports is as a sucker's game, one with many more losers than winners. Notre Dame, a great football team before it was a great university, is the prototype for all schools hoping to hitch a ride on the back of a popular sports team. Duke certainly has become more celebrated and academically selective in the years its basketball team has been a perennial Final Four participant. But Notre Dame and Duke are exceptions. For every Notre Dame and Duke, there are many more like Rutgers and U.A.B., schools that spend millions in a hopeless mission to reach the top.

The University of South Florida, nonetheless, 15 wants in on the gamble and in on the perceived spoils. The new gospel there is that football is "the tip of the marketing sword." I heard the phrase from several administrators at U.S.F. Vicki Mitchell explained the concept to me. She had directed a highly successful university-wide fund-raising campaign, but in May, not long after the team jumped to Division I-A, she moved to the athletic department to raise money specifically for sports. Under Mitchell, the office devoted to sports fund-raising was ramped up from three staff members to eight, and in the first three months of this fiscal year she and her team brought in $1.6 million, just $200,000 less than the total raised in the previous 12 months. "The easiest way to build a U.S.F. brand is to build an athletic program that is known, and that means football," Mitchell said. "Maybe that's not what the university wants to be known for, but it's reality."

Nearly two decades ago, the exploits of the Boston College quarterback Doug Flutie and the success of the team were credited with increasing applications by 25 percent and transforming B.C. from a regional to a national university. The syndrome was even given a name: the Flutie effect. That's the kind of magic U.S.F. is trying to catch.

U.S.F. didn't play football at any level until 1997. Its founding president, John Allen, who presided over the university from 1957 to 1970, was that rare thing in football-crazed Florida—a staunch opponent of the sport. In the 1980's, U.S.F. alumni and Tampa businessmen began pushing for football, and the U.S.F. administration began lobbying a reluctant state Board of Regents for a team. In 1993, the outgoing president, Frank Borkowski, in his final weeks at U.S.F. and with the Regents' decision on football pending, hired Lee Roy Selmon—a former N.F.L. star and one of the most admired men in Tampa—to lead football fund-raising. That was the pivotal moment. "I was in a pretty tight box," recalls Borkowski, now chancellor at Appalachian State University. "The Regents did not want us to have a team." But to deny football would have been a slap to Selmon.

Jim Leavitt was hired in 1995, two years before the University of South Florida Bulls played their first game. From the start, the university intended to move quickly to the N.C.A.A.'s highest level and eventually challenge football factories like Florida State, the University of Florida and the University of Miami. By the time the current U.S.F. president, Judy Genshaft, arrived in 2000, the program was in full bloom. Genshaft's term has so far been marked by a thorny dispute spawned by her suspension of Sami Al-Arian, a tenured professor of computer science, over charges that he had ties to terrorism. Compared to the fallout from that, football has been pure pleasure.

Genshaft, who attends the team's games and keeps a jersey in her office with her name on the back, was an undergraduate at Wisconsin and a long-time administrator at Ohio State. "I know big sports," she says, "and I love big sports. It brings more visibility, more spirit, more community engagement. Even researchers coming to us from other big universities, they are expecting sports to be part of campus life."

The rationales put forth for big-time sports are not 20 easily proved or disproved. One example is the assumption that successful teams spur giving to the general funds of universities. "The logic is reasonable enough," Zimbalist wrote in "Unpaid Professionals." "A school goes to the Rose Bowl or to the Final Four. Alumni feel proud and open up their pocketbooks." But Zimbalist looked at the available evidence and concluded that winning teams, at best, shake loose dollars given specifically for sports. And only for a time; when on-field fortunes reverse, or a scandal occurs, the money often dries up.

Genshaft says that U.S.F. can play football at the highest level without financial or ethical ruin. "It's a risk and it is expensive," she says. "But we've decided that football is part of who we are and where we're going."

But others see disaster as the only possible result. At Rutgers, the sports program has split the campus community and spawned an angry and unusually organized opposition. "The reality of sports at this level is it can't be done right," says William C. Dowling, an English professor and one of the leaders of the Rutgers 1,000. "It's not possible, anywhere, even at the so-called best places. Look at the differences in SAT levels."

One study showed the SAT scores of football players at Division I-A schools to be 271 points lower than incoming nonathletes. "You have kids brought to campus and maybe, *maybe* they could be real students if they studied 60 hours a week and did nothing else,"

Dowling says. "But everyone knows that's not happening. It's not their fault. They've been lied to in high school, all these African-American kids who get told that playing ball is their way up in society, even though it's never been that for any other ethnic group in America. It's dishonest. It's filthy."

When Vicki Mitchell pitches U.S.F. donors, however, she sells the program as if it were in a state of grace—unsullied by scandal, at least so far, and still operating with a degree of fiscal sanity. She begins by painting a picture of what life is like at the really big football powers. To secure a season ticket at one of those schools in a desirable part of the stadium, if that's even possible, can set a donor back tens of thousands of dollars. "I'll say to someone: 'You're a sports fan. You need to get on board, because everyone knows what it costs at those other places. Our aspirations are no less, but we're not there yet. We're young. We're fun. We're a growth stock. Get in now while it's still affordable.'"

I met head coach Jim Leavitt for the first time just a 25 few days before the biggest home game in the history of University of South Florida football. The opponent, Southern Mississippi, was the strongest team ever to visit U.S.F. and a favorite to break its 15-game home winning streak. U.S.F. had lost an early-season road game at Oklahoma, then the second-ranked team in the nation, but outplayed the powerful Sooners for long stretches. Leavitt's team was surging in the national polls; the New York Times computer rankings would place it as high as 18th in the nation, ahead of such tradition-rich football powers as Tennessee, Florida State, Auburn, Clemson and Nebraska. These accomplishments, for a program playing just its sixth season, were nothing short of astounding.

As the showdown against Southern Mississippi loomed, two things obsessed Leavitt: winning the game, and money. "The kind of money we need is big, big money," he said to me not long after saying hello. He kept returning to the same point. "We have what we need for a beginning program, but we're not a beginning program anymore." Then: "I don't know what this program will look like in the future. It can be big. But you've got to have money. You've got to have facilities. If you don't, it ain't gonna happen."

Leavitt, 46, grew up in nearby St. Petersburg. He was a high-school sports star, a defensive back at the University of Missouri, then an assistant coach at several universities before he came home to be the first coach of U.S.F. football.

Leavitt has won praise not just for winning, but also for doing so on the cheap. He and his nine assistant coaches work out of a complex of four trailers, in front of which Leavitt erected a split-rail fence "to make it look like the Ponderosa." Leavitt proudly told me that the couch in his office, on which he sometimes lies down for the night, is a $700 vinyl number rather than one of those $5,000 leather cruise ships to be found in the offices of so many other coaches.

This era of frugality, though, has just ended. In early November, the university unveiled drawings for a long-hoped-for training and office complex that will be as big as a football field — 104,000 square feet over two floors that will serve most of the university's men's and women's teams but will be dominated by football.

Leavitt views this as natural and right. He tells me about Oklahoma, coached by his close friend Bob Stoops, which already has "an outrageous setup, everything you can imagine," and has just raised yet another $100 million. "I imagine they'll tell you it's not for football only, and I would assume it's not," Leavitt says. "But I'm pretty sure football will get what it needs first. As it should, in my opinion."

Like many football coaches, Leavitt is no fan of Title IX regulations that mandate equal opportunity for female athletes. "Don't get me wrong," he says, "I am a big proponent of women's sports. I want us to be great at women's sports. But football should be separate from the Title IX thing, because nobody else operates like we do. We're revenue-producing."

To build the U.S.F. athletic complex will cost as much as $15 million. To furnish it — starting with $425,000 in weight-training equipment, a $65,000 hydrotherapy tub, portable X-ray machines, satellite uplinks and downlinks, trophy cases for a U.S.F. sports hall of fame in the atrium entrance — will cost up to $5 million more.

Despite aggressive fund-raising, private pledges for this facility have reached only $5 million, so it will be built on borrowed money. The construction bond will be backed partly by the "athletic fee" charged to students, which for those who attend full time has reached $224 a year — a fairly substantial add-on to a tuition of only $2,159.

Mitchell says the university considers students "its biggest donor," and student leaders are, in fact, courted like boosters. In October, the student government president and vice president flew on a private jet with President Genshaft to the big game at Oklahoma.

U.S.F. calculates that the football team brings in, roughly, $4 million in revenue and spends about the same amount. But as in most athletic departments, the accounting makes no attempt to measure the true resources used.

One day, I stood in a humid basement room and watched the laundry — muddy Bulls jerseys and pants, T-shirts, sweat socks, wrist- and headbands, jockstraps — from 105 football players being cleaned. Several colossal washers and dryers were fed by three athletic-department employees. They perform this task early August through late November, six days a week, 10 hours a day.

None of this — the salaries, the utility costs, the $8,000 a year just in laundry detergent — is charged against football. Nor is there any attempt to break out football's share of such costs as sports medicine, aca-

---

The University of South Florida wants in on the gamble. The new gospel there is that football is "the tip of the marketing sword."

---

demic tutoring, strength and conditioning, insurance, field upkeep or the rest of its share of the more than $5 million in general expenses of the athletic department not assigned to a specific sport.

In the papers I was shown, I also could find no evidence that a $2 million fee to join Conference USA (which is not a B.C.S. conference) as a football-playing member in 2003 was accounted for in football's expense ledger. The money was borrowed from the university's general endowment, and the athletic department is paying the interest.

So when Jim Leavitt says that his football team is revenue-producing, that should not be understood as profit-generating. I would not pretend to know what football really costs at U.S.F., but it's clearly a lot more than $4 million, maybe even twice that. And another big bill is about to come due: Leavitt's next contract.

When the local sportswriters ask Leavitt about his contract, he gives carefully bland responses. He doesn't have an agent, and it could be argued that with his fawning press, he hardly needs one. The articles clearly please him. One day he says to me: "The Tampa paper is going to have another piece coming up on my salary. But you know, I don't pay too much attention. I don't deserve anything. I'm just glad I have a job. I'm blessed.

"And I mean that. I have zero interest in leaving here. But then people say to me, 'What if you were offered $1 million to go somewhere else?' Well, then I'd probably leave. Let's be realistic."

I asked him what he thought his market value was, and he did not hesitate. "About $500,000 or $600,000," he said. "At least."

The biggest of the big-time college sporting events are intoxicating. The swirl of colors, the marching bands, the deafening roars, the over-the-top political incorrectness—Florida State's Seminole mascot riding in on horseback; a Mississippi State coach some years back, on the eve of a game against the Texas Longhorns, castrating a bull. The whole thing is a little reminiscent of what I've heard some Catholic friends of mine say: even if you're a little ambivalent about the message, the pageantry will get you every time.

In college sports, the heady mix of anticipation, adrenaline, camaraderie and school pride is the gloss over the grubby reality. Pro sports operates within some financial parameters, governed by a profit motive. College sport, by contrast, is a mad cash scramble with squishy rules. Universities run from conference to conference, chasing richer TV deals; coaches from school to school, chasing cash. It's a game of mergers and acquisitions—of running out on your partners before they run out on you.

It's understandable why universities with hundreds of millions already invested in sports can't find a way out. Far less understandable is why a school like U.S.F. would, with eyes wide open, walk in. "I felt then and still feel that U.S.F. could be a model football program," says Frank Borkowski, the former president. "One with clear policies and rules, attractive to bright students, that would not go the way of so many programs—a corrupt way."

But the whole framework of college sports, with its out-of-control spending and lax academic and ethical standards, is rotten; it's difficult to be clean within it. The "student athletes," as the N.C.A.A. insists on calling them, feel the hypocrisy. When one is caught taking the wrong thing from the wrong person—not the usual perks but actual money—what ensues is a "Casablanca"-like overabundance of shock, then a bizarre penalty phase that almost always punishes everyone but the guilty parties. Thus, when the University of Michigan finally acknowledged this fall that some members of its famed "Fab Five" basketball teams of the early 1990's may have accepted payments from a booster, the university tried to get out in front of N.C.A.A. sanctions by disqualifying this year's team—whose players were about 8 years old in the Fab Five years—from participating in the 2003 N.C.A.A. tournament.

College sport could not survive if it were viewed only as mass entertainment. On another level, it serves as a salvation story. The enterprise rests mostly on a narrative of young men pulled from hopeless situations, installed at universities, schooled in values by coaches and sent off into the world as productive citizens.

"We encourage the players to be as much a part of normal campus life as possible," said Phyllis LaBaw, the associate athletic director for academic support. But no one pretends that they really are much like the typical U.S.F. student.

Nearly 70 percent of the U.S.F. football team is black on a campus that is otherwise 70 percent white. (Only 11 percent of U.S.F. students are black; the rest of the minority population is Hispanic and Asian and Native American.) The football players tend to be poorer than other students and more in need of academic help.

To be a football player at U.S.F., or an athlete of any [50] kind, is like taking your mother to school with you — or several mothers. Academic counselors meet with athletes at least weekly. They sometimes follow them right to the door of a classroom, which in the trade is known as "eye-balling" a player to class. Where a lot of players are grouped in one class, tutors sometimes sit in and take notes. Counselors communicate directly with professors. "We don't ever ask for favors," LaBaw said. "But professors do provide us with information, which is vital."

Football players who miss a class or a mandatory study session get "run" by coaches — meaning they must show up on the practice field at 6 A.M. to be put through a series of sprints by a coach who is not happy to be there at that hour. "It is very punitive," LaBaw said.

LaBaw's department employs four full-time counselors and about 40 tutors and has an annual budget of $400,000. The staff serves all 450 intercollegiate athletes at U.S.F., so the 105 football players are less than a quarter of the clients — but as is the case with so much else, football sucks up more resources than its raw numbers would indicate. "They need more help," LaBaw said of the footballers, "but what we're doing works. Last year our football players had a mean G.P.A. of 2.52, which if we were already in Conference USA would have been the best in the conference — including Army."

LaBaw is part den mother, part drill sergeant — loving and supportive or confrontational and blunt, depending on the needs of the moment. Under her desk, she keeps a big box; when the season began, it had 5,000 condoms in it, all different colors. She hands them out like lollipops along with however much sex education she can blurt out.

Her effort, while well intentioned, is a version of closing the barn door after the horses have run out. Of the 105 players on U.S.F.'s football team — most of them between 18 and 23 years old — about 30 are fathers and many have produced multiple children. "I would say there's a total of 60 children from this team, and that's a conservative estimate," said LaBaw. "It's amazing how quickly it occurs, usually in the first year. Or they come to school already fathers."

What this means is that the recipients of Lee Roy [55] Selmon's scholarship program for needy young men are recreating the need that many of them came from — children living in poverty, without fathers at home. With their five hours per day of football-related activity on top of class and studying, the fathers have no time even to change a diaper, let alone work to financially support their children. Most of the children live with their mothers or aunts or grandmothers. Some who are nearby spend the day at the university's day-care center, yet another cost of college football since the service is offered virtually free to U.S.F. students.

On Dec. 12, the University of South Florida ripped up Jim Leavitt's contract and signed him to a new five-year deal that more than doubled his salary. If he keeps winning, he probably won't make it to the final year of this contract, either, when he's scheduled to make nearly $700,000. U.S.F. will have to pay more to keep him, or other programs will come looking to steal him away. That's how it is when you decide to play with the big boys. The bills just keep on getting bigger.

Is Sokolove's purpose here to inform? To explore? To convince? something else? See Chapter 1 to decide.

LINK TO P. 6 ···

RESPOND •

1. Why does Sokolove contend that "(college) football is a sucker's game"? What specific arguments does he make? What evidence does he marshal to support his claims? How convincing do you find these arguments and the evidence offered? To the extent that you accept Sokolove's position, try to explain why college football is so appealing to so many groups.

2. How is this excerpt a causal argument (Chapter 11)? Find at least one example of each of the three kinds of causal arguments (cause → effect(s), effects ← cause(s), and causal chain) in the excerpt, and evaluate its effectiveness.

3. In what ways is Sokolove's argument a case study in competing values? Which specific values are involved? How does he create an argument based on values? (Chapter 5 will help you answer this question.)

4. Sports — especially intercollegiate athletics — play a role in U.S. college life that they play in the college life of no other country, and in the world of intercollegiate athletics, football is king. What is especially American about college football? How would America — especially American colleges and universities — be different without college football? (As Sokolove's article implies, the absence of football would involve much more than an absence of stadiums, cheerleaders and bands, and pep rallies. It would extend to many aspects of campus life, including fund-raising, and the life of society at large.) **Write an essay** in which you describe America without college football. You'll likely want to limit your discussion to three or four specific differences and their consequences, rather than trying to catalog all the differences. (Note that your essay will, in many ways, be a definition.)

5. **Write an essay** in which you construct a comparative evaluative argument examining whether or not the disadvantages of college football outweigh the advantages. Sokolove has amply sketched many of the disadvantages, but you will need to develop the possible advantages. In order to do so, you may well need to do some research, perhaps about the college or university you attend. Successful arguments, regardless of the stance they take, will not rely on empty appeals to the worth of values like "sportsmanship" or "competition" but will treat the relevant issues in more analytic detail.

chapter twenty-six

Who Owns What?

You die tomorrow. Who owns your body? What about its parts—the kidneys or eyes or heart or skin or bone marrow? And what if you've left sperm in a sperm bank, eggs in an egg bank, or fertilized embryos stored for future implantation? How about the white blood cells in your spleen, which might become the source of a medical discovery that stands to make some scientific researchers and enterprising capitalists very wealthy? And who owns your bones when you're no longer alive? How long do those claims of ownership endure? Months? Years? Forever? Easy questions, you might think, and you just might be wrong.

And what about words and ideas? Can anyone be said to own them? Under what circumstances? If they're said in private and not recorded? If they're so well known that even schoolchildren can recite them? In this chapter, we examine what quickly becomes a complex problem, *who owns what*, by looking at two very different sets of issues—first, ownership of the body and its parts; second, ownership of words and ideas, one form of "intellectual property." As the arguments here demonstrate, there is little agreement among the many competing parties who have an interest in ownership about much of anything—except, perhaps, the importance of whatever they're fighting over.

The arguments in this chapter challenge us to rethink assumptions we might hold about the nature of individual and communal ownership and to recognize the changing nature of each. They force us to consider the competing interests of the individual and the community, the individual and society, and the individual and social institutions like medicine, law, and even art. Especially because our society is simultaneously democratic (valuing "equality") and capitalist (valuing private ownership and financial profit), questions of ownership cannot help but become questions of how we, as Americans, define the nature of the self in our society.

www.
For additional readings on
Who Owns What?, visit
bedfordstmartins.com
/everythingsanargument.

This cluster of arguments provides a spectrum of attitudes about **who owns the body and its parts and who owns life.** The opening readings ask about the ethics of soliciting egg donors (tall, blonde, SAT scores over 1400, and athletic, please), sometimes for astounding fees like $25K. We reproduce two ads for such donors. (Remember that *donor* is derived historically from the Latin verb "to give," not the one meaning "to sell"!) These ads are followed by two overlapping but different accounts of the stir the ads raised when they first began to appear on college campuses. These articles, by Gina Kolata and David Lefer, ask whether women should sell their eggs to the highest bidder. (It's worth noting that businesses in many cities also offer men compensation for their sperm. Once again, not all men need apply: the couples or women buying these sperm want to know all sorts of things about the man who produced them—his hobbies, medical history, hair color, hand span, and so on.)

The next two essays represent pro/con arguments about the question of who owns life and the ethics of physician-assisted suicide. Faye Girsh's "Should Physician-Assisted Suicide Be Legalized? Yes!" makes her stance quite clear, as does Joe Loconte's "Hospice, not Hemlock." (Loconte's allusion to hemlock recalls not only the poisonous drink with which Socrates ended his life, but, more important, the Hemlock Society, which advocates death with the help of a physician.) Clearly, Girsh and Loconte have different ideas about whether individuals in some sense "own" their own lives.

The final two pieces in the cluster consider property of a very different sort, ancestral remains, offering differing perspectives on Harvard University's decision to repatriate the remains of Native Americans, purchased early last century, by returning them to the Jemez Pueblo nation, which claims the sanctity of the body and, hence, bodily remains, for generations, for centuries — indeed, forever. The first of the texts, James Bandler's "A Long Journey Home," appeared in the *Boston Globe*, the major newspaper in the large city closest to Harvard; the second, Miguel Navrot's "Ancestors Return Home," was published in the *Albuquerque Journal*, the major newspaper serving the area that includes the pueblo to which the remains were returned. These two texts report on the same basic story, but from different perspectives and for different communities. As a result, you'll see that they tell somewhat different stories about what happened, why, what it meant, and for whom.

In some of the cases examined in these readings, ownership of bodies or their parts, living or not, is seen as resting with a community and serving, in some way, to strengthen bonds among the living members of that community. Other cases, especially those relating to eggs, seem to pit individual against individual — and perhaps the market. All of them make clear that questions about who owns the body and its parts are anything but simple.

◄ *Here are two ads of a sort that became the subject of controversy in 1999: ads soliciting egg donors from particular categories of women. The controversy began when such an ad appeared in student newspapers at Stanford, MIT, CIT, Harvard, and Yale late in February 1999. Similar ads have since appeared in student newspapers at other universities as well as in many popular magazines.*

Though brief, the text in each of these ads relies on multiple lines of argument. What sorts of

▼ *Gina Kolata writes regularly on science and medicine for the* New York Times. *She is the winner of numerous writing awards and author of several books, including* The Baby Doctors: Probing the Limits of Fetal Medicine *(1990);* Sex in America: A Definitive Survey *(with Edward Laumann, John Gagnon, and Robert Michaels) (1995); and* Clone: The Road to Dolly and the Path Ahead *(1999). In 1971, she dropped out of the doctoral program in microbiology at MIT to pursue a writing career. In this news article, Kolata offers the* New York Times's *initial discussion of the ad first run at Stanford, Yale, MIT, CIT, and Harvard in February 1999, presenting factual information about the ad and reporting responses from an attorney, the director of an assisted-reproduction program at a major hospital, and a medical ethicist.*

$50,000 Offered to Tall, Smart Egg Donor

GINA KOLATA

The advertisements started appearing last week in newspapers at the nation's top schools—Ivy League colleges, Stanford University, the Massachusetts Institute of Technology, the California Institute of Technology.

"Egg Donor Needed," the advertisements said, adding, "Large Financial Incentive." The advertisements called for a 5-foot-10, athletic woman who had scored at least 1400 on her Scholastic Achievement Test and who had no major family medical problems. In return for providing eggs, she would receive $50,000.

Already, more than 200 women have responded to what is believed to be the largest amount of money offered for a woman's eggs. Darlene Pinkerton, who with her lawyer-husband, Thomas Pinkerton, placed the advertisement on behalf of an infertile couple, said that most respondents were from Ivy League institutions and that she was starting to get calls from women in countries as far away as Finland and New Zealand. Women from state colleges and universities are calling, Ms. Pinkerton said, as are women who are too short or whose S.A.T. scores are too low.

When she ran the same advertisement in October, without mentioning the price the couple would pay, Ms. Pinkerton said, she got only six responses.

Until now, ethicists argued whether $5,000 was too much to pay for an egg donor. They debated whether it was coercive for couples to ask for S.A.T. scores or height or favorite books when they sought egg donors. But, some ethicists say, a $50,000 price, in a donor market that just a year ago was reeling from offers of $7,500 for donors, makes them wonder whether the business is getting out of control.

The couple offering $50,000 wants to remain anonymous, Ms. Pinkerton said. But, she said, they decided to offer $50,000 "because they can."

The couple also realized that it might be hard to find a donor who met their criteria. They are "highly educated," Ms. Pinkerton said, and want a child who can be highly educated as well. They are tall, so they want a child who is tall.

"We have heard that only one percent of the college population is over 5-feet-10 inches with over 1400 S.A.T. scores," Ms. Pinkerton said.

Lori Andrews, a professor at Chicago-Kent College of Law, is taken aback by the heights that payments are reaching. "I think we are moving to children as consumer products," Ms. Andrews said.

5

649

"When prices for donors reach $50,000, it gets to be a meaningful, life-altering sum," she said. 10

Dr. Mark Sauer, who directs the assisted-reproduction program at Columbia University's College of Physicians and Surgeons in New York, said he found women, even Ivy League women, who were willing to donate their eggs for $5,000. And so, Dr. Sauer asks, why would a couple want to pay $50,000?

"I can understand the motive for the donor—it's like winning the lottery," Dr. Sauer said.

After all, he said, it takes just three to four weeks to produce eggs. The donor takes fertility drugs to stimulate her ovaries to produce more than a dozen eggs, has regular ultrasound exams so a doctor can follow the eggs' development, and then is anesthetized while a doctor aspirates the eggs from her ovaries through a needle.

But, Dr. Sauer asked, what are the egg recipients thinking when they offer to pay so much for a donor with such specific traits?

"What genetics textbook did they read," he asks, that would tell them that they could order up a tall, smart, athletic child by paying $50,000 for a donor? 15

But other experts say they fail to see what is so wrong with looking for specific traits in a donor and paying $50,000 for them. Dr. Norman Fost, who directs the program in medical ethics at the University of Wisconsin in Madison, said it was not so crazy to ask for height and S.A.T. scores.

Dr. Fost said he worried more about parents who tried to engineer their children after they were born, pushing them to get perfect grades and to take endless S.A.T. tutoring courses.

"I don't think that genetic engineering is any more pernicious," he said.

As for the $50,000 payment to the egg donor, why not? "It's like offering someone a million dollars to play professional football," Dr. Fost said. "You are perfectly free to walk away from it. People make these choices all their lives."

In the end, he said, "whether children are valued and how they are treated has very little to do with how they are conceived." 20

Kolata's evidence comes mainly from interviews with "experts." This strategy works especially well for arguments based on character; check out Chapter 6 for more suggestions on using arguments based on character.

·······················LINK TO P. 90

RESPOND •

1. Do you agree with Dr. Norman Fost's statement that parents' efforts at "engineering" children after they're born are worse than engineering their conception (paragraphs 17–18)? Why or why not?

2. How do you respond to Fost's claim that "[y]ou are perfectly free to walk away from [the $50,000]" (paragraph 19)? Is his claim true or relevant in all cases? Why or why not?

3. How does Kolata describe the procedure used for egg extraction? Do you think her article gives an accurate summary of this procedure? (You might consult another characterization of the process, one presented in far less neutral terms, that appears in Rebecca Mead's "Eggs for Sale," *The New Yorker,* August 9, 1999, pp. 55–56.) How does Kolata's discussion of the procedure serve her rhetorical purpose?

4. How should the going rate for donated eggs be established? Should there be a "free market" with no regulation or intervention by government bodies or professional organizations? Why or why not? If there were to be a fixed rate of compensation for donors, what criteria should be used to establish that rate? **Write an essay** exploring these issues.

▼ *David Lefer is a staff writer for the* New York Daily News, *a newspaper that targets a different audience from the* New York Times. *In this article on the controversy following in the wake of the first smart-egg ad, Lefer focuses on the responses of several potential egg donors, the director of the center for reproductive medicine and fertility at a majority university, an NCAA spokesperson, a sociologist who specializes in biotechnology, and an Ivy League admissions officer.*

An Ad for Smart Eggs Spawns Ethics Uproar

DAVID LEFER

An advertisement seeking egg donors among the nation's tallest and smartest college women has resulted in a flaring controversy on some of the nation's top campuses. Athletic officials even have suggested that women accepting money for eggs might violate intercollegiate eligibility rules.

The so-called smart-egg ad, placed in school newspapers from Harvard and Yale to Stanford and the California Institute of Technology, offered the unprecedented sum of $50,000 for the ova of healthy, athletic women who stand taller than 5-foot-10 and have SAT scores greater than 1400. The anonymous couple who paid for the ad is said to be tall, well-educated and wealthy enough to pay for such a super egg.

So far, say the couple's Los Angeles–based lawyers, between 200 and 300 hopefuls have volunteered to donate eggs. Still, reaction to the ads on campuses has provoked heated debate among students, doctors and ethicists about the morality of donating eggs for big bucks.

EGG DONOR NEEDED

LARGE FINANCIAL INCENTIVE

Intelligent, Athletic Egg Donor Needed

For Loving Family

You must be at least 5'10"

Have a 1400+ SAT score

Possess no major family medical issues

$50,000

Free Medical Screening

All Expenses Paid

Columbia University student Brie Cokos. An advertisement offering $50,000 for the eggs of tall, brainy women like Cokos for a couple seeking to have a baby has caused controversy on the nation's top college campuses.

"People are really split on the issue," said Megan Bramlette, a 6-foot-1 freshman on Columbia University's women's basketball team who scored high on her SATs. "Some people are totally morally opposed to it. Others say, 'For $50,000, I'd do just about anything.'"

"I think it's a coercive amount of money," said Dr. Zev Rosenwaks, director of the Center for Reproductive Medicine and Fertility at Cornell University. "This is something that should not be done."

"College students don't have a concept of that amount of money," said a 6-foot senior on Harvard's women's basketball team with SAT scores higher than 1400.

Brie Cokos, a 5-foot-11 sophomore biology major at Columbia University who scored 1410 on her SATs, said she doesn't think she could go through with donating her eggs. But she admits the money is enticing.

"For that amount of money, why would you not at least find out what all this is about?" she said. "For one thing, my loans would be out of the way."

Despite the extraordinary sum involved, there might be another hitch in getting student athletes to participate. Although the National Collegiate Athletic Association has no policy on egg donations, an NCAA spokesman confirmed that any student who receives money based directly or indirectly on athletic ability would be ineligible for play.

"If you say you can't play basketball anymore, that's going to take a lot of people out of the running," said Columbia's Bramlette.

Religious beliefs also would keep some students from donating eggs.

"I'm a Catholic, and I would probably have to see what the Church would say about it," said a 6-foot-1 Harvard senior with SATs of more than 1400. Money aside, doctors and ethicists are quick to point out that exceptional genes don't necessarily produce exceptional offspring.

"[The offer] reflects an extraordinarily naive view of genetics that you can pay for a certain kind of heredity and think that it will come out exactly as you planned," said Dorothy Nelkin, a professor of sociology at New York University who specializes in the ethics of biotechnology and genetics.

But at least one Ivy League admissions officer already foresees the possibility that the smart-egg controversy might be around for some time.

"If there are two applicants for admission and one space, would the person who came from a Harvard egg get the spot?" asked Marlyn McGrath-Lewis, admissions director for Harvard and Radcliffe colleges.

"The only good news is it will be another 18 years before we really have to deal with this."

Lefer's article raises many questions, many of which are causal in nature, including one about the consequences for college athletes who accept payment for their ova. See more about causal arguments in Chapter 11.

···································· **LINK TO P. 205**

RESPOND •

1. The technology permitting human egg donation raises a number of ethical issues, yet many of the negative responses touched off by the smart-egg ads focused on the high payment involved. Which, if any, of the ethical questions would a legally set fixed rate resolve? Would you support such a move? Why or why not?

2. Why do you think Lefer includes comments from McGrath-Lewis about the "Harvard egg" applicant (paragraph 15) and the issue of legacy admission, that is, preference in the admissions process because one's parents or other relatives attended a school? Assuming that legacy admission will continue to exist, should admissions committees include in the pool of legacy applicants those who can demonstrate that the egg donor or sperm donor who helped give them life is an alum? Should, for example, admissions committees be privy to such information? Should they be able to ask for it? Should they refuse to consider it? Why or why not?

3. Do you think tall, athletic, and intelligent couples are more entitled to solicit eggs from a tall, athletic, and intelligent donor than prospective parents who may be short, clumsy, and less than brilliant? Why or why not?

4. Read Gina Kolata's article on smart-egg ads (p. 649), noting the similarities with and differences from Lefer's piece. **Write an essay** in which you compare and contrast the two articles, focusing particularly on the sources each writer consulted, her or his ultimate purposes, and her or his likely audience.

5. **Write a proposal** in which you define and propose how best to regulate the business of "eggs for sale." A likely part of the justification for your proposal will be your own beliefs about this practice.

In this essay, Faye Girsh, executive director of what was the Hemlock Society, a nonprofit organization seeking to help legalize "voluntary physician aid in dying for terminally ill consenting adults," argues that physician-assisted suicide should be legalized in the United States. (In July 2003, the Hemlock Society changed its name to End-of-Life Choices <endoflifechoices.org>.) According to the society's Web page at the time this essay first appeared, "Hemlock believes that people who wish to retain their dignity and choice at the end of life should have the option of a peaceful, gentle, certain and swift death in the company of their loved ones. The means to accomplish this is with legally prescribed medication as part of the continuum of care between a patient and a doctor." We found Girsh's article on the Web, but it was originally published in 1999 in Insight on the News, a weekly news magazine covering politics and cultural issues for a national audience. As you read, pay special attention to how Girsh deals—or fails to deal—with potential counterarguments.

Socrates drinking hemlock and thus ending his life. Accused by Athenian authories of "impropriety," most likely because they disagreed with his political affiliations and ideas about education, Socrates was sentenced to die. During and after his trial, he refused to take actions that might have resulted in a lighter sentence because he viewed such actions as compromising; similarly, he did not escape from jail although he easily might have. Instead, he drank hemlock (to the despair of friends), thus forcing the Athenians to face the unjust consequences of their decision.

Should Physician-Assisted Suicide Be Legalized? Yes!

FAYE GIRSH

Q: Should physician-assisted suicide be legalized by the states?
Yes: Don't make doctors criminals for helping people escape painful terminal illnesses.

Many people agree that there are horrifying situations at the end of life which cry out for the help of a doctor to end the suffering by providing a peaceful, wished-for death. But, opponents argue, that does not mean that the practice should be legalized. They contend that these are the exceptional cases from which bad law would result.

I disagree. It is precisely these kinds of hard deaths that people fear and that happen to 7 to 10 percent of those who are dying that convince them to support the right to choose a hastened death with medical assistance. The reason that polls in this country—and in Canada, Australia, Great Britain and other parts of Europe—show 60 to 80 percent support for legalization of assisted suicide is that people want to know they will have a way out if their suffering becomes too great. They dread losing control not only of their bodies but of what will happen to them in the medical system. As a multiple-sclerosis patient wrote to the Hemlock Society: "I feel like I am just rotting away. . . . If there is something that gives life meaning and purpose it is this: a peaceful end to a good life before the last part of it becomes even more hellish."

Even with the best of hospice care people want to know that there can be some way to shorten a tortured dying process. A man whose wife was dying from cancer wrote, "For us, hospice care was our choice. We, however, still had 'our way,' also our choice, as 'our alternative.' We were prepared. And the 'choice' should be that of the patient and family."

It is not pain that causes people to ask for a hastened death but the indignities and suffering accompanying some terminal disorders such as cancer, stroke and AIDS. A survey in the Netherlands found that the primary reason to choose help in dying was to avoid "senseless suffering."

Hospice can make people more comfortable, can bring spiritual solace and can   5 work with the family, but—as long as hospice is sworn neither to prolong nor hasten death—it will not be the whole answer for everyone. People should not have to make a choice between seeking hospice care and choosing to hasten the dying process. The best hospice care should be available to everyone, as should the option of a quick, gentle, certain death with loved ones around when the suffering has become unbearable. Both should be part of the continuum of care at the end of life.

We have the right to commit suicide and the right to refuse unwanted medical treatment, including food and water. But what we don't have—unless we live in Oregon—is the right to get help from a doctor to achieve a peaceful death. As the trial judge in the Florida case of Kirscher vs. McIver, an AIDS patient who wanted his doctor's help in dying, said in his decision: "Physicians are permitted to assist their terminal patients by disconnecting life support or by prescribing medication to ease their starvation. Yet medications to produce a quick death, free of pain and protracted agony, are prohibited. This is a difference without distinction."

The Oregon example has shown us that, although a large number of people want to know the choice is there, only a small number will take advantage of it. During the first eight months of the Oregon "Death with Dignity" law, only 10 people took the opportunity to obtain the medications and eight used them to end their lives. In the Netherlands it consistently has been less than 5 percent of the total number of people who die every year who choose to get help in doing so from their doctor.

In Switzerland, where physician-assisted death also is legal, about 120 people die annually with the help of medical assistance. There is no deluge of people wanting to put themselves out of their misery nor of greedy doctors and hospitals encouraging that alternative. People want to live as long as possible. There are repeated testimonials to the fact that people can live longer and with less anguish once they know that help will be available if they want to end it. Even Jack Kevorkian, who says he helped 130 people die since 1990, has averaged only 14 deaths a year.

To the credit of the right-to-die movement, end-of-life care has improved because of the push for assisted dying. In Oregon, end-of-life care is the best in the country: Oregon is No. 1 in morphine use, twice as many people there use hospice as the national average and more people die at home than in the hospital. In Maine there will be an initiative on the ballot in 2000 to legalize physician aid in dying, and in Arizona a physician-assisted-dying bill has been introduced. In both states the Robert Wood Johnson Foundation has awarded sizable grants to expand hospice care and to improve end-of-life care.

It is gratifying that the specter of assisted dying has spurred such concern for care at the end of life. Clearly, if we take the pressure off, the issue will disappear back into the closet. No matter how good the care gets, there still will be a need to have an assisted death as one choice. The better the care gets, the less that need will exist.   10

The pope and his minions in the Catholic Church, as well as the religious right, announce that assisted dying is part of the "culture of death." Murder, lawlessness, suicide, the cheapening of life with killing in the media, the accessibility of guns, war—those create a culture of death, not providing help to a dying person who repeatedly requests an end to his or her suffering by a day or a week. Not all religious people believe that. The Rev. Bishop Spong of the Episcopal Diocese of Newark, N.J., said: "My personal creed asserts that every person is sacred. I see the holiness of life enhanced, not diminished, by letting people have a say in how they choose to die. Many of us want the moral and legal right to choose to die with our faculties intact, surrounded by those we love before we are reduced to breathing cadavers with no human dignity attached to our final days. Life must not be identified with the extension of biological existence. Assisted suicide is a life-affirming moral choice."

The Catholic belief that suicide is a sin which will cause a person to burn in hell is at the root of the well-financed, virulent opposition to physician aid in dying. This has resulted in expenditures of more than $10 million in losing efforts to defeat the two Oregon initiatives and a successful campaign to defeat the

A word like *minions* carries a strong connotation. Sometimes the choice of such a powerful word is an effective rhetorical strategy, but other times less potent words are more effective. Check out the section on the dangers of unduly slanted language in Chapter 14 for suggestions on word choice.

···LINK TO P. 297

recent Michigan measure. And $6 million was spent in Michigan, most of which came from Catholic donors, to show four TV ads six weeks before voters saw the issue on the 1998 ballot. The ads never attacked the concept of physician aid in dying, but hammered on the well-crafted Proposal B. Surely that money could have been spent to protect life in better ways than to frustrate people who have come to terms with their deaths and want to move on. The arguments that life is sacred and that it is a gift from God rarely are heard now from the opposition. Most Americans do not want to be governed by religious beliefs they don't share, so the argument has shifted to "protection of the vulnerable and the slippery slope." Note, however, that the proposed death-with-dignity laws carefully are written to protect the vulnerable. The request for physician-assisted death must be voluntary, must be from a competent adult and must be documented and repeated during a waiting period. Two doctors must examine the patient and, if there is any question of depression or incompetence or coercion, a mental-health professional can be consulted. After that it must be up to the requester to mix and swallow the lethal medication. No one forces anyone to do anything!

The same arguments were raised in 1976 when the first "living-will" law was passed in California. It again was raised in 1990 when the Supreme Court ruled that every American has the right to refuse medical treatment, including food and hydration, and to designate a proxy to make those decisions if they cannot. This has not been a downhill slope in the last 22 years but an expansion of rights and choices. It has not led to abuse but rather to more freedom. Those who raise the specter of the Nazis must remember that we are in greater danger of having our freedoms limited by religious dogma than of having them expanded so that more choices are available. When the state dictates how the most intimate and personal choices will be made, based on how some religious groups think it should be, then we as individuals and as a country are in serious trouble.

One observer said about the Oregon Death with Dignity law: "This is a permissive law. It allows something. It requires nothing. It forbids nothing and taxes no one. It enhances freedom. It lets people do a little more of what they want without hurting anyone else. It removes a slight bit of the weight of government regulation and threat of punishment that hangs over all of us all the time if we step out of line."

Making physician aid in dying legal as a matter of public policy will accomplish   15
several objectives. Right now we have a model of prohibition. There is an

underground cadre of doctors—of whom Kevorkian is the tip of the iceberg—who are helping people die. The number varies, according to survey, from 6 to 16 percent to 20 to 53 percent. The 53 percent is for doctors in San Francisco who work with people with AIDS where networks for assisted dying have existed for many years. This practice is not regulated or reported; the criteria and methods used are unknown. There is some information that the majority of these deaths are done by lethal injection. Millions of viewers witnessed on *60 Minutes* the videotape of Kevorkian using this method to assist in the death of Thomas Youk. If the practice is regulated, there will be more uniformity, doctors will be able to and will have to obtain a second opinion and will have the option of having a mental-health professional consult on the case. Most importantly for patients, they will be able to talk about all their options openly with their health-care providers and their loved ones.

Another consequence is that desperately ill people will not have to resort to dying in a Michigan motel with Kevorkian's assistance, with a plastic bag on their heads, with a gun in their mouth or, worse, botching the job and winding up in worse shape and traumatizing their families. They won't have to die the way someone else wants them to die, rather than the way they choose. As Ronald Dworkin said in *Life's Dominion*: "Making someone die in a way others approve, but he believes a horrifying contradiction of his life, is a devastating, odious form of tyranny."

RESPOND●

1. Briefly summarize Girsh's arguments for legalizing physician-assisted suicide as well as her counterarguments against those who oppose such legalization. Although she does not explicitly mention changing technology as an impetus for physician-assisted suicide, how is the existence of such technology invoked in the text?

2. What sorts of appeals does Girsh use in constructing her argument? List the specific appeals that she uses, providing examples from the text. How effective are they? On the basis of these appeals, what sorts of readers might you deduce Girsh expects to read her article?

3. How effectively does Girsh deal with the opposition to legalizing physician-assisted suicide? (Note that this opposition might take several forms—those who oppose it in principle, those who argue that physician-assisted suicide is unnecessary if adequate hospice care is provided, etc.) How fairly does she characterize and deal with opposing views and concerns in general? What is the likelihood that Girsh's arguments will persuade readers who do not already agree with her position? Why? What is the likelihood that Girsh will persuade religious readers, particularly those who are Catholic (given her comments in paragraphs 11–12)?

4. Girsh formulates her argument as the "correct" answer to a purely legal question about physician-assisted suicide. In a collection of papers, *Physician-Assisted Suicide: Expanding the Debate* (1998), the editors, Margaret P. Battin, Rosamond Rhodes, and Anita Silvers, argue that the issue is much larger than a legal question, encompassing what they label the philosophical landscape; the clinical or medical landscape; the social, political, economic, and public policy landscape; and the religious landscape. **Write an essay** in which you define what you see as the most appropriate terms in which to formulate questions about whether humans "own" the right to end their life in cases of terminal illness, evaluating the potential consequences of the various questions you devise.

▼ *Joe Loconte is author of* Seducing the Samaritan: How Government Contracts Are Reshaping Social Services *(1997) and deputy editor of* The Journal of American Citizenship, *the source from which this reading was excerpted. The original article appeared in March–April 1998. As this reading's title implies, it makes a strong argument for the use of hospice treatment for the terminally ill and against physician-assisted suicide.*

Hospice, Not Hemlock

JOE LOCONTE

In the deepening debate over assisted suicide, almost everyone agrees on a few troubling facts: Most people with terminal illnesses die in the sterile settings of hospitals or nursing homes, often in prolonged, uncontrolled pain; physicians typically fail to manage their patients' symptoms, adding mightily to their suffering; the wishes of patients are ignored as they are subjected to intrusive, often futile, medical interventions; and aggressive end-of-life care often bankrupts families that are already in crisis.

TOO MANY PEOPLE IN AMERICA
ARE DYING A BAD DEATH

The solution, some tell us, is physician-assisted suicide. Oregon has legalized the practice for the terminally ill. Michigan's Jack Kevorkian continues to help willing patients end their own lives. The prestigious *New England Journal of Medicine* has come out in favor of doctor-assisted death. Says Faye Girsh, the director of the Hemlock Society: "The only way to achieve a quick and painless and certain death is through medications that only a physician has access to."

This, we are told, is death with dignity. What we do not often hear is that there is another way to die — under the care of a specialized discipline of medicine that manages the pain of deadly diseases, keeps patients comfortable yet awake and alert, and surrounds the dying with emotional and spiritual support. Every year, roughly 450,000 people die in this way. They die in hospice.

"The vast majority of terminally ill patients can have clarity of mind and freedom from pain," says Martha Twaddle, a leading hospice physician and medical director at the hospice division of the Palliative Care Center of the North Shore, in Evanston, Illinois. "Hospice care helps liberate patients from the afflictions of their symptoms so that they can truly live until they die."

The hospice concept rejects decisions to hasten 5
death, but also extreme medical efforts to prolong life for the terminally ill. Rather, it aggressively treats the symptoms of disease — pain, fatigue, disorientation, depression — to ease the emotional suffering of those near death. It applies "palliative medicine," a team-based philosophy of caregiving that unites the medical know-how of doctors and nurses with the practical and emotional support of social workers, volunteer aides, and spiritual counselors. Because the goal of hospice is comfort, not cure, patients are usually treated at home, where most say they would prefer to die.

"Most people nowadays see two options: A mechanized, depersonalized, and painful death in a hospital or a swift death that rejects medical institutions and technology," says Nicholas Christakis, an assistant professor of medicine and sociology at the University of Chicago. "It is a false choice. Hospice offers a way out of this dilemma."

HOSPICE OR HEMLOCK?

If so, there remains a gauntlet of cultural roadblocks. Hospice is rarely mentioned in medical school curricula. Says Dale Smith, a former head of the American Academy of Hospice and Palliative Medicine, "Talk to any physician and he'll tell you he never got any training in ways to deal with patients at the end of life."

The result: Most terminally ill patients either never hear about the hospice option or enter a program on the brink of death. Though a recent Gallup Poll shows that nine out of 10 Americans would choose to die at home once they are diagnosed with a terminal disease, most spend their final days in hospitals or nursing homes.

And, too often, that's not a very good place to die. A four-year research project funded by the Robert Wood Johnson Foundation looked at more than 9,000 seriously ill patients in five major teaching hospitals. Considered one of the most important studies on medical care for the dying, it found that doctors routinely subject patients to futile treatment, ignore their specific instructions for care, and allow them to die in needless pain.

"We are failing in our responsibility to provide 10 humane care for people who are dying," says Ira Byock, a leading hospice physician and the author of *Dying Well.* George Annas, the director of the Law, Medicine and Ethics Program at Boston University, puts it even more starkly: "If dying patients want to retain some control over their dying process, they must get out of the hospital."

Since the mid-1970s, hospice programs have grown from a mere handful to more than 2,500, available in nearly every community. At least 4,000 nurses are now nationally certified in hospice techniques. In Michigan — Kevorkian's home state — a statewide hospice program cares for 1,100 people a day, regardless of their ability to pay. The Robert Wood Johnson Foundation, a leading health-care philanthropy, has launched a $12-million initiative to improve care for the dying. And the American Medical Association, which did not even recognize hospice as a medical discipline until 1995, has made the training of physicians in end-of-life care one of its top priorities.

There is a conflict raging in America today over society's obligations to care for its most vulnerable. Says Charles von Gunten, a hospice specialist at Northwestern Memorial Hospital, in Chicago, "It is fundamentally an argument about the soul of medicine." One observer calls it a choice between hospice or hemlock — between a compassion that "suffers with" the dying, or one that eliminates suffering by eliminating the sufferer.

A NEW VISION OF MEDICINE

The modern hospice movement was founded by English physician Cicely Saunders, who, as a nurse in a London clinic, was aghast at the disregard for the emotional and spiritual suffering of patients near death. In 1967, she opened St. Christopher's Hospice, an in-patient facility drawing on spiritual and practical support from local congregations.

"She wanted to introduce a distinctly Christian vision to mainstream medicine," says Nigel Cameron, an expert in bioethics at Trinity International University, in Deerfield, Illinois. The staples of the hospice philosophy quickly emerged: at-home care; an interdisciplinary team of physicians, nurses, pharmacists, ministers, and social workers; and a heavy sprinkling of volunteers.

Saunders's vision got a boost from *On Death and* 15 *Dying,* Elisabeth Kübler-Ross's book based on more than 500 interviews with dying patients. The study, in which the author pleaded for greater attention to the psychosocial aspects of dying, became an international bestseller. By 1974, the National Cancer Institute had begun funding hospices; the first, in Branford, Connecticut, was regarded as a national model of home care for the terminally ill.

Early hospice programs were independent and community-run, managed by local physicians or registered nurses. Most operated on a shoestring, relying on contributions, patient payments, and private insurance. Many were relatively spartan, consisting of little more than a nurse and a social worker making home visits.

Religious communities were early and natural supporters. "The questions people ask at the end of life are religious questions," says Rabbi Maurice Lamm, the president of the National Institute for Jewish Hospice, "and they must be answered by somebody who knows the person's faith." Synagogues, which usually support visitation committees for the sick, formed commissions to establish a Jewish presence in hospitals offering hospice care. The Catholic Church took a leadership role: Through its hospitals, health-care systems, and parishes, it began providing hospice beds, nurses, and priests.

A hospice patient at home during the final months of her life

By the mid-1980s, the movement started to take off. As hospital costs escalated, Medicare joined a growing number of insurance companies that offered reimbursement for hospice's home-care approach. In 1985, President Ronald Reagan signed legislation making the Medicare hospice benefit a permanent part of the Medicare program.

Today nearly 80 percent of hospices qualify. Medicare picks up most of the bill for services, from pain medications to special beds. The majority of managed-care plans offer at least partial coverage, and most private insurance plans include a hospice benefit. Since becoming a part of Medicare, hospice has seen a four-fold increase in patients receiving its services.

REDEFINING AUTONOMY

The starting place for any hospice team is the patient: 20 What kind of care does he or she really want? "It's not about our goals for a patient," says Dorothy Pitner, the president of the Palliative Care Center of the North Shore, which cares for about 200 people a day in Chicago's northern suburbs. "They tell us how they define quality of life, and then together we decide the course of action."

This is how hospice respects patient autonomy: not by hastening death, but by working closely with patients and families to weigh the costs and benefits of care. "Patients have the right to refuse unwanted, futile medical care," says Walter Hunter, the chairman of the National Hospice Ethics Committee. "But the right to refuse care does not mean the right to demand active assistance in dying."

Though physicians and medical directors may make only a few visits to a patient's home over the course of an illness, they supervise all caregiving decisions by the hospice teams. No one fills a prescription, inserts a tube, or gives medication without their OK. The central task of getting a person's pain under control falls to doctors, working closely with pharmacists.

Registered nurses serve as case managers. Usually they are the first to enter the home of the dying, make an assessment, and describe symptoms to physicians. They visit the home weekly and are on call 24 hours a day for emergencies. Nurses, along with nurse's aides, not only act as the go-between for families and physicians; they also bear much of the burden for making sure patients are comfortable, from administering drugs to drawing blood to suggesting medications or therapies.

Volunteers are also important to that work. For several hours a week they help out at home, cooking or doing household chores, keeping an eye on bed-ridden patients, or just listening as family members struggle with grief. Last year, about 100,000 volunteers joined 30,000 paid staff in hospices nationwide. They are, as one veteran caregiver puts it, the "sponges" in the mix, soaking up some of the anguish that accompanies death and dying.

THE DEATH WISH

Hospice care usually begins where traditional medi- 25 cine ends: when it becomes clear that a person's illness will not succumb to even the most heroic of medical therapies. "This is the toughest problem for doctors and families, the issue of letting go," says Alan Smookler, the Palliative Care Center's assistant medical director. "There's a lot of technology out there—feeding tubes, antibiotics, oxygen, ventilators, dialysis—and the hardest problem is saying that these interventions are no longer beneficial."

Hospice [of the Florida Suncoast] president Mary Labyak says many people come in eager to hasten their own deaths, but almost always have a change of heart. Of the 50,000 patients who have died under the group's care, she says, perhaps six have committed suicide. "The public perception is that people are [choosing suicide] every day. But these are people in their own homes, they have the means, they have lots of medication, and they don't choose death."

Hardly anything creates a more frightening sense of chaos than unrelieved pain and suffering. "We know that severe pain greatly reduces people's ability to function," says Patricia Berry, the director of the Wisconsin Cancer Pain Initiative. "If we don't control symptoms, then people can't have quality of life, they can't choose what they want to do or what to think about."

Hospice has understood this connection between pain and overall well-being from the start. After conventional treatments fail, says Martha Twaddle, "you'll often hear doctors say 'there's nothing left to do.' There's a lot left to do. There is a lot of aggressive care that can be given to you to treat your symptoms."

Hardly anyone doubts that more energetic caregiving for the dying is in order. A 1990 report from the National Cancer Institute warned that "undertreatment of pain and other symptoms of cancer is a serious and neglected public health problem." The New York State Task Force on Life and the Law, in arguing against legalizing assisted suicide, cited the "pervasive failure of our health-care system to treat pain and diagnose and treat depression."

The best studies show that most doctors still 30 undertreat pain and that most people with chronic and terminal illnesses experience needless suffering. A survey was taken a few years ago of 1,177 U.S. physicians who had cared for more than 70,000

patients with cancer during the previous six months. Eighty-five percent said the majority of cancer patients with pain were undermedicated; nearly half of those surveyed rated their own pain management techniques as fair or very poor.

A DEBT TO HOSPICE

The pain-control approach of hospice depends on an aggressive use of opioid drugs — narcotics such as morphine, fentanyl, codeine, or methadone. Despite the effectiveness of these drugs in clinical settings, euthanasia supporters often ignore or contest the results. Timothy Quill, a leading advocate of doctor-assisted suicide, writes that "there is no empirical evidence that all physical suffering associated with incurable illness can be effectively relieved."

Ira Byock, the president of the American Academy of Hospice and Palliative Medicine, says that's medical bunk. A 20-year hospice physician, Byock has cared for thousands of patients with terminal disease. "The best hospice and palliative-care programs have demonstrated that pain and physical suffering can always be alleviated," he says. "Not necessarily eliminated, but it can always be lessened and made more tolerable." Physicians and other authorities outside the hospice movement agree that most pain can be controlled. Authors of the New York Task Force report assert that "modern pain relief techniques can alleviate pain in all but extremely rare cases."

LIVING UNTIL THEY DIE

Even the goal of easing people's suffering, as central as it is to hospice care, is not an end in itself. The aim of comfort is part of a larger objective: to help the terminally ill live as fully as possible until they die. This is where hospice departs most pointedly both from traditional medicine and the advocates of assisted suicide.

Loconte's article makes an evaluation argument by examining the question, "What is a good death?" Chapter 10 explains other ways of using evaluation arguments.

················· **LINK TO P. 174**

Hospice, by shining a light on the emotional and spiritual aspects of suffering, is challenging the medical community to re-examine its priorities. The period at the end of life, simultaneously ignored and micro-managed by conventional approaches, can be filled with significance. To neglect it is to diminish ourselves. "Spiritual inattentiveness in the face of dying and death can lead to the sad spectacle of medical technology run amok," says Laurence O'Connell, the president of the Park Ridge Center, a medical ethics think tank in Chicago.

Those who have spent years tending to the dying say there is a mystery at life's end, one that seems to defy the rules of medicine. Walter Hunter, a medical director at the Hospice of Michigan, recalls a patient with end-stage kidney disease who entered hospice and quickly asked to be taken off the hemodialysis (a kidney machine) needed to keep her alive. Conventional medical wisdom put her life expectancy at two to three weeks without the technology, but the woman said she was eager to die.

Eight months later she was still alive. She asked Hunter, then her primary doctor, why she was still breathing. "I don't know," the doctor replied. "According to the textbooks, you should be dead."

Hospice staff had been busy in those months, keeping the patient comfortable, providing emotional and spiritual support. They later learned that just two days before the woman died, she had reconciled with one of her estranged children.

Sharon McCarthy has been a social worker at the Palliative Care Center of the North Shore for 18 years. She has cared for thousands of dying patients, getting a ringside seat to the grief of countless families. For the vast majority, she says, hospice provides the window of opportunity to get their lives in order. One of the most common desires: forgiveness, both extended and received. "There's a lot of nonphysical pain that goes on when these things aren't done." Says Mary Sheehan, director of clinical services and a 12-year veteran in hospice: "Ninety-nine percent of the time they have unfinished business."

SAVING THE SOUL OF MEDICINE

Hospice or hemlock: Though both end in death, each pursues its vision of a "good death" along radically different paths. At its deepest level, the hospice philosophy strikes a blow at the notion of the isolated individual. It insists that no one dies in a vacuum. Where one exists, hospice physicians, nurses, and social workers rush in to help fill it.

For many hospice staff and supporters, such work is motivated and informed by a deeply moral and religious outlook. "I do not work within a specific religious context," writes Byock in *Dying Well*, "but I find more than a little truth in the spiritual philosophies of Christianity, Buddhism, and Judaism." Karen Bell, the hospice director of the Catholic-run Providence Health System in Portland, Oregon, says her organization is propelled by religious values. "The foundational principle is that life has a meaning and value until the very end, regardless of a person's physical condition or mental state."

Faith communities have always been involved in caring for the desperately ill, founding hospitals, clinics, medical schools, and so on. Though not usually connected to religious institutions, nearly all hospice programs make spiritual counseling available; rabbis, chaplains, and ecumenical ministers make frequent home visits and regularly attend hospice team meetings.

For many religious physicians, tackling the issue of personal autonomy is a crucial step in end-of-life care. "This is the Christian answer to whose life it is: 'It is not your own; you were bought at a price,'" says Yale University Medical School's Dr. Diane Comp, quoting the apostle Paul. "But if we are not in control of our lives, then we need companionship. We need the companionship of God and the companionship of those who reflect the image of God in this broken world."

Leon Kass, a physician and philosopher at the University of Chicago, says the religiously inspired moral vigor of hospice sets itself squarely against the movement for assisted death. "Hospice borrows its energy from a certain Judeo-Christian view of our obligations to suffering humanity," he says. "It is the idea that company and care, rather than attempts at cure, are abiding human obligations. These obligations are put to the severest test when the recipient of care is at his lowest and most unattractive."

We seem, as a culture, to be under such a test, and the outcome is not at all certain. Some call it a war for the soul of medicine. If so, hospice personnel could be to medical care what American GIs were to the Allied effort in Europe—the source of both its tactical and moral strength and, eventually, the foot soldiers for victory and reconstruction.   ∎

RESPOND ●

1. What seem to be Loconte's purposes in writing this essay? Does he seem more concerned with arguing against physician-assisted suicide or arguing for hospice care? What evidence can you cite for your claim? Are the two mutually exclusive? Why or why not?

2. How do you imagine Faye Girsh ("Should Physician-Assisted Suicide Be Legalized? Yes!" p. 654) would respond to Loconte's essay? Which of his claims in particular would she find most problematic? Why? Loconte paints an especially positive and trouble-free view of hospice care. Might there be problems (or potential problems) he is ignoring or overlooking? How do you respond to Loconte's essay? Does he persuade you of his position? Why or why not?

3. *The Journal of American Citizenship* is published by the Heritage Foundation, a conservative think tank. Does Loconte's essay strike you as "conservative" in any way? Why or why not? Can you imagine people who might label themselves "liberals" sharing many (or all) of Loconte's views? Why or why not?

4. Loconte's essay, like the previous one by Girsch, seeks to answer a profound question: Who "owns" human life in cases of terminal illness? Both have rejected what is often called the biomedical model of death and dying, which emphasizes keeping an individual alive as long as is humanly possible, as if to claim that "science" doesn't own human life in these cases—or shouldn't. Girsch opts for freedom for the individual, provided care is taken to ensure that choices are freely made, while Loconte argues for hospice care as a third alternative to both physician-assisted suicide and the biomedical model of death and dying. Write an essay in which you evaluate the evidence offered by each author to support her or his position. Be sure to discuss why each author uses the sorts of evidence that she or he does (e.g., Loconte closes by discussing matters of religious faith).

▼ This story appeared on May 19, 1999, on the first page of the metro/regional news section of the Boston Globe. James Bandler reports on the return of two thousand skeletal remains of the Pecos Pueblo people to New Mexico by Harvard's Peabody Museum of Archeology and Ethnology, some eighty-four years after they were unearthed in 1916. As you read, think about who might make up the readership of the Boston newspaper and what interest that audience might have in the event reported here.

A Long Journey Home

Decades after Dig, Remains Returning to N.M. Tribe

JAMES BANDLER

Alfred V. Kidder offered 50 cents to the man who found the first skeleton.

It was 1916, and Kidder, a pipe-smoking archeologist fresh out of Harvard's graduate school, stood atop a rocky knoll overlooking New Mexico's Pecos Valley. On this tongue of land, Kidder's team had begun unearthing the ruins of an American Indian pueblo.

The Pecos dig, later hailed by scholars as the coming of age of American archeology, would propel Kidder into prominence in his field. It would create one of the most important collections of human remains in the United States, leading to groundbreaking research in the study of osteoporosis.

But it would also cause wrenching pain to the descendants of the Pecos Indians whose remains were exhumed. Today, with the return of the remains to New Mexico imminent, they regard the excavation as a desecration, and they wonder how anyone could have so thoughtlessly violated holy ground.

But on that early summer day as his team picked through the red soil, Kidder had his mind on more temporal matters. He was thinking about bones. "I was very anxious, of course, to find skeletons, because they would lead to pottery," Kidder wrote in his memoirs. "We began to find skeletons pretty soon." [5]

On the second day of digging, a single skeleton was uncovered. Kidder reduced the reward to 25 cents. The more they dug, the more skeletons they discovered, and the finder's fee was lowered to a dime.

"I finally said if they found any more skeletons, I would fine them," Kidder recalled years later. "That rubbish heap was literally full of skeletons."

That "rubbish heap," actually a resting place where the Pecos buried their dead alongside ordinary objects, and the hundreds of rooms next to it ultimately yielded more than 2,000 human remains. The Kidder excavation also took thousands of artifacts, including ceramic vessels, shell pendants, and effigies. The bones and artifacts date from the 12th century to the 1830s.

While most of the bones were taken to Harvard's Peabody Museum of Archeology and Ethnology, the artifacts have been kept at Phillips Academy of Andover's Robert Peabody Museum of Archeology, which sponsored Kidder's excavation.

Yesterday, 84 years after Kidder began his work in Pecos, the remains and remaining artifacts finally started their journey home after a ceremony at the Harvard museum. On Saturday there will be a private reburial ceremony in Pecos, N.M., marking the largest repatriation of American Indian remains. [10]

"It's a phenomenal event," said William Whatley, tribal preservation officer for the Pueblo of Jemez, a tribe that traces its lineage to the Pecos Pueblo. "It's a closing of the circle."

Is Whatley being literal or metaphorical about the closing of the circle? It could be argued both ways; check out Chapter 14 to help you decide.

LINK TO P. 288 ·······························

The reburial ends years of negotiations between tribal officials and the two museums—a process that began four years after the passage of the federal Native American Graves Protection and Repatriation Act in 1990. The law requires museums to inventory their collections of items that might have sacred or special tribal significance and to return them to those tribes that can make strong claims.

Jemez tribal representatives paid their first visit to Harvard's Peabody Museum in 1996. They were led to a sprawling, two-storied storage room filled with thousands of boxes of human remains. The Pecos remains occupied nearly the entire second level of the room—and the sight of them caused the tribal leaders to weep. The tribal leaders then consulted the spirits of the ancestors, Whatley said. The answer, he said, was unequivocal: "We want to go home."

Anthropologists and medical researchers have regarded the Pecos collection as a scientific treasure. The bones, by and large, are in remarkably good condition, and the collection, which is demographically representative of a single population, is large enough to be statistically significant. The bones have been studied by dozens of researchers, from eugenicists in the 1930s who equated cranial size with intelligence, to scientists who have engaged in more legitimate inquiries—everything from head injuries to tooth decay.

One of the most significant pieces of research was performed by Johns Hopkins University anthropologist Christopher Ruff. His studies demonstrated that exercise could strengthen aging bones by enlarging them to compensate for the shrinkage associated with osteoporosis.

Ruff called the repatriation of the bones a "significant loss to science," but he said he also understands the fiercely emotional sentiments of the Jemez people.

The Jemez, who say their ancestors migrated from Pecos Pueblo in 1838, said they are glad some good came from the bones' presence at Harvard. But they said no amount of scientific research would compensate for Kidder's desecration. "It's our belief that no one has the right to disturb the graves of another man's ancestors," Whatley said.

Yet Whatley said the tribe bore no animosity toward Kidder, Harvard, or Andover. He said Harvard's Peabody Museum curators had handled the remains with the care of parents. Representatives from both the Harvard and Andover museums, he said, would be invited to Pecos for the May 22 ceremony. "Even though it's a private family funeral, those representatives will be standing side by side with us," Whatley said. "They're considered family."

As for Kidder, he died of heart failure in 1963 after an illustrious career and was buried in Mount Auburn Cemetery. But his story didn't end there.

Before she died, Kidder's wife, Madeleine, requested that upon her death, her husband's remains be exhumed from his grave in Cambridge, cremated, and reburied in New Mexico, next to hers. Today, a simple, flat stone by a stream bed marks the grave, a half mile or so from the site of Kidder's famous dig.

"It was a place he deeply loved," said Kidder's only surviving son, James. "He was repatriated, too."

15

20

RESPOND ●

1. Bandler describes the first visit made by Jemez tribal representatives to the Harvard museum to begin negotiating for the repatriation of their Pecos ancestors' remains, writing that "the sight of [the remains] caused the tribal leaders to weep" (paragraph 13). Do you think this statement is an argument of emotion? Why or why not? Are there any arguments of emotion in this article? What are they?

2. "A Long Journey Home" appeared in the regional news section of a Boston newspaper, near where Harvard University is located. Compare it with Miguel Navrot's "Ancestors Return Home" (p. 670), which appeared in the *Albuquerque Journal* a few days after Bandler's article was published in the *Globe*. Which events or features of the story does each author and newspaper choose to emphasize? Why might the authors and newspaper editors have made these choices? What is the central argument of each piece?

3. Why do you think Bandler ends his article with an anecdote about archaeologist Alfred Kidder? Is the anecdote relevant? What does it contribute to the article as a whole?

4. What basic assumptions permitted early twentieth-century researchers, scholars, and speculators in archaeology to think it was acceptable to "own" human remains? What factors do you think may have led more recent researchers, scholars, and the general public to rethink these assumptions? Would you visit a museum to see an exhibit of Egyptian mummies or of the remains of people from various social groups, including your own? Why or why not?

5. This article and the following one present two perspectives on the return of skeletal remains from the Peabody Museum at Harvard to the Native American groups as mandated by a 1990 law. The question of possession of cultural artifacts or human remains by a museum and the claim of ownership by various groups is far larger than arguments between groups and museums within national boundaries. For example, Greece continues to press Britain for the return of the Elgin Marbles, the marble pediments that decorated the Parthenon; Jewish families around the world continue to try to locate and repossess art that was stolen from them during the Holocaust; and the 2003 war with Iraq led to criticism of the United States by many here and abroad because the treasures of the Iraqi National Museum, many of which document the rise of human civilization in Mesopotamia, were not protected by U.S. forces from looters and thieves, even though other buildings and areas claimed to be of "strategic significance" were. These cases raise complex questions about the ownership of things—artifacts, manuscripts, works of art—part of whose value is associated with their historical significance or cultural value. Using the Internet, research one of these cases or another one with which you are familiar, and **write an essay** in which you evaluate the relative claims of each party. In weighing the relevant issues, you may wish to consider the conditions under which an artifact should be considered property of a nation, property of a group, or property of an individual.

▼ *This story about the repatriation of ancestral remains to the Jemez Pueblo appeared on May 23, 1999, on the front page of the* Albuquerque Journal, *a daily newspaper with the largest circulation in New Mexico. Another article of similar length covering this event appeared on the front page on May 17, the day that the remains left Massachusetts. As you read, look for ways in which Miguel Navrot is writing to a local audience.*

Ancestors Return Home

Jemez Pueblo Turned Out in Force as Bones of Almost 2,000 Native Americans Were Reburied Saturday

MIGUEL NAVROT

PECOS NATIONAL HISTORICAL PARK—Escorted by hundreds of tribal officials, elders and members, the ancestral remains of nearly 2,000 Native Americans returned home Saturday. Their return, touted as the largest act of Native American repatriation in the nation's history, capped years of work among tribal leaders, museum administrators and government officials.

The remains and hundreds of artifacts had been exhumed from Pecos Pueblo roughly 75 years ago by archaeologist Alfred V. Kidder, and some date back to the 12th century.

"This repatriation is a very, very important political victory, not only for the Pueblo of Jemez, but for all Native Americans across the United States," said 2nd Lt. Gov. Ruben Sando of Jemez after Saturday's private burial ceremony.

Saturday's reburial of ancestors of the Pecos, Comanche, Kiowa, Apache, Navajo and other Native

A TIME OF JOY: Dolores Toya, from Jemez Pueblo, celebrates the return of American Indian remains to Pecos National Historical Park on Saturday.

Americans brought a dramatic end to the Jemez quest to reinter the remains. Many of the Jemez people trace their ancestry to the last of the Pecos survivors who abandoned the site in 1838.

The remains and artifacts arrived 5 at the park under escort of law enforcement and more than 600 tribal officials, elders, members and invited guests, who walked just over a mile to the park entrance under Saturday's early morning sun. Boxed in cardboard, the remains and artifacts had been trucked from Massachusetts last week in a tractor-trailer.

The procession into the park stretched about the length of a football field as walkers brimmed over the sides of two-lane N.M. 63. A delegation of tribal officials and elders, clad in brightly colored traditional clothing, walked at the head.

Bearing the Pecos Pueblo Governor's Cane given to the pueblo while Spain claimed possession of present-day New Mexico, Sando led the walk, eyes fixed straight ahead throughout. Tribal member Ada Romero walked near the procession front, sprinkling corn meal along the path from a small woven basket she carried.

Saturday's procession also marked the final leg of a four-day march by hundreds of Jemez members from their pueblo to the national park. Tribal officials calculated the distance of the trek at 100 miles over sand, rocks, sun-baked asphalt, sections of the Santa Fe River and stretches of road under construction.

The journey left walkers with blistered and bruised feet, although many, like Jemez resident Julian Vigil, said they weren't concerned with pain Saturday.

"It's a sacrifice," Vigil said. "It's a 10 sacrifice for our people, and a sacrifice for our ancestors."

Elvera Gachupin, a cousin to tribal Gov. Raymond Gachupin, spoke of the walkers' arrival at Pecos. "I'm proud of our accomplishment," she said. "I'm very happy about what we've done. I'm sore, I guess, but I'm happy."

Upon their approach to the park gate, procession participants followed the truck into a closed-off section for private burial rites for the remains and artifacts.

Following the ceremonies, participants gathered for acknowledgments of the work that went into the event. An emotional Sando, whose voice halted occasionally during his speech, said Saturday's reburial symbolized a new beginning for the Jemez people.

"Our ancestors and other tribes who were born here, played here, sang and danced along this beautiful Pecos River valley and mountain, who were taken away for so many years, are now home," Sando said. "I guarantee to all of you that they are joyously happy, as we all are."

Reclaiming the remains was a 15 long, quiet process for the tribe. In September 1991, then-Gov. Jose Toledo, other officials and tribal archaeologist William Whatley began formal meetings with the park service about returning the skeletal remains dug up in the 1910s and 1920s at the long-deserted pueblo. Their meetings began shortly after then-President George Bush signed the Native Amer-

ican Graves Protection and Repatriation Act of 1990 into law.

Tribal leaders pursued their goal with tribal and federal officials and museum representatives for nearly eight years, telling few outsiders of their efforts.

Last month, those efforts finally paid off.

"We have completed that journey," Gov. Gachupin said Saturday. "This may be a political victory for our people, and maybe for all Native American people throughout the country."

The remains had been kept for study at the Peabody Museum of Archaeology and Ethnology.

Michele Morgan, an associate of 20 osteology at Peabody, said that unlike some other acts of repatriation the museum is working on, no disputes arose as to the rightful owners of the "Pecos Collection."

"The Jemez case presents no real gray areas for us," Morgan said in a recent interview. The museum, mandated by federal law to return sections of its collection to the rightful Native American owners, also is compelled to ensure remains and artifacts go to the proper people.

"That's what can take more time than (we) or the tribes would sometimes like," Morgan added.

The eight years of work by the Jemez people, though, have yielded more than just the return of their ancestral remains, Sando said.

"It proves on a very large scale that Native Americans do have rights to the artifacts, objects and human remains that have been taken from their ancestral lands."

RESPOND ●

1. The readership of the *Albuquerque Journal* would certainly include many Native American and other readers supportive of the goal of the Pueblo of Jemez, but there would also likely be a significant number of readers who are not sympathetic to Native American claims. Although this article appeared on the front page of a daily newspaper, it may not necessarily assume a neutral stance on the event. Does Navrot take a position in this article? How do you know? Give evidence from the text to support your answer.

2. Compare Navrot's article with the preceding article on the same event published in the *Boston Globe*. Note that both articles quote Jemez official William Whatley; the Boston article identifies Whatley as "tribal preservation officer," while the Albuquerque article identifies him as "tribal archaeologist." (Whatley holds both offices, and both titles are accurate.) Why might each paper have chosen the single title that it did to identify Whatley? What are the denotative differences in meaning between the two titles? The connotative differences?

3. Anthropologist Christopher Ruff, who had used the Pecos remains for medical research, is quoted in the previous article as saying that "the repatriation of the bones [is] a 'significant loss to science'" (paragraph 16). Do you think the needs of science would ever prevail over Native Americans' right to own their ancestors' remains? (You'll likely find that this is not a simple "yes" or "no" situation.) Under what conditions, if any, would science have a legitimate claim to human remains? Within a certain time period after death? Whose remains? Would some types of research have more legitimate claims than others? **Write an essay** in which you propose research guidelines that would address these questions and argue for the adoption of your guidelines. What types of argument will you rely on to make your case? What authorities will you want to quote?

Use the criteria for assessing sources in Chapter 21 to determine if Navrot's article would be a good source for a paper on the repatriation of Native American remains. Would it be a good source for a paper on Jemez history? On the Peabody Museum?

LINK TO P. 412

The second cluster of arguments in this chapter deals with issues of intellectual property and, more specifically, **who owns words and ideas.** You've likely never given it much thought, but about 20 percent—one-fifth—of the price you paid for this textbook went to cover the cost of intellectual property—not just royalties paid to the book's authors but also permission fees paid to the authors, photographers, and artists to reprint the arguments you're analyzing. In fact, some texts and illustrations were not used in this book because the cost of using them—the price to be paid for reproducing the intellectual property—was simply too high.

The cluster begins with an excerpt from Charles C. Mann's essay "Who Will Own Your Next Good Idea?" The essay originally appeared in *The Atlantic Monthly* and serves as a quick overview of the sorts of issues associated with intellectual property. The second essay by Megan Elizabeth Murray, a law student at the time the piece was written, questions who owns the right to define the term *affirmative action*. Next comes a cartoon representing a very real conflict in the realm of intellectual property—the rights of musical artists and those of techno-savvy consumers who download music from the Internet. Peter Mandaville then examines how access to information technology is "changing the boundaries of religious knowledge" and reconfiguring the ownership of authority to interpret the religious tradition for Muslims.

The remainder of the cluster offers a case study in intellectual property by focusing on reactions to a court case involving the estate of Dr. Martin Luther King Jr. and the Columbia Broadcasting Service (CBS). Whereas CBS contends that Dr. King's "I Have a Dream" speech (reprinted in this book in Chapter 28) is in the public domain—that is, that anyone can reproduce the words without seeking permission or paying royalties—the King family contends that it is not and that CBS must pay the estate for its use of excerpts from the speech. Do King's words belong to the estate, or do they belong to us all—not merely in some abstract sense but in the very real sense that we can use them, even as the basis for seeking profit? We begin with Bill Rankin's "King's Speech: Who Owns Soul-Stirring Words?" from the *Atlanta Journal and Constitution*, which serves the city that in many ways claims Dr. King as its own. Rankin's discussion of the issue elicited a letter to the editor from Margaret Curtis, who argues that the King family does not own King's words. Ellen Goodman, the nationally syndicated columnist who regularly writes for the *Boston Globe* and whose column also appears in the *Journal and Constitution*, weighs in on the issue with "Who Owns Dr. King's Words?" Like Rankin's article, Goodman's column elicited a response, and Thomas Burnett disagrees with Goodman's position in his letter, which is titled "Promoting an Extreme Case of Sharing."

As all the readings in this cluster demonstrate, new technologies and new means of mechanically reproducing words, sounds, and images have brought a burgeoning interest in intellectual property: it's not just about plagiarism anymore.

Who Will Own Your Next Good Idea?

CHARLES C. MANN

> Some corporations want to lock up copyright even tighter. Some naive intellectuals want to abandon copyright altogether. Where is a "do-nothing" Congress now that we need one?

About twelve years ago I walked past a magazine kiosk in Europe and noticed the words *"temple des rats"* on the cover of a French magazine. Rat temple! I was amazed. A few months before, a friend of mine had traveled to northwestern India to write about the world's only shrine to humankind's least favorite rodent. The temple was in a village in the Marusthali Desert. That two Western journalists should have visited within a few months of each other stunned me. Naturally, I bought the magazine.

◀ Charles C. Mann wrote the article from which this excerpt was taken for the September 1998 issue of The Atlantic Monthly, *a magazine that offers in-depth coverage of current events, arts, politics, and technology. Mann explores issues surrounding copyrights, a U.S. institution established in the Constitution and now being complicated by recent technological developments. Every one of us has a large stake in how these issues of copyright are resolved—either as authors/ artists, or as readers and consumers, or often as both. As you read, think about what interest(s) Mann may be representing in this article.*

The article began with a Gallic tirade against the genus *Rattus*. *Le spectre du rat, le cauchemar d'humanité! Quel horreur!*—that sort of thing. Then came the meat: an interview, in Q&A form, with a "noted American journalist" who had just gone to the rat temple. The journalist, who was named, was my friend. No such interview had occurred: the article was a straight translation, with fake interruptions by the "interviewer" such as *"Vraiment?"* and *"Mon Dieu!"*

I was outraged. To my way of thinking, these French people had ripped off my friend. I telephoned him immediately; he had the same reaction. Expletives crackled wildly across the Atlantic. Reprinting his copyrighted article without permission or payment was the same, we decided, as kicking down his door and stealing his CD player.

We were wrong. Although the magazine had done my friend wrong, what was stolen was not at all like a CD player. CD players are physical property. Magazine articles are *intellectual* property, a different matter entirely. When thieves steal CD players, the owners no longer have them, and are obviously worse off.

But when my friend's writing was appropriated, he still had the 5 original manuscript. What, then, was stolen? Because the article had been translated, not one sentence in the French version appeared in the original. How could it be considered a copy? Anomalies like this are why intellectual property has its own set of laws.[1]

Intellectual property is knowledge or expression that is owned by someone. It has three customary domains: copyright, patent, and trademark (a fourth form, trade secrets, is sometimes included). Copyrighted songs, patented drugs, and trademarked soft drinks have long been familiar denizens of the American landscape, but the growth of digital technology has pushed intellectual property into new territory. Nowadays one might best define intellectual property as anything that can be sold in the form of zeroes and ones. It is the primary product of the Information Age. All three forms of intellectual property are growing in importance, but copyright holds pride of place. In legal terms, copyright governs the right to make copies of a given work. It awards limited monopolies to creators on their creations: for a given number of years no one but Walt Disney can sell Mickey Mouse cartoons without permission. Such monopolies, always valuable, are increasingly lucrative. For the past twenty years the copyright industry has grown almost three times as fast as the economy as a whole, according to the

International Intellectual Property Alliance, a trade group representing film studios, book publishers, and the like. Last year, the alliance says, copyrighted material contributed more than $400 billion to the national economy and was the country's single most important export.[2]

These figures may actually understate the value of copyright. Today it is widely believed that personal computers, cable television, the Internet, and the telephone system are converging into a giant hose that will spray huge amounts of data — intellectual property — into American living rooms. As this occurs, according to the conventional scenario, the economic winners will be those who own the zeroes and ones, not those who make the equipment that copies, transmits, and displays them. Because copyright is the mechanism for establishing ownership, it is increasingly seen as the key to wealth in the Information Age.

At the same time, the transformation of intellectual property into electronic form creates new problems. If the cost of manufacturing and distributing a product falls, economic forces will drive down its price, too. The Net embodies this principle to an extreme degree. Manufacturing and distribution costs collapse almost to nothing online:

What kind of figurative language is Mann using with his image of a giant hose? See Chapter 14 to help you find the answer.

LINK TO P. 288 ······································

zeroes and ones can be shot around the world with a few clicks of a mouse. Hence producers of digital texts, music, and films will have trouble charging anything at all for copies of their works—competitors can always offer substitutes for less, pushing the price toward the vanishing point.

In addition, creators must deal with piracy, which is vastly easier and more effective in the digital environment. People have long been able to photocopy texts, tape-record music, and videotape television shows. Such leakage, as copyright lawyers call it, has existed since the first day a reader lent a (copyrighted) book to a friend. With the rise of digital media, the leakage threatens to turn into a gush. To make and distribute a dozen copies of a videotaped film requires at least two videocassette recorders, a dozen tapes, padded envelopes and postage, and considerable patience. And because the copies are tapes of tapes, the quality suffers. But if the film has been digitized into a computer file, it can be E-mailed to millions of people in minutes; because strings of zeroes and ones can be reproduced with absolute fidelity, the copies are perfect. And online pirates have no development costs—they don't even have to pay for paper or blank cassettes—so they don't really have a bottom line. In other words, even as digital technology drives the potential value of copyright to ever greater heights, that same technology threatens to make it next to worthless.

This paradox has engendered two reactions. One is to advocate 10 eliminating copyright altogether. Led by a small but surprisingly influential cadre of libertarian futurists, anti-copyrightists believe that the increased ease of copying effectively obviates the © symbol and all it entails. "Information wants to be free"—a phrase apparently coined by the writer Stewart Brand—is the apothegm° of choice here. In this view, copyright restricts what people can do with the intellectual property coming through the wires. Futilely but dangerously, it tries to fence the electronic frontier. It unjustly creates monopolies in the basic commodity of the Information Age. It is a relic of the past and should be expunged.

The other, opposing reaction is to strengthen the hand of copyright owners. Realizing the growing economic import of copyright, Congress is rapidly trying to overhaul the nation's intellectual-property regime. The changes would give copyright owners more control for longer times; some would make it a crime to work around copyright-protection

apothegm: a short, pithy saying.

schemes. A different tack is being taken by state governments, which may bypass copyright altogether by amending the laws governing sales contracts. If they succeed, copyright owners will be able to ask individual customers to agree to contracts regulating the zeroes and ones flowing into their homes. *Before we send this vintage episode of Sein-feld to your computer, please read the following conditions and terms, paying careful attention to the clauses that forbid taping or replaying the program even once. After you click "OK," the transmission will start.*

Because I make much of my living from copyright, I find the to-and-fro fascinating, and have a vested interest in the results. But issues bigger than the financial status of writers are involved. Copyright is the regulatory authority for the marketplace of ideas. It lays out the economic ground rules to create the hubbub of debate that the Founders believed necessary for democracy—one reason that they included copyright in the Constitution (Article I, Section 8, instructs Congress to "secur[e] for limited Times to Authors and Inventors the exclusive Right to their Respective Writings and Discoveries"). Copyright law allows Michael Jackson to make a fortune from the Beatles catalogue, and Bill Gates to add to his untold wealth by licensing electronic reproductions of the photographs of Ansel Adams. But its real purpose is to foster ever more ideas and ever more innovation from ever more diverse sources. When, in 1790, George Washington asked Congress to enact copyright legislation, he argued that it would increase the national stock of knowledge. And knowledge, he said, is "the surest basis of public happiness."

Today the marketplace of ideas is being shaken up by the competing demands of technology, finance, and law. Large sums of money are at stake. Change seems inevitable. One way or another, we will lay a new institutional foundation for literary culture in the United States. How we do it will play a big role, according to the logic of the Founders, in determining our future well-being. It would be comforting to believe that decisions will be made thoughtfully and well. But little evidence suggests this is true. Indeed, we may be heading into a muddle that it will take us a long time to escape.

NOTES

1. A translation is not a copy? Could anyone believe this? In 1853 Harriet Beecher Stowe sued to stop an unauthorized German translation of *Uncle*

Tom's Cabin — and lost. Copyright, ruled Judge Robert Grier, applies only to the "precise words." Calling a translation "a copy of the original," he opined, is "ridiculous." Only in 1870 did Congress include translations in the Copyright Act.

2. "Most people do not realize the extent to which copyright pervades their lives," says L. Ray Patterson, a professor at the University of Georgia School of Law and the author of a standard history of copyright. "They get their education from copyrighted books, they get their news from copyrighted papers and TV programs, they get their jobs from copyrighted want ads, they get their entertainment from copyrighted music and motion pictures — every aspect of life is affected by the law of copyright."

RESPOND.

1. Mann suggests two thumbnail definitions of *intellectual property* in paragraph 6—the traditional "knowledge or expression that is owned by someone," and the more current "anything that can be sold in the form of zeroes and ones." What kind of definition does each one represent—a formal definition, an operational definition, or a definition by example? What are the fundamental differences between Mann's two definitions? Are they mutually exclusive? Do you think one definition is more accurate than the other? Why or why not?

2. Although Mann has a strong personal stake in the outcome of the copyright debate (as he notes in paragraph 12), he doesn't take a clear position in this article. Why might he have chosen not to do so?

3. Two of the hottest intellectual property issues in the country since the last edition of this book in 2001 have both involved events on college campuses. The first was downloadable music, and the other involved having copies of software for which one doesn't have a license. In responding to these situations, some schools have blocked access to certain Internet music sites while others have confiscated students' computers and punished those found to have unlicensed software. (One reason we have no readings on either of these subjects is that the events and court rulings continue to occur so rapidly that any article we'd have included would have been hopelessly out of date by the time you read these words.) Using the Internet, investigate one of these cases; then, **write an essay** in which you evaluate the arguments used by each side. Mann's discussion of the issues should help you clarify your thinking.

4. How the copyright debate is ultimately resolved will depend in part on a determination of what constitutes intellectual property. Using the guidelines in Chapter 9 for developing arguments of definition, **write an essay** in which you draw the boundaries of intellectual property as you see them. (Your responses to question 1 will likely help you get started.)

▶ *The following essay by Megan Elizabeth Murray is from* The Diversity Hoax *(1999), a collection of essays written by students at Boalt Hall, the law school at U. C. Berkeley, during the troubled year following the passage of Proposition 209 forbidding affirmative action in admissions. Of particular interest in this piece is Murray's reminder that public debates can take place in the most private of places—bathroom stalls.*

News from the Ladies' Room

MEGAN ELIZABETH MURRAY

This piece was written from my heart. It is not prize-winning writing. It is not first-rate storytelling. It is how I feel, poured out onto paper with little editing. It is the true experience of a second-year Boalt Hall student.

Diversity. What a joke. Webster's dictionary defines diversity as, "quality, state, fact, or instance of being different or dissimilar; varied." Boalt diverse? Not even close. On the biggest issue facing the university today, affirmative action, only one voice is heard. That is the voice of the tyrannical few.

Boalt is the most homogenous place I have been. Everywhere I look I see signs and stickers about the racist regime of Proposition 209. In every class I hear how each and every regulatory scheme is racist—even organ transplant distribution schemes (how dare they prefer donees with the same blood type?). Half the student body wears T-shirts that say "Educate, Don't Segregate." I do not believe a word of it. Yet, I virtually never speak up. Why is that? I am one of the most outspoken people around. I have never shied away from making outrageous remarks. I am the one who will shout out that the emperor is wearing no clothes. But for some reason, I stay silent at Boalt. I stay silent because the atmosphere is so hostile. I stay silent because the arguments are irrational.

The latest sign posted talks about declining minority admissions to the school. It says, and I really do quote, "No more of this shit." This is what is hanging in my face when I go to check my mailbox at school. The only thing I ever see in the weekly bulletin from the Dean's office to the students is that it is against school rules for anyone to remove such signs. There is never a word about the profanity or the attacking nature of the signs. So I get to walk around my own school with messages cursing about the racism of school policies. Of course, these same signs make no mention of the decline in applications for minorities. It is awfully hard to get admitted if you do not apply. However, I know that if I put up a sign mentioning that, it would be torn down in a heartbeat, and no one would do a thing about it.

There are other signs. There are ones referring to 209 as "racist legislation" and implying that all of us who voted for it are racist. Slap an ugly label like that on us, combine it with an irrational refusal to listen to opposing arguments, and none of us are going to speak.

The stickers have to be the best, though. In every bathroom stall, on   5 almost every locker, and in all kinds of odd places, like the middle of walls, there are stickers again calling Proposition 209 racist, and rallying to support affirmative action. Stickers are not removed nearly as easily as posters. Believe me. I have tried. I have never been one to criticize others for speaking. All year I have fought the urge to tear these signs and posters and stickers off the walls. My feeling has been that it is everyone's prerogative to speak how they please. After many months it finally got to me, though, and I tried to take a sticker off the stall door in a bathroom. Forget it. They will have to be sanded off, literally.

I gave up for a while after that. I decided it was my conscience telling me it was the wrong thing to do. It was not my place. So I dropped it. A few weeks later, though, I got really steamed. In a stall, someone had partially torn off a sticker. It left a white sheet of backing paper behind. Someone had written on that sheet, "Affirmative action is racism." The next person had scribbled over it. What right did that person have, I thought, to cross it out? My whole philosophy of leaving everything behind had been premised on the belief that we all have a right to speak, but here the very people whose rights I was trying to respect were not respecting the rights of others. So, I stooped as low as I ever have. I wrote on the leftover sticker. I could not believe I did it, because I am one of those goody two-shoes who would never vandalize or deface property. I suppose I justified it by thinking that I only wrote on the sticker, not the wall. I still felt guilty, though. I did. I do not anymore.

What I wrote was, "You can't ignore the truth by scratching it out. Affirmative action is racism." I checked back a few weeks later. Someone had written, and again, I apologize for the profanity, "You fucking idiot! Prop. 209 allows the racist regime to continue." I stopped feeling guilty right then and there. Why have I been so careful in respecting the rights of people whose arguments consist of name-calling and

profanity? I suddenly felt obligated to respond. Maybe that is what they wanted. I do not know. All I know is that suddenly, writing on the leftover sticker on a bathroom wall was not vandalism. It was almost a right I had to respond to being torn down.

So, I wrote back. First, I circled "fucking idiot" and wrote, "Brilliant," next to it. Then I went to the end of the last woman's message and wrote, "NO. Giving one race preference over another is RACISM." I used up the sticker on that message. I have not heard back. Maybe she feels the same way I do about vandalizing the wall. Maybe she can only bring herself to write on the sticker, too. Maybe I should bring in a new sticker. I would feel terrible about sticking it on in the first place though. They don't come off.

My bathroom experience sums up my frustration with the lack of true diversity at Boalt. How can we call the school diverse when a segment of the population speaks out only in bathroom stalls? This school touts itself as one of the best in the country. How can that be when students are not truly free to speak and share ideas? How can meaningful intellectual discourse take place when every word is chosen so carefully so as not to offend? It cannot. How can a school claim to be one of the best when no meaningful discourse takes place? It cannot. Those of us who believe in Proposition 209, who believe that racial preference is racist, and who are proud card-carrying Republicans lurk about in the shadows. We are not holding rallies, wearing T-shirts, or posting profanity-filled signs. Yet we are here. You would not know it from listening in classes or reading posters around school, but we are here. True diversity can only come about if we come out of the stalls and show our faces.

RESPOND •

1. What is Murray's thesis? How does she go about supporting it? Specifically, what sorts of arguments among students at Boalt Hall does she cite to support her claim about the intolerance of diversity at Berkeley Law School? How do you respond to this argument? Does it surprise or shock you, for example? Does it make you laugh or shake your head in disbelief? Why or why not?

2. What sort of ethos does Murray attempt to create for herself in this essay? How does that ethos contribute to or detract from her thesis?

3. Murray describes an interesting kind of debate—one that is public but anonymous, taking place in college rest rooms via graffiti written on the stalls. What are the features or characteristics of effective graffiti arguments in men's or women's rest rooms? How does the physical situation influence the criteria for effective argument? Why, according to Murray, do some arguments take place only via bathroom graffiti? Is this fact good or bad? Why?

4. **Write an essay** in which you compare and contrast the values espoused by Murray in this reading and by Gordon Marino in "Me? Apologize for Slavery?" (p. 806). (Note that you can only make assumptions about Marino's views on affirmative action in college admissions policy and Murray's stance on White America's need to apologize for slavery, but you can come to some conclusions about how the two authors espouse very similar—and very different—values in these readings.)

5. Murray's essay raises complicated questions about who "owns" words—that is, who has the right to define them, especially in public discourse. Her specific example involves defining "racism" (or, you might want to argue, "diversity"), but the meanings of many words in American society are hotly contested, as with "equality," "Christian," "patriotism," "fair," and "Democrat" (to list only five). Dictionaries are little help here because what ultimately matters is how people use the word, especially in public discourse. **Write an essay** examining and evaluating the competing definitions for one such word. Like many complex arguments, your essay will involve aspects of a definition essay because you must delineate the different meanings assigned to the word you choose by various groups. Ultimately, the major purpose of the essay will be evaluative because you will be demonstrating why one of the ways the term is used in public debate is preferable to others.

"Wow, thanks. I'm a big fan. I've downloaded all your stuff."

RESPOND.

1. What makes this cartoon humorous? What argument(s) is it making?

2. Have you ever considered downloading music as an intellectual property issue? What are the intellectual property issues in downloading a song—from the perspective of the downloader? The owner of the Web site providing the songs? The recording company? The recording artist? Research the pros and cons of downloading intellectual property using an Internet search engine, and **write an essay** in which you argue for or against the practice of downloading. (If you have not read the excerpt from Charles C. Mann's "Who Will Own Your Next Good

Digital Islam:
Changing the Boundaries of Religious Knowledge?

PETER MANDAVILLE

The phenomenal popularization and transnational propagation of communications and information technologies (hereafter referred to as IT) in recent years has generated a wide range of important questions in the context of Islam's sociology of knowledge. How have these technologies transformed Muslim concepts of what Islam is and who possesses the authority to speak on its behalf? Moreover, how are they changing the ways in which Muslims imagine the boundaries of the *umma*°?

   The book, pamphlet, and newsletter were taken up with urgency by Muslims in the nineteenth century in order to counter the threat posed to the Islamic world by European imperialism. The *'ulama*° were initially at the forefront of this revolution, using a newly expanded and more widely distributed literature base to create a much broader constituency for their teachings. An inevitable side-effect of this phenomenon, however, was the demise of their stranglehold over the production and dissemination of religious knowledge. Muslims found it increasingly easy to bypass formally-trained religious scholars in the search for authentic Islam and for new ways of thinking about their religion. The texts were in principle now available to anyone who could read them; and to read is, of course, to interpret. These media opened up new spaces of religious contestation where traditional sources of authority could be challenged by the wider public. As literacy rates began to climb almost exponentially in the twentieth century, this effect was amplified even further. The move to print technology hence meant not only a new method for transmitting texts, but also a new idiom of selecting, writing and presenting works to cater to a new kind of reader.[1]

   Contemporary Muslims have been speculating about the utility of electronic information technology in the organization of religious knowledge for some time now. Abdul Kadir Barkatulla, director of London's Islamic Computing Centre, explains that he first became

◀ This essay examines how information technology is changing the ways Muslims understand their faith. It asks who owns the interpretation of religious texts, a question that might be asked of any religious community. As it demonstrates, Muslim believers, like those of all religions, seek to understand the meanings of their faith as the world continues to change. This essay first appeared as the cover story in the March 1999 issue of the ISIM Bulletin, the quarterly newsletter of the International Institute of the Study of Islam in the Modern World, located in Leiden, the Netherlands. Peter Mandaville, at that time a lecturer in international relations in the Department of Politics and International Relations at the University of Kent, Canterbury, United Kingdom, currently teaches at George Mason University in Virginia. As you read, consider the various ways in which Muslim communities interpret their sacred texts and what each assumes about the ownership of ideas and interpretation.

umma: the community or nation of Muslim believers

'ulama: religious scholars (plural of *'alim*)

hadith: the recorded sayings of the Prophet Mohammad

tafsir: tradition of commentary on the Qur'an across the centuries

fiqh: Islamic jurisprudence, that is, Islamic law

attracted to computer-mediated data storage in his capacity as a scholar of *hadith,*° a field which involves the archiving and retrieval of thousands upon thousands of textual references. The CD-ROM has provided an invaluable medium for his work. The entire Qur'an (including both text and recitation) along with several collections of *hadith*°, *tafsir*°, and *fiqh*° can easily fit on a single disc. Barkatulla sees this development as having the greatest relevance for those Muslims who live in circumstances where access to religious scholars is limited, such as in the West. For him, such CD-ROM selections offer a useful alternative. "IT doesn't change the individual's relationship with his religion," he says, "but rather it provides knowledge supplements and clarifies the sources of information such that Muslims can verify the things they hear for themselves." Barkatulla sees IT as a useful tool for systematizing religious knowledge, but—crucially—only pre-existing juridical opinions. In his terms, IT is only for working with knowledge that has already been "cooked," and not for generating new judgements. There are, however, those who disagree with him. Sa'ad al-Faqih, for example, leader of the London-based "Movement for Islamic Reform in Arabia" and another keen advocate of information technology, believes that the average Muslim can now revolutionize Islam with just a basic understanding of Islamic methodology and a CD-ROM. In his view, the technology goes a long way to bridging the "knowledge gap" between an *'alim*° and a lay Muslim by placing all of the relevant texts at the fingertips of the latter. "I am not an *'alim,*" he

'alim: religious scholar (literally, 'knowing, learned'; plural *'ulama*)

Does Mandaville assume that you share certain values with him? How do you know? Chapter 3 discusses how writers establish credibility by highlighting shared values.

···LINK TO P. 56

says, "but with these tools I can put together something very close to what they would produce when asked for a *fatwa°*."

fatwa: formal legal opinion issued by Muslim religious scholars

That is certainly not to say, however, that the 'ulama have been entirely marginalized. In fact, some religious scholars have become quite enthusiastic about computer technology themselves. "Traditional centers of Islamic learning (such as al-Azhar in Cairo and Qom in Iran) did not respond to the opportunities offered by IT for about ten years," Barkatulla observes, "but now they are forced to." He alludes to something like a "race to digitize Islam" among leading centers of religious learning around the world. Because the modern religious universities have developed comprehensive information systems, the more conservative, traditional institutions are now forced to respond in kind in order to keep up with the times. At the Center for Islamic Jurisprudence in Qom, Iran, several thousand texts, both Sunni and Shi'i, have been converted to electronic form. While Sunni institutions tend to ignore Shi'i texts, the Shi'a centers are digitizing large numbers of Sunni texts in order to produce databases which appeal to the Muslim mainstream, and hence capture a larger share of the market for digital Islam.

Neither has the rise of electronic "print Islam" eradicated the saliency of the oral tradition. Electronic media are as adept with sound as they are with the written word. Certainly we have heard much about the role of audio cassettes in Iran's Islamic revolution, where recordings of Khomeini's sermons were smuggled over from his Neauphle-le-Chateau headquarters near Paris and, much to the Shah's dismay, widely distributed in Iran. The Friday sermon, or *khutba*, is today recorded at many mosques throughout the Muslim world and the distribution of these recordings along with addresses by prominent ideologues, consciously emulating the rhetoric of influential modern Muslim thinkers such as Sayyid Qutb, Ali Shariati, and Abu'l Ali Mawdudi, serves to politicize Islam before an audience of unprecedented proportions. Recordings of sermons by dissident Saudi 'ulama, such as Safar al-Hawali and Salman al-'Awda, also circulate widely both inside and outside the Kingdom, and this marks the first time that material openly critical of the Saudi regime has been heard by relatively large sections of that country's population. The website of a London-based Saudi opposition group has also made Salman al-'Awda's sermons available over the Internet using the latest audio streaming technology.[2] "Now that media technology is increasingly able to deal with other symbolic modes," notes the anthropologist Ulf Hannerz, "we may wonder whether imagined communities are increasingly moving beyond words."[3]

It is perhaps on the Internet, however, that some of the most interesting things are happening. Can we meaningfully speak today about the emergence of new forms of Islamic virtual community? To begin with, we need to make sure that we have a more nuanced understanding of those Muslim identities which use the Internet. We cannot start talking about new forms of diasporic° Muslim community simply because many users of the Internet happen to be Muslims. Noting that in many instances Muslim uses of the Internet seem to represent little more than the migration of existing messages and ideas into a new context, Jon Anderson rightfully warns that "new talk has to be distinguished from new people talking about old topics in new settings."[4] Yet we also have to acknowledge the possibility that the hybrid discursive spaces of the Muslim Internet can give rise, even inadvertently, to new formulations and critical perspectives on Islam and the status of religious knowledge. As regards notions of political community in Islam, there is also the Internet's impact on "center-periphery" relations in the Muslim world to be examined. A country such as Malaysia, usually considered to be on the margins of Islam both in terms of geography and religious influence, has invested heavily in information and networking technologies. As a result, when searching on the Internet for descriptions of programs which offer formal religious training, one is far more likely to encounter the comprehensive course outlines provided by the International Islamic University of Malaysia than to stumble across the venerable institutions of Cairo, Medina, or Mashhad.

It is usually amongst the diasporic Muslims of the Western world that we find the Internet being appropriated for political purposes. The American media has recently been full of scare-mongering about "radical fundamentalists" who use the United States as a fundraising base for their overseas operations. Reports often cite the Internet as a primary tool for the dissemination of propaganda by Islamic militants. A more sober examination of the situation, however, reveals that very few of the Muslim groups who have a presence on the Internet are involved in this sort of activity. Moreover, there are also those who argue that the Internet has actually had a moderating effect on

diasporic: those (here Muslims) who have been dispersed or spread (here, across the Western world, having once been concentrated in places where Islam was the dominant religion)

Islamist discourse. Sa'ad al-Faqih, for example, believes that Internet chat rooms and discussion forums devoted to the debate of Islam and politics serve to encourage greater tolerance. He believes that in these new arenas one sees a greater convergence in the center of the Islamist political spectrum and a weakening of its extremes.

Thus, for the overwhelming majority of Muslims who seek Islam online, the Internet is a forum for the conduct of politics *within* their religion. In the absence of sanctioned information from recognized institutions, Muslims are increasingly taking religion into their own hands. Through various popular newsgroups and e-mail discussion lists, Muslims can solicit information about what "Islam" says about any particular problem. Not only that, notes al-Faqih, "but someone will be given information about what Islam says about such and such and then others will write in to correct or comment on this opinion/ interpretation." Instead of having to go down to the mosque in order to elicit the advice of the local *mullah°*, Muslims can also now receive supposedly "authoritative" religious pronouncements via the various e-mail *fatwa* services which have sprung up in recent months. The Sheikhs of al-Azhar are totally absent, but the enterising young *mullah* who sets himself up with a colorful website in Alabama suddenly becomes a high-profile representative of Islam for a particular constituency.[5] Due to the largely anonymous nature of the Internet, one can also never be sure whether the "authoritative" advice received via these services is coming from a classically-trained religious scholar or an electrical engineer moonlighting as an amateur *'alim*.

mullah: Muslim religious scholar specializing in the interpretation of Islamic law and theology (used chiefly in parts of the Muslim world where Persian, Turkish, and Urdu are spoken)

More than anything else, the Internet and other information technologies provide spaces where diasporic Muslims can go in order to find others "like them." It is in this sense that we can speak of the Internet as allowing Muslims to create a new form of imagined community, or a re-imagined *umma*. The Muslim spaces of the Internet hence offer a reassuring set of symbols and a terminology which attempt to reproduce and recontextualize familiar settings and terms of discourse in locations far remote from those in which they were originally embedded. As has become apparent, the encounter between Islam and the transnational technologies of communication is as multifaceted as the religion itself. The rise of IT has led to considerable intermingling and dialogue between disparate interpretations of what it means to be "Islamic" and the politics of authenticity which inevitably ensue from this also serve to further fragment traditional sources of authority, such that the locus of "real" Islam and the identity of those who are permitted to speak on its behalf become ambiguous. This, in many ways, is an Islam with a distinctly modern, or perhaps even *post*-modern ring to it. The vocabulary here is eclectic, combining soundbites of religious knowledge into novel fusions well suited to complex, transnational contexts. Most importantly, the changing connotations of authority and authenticity in digital Islam appear to be contributing to the critical re-imagination of the boundaries of Muslim politics.

NOTES

1. Geoffrey Roper (1995), "Faris al-Shidyaq and the Transition from Scribal to Print Culture in the Middle East," in: George N. Atiyeh (ed.), *The Book in the Islamic World: The Written Word and Communication in the Middle East,* Albany: SUNY Press, 1995, p. 210.
2. See http://www.miraserve.com/
3. Ulf Hannerz (1996), *Transnational Connections: Culture, People, Places,* London: Routledge, p. 21.
4. Jon Anderson (1996), "Islam & the Globalization of Politics." Paper presented to the Council on Foreign Relations Muslim Politics Study Group, New York City, June 25, 1996, p. 1.
5. Some of these sites are registering several thousand hits per day. Their users are often "nomadic," spending several days or weeks in one discussion forum before moving on to populate another site.

RESPOND •

1. Although this essay is largely informative in purpose, we can say that it offers an argument about how information technology is changing the ways in which Muslims understand the nature of their community, or *umma*. Which specific technologies does Mandaville discuss, and what are the consequences of each for questions of interpretation—and thus the "ownership"—of religious authority?

2. In what ways does this article demonstrate the diversity of Islamic thought? Of Muslims' responses to technology, on the one hand, and to the modern world, on the other?

3. How does Mandaville develop his argument? You'll want to read each paragraph carefully, examining it to see how the author is using it to contribute to his main point. Also consider how he links paragraphs together. In answering this question, you should produce a sentence outline for the article, with one or two sentences for each paragraph. Your sentence for the paragraph beginning "The book, pamphlet, and newsletter," paragraph 1 of the article, might read like this one: "In paragraph 1, Mandaville uses historical information to show how nineteenth-century Muslim leaders used the available print technology to fight against European colonialism; one effect of this action was to create new opportunities for Muslims to interpret religious texts for themselves." (Note that this technique is a good one for understanding texts that you find difficult at first.)

4. Using the information provided about where this article first appeared and the text itself, whom do you imagine to be Mandaville's intended readers? Who are his invoked readers? How can we determine his invoked readers by carefully examining his text—what it does (and does not) say about Islam and how Mandaville presents his argument. (Chapter 3 discusses intended and invoked readers.)

5. If you consider yourself to be a member of a religious community, **write an essay** in which you define how members of that local community create interpretations of its texts and traditions. In other words, how do members of the community distinguish between "good" and "bad" (or "true" or "false") interpretations? Who "owns" the authority to offer interpretations? To evaluate them? If you do not consider yourself a member of a religious community, interview someone who is to find out her or his understanding of how processes of interpretation work in that community, and **write an essay** based on what you learn.

▼ *The next four arguments all appeared in 1999, between May 12 and May 20, in the* Atlanta Journal and Constitution, *the largest-circulation daily newspaper in the city where the Martin Luther King Jr. Center for Non-violent Social Change is located. All four texts deal with a then-pending federal appeals court case to determine who owns the rights to King's famous 1963 "I Have a Dream" speech (p. 811). The first article, by Bill Rankin, appeared as a front-page news story. Margaret Curtis's letter to the editor responded to Rankin's article. The third piece, "Who Owns Dr. King's Words?" was written by nationally syndicated columnist Ellen Goodman. Thomas Burnett's letter to the editor responds to Goodman's column. As you read, try to determine what the central issues of the controversy are and to consider the extent to which the four authors bring other issues into the debate. In July 2000, CBS and the King family reached an agreement so that both parties can use the speech. CBS agreed to make a contribution of an undisclosed amount to the King Center and to provide the estate with footage for its own use. The settlement does not, however, resolve the issue of who ultimately owns King's words.*

King's Speech
Who Owns Soul-Stirring Words?

BILL RANKIN

When the Rev. Martin Luther King Jr. spoke to a divided nation from the steps of the Lincoln Memorial more than 35 years ago, he wanted his oratory to reach as many people as possible.

His "I Have a Dream" speech, climaxing the March on Washington, not only ignited a crowd of more than 200,000 people on the Washington Mall, it was broadcast live to millions of television viewers. But today the family of the slain civil rights leader is waging a court battle to control the rights to King's legacy, including the famous Aug. 28, 1963, speech.

Before the 11th U.S. Circuit Court of Appeals in Atlanta on Tuesday, a lawyer for the family asked a three-judge panel to rule that the rights to the speech belong to King's estate and should not be used by others who want to profit from it. The lawsuit by the King estate against CBS News was dismissed by a district court, which said King forfeited his rights to the speech because it was widely disseminated. It could be several months before the appeals panel decides, but it is not a debate that is likely to fade.

"This is more than an argument of free speech vs. copyright law. It is a battle over who will profit from one of the most widely quoted pieces of this century's oratory," said David Garrow, a King historian and Emory University professor.

The First Amendment and copyright claims set forth in the suit 5

by CBS and the King estate, respectively, are "the kind of case in which an historian can laugh at the arguments made by both sides," he said.

CBS is accused in the pleadings of also profiting from the speech by licensing the use of its archival film at rates of up to $2,500 per minute.

Garrow added, "If the Kings are able to successfully beat up on CBS, which may deserve it a little, the end result of a King victory could be to further restrict and constrict public access to King's work."

That is not the intention of the Kings or the Martin Luther King Jr. Center for Nonviolent Social Change, said Dexter Scott King, the center president.

"We're simply following my father's conduct and trying to respect his wishes and intent," he said outside the courthouse. "My father's actions and his conduct were to protect the speech. He filed for many copyrights for his works. This is a very important case."

King's widow, Coretta Scott King, 10 sat with her son on the front row of the courtroom during Tuesday's hourlong arguments.

Over the past few years, the King family has moved aggressively to protect King's legacy. It has brought a lawsuit to prevent companies from using King's image on refrigerator magnets. It lost a lawsuit in 1993 seeking to remove thousands of

King's personal papers from his alma mater, Boston University, and bring them back to Atlanta.

Henry Hampton, who produced "Eyes on the Prize," the public television series on the civil rights movement, was sued and later settled with the King estate. When USA Today reprinted the "I Have a Dream" speech in 1993 to mark the 30th anniversary of the March on Washington, it, too, was sued and also settled with the family.

By holding the copyrights, the family can prevent the misuse of King's works, said Ray Patterson, a copyright law professor at the University of Georgia. If the court rules the "I Have a Dream" speech is in the public domain, anyone could use the speech for any purpose, he said.

Nine minutes — or 62 percent — of the speech were broadcast in "The 20th Century with Mike Wallace," a documentary that CBS produced in 1994 with the cable network Arts & Entertainment. The documentary, in which the civil rights movement was featured in one segment, was broadcast and sold as a boxed set by A&E.

The King family filed suit against 15 CBS in November 1996, saying the network infringed upon the family's copyright. But in a ruling last summer, U.S. District Judge William O'Kelley dismissed the lawsuit.

"As one of the most public and most widely disseminated speeches in history, it could be the poster child for general publications," O'Kelley wrote.

Many of the key passages in "I Have a Dream" — about 600 words that are among the most quoted — were not in the advance text given to reporters. The trademark "I have a dream" phrase and the thoughts that follow from it were not in that text, nor were the passages introduced with "let freedom ring." It is the use of these specific words, among others, that has prompted the King family to sue organizations that reprint or replay them without their permission.

Newspaper articles like this one often incorporate quotations. See Chapter 21 for a guide to the proper form and procedure for using quotations in your work.

·······················LINK TO P. 418

Kings Don't Own Words

On first hearing the Rev. Martin Luther King's "I Have a Dream" speech, my startled reaction was, "God is speaking through that man!" I have no problem with the King family's desire to prosper ("King's speech: Who owns soul-stirring words?" Page One, May 12). Blacks have too long been denied a fair reward for their labor, but trying to copyright King's speech is like trying to copyright the Bible, from which much of his speech is borrowed. Even the phrase "let freedom ring" did not originate with him. How can the speech be divided into which part was his invention and which was not? More important, any attempt to copyright and profit from that speech trivializes and dishonors something many believe is sacred.

– Margaret Curtis

Curtis is a homemaker living in Vinings.

Joseph Beck, a King family lawyer, told the federal appeals court Tuesday that King registered the speech with the U.S. Copyright Office a month after giving the speech and also successfully sued a company in 1964 that sought to sell tapes of the speech in its entirety.

"His conduct shows an attitude to protect his work," Beck said. Simply giving the speech to such a large audience also did not cause the copyright to be forfeited, Beck said, adding, "When someone makes a speech in public, one doesn't have to stand up and say, 'All rights reserved.'"

During the hearing, Judges Lanier Anderson III and Paul Roney expressed concern that King had allowed an advance copy of his speech to be handed out to the news media and that the Southern Christian Leadership Council, of which King was president, later reprinted the entire speech in its newsletter, without listing any copyright protection.

"It's hard for me to believe that Dr. King didn't know what was in that newsletter . . . when the speech itself was published in its entirety," Anderson said. "It would have only been a matter of courtesy . . . to make sure it's all right with him, would it not?"

Beck said he believes that King did not authorize the publication in the newsletter. As for the advance text, the most well-known passages of the speech were not in it because they were in King's extemporaneous remarks, Beck added, noting that CBS broadcast 90 percent of the ad-libbed portion in the A&E program.

The newsletter shows King did not move to protect his copyright of the speech, Floyd Abrams, a lawyer for CBS, told the court.

After the hearing, Beck responded sharply to questions as to whether the King family is seeking to profit from King's legacy.

The King family routinely provides the speech free for use by schools, but CBS charges as much as $2,500 a minute for its broadcast rights to the speech, he said. "Let's talk about who's being greedy here," he said.

CBS, which taped and broadcast the "I Have a Dream" speech, licenses segments or "clips" of the speech. . . . The network charges $2,500 a minute for the clips to private entities and $1,000 a minute to churches, schools and other non-profits.

Who Owns Dr. King's Words?

ELLEN GOODMAN

At first it sounds like a question for a panel of philosophers: Who owns a dream? What happens when a vision that's formed in the words of one person is released like a balloon into the air to be shared with everyone? Whose property is it then?

The dream in this case was described by Martin Luther King Jr. Standing before a crowd of 200,000 at the Lincoln Memorial on that August day in 1963, he found the language to match the moment. "I Have a Dream," he told the country in a speech that became a part of our collective eloquence, as much a part of our heritage as the Gettysburg Address.

Dr. King had a gift. Now people are wrangling over the value of that gift.

Today the question of dreamers and owners, words and property, history and money, has been set before a

Coretta Scott King, widow of Martin Luther King Jr.

panel of three judges in Atlanta. The King family is asking an appeals court to rule that CBS must pay them to use the dream speech in a documentary sold on videotape. They claim that they — not the public — own Dr. King's words.

> ## "He had a gift. Now people are wrangling over the value of it."

For years, the King family has been protective or litigious — choose one or the other. They sued and settled with Henry Hampton, who produced the "Eyes on the Prize" documentary. They sued and settled with USA Today. They regard themselves as keepers of the legacy . . . and the accounting books.

In 1963, no one would have believed there was money to be made from civil rights history. In his lifetime Dr. King was interested in justice, not profit. His family at times lived on the salary of a $6,000-a-year minister. He contributed everything, even his Nobel Prize money, to the Southern Christian Leadership Conference.

When Dr. King was assassinated, the sum total of his estate was a $50,000 insurance policy bought for

him by Harry Belafonte. That, plus his words.

These words are what the family lawyers call "intellectual property." It's property that will soon be worth an estimated $50 million from multimedia deals, licensing, and real estate.

I do not mean to suggest that the family is in the protection racket solely for the money. Schools are granted the use of the "Dream Speech" freely. At the same time, one of the many lawsuits was against a company that wanted to use Dr. King's image on refrigerator magnets.

It's not surprising that the family would resist the trivialization of a man's magnetism into a refrigerator magnet. It's far too easy in our culture to slip from being a martyr on a pedestal to a pop icon on a T-shirt.

While we are talking about King and commercialism, it is fair to ask the difference between the family profit — much of which goes to the Center for Nonviolent Social Change in Atlanta — and CBS's profit.

But nevertheless there is still the little matter of public history and private property.

In the appeals court, the case will not be decided on the grounds of greed but of copyright law and free speech. On the one hand Dr. King gave the press advance copies of the speech; on the other hand, the most eloquent passages were extemporaneous. On the one hand he copyrighted

Promoting an Extreme Case of Sharing

If syndicated columnist Ellen Goodman is not a Democrat, she would make a good one ("Who Owns Dr. King's Words?"). She wants to take something owned by a private party (the King family) and convert it to public use — without paying for it, of course. If Goodman owned the rights to something worth $50 million, would she give it to the public?

– Thomas R. Burnett

Burnett, of Chamblee, is an environmental engineer.

the speech after it was given; on the other hand he characterized it as "a living petition to the public and the Congress."

Those of us who work with words for a living understand the desire to control our ephemeral "product." We are sensitive to the notion of intellectual property and do not take kindly to bootlegged editions of CDs or books or software that show up on black markets.

But Martin Luther King Jr. was 15 not a rock star. Or a software de-

signer. He was a preacher, a leader, a prophet, a martyr. He was, in every sense of the word, a public figure.

One day, 36 years ago, he gave voice to our collective idealism and words to our best collective yearnings: "I have a dream that my four little children will one day live in a nation where they will not be judged by the color of their skin but by the content of their character."

This is not a private dream. It doesn't belong to his family estate. It belongs to all of us.

Why does Goodman use *our* and *us* at the end? See Chapter 3 for details on ways of using language to build common ground.

LINK TO P. 58

RESPOND●

1. The front-page news story by Rankin reports on a court case and gives some background information. Everything in the article is factual, and Rankin does not overtly display any particular point of view. Do you think the article is completely neutral? What evidence do you have for your conclusion? As a staff writer for the *Atlanta Journal and Constitution*, Rankin wrote this article expressly for an Atlanta audience. What features of Rankin's article reveal his awareness of a local audience?

2. In her letter to the editor, Curtis comments on selected elements of the case while ignoring others. Do you think she addresses the central issues of the controversy? Why or why not? What do you see as the central issues of the case? How does Curtis employ an argument of values in her letter? Do you think her argument is effective? Why or why not?

3. In his short letter, Burnett uses humor—sarcasm, in fact—to make his point. How does the humor contribute to his argument? Is it persuasive for you? Why or why not? How would not using humor have affected the effectiveness of Burnett's argument?

4. Goodman and Burnett both frame the controversy in terms of money and profit. Do you think this representation of the issue is an accurate one? Why or why not?

5. The *Atlanta Journal and Constitution* prints the occupation of its letter writers. Why might the paper want to include that information? Does occupational information about Curtis and Burnett influence your evaluation of the letters? Should it? Why or why not?

6. The three overtly opinion pieces—by Curtis, Goodman, and Burnett— approach the controversy as a conflict between the King estate and the public interest, with little consideration of CBS, the other party in the lawsuit. Goodman briefly mentions CBS once in her column in paragraph 11 while neither Curtis nor Burnett makes any reference to CBS at all. Why did these writers not discuss CBS? How, if at all, is the public interest involved in this case? Should "public interest" be used to resolve the controversy? Why or why not?

7. Professor David Garrow is cited in Rankin's article asserting, "This is more than an argument of free speech vs. copyright law. It is a battle over who will profit from one of the most widely quoted pieces of this century's oratory" (paragraph 4). Do you agree? Why or why not? Should the status of Dr. King, his role in American history, or the national significance of this speech be a factor in how the judge interprets the law? Why or why not? **Write an essay** in which you explore the role that the literary, social, or historical importance of a work might or should play in arguments about ownership of intellectual property like "I Have a Dream."

8. Who should own Dr. King's words and why? All of his words or some of them? **Write an essay** responding to these questions. As you plan your essay, give special consideration to the kinds of arguments you use and to your reasons for using them.

chapter twenty-seven

Language(s) and Identities

Language isn't just a tool for communicating. It also works as a symbol we use to create identities for ourselves as individuals and as members of myriad social groups. The ways we use language, whether spoken, signed, or written, tell others who we are or want to be— and who we don't want to be mistaken for. Take a moment to list ten groups you belong to. Odds are that all these groups are in some way defined by the language they use.

The arguments in this chapter examine the topic of languages and identities from many perspectives. The questions raised here ask you to consider the roles that language in general and specific varieties of language in particular play in how you tell the world who you are and how you want to be perceived. The chapter begins with several arguments that consider the connection between language and identity. Is there a link between patriotism and the way you speak English? Should bilingualism be encouraged in the United States? Are laws mandating signs in English good or bad—and for whom? Can a person come to be proud of speaking many different "Englishes"—or other language varieties? What do attitudes Americans hold about Ebonics tell us about ourselves and our society? About what we do and don't know about the history of American English? Do women and men use language differently? Does it matter? What role has language played in creating "America"?

The second half of the chapter offers a cluster of readings about being bilingual in the United States. Now, more than at any time in the recent past, our country has many bilinguals, whether immigrants born elsewhere or bilinguals growing up here in immigrant families or in traditionally bilingual communities. These readings provide a sample of the experiences of bilinguals who claim America as their home.

"Don't believe everything you think." Or so states one of our favorite bumper sticker arguments. The arguments in this chapter should challenge you to recognize—and reexamine—some of your assumptions about language and identity, yours and everyone else's.

www.
For additional readings on **Language(s) and Identities,** visit bedfordstmartins.com /everythingsanargument.

▶ *This pledge was distrib-uted by the Chicago Women's Club American Speech Com-mittee to the schoolchildren of the city in 1918.*

Pledge for Children

CHICAGO WOMEN'S CLUB

I love the United States of America. I love my country's flag. I love my country's language. I promise:

1. That I will not dishonor my country's speech by leaving off the last syllables of words.

2. That I will say a good American "yes" and "no" in place of an Indian grunt "um-hum" and "nup-um" or a foreign "ya" or "yeh" and "nope."

3. That I will do my best to improve American speech by avoiding loud, rough tones, by enunciating clearly, and by speaking pleasantly, clearly, and sincerely.

4. That I will learn to articulate correctly as many words as possible during the year.

Not all arguments based on values are as overt as this one. See examples of more subtle arguments in Chapter 5.

···LINK TO P. 78

RESPOND •

1. What sorts of arguments are being made by this pledge? In other words, how is Americanness defined in general? With respect to lan-guage use in particular? According to the pledge, how does the "ideal American," or the American who loves his or her country, speak?

2. According to the criteria of the pledge, do you qualify as an "ideal American"? Does that trouble you in any way? Why or why not? How do you think you'd respond if you'd been given such a pledge as, say, an eighth grader? Why?

3. Consider the table on p. 703, which presents statistics about immi-grants in Chicago in 1900, 1910, 1920, and 1990. At the time the pledge was issued, many of the immigrants living in Chicago had come from

Germany, Austria, Poland, and Russia and, to a far lesser extent, Ireland, Sweden, and Italy. Upon arrival, they were generally poor and uneducated. How do these figures, along with the 1918 pledge, construct an argument? What, specifically, is the argument?

Immigrants in Chicago

Year	Population	Foreign Born	Foreign-born Stock*
1900	1,698,575	35%	77%
1910	2,185,283	36%	78%
1920	2,701,705	30%	72%
1990	2,783,726	17%	Not Available

*Foreign-born stock = Immigrants from other countries and their U.S.-born children.

4. **Write an essay** analyzing the goals of the pledge in the historical context of the census data presented. Is the pledge, for example, a case of forensic, epideictic, or deliberative rhetoric? Why?

▼ *Ariel Dorfman teaches literature and Latin American studies at Duke University. One of his books,* Heading South, Looking North: A Bilingual Journey *(1998), which appeared in both English and Spanish, expands on issues raised in this piece. The essay reprinted here originally appeared in the* New York Times *in June 1998.*

If Only We All Spoke Two Languages

ARIEL DORFMAN

DURHAM, N.C.—Ever since I came to settle in the United States 18 years ago, I have hoped that this nation might someday become truly multilingual, with everyone here speaking at least two languages.

I am aware, of course, that my dream is not shared by most Americans: if the outcome of California's referendum on bilingual education earlier this month is any indication, the nation will continue to stubbornly prefer a monolingual country. California voters rejected the bilingual approach—teaching subjects like math and science in the student's native language and gradually introducing English. Instead, they approved what is known as the immersion method, which would give youngsters a year of intensive English, then put them in regular classrooms.

The referendum was ostensibly about education, but the deeper and perhaps subconscious choice was about the future of America. Will this country speak two languages or merely one?

The bilingual method, in spite of what its detractors claim, does not imprison a child in his or her original language. Rather, it keeps it alive in order to build bridges to English. The immersion method, on the other hand, wants youngsters to cut their ties to the syllables of their past culture.

Both methods can work. I should know. I have endured them both. But my experience was unquestionably better with bilingual education. 5

I first suffered the immersion method in 1945 when I was 2½ years old. My family had recently moved to New York from my native Argentina, and when I caught pneumonia, I was interned in the isolation ward of a Manhattan hospital. I emerged three weeks later, in shock from having the doctors and nurses speak to me only in English, and didn't utter another word in Spanish for 10 years.

That experience turned me into a savagely monolingual child, a xenophobic all-American kid, desperate to differentiate himself from Ricky Ricardo° and Chiquita Banana.° But

Ricky Ricardo: the husband of Lucy in *I Love Lucy,* a TV series in the 1950s. In real life, Lucille Ball (1911–1989), who played Lucy, and Desi Arnez (1917–1986), who played Ricky, were married from 1940 to 1960. Arnez had immigrated to the United States at age 16 from Cuba.

Chiquita Banana: a brand of banana; the reference here is to commercials from the 1950s that included a dancing banana and/or a woman, both wearing large-brimmed hats full of fruit. See and hear them at <chiquita.com/discover /media/origjingle.wav>.

when my family moved to Chile in 1954, I could not continue to deny my heritage. I learned Spanish again in a British school in Santiago that used the gradualist method. Thus I became a bilingual adolescent.

Later, during the ideologically charged 1960's, I foolishly willed myself to become monolingual again, branding English as the language of an imperial power out to subjugate Latin America. I swore never to speak or write in English again. The 1973 military coup in Chile against the democratically elected Government of Salvador Allende Gossens sent me into exile—and back into the arms of English, making me into this hybrid creature who now uses both languages and writes a memoir in English and a play in Spanish as if it were the most ordinary thing to do.

I have developed a linguistic ambidexterity that I will be the first to admit is not at all typical. Even so, it is within reach of others if they start early enough, this thrilling experience of being dual, of taking from one linguistic river and then dipping into the other, until the confluence of the two vocabularies connects distant communities. This is an experience I wish all Americans could share.

Or maybe I would be satisfied if 10 voters in this country could understand that by introducing children from other lands to the wonders of English while leaving all the variety

---

Bilingualism as a bridge to other cultures.

---

and marvels of their native languages intact, the American experience and idiom are fertilized and fortified.

If people could realize that immigrant children are better off, and less scarred, by holding on to their first languages as they learn a second one, then perhaps Americans could accept a more drastic change. What if every English-speaking toddler were to start learning a foreign language at an early age, maybe in kindergarten? What if these children were to learn Spanish, for instance, the language already spoken by millions of American citizens, but also by so many neighbors to the South?

Most Americans would respond by asking why it is necessary at all to learn another language, given that the rest of the planet is rapidly turning English into the lingua franca of our time. Isn't it easier, most Americans would say, to have others speak to us in our words and with our grammar? Let them make the mistakes and miss the nuances and subtleties while we occupy the more powerful and secure linguistic ground in any exchange.

But that is a shortsighted strategy. If America doesn't change, it will find itself, let's say in a few hundred years, to be a monolingual nation in a world that has become gloriously multilingual. It will discover that acquiring a second language not only gives people an economic and political edge, but is also the best way to understand someone else's culture, the most stimulating way to open your life and transform yourself into a more complete member of the species.

No tengan miedo. Don't be afraid.

Your children won't be losing 15 Shakespeare. They'll just be gaining Cervantes.

Dorfman is obviously making a proposal argument, but how good is it as a proposal? Use the criteria under "Developing Proposals" in Chapter 12 to decide.

LINK TO P. 243

RESPOND •

1. What event motivated Dorfman to write this essay? What seems to be his ultimate argument: that the United States should be multilingual (or encourage multilingualism), that it should be bilingual (or encourage bilingualism), or that it should become bilingual in English and Spanish (or encourage such bilingualism)? What evidence can you provide for your position?

2. What experiences led to Dorfman's bilingualism? How are his experiences similar to or different from those of the typical immigrant to the United States? Why is this question in particular important when thinking about generalizing Dorfman's experiences to other situations?

3. Supporters of the California referendum on bilingual education would likely argue that immigrants are free to speak, use, and pass on to their children any languages other than English that they might speak but that they should not expect publicly funded schools to teach their children these languages. Does Dorfman anticipate or respond in any way to this criticism? If he does not, why not? Can an argument that does not address the concerns of those taking an opposing view still be effective? Give reasons for your answer.

4. Those who write about bilingual education distinguish among three types of programs: *transitional programs,* which seek to help children make the transition from the home language to the school language as quickly as possible; *maintenance programs,* which seek to produce bilinguals able to speak and write both the language of the school and that of the home community; and *enrichment programs,* which enable students who already speak the language of the school to learn a second language that they (or their parents) believe will be of use to them. (Legally mandated bilingual programs in the United States are transitional programs.) **Write an essay** evaluating the advantages and disadvantages of each of the three kinds of programs for the individual, the community, and the society. (Note that you are not being asked to support bilingual education for this or any other country; rather, you're being asked to evaluate objectively the different kinds of bilingual programs.)

Mute in an English-Only World

CHANG-RAE LEE

When I read of the troubles in Palisades Park, N.J., over the proliferation of Korean-language signs along its main commercial strip, I unexpectedly sympathized with the frustrations, resentments and fears of the longtime residents. They clearly felt alienated and even unwelcome in a vital part of their community. The town, like seven others in New Jersey, has passed laws requiring that half of any commercial sign in a foreign language be in English.

Now I certainly would never tolerate any exclusionary ideas about who could rightfully settle and belong in the town. But having been raised in a Korean immigrant family, I saw every day the exacting price and power of language, especially with my mother, who was an outsider in an English-only world.

In the first years we lived in America, my mother could speak only the most basic English, and she often encountered great difficulty whenever she went out.

We lived in New Rochelle, N.Y., in the early 70's, and most of the local businesses were run by the descendants of immigrants who, generations ago, had come to the suburbs from New York City. Proudly dotting Main Street and North Avenue were Italian pastry and cheese shops, Jewish tailors and cleaners and Polish and German butchers and bakers. If my mother's marketing couldn't wait until the weekend, when my father had free time, she would often hold off until I came home from school to buy the groceries.

Though I was only 6 or 7 years old, she insisted that I go out shopping with her and my younger sister. I mostly loathed the task, partly because it meant I couldn't spend the afternoon playing catch with my friends but also because I knew our errands would inevitably lead to an awkward scene, and that I would have to speak up to help my mother. 5

I was just learning the language myself, but I was a quick study, as children are with new tongues. I had spent kindergarten in almost complete silence, hearing only the high nasality of my teacher and

◄ Chang-rae Lee is author of Native Speaker (1995), a powerful novel about language as a locus of identity, especially for immigrants and their children, in which the protagonist, a Korean American, tries to make sense of who he is—and isn't. In "Mute in an English-Only World," which was published on the op-ed page of the New York Times in 1996, Lee writes of his mother's experience as a nonnative speaker of English, using her situation to offer an unexpected perspective on a Palisades Park law requiring that commercial signs be written at least half in English.

Do you think Lee's article is an example of an argument from the heart? Check out Chapter 4 to find out exactly what such arguments are—and aren't.

LINK TO P. 65 ···

Tim Bower

comprehending little but the cranky wails and cries of my classmates. But soon, seemingly mere months later, I had already become a terrible ham and mimic, and I would crack up my father with impressions of teachers, his friends and even himself. My mother scolded me for aping his speech, and the one time I attempted to make light of hers I rated a roundhouse smack on my bottom.

For her, the English language was not very funny. It usually meant trouble and a good dose of shame, and sometimes real hurt. Although she had a good reading knowledge of the language from university classes in South Korea, she had never practiced actual conversation. So in America, she used English flashcards and phrase books and watched television with us kids. And she faithfully carried a pocket workbook illustrated with stick-figure people and compound sentences to be filled in.

But none of it seemed to do her much good. Staying mostly at home to care for us, she didn't have many chances to try out sundry words and phrases. When she did, say, at the window of the post office, her readied speech would stall, freeze, sometimes altogether collapse.

One day was unusually harrowing. We ventured downtown in the new Ford Country Squire my father had bought her, an enormous station wagon that seemed as long—and deft—as an ocean liner. We were shopping for a special meal for guests visiting that weekend, and my mother had heard that a particular butcher carried fresh oxtails— which she needed for a traditional soup.

We'd never been inside the shop, but my mother would pause 10 before its window, which was always lined with whole hams, crown roasts and ropes of plump handmade sausages. She greatly esteemed the bounty with her eyes, and my sister and I did also, but despite our desirous cries she'd turn us away and instead buy the packaged links at the Finast supermarket, where she felt comfortable looking them over and could easily spot the price. And, of course, not have to talk.

But that day she was resolved. The butcher store was crowded, and as we stepped inside the door jingled a welcome. No one seemed to notice. We waited for some time, and people who entered after us were now being served. Finally, an old woman nudged my mother and waved a little ticket, which we hadn't taken. We patiently waited again, until one of the beefy men behind the glass display hollered our number.

My mother pulled us forward and began searching the cases, but the oxtails were nowhere to be found. The man, his big arms crossed, sharply said, "Come on, lady, whaddya want?" This unnerved her, and she somehow blurted the Korean word for oxtail, soggori.

The butcher looked as if my mother had put something sour in his mouth, and he glanced back at the lighted board and called the next number.

Before I knew it, she had rushed us outside and back in the wagon, which she had double-parked because of the crowd. She was furious, almost vibrating with fear and grief, and I could see she was about to cry.

She wanted to go back inside, but now the driver of the car we were 15 blocking wanted to pull out. She was shooing us away. My mother, who had just earned her driver's license, started furiously working the pedals. But in her haste she must have flooded the engine, for it wouldn't turn over. The driver started honking and then another car began honking as well, and soon it seemed the entire street was shrieking at us.

In the following years, my mother grew steadily more comfortable with English. In Korean, she could be fiery, stern, deeply funny and ironic; in English, just slightly less so. If she was never quite fluent, she gained enough confidence to make herself clearly known to anyone, and particularly to me.

Five years ago, she died of cancer, and some months after we buried her I found myself in the driveway of my father's house, washing her sedan. I liked taking care of her things; it made me feel close to her. While I was cleaning out the glove compartment, I found her pocket English workbook, the one with the silly illustrations. I hadn't seen it in nearly 20 years. The yellowed pages were brittle and dog-eared. She had fashioned a plain-paper wrapping for it, and I wondered whether she meant to protect the book or hide it.

I don't doubt that she would have appreciated doing the family shopping on the new Broad Avenue of Palisades Park. But I like to think, too, that she would have understood those who now complain about the Korean-only signs.

I wonder what these same people would have done if they had seen my mother studying her English workbook—or lost in a store. Would they have nodded gently at her? Would they have lent a kind word?

RESPOND•

1. Throughout the piece, Lee offers numerous insights into the strategies those who do not speak English well use to negotiate American society. List some of these strategies along with their consequences for people like Lee's mother and their loved ones.

2. One of the interesting things about this essay from a rhetorical perspective is the way in which Lee bucks reader expectations. Many readers would assume that the son of an immigrant, writing about his mother's struggles with English, would oppose a law mandating the use of English in signs. How and why does Lee challenge reader expectations? How does this use of his mother's experiences contribute to his ethos and authority?

3. Read Ariel Dorfman's essay, "If Only We All Spoke Two Languages" (p. 704), which also discusses bilingualism in American society. Then, **write a dialogue** representing the conversation Lee and Dorfman might have about bilingualism in the United States. Lee became bilingual because he grew up in an immigrant household while Dorfman learned English under different circumstances. What, if anything, might the authors share in terms of experience or stance? How and why might they differ? The conversation you construct should take the form of an argument—perhaps exploratory, perhaps antagonistic.

4. Lee's essay describes a series of events relating to language that were embarrassing for his mother (and, one imagines, sometimes for the author himself). **Write an essay** about an experience in your life when you were embarrassed by someone's use or misuse of a particular language. Reflecting on the experience, discuss what you learned from the experience about yourself and about language and identity.

Mother Tongue

AMY TAN

I am not a scholar of English or literature. I cannot give you much more than personal opinions on the English language and its variations in this country or others.

I am a writer. And by that definition, I am someone who has always loved language. I am fascinated by language in daily life. I spend a great deal of my time thinking about the power of language—the way it can evoke an emotion, a visual image, a complex idea, or a simple truth. Language is the tool of my trade. And I use them all—all the Englishes I grew up with.

Recently, I was made keenly aware of the different Englishes I do use. I was giving a talk to a large group of people, the same talk I had already given to half a dozen other groups. The nature of the talk was about my writing, my life, and my book, *The Joy Luck Club.* The talk was going along well enough, until I remembered one major difference that made the whole talk sound wrong. My mother was in the room. And it was perhaps the first time she had heard me give a lengthy speech—using the kind of English I have never used with her. I was saying things like, "The intersection of memory upon imagination" and "There is an aspect of my fiction that relates to thus-and-thus"—a speech filled with carefully wrought grammatical phrases, burdened, it suddenly seemed to me, with nominalized forms, past perfect tenses, conditional phrases—all the forms of standard English that I had learned in school and through books, the forms of English I did not use at home with my mother.

Just last week, I was walking down the street with my mother, and I again found myself conscious of the English I was using, the English I do use with her. We were talking about the price of new and used furniture and I heard myself saying this: "Not waste money that way." My husband was with us as well, and he didn't notice any switch in my English. And then I realized why. It's because over the twenty years we've been together I've often used that same kind of English with him, and sometimes he even uses it with me. It has become our language of intimacy, a different sort of English that relates to family talk, the language I grew up with.

So you'll have some idea of what this family talk I heard sounds like, I'll quote 5 what my mother said during a recent conversation which I videotaped and then transcribed. During this conversation, my mother was talking about a political gangster in Shanghai who had the same last name as her family's, Du, and how the gangster in his early years wanted to be adopted by her family which was rich by comparison. Later, the gangster became more powerful, far richer than my mother's family, and one day showed up at my mother's wedding to pay his respects. Here's what she said in part:

"Du Yusong having business like fruit stand. Like off the street kind. He is Du like Du Zong—but not Tsung-ming Island people. The local people call putong, the river east side, he belong to that side local people. That man want to ask Du Zong father take him in like become own family. Du Zong father wasn't look down on him, but didn't take seriously, until that man big like become mafia. Now important person, very hard to inviting him. Chinese way, came only to show respect, don't stay for dinner. Respect for making big celebration, he shows up. Mean gives lots of respect. Chinese custom. Chinese social life that way. If too important won't have to stay too long. He come to my wedding. I didn't see, I heard it. I gone to boy's side, they have YMCA dinner. Chinese age I was 19."

You should know that my mother's expressive command of English belies how much she actually understands. She reads the Forbes report, listens to Wall Street Week, converses daily with her stockbroker, reads all of Shirley MacLaine's books with ease—all kinds of things I can't begin to understand. Yet some of my friends tell me they understand fifty percent of what my mother says. Some say they understand eighty to ninety percent. Some say they understand none of it, as if she were speaking pure Chinese. But to me, my mother's English is perfectly clear, perfectly natural. It's my mother tongue. Her language, as I hear it, is vivid, direct, full of observation and imagery. That was the language that helped shape the way I saw things, expressed things, made sense of the world.

Lately, I've been giving more thought to the kind of English my mother speaks. Like others, I have described it to people as "broken" or "fractured" English. But I wince when I say that. It has always bothered me that I can think of no way to describe it other than "broken," as if it were damaged and needed to be fixed, as if it lacked a certain wholeness and soundness. I've heard other terms used, "limited English," for example. But they seem just as bad, as if everything is limited, including people's perception of the limited English speaker.

I know this for a fact, because when I was growing up, my mother's "limited" English limited my perception of her. I was ashamed of her English. I believed that

Tan's open, informal style may make you feel as if you are part of a conversation among friends, but her speech is carefully prepared in ways that casual conversation rarely is. See Chapter 17 to learn some of the techniques that Tan uses so effectively.

LINK TO P. 348 ·····················

her English reflected the quality of what she had to say. That is, because she expressed them imperfectly her thoughts were imperfect. And I had plenty of empirical evidence to support me: the fact that people in department stores, at banks, and at restaurants did not take her seriously, did not give her good service, pretended not to understand her, or even acted as if they did not hear her.

My mother has long realized the limitations of her English as well. When I was 10 fifteen, she used to have me call people on the phone to pretend I was she. In this guise, I was forced to ask for information or even to complain and yell at people who had been rude to her. One time it was a call to her stockbroker in New York. She had cashed out her small portfolio and it just so happened we were going to go to New York the next week, our very first trip outside California. I had to get on the phone and say in an adolescent voice that was not very convincing, "This is Mrs. Tan."

And my mother was standing in the back whispering loudly, "Why he don't send me check, already two weeks late. So mad he lie to me, losing me money."

And then I said in perfect English, "Yes, I'm getting rather concerned. You had agreed to send the check two weeks ago, but it hasn't arrived."

Then she began to talk more loudly, "What he want, I come to New York tell him front of his boss, you cheating me?" And I was trying to calm her down, make her be quiet, while telling the stockbroker, "I can't tolerate any more excuses. If I don't receive the check immediately, I am going to have to speak to your manager when I'm in New York next week." And sure enough, the following week there we were in front of this astonished stockbroker, and I was sitting there red-faced and quiet, and my mother, the real Mrs. Tan, was shouting at his boss in her impeccable broken English.

We used a similar routine just five days ago, for a situation that was far less humorous. My mother had gone to the hospital for an appointment, to find out about a benign brain tumor a CAT scan had revealed a month ago. She said she had spoken very good English, her best English, no mistakes. Still, she said, the hospital did not apologize when they said they had lost the CAT scan and she had come for nothing. She said they did not seem to have any sympathy when she told them she was anxious to know the exact diagnosis since her husband and son had both died of brain tumors. She said they would not give her any more information until the next time and she would have to make another appointment for that. So she said she would not leave until the doctor called her daughter. She wouldn't budge. And when the doctor finally called her daughter, me, who spoke in perfect English—lo and behold—we had assurances the CAT scan would be found, promises that a conference call on Monday would be held, and apologies for any suffering my mother had gone through for a most regrettable mistake.

I think my mother's English almost had an effect on limiting my possibilities in life 15 as well. Sociologists and linguists probably will tell you that a person's developing language skills are more influenced by peers. But I do think that the language spoken in the family, especially in immigrant families which are more insular, plays a large role in shaping the language of the child. And I believe that it affected my results on achievement tests, IQ tests, and the SAT. While my English skills were never judged as poor, compared to math, English could not be considered my strong suit. In grade school, I did moderately well, getting perhaps *B*s, sometimes *B+*s in English, and scoring perhaps in the sixtieth or seventieth percentile on achievement tests. But those scores were not good enough to override the opinion that my true abilities lay in math and science, because in those areas I achieved *A*s and scored in the ninetieth percentile or higher.

This was understandable. Math is precise; there is only one correct answer. Whereas, for me at least, the answers on English tests were always a judgment call, a matter of opinion and personal experience. Those tests were constructed around items like fill-in-the blank sentence completion, such as "Even though Tom was _____, Mary thought he was _____." And the correct answer always seemed to be the most bland combinations of thoughts, for example, "Even though Tom was shy, Mary thought he was charming," with the grammatical structure "even though" limiting the correct answer to some sort of semantic opposites, so you wouldn't get answers like "Even though Tom was foolish, Mary thought he was ridiculous." Well, according to my mother, there were very few limitations as to what Tom could have been, and what Mary might have thought of him. So I never did well on tests like that.

The same was true with word analogies, pairs of words, in which you were supposed to find some sort of logical, semantic relationship—for example, "sunset" is to "nightfall" as _____ is to _____. And here, you would be presented with a list of four possible pairs, one of which showed the same kind of relationship: "red" is to "stoplight," "bus" is to "arrival," "chills" is to "fever," "yawn" is to "boring." Well, I could never think that way. I knew what the tests were asking, but I could not block out of my mind the images already created by the first pair, "sunset is to nightfall"—and I would see a burst of colors against a darkening sky, the moon rising, the lowering of a curtain of stars. And all the other pairs of words—red, bus, stoplight, boring—just threw up a mass of confusing images, making it impossible for me to sort out something as logical as saying: "A sunset precedes nightfall" is the same as "a chill precedes a fever." The only way I would have gotten that answer right would have been to imagine an associative situation, for example, my being disobedient and staying out past sunset, catching a chill at night, which turns into feverish pneumonia as punishment, which indeed did happen to me.

I have been thinking about all this lately, about my mother's English, about achievement tests. Because lately I've been asked, as a writer, why there are not more Asian-Americans represented in American literature. Why are there few Asian-Americans enrolled in creative writing programs? Why do so many Chinese students go into engineering? Well, these are broad sociological questions I can't begin to answer. But I have noticed in surveys—in fact, just last week—that Asian students, as a whole, always do significantly better on math achievement tests than in English. And this makes me think that there are other Asian-American students whose English spoken in the home might also be described as "broken" or "limited." And perhaps they also have teachers who are steering them away from writing and into math and science, which is what happened to me.

Fortunately, I happen to be rebellious in nature, and enjoy the challenge of disproving assumptions made about me. I became an English major my first year in college after being enrolled as pre-med. I started writing non-fiction as a freelancer the week after I was told by my former boss that writing was my worst skill and I should hone my talents toward account management.

But it wasn't until 1985 that I finally began to write fiction. And at first I wrote 20 using what I thought to be wittily crafted sentences, sentences that would finally prove I had mastery over the English language. Here's an example from the first draft of a story that later made its way into *The Joy Luck Club,* but without this line: "That was my mental quandary in its nascent state." A terrible line, which I can barely pronounce.

Fortunately, for reasons I won't get into today, I later decided I should envision a reader for the stories I would write. And the reader I decided upon was my mother, because these were stories about mothers. So with this reader in mind—and in fact, she did read my early drafts—I began to write stories using all the Englishes I grew up with: the English I spoke to my mother, which for lack of a better term, might be described as "simple"; the English she used with me, which for lack of a better term might be described as "broken"; my translation of her Chinese, which could certainly be described as "watered down"; and what I imagined to be her translation of her Chinese if she could speak in perfect English, her internal language, and for that I sought to preserve the essence, but not either an English or a Chinese structure. I wanted to capture what language ability tests can never reveal: her intent, her passion, her imagery, the rhythms of her speech and the nature of her thoughts.

Apart from what any critic had to say about my writing, I knew I had succeeded where it counted when my mother finished reading my book, and gave me her verdict: "So easy to read."

RESPOND ●

1. How have Tan's attitudes toward her mother's English changed over the years? Why? Have you had similar experiences with your parents or other older relatives?

2. Why, ultimately, is Tan suspicious of language ability tests? What are her complaints? What sorts of evidence does she offer? Do you agree or disagree with her argument? Why?

3. Tan's text was written to be read aloud by the author herself. In what ways might this fact be important? (You may wish to consult Chapter 17 on the features of spoken arguments.) What would it be like, for example, to have heard Tan deliver this text? How would such an experience have been different from reading it on the page? Had Tan written the piece to be read silently by strangers—as her novels are, for example—how might she have altered it? Why?

4. What does Tan mean when she claims that she uses "all the Englishes [she] grew up with"? What are these Englishes? What are her problems in giving them labels? Do you agree with Tan's implied argument that we should use all our Englishes and use them proudly? Why or why not? Are there any limits to this position? If so, what are they? **Write an essay** evaluating Tan's position. (In preparing for this assignment, you might think about the Englishes that you know and use. Do they all have recognizable names or convenient labels? Do you associate them with certain people or places or activities? What does each represent to you? About you? Do you have ambivalent feelings about any of them? Why?)

▶ *David D. Troutt is a professor at the Rutgers School of
Law at Newark and also
author of a collection of short
stories, The Monkey Suit
(1998), based on famous legal
cases involving African Americans. In this essay, he seeks
to analyze why the actions of
the Oakland school board
regarding Ebonics caused
such an uproar in Black and
non-Black communities. This
article originally appeared
in January 1997 in the Los
Angeles Times.*

Defining Who We Are in Society

DAVID D. TROUTT

When passing a controversial resolution to help black schoolchildren
learn standard English through Ebonics, the speech patterns many use
at home, the Oakland School District reminded the nation of what language means to us. It is our very beginning. Once we as toddlers are
given the gift of the communicating self, we can forever discover, learn
and expand in a world of common symbols.

Perhaps nothing defines us more than our linguistic skills; nothing
determines as much about where we can and cannot go. How we talk
may be the first—and last—clue about our intelligence and whether
we're trusted or feared, heard or ignored, admitted or excluded.

But we treat our fluency like property. Depending where we are,
our ability to speak in certain ways entitles us to access, membership
and social riches, such as employment or popularity. As a culture, the
greatest benefits go to those who write and speak in standard English,
ways identified by most of us as "white," specifically middle-class
white.

But participating in the benefits of communication doesn't require
being white. It only requires that people around us—wherever we
are—understand what we're saying. Ebonics merely validates the distinctive talk among people on a margin far from the majority's view of
competence and invites them in. It recognizes that a voice developed
amid inequality does not bespeak inferiority.

The problem with Ebonics is not that it will teach children what 5
they already know, which, as critics point out, would be silly. The problem is that its public acceptance might throw into question claims of
ownership to intelligence and belonging. After all, Ebonics is not as
much the language of blackness as it is the only dialect of persistently
poor, racially segregated people—the so-called black underclass. It is
the dumbness against which all smartness is measured. But if we
reached consensus that Ebonics is a real linguistic system born of difference whose use in schools may facilitate inclusion for children of
the excluded, we must deal frankly with the exclusion itself.

718

Ebonics therefore becomes a troubling measure of separation. For many whites, it measures the contradictions of colorblind convictions. For many blacks, Ebonics measures the complications of assimilation and the resiliency of shame.

The ridicule and disparagement on talk radio confirm why an Ebonics program makes sense. Many whites have used the issue as an opportunity to vent racist jokes ordinarily kept underground or in sports bars. Others invoke it in order to restrict black cultural influences, such as banning rap music or canceling TV shows in which black characters use slang.

Meanwhile, more serious mainstream criticism sees the colorblind vision of the republic at stake. Suddenly interested in the achievement of poor black schoolchildren, pundits, federal officials and policymakers unanimously condemn Ebonics for lowering standards. Inadvertently echoing English-only advocacy, they argue that Oakland's resolution would replace children's individuality with militant group identification and promote black "separatism." The Standard English language, they say, belongs to all of us.

Such hypocrisy is hard to beat. Of course, language, like intelligence, is no group's personal property. But despite the well-meaning ring of colorblind ideals, you cannot demand sameness of language while perpetuating segregated education. Privately, any master of the language will admit, the best thing you can do for your kids is get them into schools with the tiniest percentage of (poor) blacks. Thus, it is no coincidence that the public school districts experimenting with Ebonics have long been abandoned by white parents. In fact, many public schools are funded by property taxes, making direct the connection between residential and education segregation. This separatism is quite normal. It is how social advantages are reproduced. But you can't enjoy them at a distance and demand conformity, too.

Since the Supreme Court declared separate-but-equal school facili- 10 ties unconstitutional in Brown vs. Board of Education,° most urban school districts have become more, not less, segregated. Moreover, as wealth and resources develop the suburbs, the residential segregation that accompanies separate schooling has produced a degree of racial isolation among inner-city blacks that approaches complete homogeneity.

Brown v. Board of Education: landmark 1954 U.S. Supreme Court decision that declared segregated schooling unconstitutional and put an end to the doctrine of "separate but equal."

Notice how Troutt makes value-based arguments by invoking the authority of respected Black writers. Arguments based on values often work in combination with arguments based on character; see Chapters 5 and 6 for more on both kinds of argument.

························· LINK TO PP. 78 AND 88

Frederick Douglass: African American orator, autobiographer, and journalist (1818–1895), much involved in the abolitionist movement and considered by many to have been the most significant Black American writer and speaker of the nineteenth century.

To be sure, the Oakland resolution's description of Ebonics as a "primary" language was unfortunate. Such a language would not be English, and non-English cannot be criticized for being "bad English." It is enough that Ebonics has a distinct lexicon and grammatical rules that are spoken exclusively by some blacks. It then qualifies as a reliable measurement of the gulf between many poor blacks and the middle-class world where Standard English is spoken.

Recognition of this fact by sociolinguists and its application in school settings are at least three decades old. In addition to Los Angeles and Oakland, schools in Michigan, Texas and New York use what scholars call Black English Vernacular (BEV) as a teaching tool. The principle is hardly new: Begin teaching from where students are and bridge the familiar with the untried.

Another principle at work, however, is assimilation. If Ebonics measures distance, it also measures a closeness more successful blacks have to mainstream culture. Formally educated blacks who use both Standard English and Ebonics depending on social context, or "code switching," remain close to two worlds that seem at odds with each other. For white co-workers, they may introduce black English idioms into common parlance. Among less-assimilated family and friends, they may be ostracized for "talking white." As a result, they often both bemoan and boast of their bidialectalism. It is a mark of cross-cultural identification, involving a complicated mix of pride, achievement and lingering shame.

Jesse Jackson illustrated this when he immediately denounced the Oakland resolution as an "unacceptable surrender," then, soon after, changed his mind. His first reaction honored a long, revolutionary tradition of black educators teaching Standard English to children at a time when white institutions and hate groups forcibly and deliberately denied us the written and spoken language. Much of the NAACP's legacy—including the Brown decision—was built on such demands for access. It is not surprising, then, that its current director, Kweisi Mfume, denounced Ebonics by resurrecting the memory of Frederick Douglass,° the freed slave who taught himself to read five languages.

Jackson inherits that tradition of civil-rights leadership. He under- 15 stands how the social benefits of assimilation come primarily through language acquisition. Surely, he also recognizes a deep-seated shame many blacks feel at the persistent inability of less-advantaged blacks to cross over and speak both tongues. The public and institutional denigration of black speech patterns for so long contributes to an undeniable sense of stigma against which blacks from a variety of class backgrounds still struggle.

But in his second reaction, Jackson must have resolved that Ebonics does not dignify some shameful difference. If done right, it should validate, then transcend difference. This reaction also enjoys a long tradition in black culture, as illustrated by the diverse work of writers such as Zora Neale Hurston° and Amiri Baraka.° Many wrote powerfully in Standard English, only to return at times to black dialect and write just as beautifully there.

Although Ebonics may prove valuable in teaching underperforming black children Standard English, implementing Ebonics programs probably shouldn't be confused with bilingualism. This would create potential competition for scarce funds between blacks and students for whom English is not a primary language. Hopefully, we will find a better way than pitting outsiders against outsiders. There are important differences in the experience of a Guatemalan or Vietnamese third-grader, who returns from school to immigrant parents. The stigma may not result from associating her language with ignorance, but the unkindness is just as real.

Instead, the Ebonics debate should heighten our appreciation of differences among us, as well as the special difficulties faced by students on the margins, who, along with their families, are trying, against long odds, to belong.

Zora Neale Hurston: African American writer (1891–1960) who wrote novels and short stories as well as book-length folklore and anthropological studies of African American, Haitian, and Jamaican culture.

Amiri Baraka: African American writer, political activist, and theatrical director (1934–) especially known for his influence on Black American writers of the last third of the twentieth century who, following his example, proudly drew on their own cultural heritage.

RESPOND.

1. Troutt begins with the assertion that "[p]erhaps nothing defines us more than our linguistic skills" (paragraph 2). Throughout the rest of the essay, what evidence does he offer for such a strong assertion?

2. According to Troutt, how did the responses of Blacks and Whites to the Ebonics controversy differ? What were the origins and consequences of these differences? Again, what sorts of evidence does Troutt offer to support his position? How, specifically, does he use the example of Jesse Jackson to demonstrate the ambivalence of most African Americans toward Ebonics?

3. Troutt argues that American society is not exactly honest about Standard English. "As a culture, the greatest benefits go to those who write and speak in Standard English," but, according to Troutt, these "ways [of using language are] identified by most of us as 'white,' specifically middle-class white" (paragraph 3). At the same time, "[t]he Standard English language, they say, belongs to all of us" (paragraph 8). Does Standard English belong to everyone? To what extent is it linked implicitly or explicitly to issues of class and ethnicity (and perhaps other axes of social difference such as gender or region)? **Write an essay** in which you explore the ownership of Standard English.

▼ *John Rickford teaches linguistics and directs the Center for African American Studies at Stanford University. A native speaker of Guyanese Creole, Rickford has devoted much research to documenting the links among various Caribbean creoles and their links to the language used by African Americans. In this essay, which originally appeared in* Discover *in 1997, he explains how linguists look at Ebonics and why.*

Suite for Ebony *and* Phonics

JOHN RICKFORD

To James Baldwin, writing in 1979, it was "this passion, this skill . . . this incredible music." Toni Morrison, two years later, was impressed by its "five present tenses" and felt that "the worst of all possible things that could happen would be to lose that language." What these novelists were talking about was Ebonics, the informal speech of many African Americans, which rocketed to public attention a year ago this month after the Oakland School Board approved a resolution recognizing it as the primary language of African American students.

The reaction of most people across the country—in the media, at holiday gatherings, and on electronic bulletin boards—was overwhelmingly negative. In the flash flood of e-mail on America Online, Ebonics was described as "lazy English," "bastardized English," "poor grammar," and "fractured slang." Oakland's decision to recognize Ebonics and use it to facilitate mastery of Standard English also elicited superlatives of negativity: "ridiculous, ludicrous," "VERY, VERY STUPID," "a terrible mistake."

However, linguists—who study the sounds, words, and grammars of languages and dialects—though less rhapsodic about Ebonics than the novelists, were much more positive than the general public. Last January, at the annual meeting of the Linguistic Society of America, my colleagues and I unanimously approved a resolution describing Ebonics as "systematic and rule-governed like all natural speech varieties." Moreover, we agreed that the Oakland resolution was "linguistically and pedagogically sound."

Why do we linguists see the issue so differently from most other people? A founding principle of our science is that we describe *how* people talk; we don't judge how language should or should not be used. A second principle is that all languages, if they have enough speakers, have dialects—regional or social varieties that develop when people are separated by geographic or social barriers. And a third principle, vital for understanding linguists' reactions to the Ebonics controversy, is that all languages and dialects are systematic and rule-governed. Every human language and dialect that we have studied to date—and we have studied thousands—obeys distinct rules of grammar and pronunciation.

What this means, first of all, is that Ebonics is not 5 slang. Slang refers just to a small set of new and usually short-lived words in the vocabulary of a dialect or language. Although Ebonics certainly has slang words—such as *chillin* ("relaxing") or *homey* ("close friend"), to pick two that have found wide dissemination by the media—its linguistic identity is described by distinctive patterns of pronunciation and grammar.

723

But is Ebonics a different language from English or a different dialect of English? Linguists tend to sidestep such questions, noting that the answers can depend on historical and political considerations. For instance, spoken Cantonese and Mandarin are mutually unintelligible, but they are usually regarded as "dialects" of Chinese because their speakers use the same writing system and see themselves as part of a common Chinese tradition. By contrast, although Norwegian and Swedish are so similar that their speakers can generally understand each other, they are usually regarded as different languages because their speakers are citizens of different countries. As for Ebonics, most linguists agree that Ebonics is more of a dialect of English than a separate language, because it shares many words and other features with other informal varieties of American English. And its speakers can easily communicate with speakers of other American English dialects.

Yet Ebonics is one of the most distinctive varieties of American English, differing from Standard English — the educated standard — in several ways. Consider, for instance, its verb tenses and aspects. ("Tense" refers to *when* an event occurs, "aspect" to *how* it occurs, whether habitual or ongoing.) When Toni Morrison referred to the "five present tenses" of Ebonics, she probably had usages like these — each one different from Standard English — in mind:

1. He runnin. ("He is running.")
2. He be runnin. ("He is usually running.")
3. He be steady runnin. ("He is usually running in an intensive, sustained manner.")
4. He bin runnin. ("He has been running.")
5. He BIN runnin. ("He has been running for a long time and still is.")

In Standard English, the distinction between habitual or nonhabitual events can be expressed only with adverbs like "usually." Of course, there are also simple present tense forms, such as "he runs," for habitual events, but they do not carry the meaning of an ongoing action, because they lack the "-ing" suffix. Note too that "bin" in example 4 is unstressed, while "BIN" in example 5 is stressed. The former can usually be understood by non-Ebonics speakers as equivalent to "has been" with the "has" deleted, but the stressed BIN form can be badly misunderstood. Years ago, I presented the Ebonics sentence "She BIN married" to 25 whites and 25 African Americans from various parts of the United States and asked them if they understood the speaker to be still married or not. While 23 of the African Americans said yes, only 8 of the whites gave the correct answer. (In real life a misunderstanding like this could be disastrous!)

Word pronunciation is another distinctive aspect of dialects, and the regularity of these differences can be very subtle. Most of the "rules" we follow when speaking Standard English are obeyed unconsciously. Take for instance English plurals. Although grammar books tell us that we add "s" to a word to form a regular English plural, as in "cats" and "dogs," that's true only for writing. In speech, what we actually add in the case of "cat" is an *s* sound; in the case of "dog" we add *z*. The difference is that *s* is voiceless, with the vocal cords spread apart, while *z* is voiced, with the vocal cords held closely together and noisily vibrating.

Now, how do you know whether to add *s* or *z* to 10 form a plural when you're speaking? Easy. If the word ends in a voiceless consonant, like "t," add voiceless *s*. If the word ends in a voiced consonant, like "g," add voiced *z*. Since all vowels are voiced, if the word ends in a vowel, like "tree," add *z*. Because we spell both plural endings with "s," we're not aware that English speakers make this systematic difference every day, and I'll bet your English teacher never told you about voiced and voiceless plurals. But you follow the "rules" for using them anyway, and anyone who doesn't — for instance, someone who says "bookz" — strikes an English speaker as sounding funny.

One reason people might regard Ebonics as "lazy English" is its tendency to omit consonants at the ends of words—especially if they come after another consonant, as in "tes(t)" and "han(d)." But if one were just being lazy or cussed or both, why not also leave out the final consonant in a word like "pant"? This is not permitted in Ebonics; the "rules" of the dialect do not allow the deletion of the second consonant at the end of a word unless both consonants are either voiceless, as with "st," or voiced, as with "nd." In the case of "pant," the final "t" is voiceless, but the preceding "n" is voiced, so the consonants are both spoken. In short, the manner in which Ebonics differs from Standard English is highly ordered; it is no more lazy English than Italian is lazy Latin. Only by carefully analyzing each dialect can we appreciate the complex rules that native speakers follow effortlessly and unconsciously in their daily lives.

Who speaks Ebonics? If we made a list of all the ways in which the pronunciation and grammar of Ebonics differ from Standard English, we probably couldn't find anyone who always uses all of them. While its features are found most commonly among African Americans (*Ebonics* is itself derived from "ebony" and "phonics," meaning "black sounds"), not all African Americans speak it. The features of Ebonics, especially the distinctive tenses, are more common among working-class than among middle-class speakers, among adolescents than among the middle-aged, and informal contexts (a conversation on the street) rather than formal ones (a sermon at church) or writing.

The genesis of Ebonics lies in the distinctive cultural background and relative isolation of African Americans, which originated in the slaveholding South. But contemporary social networks, too, influence who uses Ebonics. For example, lawyers and doctors and their families are more likely to have more contact with Standard English speakers—in schools, work, and neighborhoods—than do blue-collar workers and the unemployed. Language can also be used to reinforce a sense of community. Working-class speakers, and adolescents in particular, often embrace Ebonics features as markers of African American identity, while middle-class speakers (in public at least) tend to eschew them.

Some Ebonics features are shared with other vernacular varieties of English, especially Southern white dialects, many of which have been influenced by the heavy concentration of African Americans in the South. And a lot of African American slang has "crossed over" to white and other ethnic groups. Expressions like "givin five" (slapping palms in agreement or congratulation) and "Whassup?" are so widespread in American culture that many people don't realize they originated in the African American community. Older, nonslang words have also originated in imported African words. *Tote*, for example, comes from the Kikongo word for "carry," *tota,* and *hip* comes from the Wolof word *hipi,* to "be aware." However, some of the distinctive verb forms in Ebonics— he run, he be runnin, he BIN runnin—are rarer or nonexistent in white vernaculars.

How did Ebonics arise? The Oakland School 15 Board's proposal alluded to the Niger-Congo roots of Ebonics, but the extent of that contribution is not at all clear. What we do know is that the ancestors of most African Americans came to this country as slaves. They first arrived in Jamestown in 1619, and a steady stream continued to arrive until at least 1808, when the slave trade ended, at least officially. Like the forebears of many other Americans, these waves of African "immigrants" spoke languages other than English. Their languages were from the Niger-Congo language family, especially the West Atlantic, Mande, and Kwa subgroups spoken from Senegal and Gambia to the Cameroons, and the Bantu subgroup spoken farther south. Arriving in an American milieu in which English was dominant, the slaves learned

English. But how quickly and completely they did so and with how much influence from their African languages are matters of dispute among linguists.

The Afrocentric view is that most of the distinctive features of Ebonics represent imports from Africa. As West African slaves acquired English, they restructured it according to the patterns of Niger-Congo languages. In this view, Ebonics simplifies consonant clusters at the ends of words and doesn't use linking verbs like "is" and "are"—as in,

> **Media uproar over Ebonics missed the point. What's really important is not what kind of language Ebonics isn't, but what kind it is.**

for example, "he happy"—because these features are generally absent from Niger-Congo languages. Verbal forms like habitual "be" and BIN, referring to a remote past, it is argued, crop up in Ebonics because these kinds of tenses occur in Niger-Congo languages.

Most Afrocentrists, however, don't cite a particular West African language source. Languages in the Niger-Congo family vary enormously, and some historically significant Niger-Congo languages don't show these forms. For instance, while Yoruba, a major language for many West Africans sold into slavery, does indeed lack a linking verb like "is" for some adjectival constructions, it has another linking verb for other adjectives. And it has *six* other linking verbs for nonadjectival constructions, where English would use "is" or "are." Moreover, features like dropping final consonants can be found in some vernaculars in England that had little or no West African influence. Although many linguists acknowledge continuing African influences in some Ebonics and American English words, they want more proof of its influence on Ebonics pronunciation and grammar.

A second view, the Eurocentric—or dialectologist—view, is that African slaves learned English from white settlers, and that they did so relatively quickly and successfully, retaining little trace of their African linguistic heritage. Vernacular, or non-Standard features of Ebonics, including omitting final consonants and habitual "be," are seen as imports from dialects spoken by colonial English, Irish, or Scotch-Irish settlers, many of whom were indentured servants. Or they may be features that emerged in the twentieth century, after African Americans became more isolated in urban ghettos. (Use of habitual "be," for example, is more common in urban than in rural areas.) However, as with Afrocentric arguments, we still don't have enough historical details to settle the question. Crucial Ebonics features, such as the absence of linking "is," appear to be rare or nonexistent in these early settler dialects, so they're unlikely to have been the source. Furthermore, although the scenario posited by this view is possible, it seems unlikely. Yes, African American slaves and whites sometimes worked alongside each other in households and fields. And yes, the number of African slaves was so low, especially in the early colonial period, that distinctive African American dialects may not have formed. But the assumption that slaves rapidly and successfully acquired the dialects of the whites around them requires a rosier view of their relationship than the historical record and contemporary evidence suggest.

A third view, the creolist view, is that many African slaves, in acquiring English, developed a pidgin language—a simplified fusion of English and African languages—from which Ebonics evolved. Native to none of its speakers, a pidgin is a mixed language, incorporating elements of its users' native languages but with less complex grammar and fewer words than either parent language. A pidgin language emerges to facilitate communication between speakers who do not share a language; it becomes a creole language when it takes root and becomes the primary tongue among its users. This often occurs among the children of pidgin speakers — the vocabulary of the language expands, and the simple grammar is fleshed out. But the creole still remains simpler in some aspects than the original languages. Most creoles, for instance, don't use suffixes to mark tense ("he walk*ed*"), plurals ("boy*s*"), or possession ("John*'s* house").

Creole languages are particularly common on the islands of the Caribbean and the Pacific, where large plantations brought together huge groups of slaves or indentured laborers. The native languages of these workers were radically different from the native tongues of the small groups of European colonizers and settlers, and under such conditions, with minimal access to European speakers, new, restructured varieties like Haitian Creole French and Jamaican Creole English arose. These languages do show African influence, as the Afrocentric theory would predict, but their speakers may have simplified existing patterns in African languages by eliminating more complex alternatives, like the seven linking verbs of Yoruba I mentioned earlier.

Within the United States African Americans speak one well-established English creole, Gullah. It is spoken on the Sea Islands off the coast of South Carolina and Georgia, where African Americans at one time constituted 80 to 90 percent of the local population in places. When I researched one of the South Carolina Sea Islands some years ago, I recorded the following creole sentences. They sound much like Caribbean Creole English today:

1. E. M. run an gone to Suzie house. ("E. M. went running to Suzie's house.")
2. But I does go to see people when they sick. ("But I usually go to see people when they are sick.")
3. De mill bin to Bluffton dem time. ("The mill was in Bluffton in those days.")

Note the creole traits: the first sentence lacks the past tense and the possessive form; the second sen-

tence lacks the linking verb "are" and includes the habitual "does"; the last sentence uses unstressed "bin" for past tense and "dem time" to refer to a plural without using an *s*.

What about creole origins for Ebonics? Creole speech might have been introduced to the American colonies through the large numbers of slaves imported from the colonies of Jamaica and Barbados, where creoles were common. In these regions the percentage of Africans ran from 65 to 90 percent. And some slaves who came directly from Africa may have brought with them pidgins or creoles that developed around West African trading forts. It's also possible that some creole varieties — apart from well-known cases like Gullah — might have developed on American soil.

This would have been less likely in the northern colonies, where blacks were a very small percentage of the population. But blacks were much more concentrated in the South, making up 61 percent of the population in South Carolina and 40 percent overall in the South. Observations by travelers and commentators in the eighteenth and nineteenth centuries record creole-like features in African American speech. Even today, certain features of Ebonics, like the absence of the linking verbs "is" and "are," are widespread in Gullah and Caribbean English creoles but rare or nonexistent in British dialects.

My own view is that the creolist hypothesis incorporates the strengths of the other hypotheses and avoids their weaknesses. But we linguists may never be able to settle that particular issue one way or another. What we can settle on is the unique identity of Ebonics as an English dialect.

So what does all this scholarship have to do with the Oakland School Board's proposal? Some readers might be fuming that it's one thing to identify Ebonics as a dialect and quite another to promote its usage. Don't linguists realize that nonstandard dialects are stigmatized in the larger society, and that Ebonics speakers who cannot shift to Standard

English are less likely to do well in school and on the job front? Well, yes. The resolution we put forward last January in fact stated that "there are benefits in acquiring Standard English." But there is experimental evidence both from the United States and Europe that mastering the standard language might be easier if the differences in the student vernacular and Standard English were made explicit rather than entirely ignored.

To give only one example: At Aurora University, outside Chicago, inner-city African American students were taught by an approach that contrasted Standard English and Ebonics features through explicit instruction and drills. After eleven weeks, this group showed a 59 percent reduction in their use of Ebonics features in their Standard English writing. But a control group taught by conventional methods showed an 8.5 percent increase in such features.

This is the technique the Oakland School Board was promoting in its resolution last December. The approach is not new; it is part of the 16-year-old Standard English Proficiency Program, which is being used in some 300 California schools. Since the media uproar over its original proposal, the Oakland School Board has clarified its intent: the point is not to teach Ebonics as a distinct language but to use it as a tool to increase mastery of Standard English among Ebonics speakers. The support of linguists for this approach may strike nonlinguists as unorthodox, but that is where our principles — and the evidence — lead us.   ∎

RESPOND •

1. In light of Rickford's argument, what do the following sentences from p. 727 mean: "Media uproar over Ebonics missed the point. What's really important is not what kind of language Ebonics isn't, but what kind it is"?

2. What are the three theories of the origins of Ebonics that Rickford discusses? How effectively does he summarize each theory? (In other words, how clear an idea do you have of what each theory argues?) What does he say are the strengths and weaknesses of each? How persuasive is he in arguing for the creolist view, given the evidence he offers? Do you think Rickford assumes you will agree with him? Why or why not?

3. As Rickford notes, linguists contend that they study language scientifically. Assuming they do, how much knowledge about language or linguistics do you find in the other pieces about Ebonics in this cluster? What, in your opinion, accounts for the fact that the knowledge claimed by linguists, as scientists, is generally absent from public debates about language?

4. What does Rickford's final sentence mean? How does it support his own position and that of other linguists? How does it indirectly criticize the negative responses to the Ebonics resolution summarized in paragraph 2 of the essay? **Write an essay** evaluating the evidence Rickford provides for taking a linguistically informed stance on Ebonics.

Rickford constructs his argument on a very emotionally loaded subject using evidence based on fact and reason — historical fact, statistics, and studies. Find out about other kinds of fact- and reason-based evidence in Chapter 7.

LINK TO P. 100

▶ *Deborah Tannen, a socio-*
linguist who teaches at
Georgetown University, is
the author of several popular
books, including the best-
selling You Just Don't Understand: Women and Men in
Conversation *(1990),* Talking
from 9 to 5: Women and
Men at Work *(1994), and*
The Argument Culture:
Stopping America's War of
Words *(1998); and numerous*
scholarly works. In this essay,
which appeared in 1991 in the
Chronicle of Higher Education, *a weekly newspaper that*
deals with issues of interest to
college and university admin-
istrators and faculty, she
applies some of her research
findings to classrooms, in-
cluding her own. Notice how
Tannen characterizes the
differences between female
and male conversational
styles and how she sees
evidence of these styles in
the college classroom.

Teachers' Classroom Strategies Should Recognize That Men and Women Use Language Differently

DEBORAH TANNEN

When I researched and wrote my latest book, *You Just Don't Understand: Women and Men in Conversation,* the furthest thing from my mind was reevaluating my teaching strategies. But that has been one of the direct benefits of having written the book.

The primary focus of my linguistic research always has been the language of everyday conversation. One facet of this is conversational style: how different regional, ethnic, and class backgrounds, as well as age and gender, result in different ways of using language to communicate. *You Just Don't Understand* is about the conversational styles of women and men. As I gained more insight into typically male and female ways of using language, I began to suspect some of the causes of the troubling facts that women who go to single-sex schools do better in later life, and that when young women sit next to young men in classrooms, the males talk more. This is not to say that all men talk in class, nor that no women do. It is simply that a greater percentage of discussion time is taken by men's voices.

The research of sociologists and anthropologists such as Janet Lever, Marjorie Harness Goodwin, and Donna Eder has shown that girls and boys learn to use language differently in their sex-separate peer groups. Typically, a girl has a best friend with whom she sits and talks, frequently telling secrets. It's the telling of secrets, the fact and the way that they talk to each other, that makes them best friends. For boys, activities are central: Their best friends are the ones they do things with. Boys also tend to play in larger groups that are hierarchical. High-status boys give orders and push low-status boys around. So boys are expected to use language to seize center stage: by exhibiting their skill, displaying their knowledge, and challenging and resisting challenges.

These patterns have stunning implications for classroom interaction. Most faculty members assume that participating in class discussion is a necessary part of successful performance. Yet speaking in a classroom is more congenial to boys' language experience than to girls', since it entails putting oneself forward in front of a large group of people, many of whom are strangers and at least one of whom is sure to judge speakers' knowledge and intelligence by their verbal display.

Another aspect of many classrooms that makes them more hos- 5 pitable to most men than to most women is the use of debate-like formats as a learning tool. Our educational system, as Walter Ong argues persuasively in his book *Fighting for Life* (Cornell University Press, 1981), is fundamentally male in that the pursuit of knowledge is believed to be achieved by ritual opposition: public display followed by argument and challenge. Father Ong demonstrates that ritual opposition—what he calls "adversativeness" or "agonism"—is fundamental to the way most males approach almost any activity. (Consider, for example, the little boy who shows he likes a little girl by pulling her braids and shoving her.) But ritual opposition is antithetical to the way most females learn and like to interact. It is not that females don't fight, but that they don't fight for fun. They don't *ritualize* opposition.

Anthropologists working in widely disparate parts of the world have found contrasting verbal rituals for women and men. Women in completely unrelated cultures (for example, Greece and Bali) engage in ritual laments: spontaneously produced rhyming couplets that express their pain, for example, over the loss of loved ones. Men do not take part in laments. They have their own, very different verbal ritual: a contest, a war of words in which they vie with each other to devise clever insults.

When discussing these phenomena with a colleague, I commented that I see these two styles in American conversation: Many women bond by talking about troubles, and many men bond by exchanging playful insults and put-downs, and other sorts of verbal sparring. He exclaimed: "I never thought of this, but that's the way I teach: I have students read an article, and then I invite them to tear it apart. After we've torn it to shreds, we talk about how to build a better model."

This contrasts sharply with the way I teach: I open the discussion of readings by asking, "What did you find useful in this? What can we use in our own theory building and our own methods?" I note what I see as weaknesses in the author's approach, but I also point out that

the writer's discipline and purposes might be different from ours. Finally, I offer personal anecdotes illustrating the phenomena under discussion and praise students' anecdotes as well as their critical acumen.

These different teaching styles must make our classrooms wildly different places and hospitable to different students. Male students are more likely to be comfortable attacking the readings and might find the inclusion of personal anecdotes irrelevant and "soft." Women are more likely to resist discussion they perceive as hostile, and, indeed, it is women in my classes who are most likely to offer personal anecdotes.

A colleague who read my book commented that he had always taken 10 for granted that the best way to deal with students' comments is to challenge them; this, he felt it was self-evident, sharpens their minds and helps them develop debating skills. But he had noticed that women were relatively silent in his classes, so he decided to try beginning discussion with relatively open-ended questions and letting comments go unchallenged. He found, to his amazement and satisfaction, that more women began to speak up.

Though some of the women in his class clearly liked this better, perhaps some of the men liked it less. One young man in my class wrote in a questionnaire about a history professor who gave students questions to think about and called on people to answer them: "He would then play devil's advocate . . . *i.e.*, he debated us. . . . That class *really* sharpened me intellectually. . . . We as students do need to know how to defend ourselves." This young man valued the experience of being attacked and challenged publicly. Many, if not most, women would shrink from such "challenge," experiencing it as public humiliation.

A professor at Hamilton College told me of a young man who was upset because he felt his class presentation had been a failure. The professor was puzzled because he had observed that class members had listened attentively and agreed with the student's observations. It turned out that it was this very agreement that the student interpreted as failure: Since no one had engaged his ideas by arguing with him, he felt they had found them unworthy of attention.

So one reason men speak in class more than women is that many of them find the "public" classroom setting more conducive to speaking, whereas most women are more comfortable speaking in private to a small group of people they know well. A second reason is that men are more likely to be comfortable with the debate-like form that discussion may take. Yet another reason is the different attitudes toward speaking in class that typify women and men.

Students who speak frequently in class, many of whom are men, assume that it is their job to think of contributions and try to get the floor to express them. But many women monitor their participation not only to get the floor but to avoid getting it. Women students in my class tell me that if they have spoken up once or twice, they hold back for the rest of the class because they don't want to dominate. If they have spoken a lot one week, they will remain silent the next. These different ethics of participation are, of course, unstated, so those who speak freely assume that those who remain silent have nothing to say, and those who are reining themselves in assume that the big talkers are selfish and hoggish.

When I looked around my classes, I could see these differing ethics 15 and habits at work. For example, my graduate class in analyzing conversation had 20 students, 11 women and 9 men. Of the men, four were foreign students: two Japanese, one Chinese, and one Syrian. With the exception of the three Asian men, all the men spoke in class at least occasionally. The biggest talker in the class was a woman, but there were also five women who never spoke at all, only one of whom was Japanese. I decided to try something different.

I broke the class into small groups to discuss the issues raised in the readings and to analyze their own conversational transcripts. I devised three ways of dividing the students into groups: one by the degree program they were in, one by gender, and one by conversational style, as closely as I could guess it. This meant that when the class was grouped according to conversational style, I put Asian students together, fast talkers together, and quiet students together. The class split into groups six times during the semester, so they met in each grouping twice. I told students to regard the groups as examples of interactional data and to note the different ways they participated in the different groups. Toward the end of the term, I gave them a questionnaire asking about their class and group participation.

I could see plainly from my observation of the groups at work that women who never opened their mouths in class were talking away in the small groups. In fact, the Japanese woman commented that she found it particularly hard to contribute to the all-woman group she was in because "I was overwhelmed by how talkative the female students were in the female-only group." This is particularly revealing because it highlights that the same person who can be "oppressed" into silence in one context can become the talkative "oppressor" in another. No one's conversational style is absolute; everyone's style changes in response to the context and others' styles.

Some of the students (seven) said they preferred the same-gender groups; others preferred the same-style groups. In answer to the question "Would you have liked to speak in class more than you did?" six of the seven who said Yes were women; the one man was Japanese. Most startlingly, this response did not come only from quiet women; it came from women who had indicated they had spoken in class never, rarely, sometimes, and often. Of the 11 students who said the amount they had spoken was fine, 7 were men. Of the four women who checked "fine," two added qualifications indicating it wasn't completely fine: One wrote in "maybe more," and one wrote, "I have an urge to participate but often feel I should have something more interesting/relevant/wonderful/intelligent to say!!"

I counted my experiment a success. Everyone in the class found the small groups interesting, and no one indicated he or she would have preferred that the class not break into groups. Perhaps most instructive, however, was the fact that the experience of breaking into groups, and of talking about participation in class, raised everyone's awareness about classroom participation. After we had talked about it, some of the quietest women in the class made a few voluntary contributions, though sometimes I had to insure their participation by interrupting the students who were exuberantly speaking out.

Americans are often proud that they discount the significance of 20 cultural differences: "We are all individuals," many people boast. Ignoring such issues as gender and ethnicity becomes a source of pride: "I treat everyone the same." But treating people the same is not equal treatment if they are not the same.

The classroom is a different environment for those who feel comfortable putting themselves forward in a group than it is for those who find the prospect of doing so chastening, or even terrifying. When a professor asks, "Are there any questions?," students who can formulate statements the fastest have the greatest opportunity to respond. Those who need significant time to do so have not really been given a chance at all, since by the time they are ready to speak, someone else has the floor.

In a class where some students speak out without raising hands, those who feel they must raise their hands and wait to be recognized do not have equal opportunity to speak. Telling them to feel free to jump in will not make them feel free; one's sense of timing, of one's rights and obligations in a classroom, are automatic, learned over years of interaction. They may be changed over time, with motivation and effort, but they cannot be changed on the spot. And everyone assumes his or her own way is best. When I asked my students how the class could be changed to make it easier for them to speak more, the most talkative woman said she would prefer it if no one had to raise hands, and a foreign student said he wished people would raise their hands and wait to be recognized.

My experience in this class has convinced me that small-group interaction should be part of any class that is not a small seminar. I

Tannen is using personal experience as evidence, but she's also presenting evidence from surveys and questionnaires she systematically conducted with her own students. Read more in Chapter 18 about what counts as evidence.

LINK TO P. 367 ···························

also am convinced that having the students become observers of their own interaction is a crucial part of their education. Talking about ways of talking in class makes students aware that their ways of talking affect other students, that the motivations they impute to others may not truly reflect others' motives, and that the behaviors they assume to be self-evidently right are not universal norms.

The goal of complete equal opportunity in class may not be attainable, but realizing that one monolithic classroom-participation structure is not equal opportunity is itself a powerful motivation to find more-diverse methods to serve diverse students—and every classroom is diverse.

RESPOND●

1. To what extent do you agree with Tannen's characterization of female and male conversational styles? With her discussion of the consequences of these different styles on classroom interaction? Why?

2. Do you prefer classes in which the "male" or "female" style of interaction, as described by Tannen, is rewarded? Why? How do you respond when you are in a classroom where the kind of interactional style you do not prefer is rewarded? If you are male and prefer the "female" style of interaction or if you are female and prefer the "male" style of interaction, should you be worried? Why or why not?

3. Tannen claims that "[o]ur educational system . . . is fundamentally male in that the pursuit of knowledge is believed to be achieved by . . . argument and challenge" (paragraph 5). Similar claims have been made about the style of argumentation required of college students and that required of professors in their research. To what extent do you agree? Why or why not?

4. Describe Tannen's own style of argumentation. Is it antagonistic or adversarial? Does it seek common ground? Is it absolutist ("There is only one right answer, and I have it")? Why or why not?

5. In paragraph 23, Tannen argues that "small-group interaction should be part of any class that is not a small seminar." Do you agree or disagree? To what extent? Why? Using personal experience, and what you have learned from this article, **write an essay** in which you respond to Tannen's argument about including small-group interaction in all classes. Be careful to discuss not only its benefits but also any drawbacks you might see.

▼ *In this column from the June 1999 issue of* Sports Illustrated, *Steve Rushin describes and critiques one aspect of what we might term "the American character." Crucially, the patterns of behavior he criticizes are linguistic in nature, involving ways we use language to create our identities. As you read, pay special attention to the sorts of examples Rushin uses to support his claim that the United States has become "Wise Guy Nation."*

Hip Unchecked

In Sports and on TV, Sarcasm and Cynicism Are Drowning Out Sincerity and Compassion

STEVE RUSHIN

LAST WEEK, at an amusement park in middle America, I saw a seven-year-old boy in a basketball-themed T-shirt that read KNOW YOUR ROLE — SHUT YOUR MOUTH. Within minutes came another kid, maybe 12, in a trash-talking T-shirt that said YOU SHOULD BE IN A MUSEUM — YOU'RE GETTIN' WAXED. Moments later, yet another child walked world-wearily by in a T-shirt that commanded SPEAK TO MY AGENT. He was, at most, five years old.

All day these pip-squeaks passed, like the little boy in a T-shirt manufactured by the No Fear, Inc. apparel company, one that declared IF YOU CAN'T WIN, DON'T PLAY. (He was holding his father's hand.) Retreating to my hotel, I switched on ESPN2 in time to see a commercial in which a man dressed as a giant Slim Jim was yelling, "Eat me!" Flipping to *The Late Late Show* on CBS, I watched former ESPN anchor Craig Kilborn read a phony news item about drug agents seizing several tons of

cocaine before it reached its intended destination of — smirk, leer, arched eyebrow — "Darryl Strawberry's left nostril." So ended an unremarkable day in the life of America, where every citizen is a snarky, cynical, hipper-than-thou, irony-dripping icon of comedy and cool.

I don't know when, exactly, everyone became a smart-ass, only that it has happened. "Everybody I know is sarcastic all the time, in everything they say," a guy named Scott Dikkers recently told *The New Yorker.* Dikkers is editor-in-chief of — what else? — a satirical newspaper called *The Onion,* and he and I seem to know all the same people. In sports the smart-aleck attitude is inescapable, be it on *SportsCenter,* in ads for EA Sports, or wherever two sportswriters gather — invariably to make fun of everyone, including each other.

It is exhausting, all this clever contempt for everything. I have seen major league baseball trainers wearing T-shirts bearing the slogan I WILL GIVE TREATMENT, NOT SYMPATHY. On such seemingly minor everyday messages — call them incidental incivilities — a popular culture has been built.

So remind me: Why is it wrong to give sympathy   5 to someone who might need it? What is uncool about occasional earnestness, sincerity or genuine human emotion? Does every TV commercial have to be a winking, we-know-that-you-know-that-this-is-a-cheesy-commercial commercial? With the spoofed-up news on *The Daily Show with Jon Stewart,* and "Headlines" on *The Tonight Show,* and the mock newscast on *The Late Late Show,* and the mock newscast on *Dennis Miller Live,* and the mock newscast on *Saturday Night Live,* television now broadcasts more news parodies than actual news programs. We have become Wise Guy Nation. On our one-dollar bill George Washington ought to smirk like Mona Lisa. On the five, Lincoln's fingers could form a *W,* the international symbol for *whatever.*

In an interview broadcast during halftime of the Knicks-Pacers playoff game on NBC last Friday night, Indiana guard Mark Jackson spoke movingly about the recent death of his father. It was telling that Jackson felt it necessary to point out, "There's no shame in crying and saying 'I love him to death.'"

You wouldn't think so. But people now feel shame for their virtues (e.g., loving one's parents) and no shame for their sins (e.g., loving one's White House intern). Losers — socially or athletically — deserve ridicule. As I left the amusement park last week, I saw an adult in a T-shirt that bore the image of a high school wrestler and the following slogan across the chest: WIN WITH HUMILITY, LOSE WITH DIGNITY.

The earnest and simple sentiment gave me hope, so I nodded solemnly as the man passed. Only then did I see the back of his shirt. It read BUT DON'T LOSE!

■

Rushin's article is about values, but is his appeal based on values? Emotion? A combination? Check out Chapters 4 and 5 to help you decide.

·········· LINK TO PP. 65 AND 78

RESPOND ●

1. How well does the article's subtitle — "In Sports and on TV, Sarcasm and Cynicism Are Drowning Out Sincerity and Compassion" — summarize Rushin's argument? Why do you think that Rushin does not include an explicit thesis in his essay? How might doing so have altered the tone of the piece?

2. How would you describe the tone of Rushin's essay? To what extent does his tone enact the very attitudes and behaviors he is criticizing? Do you think the tone contributes to or detracts from his argument? Why or why not?

3. Nearly all of Rushin's examples involve males. Is the pattern of behavior Rushin describes and criticizes "a guy thing" or "an American thing"? Why? (Imagine, for example, how Deborah Tannen (p. 730) might respond to this piece.)

4. Rushin claims in paragraph 7 that "people now feel shame for their virtues . . . and no shame for their sins. . . ." **Write an essay** supporting or rejecting this claim.

According to the 2000 census, there are more foreign-born Americans in the United States today than at any time in our country's history. (At the same time, the percentage of foreign-born Americans is much lower than it was early in the twentieth century, as the article by Janny Scott, which opens this cluster, demonstrates.) This large influx of foreign-born Americans means that a growing number of the population are bilingual, either because they grew up elsewhere speaking a language other than English and now use English here, or because they grew up in bilingual families (and, often, communities) here in the States. In this cluster, we offer a range of perspectives about **being bilingual in the United States,** which are ultimately opinions about issues of language and identity.

Following Scott's article are excerpts from the 2002 National Survey of Latinos conducted by the Henry J. Kaiser Family Foundation and the Pew Hispanic Center. The excerpts presented here deal specifically with attitudes among Latinos about Spanish, English, and identity. The remainder of the cluster presents personal accounts of bilingualism in this country. Myriam Marquez, a Cuban American columnist, Sandra Cisneros, a Mexican American novelist, and Marjorie Agosín, a professor of Spanish, poet, human rights activist, and refugee from Chile, provide complementary points of view on what it means to speak Spanish and English in our country as they write about showing respect, making love, and recapturing a lost past. They remind us that languages and their meanings for those who speak them are multiple, overlapping, and often conflicting. An excerpt from Lan Cao's novel *Monkey Bridge* describes the situation of a Vietnamese adolescent girl who, because she absorbs English and comes to understand American culture quickly, must "parent" her mother, who finds things like supermarkets disorientingly foreign. Thus it describes a common situation among immigrant children, who become cultural translators and interpreters for their parents, a role reversal that turns traditional notions of parent/child relations on their head. Cao, an immigrant herself, is now a law professor. The cluster closes with an essay by a college senior who comes to realize that like it or not, the Chinese language is an inescapable part of who she is.

If you're bilingual, these readings give you a chance to think about who you are and how your experiences compare with those of other Americans who speak more than one language. If you don't already speak another language, there's still time: monolingualism isn't a terminal disease, as a favorite bumper sticker proclaims! Even as English becomes "the" world language, learning another language changes the way you understand yourself and the world. In the meantime, these readings offer you the chance to learn things about the life of a growing number of Americans that you may otherwise never know.

▼ *This February 2002 news article appeared in the* New York Times. *Using data from the 2000 census, its author, Janny Scott, puts recent immigration to the United States in a historical context. In this short piece, she not only provides a great deal of information about recent immigration, using facts and figures, but also explores what the significance of such immigration might be for the country as a whole. As you read, think about the consequences of the situation described for bi- and multilingualism in the United States now, in the past, and in our country's future.*

Foreign Born in U.S. at Record High

Census Puts Number at 56 Million, with Mexico Chief Supplier

JANNY SCOTT

The number of foreign-born residents and children of immigrants in the United States has reached the highest level in history, according to a Census Bureau report released yesterday. It found that the number had leapt to 56 million from 34 million in the last three decades.

Mexico accounted for more than a quarter of all the foreign-born residents, the bureau's analysis of data from its March 2000 Current Population Survey showed. That share is the largest any country has held since the 1890 census, when about 30 percent of the country's foreign-born population was from Germany.

The study found that, on average, foreign-born residents were much more likely than native Americans to live in or around a handful of big cities. They were almost equally likely to be in the labor force. But foreign-born residents earned less and were less likely to have health insurance than native Americans.

While the number of foreign-born residents and their children is higher than ever, their percentage in the population is not. In the 1910 census, that group made up 35 percent of the population, compared with 20 percent in 2000, a spokesman for the Census Bureau said.

The report brings together data on the age, sex and birthplaces of the foreign born, their education levels, jobs and earnings. In doing so, it makes clear the near impossibility of generalizing about immigrants and the immigrant experience.

For example, while only 33.8 percent of residents over age 25 and born in Mexico had completed high school, 95 percent of those born in Africa had. While the median household income for those born in Latin America was $29,338, it was $51,363 for those from Asia, well above that of native Americans.

The proportion of married couples with children under 18 ranged from 35 percent for residents born in Europe to 73.4 percent for those from Latin America. The proportion of nat-

California leads in foreign-born residents, with New York second.

uralized citizens varied widely, from 52 percent of those born in Europe to 21.1 percent of those born in Central America.

"The big question is how the second generation is going to do," said Nancy Foner, a professor of anthropology at the State University of New

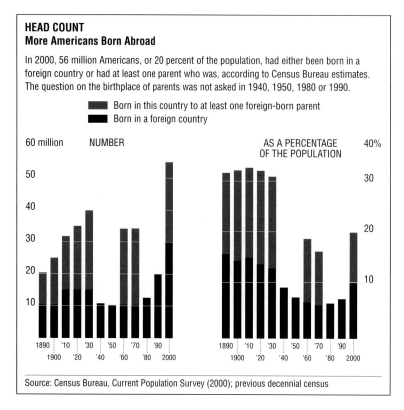

HEAD COUNT
More Americans Born Abroad

In 2000, 56 million Americans, or 20 percent of the population, had either been born in a foreign country or had at least one parent who was, according to Census Bureau estimates. The question on the birthplace of parents was not asked in 1940, 1950, 1980 or 1990.

■ Born in this country to at least one foreign-born parent
■ Born in a foreign country

Source: Census Bureau, Current Population Survey (2000); previous decennial census

York at Purchase and the author of "From Ellis Island to JFK: New York's Two Great Waves of Immigration" (Yale, 2000). "And how the presence of large proportions of Asians, Latinos and black immigrants are changing Americans' notions of race."

The Census Bureau study found that the foreign-born population

Did Scott choose appropriate evidence and use it effectively? Use the criteria given in Chapter 18 to determine your answer.

LINK TO P. 367

was heavily concentrated in California, New York, Florida, Texas, New Jersey and Illinois; those six states accounted for 70.4 percent of the total. Nearly 55 percent lived in the nine metropolitan areas with populations of five million or more.

California led the nation with the highest percentage of foreign-born residents with 25.9 percent, followed by New York State with 19.6. The metropolitan areas with the largest percentage of foreign-born popula-

tions were Los Angeles with 29.6 percent and New York with 22.8.

In New York City, said John H. Mollenkopf, a demographer at the City University of New York, 43 percent of the residents are foreign born and another 9.2 percent are the children of two foreign-born parents. In 1900, Professor Mollenkopf said, only 23 percent of New Yorkers had native-born parents.

The Census Bureau's report put at 55.9 million the number of people of so-called foreign stock, which includes 28.4 million foreign born, 14.8 million native born with two foreign-born parents, and 12.7 million of mixed parentage. That group is likely to grow, in part because the proportion of births to foreign-born women rose to 20.2 percent in 1999 from 6 percent of all births in 1970, the report said.

While the median ages of the foreign-born and native populations barely differed, foreign-born residents fell disproportionately between the ages of 25 and 54. The percentage of foreign-born residents in that age group was 58.7, compared with 41.7 percent of native Americans.

"In some ways, it has complemented the baby boom," Dianne Schmidley, a Census Bureau statistician and author of the report, said of the rise of the foreign born. "Every discussion you hear about the baby boom and the effect of the baby boom—all that has been made greater by the addition of those young adults."

Flag of faces, Ellis Island

RESPOND●

1. Like many news articles, Scott's argument is informative: her goal is to inform readers of the *Times* about the topic of immigration from several perspectives. Make a list of the specific generalizations she makes and the sorts of evidence she cites for them. (Chapter 18 on what counts as evidence may prove helpful in answering this question.) What consequences might these generalizations have for bi- or multilingualism in the United States? Why?

2. A particularly interesting aspect of this article is its use of visual information in the two graphs in "Head Count." As you can see, one bar graph shows (for the past 110 years) the number of people in the United States born in another country or having at least one foreign-born parent, while the other shows the percentage of the total population each group represents for each ten-year cohort. What do we learn from each graph? From the two graphs together? Why is it important to consider both kinds of historical information in understanding immigration? In understanding bi- or multilingualism in the United States?

3. As "Head Count" notes, the Census Bureau did not ask questions about the birthplace of parents in 1940, 1950, 1980, or 1990. What challenges does this fact present for students of immigration? Of American bi- or multilingualism?

4. Using the Internet, find information from the 2000 census about immigration to your hometown and state (try <census.gov>). Who moved to your hometown and state in the 1990s? Where did they come from? What consequences might these new arrivals have on bi- or multilingualism there? **Write a short essay** describing the demographic changes to your hometown or state during the 1990s, and speculate on the consequences these changes have had for the linguistic situation there.

▼ *This selection offers excerpts from the Pew Hispanic Center/Kaiser Family Foundation's "2002 National Survey of Latinos." (The entire report is available at <pewhispanic.org>.) Noting a 142 percent increase in the number of Hispanics between the 1980 and 2002 U.S. censuses, the survey set out "to capture the diversity of the Latino population." To do so, a total of 2,929 adult Latinos from various backgrounds were carefully chosen and sampled, along with 171 African Americans and 1,008 Whites, whose responses were used as a basis for comparison in some questions. The survey uses the phrase "foreign born" to refer to those born outside the fifty states of the Union; hence, those born in Puerto Rico, a U.S. commonwealth, although citizens, are considered foreign born because of the Spanish-dominant nature of Puerto Rican culture. Native-born Latinos are referred to as "U.S.-born Latinos." The survey relies on self-report data about one's ability to speak and read Spanish and/or English.*

The excerpts included here, which come from various places in the report, are those that deal most directly with questions of language(s) spoken. First, we present the "Executive Summary," which offers an overview of the results of the study. Next, we present the two primary observations about assimilation and language. Finally, we present a series of more detailed observations, along with data from the survey to support the claims made. As you read, notice how each contributes to the complex picture of language issues among Hispanics.

2002 National Survey of Latinos

PEW HISPANIC CENTER/KAISER FAMILY FOUNDATION

EXECUTIVE SUMMARY

The Pew Hispanic Center/Kaiser Family Foundation 2002 *National Survey of Latinos* comprehensively explores the attitudes and experiences of Hispanics on a wide variety of topics. This survey was designed to capture the diversity of the Latino population by including almost 3,000 Hispanics from various backgrounds and groups so that in addition to describing Latinos overall, comparisons can be made among key Hispanic subgroups as well.

We find that as a whole, the Hispanic population of the United States holds an array of attitudes, values and beliefs that are distinct from those of non-Hispanic whites and African Americans. Even Latinos who trace their ancestry in the United States back for several generations express views that distinguish them from the non-Hispanic native-born population.

However, there is no single, homogeneous Latino opinion. A diversity of views exists among Latinos, and the differences between the foreign born, regardless of their country of origin, and the native born and those between the English dominant and the Spanish dominant are most notable. In fact, the survey presents a multifaceted representation of a population undergoing rapid change due to immigration that includes individuals at many different stages in the process of assimilation to English and American ways. The survey, however, renders a portrait of a people at a given moment in time—the late spring of 2002—rather than serving as a prediction for a certain future. Nonetheless, the survey results help resolve a sometimes argumentative though frequently-asked question: Are Latino newcomers undergoing the melting pot experience, or are they and their offspring maintaining their native cultures and becoming an ethnic group that is different from the mainstream? The answer is: Both, to some extent.

For example, an examination of Latinos' attitudes on social issues shows that immigrants hold a range of views on matters like gender roles, abortion and homosexuality that are somewhat more conservative than those of most non-Hispanic whites. Meanwhile native-born Latinos, including the children of immigrants, express attitudes that are more squarely within the range of views voiced by non-Hispanics. Nonetheless, some elements of this social conservatism and, in particular, a strong attachment to family is evident among Latinos who predominantly speak English and are generations removed from the immigrant experience.

Immigration is also an important factor in shaping Latinos' sense of their social identity. The survey reveals a robust attachment to countries of origin, and while this attachment is naturally strongest among the foreign born, it also extends to their U.S.-born children and even somewhat among Hispanics whose families are long-time U.S. residents. Social identity for Latinos, however, is much more complex and fluid than simply a connection to an ancestral homeland. Native-born Latinos also use the term "American" to describe themselves more than terms like "Mexican" or "Cuban." Use of the terms "Latino" or "Hispanic," which encompass all national origin groups, adds another crosscurrent. Respondents use these broader terms to distinguish themselves from non-Hispanics, but in large numbers they also say that Latinos of different countries of origin share no common culture.

The survey also sheds considerable light on the experiences that Latinos have in the United States. Focusing particularly on experiences with discrimination, their economic and financial situations and experiences with the health care system, the survey finds a diversity of experiences largely reflective in differences between native and foreign born and differences between English and Spanish dominant.

Overall, the findings suggest the need for new ways of thinking about the Hispanic population in this country. It is neither monolithic nor a hodgepodge of distinct national origin groups. Rather, Latinos share a range of attitudes and experiences that set them apart from the non-Hispanic population. Yet this common culture embraces a diversity of views that is most evident in the contrasts between immigrants and the native born. The survey argues for a more dynamic approach in regard to Latinos because this is a population undergoing constant change due to immigration. Regardless of nativity or country of origin, Hispanics who reside in the United States are engaging the English language and American ways to various degrees. Yet, simultaneously, newly arrived immigrants are bringing new energy to Spanish and to attitudes shaped in Latin America. In interpreting the survey results it is important to keep in mind that these two processes—assimilation and immigration—are taking place side-by-side in Latino communities, often within a single family.

SURVEY HIGHLIGHTS

- Hispanics, particularly those who are Spanish speakers, feel very strongly that Hispanics must learn English in order to be successful in the United States.
- Spanish remains the dominant language in the adult Hispanic population. English, however, clearly gains ground even within immigrant households. The second generation—the U.S.-born children of immigrants—predominantly speak English or are bilingual. Indeed, Hispanic parents, even those who are immigrants, report that English is the language their children generally use when speaking to their friends.

Additional Key Demographic Differences

Primary Language

As might be expected, native-born Latinos are much
more likely than foreign-born Latinos to speak English as their primary language (61% vs. 4%) or to be
bilingual (35% vs. 24%), while foreign-born Latinos
are much more likely than native-born Latinos to be
Spanish dominant (72% vs. 4%). (Table 1.1)

AGE AT IMMIGRATION

Definition

Respondents who were born outside of the United
States were asked their age at the time they immigrated to the United States (Puerto Ricans born on
the island were not asked this question and are not
included in these groups). Based on their responses
they were categorized into four groups: those who
arrived when they were age 10 or younger, ages 11–17,
ages 18–25, and those who arrived when they were
age 26 or older.

Foreign-born Latinos are more likely to report
having immigrated to the United States at an older
age.

Additional Key Demographic Differences

Primary Language

Those who arrived when they were very young, in this
case age 10 or younger, may have experiences more
similar to Hispanics who were born in the United
States than to others who are foreign-born. In particular, foreign-born Hispanics who arrive at a young
age are much more likely to speak English as adults
and will have received a majority of their education
from American schools. In contrast, foreign-born
Hispanics who arrived when they were older, particularly those who arrived when they are already into
adulthood, in this case age 26 and older, are more
likely to be Spanish dominant than those who arrived
when they were younger. (Table 1.2)

As noted above, a large majority (72%) of first
generation or foreign-born Latinos are Spanish dominant; about one in four (24%) is bilingual while only
4% are English dominant. In contrast, second generation Latinos are mostly divided between those who
are English dominant (46%) and those who are bilingual (47%). Third generation or higher Hispanics are
largely English dominant (78%). While a few Hispanics whose families have been in the United States for
multiple generations are bilingual (22%), none indicate that they are Spanish dominant. (Table 1.3)

PRIMARY LANGUAGE

Definition

Respondents were asked a series of four questions
about their language ability. They were asked about
their ability to carry on a conversation in Spanish and
to carry on a conversation in English ("Would you say

Table 1.1 Primary Language, by Foreign/Native-Born Latinos

	Foreign-Born Latinos	Native-Born Latinos
English-Dominant	4%	61%
Bilingual	24	35
Spanish-Dominant	72	4

Table 1.2 Primary Language among Foreign-Born Latinos, by Age at Immigration to the United States

	Age at Immigration to the United States among Foreign-Born Latinos			
	10 years or younger	Ages 11–17	Ages 18–25	Ages 26+
English-Dominant	18%	4%	1%	2%
Bilingual	70	31	15	10
Spanish-Dominant	11	66	84	89

Table 1.3 Primary Language among Latinos, by Generation in the United States

	Generation in the United States		
	1st Generation	2nd Generation	3rd Generation and Higher
English-Dominant	4%	46%	78%
Bilingual	24	47	22
Spanish-Dominant	72	7	–

Table 1.4 Primary Language among Latinos

	Percentage of Latino Adults
English-Dominant	25%
Bilingual	28
Spanish-Dominant	47

you can carry on a conversation in Spanish/English, both understanding and speaking—very well, pretty well, just a little, or not at all?") and questions about their ability to read in English and in Spanish ("Would you say you can read a newspaper or book in Spanish/English—very well, pretty well, just a little, or not at all?"). Based on their answers to these four questions, respondents were divided into three language groups: English dominant, bilingual, and Spanish dominant. Using these divisions, almost half (47%) of Hispanics are categorized as "Spanish dominant." The remaining half of Latinos split between those who are English dominant (25%) and those who are bilingual (28%). (Table 1.4)

Throughout the report English-dominant Latinos are also referred to as those "who predominantly speak English" and Spanish-dominant Latinos are also referred to as those "who predominantly speak Spanish." This wording is used for brevity. Please note, however, that the variables used to establish language dominance included both reading and speaking ability.

Primary Language

Hispanics associated with different countries of origin have differences in the primary language they speak. Hispanics from "other" countries are much more likely than other groups to be English dominant. Puerto Ricans also stand out as being much more likely than other groups to speak English predominantly or to be bilingual.

In contrast, Latinos from Central America, El Salvador, and the Dominican Republic are more likely than Puerto Ricans, Mexicans and Hispanics from "other" countries to be Spanish dominant. (Table 1.5)

Table 1.5 Dominant Language among Latinos, by Country of Origin

	Country of Origin								
	Mexican	Puerto Rican	Cuban	Total Central American	Total South American	Salvadoran	Dominican	Colombian	All Other
English-Dominant	23%	39%	17%	10%	12%	12%	6%	12%	70%
Bilingual	26	40	30	25	34	25	34	30	27
Spanish-Dominant	51	21	53	65	54	63	61	58	3

ASSIMILATING TO THE UNITED STATES

Language Assimilation

Hispanics, whites, and African Americans all agree that adult Hispanic immigrants need to learn to speak English to succeed in the United States. Hispanics who speak Spanish primarily and those born outside of the United States are particularly likely to hold this view. (Chart 1.1)

- About nine in ten (89%) Latinos indicate that they 20 believe immigrants need to learn to speak English to succeed in the United States. Similar numbers of whites (86%) and African Americans (86%) agree. Far fewer (10%) Latinos believe immigrants can succeed if they only speak Spanish.
- Slightly more Spanish-dominant (92%) compared to bilingual (88%) or English-dominant (86%) Latinos believe immigrants need to learn to speak English to succeed in the United States. Similarly, foreign-born Latinos are slightly more likely than U.S.-born Latinos to feel English language skills are necessary for success (91% vs. 86%).

In many ways, Spanish remains the dominant language among adult Hispanics. Not only do more Latinos speak and read Spanish than English, but also it is spoken more in the home and used a great deal at work. In addition, Spanish language media are important sources of news for many. (Chart 1.2)

- Overall, a very large majority (86%) of Hispanics report that they can carry on a conversation in Spanish both understanding and speaking "very" (74%) or "pretty" (12%) well, while a significant minority (40%) speaks and understands "just a little" (29%) or no (11%) English.
- Similarly, Latinos are more likely to say they can read a newspaper or book at least pretty well in Spanish than in English (74% vs. 58%). A significant number (42%) indicate that they read "just a little" or no English.
- In addition, a slight majority (53%) of Hispanics 25 report they predominantly speak Spanish at home. About one in five (19%) says Spanish and English are spoken equally in their homes, while 28% say they predominantly speak English at home.
- While almost half (48%) of Latinos who are employed say they predominantly speak English at work, Spanish is also used a great deal in the workplace. More than half (52%) of employed Hispanics report that they speak Spanish at work at least some of the time. This includes about one in four (26%) Hispanics who report speaking predominantly Spanish at work, including 14% who report that they *only* speak Spanish at work. About one in four (26%) say they speak both Spanish and English equally.

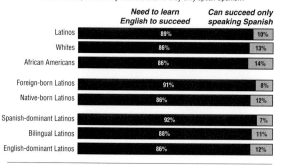

Chart 1.1: English Seen as Necessary for Success in the United States

Do you think adult Latino immigrants need to learn English to succeed in the United States, or can they succeed even if they only speak Spanish?

	Need to learn English to succeed	Can succeed only speaking Spanish
Latinos	89%	10%
Whites	86%	13%
African Americans	86%	14%
Foreign-born Latinos	91%	8%
Native-born Latinos	86%	12%
Spanish-dominant Latinos	92%	7%
Bilingual Latinos	88%	11%
English-dominant Latinos	86%	12%

Note: "Don't know" responses not shown.
Source: Pew Hispanic Center/Kaiser Family Foundation *National Survey of Latinos.* December 2002 (conducted April–June 2002).

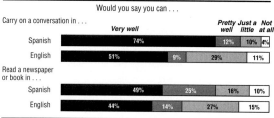

Chart 1.2: Spanish More Dominant Than English among Latinos Overall

Would you say you can . . .

	Very well	Pretty well	Just a little	Not at all
Carry on a conversation in . . .				
Spanish	74%	12%	10%	4%
English	51%	9%	29%	11%
Read a newspaper or book in . . .				
Spanish	49%	25%	16%	10%
English	44%	14%	27%	15%

Note: "Don't know" responses not shown.
Source: Pew Hispanic Center/Kaiser Family Foundation *National Survey of Latinos.* December 2002 (conducted April–June 2002).

Chart 1.3: Language Spoken in Various Situations among Latinos Overall

What language do you . . .

	Predominantly Spanish	Both Equally	Predominantly English
Speak at home	53%	19%	28%
Speak at Work (among those who are employed)	26%	26%	48%
Watch TV or listen to the radio	38%	26%	36%

What language do your children . . . (among those with children)

Speak with their friends	17%	26%	58%

Note: "Don't know" responses not shown.
Source: Pew Hispanic Center/Kaiser Family Foundation *National Survey of Latinos*. December 2002 (conducted April–June 2002).

- Spanish language media are an important source of broadcast news for a majority of Latinos: 38% of Latinos report that they usually listen to and predominantly watch Spanish language news programs, including one in four who *only* tune in to Spanish language broadcasts. An additional 26% report that they get their news from both Spanish and English news sources equally. Older Latinos rely on the Spanish language media most heavily while younger, those who are better-educated and those who are more affluent are more likely to get their broadcast news in English.

While Spanish remains the dominant language in the adult Hispanic population, English gains ground even within immigrant households. The second generation—the U.S.-born children of immigrants—is either bilingual or predominantly speaks English. Indeed, Hispanic parents, even those who are immigrants, report that English is the language their children generally use when their children are speaking to their friends. (Chart 1.3)

- Only 7% of second generation Latinos are Spanish dominant, while the rest are divided between those who are bilingual (47%) and those who are English dominant (46%). Those whose parents were born in the United States (third generation and higher) are much more likely to speak English predominantly (78%), while about one in five (22%) are bilingual.
- Over half (58%) of Latinos with children say their children usually speak English with their friends, including 36% who only speak English. About one in four (26%) says their children speak both Spanish and English equally with their friends, while 17% report their children speak predominantly Spanish, including 13% who *only* speak Spanish.
- English is making inroads among immigrant households. Among foreign-born parents, 45% say their children communicate with their friends predominantly in English and another 32% say their children use both English and Spanish equally. Just 18% of immigrant parents say that their children *only* speak Spanish with their friends.

How do the authors of this study use their evidence to make an argument? See Chapter 21 on Evaluating and Using Sources for more on summarizing and other ways of using sources to bolster an argument.

LINK TO P. 416

RESPOND.

1. What is your response to this information? Were you already aware of the situation described in the report, or did this selection present you with information or perspectives that were new? How? Why?

2. This report from the Pew Hispanic Center/Kaiser Family Foundation represents an increasingly common genre of writing: the presentation of quantitative information in summary form so that it can be used by many sorts of researchers for many purposes. How have the creators of this report written it with the users in mind? In other words, what features of the text help readers with respect to understanding and using the data? How?

3. What does this report teach us about language among Americans who identify as Latino or Hispanic? About bilingualism? About identity?

4. **Write a summary** of the information presented in this selection that you might use in a research paper on language in the Hispanic community. Specifically, you will need to choose two or three main points that you believe are most relevant, state them and the relationships among them clearly, and provide data from the report to support your claim. You'll also need to use the proper documentation. (Chapter 22, page 424, will help you with questions on documentation.) Obviously, one can use the facts and observations presented in the report to support many different sorts of arguments. At the same time, the facts and observations made in the report cannot be used as evidence for certain claims about language in the Hispanic community.

▼ *Myriam Marquez writes regularly for the* Orlando Sentinel, *and her columns are syndicated nationally. (We ran across this one in July 1999 in the* Austin American Statesman.) *In this op-ed piece, Marquez explains why she, a Cuban American who grew up in Miami, and her family use Spanish in public within the earshot of people who don't speak Spanish. As you read, consider the ways in which Marquez relies on arguments based on values, arguments from the heart, arguments based on character, and arguments based on reason to make her point.*

Why and When We Speak Spanish in Public

MYRIAM MARQUEZ

When I'm shopping with my mother or standing in line with my stepdad to order fast food or anywhere else we might be together, we're going to speak to one another in Spanish.

That may appear rude to those who don't understand Spanish and overhear us in public places.

Those around us may get the impression that we're talking about them. They may wonder why we would insist on speaking in a foreign tongue, especially if they knew that my family has lived in the United States for 40 years and that my parents do understand English and speak it, albeit with difficulty and a heavy accent.

Let me explain why we haven't adopted English as our official family language. For me and most of the bilingual people I know, it's a matter of respect for our parents and comfort in our cultural roots.

It's not meant to be rude to others. 5 It's not meant to alienate anyone or to Balkanize America.

It's certainly not meant to be un-American—what constitutes an "American" being defined by English speakers from North America.

Being an American has very little to do with what language we use during our free time in a free country. From its inception, this country was careful not to promote a government-mandated official language.

We understand that English is the common language of this country and the one most often heard in international-business circles from Peru to Norway. We know that, to get ahead here, one must learn English.

But that ought not mean that somehow we must stop speaking in our native tongue whenever we're in a public area, as if we were ashamed of who we are, where we're from. As if talking in Spanish—or any other language, for that matter—is some sort of litmus test used to gauge American patriotism.

Throughout this nation's history, 10 most immigrants—whether from Poland or Finland or Italy or wherever else—kept their language through the first generation and, often, the second. I suspect that they spoke among themselves in their native tongue—in public. Pennsylvania even provided voting ballots written in German during much of the

1800s for those who weren't fluent in English.

In this century, Latin American immigrants and others have fought for this country in U.S.-led wars. They have participated fully in this nation's democracy by voting, holding political office and paying taxes. And they have watched their children and grandchildren become so "American" that they resist speaking in Spanish.

You know what's rude?

When there are two or more people who are bilingual and another person who speaks only English and the bilingual folks all of a sudden start speaking Spanish, which effectively leaves out the English-only speaker. I don't tolerate that.

One thing's for sure. If I'm ever in a public place with my mom or dad and bump into an acquaintance who doesn't speak Spanish, I will switch to English and introduce that person to my parents. They will respond in English, and do so with respect.

Who are Marquez's intended readers? Who are her invoked readers? Her real readers? See Chapter 3 for more on how writers address audiences.

······················ LINK TO P. 51

RESPOND •

1. How does Marquez explain and justify her behavior and that of many immigrants, including Spanish-speaking immigrants? What fear does she acknowledge on the part of those who don't speak Spanish? How does she seek to respond to it?

2. What are the specific ways in which Marquez relies on arguments based on values, arguments from the heart, arguments based on character, and arguments based on reason to make her point? What values does Marquez appeal to when she explains why bilinguals like her speak Spanish in public?

3. The last three paragraphs of this essay represent a clear shift in tone and emphasis from the rest of this selection, especially the previous few paragraphs. What is their purpose? Do you find that they contribute to or detract from the overall effect of the selection? Why?

4. **Write an essay** in which you define and evaluate the notion of public space with respect to speaking languages other than English as presented by Marquez. As Marquez notes, for her and many Americans, the public space is not a space where only English can be spoken. At the same time, there are limits to what is permissible. Thus you will need to define the public space with respect to language in the terms Marquez uses and then evaluate her definition or characterization of that space, depending on your own values and experiences.

I'd Never Made Love in Spanish Before

SANDRA CISNEROS

I'd never made love in Spanish before. I mean not with anyone whose *first* language was Spanish. There was crazy Graham, the anarchist labor organizer who'd taught me to eat jalapeños and swear like a truck mechanic, but he was Welsh and had learned his Spanish running guns to Bolivia.

And Eddie, sure. But Eddie and I were products of our American education. Anything tender always came off sounding like the subtitles to a Buñuel° film.

But Flavio. When Flavio accidentally hammered his thumb, he never yelled "Ouch!" he said "¡Ay!" The true test of a native Spanish speaker.

¡Ay! To make love in Spanish, in a manner as intricate and devout as la Alhambra.° To have a lover sigh *mi vida, mi preciosa, mi chiquitita,* and whisper things in that language crooned to babies, that language murmured by grandmothers, those words that smelled like your house, like flour tortillas, and the inside of your daddy's hat, like everyone talking in the kitchen at the same time, or sleeping with the windows open, like sneaking cashews from the crumpled quarter-pound bag Mama always hid in her lingerie drawer after she went shopping with Daddy at the Sears.

That language. That sweep of palm leaves and fringed shawls. That 5 startled fluttering, like the heart of a goldfinch or a fan. Nothing sounded dirty or hurtful or corny. How could I think of making love in English again? English with its starched *r*'s and *g*'s. English with its crisp linen syllables. English crunchy as apples, resilient and stiff as sailcloth.

But Spanish whirred like silk, rolled and puckered and hissed. I held Flavio close to me, in the mouth of my heart, inside my wrists.

Incredible happiness. A sigh unfurled of its own accord, a groan heaved out from my chest so rusty and full of dust it frightened me. I was crying. It surprised us both.

"My soul, did I hurt you?" Flavio said in that other language.

I managed to bunch my mouth into a knot and shake my head "no" just as the next wave of sobs began. Flavio rocked me, and cooed, and rocked me. *Ya, ya, ya.* There, there, there.

◀ *Sandra Cisneros is a Mexican American writer who lives in San Antonio. At press time, her most recent novel was* Caramelo *(2002). Born in Chicago in 1954, she is the recipient of a number of important awards, including a MacArthur Foundation fellowship. In this short excerpt from* Woman Hollering Creek and Other Stories *(1991), Cisneros helps readers understand how bilinguals experience the languages they know. As you read, note how Cisneros uses careful description to make her argument.*

Buñuel: Spanish filmmaker (1900–1983), famous for his Surrealist images and groundbreaking, often bizarre, visual imagery.

la Alhambra: from an Arabic word meaning "red palace"; la Alhambra was the palace, citadel, gardens, fortress, and home of the Nasrid sultans in the thirteenth and fourteenth centuries in Grenada in the south of Spain.

Which tropes of figurative language does Cisneros use in her essay? See descriptions of the different types of figurative language in Chapter 14 to help you figure out your answer.

············LINK TO P. 288

I wanted to say so many things, but all I could think of was a line I'd 10 read in the letters of Georgia O'Keeffe years ago and had forgotten until then. Flavio . . . did you ever feel like flowers?

RESPOND •

1. For Cisneros—and one can likely claim it for all bilinguals—the languages she knows are not equal in some sense. Rather, each language is associated with different worlds of experience. What does Spanish connote for the narrator in Cisneros's text? What does English connote? Where would such connotations come from?

2. Whereas Myriam Marquez wrote about the use of Spanish in public, Cisneros writes about the use of Spanish in the most private of contexts. Are there things Marquez and Cisneros (or at least her narrator) would agree about? What might they be? Why?

3. One resource bilingual writers have is codeswitching: switching between the languages they know. In this excerpt, we see the simple noun phrase "la Alhambra" (paragraph 4) from Spanish, which we can correctly understand even if we know no Spanish. We also see the phrase "Ya, ya, ya" (paragraph 9), which is followed immediately by the English equivalent, "There, there, there." Yet we also find the phrases "mi vida, mi preciosa, mi chiquitita" (paragraph 4), which we may not be able to figure out the meanings of. (In fact, the phrases translate literally as "my life, my precious [one], my dearest little [one]"—things native speakers of English wouldn't normally say to one another, even when being intimate. Such phrases are perfectly normal among speakers of Spanish.) Why might writers purposely create texts that include parts readers may not be able to understand? Why would such a strategy be especially effective when talking about intimacies like making love?

4. Likely all humans have an affective or emotional attachment to one or more languages or language varieties, most often one associated with childhood. **Create a text** in which you explore and define the meaning of some language or language variety—a regional, social, or ethnic variety of English, for example—for you. Your text can take the form of an essay, or you may wish to create a sketch more like Cisneros's (though you needn't write about anything so intimate as love making!). In it, seek to help readers—both those who know that language variety and those who don't—understand its meanings and significance for you.

▼ *Marjorie Agosín is a professor of Spanish at Wellesley College in Massachusetts and an award-winning writer and human rights activist. She was reared in Chile, the country to which her grandparents had moved early in the twentieth century at a time when Jews faced persecution in parts of Europe. Her family moved to the United States in the 1970s, when Augusto Pinochet took over the Chilean government. In this essay, which originally appeared in* Poets & Writers *in 1999 and was translated by Celeste Kostopulos-Cooperman, Agosín explains why she, as a political exile, "writes only in Spanish and lives in translation."*

Always Living in Spanish

Marjorie Agosín

Recovering the Familiar, Through Language

In the evenings in the northern hemisphere, I repeat the ancient ritual that I observed as a child in the southern hemisphere: going out while the night is still warm and trying to recognize the stars as it begins to grow dark silently. In the sky of my country, Chile, that long and wide stretch of land that the poets blessed and dictators abused, I could easily name the stars: the three Marias, the Southern Cross, and the three Lilies, names of beloved and courageous women.

But here in the United States, where I have lived since I was a young girl, the solitude of exile makes me feel that so little is mine, that not even the sky has the same constellations, the trees and the fauna the same names or sounds, or the rubbish the same smell. How does one recover the familiar? How does one name the unfamiliar? How can one be another or live in a foreign language? These are the dilemmas of one who writes in Spanish and lives in translation.

Since my earliest childhood in Chile I lived with the tempos and the melodies of a multiplicity of tongues: German, Yiddish,° Russian, Turkish, and many Latin songs. Because everyone was from somewhere else, my relatives laughed, sang, and fought in a Babylon of languages. Spanish was reserved for matters of extreme seriousness, for commercial transactions, or for illnesses, but everyone's mother tongue was always associated with the memory of spaces inhabited in the past: the shtetl,° the flowering and vast Vienna avenues, the minarets of Turkey, and the Ladino° whispers of Toledo. When my paternal grandmother sang old songs in Turkish, her voice and body assumed the passion of one who was there in the city of Istanbul, gazing by turns toward the west and the east.

Destiny and the always ambiguous nature of history continued my family's enforced migration, and because of it I, too, became one who had to live and speak in translation. The disappearances, torture, and clandestine deaths in my country in the early seventies drove us to the United States, that other America that looked with

Yiddish: Germanic language, much influenced by Hebrew and Aramaic, spoken by Ashkenazi Jews in Central and Eastern Europe and their descendents. In the nineteenth century, it was found in most of the world's countries with an Ashkenazi population, including the U.S. Yiddish is written in the Hebrew alphabet.

shtetl: a small Jewish village or town in Eastern Europe (originally, a Yiddish word meaning "little town").

Ladino: a nearly extinct Romance language, based on archaic Castilian Spanish, spoken by Sephardic Jews in the Balkans, North Africa and the Middle East, Turkey, and Greece. It originated in Spain and was carried elsewhere by the descendents of Jews exiled from there during the Inquisition.

suspicion at those who did not speak English and especially those who came from the supposedly uncivilized regions of Latin America. I had left a dangerous place that was my home, only to arrive in a dangerous place that was not: a high school in the small town of Athens, Georgia, where my poor English and my accent were the cause of ridicule and insult. The only way I could recover my usurped country and my Chilean childhood was by continuing to write in Spanish, the same way my grandparents had sung in their own tongues in diasporic° sites.

The new and learned English language did not fit with the visceral emotions and themes that my poetry contained, but by writing in Spanish I could recover fragrances, spoken rhythms, and the passion of my own identity. Daily I felt the need to translate myself for the strangers living all around me, to tell them why we were in Georgia, why we ate differently, why we had fled, why my accent was so thick, and why I did not look Hispanic. Only at night, writing poems in Spanish, could I return to my senses, and soothe my own sorrow over what I had left behind.

This is how I became a Chilean poet who wrote in Spanish and lived in the southern United States. And

then, one day, a poem of mine was translated and published in the English language. Finally, for the first time since I had left Chile, I felt I didn't have to explain myself. My poem, expressed in another language, spoke for itself . . . and for me.

Sometimes the austere sounds of English help me bear the solitude of knowing that I am foreign and so far away from those about whom I write. I must admit I would like more opportunities to read in Spanish to people whose language and culture is also mine, to join in our common heritage and in the feast of our sounds. I would also like readers of English to understand the beauty of the spoken word in Spanish, that constant flow of oxytonic° and paraoxytonic° syllables (*Verde que te quiero verde*°), the joy of writing—of dancing—in another language. I believe that many exiles share the unresolvable torment of not being able to live in the language of their childhood.

I miss that undulating and sensuous language of mine, those baroque descriptions, the sense of being and feeling that Spanish gives me. It is perhaps for this reason that I have chosen and will always choose to write in Spanish. Nothing else from my childhood world remains. My country seems to be frozen in gestures of silence and oblivion. My relatives have died, and I have grown up not knowing a young generation of cousins and nieces and nephews. Many of my friends were disappeared, others were tortured, and the most fortunate, like me, became guardians of

memory. For us, to write in Spanish is to always be in active pursuit of memory. I seek to recapture a world lost to me on that sorrowful afternoon when the blue electric sky and the Andean cordillera° bade me farewell. On that, my last Chilean day, I carried under my arm my innocence recorded in a little blue notebook I kept even then. Gradually that diary filled with memoranda, poems written in free verse, descriptions of dreams and of the thresholds of my house surrounded by cherry trees and gardenias. To write in Spanish is for me a gesture of survival. And because of translation, my memory has now become a part of the memory of many others.

Translators are not traitors, as the proverb says, but rather splendid friends in this great human community of language.

---

diasporic: relating to a diaspora, or dispersion of a group of people across a large geographic area to which they are not native.

oxytonic: with main stress on the final or single syllable of a word.

paraoxytonic: with main stress on the next-to-last syllable of a word.

Vérde qué té quiéro vérde: (translation [stressed syllables marked]: "Green. How I want you green," the opening line of a famous poem by Federico García Lorca), an illustration of stress falling on oxytonic and paraoxytonic syllables.

cordillera: mountain ranges consisting of more or less parallel chains of peaks.

Argosín uses her personal experiences as an exile in the United States to argue about her reasons for continuing to write in Spanish. Check out what Chapter 18 has to say about using personal experience in your writing.

·· **LINK TO P. 375**

ENGLISH

MARJORIE AGOSÍN translated by Monica Bruno

I discovered that English
is too skinny,
functional,
precise,
too correct,
meaning
only one thing.
Too much wrath,
too many lawyers and sinister policemen,
too many deans at schools for small females,
in the Anglo-Saxon language.

II

In contrast Spanish
has so many words to say come with me friend,
make love to me on
the *césped,* the *grama,* the *pasto.*[1]
Let's go party,[2]
at dusk, at night, at sunset.
Spanish
loves
the unpredictable, it is
dementia,
all windmills° and velvet.

III

Spanish
is simple and baroque,

Landscape of Chile

windmills: an allusion to Don Quixote, who tilted at windmills on his old nag, imagining them to be giants.

---

[1]All three words mean *grass* in English.
[2]The Spanish version of this poem uses two phrases which mean *to party*: *de juerga* and *de fiesta.*

(Pablo) Neruda: Pen name of the Nobel prize-winning Chilean poet, politician, and diplomat (1904–1973), considered by many to be the finest Latin American poet of the twentieth century.

Federico García Lorca: Spanish poet and playwright (1898–1936); a sympathizer with leftist causes and a homosexual, Lorca was executed by a Nationalist firing squad early on in the Spanish Civil War under mysterious circumstances. Lorca penned "Verde, que te quiero verde," cited by Agosín in her essay.

Don Quixote: the hero of Miguel de Cervantes's comic and satiric novel of the same name; the novel was originally published in two volumes in 1605 and 1615. The novel concerns Quixote, who, having read too many courtly romances, goes off to find adventure. Quixote's name and the adjective "quixotic" are often applied to someone who, inspired by high (but often false) ideals, pursues an impossible project or task.

Violeta Parra: Chilean folksinger (1917–1967) most often associated with "La Nueva Cancion," a new style of Chilean and Latin American popular music, much influenced by folk traditions. Her best-known work is perhaps "Gracias à la Vida," "Thanks to Life."

(continued on page 759)

a palace of nobles and beggars,
it fills itself with silences and the breaths of dragonflies.
Neruda's° verses
saying "I could write the saddest verses
tonight,"
or Federico° swimming underwater through the greenest of
   greens.

IV

Spanish
is Don Quijote° maneuvering,
Violeta Parra° grateful
spicy, tasty, fragrant
the rumba, the salsa, the cha-cha.
There are so many words
to say
naive dreamers
and impostors.
There are so many languages in our
language: Quechua,° Aymará,° Rosas chilensis,° Spanglish.°

V

I love the imperfections of
Spanish,
the language takes shape in my hand:
the sound of drums and waves,
the Caribbean in the radiant foam of the sun,
are delirious upon my lips.
English has fallen short for me,
it signifies business,
law
and inhibition,
never the crazy, clandestine,
clairvoyance of
love.

RESPOND●

1. Why does Agosín write only in Spanish? How do her reasons for using Spanish compare with those of Marquez and Cisneros? How does she regard using Spanish as relating to her ancestry as a Jew?

2. What sort of experiences did Agosín have while trying to learn English? How typical do you think her experiences were? In other words, how do Americans who are native speakers of English treat nonnative speakers of English? How did Spanish represent a source of strength and consolation to Agosín during the period when she was learning English?

3. What does Spanish represent for Agosín? Why would it represent these things for her?

4. As the selections by Marquez, Cisneros, and Agosín make clear, even though Spanish does not mean the same thing to everyone who speaks it, its various meanings remain significant to many Americans whose ancestors can be traced somehow to the Spanish-speaking world. The selections by these writers, along with the survey data from the Pew Heritage Center/Kaiser Family Foundation (p. 744), also make clear that for many Hispanics, to lose Spanish would be to lose a fundamental part of their identity as individuals and as members of larger groups. Using these texts, perhaps personal experience, and perhaps discussions you have with people who claim to be bilingual or bidialectal (i.e., to speak a dialect of English other than Standard English, the variety expected and rewarded at school), **write an essay** in which you seek to define the role of language(s) in the creation of individual and group identity.

Quechua: the language of the former Inca empire and the major indigenous language of the central Andes today.

Aymará: one of the major indigenous languages of Bolivia.

Rosas chilensis: Latin species name for a rose indigenous to Chile.

Spanglish: popular label for the practice of switching between Spanish and English within a conversation or sentence, as many bilingual Hispanics do when they speak with other bilinguals.

▶ *Lan Cao is currently Cabell*
Professor of Law at the
Marshall-Wythe School of
Law at the College of William
and Mary. She is the author
of Monkey Bridge *(1997), the*
novel from which this excerpt
comes. (A monkey bridge is a
spindly bamboo bridge used
by Vietnamese peasants.) The
novel recounts the experiences
of a young woman who, like
Lan Cao, came to the United
States fleeing the Vietnam
War. Cao herself arrived here
in 1975.

At this point in the novel
the narrator, an adolescent
girl, and her mother have
moved to the States, having
had to leave behind the girl's
maternal grandfather—their
only other living relative. The
girl had arrived before the
mother and had stayed with
an American colonel her fam-
ily had befriended while he
was in Vietnam. He and his
wife are the Uncle Michael
and Aunt Mary referred to in
the text. This excerpt begins
with a comparison of Ameri-
can and Asian markets but
quickly moves to more com-
plex topics. As you read, try to
put yourself in Lan Cao's posi-
tion. For some readers, it will
be an all too familiar one; for
others, it may be an almost
unimaginable one.

The Gift of Language

LAN CAO

I discovered soon after my arrival in Falls Church that everything, even the simple business of shopping the American way, unsettled my mother's nerves. From the outside, it had been an ordinary building that held no promises or threats beyond four walls anchored to a concrete parking lot. But inside, the A & P brimmed with unexpected abundance. Built-in metal stands overflowed with giant oranges and grapefruits meticulously arranged into a pyramid. Columns of canned vegetables and fruits stood among multiple shelves as people well rehearsed to the demands of modern shopping meandered through the fluorescent aisles. I remembered the sharp chilled air against my face, the way the hydraulic door made a sucking sound as it closed behind.

My first week in Connecticut with Uncle Michael and Aunt Mary, I thought Aunt Mary was a genius shopper. She appeared to have the sixth sense of a bat and could identify, record, and register every item on sale. She was skilled in the art of coupon shopping—in the American version of Vietnamese haggling, the civil and acceptable mode of getting the customers to think they had gotten a good deal.

The day after I arrived in Farmington, Aunt Mary navigated the cart—and me—through aisles, numbered and categorized, crammed with jars and cardboard boxes, and plucked from them the precise product to match the coupons she carried. I had been astonished that day that the wide range of choices did not disrupt her plan. We had a schedule, I discovered, which Aunt Mary mapped out on a yellow pad, and which we followed, checking off item after item. She called it the science of shopping, the ability to resist the temptations of dazzling packaging. By the time we were through, our cart would be filled to the rim with cans of Coke, the kinds with flip-up caps that made can openers obsolete, in family-size cartons. We had chicken and meat sealed in tight, odorless packages, priced and weighed. We had fruits so beautifully polished and waxed they looked artificial. And for me, we had mangoes and papayas that were still hard and green

Bilingual outreach worker helping Vietnamese shoppers in the United States.

but which Aunt Mary had handed to me like rare jewels from a now extinct land.

But my mother did not appreciate the exacting orderliness of the A & P. She could not give in to the precision of previously weighed and packaged food, the bloodlessness of beef slabs in translucent wrappers, the absence of carcasses and pigs' heads. In Saigon, we had only outdoor markets. "Sky markets," they were called, vast, prosperous expanses in the middle of the city where barrels of live crabs and yellow carps and booths of ducks and geese would be stacked side by side with cardboard stands of expensive silk fabric from Hong Kong. It was always noisy there—a voluptuous mix of animal and human sounds that the air itself had assimilated and held. The sharp acrid smell of gutters choked by the monsoon rain. The unambiguous odor of dried horse dung that lingered in the atmosphere, partially camouflaged by the fat, heavy scent of guavas and bananas.

My mother knew the vendors and even the shoppers by name and 5
would take me from stall to stall to expose me to her skills. They were
all addicted to each other's oddities. My mother would feign indifference and they would inevitably call out to her. She would heed their
call and they would immediately retreat into sudden apathy. They
knew my mother's slick bargaining skills, and she, in turn, knew how
to navigate with grace through their extravagant prices and rehearsed
huffiness. Theirs had been a mating dance, a match of wills.

Toward the center of the market, a man with a spotted boa con-
strictor coiled around his neck stood and watched day after day over
an unruly hodgepodge of hand-dyed cotton shirts, handkerchiefs, and
swatches of white muslin; funerals were big business in Vietnam. To
the side, in giant paper bags slit with round openings, were canaries
and hummingbirds which my mother bought, one hundred at a time,
and freed, one by one, into our garden; it was a good deed designed to
generate positive karma for the family. My mother, like the country
itself, was obsessed with karma. In fact, the Vietnamese word for
"please," as in "could you please," means literally "to make good
karma." "Could you please pass the butter" becomes "Please make good
karma and pass me the butter." My mother would cup each bird in her
hand and set it on my head. It was her way of immersing me in a well-
spring of karmic charm, and in that swift moment of delight when the
bird's wings spread over my head as it contemplated flight, I believed
life itself was utterly beautiful and blessed.

Every morning, we drifted from stack to stack, vendor to vendor.
There were no road maps to follow—tables full of black market Prell
and Colgate were pocketed among vegetable stands one day and jars
of medicinal herbs the next. The market was randomly organized, and
only the mighty and experienced like my mother could navigate its
patternless paths.

But with a sense of neither drama nor calamity, my mother's ability
to navigate and decipher simply became undone in our new life. She
preferred the improvisation of haggling to the conventional certainty
of discount coupons, the primordial messiness and fishmongers' stink
of the open-air market to the aroma-free order of individually wrapped
fillets.

Now, a mere three and a half years or so after her last call to the sky
market, the dreadful truth was simply this: we were going through life

in reverse, and I was the one who would help my mother through the hard scrutiny of ordinary suburban life. I would have to forgo the luxury of adolescent experiments and temper tantrums, so that I could scoop my mother out of harm's way and give her sanctuary. Now, when we stepped into the exterior world, I was the one who told my mother what was acceptable or unacceptable behavior.

All children of immigrant parents have experienced these 10 moments. When it first occurs, when the parent first reveals the behavior of a child, is a defining moment. Of course, all children eventually watch their parents' astonishing return to the vulnerability of childhood, but for us the process begins much earlier than expected.

"We don't have to pay the moment we decide to buy the pork. We can put as much as we want in the cart and pay only once, at the checkout counter." It took a few moments' hesitation for my mother to succumb to the peculiarity of my explanation.

And even though I hesitated to take on the responsibility, I had no other choice. It was not a simple process, the manner in which my mother relinquished motherhood. The shift in status occurred not just in the world but in the safety of our home as well, and it became most obvious when we entered the realm of language. I was like Kiki, my pet bird in Saigon, tongue untwisted and sloughed of its rough and thick exterior. According to my mother, feeding the bird crushed red peppers had caused it to shed its tongue in successive layers and allowed it to speak the language of humans.

Every morning during that month of February 1975, while my mother paced the streets of Saigon and witnessed the country's preparation for imminent defeat, I followed Aunt Mary around the house, collecting words like a beggar gathering rain with an earthen pan. She opened her mouth, and out came a constellation of gorgeous sounds. Each word she uttered was a round stone, with the smoothness of something that had been rubbed and polished by the waves of a warm summer beach. She could swim straight through her syllables. On days when we studied together, I almost convinced myself that we would continue that way forever, playing with the movement of sound itself. I would listen as she tried to inspire me into replicating the "th" sound with the seductive powers of her voice. "Slip the tip of your tongue between your front teeth and pull it back real quick," she would coax and coax. Together, she and I sketched the English language, its curi-

Khe Sanh: a remote United States Marine base in Vietnam. On January 21, 1968, troops from the North Vietnamese Army launched an attack on the base, starting a seventy-seven day battle that is often considered one of the most brutal of the entire Vietnam War.

Tet Offensive: a surprise attack launched on over a hundred South Vietnamese cities and towns by 70,000 North Vietnamese Army troops during the truce declared to celebrate Tet, the Vietnamese New Year. While it cost the lives of many North Vietnamese troops and left their military unstable, the Offensive is often considered a public relations defeat for the United States, as it made North Vietnam's military seem stronger than many believed and reduced the American public's drive to continue fighting the war.

Ho Chi Minh Trail: a complex network of paths, roads, and jungle trails leading from the panhandle of northern Vietnam through Laos and Cambodia and into southern Vietnam. The Trail was used throughout the Vietnam War to resupply the North Vietnamese military with food and weaponry, to transport soldiers into South Vietnam, and as a base to launch close-range attacks on South Vietnam.

ous cadence and rhythm, into the receptive Farmington landscape. Only with Aunt Mary and Uncle Michael could I give myself an inheritance my parents never gave me: the gift of language. The story of English was nothing less than the poetry of sound and motion. To this day, Aunt Mary's voice remains my standard for perfection.

My superior English meant that, unlike my mother and Mrs. Bay, I knew the difference between "cough" and "enough," "bough" and "through," "trough" and "thorough," "dough" and "fought." Once I made it past the fourth or fifth week in Connecticut, the new language Uncle Michael and Aunt Mary were teaching me began gathering momentum, like tumbleweed in a storm. This was my realization: we have only to let one thing go—the language we think in, or the composition of our dream, the grass roots clinging underneath its rocks—and all at once everything goes. It had astonished me, the ease with which continents shift and planets change course, the casual way in which the earth goes about shedding the laborious folds of its memories. Suddenly, out of that difficult space between here and there, English revealed itself to me with the ease of thread unspooled. I began to understand the levity and weight of its sentences. First base, second base, home run. New terminologies were not difficult to master, and gradually the possibility of perfection began edging its way into my life. How did those numerous Chinatowns and Little Italys sustain the will to maintain a distance, the desire to inhabit the edge and margin of American life? A mere eight weeks into Farmington, and the American Dream was exerting a sly but seductive pull.

By the time I left Farmington to be with my mother, I had already 15 created for myself a different, more sacred tongue. Khe Sanh,° the Tet Offensive,° the Ho Chi Minh Trail°—a history as imperfect as my once obviously imperfect English—these were things that had rushed me into the American melting pot. And when I saw my mother again, I was no longer the same person she used to know. Inside my new tongue, my real tongue, was an astonishing new power. For my mother and her Vietnamese neighbors, I became the keeper of the word, the only one with access to the light-world. Like Adam, I had the God-given right to name all the fowls of the air and all the beasts of the field.

The right to name, I quickly discovered, also meant the right to stand guard over language and the right to claim unadulterated authority. Here was a language with an ocean's quiet mystery, and it would be up to me to render its vastness comprehensible to the newcomers around me. My language skill, my ability to decipher the nuances of American life, was what held us firmly in place, night after night, in our Falls Church living room. The ease with which I could fabricate wholly new plot lines from TV made the temptation to invent especially difficult to resist.

And since my mother couldn't understand half of what anyone was saying, television watching, for me, was translating and more. This, roughly, was how things went in our living room:

The Bionic Woman had just finished rescuing a young girl, approximately my age, from drowning in a lake where she'd gone swimming against her mother's wishes. Once out of harm's way, Jaime made the girl promise she'd be more careful next time and listen to her mother.

Translation: the Bionic Woman rescued the girl from drowning in the lake, but commended her for her magnificent deeds, since the girl had heroically jumped into the water to rescue a prized police dog.

"Where's the dog?" my mother would ask. "I don't see him."   20

"He's not there anymore, they took him to the vet right away. Remember?" I sighed deeply.

"Oh," my mother said. "It's strange. Strong girl, Bionic Woman."

The dog that I convinced her existed on the television screen was no more confusing than the many small reversals in logic and the new identities we experienced her first few months in America.

"I can take you in this aisle," a store clerk offered as she unlocked a new register to accommodate the long line of customers. She gestured us to "come over here" with an upturned index finger, a disdainful hook we Vietnamese use to summon dogs and other domestic creatures. My mother did not understand the ambiguity of American hand gestures. In Vietnam, we said "Come here" to humans differently, with our palm up and all four fingers waved in unison—the way people over here waved goodbye. A typical Vietnamese signal beckoning someone to "come here" would prompt, in the United States, a "goodbye," a response completely opposite from the one desired.

"Even the store clerks look down on us," my mother grumbled as we 25 walked home. This was a truth I was only beginning to realize: it was not the enormous or momentous event, but the gradual suggestion of irrevocable and protracted change that threw us off balance and made us know in no uncertain terms that we would not be returning to the familiarity of our former lives.

It was, in many ways, a lesson in what was required to sustain a new identity: it all had to do with being able to adopt a different posture, to reach deep enough into the folds of the earth to relocate one's roots and bend one's body in a new direction, pretending at the same time that the world was the same now as it had been the day before. I strove for the ability to realign my eyes, to shift with a shifting world and convince both myself and the rest of the world into thinking that, if the earth moved and I moved along with it, that motion, however agitated, would be undetectable. The process, which was as surprising as a river reversing course and flowing upstream, was easier said than done.

RESPOND.

1. What is your initial response to this excerpt from Cao's novel? Given the mother's cultural expectations, which she has brought from Vietnam, is it logical for her to respond as she does? In what senses is Cao forced to parent her mother?

2. How does Cao construct the argument she makes here? What sorts of evidence does she rely on? How does she use language effectively to convey her ideas? (Chapters 14 and 18, respectively, will help you answer these questions.)

3. The tale that Cao tells has been told many times in the writings of immigrants, especially those who arrive in the United States as children with parents who speak little or no English. What are the consequences for family life? How does language become a source of power for the child? How does this power disrupt traditional patterns of family life?

4. Cao, like many immigrant children, lost much of her native language— Vietnamese—as well as French, another language widely spoken by educated Vietnamese at that time. (France had colonized Vietnam for many years prior to the war.) The decline in her ability to use these languages had negative repercussions for her relationship with her parents. As she commented in an interview given while she was a visiting law professor at Duke University, "The more educated I became, the more separate I was from my parents. I think that is a very immigrant story." Even native speakers of English who are not from middle-class backgrounds often report similar situations in their own lives. Should such separation from one's home community be a necessary consequence of education for native or nonnative speakers of English in the United States? Why or why not? Might there be ways to prevent it? Are there benefits to preventing it? Should such efforts be made? Why? **Write an essay** in which you tackle these questions. Your essay will likely include features of evaluative, causal, and proposal arguments. If the situation described is unfamiliar to you, you might make a point of interviewing people who know about it firsthand.

▶ *Andrea Lo is a senior math major at the University of Texas at Austin, where she is in the Plan II Honors Program. She wrote this essay in a course entitled "Arguing about Language," which used the earlier edition of this book supplemented with additional readings focusing on popular debates about language and language issues. As you read, notice how Lo uses language—or the lack of it— to define who she is and isn't.*

Finding Myself through Language

ANDREA LO

"Wo men dou shi zhong guo ren." *We are all Chinese*. These were the lyrics to the first song I learned at Chinese Sunday school. It's a song that brings a sense of national and cultural pride to millions of Chinese around the world. But for me, it was a song that represented a national and cultural identity of which I didn't want to be—and indeed of which I *wasn't*—a part. I was not Chinese. Growing up in the American school system, I recited the Pledge of Allegiance each day and sang the American national anthem every Monday morning. I was born of Chinese blood, but I was born and raised in the USA. I was Chinese-*American*, and I was adamant in making that distinction.

Of course I couldn't drop the "Chinese" altogether. People always questioned my nationality based on my appearance, which was something I could never change. Even if I dyed my hair blonde and wore blue contact lenses, nobody would believe I was anything but Asian. So I settled for "Chinese-American," using the word "Chinese" as if it was simply a qualifier to account for my physical appearance. "I'm American even though I look Chinese." If it had been grammatically acceptable, I probably even would have said I was "chinese-American"—with a lowercase "c"—after all my efforts to minimize that portion of my identity that fell before the hyphen. And, indeed, I expended a great deal of energy on this project.

I rejected numerous aspects of Chinese culture. I refused to watch the Chinese soap operas and Hong Kong dramas that my parents and grandparents loved. I grew to dislike Chinese furniture and Chinese art, and I dreaded learning about any era in China's expansive history. I even began to feel uncomfortable around my group of friends, who were often peers from Chinese school or children of my parents' close friends and therefore of Asian descent like me. Terms like "Asian pride" were popular with my Asian friends, who scrawled it across their notebooks and shouted it out in the hallways, but those words made me cringe. I didn't want to get "stuck" in the Asian crowd and be stigmatized or stereotyped because of them.

Closed sign (in Chinese and English)

Most importantly, however, I rejected the Chinese language. As is the experience for many American children of non-English-speaking parents, I was ashamed of my parents' native tongue. I clearly remember the day in elementary school when I had to present my family tree to the class. All of the other children were talking about Adams and Walkers and Johnsons. One boy could even trace his lineage back to Johnny Appleseed. But my family tree was full of strange names like Sau Kam Siu and Wing Wa Lo that nobody—except me—could pronounce properly or gracefully, let alone recognize. I could feel my ears burning as I read out the names of my family members and heard the snickers of my classmates. They were laughing because my family's names were Chinese. Perhaps this is understandable. People tend to laugh at things that sound odd to them, and surely a foreign language can sound strange to one's ears. But for me at the time, my classmates' laughter was a signal of exclusion. If Chinese names were "different," then, by extension, so was I.

This experience and others, like the time a boy shouted "Ching 5
chang chong" when he passed me on the track during gym, made me

embarrassed about the Chinese language. I made the conscious effort to *avoid* learning it with the hope that I would never be associated with it or humiliated by it again. When my parents spoke to me at home in Cantonese, I would no longer respond to them in the same language. Instead, I would insist on speaking in English. In Chinese Sunday school—which I was forced to attend—I exerted effort only to get a good grade but not to learn the language. My grades were a quantitative measure that my parents could manipulate by praising or punishing me. My actual retention of the language was something over which they had no control. Therefore, I would memorize Chinese characters on Saturday night, regurgitate them the following morning, and promptly forget about them for the rest of the week. In this way, then, I tried to distance myself from the language that had been the source of so much humiliation. I threw away Chinese and embraced English, hoping that in doing so I could erase all my Chinese connections.

Soon, my knowledge of Mandarin consisted only of those words that I had involuntarily retained from Chinese school lessons. My spoken Cantonese was so poor that I could no longer hold an extended conversation with my own grandparents, who speak only Cantonese. My rejection of the Chinese language had thus severed my ties to members of my own family. However, it never succeeded in guaranteeing my acceptance as an American. For example, my elementary and middle-school classmates could observe that I couldn't converse in Chinese with new students who came from Taiwan or Hong Kong. Yet in the ninth grade, when I told them about my upcoming move to China for my father's job, few could understand my fear of going to this new country. They assumed that for me it would be like "going home."

Moving to Beijing made my struggle to establish an American identity even more difficult. There, despite the fact that, for once, I looked like the millions of people around me, I felt like I was in a sea of foreigners. I felt like I was the American in a crowd of Chinese faces. But the Chinese in Beijing didn't consider me to be American. For them, anybody of Chinese blood was a Chinese person. I just didn't make a very "good" Chinese person because I didn't know how to speak "my" language. I was reprimanded by everybody from my parents' coworkers to our telephone repairman for not knowing how to speak my "native" tongue. Many white Americans or other Caucasian foreigners in Beijing didn't see me as an American, either. I was just one of the many indistinguishable faces in the vast Chinese sea.

In Asia, then, as in the United States, cultivating an ignorance of the Chinese language was not sufficient for me to reject my Chinese identity or to establish an American one. I, therefore, placed more emphasis on my knowledge of and fluency in English in order to justify my claim to being American. I attended international schools with students from all around the world, yet I gravitated towards the native English speakers when building my social networks. I volunteered to teach conversational English in local Hong Kong schools, making sure to tell my students from the first day that I didn't speak Cantonese, that I was a native speaker of English, and that I wasn't from Hong Kong: I was American.

I wasn't the only one in my family to use English in this way. Walking through the street markets in China, I noticed my brother would always make a comment in English about a piece of clothing or an interesting piece of art each time a Caucasian person would pass by. More often than not, my brother's comment would cause the Caucasian person to look our way in surprise. It didn't matter if the person was American or not. My brother's intention was solely to differentiate himself from the rest of the Chinese around him. He wanted people to know he was American, and he demonstrated this fact by speaking fluent English with a clearly American accent.

I returned to the U.S. after three-and-a-half years in Asia. After   10 learning of my experiences, people would often ask me if I were fluent in Chinese. Before my trip to China, I was often expected to speak Chinese simply because I looked Chinese. Now, people expected me to speak Chinese because I had spent a significant amount of time in China. I used to have a reason for my ignorance, but now I no longer did. I had no excuse for spending more than three years in a foreign country and never learning its language.

I realized that in my determination to reject learning about Chinese culture as *my* culture, I had also rejected learning about it as a *new* culture. I had buried myself in the international communities, emphasizing each of my ties to American culture. Meanwhile, I had failed to explore the local communities that were just around the corner. I had been so caught up in using language to create my own identity that I had ignored its utility in learning about others. Knowing how to speak

Chinese, regardless of my ethnic background, could have enabled me to speak with people of the local culture, to learn from them about their beliefs, their values, and their way of life. It could have helped me to learn about their history and their politics and to develop meaningful relationships with them on a more personal level. I denied myself of all these opportunities simply by rejecting the language.

I also realize now that the culture I failed to learn about while living in China is an inseparable part of my own heritage. The Chinese names on my family tree aren't just names—they are my family and my history. They are indeed "different" from typically Caucasian names, and I am indeed "different" from Caucasians, but this fact should not be the source of shame. Adopting a family with names that are easier to pronounce or changing the history of which my family was a part will not make me feel any more accepted in this predominantly Caucasian society. I was born in America to Chinese parents. Because of that, both the American and Chinese cultures have helped to shape who I am. Growing up, I used language in an attempt to reject one and adopt the other. But I understand now that renouncing the Chinese language can never erase my Chinese heritage, nor can embracing the English language uniquely write me a new personal history.

I still choose to make the distinction that I'm not Chinese but Chinese-American. The "Chinese," however, is no longer a qualifier to account for my appearance. Instead, it's a part of me that is equal in importance to the "American" that follows. Of course, I still have much to learn about Chinese culture and about my own family's Chinese background in order to discover how these cultural influences have shaped my own behavior and identity. But now I know exactly where to begin in this exploration. I should begin with the part of the culture that I once tried the hardest to reject. The place for me to begin is in the language. I may not be able to become literate in Chinese quickly or easily, but I hope to at least regain my fluency in the language. Learning to speak Cantonese will allow me to rebuild connections with my family members. It will give me a greater understanding of Hong Kong life and culture—the life and culture that my own parents and grandparents experienced before coming to America. If nothing else, learning to speak Cantonese will be a constant reminder of that part of my identity that I was once so keen to ignore and that I am now so lucky to still have the opportunity to embrace.

Among the elements in Lo's finely crafted essay are definition arguments exploring what it means to be labeled *Chinese* and *American*. See Chapter 9 for more on making definition arguments.

·· LINK TO P. 147

RESPOND •

1. How does this essay recount Lo's changing understanding of her own identity and the roles that language and labels have played in it? In what ways has she let Chinese define her identity, even as (or perhaps because) she struggled against it?

2. What might Lo's comment in paragraph 2 that "'I'm American even though I look Chinese'" mean? After all, she was born in the United States. What does an American look like? What does it mean when Americans say "You don't look American" to someone like Lo?

3. One memorable aspect of this essay is its use of crisp detail. Choose three specific examples of detail that Lo uses, explaining how each contributes to her point, both in the paragraph in which the detail occurs and in the essay overall.

4. Lo's essay focuses on the knowledge and use of a language other than English—perhaps one of the most salient examples of negotiating an identity through language in the United States, where the majority of citizens seem to take pride in being monolingual. Yet all Americans must, in some sense, find themselves through language. **Write an essay** in which you recount your own efforts to do so—to understand the varieties of language or the languages to which you have had access in your life as well as, perhaps, your efforts to change them. There will likely be aspects of definitional, evaluative, and causal argumentation in your essay—and perhaps a proposal about the future, as there is for Lo.

chapter twenty-eight

Beliefs and Stances

What does it mean to take a stance on an issue, especially a controversial one, in a society as diverse and pluralistic as the United States? Does the American commitment to freedom of religion include the right to talk about or practice one's religion publicly? Or does freedom of religion mean freedom from religious discourse of any kind in a public setting? What if some people's religious beliefs conflict with the commitments of others? What does it mean to be patriotic in America today? Can one be critical of the country, even when it is at war, or does patriotism demand agreement with the government's decisions? Do patriots follow rules and honor commitments, even if doing so means they are no longer true to what they really believe?

The arguments in this chapter call upon you to consider these issues. Regardless of your own ideological commitments, these readings will force you to examine those commitments and the ways in which you argue for them. Is your argumentative strategy to silence those with opposing views, figuratively or literally? Do you seek to "defeat" those with whom you disagree? Do you instead agree to disagree? Or do you seek common ground in order to find "win-win" solutions to what would otherwise remain disagreements? How can you—as an individual and as a member of society—determine what might be appropriate responses in particular situations?

The chapter begins with a cluster of readings about religious beliefs of all sorts in the public arena. It is followed by a cluster of arguments about patriotism, especially in time of war.

www.
For additional readings on
Beliefs and Stances,
visit bedfordstmartins.com
/everythingsanargument.

One thing distinguishing the United States from perhaps all other countries is its constitutional separation of church and state. There is no "state religion," and Americans aren't required to pay dues or taxes to any religious institution. Indeed, most Americans—even (or especially) those who are religious—are generally happy with that state of affairs because they don't want others dictating what they should believe or practice. At the same time, we cannot deny that "In God We Trust" appears on all American currency (a practice begun in 1861 with the two-cent piece and extended to all coins in 1908 and all currency in 1955) nor that if businesses close, they generally do so on Sundays and holidays associated with the Christian tradition.

These facts remind us that there is little common ground among Americans on the proper role of **religious beliefs in the public arena.** Should the government be neutral on matters of faith and religion? Should it vigorously protect the rights of those who are religious? Of those who are not? Of the majority? Of the minority? Is it possible to protect simultaneously the rights of those who are *and* are not religious? Of the majority *and* the minority? These unresolved questions will likely exist as long as this country does.

The arguments in this cluster all focus in some way on matters of religious belief and their expression in the public arena. Sometimes the audience for that expression is limited to members of the writer's community of faith; often it is much larger, encompassing the entire society. The issues raised, however, certainly extend beyond the particular texts. How does America compare with other countries with respect to matters of religious faith? Does the freedom to espouse one's religious beliefs entail a commitment to the right of others to espouse the beliefs of other religions — or even no religion at all? What happens if religious practice conflicts with commitments to concepts like equality? Should cartoonists of a particular faith be surprised if some newspapers refuse to print their cartoons when they explicitly espouse that faith? How do the children of immigrants who practice a minority religion make sense of who they are in a culture quite different from the one in their parents' homeland? How do gay men and lesbians engage with religious traditions that promote a decidedly negative view of homosexuality and homosexuals? How does a White fundamentalist Christian seek to persuade other White fundamentalists that they, on religious grounds, should apologize to African Americans for slavery? Should jurists' interpretation of the Christian God as the ultimate arbiter of justice matter in American courts? Should Muslim women have to worry if they veil themselves publicly?

As the response to each round of Supreme Court rulings reminds us — whether the cases concern abortion, prayer at graduation ceremonies, or the right of the Boy Scouts to reject gay men as scout leaders — religious beliefs have always been present in our country's public debate, and it's likely they'll stay there. For that reason alone, it's in everyone's best interest to spend some time evaluating how such beliefs manifest themselves in our public discourse and how they work as parts of arguments.

The two-year Pew Global Attitudes Project, sponsored by the Pew Charitable Trust with additional funding from the William and Flora Hewlett Foundation, represents "a series of worldwide public-opinion surveys that will measure the impact of globalization, modernization, rapid technological and cultural change and the September 11 terrorist events on the values and attitudes of more than 38,000 people in 44 countries worldwide." Here, we present the opening pages of a December 2002 report on attitudes toward religion and its importance in people's lives around the world. As the text and accompanying charts — a defining characteristic of social science writing — clearly illustrate, the United States is unique among wealthy nations in the high percentage of people reporting that religion is very important in their life. Should we be surprised that religious beliefs play a significant role in public life in our country?

Among Wealthy Nations . . ., U.S. Stands Alone in Its Embrace of Religion

PEW GLOBAL ATTITUDES PROJECT

Religion is much more important to Americans than to people living in other wealthy nations. Six-in-ten (59%) people in the U.S. say religion plays a *very* important role in their lives. This is roughly twice the percentage of self-avowed religious people in Canada (30%), and an even higher proportion when compared with Japan and Western Europe. Americans' views are closer to people in developing nations than to the publics of developed nations.

The 44-nation survey of the *Pew Global Attitudes Project* shows stark global regional divides over the personal importance of religion.[1] In Africa, no fewer than eight-in-ten in any country see religion as very

important personally. Majorities in every Latin American country also subscribe to that view, with the exception of Argentina. More than nine-in-ten respondents in the predominantly Muslim nations of Indonesia, Pakistan, Mali and Senegal rate religion as personally very important. In Turkey and Uzbekistan, however, people are more divided over religion's importance.

Secularism is particularly prevalent throughout Europe. Even in heavily Catholic Italy fewer than three-in-ten (27%) people say religion is very important personally, a lack of intensity in belief that is consistent with opinion in other Western European nations. Attitudes are comparable in former Soviet bloc countries. In the Czech Republic, fully 71% say religion has little or no importance in their lives — more than any nation surveyed — while barely one-

---

[1]Question wording: How important is religion in your life — very important, somewhat important, not too important, or not at all important?

in-ten (11%) say it is very important. And in Poland, the birthplace of the Pope and where the Catholic Church played a pivotal role during the communist era, just 36% say religion is very important.

The Global Attitudes study correlated views on religion with annual per capita income and found that wealthier nations tend to place less importance on religion—with the exception of the United States. This is seen most clearly in Asia, where publics in the two wealthiest nations surveyed—Japan and South Korea—are far less likely to cite religion as personally important than those in poorer nations of the region. The lone exception is Vietnam, however, where just 24% of the public view religion as very important. (Questions on the personal importance of religion were not permitted in China, and were deemed too sensitive to ask in Egypt, Jordan and Lebanon.)

Religion Very Important

Country	Percent
N. America	
U.S.	59%
Canada	30%
West Europe	
G Britain	33%
Italy	27%
Germany	21%
France	11%
East Europe	
Poland	36%
Ukraine	35%
Slovakia	29%
Russia	14%
Bulgaria	13%
Czech	11%
Conflict Area	
Pakistan	91%
Turkey	65%
Uzbek.	35%
Latin America	
Guatem.	80%
Brazil	77%
Honduras	72%
Peru	69%
Bolivia	66%
Venez.	61%
Mexico	57%
Argentina	39%
Asia	
Indonesia	95%
India	92%
Phillip.	88%
Bangla.	88%
Korea	25%
Vietnam	24%
Japan	12%
Africa	
Senegal	97%
Nigeria	92%
Iv. Coast	91%
Mali	90%
S. Africa	87%
Kenya	85%
Uganda	85%
Ghana	84%
Tanzania	83%
Angola	80%

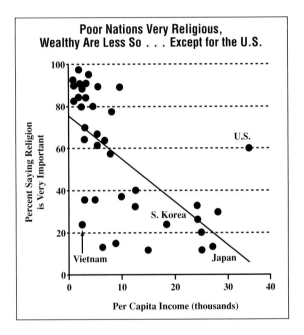

Poor Nations Very Religious, Wealthy Are Less So . . . Except for the U.S.

This report offers an evaluative argument that compares the importance of religion in the lives of people in the United States, and in those from other nations. For more about constructing evaluative arguments, see Chapter 10.

LINK TO P. 174 ·····················

RESPOND.

1. Does the information contained in this brief introductory section to the Pew Global Attitudes Project surprise you in any way? Why or why not? In your opinion, what might account for the unusual attitudes and behavior of Americans in comparison to citizens of other wealthy nations that the United States often sees as its peers and allies?

2. What do we learn about China, Egypt, Jordan, and Lebanon in this text? Why might these governments not want their citizens discussing religion? (You may need to do some research to find out something about these countries, their demographic makeup, and their history.)

3. As mentioned in the headnote, social scientists often rely on charts, tables, figures, and diagrams to do much of their work for them. Not only do they generally contain a great deal of information that is never discussed explicitly in the text, but they also permit the reader to check conclusions drawn in the text against the visual display, whether it is a chart (like the ones used in this excerpt) or a table, figure, or diagram. What sorts of additional observations not already mentioned in the text can you make on the basis of information included in the two charts?

   (The second chart, "Poor Nations Very Religious, Wealthy Are Less So . . . Except for the U.S.," may be difficult for you to read at first. It represents the results of the correlation, or statistical relationship, between wealth, as measured by annual per capita income, and importance reportedly placed on religion, as measured in terms of percentage of answers of "very important" to the question given in footnote 1. The horizontal sloping line in the chart, the regression line, represents a perfect negative correlation: if greater wealth in a country always meant comparably less importance reportedly attached to religion, all the dots or data points, each representing a country, would fall along this line. The closer the data point representing a country is to the line, the tighter the negative relationship between the wealth and importance of religion. Outliers, those data points farthest from the regression line, represent exceptions—for example, Vietnam and the United States in this case.)

4. **Write an essay** in which you evaluate your own responses to this text. Following question 1, you may discuss your surprise (or lack of it) or some other emotional response that you had: chagrin, dismay, happiness. As Chapter 10 reminds us, good evaluative arguments are based on explicit criteria. Hence you will need to examine your own assumptions about the United States and the larger world and about religion in public life.

In "The Ethicist," a weekly advice column in the New York Times that is also syndicated nationally, Randy Cohen helps readers make sense of dilemmas they encounter in their daily lives. Since the late nineteenth century, Americans have turned to newspaper columnists for advice; from the perspective of argumentation, columnists evaluate situations (Chapter 10) and offer readers proposals about potential courses of action they might take—or should have taken (Chapter 12). In this specific case, a New Yorker asked how she might balance her opposition to what she perceived as an act of sexism committed in the name of religion with her commitment to others' right to religious expression.

Read the query, read Cohen's response, and decide whether you agree or disagree with Cohen's analysis. Then, read on to see what readers of the Times had to say about Cohen's analysis and advice. The letters to the editor about this specific column spanned several weeks, with readers ultimately responding to other readers' letters. The first three letters appeared three weeks after the initial column with the editorial comment, "The Ethicist was reprimanded by hundreds of Orthodox Jews, outraged at criticism of a religious rule banning a handshake between the sexes." (Interestingly, among the published letter writers criticizing Cohen, several have last names that are traditionally Jewish, but none identifies him- or herself as Orthodox. One wonders if the editors of the Times had sufficient evidence for their claim.) The last three letters appeared two weeks after the initial letters were printed.

Between the Sexes

THE ETHICIST
RANDY COHEN

The courteous and competent real-estate agent I'd just hired to rent my house shocked and offended me when, after we signed our contract, he refused to shake my hand, saying that as an Orthodox Jew he did not touch women. As a feminist, I oppose sex discrimination of all sorts. However, I also support freedom of religious expression. How do I balance these conflicting values? Should I tear up our contract?

　　　　　　　　J.L., NEW YORK

This culture clash may not allow you to reconcile the values you esteem. Though the agent dealt you only a petty slight, without ill intent, you're entitled to work with someone who will treat you with the dignity and respect he shows his male clients. If this involved only his own person—adherence to laws concerning diet or dress, for example—you should of course be tolerant. But his actions directly affect you. And sexism is sexism, even when motivated by religious convictions. I believe you should tear up your contract.

Had he declined to shake hands with everyone, there would be no problem. What he may not do, however, is render a class of people untouchable. Were he, say, an airline ticket clerk who refused to touch Asian-Americans, he would find himself in hot water and rightly so. Bias on the basis of sex is equally discreditable.

Some religions (and some civil societies) that assign men and women distinct spheres argue that while those two spheres are different, neither is inferior to the other. This sort of reasoning was rejected in 1954 in the great school desegregation case, Brown v. Board of Education, when the Supreme Court declared that separate is by its very nature unequal. That's a pretty good ethical guideline for ordinary life.

There's a terrific moment in "Cool Hand Luke," when a prison guard about to put Paul Newman in the sweatbox says—I quote from memory—"Sorry, Luke, just doing my job." Newman replies, "Calling it your job don't make it right, boss." Religion, same deal. Calling an offensive action religious doesn't make it right.

LETTERS IN RESPONSE TO COHEN'S ADVICE

As a Jew, a feminist and a future rabbi, I share the Ethicist's contempt for discriminatory religious norms and practices (Oct. 27). However, the practice of "shomer negiah"—of refraining from engaging in any physical contact with members of the opposite sex who are not family—does not fall into this category. Had the Ethicist done his research, he would have known that the laws of negiah apply equally to both sexes and do not render either women or men peculiarly "untouchable." These laws are based on the belief that platonic male-female contact can easily degenerate into sexual impropriety.

Whether or not one agrees with this logic, it does not lend itself to an accusation of sexism. The real disgrace is that the Ethicist answered this query without educating himself about the religious practice upon which it is based and without consulting Jewish authorities who could assist him in this endeavor.

CARA WEINSTEIN ROSENTHAL
South Orange, N.J.

The Orthodox Jew who refused to shake a woman's hand after signing a real-estate contract was wrongfully accused of sexism and of acting without the "dignity and respect he shows his male clients." Rather, it was out of respect to his own wife and to other women that the man did not extend his hand; his intent was to elevate and sanctify the relationship between men and women, which is all too often trivialized.

HELEN POGRIN
New York

A real-estate agent is hired to rent a house, and the woman who hires him wants to tear up the contract because his religious beliefs prevent him from shaking hands? The agent was courteous and competent. What more did she want? The prohibition of physical contact between unrelated men and women has nothing to do with sexism. Religious freedom is a constitutional and moral right. No one should understand that more than the Ethicist.

ROBERT M. GOTTESMAN
Englewood, N.J.

Randy Cohen sure unleashed the 10 Furies (Letters, Nov. 17, responding to the Ethicist from Oct. 27). Actually, Cohen has a good point, and his critics protest too much. Orthodox

Judaism hardly treats women as equal to men. Orthodox men regularly express in prayer their gratitude to God for not having made them women. I suspect that the prohibition against touch isn't all that egalitarian either. After all, it is women who are viewed as impure for large segments of their lives.

EVA LANDY
Barrington, R.I.

Our rabbi—who is modern and egalitarian—gave a sermon on the Ethicist column, and he carefully drew the distinction between a religious belief and a discriminatory act. One question I have heard frequently: had the religion in question been one less familiar to the writer—say, Islam—would Cohen have given such a glib response without checking with religious experts and without considering both parties' sensitivities?

PAUL BERMAN
Edison, N.J.

As a Jewish woman, respectful but nonobservant, I can understand the discomfort of the woman who was offended. As a lawyer, however, I know that discomfort is never cause for breaking a contract.

MARGARET R. LOSS
New York

In order for his readers to trust his advice, Cohen must first convince them of his credibility as "The Ethicist." See Chapter 3 for more on how authors establish credibility with their audiences.

LINK TO P. 56

RESPOND •

1. Do you agree or disagree with Randy Cohen's analysis of the situation J.L. describes? In other words, did the Orthodox Jew's refusal to shake hands with a woman who was not a relative by blood or marriage constitute an act of sexism in terms of the intentions of the real estate agent or its effect upon his client? Should J.L., as Cohen suggests, have torn up the contract? Why or why not?

2. Evaluate the responses to Cohen's column. What sorts of arguments—those from the heart, those based on values, those based on character, or those based on fact and reason—do the letter writers use? Which specific arguments do you find most persuasive? Why?

3. How should a pluralistic society like ours accommodate religious expression when that expression violates—or appears to violate, in the eyes of some—other principles that are important, such as gender equality? **Write a proposal argument** (Chapter 12) in which you offer criteria for balancing these two when they are in conflict. Note that the case described here involves an individual's providing a contractual service to another; the range of such conflicts is, in fact, much broader. Thus you may wish to write about the case Cohen describes, or you may prefer to research other cases, which may have involved, for example, such issues as the right of parents who are Christian Scientists to deny or limit medical care for their children and the display of religious symbols such as menorahs or Christmas trees in various public places. The most effective proposals will be those that demonstrate they have dealt with the case they examine in its complexity.

Nationally syndicated columnist Leonard Pitts writes about politics, culture, and everyday life. He has won several journalism awards for his outstanding columns and has written a book, Black Men and the Journey to Fatherhood (1999). In this column, which appeared in major U.S. newspapers in late April 1999, Pitts examines a controversy about religious themes in public discourse generally and in newspaper comics specifically by focusing on the work of Johnny Hart, some of whose cartoons are reprinted following this selection (p. 786). As you read, notice the way Pitts's writing style works as a rhetorical tool.

A Little Matter of Faith

LEONARD PITTS

Ordinarily, Johnny Hart is not a guy I'd be rushing to defend.

Politically speaking, he's a little to the right of Attila the Hun. Adheres to an unswervingly literal interpretation of the Bible. Believes God may have been behind the assassination of Israeli Prime Minister Yitzhak Rabin as punishment for negotiating holy land away. Thinks Muslims, Jews and gays are on the afterlife express to hell. Not exactly on the same page, Johnny Hart and I. Till now.

It seems that in the last few years, Hart — creator of a popular comic strip called "B.C." that runs in many newspapers — has been at the center of a minor media controversy. Angry readers have complained. And some of the more than 1,200 newspapers that carry his work have either dropped it entirely or reserved the right to excise strips they don't like. Count among them such powerhouses as the *Chicago Sun-Times*, the *Los Angeles Times* and the *Washington Post*.

You might be wondering what Hart did to raise such a stink. According to a profile that recently ran in the *Post*, the answer is simple: He mentioned Jesus. Meaning that from time to time, particularly around the religious holidays, Hart uses the comic strip as a forum for Christian doctrine: birth, death, resurrection, salvation.

That, apparently, is more than 5 some folks can stand.

It's a funny thing about the funny pages. People don't like it when you mess with 'em. That's why so many strips seem to unfold in some dimension beyond time, an eternal '50s where nothing changes and safe, inoffensive gags recycle without end.

In such an environment, it doesn't take much to stir controversy. Garry Trudeau's "Doonesbury" does it with pointed sociopolitical satire. Lynn Johnston's "For Better or for Worse" does it with a recurring character who's gay. And Johnny Hart does it by talking Jesus. Which seems to illustrate the looming difficulty we have with discussing issues of faith.

It's a private matter, we say, but there's a certain hypocrisy in that argument, given that we discuss private matters in public forums all the time. What's it say to you that some of us find it easier to discuss penile implants than the fact that some people believe a man named Jesus was killed and then lived again? Or that others believe their ancestors were led from slavery to freedom by a man named Moses? Or that still others believe an angel imparted divine wisdom to a man named Mohammed?

I'm not here to argue the verities of faith. The point I'm trying to make has nothing to do with what people believe. Rather, it deals with the fact that people believe. Believe overwhelmingly, according to the polls. In a higher power, a force, a man or woman upstairs, a God.

Media—from the funny pages to 10 the 6 o'clock news—often seem ill at ease with that. Outside the easy hooks—Islamic terrorists, Christian zealots—they tend to pass the subject in silence, for reasons I'm not sure I understand. But I certainly understand the result: Media miss a large portion of the lives they purport to reflect.

I appreciate the misgivings of newspaper editors regarding Hart. They have a right—an obligation— to police their pages for inappropriate content. And there have been times his work teetered uncomfortably close to sheer proselytizing. Other times when it was, arguably, ugly toward those who don't believe as he does.

I'm convinced, however, that the larger part of media—and public— disaffection with Hart's work has less to do with how he says what he says than that he says it at all. That he transgresses the unspoken rule by which issues of faith are not to be openly discussed.

But the American creed of free speech has always demanded that we consider more views, not fewer. Has always held that the ability to countenance diverse opinions is a source of strength, not a sign of weakness. Guided by that principle, we've survived some pretty extreme characters.

I have to believe we can survive Jesus, too.

RESPOND ●

1. Why does Pitts, a religious believer who generally does not agree with Johnny Hart's religious beliefs, defend the cartoonist's right to use religion explicitly as a theme in his cartoons? What sorts of arguments does Pitts make? What sorts of evidence does he offer for his claims? How effective are they? What does Pitts mean in his final sentence when he writes, "I have to believe we can survive Jesus, too"?

2. Pitts's column is written in a very casual style: the reader can easily imagine him *saying* more or less exactly what he has written. He achieves this conversational tone by using sentence fragments and syntax that sound much like that of everyday speech. Rewrite paragraphs 6–9 in a style appropriate for an academic essay, recasting fragments into complete sentences, altering at least some of the informal syntax, and perhaps making other changes as well.

3. Among Pitts's arguments is the claim (paragraph 10) that with a few key exceptions, the media ignore religion and religious believers because they are "ill at ease" with religious belief. (Note that Pitts makes two separate but related claims here—he claims that the media ignore matters of faith and he offers his analysis of their reason for doing so.) Do you agree? Why or why not? **Write a column** of about five hundred words for a newspaper you regularly read addressing the paper's coverage of matters relating to faith or beliefs, and support or critique its current practice with respect to these topics.

Causal arguments often focus on the claim that something *will* happen; here Pitts is arguing that a particular result *won't* occur. See more about how to formulate a causal argument in Chapter 11.

LINK TO P. 205

B.C. is an award-winning comic strip drawn by Johnny Hart since 1958. The B.C. cartoons reprinted here address directly matters of faith from a decidedly Christian perspective. The title of the strip is, of course, part of Hart's argument. As you study these cartoons, consider how readers from a range of faiths and with a range of attitudes about the role of religious belief in public life might respond to them and their appearance in newspapers across the United States.

How does Hart use symbols in the arguments B.C. makes? See more about visual arguments in Chapter 15.

LINK TO P. 301

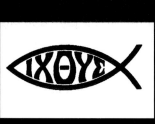

1. What is Hart's argument in each cartoon? Who is the intended audience? The invoked audience? The "real" or actual audience? (See Chapter 3.) How do you know? (Consider, for example, how members of each of the following groups might respond to the cartoons: evangelical Christians; Christians who find evangelism offensive or at least unwarranted; members of other faiths; atheists and others who believe there should be no mention of religious beliefs in public forums; those who believe that certain religious groups should have the right to mention their beliefs, even if others may find the beliefs offensive; and those who believe that "free speech" means all people can say anything they like.)

2. What are the meaning and history of the symbol that appears in the last panel of the fourth cartoon (which is a visual argument based on a Greek acronym)? This symbol often appears affixed to the rear end of automobiles, and it has given rise to at least two other "arguments," both of which are also often stuck to cars: a fish with small feet that has the name DARWIN written inside, and a fish with the word GEFILTE written inside. Explain each of the three arguments, discussing the sort of people who are likely to display each one on their cars. How effective are the two arguments that allude to the original one? How effectively do they use humor? To what ends? What is the purpose of making such arguments (that is, why do people affix such symbols to their automobiles in the first place)?

3. In "A Little Matter of Faith" (p. 784), Leonard Pitts points out that some newspapers no longer carry Hart's *B.C.* cartoons or "reserve . . . the right to excise strips they don't like" (paragraph 3). This decision was made in response to readers' complaints about the cartoons' overtly Christian content. **Write an essay** in which you respond to the question of whether such a decision constitutes censorship, good business, or something else. The most well-reasoned responses will not be those that merely reply "yes" or "no" but those that address both (1) the limits placed on the expression of religious faith in forums like the comics of a commercial newspaper and (2) the heterogeneous nature of U.S. society with respect to matters of faith and their public discussion.

▼ *In "A Hindu Renaissance," a feature article written in May 1999 for the* Dallas Morning News and Observer, *staff writer Deborah Kovach Caldwell examines the situation of immigrants who practice a minority religion in this country. As she notes, the experiences of immigrants and their children are quite different with respect to the religion, its practice, and its meanings in their lives. If you are a recent immigrant to the United States, compare your experiences with those detailed by Caldwell; if your family has been in the United States for generations, imagine what it would be like to immigrate to a country where the dominant religious traditions differ from your own or those with which you are familiar.*

A Hindu Renaissance

DEBORAH KOVACH CALDWELL

COPPELL, Texas—A few years ago, Manmadhan and Radha Nair enclosed the patio off their trim suburban ranch house and turned it into a Hindu oasis.

The white-tiled room is a tranquil place for lighting candles, draping deities—Vishnu, Shiva, Ganapathi and others—with garlands and offering rose water and grapes.

They wouldn't have considered such a room 20 years ago.

"Honestly, we were kind of embarrassed," said Manmadhan Nair, 45, who likes to be called Mike. "We were a little worried whether we could expose this kind of thing to other people."

Then their born-and-reared-in-America teenage kids came along. [5]

For more than a generation, most of the nation's approximately 1.5 million Hindus—the vast majority of them Indian immigrants—have paid little attention to their ancient faith. Busy building careers and families, they've tried to blend into America. But now the first generation of American-born Indians is coming of age. They are forcing their baby-boomer parents to reckon with a long-neglected faith.

Prayer rooms like the Nairs' are appearing in subdivisions everywhere. Nationwide, a wave of Hindu temple construction is going on; perhaps 1,000 communities are in various stages of planning or construction, according to observers. About 200 temples have already been built.

Devotees are starting the Hindu version of Bible studies and Sunday schools, unheard of in India.

There is a Web site—http://www.hindunet.org/—aimed at the young. And there is a glossy monthly called *Hinduism Today* that bills itself as a leader in the Hindu "renaissance." On campuses, Hindu awareness groups are popping up. There is even a small organization called the American Hindu Anti-Defamation Council.

What is going on? [10]

"Religion is becoming very important for the second generation because that is the way immigrants maintain ethnic identity," said Prema Kurien, a sociology professor at the University of Southern California who studies Indian immigration. "They first tried to be just American, and they weren't accepted as just American. This is a reaction to that."

But older Hindus are also in the midst of an intense struggle over how to make the religion attractive to their youth. Young Hindus want to know why they should practice the faith, but their parents often don't know the answer. Most baby-boomer Hindus learned only the rituals, not the theology, when they were growing up in India.

The Gen-Xers want more. And they, too, are struggling. Those who've learned the faith from their parents want to keep it. But every day

789

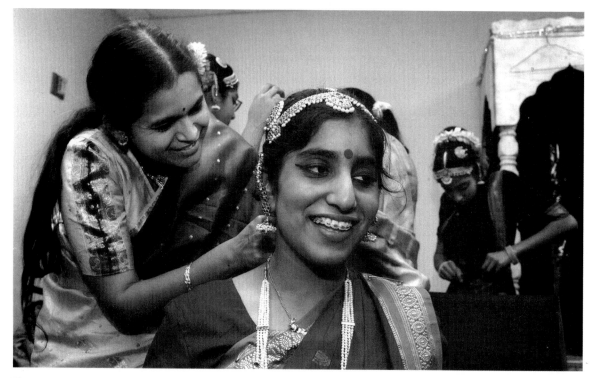

Three generations of Hindu women prepare for a ceremony in a Dallas/Fort Worth temple.

they battle against two opposing forces: American culture and their parents' Indian ways.

Some Hindus believe that if they can rejuvenate their faith, it can become an important new American force, like Islam. Everyone agrees, however, that the path will be difficult.

CULTURE VS. FAITH

Manish Nair, 16, plopped in a chair 15 in his living room on a Saturday afternoon. He wore shorts and a T-shirt but said when he goes to the temple, he wears a "juba" — loose-fitting pants and a shirt.

"Religiously, I'm settled," he said. "I'd like to follow Hinduism. But culturally, it's hard. What we do in the home is completely different from what I do out there."

He eats meat outside his house — a practice that goes against Hindu teaching. On the other hand, he doesn't expect to date; it is simply not done in India. And he intends to marry an Indian woman.

His father sat next to him, smiling his approval.

"Mike" Nair came to the United States from India in 1980. After graduating from the University of North

Texas in 1989, he went to work for J.C. Penney as a systems analyst.

He and his wife, Radha, who is 42 20 and owns a home health care business, also have a daughter, Asha, 13.

In the early years, the Nairs found it difficult to keep up the daily prayers; they were busy coping with jobs, a young family and the overwhelming American culture. So for a while, they let the rituals slide.

Then the children got older.

"They have pushed us a lot," Nair said. "We picked up all our knowledge of Hinduism from our parents, and we felt if we were not giving it to our children, a great culture would be lost. It's our moral duty to show them."

Asha has become heavily involved in Hindu classical dance and practices in the prayer room. Before school and work each day, the Nairs bathe; then they pray in their special room. At the end of the day they repeat the process.

"It's a very sacred place in this home," Nair said.

Still, the disconnect between the two cultures is sometimes wearying.

"I bring my friends home and they ask, 'Why do you worship elephants?'" Manish said, referring to the god Ganapathi, with his elephant face.

Manish hopes Hinduism lasts into the next generation in America—but he isn't sure it will.

"It's hard to keep up the traditions and values," he said. "You're being pulled between two societies."

RITUALS VS. BELIEFS

That is the anxiety for Hindus. Even though some Hindu families like the Nairs are working to create a vibrant faith in America, many Hindu leaders worry that their numbers are small.

"What good things we have, I don't know if we'll preserve them," says Dr. Asmukh Shah, 73, a cardiovascular surgeon who came to the United States 40 years ago.

Nearly 20 years ago, Shah organized a local group that got together to read the Bhagavad Gita, a Hindu scripture. Today, Shah leads weekly religion classes at the Dallas/Fort Worth Hindu Temple in Irving. But out of an estimated local Hindu population of 20,000, only 150 people come, he said. On festival days, perhaps 2,000 people show up.

Perhaps that is because understanding Hinduism is so difficult. It is a complex 5,000-year-old village tradition with various beliefs across India. Most Indians learn the faith from their families during rituals passed down through generations. As a result, most Hindus don't understand their faith as a system of ideas.

That leads to another of Hinduism's unique challenges: It isn't demanding or rule-bound. One of the few ideas around which Hindus rally is that "You can have what you want." Hindus are taught to lead moderate, generous lives, but they are not given a list of do's and don'ts. That is one reason Hinduism has historically been tolerant of other religions.

But in the West, this causes a problem because Christianity, Judaism and Islam are all faiths with more rigid boundaries—and thus a lack of understanding of a looser set of beliefs.

Hindu observers worry the faith won't adapt to American culture.

Most Hindu priests are trained only in leading rituals—which don't interest the vast majority of American Hindus, observers say. Most Hindu leaders have no training in teaching, counseling or programming, according to Arumugaswami, managing editor of *Hinduism Today.* He and others believe an American-style menu of services like classes and activities will draw Hindus.

"We need to adapt our religion to another country," he said. "That's what other religions did. But we're not even in a good position to convert our own people."

Hinduism Today recently published an article about the organizing efforts of American Muslims, and added an editor's note suggesting Hindus could learn from those efforts. In many ways Islam, which claims about 6 million American adherents, was in Hinduism's situation a decade ago.

But the road ahead will be harder for Hindus, experts say.

"The Hindu community is not anywhere near as well-organized as Muslims," says Diana Eck, director of the Pluralism Project at Harvard University and an expert on Hinduism. "The Islamic community has a very large national infrastructure, and also they've prioritized Islamic education over and above building religious institutions like mosques. And there is also a core teaching to Islam that makes it a bit easier for young Muslims to get hold of.

"I don't know that you'll ever see American Hindus with the same kind of assertiveness," she said.

TWO WORLDS

When Mallika Rao was small, she dreamed of painting herself white and having white children.

"I wanted to fit in," said Mallika, 15, a sophomore at Ursuline Academy in Dallas.

That feeling has disappeared. But Mallika and her brother, Siddartha, a 17-year-old junior at St. Mark's School in Dallas, still struggle.

They talk to their parents about Hinduism occasionally, but they get frustrated because their parents don't understand what it's like to be a questioning American teenager.

Mallika eats meat, although her brother does not. They both plan to date, and they both go to parties — and feel a little guilty about it.

Sometimes they make fun of their elders' Indian accents, and that makes them feel guilty, too. They're embarrassed when their mother wears saris to school functions but they're not sure why.

Still, they sense an emergence of Hindu pride.

"All of a sudden there is this big 50 rush of people liking Indian stuff," said Mallika.

One of her friends sports a bindi, the brown dot many Indian women wear to represent the third eye of Shiva, the protective goddess. She notices popular musicians also wearing bindis.

Mallika's mother, Dallas neurologist Dr. Kalpana Rao, said she ran into a white American middle-schooler at an Indian restaurant recently. The boy pointed to a bronze statue and said, "That's Shiva, right?" He was correct.

For Rao, 47, the emergence of pop Hinduism isn't surprising. The world is getting smaller, after all, she said.

Rao believes that while American Hindus are struggling to keep the faith, so are Indians.

Rao remembered her grandmother's rigid Hindu practices: She forced everyone to bathe before they entered the kitchen, where she wore a special sari. But her parents didn't practice such rituals, and she doesn't either.

"India is changing and so are we," 55 she said. "If there is going to be a Hindu renaissance, it's going to be more in a practical sense."

But how?

In small pockets around America, change is happening.

According to Kurien of the University of Southern California, temples are beginning to hold rituals and special celebrations on Sundays, when most people aren't working. Many American temples, including the one in Irving, practice a kind of "ecumenical Hinduism." They display deities popular in various parts of India to satisfy their diverse congregations. The Irving temple has three priests, each from a different Indian region.

And some communities, including the Irving temple, have started offering American-style celebrations,

such as Graduation Day or Mother's Day — all unheard of in India.

But more needs to happen, said 60 Gurumurthy Kalyanaram, 42, a Dallas marketing consultant.

"How are these temples going to survive?" he said, gesturing as he ate lunch at India Palace restaurant in North Dallas. "We are not telling the next generation what we're about."

Kalyanaram wants to see more programs at the temple and more discussion groups to help Hindus understand their tradition.

"I'm hopeful about the younger generation," he said. "The great joy of being born in this country and not being constrained is that you rediscover Hindu thought in a meaningful way. But the anxiety is this: Between that generation and the older generation there is a gap of about 20 years — the baby boomers who immigrated here. That generation is anchored neither in the joy of Hindu thought nor in the rituals."

And that leaves the difficult question.

"Who," he asked, "is going to 65 bridge this gap?"

Not all causal arguments are intended to convince or persuade. We can interpret Caldwell's article as an argument to explore. See more about the many purposes of arguments in Chapter 1.

········· LINK TO P. 3

RESPOND•

1. According to the Hindus interviewed by Caldwell, what sorts of tensions do U.S. immigrants who practice a minority religion face? How do these tensions manifest themselves in different ways for different generations of immigrants? How do the faiths of immigrants become adapted to American culture? What, ultimately, is Caldwell's argument?

2. As in most feature articles, much of Caldwell's support for her argument comes from testimony. What sorts of testimony does she use, and how effectively do these testimonies work to support her argument?

3. Investigate the issues discussed in this article by interviewing two or three people whose families immigrated to this country within the past few decades, or people who were born in the United States but have lived in another country or culture where the predominant religion was not their own. Ask them to describe the accommodations they had to make and the conflicts they experienced—perhaps internal conflicts or conflicts with family members or people in the home community—with respect to matters of religious faith and practice. **Write an essay** in which you report on and analyze the situations of the people you have interviewed.

▶ Ed Madden teaches in the
English Department at the
University of South Carolina.
A scholar and poet, he is also
a committed Christian. This
letter, written in 1997, originally circulated as email; the
version reprinted here was
forwarded to one of the
authors from a friend rather
than coming directly from
Madden. Readers from the
Christian tradition will be
well aware of the importance
of the epistolary tradition in
their faith. Most of the books
of the New Testament began
as letters written to distant
churches or believers,
prompted by particular historical events. The event that
prompted Madden's letter was
the controversy following Ellen
DeGeneres's coming out on the
Ellen show in 1997.

An Open Letter to My Christian Friends

ED MADDEN

An open letter to my Christian friends, and to my Harding University brothers and sisters, after reading many email messages and forwardings about "Ellen":

I, like many young Christian men and women, grew up in a loving and warm Christian home, attended an active and devoted rural church, went to a spiritu-ally enriching Christian college, and spent a great deal of my life devoted to the work of Christ. As a high school student I won the state Bible bowl competi-tions several years in a row and played an active leadership role in my church. As a college student I went on mission trips to Europe, and actively pursued study of the Bible. As a graduate student I took time to attend (and graduate from) a Christian seminary, and I worked with the educational programs of my church.

Like many young men and women, though, I also grew up knowing that I was different, realizing later that that difference was and is homosexual orientation. And I spent a great part of my life learning how to lie, how to deceive, and how to hate myself. Sexual issues were rarely discussed in my church and family, except in cases of condemnation, and homosexuality was even more rarely discussed, except as something absolutely abhorrent, unspeakable, and dis-gusting. When you're a little kid, and when you are beginning to sense that the difference you feel from your culture is something so hated, you learn your les-sons well. Often you spend your time working for God's favor and praying for change. Sometimes you spend your time cultivating the favor of your parents, knowing that there is something about you that they might (and often do) reject. Sometimes you cultivate asexuality, and avoid love or devotion altogether. Sometimes you date women to keep up appearances. Always you learn to be silent. Always you learn to lie, when necessary. Always you learn how to hate yourself.

After I left Harding University, a good Christian school that was essential to my spiritual development, I decided to be honest, both with myself and others. I have known I was gay at least since I was eight years old, if not before. I spent most of my life learning to hide my feelings, or worse, learning to fake feelings

I didn't have. I tried to become engaged, in an act of desperation. I felt almost suicidal when my girlfriend (wisely) broke up with me—she seemed my last hope, my last bargaining chip with God.

I spent a great deal of time in reading and prayer, trying to understand. I do not   5 fit the usual right-wing or pathological explanations of homosexuality. I was never abused as a child. I did not have a smothering mother, nor did I have an especially distant father. Nor did I *choose* to be gay. My orientation is a preconscious condition, not a willful choice or a perverse preference. I realized that being gay is not a choice; being honest is. I prayed and prayed for God to change me. He did: he changed my mind.

I left the Church of Christ for the Methodist Church, a church at least willing to discuss the issue and have compassion and understanding for gay and lesbian Christians. I may have been wrong about the Church of Christ, and your particular church may be different, but my only sense of things there was that it was a church that refused to deal with the issue, a group that felt a compulsion to silence those who wished to address it, and a community that demonized those who, by no choice of their own, found themselves to be lesbian or gay. You were rejected, that is, unless you were dying of AIDS, and then you were welcomed back into the church as a prodigal son. Dying as a precondition for acceptance.

It was also a church in which homosexuality was treated simply as a behavior, not as a condition, much less an identity. The experience of most gays and lesbians is that being gay is not something we do. It's who we are, regardless of what we do. The failure of our community to recognize that distinction (it's not what you do, it's who you are) only complicates our attempts to deal with the issue as gay or lesbian Christians. Furthermore, homosexuality is more often than not treated as the worst sin, an unforgivable sin, something unspeakable. It is demonized, pathologized, and silenced. And those of us who grow up knowing we are gay or lesbian, but also knowing we are Christian, find ourselves in an impossible situation. We are both part of the community, and we are its object of hatred.

For example, when I once worked with preteen boys on a biblical drama, a "parable project" in which we acted out parables from the gospels, those little boys made it clear to me that early on we learn in Christian families that homosexuals are people to be hated. We were modernizing the parables for them to act out (the kids wrote the scripts, planned the costumes, worked on props, and

talked about the important Christian lessons being taught). We were working on the parable of the good Samaritan.° My female co-teacher and I talked about the Jewish contempt for the Samaritans, and suggested that they come up with a modern equivalent. Since the church was a progressive urban church, the boys did not choose the obvious parallels of racism or even religious hatred. Without any prompting, they suggested two groups that people (including their parents, they said) hate or despise: homeless people and gay men. Although they chose to act out the parable using a homeless man as a good Samaritan, which was probably the wisest choice given the context, I learned the lesson that they had also learned all too well: it is okay for Christians to despise and hate homosexuals. Wisdom from the mouths of children.

good Samaritan: one of Jesus's parables (Luke 10:25–37) told in answer to the question, "Who is my neighbor?" The parable recounts how both a priest and a religious man walked past a man who had been robbed and left to die by the side of the road, offering no assistance, while a Samaritan, a member of the group most despised by Jesus's listeners, stopped to offer assistance. When Jesus asked the questioner which of these men had acted as a neighbor, the petitioner responded, "The one who showed mercy." Jesus then told him to go and do likewise.

(Read Bette Greene's adolescent novel *The Drowning of Stephan Jones*, based on a true story, about teenage boys killing a gay man, and justifying that murder with the hatred they learned in their Christian communities.)

When I decided to be honest with my family, I further learned how Christian and 10 family values are acted out when you happen to be gay. What are those family values? That honesty has a cost. That family love is conditional. That brother may reject brother. That the use of scripture is selectively enforced. (Although Jesus has a lot to say about greed, homosexuality is the condition that requires that you reject your own loved ones.) That dishonesty is a virtue. (I was told that I should spend my life lying, that I should "lie to [my] grave.") That homosexual is the worst possible thing one can be. (If only, as one family member said, I could be addicted to drugs or had murdered someone, they could deal with that.)

My students tell me horror stories. One kid's father asked him to leave his house when he found out that his son was gay. While this student was hurriedly packing up some things and preparing to leave, he decided to run to the hallway and grab a family photo. All the photos with him in them were gone, and his father was in the backyard destroying them. The last words he ever heard from his brother, a respected Southern Baptist minister, were: "I hope you get AIDS and die like all the other faggots." Another kid I know had his father write to him: "Tell me if you're ever coming home, so that I can leave town." Another man I know opened his mail in January to find that his father had returned to him all the Christmas gifts he had sent to him, all of them unopened.

The ultimate value most gay kids learn in the church is dishonesty. We learn that being dishonest, lying, is a good Christian practice. How many closeted gay men have I known who have stayed in the church, only on the condition of their own dishonesty? If they are honest, they will be rejected, stigmatized, effectively driven away. If they remain closeted, they can stay in the church. They may secretly "fall" with a frequency that would appall most of their companions, they may indulge in bad sexual behavior. Or they may remain celibate and silent and perpetuate the stigma and the lie that we are not part of the Christian community. Or they may even marry to keep up appearances. They are good citizens of the church, good brethren, and good liars. Those of us who try to live with honesty and integrity, who wish to be honest about who we are, are often rejected by our families, despised and rejected by our communities, and sometimes silenced by our churches.

I realize some gay men and lesbians may try to change, or deny and repress the deep fact of their orientation. I respect them for their decisions. But what if they were allowed to be honest?

It is no wonder that 1/3 of teenage suicides can be tied to issues of sexual identity. Many of us know we are gay, and we imagine ourselves therefore fully deserving of hatred and rejection, even though we may have never had sex or fallen in love. We hear of the "lifestyle" we lead that deserves condemnation, even though we may never wear leather, dress in drag, or pursue anonymous or promiscuous sex. And, as the outrage about "Ellen" demonstrates, our friends and companions make it clear that discussion about or even awareness of homosexuality is something to be silenced. It is a chilling monologue, not a conversation, that results: "Hate yourself!" "Shut up!" Or, more often than not, "Leave."

Regardless of what you think about homosexuality, please remember that you   15
know homosexuals and lesbians, whether you are aware of them or not. Remember that most of us experience our sexual orientation as an essential part of who we are, an identity, not an isolated act or a behavioral choice. Remember that some of us found ourselves rejected by our families and our churches, and many of us have not experienced compassion or understanding from the Christian communities in which we grew up. Remember that most of us were, in fact, forced to find other communities in order to be honest people.

Remember that there are lots of frightened gay teenagers, who are studiously learning how to hate themselves and how to lie, who have all their self-hatred and fear affirmed every time they hear messages of demonization rather than messages of compassion. Remember that lots of other teenage kids have grown up in a Christian community that taught them that it is perfectly accept-able to despise and hate gays and lesbians, even if they're in your own family, and it is perfectly within the bounds of Christian love to reject your own brother or sister if they happen to be gay or lesbian.

We are your invisible sons and daughters, your invisible brothers and sisters. Please at least think about that.

In Christian love,

Ed

RESPOND •

1. What sort of ethos does Madden establish for himself as author? How does he do so? What do you believe Madden is asking of his audience? In other words, what does he hope the outcome of his letter will be? Why? What is the tone of his letter? Is it effective, given the writer's purpose and argument? Why or why not?

2. In paragraph 7, Madden writes, "We [gay and lesbian Christians] are both part of the community, and we are its object of hatred," a point to which he returns in the letter's closing paragraphs. Why does he char-acterize the situation of lesbian and gay Christians in this way? Can you think of other groups about whom a similar claim could be made?

3. Think of Madden's letter as an apology, in the original sense of the term—that is, a genre that aims to explain or justify a strongly held idea or position about a matter of importance. Madden's letter addresses a particular situation about which he feels a need to take a stand and to do so honestly, though he is aware that doing so will likely cost him a great deal. Part of the power of his letter comes from the nature of the situation and how it is viewed by our society at this time. **Write a letter** in which you explain to someone—a friend, your parents, a teacher, for example—why you have been moved to take a stance on some issue with which they disagree.

Journey toward Wholeness: Reflections of a Lesbian Rabbi

LA ESCONDIDA

▶ *The author of this excerpt explains why she, a lesbian rabbi, has chosen to use the pseudonym La Escondida ("the hidden one") in writing this essay, which originally appeared in* Twice Blessed: On Being Lesbian, Gay, and Jewish *(1989), one of the earliest collections of writings by lesbians and gay men of faith.*

crypto-: hidden, secret.

Recently, I heard a report on National Public Radio about "the secret Jews of New Mexico," remnants of the Marranos, the crypto-Jews° of late medieval Spain who hid their Jewish identities in order to escape persecution at the hands of the Spanish Inquisition. These New Mexican Jews, outwardly Catholics, call themselves "los escondidos" (the hidden ones). They still live in secret, quietly teaching their children ancient Jewish rituals, quietly observing as much of Jewish practice as they know after centuries of separation from mainstream Judaism. Even now, in 1988, they hide, fearful that revealing their true identities will bring them harm, fearful that someone, somewhere, will persecute them for being who they really are.

As I listened to the report, my emotions were stirred. As a student of Jewish history, I was fascinated by the tenacity of these people and their success in surviving through centuries of clandestine life, without validation and support from the larger Jewish world. As a Jew who lives much of her own life in secret, fearful of revealing all of who I am, fearful of the harm that may come to me if I do, I felt the pain and sadness of my co-religionists in New Mexico.

Because it is risky for me to reveal my true identity at this point in my career, I write this essay under a pseudonym. Like the Jews of New Mexico, I too am an "escondida," a hidden one. I am a Jew. I am a woman. I am a rabbi. I am a lesbian.

Being a Jew has always been the axis around which my life has rotated. I grew up in a deeply committed Jewish home, with ardently Zionist parents who were dedicated to the birth and growth of a Jewish homeland in which the highest ideals of social justice would be realized. My home was filled with love for the Hebrew language, a fascination with Jewish history and culture, and a deeply ingrained commitment to the survival of the Jewish people. Though not "religious" in the traditional sense, my parents were profoundly Jewish in a cultural, historical, and emotional sense. I can imagine no other way of being in the world than being a Jew who is actively and passionately connected to my people.

As an adult I spent several years in Israel, where I saw my Jewish-   5 ness in cultural, historical, and national terms. I took great pride in my people's growth, in the country we were building, in Israel's artistic flowering, in the intellectual achievements of this small nation. I thought that being a Jew and an Israeli were synonymous — and that my life was whole.

After completing my B.A. in Israel, I returned to the United States to pursue graduate studies in Jewish history. Back in America, I soon came to realize that my life as a Jew was incomplete — it had always focused on the historical and cultural evolution of my people, but I knew little about the spiritual and religious aspects of Judaism. I felt the need to connect with God, with my own soul, and with my people's faith and belief system. I realized that there was a whole world within Judaism that I hadn't yet explored and that I needed in my life. While my intellect was being nourished, my soul, too, needed to find its home within Judaism.

Simultaneous with this realization came another powerful discovery about myself: I am a lesbian. I had fallen in love with a woman. After fighting society's frightening and confusing stereotypes, I acknowledged that I had felt most comfortable and most whole throughout my life in close relationships with other girls and women. My deepest emotional attachments had always been with women, my most profound feelings of love, affection, intimate connection, and physical attraction had always been for women. With this acknowledgment, I was able to shake off the oppressive stereotypes and begin a long-term relationship with the woman whom I loved deeply.

For several years I lived a bifurcated existence. My academic and professional life as a scholar of Jewish history was entirely separate from my personal life, and my spiritual quest was done alone. Typical to the intellectual that I am, I read books about Jewish spirituality and faith, but I was not actively engaged in seeking my *own* life within the spiritual context of Judaism. Wholeness for me as a Jew was still an elusive goal.

I know now that part of the reason I didn't venture forth into a living community of Jews was that I feared being rejected as a lesbian.

Soon, to my great relief, I discovered there was a lesbian and gay outreach synagogue where I lived. I remember how I felt as my partner and I walked through the synagogue doors for the first time. The conflicts within me began to abate, as I sensed the possibility of integrating the different aspects of my being. In this modest building, I began to feel that I could be a Jew and a lesbian. I could pray as a Jew, learn as a Jew, rejoice in my loving relationship with a woman, and have others celebrate with me.

This synagogue, Beth Ameinu ("House of Our People"; the syna- 10 gogue's name is fictitious), indeed offered to me possibilities of an enriching new connection with my people. I became actively involved in the congregation, serving on the synagogue's board, as head of its ritual committee and as a frequent leader of Shabbat° services. Soon, I found that this piece of Judaism that had been missing for me, its spiritual and religious dimension, was coming alive. I no longer needed to sit alone and read books—I could pray and sing with a community as a *whole* human being: Jewish and lesbian.

Shabbat: Hebrew name for the Jewish Sabbath, from sundown Friday until sundown Saturday.

Over time, I began to feel that my professional life, though intellectually challenging, was also incomplete. As Judaism's horizons expanded for me, I felt that teaching it from a purely intellectual perspective was not enough. As a professor of Jewish history, I did not experience wholeness. In this capacity, my task was to teach Judaism in a consciously clinical and objective manner. I often felt like a disembodied mind, imparting knowledge about Judaism without also sharing its *ruach,* its spirit. It became increasingly difficult for me to offer my students a dispassionate Judaism. It simply meant too much to me to do that.

A new awareness pushed me forward on my journey. I came to realize that I wanted my professional life to reflect my deepest personal commitments: I knew that I wanted to be a rabbi. After several years of thinking seriously about the direction my life should take, and considering the life changes my decision might require, I applied to a rabbinical seminary. In my application I explained my motivations for becoming a rabbi:

> What I really want to do is help people reach the more profound spiritual dimension connected with their Judaism. I want to be able to work with other Jews to create meaningful rituals, to find their way toward their own religious/spiritual evolution. . . . I want to teach

within a Jewish context (not exclusively in a secular university) where I am not constrained by the obligation to be objective and coldly intellectual.

I want to help provide that food for the soul as well as the mind. I find that as a woman, as a feminist, there are worlds to be found within Judaism, worlds to explore, principles to be studied and challenged, a history of Jewish women to be reclaimed and a life of ritual for women to be developed. I want to be a part of that process. . . .

Now, in the final stages of my rabbinical studies, and after working for two years as a rabbi of a small congregation, these are still ideals that energize me.

Along with my idealism about becoming a rabbi have come some terribly disturbing realizations about how I must live my life as a congregational rabbi. Sadly, even as I pursue wholeness in my professional life, I have found that some of the personal integration I felt at Beth Ameinu has left me. Again I live a bifurcated life. Though I have a wonderful support system of good friends with whom I can be fully myself, the fact that I cannot be wholly honest about who I am to my congregants is painful to me. Nevertheless, despite the pain that I feel, I know that it would be professionally foolish to reveal to them who I am in my totality. If I were to come out to my congregants, in all probability I would lose my job as their rabbi. I do not believe that these warm and lovely people are ready to know that their rabbi is a lesbian.

High Holy Days: the festivals of Rosh Hashana, the Jewish New Year; Yom Kippur, the "Day of Atonement"; and the days in between.

Two years ago, I gave an impassioned sermon about AIDS to my congregation on the High Holy Days.° In the context of the emotional self-evaluation that Jews engage in at this time of year, I spoke about empathy and compassion, acceptance and marginalization—and I suggested that our congregation become involved, even in a small way, in the struggle against AIDS. I suggested that we collect food for people with AIDS who are no longer able to shop for themselves and who may be financially impoverished by the astronomical costs of medical care. My suggestion was received well by my congregants and we engaged in a fairly successful food collection. Every few weeks, I delivered the collected cans of food to the local AIDS project.

A few months after the High Holy Days, in reporting the gratitude 15 that the AIDS project had expressed to our congregation, I suggested that we might wish to let the project know that if there were Jewish people with AIDS who wished to worship in a community, the doors of our synagogue would be open to them. I was immediately confronted by a storm of reaction from my congregants, who are usually fairly receptive to my suggestions. I was told not to extend such an invitation to people with AIDS, that my congregation did not wish to be known as "the gay synagogue," and that they did not wish to be "ostracized" or "marginalized" within the larger Jewish community. I felt the pain of this incident deep within me: "If they only knew that their rabbi was a lesbian," I thought. I remained silent and accepted my congregants' instructions. I felt hurt and deeply ashamed at my inability to reveal myself to them, and to force them to confront their own prejudices. I also understood that I needed to protect myself professionally.

In the High Holy Day sermon I mentioned earlier, I spoke about a young Jewish woman with AIDS who lives in the same city where my congregation is located. Having learned about her from an article in a national magazine, I wondered out loud "if she is in a synagogue praying with a community." I wondered whether she had a community of Jews, "who will nurture her and give her the loving, the caring, the respect, and the support she needs."

I had thought seriously about *not* delivering my sermon on AIDS for fear of appearing too "outspoken," for fear of appearing too involved in an issue that was still mistakenly thought of by many as "a gay men's issue." I wondered whether I should steer clear of anything even remotely connected to gay concerns because someone might make a connection between gay issues and me. But after worrying about it for a while, I concluded that there are limits to how much one should worry about such things. I decided that as a member of an often invisible minority, I could not make myself even more invisible by remaining silent about an issue of great concern to me and to our society in general. There were limits even to my own "hiddenness." I made a conscious decision, *which stems from my identity as a lesbian,* that however controversial my sermon might be, I could not remain silent.

I will always be grateful that I gave that sermon. After services were over, a thin woman stood apart from the crowd and waited to speak with me. After almost everyone else had left, she approached me and asked to speak with me alone. Once we had gone into another room, the woman told me that *she* was the person about whom I had just spoken. Of course, I did not know that she would be in my synagogue that Yom Kippur° day. But the fact is that *she* had heard me. Taking my

Yom Kippur: the "Day of Atonement," the holiest day of the Jewish year, during which Jews fast and say prayers of penitence.

hands in hers, she said to me: "I haven't been in a synagogue in years. When I got AIDS, I was sure that God had abandoned me. But now that my life may be over soon, I felt the need to come back to my Jewish roots. I have never heard a rabbi speak the way you did today. Thank you. I want you to know that it means a great deal to me. I think you've helped me come home." We embraced and we cried together—and I offered what help I could; a listening ear, compassion, a connection with her Jewishness by a connection to me as her rabbi.

This young woman does not attend services regularly. She is now too ill to do so, but I have visited her, and we have talked. I believe that my being available to her as a rabbi is helping. In all likelihood, I will officiate at her funeral, and I hope that I can provide some solace to her family. There is deep sadness here at the loss of a fine human being. But I feel that my decisions *based on the entirety of who I am* and my work as a rabbi have been redeemed by my encounter with this woman.

There are other positive and valuable aspects to my identity as a 20 lesbian and my work as a rabbi. I believe that I am more sensitive to "the stranger who walks in our land," those Jews who sit at the edges of our communities, somewhat marginalized, somewhat outside of the mainstream. I believe that I may be more attuned to them because I, too, often feel like an outsider, unable to reveal my full self to my community. I believe that because many people judge me and my lesbian identity harshly, I may be more sensitive to judgmentalism in general. I have learned that there are many, many ways of living one's life as a decent human being—and that my responsibility is not to judge but to establish human connection.

My experience as a rabbi in a mainstream (rather than exclusively gay or lesbian) congregation has brought me great satisfaction, but it has also brought me doubts. When I dream of my work as a rabbi, I envision working with *Jews*—not exclusively young Jews, not exclusively old Jews, not exclusively gay and lesbian Jews, not exclusively heterosexual Jews. I simply want to work with *Jews*.

I often fear that I will not be given a chance (by a mainstream community that so often rejects gay people) to simply work with Jews if I come out. I fear that I will become marginal, ostracized from the general community of Jews and confined to working only with lesbian and gay Jews. While my experience at Beth Ameinu was precious to me, and I would not have traded my life in that congregation for anything, I dream of a time when there will be no need for a separate gay and lesbian congregation. As I seek wholeness for myself, an integration of all aspects of myself, I pray for such wholeness for my people as well.

I began this essay by writing about the hidden Jews of New Mexico, "los escondidos." It is my deepest hope that there will come a time when they and I will come out into the light of day and feel unthreatened, able to reveal the *totality* of our identities, able to be safe and valued in a world they know will fully accept us. May this day come speedily and in our time.

RESPOND ●

1. How does the author use the comparison of her situation with that of the Marranos to frame her essay? How does her choice of a pseudonym strengthen her association with that marginalized group? How effective are these choices, given her purposes for writing? What of the essay's title? How does it contribute to the author's argument?

2. According to La Escondida, what are the links between her sexuality and her faith? How does her identity as a lesbian influence her Jewish faith, her work as a rabbi, and Judaism? How might her faith have an impact on the lesbian and gay community?

3. What conflicts does La Escondida continue to experience with respect to her faith? Her sexual identity? The two together? Might her experiences be different if she were a gay man? Do you think that all of her conflicts would disappear if she were heterosexual? How? Why or why not?

4. How does La Escondida portray contemporary American Judaism? The Judaism she envisions as ideal? **Write an essay** in which you outline La Escondida's views on Judaism—as it exists and as it might be—as well as the values on which she bases her argument; then give your response to that argument. For example, do you find it appealing or surprising? Why or why not? You will need to acknowledge the understanding of and experience with Judaism that you bring to La Escondida's text in your essay.

▼ Gordon Marino is associate professor of philosophy at Saint Olaf College in Northfield, Minnesota. His specializations are the history of philosophy, the philosophy of religion, and the work of Danish philosopher Søren Kierkegaard (1813–1855), considered by many to be the founder of existentialism. The article reprinted here appeared in October 1998 in Christianity Today, a magazine that characterizes itself as "the definitive news voice for evangelical Christians around the world."

Me? Apologize for Slavery?
I May Not Have Owned Slaves, but I've Benefited from Their Having Been Used

GORDON MARINO

Tuskegee study of syphilis: American medical research project that has become synonymous with unethical scientific investigation. From 1932 to 1972, the U.S. Public Health Service sponsored the project, which examined the effects of untreated syphilis on a group of men, all of whom were poor African American sharecroppers. The research subjects were not informed about their health status, nor were they educated about the disease. After initial treatment proved useless, the decision was made to withhold any treatment and follow the subjects until their death in order to study the long-term effects of the disease, a decision that held even after penicillin was discovered to be an effective treatment for the disease, and after legislation mandating the disease's treatment was enacted. The study ended only in 1972, after it was the subject of articles in a Washington, D.C., newspaper.

mea culpa: expression of guilt or apology (Latin, "my fault," an expression used in the Roman Catholic Church's prayer of confession in the Latin liturgy).

Gestures of collective repentance have become popular in recent years. In 1994, the pope offered an apology for past sins committed against non-Catholics. In the summer of 1995, the Southern Baptists, who number over 15 million, voted to express a resolution of repentance that read in part, "We lament and repudiate historic acts of evil such as slavery from which we continue to reap a bitter harvest." Last year [1997], President Clinton apologized to the African Americans who were the unwitting subjects in the infamous Tuskegee study of syphilis,° and he seriously considered the possibility of apologizing for slavery in general.

Reactions to Clinton's proposed mea culpa° varied. Ward Connerly, an African-American entrepreneur, regent of the University of California, and architect of the California antiaffirmative action referendum, Proposition 209, pronounced this verdict on the idea: "Apologizing for slavery is probably one of the dumbest things anyone could do." Conversely, civil-rights leader Julian Bond maintained that an apology for slavery would be a good and important symbolic gesture.

Last summer, in between Little League baseball games in a largely white Minnesota town, I did some informal polling of my own. Though none of the people I talked to took the President's proposed apology to be an urgent matter, about half expressed mild support for the idea. Others scoffed at repenting for what they took to be ancient history. The wife of a professor commented, "Why should I apologize for something done to blacks more than a hundred years ago?" A fair question, which might be restated: "Why should I apologize for a crime that I had nothing to do with?" Or more to the point, "By what authority can I apologize for someone else's actions?" It would, after all, be hubristic° for me to think that I could repent for a mugging that I did not participate in.

As a professor of philosophy, I have encountered many white students over the years who accurately or out of paranoia believe that they are constantly being asked to feel guilty and repent for racist institutions and actions in which they themselves had no hand. When it comes to race and repentance, these students are of the Aristotelian opinion that we should only be praised or blamed for our own voluntary actions. Oddly enough, many of them feel no qualms about taking pride in the accomplishments of the various communities with which they identify—their college, church, country, or for that matter, their local major league baseball team.

This minor inconsistency aside, many of those who sneer or snarl at the suggestion of apologizing for deeds from the deep past need to consider the possibility that we may bear a moral connection to actions that we did not ourselves commit. In this regard, it would be useful to distinguish between actions that one neither commits nor profits from and actions not committed but profited from.

Suppose, for example, that unbeknownst to me, a friend of mine robs a bank and makes off with $7 million. Clearly, I am neither responsible for the robbery nor am I in a position to apologize for it. However, if after telling me about the theft, my friend offers me a million dollars of the stolen loot, and I accept it, then I am no longer innocent of the robbery, despite the fact that I had nothing at all to do with the heist. It could be argued that white people have profited from our racist past, and thus, relative to slavery, we are more like receivers of stolen goods than innocent bystanders who just happen to bear a physical likeness to slave owners.

Paradoxically enough, Americans do not shy away from admitting that we profit from access to cheap foreign labor, and yet whites find it hard to believe that we have benefited in any way from hundreds of years of free labor. Obviously, this lack of awareness would be exculpatory if, in fact, slavery and discrimination did not serve the interests of whites. However, if ignorance of being privileged is an ignorance we ourselves are responsible for producing, then we become morally reproachable receivers of stolen goods. And to be psychologically realistic, whites have a strong investment in blinkering their assessment of the broad effects of racism.

L et's return to my earlier example: assume that when I accepted the gift of a million dollars, I had no reason to think that the money had been stolen. Years later I came to understand that the funds upon which I had built a comfortable and respectable life had been pilfered from the accounts of your great-grandparents. Would the fact that many years had gone by cover the sin to such a degree that I would not bear any responsibility to the

5

hubristic: exceedingly prideful, especially the sort of pride that precedes the fall of a hero in ancient Greek tragedy.

Marino uses an extended analogy of a bank robbery to support his argument. See more about analogies in Chapter 14.

LINK TO P. 290

descendants of my great-grandparents' victims who, thanks to my ancestors, now led a distinctively unprivileged existence?

Individuals who benefit from a crime are mistaken in thinking that they have nothing to do with the crime. If responsibility does not extend from the robber baron to his children, then the material benefits of his wrongdoing can be passed along with impunity to future generations.

Once again, it is essential to distinguish between 10 cases in which one generation is entirely innocent of a transgression committed by an earlier generation and those in which the sins of the father continue to bear fruits of advantage for his descendants. Although

> **Apologies are becoming all too easy to make today. But abuse is no argument against use.**

I am not sure that a presidential apology would have the healing effects that some anticipate, I do know that white Americans have profited from slavery and discrimination. In a competitive society, whites have always had a leg up on African Americans, whether it be in hunting for a job, loan, house, or a position in a corporate firm.

Consider the Texaco scandal in 1996, when unsuspecting white corporate executives were caught on tape espousing racist sentiments. Or consider a story that a friend recently shared with me. My friend, who is about 35, recently returned to his hometown in a Detroit suburb for a class reunion at his richly integrated public high school. After the reunion, four of his old school chums convinced him to go out and play a few rounds of golf. All were corporate executives and registered Democrats. And yet, when the issue of race came up, all of them swore they would never "take the risk" of hiring an African American to fill a leadership role in their respective companies. In other words, any white applicants who sought employment in one of their firms would have a decisive advantage over all African American applicants.

I was not involved in the civil-rights struggle of the sixties. While I have huffed and puffed and shaken my head about racial injustice, I have made no significant sacrifices for the cause of racial justice. I have no special authority to preach on the matter, and yet I have lived long enough in this country to recognize by whose sweat and on whose backs this country has been built and why. Because of slavery and discrimination, African Americans have provided an endless supply of cheap labor. They still work the fields, wash white babies and white octogenarians, shake drinks in country clubs, and mop floors in the classrooms in which white folks debate about race. It was not by chance that a black woman closed my dead father's eyes. It was no accident that a black woman was there when my child first opened his blue eyes.

As a result of institutionalized racism, African Americans have been cornered into doing more than their fair share of protecting, building, and preserving this land. For that reason, I suggest that even white Americans who have cursed racism have unwillingly and perhaps unwittingly benefited from it. Thus, whites are in no position to slough off the call for an apology by insisting that they have no connection to slavery.

The Hebrew scriptures ring with intimations that blessings and blandishments can be passed on from generation to generation. The children of Abraham are blessed because of Abraham's faith. On the other side, there was clearly a time when the Israelites believed that the sins of the fathers would be punishable unto the fourth generation.

The revolutionary prophet Ezekiel inveighs against 15 the notion of cross-generational responsibility. Attempting to focus his people's attention on their individual actions, Ezekiel proclaims that if a man "has a son who sees all the sins that his father has done, considers, and does not do likewise, . . . he shall not die for his father's iniquity" (Ezek. 18:14, 17, NRSV). When we refuse to acknowledge the harm that our community has inflicted upon others, when we the unoppressed refuse to acknowledge that, at least for a time, oppression benefits those who are not forced to walk on the other side of the street, then we fail to turn away from the sin of oppression.

By turning a blind eye, the sins of the father become the sins of the more passive son. By refusing to acknowledge who has been doing what for the last four hundred years, we fail to turn away from the grievous sins of our forefathers.

There is some sense today that apologies are becoming all too easy to make. Perhaps so. But as the philosopher Stephen Toulmin° has pointed out, abuse is no argument against use. If Americans ought to feel sorry that people in our community ever permitted slavery, then we ought to be willing to say that we are sorry for slavery. Clearly, it is a sorry character who does not regret our slaveholding past.   ∎

Stephen Toulmin: British philosopher (1922–) concerned especially with the nature of practical, everyday reason; Chapter 8 discusses his model of argument.

RESPOND •

1. Marino clearly believes that White Americans should apologize to African Americans for slavery. Where and how does he use appeals to logic, emotion, values, or character? How well does he anticipate and respond to readers' potential rebuttals?

2. Assuming that most readers of *Christianity Today* are comfortable with the label "evangelical Christian," how does Marino tailor his arguments to his intended audience? What sorts of readers are invoked in the text?

3. Evaluate the likely effectiveness of his argument with a much more diverse audience—the readers of this textbook. Are you persuaded by Marino's argument? If you identify yourself as an evangelical Christian and are not persuaded by Marino's argument, how might he have argued to convince you of his position (or would such a task be impossible because of beliefs you hold)? If you do not identify yourself as an evangelical Christian and are not persuaded by Marino's argument, how might he have argued to convince you (or would such a task be impossible)?

4. Marino's argument raises complex questions about collective responsibility for the past actions of groups and even entire societies. As he notes, Americans, like people of probably all countries, are quick to claim the successes and accomplishments of groups with which they identify and quick to shun association with any of their failures or shortcomings. To what groups, if any, might Americans owe an apology? Why? If there are situations in which an apology is warranted, why is an apology sufficient? If you cannot think of any circumstances under which Americans or others might owe a group an apology, what does collective responsibility mean to you? **Write an essay** in which you explore the nature and limits of collective responsibility.

I Have a Dream

MARTIN LUTHER KING JR.

Five score years ago, a great American, in whose symbolic shadow we stand, signed the Emancipation Proclamation. This momentous decree came as a great beacon light of hope to millions of Negro slaves who had been seared in the flames of withering injustice. It came as a joyous daybreak to end the long night of captivity.

But one hundred years later, we must face the tragic fact that the Negro is still not free. One hundred years later, the life of the Negro is still sadly crippled by the manacles of segregation and the chains of discrimination. One hundred years later, the Negro lives on a lonely island of poverty in the midst of a vast ocean of material prosperity. One hundred years later, the Negro is still languishing in the corners of American society and finds himself an exile in his own land. So we have come here today to dramatize an appalling condition.

In a sense we have come to our nation's capital to cash a check. When the architects of our republic wrote the magnificent words of the Constitution and the Declaration of Independence, they were signing a promissory note to which every American was to fall heir. This note was a promise that all men would be guaranteed the inalienable rights of life, liberty, and the pursuit of happiness.

It is obvious today that America has defaulted on this promissory note insofar as her citizens of color are concerned. Instead of honoring this sacred obligation, America has given the Negro people a bad check which has come back marked "insufficient funds." But we refuse to believe that the bank of justice is bankrupt. We refuse to believe that there are insufficient funds in the great vaults of opportunity of this nation. So we have come to cash this check—a check that will give us upon demand the riches of freedom and the security of justice. We have also come to this hallowed spot to remind America of the fierce urgency of *now.* This is no time to engage in the luxury of cooling off

Martin Luther King Jr.

▶ Martin Luther King Jr. (1929–1968), winner of the 1964 Nobel Prize for peace, played a significant role in helping shape twentieth-century American history. From the mid-1950s until his assassination, he worked tirelessly for the cause of civil rights for African Americans, arguing always that nonviolence is the strongest strategy a group struggling for fairness and justice can use.

The speech printed here was delivered on August 28, 1963, at the Lincoln Memorial during the March on Washington, when a quarter of a million Americans, the majority of them African Americans, came together in the name of justice. Many Americans old enough to remember hearing the speech in 1963 are still moved to tears today when hearing recordings of it; phrases from the speech like "the content of their character" have become part of the way that Americans talk and argue, especially about matters of difference and equality. In short, King's speech reminds us of the power of words and of argument to transform a moment in time into a significant part of a country's history.

King shifts frequently and seamlessly between long, complex sentences and short, simple sentences. Remember that hearing an argument is different from reading one; listeners need frequent breaks from complexity. For more suggestions on how to construct a spoken argument, see Chapter 17.

LINK TO P. 348

or to take the tranquilizing drug of gradualism. *Now* is the time to rise from the dark and desolate valley of segregation to the sunlit path of racial justice. *Now* is the time to open the doors of opportunity to all of God's children. *Now* is the time to lift our nation from the quicksands of racial injustice to the solid rock of brotherhood.

It would be fatal for the nation to overlook the urgency of the moment and to   5 underestimate the determination of the Negro. This sweltering summer of the Negro's legitimate discontent will not pass until there is an invigorating autumn of freedom and equality. Nineteen sixty-three is not an end, but a beginning. Those who hope that the Negro needed to blow off steam and will now be content will have a rude awakening if the nation returns to business as usual. There will be neither rest nor tranquility in America until the Negro is granted his citizenship rights. The whirlwinds of revolt will continue to shake the foundations of our nation until the bright day of justice emerges.

But there is something that I must say to my people who stand on the warm threshold which leads into the palace of justice. In the process of gaining our rightful place we must not be guilty of wrongful deeds. Let us not seek to satisfy our thirst for freedom by drinking from the cup of bitterness and hatred.

We must forever conduct our struggle on the high plane of dignity and discipline. We must not allow our creative protest to degenerate into physical violence. Again and again we must rise to the majestic heights of meeting physical force with soul force. The marvelous new militancy which has engulfed the Negro community must not lead us to distrust of all white people, for many of our white brothers, as evidenced by their presence here today, have come to realize that their destiny is tied up with our destiny and their freedom is inextricably bound to our freedom. We cannot walk alone.

And as we walk, we must make the pledge that we shall march ahead. We cannot turn back. There are those who are asking the devotees of civil rights, "When will you be satisfied?" We can never be satisfied as long as our bodies, heavy with the fatigue of travel, cannot gain lodging in the motels of the highways and the hotels of the cities. We cannot be satisfied as long as the Negro's basic mobility is from a smaller ghetto to a larger one. We can never be satisfied as long as a Negro in Mississippi cannot vote and a Negro in New York believes he has nothing for which to vote. No, no, we are not satisfied, and we will not be satisfied until justice rolls down like waters and righteousness like a mighty stream.

I am not unmindful that some of you have come here out of great trials and tribulations. Some of you have come fresh from narrow cells. Some of you have come from areas where your quest for freedom left you battered by the storms of persecution and staggered by the winds of police brutality. You have been the veterans of creative suffering. Continue to work with the faith that unearned suffering is redemptive.

Go back to Mississippi, go back to Alabama, go back to Georgia, go back to 10 Louisiana, go back to the slums and ghettos of our northern cities, knowing that somehow this situation can and will be changed. Let us not wallow in the valley of despair.

I say to you today, my friends, that in spite of the difficulties and frustrations of the moment, I still have a dream. It is a dream deeply rooted in the American dream.

I have a dream that one day this nation will rise up and live out the true meaning of its creed: "We hold these truths to be self-evident: that all men are created equal."

I have a dream that one day on the red hills of Georgia the sons of former slaves and the sons of former slaveowners will be able to sit down together at a table of brotherhood.

I have a dream that one day even the state of Mississippi, a desert state, sweltering with the heat of injustice and oppression, will be transformed into an oasis of freedom and justice.

I have a dream that my four children will one day live in a nation where they will 15 not be judged by the color of their skin but by the content of their character.

I have a dream today.

I have a dream that one day the state of Alabama, whose governor's lips are presently dripping with the words of interposition and nullification, will be transformed into a situation where little black boys and black girls will be able to join hands with little white boys and white girls and walk together as sisters and brothers.

I have a dream today.

I have a dream that one day every valley shall be exalted, every hill and mountain shall be made low, the rough places will be made plain, and the crooked places will be made straight, and the glory of the Lord shall be revealed, and all flesh shall see it together.

This is our hope. This is the faith with which I return to the South. With this faith 20 we will be able to hew out of the mountain of despair a stone of hope. With this faith we will be able to transform the jangling discords of our nation into a beautiful symphony of brotherhood. With this faith we will be able to work together, to pray together, to struggle together, to go to jail together, to stand up for freedom together, knowing that we will be free one day.

This will be the day when all of God's children will be able to sing with a new meaning, "My country, 'tis of thee, sweet land of liberty, of thee I sing. Land where my fathers died, land of the pilgrim's pride, from every mountainside, let freedom ring."

And if America is to be a great nation this must become true. So let freedom ring from the prodigious hilltops of New Hampshire. Let freedom ring from the mighty mountains of New York. Let freedom ring from the heightening Alleghenies of Pennsylvania!

Let freedom ring from the snowcapped Rockies of Colorado!

Let freedom ring from the curvaceous peaks of California!

But not only that; let freedom ring from Stone Mountain of Georgia!   25

Let freedom ring from Lookout Mountain of Tennessee!

Let freedom ring from every hill and every molehill of Mississippi. From every mountainside, let freedom ring.

When we let freedom ring, when we let it ring from every village and every hamlet, from every state and every city, we will be able to speed up that day when all of God's children, black men and white men, Jews and Gentiles, Protestants and Catholics, will be able to join hands and sing in the words of the old Negro spiritual, "Free at last! free at last! thank God Almighty, we are free at last!"

RESPOND•

1. Is King's argument primarily forensic, epideictic, or deliberative (Chapter 1)? Give evidence to support your choice.

2. Investigate the 1963 March on Washington, including press coverage of King's speech. How was it received at the time? Why do you think scholars of public discourse now consider it the most significant American speech of the past century?

3. "I Have a Dream" is remembered for many reasons. As an argument, it certainly embodies appeals based on values and on character, emotional appeals, and logical appeals. Analyze each of these sorts of appeals (discussed in Chapters 4–7). First, consider the ethos King creates for himself as author and speaker. Then examine how King makes appeals to the emotions of his audiences—those present and those who heard the speech on radio or television at the time and even to those who would read or hear the speech in the future. Finally, consider the sorts of logical appeals King uses. Choose one type of appeal, and **write an essay** in which you describe and illustrate King's successful use of it in his speech.

4. The power of King's speech comes in part from his use of figurative language and the artfulness of his delivery. Both of these strengths draw on King's experience as a minister in the African American Baptist church. Analyze the speech for the types of figurative language (Chapter 14) King uses—metaphor, simile, analogy, parallelism, repetition, allusion—and for the elements of spoken argument discussed in Chapter 17. If you are able to listen to a sound clip of the speech, pay attention to how King uses breathing, phrasing, and volume strategically. **Write an essay** describing how King uses figurative language to move his audience. In order to do a thorough analysis, limit your discussion to two or three consecutive paragraphs of King's speech.

▼ *Justice Antonin Scalia has served as a member of the U.S. Supreme Court since 1986. This article, which originally appeared in* First Things: The Journal of Religion and Public Life *in May 2002, is based on earlier remarks Justice Scalia had made at a forum on religion and public life at the University of Chicago's Divinity School. In it, Scalia distinguishes between two fundamentally different ways of interpreting the U.S. Constitution, discusses the changing attitude of democratic societies to the death penalty (that is, capital punishment), and ends by disagreeing with the papal encyclical* Evangelium Vitae *and the most recent version of the Catholic catechism. As you read, note the care with which Scalia defines and illustrates the terms he uses; also, consider the ways in which these comments were written to be read aloud.*

God's Justice and Ours

ANTONIN SCALIA

Before proceeding to discuss the morality of capital punishment, I want to make clear that my views on the subject have nothing to do with how I vote in capital cases that come before the Supreme Court. That statement would not be true if I subscribed to the conventional fallacy that the Constitution is a "living document" — that is, a text that means from age to age whatever the society (or perhaps the Court) thinks it ought to mean.

In recent years, that philosophy has been particularly well enshrined in our Eighth Amendment° jurisprudence, our case law dealing with the prohibition of "cruel and unusual punishments." Several of our opinions have said that what falls within this prohibition is not static, but changes from generation to generation, to comport with "the evolving standards of decency that mark the progress of a maturing society." Applying that principle, the Court came close, in 1972, to abolishing the death penalty entirely. It ultimately did not do so, but it has imposed, under color of the Constitution, procedural and substantive limitations that did not exist when the Eighth Amendment was adopted — and some of which had not even been adopted by a majority of the states at the time they were judicially decreed. For example, the Court has prohibited the death penalty for all crimes except murder, and indeed even for what might be called run-of-the-mill murders, as opposed to those that are somehow characterized by a high degree of brutality

Eighth Amendment: "Excessive bail shall not be required, nor excessive fines imposed, nor cruel and unusual punishments inflicted."

or depravity. It has prohibited the mandatory imposition of the death penalty for any crime, insisting that in all cases the jury be permitted to consider all mitigating factors and to impose, if it wishes, a lesser sentence. And it has imposed an age limit at the time of the offense (it is currently seventeen) that is well above what existed at common law.

If I subscribed to the proposition that I am authorized (indeed, I suppose compelled) to intuit and impose our "maturing" society's "evolving standards of decency," this essay would be a preview of my next vote in a death penalty case. As it is, however, the Constitution that I interpret and apply is not living but dead—or, as I prefer to put it, enduring. It means today not what current society (much less the Court) thinks it ought to mean, but what it meant when it was adopted. For me, therefore, the constitutionality of the death penalty is not a difficult, soul-wrenching question. It was clearly permitted when the Eighth Amendment was adopted (not merely for murder, by the way, but for all felonies—including, for example, horse-thieving, as anyone can verify by watching a western movie). And so it is clearly permitted today. There is plenty of room within this system for "evolving standards of decency," but the instrument of evolution (or, if you are more tolerant of the Court's approach, the herald that evolution has occurred) is not the nine lawyers who sit on the Supreme Court of the United States, but the Congress of the United States and the legislatures of the fifty states, who may, within their own jurisdictions, restrict or abolish the death penalty as they wish.

But while my views on the morality of the death penalty have nothing to do with how I vote as a judge, they have a lot to do with whether I can or should be a judge at all. To put the point in the blunt terms employed by Justice Harold Blackmun towards the end of his career on the bench, when he announced that he would henceforth vote (as Justices William Brennan and Thurgood Marshall had previously done) to overturn all death sentences, when I sit on a Court that reviews and affirms capital convictions, I am part of "the machinery of death." My vote, when joined with at least four others, is, in most cases, the last step that permits an execution to proceed. I could not take part in that process if I believed what was being done to be immoral.

Capital cases are much different from the other life-and-death issues that my Court sometimes faces: abortion, for example, or legalized suicide. There it is not the state (of which I am in a sense the last instrument) that is decreeing death, but rather private individuals whom the state has decided not to restrain. One may argue (as many do) that the society has a moral obligation to restrain. That moral obligation may weigh heavily upon the voter, and upon the legislator who enacts the laws; but a judge, I think, bears no moral guilt for the laws society has failed to enact. Thus, my difficulty with Roe v. Wade is a legal rather than a moral one: I do not believe (and, for two hundred years, no one believed) that the Constitution contains a right to abortion. And if a state were to permit abortion on demand, I would—and could in good conscience—vote against an attempt to invalidate that law for the same reason that I vote against the invalidation of laws that forbid abortion on demand: because the Constitution gives the federal government (and hence me) no power over the matter.

With the death penalty, on the other hand, I am part of the criminal-law machinery that imposes death—which extends from the indictment, to the jury conviction, to rejection of the last appeal. I am aware of the ethical principle that one can give "material cooperation" to the immoral act of another when the evil that would attend failure to cooperate is even greater (for example, helping a burglar tie up a householder where the alternative is that the burglar would kill the householder). I doubt whether that doctrine is even applicable to the trial judges and jurors who must themselves determine that the death sentence will be imposed. It seems to me these individuals are not merely engaged in "material cooperation" with someone else's action, but are themselves decreeing death on behalf of the state.

The same is true of appellate judges in those states where they are charged with "reweighing" the mitigating and aggravating factors and determining de novo° whether the death penalty should be imposed: they are themselves decreeing death. Where (as is the case in the federal system) the appellate judge merely determines that the sentence pronounced by the trial court is in accordance with law, perhaps the principle of material cooperation could be applied. But as I have said, that principle demands that the good deriving from the cooperation exceed the evil which is assisted. I find it hard to see how any appellate judge could find this condition to be met, unless he believes retaining his seat on the bench (rather than resigning) is somehow essential to preservation of the society—which is of course absurd. (As Charles de Gaulle is reputed to have remarked when his aides told him he could not resign as President of France because he was the indispensable man: "Mon ami, the cemeteries are full of indispensable men.")

I pause here to emphasize the point that in my view the choice for the judge who believes the death penalty to be immoral is resignation, rather than simply ignoring duly enacted, constitutional laws and sabotaging death penalty cases. He has, after all, taken an oath to apply the laws and has been given no power to supplant them with rules of his own. Of course if he feels strongly enough he can go beyond mere resignation and lead a political campaign to abolish the death penalty—and if that fails, lead a revolution. But rewrite the laws he cannot do. This dilemma, of course, need not be confronted by a pro-

ponent of the "living Constitution," who believes that it means what it ought to mean. If the death penalty is (in his view) immoral, then it is (hey, presto!) automatically unconstitutional, and he can continue to sit while nullifying a sanction that has been imposed, with no suggestion of its unconstitutionality, since the beginning of the Republic. (You can see why the "living Constitution" has such attraction for us judges.)

It is a matter of great consequence to me, therefore, whether the death penalty is morally acceptable. As a Roman Catholic—and being unable to jump out of my skin—I cannot discuss that issue without reference to Christian tradition and the Church's Magisterium.°

The death penalty is undoubtedly wrong unless 10 one accords to the state a scope of moral action that goes beyond what is permitted to the individual. In my view, the major impetus behind modern aversion to the death penalty is the equation of private morality with governmental morality. This is a predictable (though I believe erroneous and regrettable) reaction to modern, democratic self-government.

Few doubted the morality of the death penalty in the age that believed in the divine right of kings. Or even in earlier times. St. Paul had this to say (I am quoting, as you might expect, the King James version):

---

de novo: Latin phrase meaning "anew, afresh"; considering the matter anew; with regard to law, the same as if a case had not been heard before and as if no decision previously had been rendered.

Magisterium: in Catholic theology, the divinely appointed authority given to the pope and bishops of the Catholic Church to teach the truths of religion.

Let every soul be subject unto the higher powers. For there is no power but of God: the powers that be are ordained of God. Whosoever therefore resisteth the power, resisteth the ordinance of God: and they that resist shall receive to themselves damnation. For rulers are not a terror to good works, but to the evil. Wilt thou then not be afraid of the power? Do that which is good, and thou shalt have praise of the same: for he is the minister of God to thee for good. But if thou do that which is evil, be afraid; for he beareth not the sword in vain: for he is the minister of God, a revenger to execute wrath upon him that doeth evil. Wherefore ye must needs be subject, not only for wrath, but also for conscience sake. (Romans 13:1–5)

This is not the Old Testament, I emphasize, but St. Paul. One can understand his words as referring only to lawfully constituted authority, or even only to lawfully constituted authority that rules justly. But the core of his message is that government—however you want to limit that concept—derives its moral authority from God. It is the "minister of God" with powers to "revenge," to "execute wrath," including even wrath by the sword (which is unmistakably a reference to the death penalty). Paul of course did not believe that the individual possessed any such powers. Only a few lines before this passage, he wrote, "Dearly beloved, avenge not yourselves, but rather give place unto wrath: for it is written, Vengeance is mine; I will repay, saith the Lord." And in this world the Lord repaid—did justice—through His minister, the state.

These passages from Romans represent the consensus of Western thought until very recent times. Not just of Christian or religious thought, but of secular thought regarding the powers of the state. That consensus has been upset, I think, by the emergence of democracy. It is easy to see the hand of the Almighty behind rulers whose forebears, in the dim mists of history, were supposedly anointed by God, or

who at least obtained their thrones in awful and unpredictable battles whose outcome was determined by the Lord of Hosts, that is, the Lord of Armies. It is much more difficult to see the hand of God—or any higher moral authority—behind the fools and rogues (as the losers would have it) whom we ourselves elect to do our own will. How can their power to avenge—to vindicate the "public order"—be any greater than our own?

So it is no accident, I think, that the modern view that the death penalty is immoral is centered in the West. That has little to do with the fact that the West has a Christian tradition, and everything to do with the fact that the West is the home of democracy. Indeed, it seems to me that the more Christian a country is, the less likely it is to regard the death penalty as immoral. Abolition has taken its firmest hold in post-Christian Europe, and has least support in the church-going United States. I attribute that to the fact that, for the believing Christian, death is no big deal. Intentionally killing an innocent person is a big deal: it is a grave sin, which causes one to lose his soul. But losing this life, in exchange for the next? The Christian attitude is reflected in the words Robert Bolt's play has Thomas More° saying to the headsman: "Friend, be not afraid of your office. You send me to God." And when Cranmer asks whether he is sure of that, More replies, "He will not refuse one who is so blithe to go to Him." For the nonbeliever, on the

---

Thomas More: beheaded in 1535 for refusing to take the oath of the Act of Succession, which would have passed the British throne to Elizabeth, a Protestant, rather than the Catholic Princess Mary. His final words were "the king's good servant, but God's first."

other hand, to deprive a man of his life is to end his existence. What a horrible act!

Besides being less likely to regard death as an utterly cataclysmic punishment, the Christian is also more likely to regard punishment in general as deserved. The doctrine of free will—the ability of man to resist temptations to evil, which God will not permit beyond man's capacity to resist—is central to the Christian doctrine of salvation and damnation, heaven and hell. The post-Freudian secularist, on the other hand, is more inclined to think that people are what their history and circumstances have made them, and there is little sense in assigning blame.

Of course those who deny the authority of a government to exact vengeance are not entirely logical. Many crimes—for example, domestic murder in the heat of passion—are neither deterred by punishment meted out to others nor likely to be committed a second time by the same offender. Yet opponents of capital punishment do not object to sending such an offender to prison, perhaps for life. Because he deserves punishment. Because it is just.

The mistaken tendency to believe that a democratic government, being nothing more than the composite will of its individual citizens, has no more moral power or authority than they do as individuals has adverse effects in other areas as well. It fosters civil disobedience, for example, which proceeds on the assumption that what the individual citizen considers an unjust law—even if it does not compel him to act unjustly—need not be obeyed. St. Paul would not agree. "Ye must needs be subject," he said, "not only for wrath, but also for conscience sake." For conscience sake. The reaction of people of faith to this tendency of democracy to obscure the divine authority behind government should not be resignation to it, but the resolution to combat it as effectively as possible. We have done that in this country (and continental Europe has not) by preserving in our

public life many visible reminders that—in the words of a Supreme Court opinion from the 1940s— "we are a religious people, whose institutions presuppose a Supreme Being." These reminders include: "In God we trust" on our coins, "one nation, under God" in our Pledge of Allegiance, the opening of sessions of our legislatures with a prayer, the opening of sessions of my Court with "God save the United States and this Honorable Court," annual Thanksgiving proclamations issued by our President at the direction of Congress, and constant invocations of divine support in the speeches of our political leaders, which often conclude, "God bless America." All this, as I say, is most un-European, and helps explain why our people are more inclined to understand, as St. Paul did, that government carries the sword as "the minister of God," to "execute wrath" upon the evildoer.

A brief story about the aftermath of September 11 nicely illustrates how different things are in secularized Europe. I was at a conference of European and American lawyers and jurists in Rome when the planes struck the twin towers. All in attendance were transfixed by the horror of the event, and listened with rapt attention to the President's ensuing address to the nation. When the speech had concluded, one of the European conferees—a religious man— confided in me how jealous he was that the leader of my nation could conclude his address with the words "God bless the United States." Such invocation of the deity, he assured me, was absolutely unthinkable in his country, with its Napoleonic tradition° of extirpating religion from public life.

It will come as no surprise from what I have said that I do not agree with the encyclical Evangelium Vitae° and the new Catholic catechism (or the very latest version of the new Catholic catechism), according to which the death penalty can only be imposed to protect rather than avenge, and that since it is (in most modern societies) not necessary for the former purpose, it is wrong.

I have given this new position thoughtful and care- 20 ful consideration — and I disagree. That is not to say I favor the death penalty (I am judicially and judiciously neutral on that point); it is only to say that I do not find the death penalty immoral. I am happy to have reached that conclusion, because I like my job, and would rather not resign. And I am happy because I do not think it would be a good thing if

American Catholics running for legislative office had to oppose the death penalty (most of them would not be elected); if American Catholics running for Governor had to promise commutation of all death sentences (most of them would never reach the Governor's mansion); if American Catholics were ineligible to go on the bench in all jurisdictions imposing the death penalty; or if American Catholics were subject to recusal° when called for jury duty in capital cases.

Napoleonic tradition: during his coronation as Emperor of France in 1804, Napoleon Bonaparte (1769–1821) famously took the crown out of the hands of the Pope and crowned himself, a symbolic demonstration that power in his empire stemmed from the state and not the church.

Evangelium Vitae: Latin title, meaning "The Gospel of Life," of a 1995 encyclical, or papal letter, defining the Church's teachings on the value and sacredness of all stages of human life, from conception to death. Papal encyclicals are always written in Latin, and their titles are the opening words of the document. They are not considered to be infallible.

recusal: a judge's voluntarily removing himself or herself from hearing a specific case because of conflict of interest, bias, or other reasons.

Justice Scalia embeds a definition argument into his article as evidence for his principal argument. See more about definition arguments and how to use them effectively in Chapter 9.

LINK TO P. 147 ·······························

RESPOND •

1. Justice Scalia devotes the first part of this article to distinguishing between those who read the Constitution as a "living document," the meaning of which changes as society "matures," and those who see it as "enduring," with a focus on its meaning at the time it was drafted. What, for Scalia, are the characteristics and consequences of each view? Which of the two views do you prefer? Why? Does either one leave you uncomfortable? Why or why not?

2. Throughout the article, Scalia makes other important distinctions: cases in which the state (that is, the government) decrees death versus those where it does not restrain death from occurring (paragraph 5), private morality versus governmental morality (paragraph 10), European versus American attitudes toward religion in public life (paragraph 14), legal versus moral matters (paragraph 17), and Christian versus post-Freudian secularist perspectives on death (paragraph 15), among others. Choose two such distinctions, and specify the basis of the distinction (in each case, a kind of definition—see Chapter 9).

3. Scalia concludes by claiming that it is a good thing for American Catholics (and, by extension, people of any faith in America) to be involved in aspects of public and political life in the United States. Do you agree or disagree? Why?

4. Scalia argues that a justice who finds the death penalty immoral should resign from the bench (paragraph 8). Do you agree or disagree? Why? Whatever your stance, you will need to do your best to anticipate and acknowledge potential rebuttals against your position.

5. Scalia claims that the state should be accorded "a scope of moral action that goes beyond what is permitted to the individual" (paragraph 10); in other words, he believes that it is a grave mistake to assume that "a democratic government, being nothing more than the composite will of its individual citizens, has no more moral power or authority than they do as individuals" (paragraph 17). **Write an essay** in the form of a proposal argument in which you propose and evaluate the consequences of each of these positions, arguing ultimately for the position you find more justifiable.

▼ Aisha Khan is the pseudonym used by a young Muslim woman living in Manchester, England. This article originally appeared as part of a series on Muslims in Britain in June 2002 in The Guardian, a daily British paper known for its liberal stance. The opening text in this cluster ("Among Wealthy Nations . . ., U.S. Stands Alone in Its Embrace of Religion") should give you important background information that will be useful in understanding Khan's argument in a British context. Although data from several sources state that the percentage of Muslims in the United Kingdom is lower than in the United States, British Muslims, most of immigrant stock, are represented by two members of Parliament and four peers in the House of Lords. However, as The Guardian's series on Muslims in Britain makes clear, many British Muslims feel they and their religion are not accepted by the larger society. (Recall that as late as World War II, Britain was overwhelmingly White.) As you read, put yourself in Khan's situation even as you imagine how she might have felt if she lived in the United States.

The Veil in My Handbag

AISHA KHAN

I see a girl in Manchester Piccadilly station. She has a full mouth, high cheekbones and velvety brown eyes. But what captivates me is the white cotton scarf covering her head. People know she is Muslim because of her veil, and I wish my appearance had the same effect.

I envy her because I am too weak to wear the veil, too scared that doors will close and that opinions will be formed long before friendships are. Islam doesn't oppress me; fear does. I live a half-life, a double-life: not quite a Muslim and not quite a westerner. My parents raised me as a Muslim. They gave me everything I wanted but I coveted the freedom enjoyed by non-Muslim friends and, because I derived no satisfaction from religion, I sought solace in hedonism.

I was 18 when I left home for university, and my limited knowledge of Islam meant I only saw negatives. Religion was bad because it stopped me from wearing what I wanted, tasting what I wanted and doing what I wanted. And what I wanted was to be like everyone in mainstream society. So I set out to have fun.

I was the toast of my friends. But I was the scourge of the Muslim community, who viewed me with pity and distaste. I remember going into a shop to buy some things I shouldn't have been buying. The man behind the counter greeted me: "Asalaam alaikum." I looked at him blankly. "I'm sorry, I don't understand you," I lied. "No, I'm sorry," he said, "I thought you were a Muslim." "I used to be," I whispered, as I left the shop, crying.

Too ashamed to talk to my parents 5 about my guilt and too impatient to unravel my dilemma to my friends, I never said anything. And the silence was devastating. I was bereft of purpose and support. My sense of isolation intensified when I saw other Muslims being part of society without compromising their faith. When people spoke about Islam, their eyes would light up and their voices resonated with pride and love. I once shared their enthusiasm, but my lifestyle was leading me so far away from religion that I could barely remember anything about it.

So I went to the university prayer room. I performed the intricate washing ritual, an act of purification and preparation. I took my place on the prayer mat to recite verses from the Koran, but my lips froze. I couldn't remember any verses—the same verses I had repeated every day as a child. I panicked. I prayed to Allah, pleading with him to let me remember. The words didn't come flooding back, but I muddled through the prayer.

I decided that I didn't want to muddle through any more and shut myself away for days, poring over books and piecing together the fragments of my knowledge. As my awareness increased, so my appetites diminished. I would go out, but I wouldn't stay out. My clothes were less revealing, but fell short of complete coverage.

Had it not been for these cosmetic changes, I would have gone through university life with my religious identity concealed. But I told people I was a Muslim and, post–September 11, this revelation prompted a tidal wave

of questions. People quizzed me about jihad—the holy war. I was reluctant to talk about it because my views were at odds with those held by most people living in the western hemisphere.

I once broached the subject of the Middle East conflict during a conversation. I explained that there was an international community of Muslims, a nation state: the ummah. Every Muslim is a member of this community so when one is murdered, it is an assault on Muslims throughout the world. I was shouted down. My peers accused me of sympathising with terrorists. I have not spoken about September 11 or jihad since.

I have left university and now feel 10 better equipped to cope with the irreconcilable differences of being British and Muslim. You can be born and raised in this country, benefit from its education and live freely and comfortably thanks to the solid British economy. But you can also be oppressed. Stay silent when your religion is being lambasted in the press. Look on helplessly when Muslims are being persecuted in their homeland and then watch them being punished

by the British asylum system. Stuff your veil into your handbag because you'll never get that job if you cover your head. Sacrifice prayer times and fasting to keep up with the crowd and stay in with the boss.

I am in my mid-20s now and loosening the ties with my past, although I still have the same friends I started university with. They know my values are changing and they respect my decision to learn more about Islam. So I have overcome one set of hurdles—the conflict between the desires of youth and the duties of religion. But I want to work as a headhunter and this line of work sits uncomfortably with the demands of my faith. Long hours, business travel and face-to-face meetings mean my values will be tested again and the disharmony will continue.

For now, I will try to pray at the appointed time instead of cramming in three or four prayers together when I get home. Nor will I break my fast. When people ask me why I'm not having lunch, I won't tell them I'm on a diet—I'll tell them I'm a Muslim.

Is Khan's purpose here to inform? To explore? To convince? Something else? See Chapter 1 to decide.

⋯⋯⋯⋯⋯⋯⋯⋯⋯⋯⋯⋯ LINK TO P. 6

RESPOND●

1. Khan's essay describes a not uncommon dilemma for many religious believers in pluralistic societies or societies in which they are members of a minority religious group: deciding how, when, and where to acknowledge publicly their religious convictions. What sorts of conflicts does Khan report? How did the events of September 11 complicate the situation of British Muslims?

2. Because the events of September 11, 2001, were perpetrated by Middle Eastern Islamic fundamentalists, American Muslims of any ethnic background and anyone who looks vaguely Middle Eastern have become the objects of intense scrutiny. (You may remember that immediately following those events, Middle Easterners, South Asians, East Asians, and even Hispanics complained that they were being hassled or worse because of their appearance; at least one American Sikh, a member of a religion with roots in India whose members wear turbans, was killed by someone who mistook him for a Muslim. Ira Berkow's article "Rower with Muslim Name Is an All-American Suspect" in Chapter 24 details a case of more recent ethnic profiling, ironic in many ways.) Were Khan living in the United States, do you think her experiences would have been any different from what they were in Britain? Why or why not?

3. **Write an essay** in which you propose how America might deal with the expression of religious commitments in public life. If your proposal is that such expressions should be permitted, what are the limits of such expression? (For example, if prayer is to be permitted in public schools, how will the rights of various groups be preserved? The relevant groups here would include members of other religious groups — including all sorts of different religious minorities — plus religious individuals who do not want prayers in school, agnostics, and atheists.) It may be useful to think about the proper balance between the rights of Americans as individuals and as groups to express their religious beliefs and the extent to which those of other faiths or no faith at all should accommodate such expression. (For example, Muslims fast from before sunrise until sunset during the month of Ramadan; at night, they usually spend time with family and friends. During this period what sorts of accommodations, if any, should, say, colleges and universities make to students who are fasting with respect to assignments and tests? Similarly, to what extent should Sunday as a holiday from work and holidays like Christmas be considered accommodations to Christians?)

The events following September 11, 2001, and particularly the war in Iraq in 2003, led Americans to consider once again in a public way what it means to be patriotic (perhaps the last round of heated public debates on this topic dates to the Vietnam War). It's understandable that events like being attacked from outside or sending troops to other countries for the express purpose of fighting lead citizens to question what it means to "love" their country or show allegiance to it. The readings in this cluster, in one sense all arguments of definition, pose the same question in various ways: **Will the real American patriot please stand up?**

The cluster opens with the transcript of a radio feature from National Public Radio in which middle-school students debate what it means to be a patriot after the events of September 11, 2001. Reading it, you'll visit two classrooms where America and patriotism are presented (and represented) in very different ways. The second selection is President Bush's speech to the joint session of Congress on the evening of September 20, 2001, an exceptionally fine example of political discourse in which Bush sought to show Americans—and the world—that the state of the American union was strong. In an essay written for *Dissent* in fall 2002, Michael Kazin argues that although liberals and those on the Left often avoid discussions of patriotism, they can and should claim to be patriotic as he recounts aspects of American history that many schoolchildren don't study. Former secretary of education William J. Bennett, claiming that the United States is "A Nation Worth Defending," defines patriotism in what we might think of as more traditional ways—ways quite different from those Kazin employs. Next, two newspaper ads—one from the Council on American-

Islamic Relations and the other from Not in Our Name, an organization opposing war with Iraq—and the Web site for Veterans Against the Iraq War claim that dissent is not disloyalty and that in fact it is often a form of patriotism—at least in America. Troy Melhus's essay questions his own patriotism as a diffident soldier in contrast to the clear moral compass of a conscientious objector Melhus had to guard during his tour of duty as a Marine. In an essay from January 2003, columnist Robert Scheer questions whether Americans aren't too quick to think of war as no more than a sporting event when, in fact, far more is at stake. Finally, shortly after the bombs began falling in Baghdad, Michael Ignatieff wrote "I Am Iraq," an essay that seeks to reframe and redefine Americans' notions of assent and dissent.

As these texts demonstrate, even though Americans may not agree on exactly what it means to be patriotic, they believe it is important to debate the issue. By the time you read these words, let us hope that Americans can worry less about security than they have had to in the years immediately following the events of September 11 and that the rebuilding of Afghanistan and Iraq is far advanced. Let us also hope that debates about the meaning of patriotism in America continue as well.

▶ *We begin this cluster of readings with the transcript of a radio program from Morning Edition, the morning news program of National Public Radio. You may wish to listen to this program as you read (or instead of reading the transcript) by going to the archives of National Public Radio at <npr.org>; the program was originally broadcast on February 6, 2003. This transcript, which contrasts how patriotism and love of America are taught in two American middle-school classrooms, represents one of a series of features on patriotism after September 11 and during a time of war, specifically, the Bush administration's War on Terrorism. As you read or listen to this transcript, think about your own experiences as a student— whether you attended school here or abroad or whether you were home-schooled—with respect to learning about patriotism and about love of the country in which you were educated or of which you feel yourself to be a member.*

Schoolchildren Debating
What It Means to Be a Patriot

MADELEINE BRAND AND BOB EDWARDS

This is MORNING EDITION from NPR News. I'm Bob Edwards.

Last fall, President Bush gave a speech about patriotism and education. He said young Americans need to know the great cause of America and why this country is worth fighting for.

President GEORGE W. BUSH: The principles we hold are the hope of all mankind. When children are given the real history of America, they will also learn to love America.

EDWARDS: But what does it mean to love America? It's a debate that gets sharper during a time of war when students in history class might ask pointed questions about current events.

As part of a series of reports, NPR's Madeleine Brand visited two schools to 5 learn how different teachers talk about patriotism, loyalty and war.

MADELEINE BRAND reporting:

In Concord, Massachusetts, on a snowy afternoon, 13-year-olds are being asked to think about something they say every day, something they probably don't think much about: the Pledge of Allegiance.

(Soundbite of someone writing on chalk board)

BRAND: Teacher Doc Miller begins the class armed with a dictionary definition.

Mr. DOC MILLER (Teacher): I looked up the word "allegiance." It said, "the duty 10 of being loyal to one's ruler, country, etc." Duty, loyal.

BRAND: Miller turns to face the class and pauses to let those two words sink in. He's been teaching eighth-grade American history for about 30 years. He wears a tie and sneakers. And he actually works up a sweat as he bounds around the room.

Mr. MILLER: Is that ringing with you? Is that getting you thinking?

BRAND: He pauses in mid-sentence to add another dictionary definition for his students to ponder; this time, the word "patriotic."

Mr. MILLER: Listen to this one: "A patriot is one who loves, supports and defends one's country." Defends one's country. Isn't that what we're about if we go to war with Iraq? And maybe it is. And this definition says, "Bang! Defend your country if you want to be a patriot." I don't know. I'm putting out questions.

BRAND: Miller says he tries hard not to tell his students what to think. He wants 15 them to learn from each other. And he says he's tried to live up to a motto he's posted in big letters on the wall behind him: Look deeply.

Mr. MILLER: Are you an American citizen?

Unidentified Girl #1: Yes.

Mr. MILLER: Do you feel loyal to your country?

Unidentified Girl #1: Yeah.

Mr. MILLER: What's that mean?   20

Unidentified Girl #1: That I would stand by it and most of its decisions.

Mr. MILLER: Hear what she said?

BRAND: Until Vietnam and Watergate, there wasn't much debate over what version of history was taught in the U.S. You studied the great documents, the great leaders and the great battles, in the process, absorbing how great America was. But the culture wars of the 1980s and '90s shook everything up. In Doc Miller's class, students like Elyse Terry now wrestle with different visions of what America is about.

ELYSE TERRY (Student): I think especially, like, post–September 11th . . .

Mr. MILLER: Yeah.   25

TERRY: . . . in America, there's this big push to be patriotic and "We are the greatest," so it's confusing about which side to lean toward.

Mr. MILLER: Boy, I see a real dilemma. It's, like, "Support your country," but you have freedom to dissent. I mean, Kimmy(ph)° jumped in and said, "Yeah, you support your country in a time of war."

ph: phonetic. Transcribers of radio and television programs often use "(ph)" to indicate that they've spelled a name, most often a person's name, as it sounds when they're not sure how it should be spelled.

Unidentified Girl #2: Right.

Unidentified Girl #3: I would.

Unidentified Girl #2: Yeah.   30

Unidentified Girl #3: You know, but that isn't for other people.

Unidentified Girl #4: But you shouldn't follow your country blindly.

Unidentified Girl #3: No, I'm not.

Unidentified Girl #4: You should look inward.

Unidentified Girl #3: I would say if we were in a war that I respected, then I would 35
respect our soldiers and I would support them.

Unidentified Girl #5: Respecting soldiers is different than respecting the government for going to war.

Mr. MILLER: Should you always just then support your soldiers, your young men and women out there defending the country?

Unidentified Girl #5: It depends.

Mr. MILLER: On what?

Unidentified Girl #5: On what you're fighting for.   40

Mr. MILLER: Uh-huh. All right.

BRAND: And while most of these students say they are patriotic, some say they are uncomfortable with the good guy–bad guy scenario that President Bush has painted regarding Iraq.

Unidentified Girl #6: I'm just going to go back to something Matty(ph) said about we and they. And she said that we don't trust them.

Mr. MILLER: Yeah.

Unidentified Girl #6: But they don't trust us. They think that we're the bad ones. 45 They think that we're evil.

Mr. MILLER: OK.

Unidentified Girl #6: So . . .

Mr. MILLER: So we ought to try to look at it through other eyes . . .

Unidentified Girl #6: Yeah.

Mr. MILLER: . . . besides just American eyes.   50

Unidentified Girl #6: Yeah.

BRAND: Doc Miller tells his students that many people think Saddam Hussein has done evil things, but he doesn't tell them what he thinks. And he refuses to make a moral judgment.

That's not the case in another classroom in another state, hundreds of miles from Concord.

Mr. JOE TRENTACOSTA (Teacher): OK. Real quick. This week, as we started out the week, we talked about your essays and what makes America great.

BRAND: Joe Trentacosta also teaches eighth-grade history in the rural town of 55 West Milford, New Jersey, at the Macopin Middle School. He's also talking to his students about patriotism and what's going on with Iraq.

Mr. TRENTACOSTA: Some of us are getting the picture that the United States is using our military force to attack and destroy. In the war in Afghanistan, what did we do almost immediately after bombing certain strategic points in Afghanistan? What then did we drop?

Unidentified Girl #7: Food.

Mr. TRENTACOSTA: Food. Now what value system makes us do something of that nature?

BRAND: The classroom looks more traditional than Doc Miller's. The desks all face front, there's a big American flag hanging in the corner. Trentacosta says it's important to let his students debate and discuss big ideas like patriotism to a point. While he says they can feel free to have differing opinions, he doesn't shy away from giving them his opinion, that America is morally superior to other countries.

Mr. TRENTACOSTA: The question is, I'm going to give you an analogy. So let's 60 say you're playing on a team, you know, call it baseball, all right? You have the best player on the team. What do you expect from that best player?

Unidentified Girl #8: To win the game for you?

Mr. TRENTACOSTA: OK. That's the guy you go to. That's the go-to guy. So what am I getting at here with our stance as Americans?

Unidentified Boy #1: Like, America, as a whole, needs to, like, set a standard for the rest of the world, like, be the role model that countries look up to?

Mr. TRENTACOSTA: I think in this country, what you'll find is that since Woodrow Wilson in, you know, the early 1900s, that we, as a nation, are the best on the team. Does that mean using military force? That's up to you. But I think we are a leader in the world through our values, through our belief in freedom.

BRAND: Trentacosta says his students may not be receiving patriotic values 65 at home, and so that responsibility falls to him. But at least one student feels this type of instruction isn't necessary. Gabrielle Stitt is wearing a gray sweat-shirt with an American flag. She says she doesn't need to be taught to love her country.

GABRIELLE STITT (Student): I mean, learning about patriotism might not help you be a patriot. You almost go with, like, an instinct. You know, I've got to protect my family and my country. So just defending what you think is right, you don't need to learn about that. You just—you have to do it.

BRAND: In Gabrielle's town, West Milford, New Jersey, September 11th still looms large. They're just an hour's drive from Lower Manhattan, and an entire wall of Trentacosta's classroom is given over to the students' drawings of World Trade Center memorials. 9/11 was also felt keenly at the Concord Middle School in Massachusetts.

Mr. MILLER: Boy, you're really hitting a chord with me. I just remember personally that day after September 11th . . .

BRAND: History teacher Doc Miller pauses in the middle of his debate on what it means to be a patriotic citizen to remember how he and his students reacted then.

Mr. MILLER: I remember saying, "Let's say the Pledge now." And I said, "I think 70 it'll mean more for us than it ever has before." And, man, did it. I mean, the class was, like, silent. Everybody said it with such respect.

BRAND: There wasn't much question about what the word "allegiance" meant then. But now, in this classroom, with war looming, there is. Miller seems to embrace that ambiguity when he returns to the definition he wrote on the chalk board at the beginning of class. "Allegiance," he asks, "what is allegiance?"

Mr. MILLER: In the morning, we say the Pledge, we say to our country, "with liberty and justice for all."

Unidentified Girl #8: Right.

Mr. MILLER: Is that true? Do we have liberty and justice for all?

Group of Students: (In unison) No.   75

Mr. MILLER: Well, then what the heck are you doing the Pledge for?

CATHERINE(ph): Because . . .

Mr. MILLER: Go, Catherine.

CATHERINE: Because you want to be loyal to the ideal and to the idea that that's sort of your goal.

Mr. MILLER: We're trying to move in that direction.   80

CATHERINE: Right.

Mr. MILLER: Yeah.

BRAND: This was the first time these students really debated what it means to be patriotic. One girl says that outside the classroom, patriotic symbols are everywhere: on TV, in ads, on bumper stickers. "You grow up," she says, "being taught America is the greatest." So class for her is a relief, a place where she can really think about what the flags and the United We Stand slogans mean and then decide for herself what she believes. Madeleine Brand, NPR News.

EDWARDS: Tomorrow, two scholars debate what a teacher's role should be during a time of war. Previous reports in this series are at npr.org.

Although this piece from National Public Radio isn't a speech delivered by a single individual, it is still a form of spoken argument and employs many of the techniques of spoken argument such as considerations of diction and syntax. Learn more of the techniques for spoken arguments in Chapter 17.

LINK TO P. 348

RESPOND.

1. This transcript contrasts two very different approaches to teaching middle-school students about patriotism. How would you characterize each approach? What are its relative strengths and weaknesses? What do you think the likely result of each approach would be? Why? Which do you prefer? Why? (If you are lucky enough to have class members who have been educated in other countries or who have been home-schooled, be sure to ask them how they learned or were taught about patriotism and its meanings.)

2. Radio and television features represent especially complex arguments. Those who create them literally use tapes of many voices to help make their argument. How would you describe the argument(s) this radio feature is trying to make? What are its functions (Chapter 1)? What is the thesis of this feature? How did its creators use a range of voices to contribute to the argument(s) being made? What functions do the various voices serve?

3. Compare the effects of reading the transcript (without hearing the audio file) and listening to the audio file (without reading the transcript). Which, in your opinion, is more effective? Why? What, if anything, is lost in the transcript of the radio feature? Does the transcript have any advantages over the audio file? If so, what are they? What does such a comparison teach you about the relationship between medium—spoken word versus written word—and creating an effective argument?

4. Conservative critics of National Public Radio complain that it is too liberal in its outlook. How might they use this transcript as evidence for their argument? How might those who disagree with the conservative critics of NPR use the transcript to refute such claims?

5. **Write an essay** in which you seek to define the goals of teaching schoolchildren about *patriotism*, a term you'll also need to define. (This transcript offers two ways of teaching children about patriotism, but there are, of course, many others.) Among the issues to consider are what you want children to learn and how they might best learn these things. You'll need to be explicit about the children you have in mind. If you are American, you'll likely want to talk about American schoolchildren. If you are from another country and have immigrated here or happen to be studying here, you may wish to write about the United States or the other country or countries where you have lived. As you plan your essay, seek to avoid empty generalities. The closing remarks by Brand in the transcript recount the story of a girl who was glad to have the opportunity to think for herself about the meaning of patriotism. Take advantage of this opportunity to do the same.

► *Only nine days after the events of September 11, 2001, President George W. Bush, the forty-third president of the United States, delivered what many consider to be his finest speech yet when he addressed both Houses of Congress, the American people, and, in many ways, the world. His speech is a perfect example of an argument about the present (Chapter 1), also known as an epideictic or ceremonial argument. Although Bush certainly looks to the past—the distant past and the events of the previous nine days—and makes promises about the future, his focus is the present: "the state of our Union," as he puts it. As you read the printed version of this speech, try to analyze it as an especially complex and effective argument; focus specifically on the ways we might divide the speech into sections, each with its own function.*

You may watch or listen to this speech at <whitehouse.gov/news/releases/2001/09>.

Address to a Joint Session of Congress and the American People, September 20, 2001

GEORGE W. BUSH

Mr. Speaker, Mr. President Pro Tempore, members of Congress, and fellow Americans:

In the normal course of events, Presidents come to this chamber to report on the state of the Union. Tonight, no such report is needed. It has already been delivered by the American people.

We have seen it in the courage of passengers, who rushed terrorists to save others on the ground—passengers like an exceptional man named Todd Beamer. And would you please help me to welcome his wife, Lisa Beamer, here tonight.

We have seen the state of our Union in the endurance of rescuers, working past exhaustion. We have seen the unfurling of flags, the lighting of candles, the giving of blood, the saying of prayers—in English, Hebrew, and Arabic. We have seen the decency of a loving and giving people who have made the grief of strangers their own.

My fellow citizens, for the last nine days, the entire world has seen for itself the state of our Union—and it is strong. 5

Tonight we are a country awakened to danger and called to defend freedom. Our grief has turned to anger, and anger to resolution. Whether we bring our enemies to justice, or bring justice to our enemies, justice will be done.

I thank the Congress for its leadership at such an important time. All of America was touched on the evening of the tragedy to see Republicans and Democrats joined together on the steps of this Capitol, singing "God Bless America." And you did more than sing; you acted, by delivering $40 billion to rebuild our communities and meet the needs of our military.

Speaker Hastert, Minority Leader Gephardt, Majority Leader Daschle and Senator Lott, I thank you for your friendship, for your leadership and for your service to our country.

And on behalf of the American people, I thank the world for its outpouring of support. America will never forget the sounds of our

National Anthem playing at Buckingham Palace, on the streets of Paris, and at Berlin's Brandenburg Gate.

We will not forget South Korean children gathering to pray outside 10 our embassy in Seoul, or the prayers of sympathy offered at a mosque in Cairo. We will not forget moments of silence and days of mourning in Australia and Africa and Latin America.

Nor will we forget the citizens of 80 other nations who died with our own: dozens of Pakistanis; more than 130 Israelis; more than 250 citizens of India; men and women from El Salvador, Iran, Mexico and Japan; and hundreds of British citizens. America has no truer friend than Great Britain. Once again, we are joined together in a great cause—so honored the British Prime Minister has crossed an ocean to show his unity of purpose with America. Thank you for coming, friend.

On September the 11th, enemies of freedom committed an act of war against our country. Americans have known wars—but for the past 136 years, they have been wars on foreign soil, except for one Sunday in 1941. Americans have known the casualties of war—but not at the center of a great city on a peaceful morning. Americans have

George W. Bush addressing the U.S. Congress

known surprise attacks—but never before on thousands of civilians. All of this was brought upon us in a single day—and night fell on a different world, a world where freedom itself is under attack.

Americans have many questions tonight. Americans are asking: Who attacked our country? The evidence we have gathered all points to a collection of loosely affiliated terrorist organizations known as al Qaeda. They are the same murderers indicted for bombing American embassies in Tanzania and Kenya, and responsible for bombing the USS Cole.

Al Qaeda is to terror what the mafia is to crime. But its goal is not making money; its goal is remaking the world—and imposing its radical beliefs on people everywhere.

The terrorists practice a fringe form of Islamic extremism that has   15 been rejected by Muslim scholars and the vast majority of Muslim clerics—a fringe movement that perverts the peaceful teachings of Islam. The terrorists' directive commands them to kill Christians and Jews, to kill all Americans, and make no distinction among military and civilians, including women and children.

This group and its leader—a person named Osama bin Laden—are linked to many other organizations in different countries, including the Egyptian Islamic Jihad and the Islamic Movement of Uzbekistan. There are thousands of these terrorists in more than 60 countries. They are recruited from their own nations and neighborhoods and brought to camps in places like Afghanistan, where they are trained in the tactics of terror. They are sent back to their homes or sent to hide in countries around the world to plot evil and destruction.

The leadership of al Qaeda has great influence in Afghanistan and supports the Taliban regime in controlling most of that country. In Afghanistan, we see al Qaeda's vision for the world.

Afghanistan's people have been brutalized—many are starving and many have fled. Women are not allowed to attend school. You can be jailed for owning a television. Religion can be practiced only as their leaders dictate. A man can be jailed in Afghanistan if his beard is not long enough.

The United States respects the people of Afghanistan—after all, we are currently its largest source of humanitarian aid—but we condemn the Taliban regime. It is not only repressing its own people, it is threatening people everywhere by sponsoring and sheltering and supplying terrorists. By aiding and abetting murder, the Taliban regime is committing murder.

And tonight, the United States of America makes the following 20 demands on the Taliban: Deliver to United States authorities all the leaders of al Qaeda who hide in your land. Release all foreign nationals, including American citizens, you have unjustly imprisoned. Protect foreign journalists, diplomats and aid workers in your country. Close immediately and permanently every terrorist training camp in Afghanistan, and hand over every terrorist, and every person in their support structure, to appropriate authorities. Give the United States full access to terrorist training camps, so we can make sure they are no longer operating.

These demands are not open to negotiation or discussion. The Taliban must act, and act immediately. They will hand over the terrorists, or they will share in their fate.

I also want to speak tonight directly to Muslims throughout the world. We respect your faith. It's practiced freely by many millions of Americans, and by millions more in countries that America counts as friends. Its teachings are good and peaceful, and those who commit evil in the name of Allah blaspheme the name of Allah. The terrorists are traitors to their own faith, trying, in effect, to hijack Islam itself. The enemy of America is not our many Muslim friends; it is not our many Arab friends. Our enemy is a radical network of terrorists, and every government that supports them.

Our war on terror begins with al Qaeda, but it does not end there. It will not end until every terrorist group of global reach has been found, stopped and defeated.

Americans are asking: Why do they hate us? They hate what we see right here in this chamber — a democratically elected government. Their leaders are self-appointed. They hate our freedoms — our freedom of religion, our freedom of speech, our freedom to vote and assemble and disagree with each other.

They want to overthrow existing governments in many Muslim 25 countries, such as Egypt, Saudi Arabia, and Jordan. They want to drive Israel out of the Middle East. They want to drive Christians and Jews out of vast regions of Asia and Africa.

These terrorists kill not merely to end lives, but to disrupt and end a way of life. With every atrocity, they hope that America grows fearful, retreating from the world and forsaking our friends. They stand against us, because we stand in their way.

We are not deceived by their pretenses to piety. We have seen their kind before. They are the heirs of all the murderous ideologies of the 20th century. By sacrificing human life to serve their radical visions — by abandoning every value except the will to power — they follow in the path of fascism, and Nazism, and totalitarianism. And they will follow that path all the way, to where it ends: in history's unmarked grave of discarded lies.

Americans are asking: How will we fight and win this war? We will direct every resource at our command — every means of diplomacy, every tool of intelligence, every instrument of law enforcement, every financial influence, and every necessary weapon of war — to the disruption and to the defeat of the global terror network.

This war will not be like the war against Iraq a decade ago, with a decisive liberation of territory and a swift conclusion. It will not look like the air war above Kosovo two years ago, where no ground troops were used and not a single American was lost in combat.

Our response involves far more than instant retaliation and isolated 30 strikes. Americans should not expect one battle, but a lengthy campaign, unlike any other we have ever seen. It may include dramatic strikes, visible on TV, and covert operations, secret even in success. We will starve terrorists of funding, turn them one against another, drive them from place to place, until there is no refuge or no rest. And we will pursue nations that provide aid or safe haven to terrorism. Every nation, in every region, now has a decision to make. Either you are with us, or you are with the terrorists. From this day forward, any nation that continues to harbor or support terrorism will be regarded by the United States as a hostile regime.

Our nation has been put on notice: We are not immune from attack. We will take defensive measures against terrorism to protect Americans. Today, dozens of federal departments and agencies, as well as state and local governments, have responsibilities affecting homeland security. These efforts must be coordinated at the highest level. So tonight I announce the creation of a Cabinet-level position reporting directly to me — the Office of Homeland Security.

And tonight I also announce a distinguished American to lead this effort, to strengthen American security: a military veteran, an effective governor, a true patriot, a trusted friend—Pennsylvania's Tom Ridge. He will lead, oversee and coordinate a comprehensive national strategy to safeguard our country against terrorism, and respond to any attacks that may come.

These measures are essential. But the only way to defeat terrorism as a threat to our way of life is to stop it, eliminate it, and destroy it where it grows.

Many will be involved in this effort, from FBI agents to intelligence operatives to the reservists we have called to active duty. All deserve our thanks, and all have our prayers. And tonight, a few miles from the damaged Pentagon, I have a message for our military: Be ready. I've called the Armed Forces to alert, and there is a reason. The hour is coming when America will act, and you will make us proud.

This is not, however, just America's fight. And what is at stake is not 35 just America's freedom. This is the world's fight. This is civilization's fight. This is the fight of all who believe in progress and pluralism, tolerance and freedom.

We ask every nation to join us. We will ask, and we will need, the help of police forces, intelligence services, and banking systems around the world. The United States is grateful that many nations and many international organizations have already responded—with sympathy and with support. Nations from Latin America, to Asia, to Africa, to Europe, to the Islamic world. Perhaps the NATO Charter reflects best the attitude of the world: An attack on one is an attack on all.

The civilized world is rallying to America's side. They understand that if this terror goes unpunished, their own cities, their own citizens may be next. Terror, unanswered, can not only bring down buildings, it can threaten the stability of legitimate governments. And you know what—we're not going to allow it.

Americans are asking: What is expected of us? I ask you to live your lives, and hug your children. I know many citizens have fears tonight, and I ask you to be calm and resolute, even in the face of a continuing threat.

I ask you to uphold the values of America, and remember why so many have come here. We are in a fight for our principles, and our first responsibility is to live by them. No one should be singled out for unfair treatment or unkind words because of their ethnic background or religious faith.

I ask you to continue to support the victims of this tragedy with 40 your contributions. Those who want to give can go to a central source of information, libertyunites.org, to find the names of groups providing direct help in New York, Pennsylvania, and Virginia.

The thousands of FBI agents who are now at work in this investigation may need your cooperation, and I ask you to give it.

I ask for your patience, with the delays and inconveniences that may accompany tighter security; and for your patience in what will be a long struggle.

I ask your continued participation and confidence in the American economy. Terrorists attacked a symbol of American prosperity. They did not touch its source. America is successful because of the hard work, and creativity, and enterprise of our people. These were the true strengths of our economy before September 11th, and they are our strengths today.

And, finally, please continue praying for the victims of terror and their families, for those in uniform, and for our great country. Prayer has comforted us in sorrow, and will help strengthen us for the journey ahead.

Tonight I thank my fellow Americans for what you have already 45 done and for what you will do. And ladies and gentlemen of the Congress, I thank you, their representatives, for what you have already done and for what we will do together.

Tonight, we face new and sudden national challenges. We will come together to improve air safety, to dramatically expand the number of air marshals on domestic flights, and take new measures to prevent hijacking. We will come together to promote stability and keep our airlines flying, with direct assistance during this emergency.

We will come together to give law enforcement the additional tools it needs to track down terror here at home. We will come together to strengthen our intelligence capabilities to know the plans of terrorists before they act, and find them before they strike.

We will come together to take active steps that strengthen America's economy, and put our people back to work.

Tonight we welcome two leaders who embody the extraordinary spirit of all New Yorkers: Governor George Pataki, and Mayor Rudolph Giuliani. As a symbol of America's resolve, my administration will work with Congress, and these two leaders, to show the world that we will rebuild New York City.

After all that has just passed—all the lives taken, and all the possi- 50 bilities and hopes that died with them—it is natural to wonder if America's future is one of fear. Some speak of an age of terror. I know there are struggles ahead, and dangers to face. But this country will define our times, not be defined by them. As long as the United States of America is determined and strong, this will not be an age of terror; this will be an age of liberty, here and across the world.

Great harm has been done to us. We have suffered great loss. And in our grief and anger we have found our mission and our moment. Freedom and fear are at war. The advance of human freedom—the great achievement of our time, and the great hope of every time—now depends on us. Our nation—this generation—will lift a dark threat of violence from our people and our future. We will rally the world to this cause by our efforts, by our courage. We will not tire, we will not falter, and we will not fail.

It is my hope that in the months and years ahead, life will return almost to normal. We'll go back to our lives and routines, and that is good. Even grief recedes with time and grace. But our resolve must not pass. Each of us will remember what happened that day, and to whom it happened. We'll remember the moment the news came—where we were and what we were doing. Some will remember an image of a fire, or a story of rescue. Some will carry memories of a face and a voice gone forever.

And I will carry this: It is the police shield of a man named George Howard, who died at the World Trade Center trying to save others. It was given to me by his mom, Arlene, as a proud memorial to her son. This is my reminder of lives that ended, and a task that does not end.

I will not forget this wound to our country or those who inflicted it. I will not yield; I will not rest; I will not relent in waging this struggle for freedom and security for the American people.

The course of this conflict is not known, yet its outcome is certain. 55 Freedom and fear, justice and cruelty, have always been at war, and we know that God is not neutral between them.

Fellow citizens, we'll meet violence with patient justice—assured of the rightness of our cause, and confident of the victories to come. In all that lies before us, may God grant us wisdom, and may He watch over the United States of America.

Thank you.

RESPOND.

1. What response do you have to this speech, especially to hearing this speech? If you heard the speech in 2001, do you remember your reaction at the time? What, specifically, accounts for the power of this speech for you and other listeners? In what ways is this a patriotic speech? Why? If you do not find the speech effective, what keeps it from being so?

2. In this question and the ones that follow, we'll seek to analyze the speech in some detail. First, go through Bush's speech circling each occurrence of "I" or "we" and underlining the verbs that occur with these pronouns. Make a list of these structures—all of the "I + *verb*" and "we + *verb*" structures—and analyze the functions they serve, that is, their effect in the speech and on the reader. (The discussion of tropes in Chapter 14 may help you here.) Obviously, the "I" refers to President Bush. Be sure to note whom the "we" refers to. (Does it, for example, always refer to all Americans? Does it ever refer to any other group—for example, subgroups of Americans or people from certain countries or cultures?) What picture do these phrases, all of the form *first-person pronoun + verb*, create of Bush? Of the American people?

3. Reread the speech. As you read, divide the speech into sections by considering the function of each paragraph—how it moves the speech along and contributes to the speech—and then grouping paragraphs that share a function. For example, you will see that paragraphs 2–5 work as a unit, demonstrating how strong the United States is despite the events of September 11. Paragraph 2 contrasts the usual occasion upon which the president addresses the joint Houses of Congress—when delivering the State of the Union address in January—with the present moment, when the American people have, through their actions, shown the state of the Union. Paragraph 3 cites the example of Todd Beamer, who led other passengers to rush the terrorists, and then introduces Beamer's wife. Paragraph 4 lists further examples: rescuers; people who have unfurled flags; people who have prayed in English, Hebrew, and Arabic; and people who have made others' grief their own. Paragraph 5 summarizes this section by noting that the world has seen the strength of the United States.

In what ways is President Bush's speech a proposal argument? See Chapter 12 to decide.

······· **LINK TO P. 238**

4. As Chapter 1 notes, arguments about the present focus on questions of values. At the same time, a speech that discusses only values remains much too general and abstract to be effective. Reread the speech once again. This time, note the ways that Bush moves beyond generalities and statements about abstract values to make the speech concrete and specific in the here and now. For example, he mentions Todd Beamer and introduces his wife, who was invited to be present at the speech (paragraph 3); he also names the countries whose citizens lost their lives in the destruction of the World Trade Center and cites specific numbers in some cases (paragraph 11). As you'll see, in nearly every paragraph Bush finds ways to use specific information to make his claims about values effective and memorable.

5. **Write an essay** in which you evaluate the contributions of the textual features discussed in response to questions 2, 3, or 4 to the overall effect of Bush's speech. Obviously, you will not need to discuss every example of each textual feature. Rather, you will want to choose the most (or perhaps least) effective examples of the features to support your point.

▼ *A professor of history at Georgetown University, Michael Kazin focuses in his research, teaching, and writing on popular social movements in U.S. politics. His most recent book, coauthored with Maurice Isserman, is America Divided: The Civil War of the 1960s (2nd ed., 2003). He also serves on the editorial board of Dissent, a quarterly magazine devoted to politics and culture found at <dissentmagazine.org>, where this essay appeared in the Fall 2002 issue. In this essay Kazin seeks to explain how and why patriotism has been a necessary part of the history of "the left" in the United States. As quickly becomes clear, he uses the label left in a way that may be unfamiliar to some readers. As he employs the term, it means not simply those who are just-left-of-center, as many Democratic politicians might be categorized today, but also those who seek more fundamental and radical changes in society. Like William Bennett, author of the following selection, "A Nation Worth Defending," Kazin is a student of our country's history—although, as you will see, he understands that history in very different ways than does Bennett. As you read, pay attention to the techniques Kazin uses to create a definition for patriotism such that those on "the left" can lay strong claim to being patriotic.*

A Patriotic Left

MICHAEL KAZIN

I love my country. I love its passionate and endlessly inventive culture, its remarkably diverse landscape, its agonizing and wonderful history. I particularly cherish its civic ideals — social equality, individual liberty, a populist democracy — and the unending struggle to put their laudable, if often contradictory, claims into practice. I realize that patriotism, like any powerful ideology, is a "construction" with multiple uses, some of which I abhor. But I persist in drawing stimulation and pride from my American identity.

Regrettably, this is not a popular sentiment on the contemporary left. Antiwar activists view patriotism as a smokescreen for U.S. hegemony,° while radical academics mock the notion of "American exceptionalism"° as a relic of the cold war, a triumphal myth we should quickly outgrow. All the rallying around the flag after September 11 increased the disdain many leftists feel for the sentiment that lies behind it. "The globe, not the flag, is the symbol that's wanted now," scolded Katha Pollitt° in The Nation. Noam Chomsky°

described patriotic blather as simply the governing elite's way of telling its subjects, "You shut up and be obedient, and I'll relentlessly advance my own interests."

Both views betray an ignorance of American history, as well as a quixotic° desire to leap from a distasteful present to a gauzy future liberated from the fetters of nationalism. Love of country was a demotic° faith long before September 11, a fact that previous lefts understood and attempted to turn to their advantage. In the United States, Karl Marx's dictum that the workers have no country has been refuted time and again. It has been not wage earners but the upper classes — from New England gentry on the Grand Tour a century ago to globe-trotting executives and cybertech professionals today — who view America with an ambivalent shrug, reminiscent of Gertrude Stein's° line, "America is my country, Paris is my hometown."

One can, like Pollitt and Chomsky, curse as jingoistic° all those "United We Stand" and "God Bless

846

Symbols of patriotism—such as the flag—can carry more than one meaning.

America" signs and hope somehow to transcend patriotism in the name of global harmony. Or one can empathize with the communal spirit that ani-

mates them, embracing the ideals of the nation and learning from past efforts to put them into practice in the service of far-reaching reform.

An earlier version of American patriotism was a   5 forerunner of the modern genre: pride in the first nation organized around a set of social beliefs rather than a shared geography and history. In its novelty, Americanism gave citizens of the new republic both a way to understand and to stand for purposes that transcended their self-interest. Of course, these purposes were not always noble ones. As historian Gary Gerstle points out in his recent book *American Crucible,* "racial nationalism" dominated much of American life through the nineteenth century and into the early decades of the twentieth. It led some white Americans to justify exterminating Indians, others to hold slaves, and still others to bar immigrants who did not possess "Anglo-Saxon" genes. But the tolerant alternative, which Gerstle calls "civic nationalism," also inspired many Americans in the modern era to help liberate Europe from fascism and Stalinism and to organize at home for social and economic justice.

For American leftists, patriotism was indispensable. It made their dissent and rebellion intelligible to

---

hegemony: using your position of strength and power to control others.

American exceptionalism: the idea that the United States is fundamentally different from the other countries it is compared to—mainly Canada and Western Europe.

Katha Pollitt: columnist for the journal *The Nation,*

college professor, and poet, known for her passionate atheism and leftist political views.

Noam Chomsky: professor of linguistics at MIT (1928–), known as one of America's most vocal leftist political critics. The author of over thirty political books, Chomsky is famous for his

critiques of United States foreign policy, governmental abuses of power, and the role of media.

quixotic: idealistic or optimistic in an unwarranted way.

demotic: of or relating to the common people.

Gertrude Stein: avant-garde writer

(1873–1946), born in the United States, who chose to move to Paris to live and work among fellow writers and artists during the period between World Wars I and II.

jingoistic: patriotic in a boasting and chauvinistic way, generally favoring an aggressive and warlike foreign policy.

their fellow citizens — and located them within the national narrative, fighting to shape a common future. Tom Paine° praised his adopted homeland as an "asylum for mankind" — which gave him a forum to denounce regressive taxes and propose free public education. Elizabeth Cady Stanton° issued a "Woman's Declaration of Rights" on the centennial of the Declaration of Independence and argued that denying the vote to women was a violation of the Fourteenth Amendment. Union activists in the Gilded Age such as Eugene Debs° and Mother Jones° accused employers of crushing the individuality and self-respect of workers. When Debs became a socialist, he described his new vision in the American idiom, as "the equal rights of all to manage and control" society. Half a century later, Martin Luther King, Jr., told his fellow bus boycotters, "If we are wrong — the Supreme Court of this nation is wrong" and proclaimed that "the great glory of American democracy is the right to protest for right."

One could easily list analogous statements from such pioneering reformers as Jane Addams and Betty Friedan, unionists Sidney Hillman and Cesar Chavez, and the gay liberationist Harvey Milk. Without patriotic appeals, the great social movements that attacked inequalities of class, gender, and race in the United States — and spread their messianic rhetoric around the world — would never have gotten off the ground.

Even slavery couldn't extinguish the promise radicals found in the American creed. On Independence Day, 1852, Frederick Douglass° gave an angry, eloquent address that asked, "What to the slave is the Fourth of July?" Every account quotes the fugitive-turned-abolitionist speaking truth to white power: "Your celebration is a sham; your boasted liberty, an unholy license; your national greatness, swelling vanity; your sounds of rejoicing are empty and heartless; your denunciations of tyrants, brass fronted impudence; your shouts of liberty and equality, hollow

mockery." But fewer commentators note that when, at the end of his speech, Douglass predicted slavery's demise, he drew his "encouragement from the Declaration of Independence, the great principles it contains, and the genius of American Institutions," as well as from a spirit of enlightenment that he believed was growing on both sides of the Atlantic. After emancipation, Douglass never stopped condemning the hypocrisy of white Americans — or continuing to base his hopes for equality on traditions he and they held in common.

Thomas Paine: political theorist and writer (1737–1809), published the pamphlet *Common Sense* in which he argued for the independence of the American colonies. His pamphlets throughout the Revolutionary War served to encourage resistance against the British colonizers.

Elizabeth Cady Stanton: leader of the women's suffrage movement (1815–1902), who helped write the bill of rights for women at the Seneca Falls women's rights convention in 1848.

Eugene Debs: labor and political leader (1855–1926), and five-time candidate for president on the

Socialist party ticket. He was sentenced to ten years in prison under the 1917 Espionage Act because of his vocal pacifism and opposition to the United States' entry into World War I.

Mother Jones: nickname for Mary Harris Jones (1830–1930), labor activist who fought for laws to end child labor and to acquire rights for garment and streetcar workers, and miners.

Frederick Douglass: a freed slave and ardent abolitionist (1818–1895) known for his powerful autobiography, in which he depicts his struggle to escape from slavery and become a freed man.

A self-critical conception of patriotism also led Americans on the left to oppose their leaders' aggressive policies abroad. Anti-imperialists opposed the conquest of the Philippines after the war of 1898 by comparing President William McKinley to King George III.° Foes of U.S. intervention in World War I demanded to know why Americans should die to defend European monarchs and their colonies in Africa and Asia. In 1917, a mass movement led by socialists and pacifists called for a popular referendum on the question of going to war. Neither group of resisters succeeded at the time, but each gained a mass hearing and saw its arguments incorporated into future policies. Congress promised independence to the Philippines sooner than colonial officials favored. And, challenged by such antiwar voices as Debs, Robert LaFollette,° and William Jennings Bryan,° Woodrow Wilson proclaimed national self-determination to be the core principle of a new world order.

A good deal that we cherish about contemporary 10 America was thus accomplished by social movements of the left, speaking out for national ideals. It may be, as the idiosyncratic Trotskyist Leon Samson argued in 1935, that Americanism served as a substitute for socialism, an ideology of self-emancipation through equal opportunity that inoculated most citizens against the class-conscious alternative. But leftists made what progress they did by demanding that the nation live up to its stated principles, rather than dismissing them as fatally compromised by the racism of the founders or the abusiveness of flag-waving vigilantes. After all, hope is always more attractive than cynicism, and the gap between promise and fulfillment is narrower for Americanism than it is for other universalist creeds such as communism, Christianity, and Islam.

It's difficult to think of any radical or reformer who repudiated the national belief system and still had a major impact on U.S. politics and policy. The movement against the Vietnam War did include activists who preferred the Vietcong's flag to the American one. But the antiwar insurgency grew powerful only toward the end of the 1960s, when it drew

---

King George III:
(1738–1820) England's monarch during the American Revolution, infamous for his insistence on taxing the colonies, and his stubborn refusal to admit to defeat in the war against the colonists.

Robert LaFollette:
(1855–1925) founder of the Progressive Movement, Republican congressman, senator, and governor of Wisconsin. In 1917 he was nearly kicked out of the Senate for disloyalty after voting against declaring war during World War I and continuing to criticize the war once the United States had entered it.

William Jennings Bryan:
(1860–1925) Congressman, three-time Democratic presidential nominee, and secretary of state to President Wilson, a position from which he resigned because of his antiwar beliefs when the United States was beginning to make motions to enter World War I.

in people who looked for leadership to liberal patriots such as King, Walter Reuther,° and Eugene McCarthy° rather than to Abbie Hoffman° and the Weathermen.°

Perhaps one exception to this rule was Malcolm X, who stated, in 1964, that he was a "victim of Americanism" who could see no "American dream," only "an American nightmare." But Malcolm was primarily a spokesman for black anger and pride, not a builder of movements or a catalyst of reforms to benefit his people.

He was, however, a prophetic figure. Soon after Malcolm's death, many on the left, of all races, began to scorn patriotic talk and, instead, to celebrate ethnic and sexual differences. In 1970, writer Julius Lester observed, "American radicals are perhaps the first radicals anywhere who have sought to make a revolution in a country which they hate." At the time, there were certainly ample reasons to consider Americanism a brutal sham. After World War II, the word itself became the property of the American Legion,° the House Un-American Activities Committee,° and the FBI. In the 1960s, liberal presidents bullied their way into Indochina in the name of what Lyndon Johnson called "the principle for which our ancestors fought in the valleys of Pennsylvania." Fierce love for one's identity group—whether black, Latino, Asian, Native American, or gay or lesbian—seemed morally superior to the master narrative that had justified war abroad and racial exclusion at home.

Yet the history of the last thirty years has also exposed the outsized flaw in such thinking. Having abandoned patriotism, the left lost the ability to pose convincing alternatives for the nation as a whole. It could take credit for spearheading a multicultural, gender-aware revision of the humanities curriculum, but the right set the political agenda, and it did so in part because its partisans spoke forcefully in the name of American principles that knit together disparate groups—anti-union businesspeople, white evangelicals, Jewish neoconservatives—for mutual ends.

In the face of such evidence, many leftists would [15] respond that civic idealism should not be confined within national borders. In a provocative 1994 essay, philosopher Martha Nussbaum argued that patriotism is "morally dangerous" because it encourages Americans to focus on their own concerns and minimize or disregard those of people in other lands. "We should regard our deliberations," she wrote, "as, first and foremost, deliberations about human problems of people in particular concrete situations, not problems growing out of a national identity that is altogether unlike that of others." Echoing her words, activists and intellectuals talk of challenging global exploitation with some form of global citizenship.

As an ethicist, Nussbaum is certainly on solid ground. Americans ought to take a massacre in Africa as seriously as one that takes place in lower Manhattan and demand that their government move rapidly to halt it. But she offers no guidance for how global leftists can get the power to achieve their laudable objectives. A planetary government is hardly on the horizon, and rich nations would no doubt hog its agenda if it were.

In the meantime, Americans who want to transform the world have to learn how to persuade the nation. At minimum, this means putting pressure on the national government, organizing coalitions of people from different regions and backgrounds, and debating citizens who think their tax money ought to be spent only at home. Disconnected as they are from any national or local constituency, global leftists now live at risk of being thrust to the margins—abstract sages of equity, operatives of nongovernmental organizations engaged in heroic but Sisyphean tasks,° or demonstrators roving from continent to continent in search of bankers to heckle.

In the wake of September 11, the stakes have been raised for the American left. Even if the "war against terrorism" doesn't continue to overshadow all other issues, it will inevitably force activists of every stripe to make clear how they would achieve security for individual citizens and for the nation. How can one seriously engage in this conversation about protecting America if America holds no privileged place in one's heart? Most ordinary citizens understandably distrust a left that condemns military intervention abroad or a crackdown at home but expresses only a pro forma concern for the actual and potential victims of terrorism. Without empathy for one's neighbors, politics becomes a cold, censorious enterprise indeed.

Walter Reuther: a major organizer and activist for trade unions; leader of the major unions including the United Automobile Workers and the AFL-CIO (1907–1970). He devoted his life to humanitarian goals, working for social welfare reforms, marching with Martin Luther King Jr. for civil rights, and vocally opposing the Vietnam War.

Eugene McCarthy: unsuccessful Democratic presidential candidate in 1968 (1916–). Known as the "peace candidate," he decided to run for president because he opposed President Lyndon B. Johnson's Vietnam policies. Although he was defeated for the nomination by Hubert Humphrey, McCarthy's vocal opposition to the war prompted a renewed discussion of the military, political, and moral implications of the United States' policies on Vietnam.

Abbie Hoffman: founder of the "Yippies," the Youth International Party (1936–1989), known for violent anti-Vietnam War activism which led to Hoffman's arrest at the 1968 Democratic National Convention. After his subsequent arrest in 1973 for cocaine possession, Hoffman disappeared, taking on aliases and undergoing plastic surgery, yet still working as an activist.

Weathermen: one of the most notorious activist groups of the 1960s, dedicated to protesting the government and the war in Vietnam. Known for their violent strategies, including building a bomb factory in a New York City townhouse and vandalizing much of Chicago's business district in a four-day protest known as the "Days of Rage," most of their most infamous members ended up in prison or dead (many from the accidental detonation of their bomb factory).

American Legion: the world's largest veterans' association, founded in 1919 by Congress and currently numbering nearly three million members worldwide.

House Un-American Activities Committee: a congressional committee (1938–1975) designed to weed out any individual or organization deemed Communist, disloyal, or subversive. The most infamous inquiries included the 1947 investigation against much of the entertainment industry in Hollywood and the 1948 Soviet espionage case against State Department official Alger Hiss. Senator Joseph McCarthy modeled his investigations of alleged Communism on this committee.

Sisyphean tasks: referring to the labors of Sisyphus in Greek mythology, condemned in Hades to push a heavy stone up a steep hill eternally and watch it roll back down just as he reached the top. Sisyphean tasks are those that demand unending and usually ineffective effort.

There's no need to mouth the Pledge of Allegiance or affix a flag pin to your lapel or handbag. But to rail against patriotic symbols is to wage a losing battle — and one that demeans us and sets us against the overwhelming majority of Americans for no worthwhile moral or political purpose. Instead, leftists should again claim, without pretense or apology, an honorable place in the long narrative of those who demanded that American ideals apply to all and opposed the efforts of those who tried to reserve them for favored groups. When John Ashcroft denies the right of counsel to a citizen accused of terrorism or a CEO cooks the books to impress Wall Street, they are soiling the flag and ought to be put on the patriotic defensive. Liberals and radicals are the only people in politics who can insist on closing the gap between America as the apotheosis° of democratic strivings and the sordid realities of greed and arrogance that often betray it.

There is really no alternative. In daily life, cultural cosmopolitanism is mostly reserved to the rich and famous. Radical environmentalists and anti-IMF crusaders seek to revive the old dream of internationalism in a version indebted more to John Lennon's "Imagine" than to V.I. Lenin's Comintern.° But three years after bursting into the headlines from the streets of Seattle, that project seems stalled indefinitely in the Sargasso Sea° that lies between rhetorical desire and political exigency.

In hope of a revival, left patriots might draw inspiration from two voices from disparate points on the demographic and ideological spectrum. During the Great Depression, the white, conservative skeptic George Santayana observed that "America is the greatest of opportunities and the worst of influences. Our effort must be to resist the influence and improve the opportunity." At the same time, Langston Hughes — black, homosexual, and communist sympathizer — expressed a parallel vision:

Let America be the dream the dreamers dreamed —
Let it be that great strong land of love
Where never kings connive nor tyrants scheme
That any man be crushed by one above . . .
O, yes,
I say it plain,
America never was America to me,
And yet I swear this oath —
America will be!

Throughout our history, and still today, the most effective way to love the country is to fight like hell to change it.

One of Kazin's strategies here is definition by example. See Chapter 9 for other kinds of definitions.

LINK TO P. 151 ⋯⋯⋯⋯⋯⋯⋯⋯⋯⋯⋯⋯⋯⋯⋯⋯⋯⋯⋯⋯

apotheosis: the perfect example, the epitome.

V.I. Lenin's Comintern: the Soviet leader's plan for global Communist revolution, established in 1919 as a gathering of representatives from over thirty Communist nations, all devoted to liberating the world from capitalist oppression.

Sargasso Sea: the body of water that covers the heart of the mysterious Bermuda Triangle, site of unexplained disappearances and reappearances of ships and airplanes.

RESPOND•

1. How does Kazin define patriotism? What sorts of definition does he give for patriotism (Chapter 9)? What does he mean when he writes of a "self-critical conception of patriotism" (paragraph 9)? How effective is he in constructing a definition of patriotism that will likely appeal to liberals and radicals? To a broader audience? Why?

2. Even though Kazin is writing to other people on the Left, he does not assume from the outset that his readers will agree with him. Rather, he writes as if he must create common ground with them. How does he accomplish this task? How does he anticipate and respond to potential rebuttals from others on the Left? In what ways could we claim that his argument is Rogerian (Chapter 1)?

3. Kazin mentions or alludes to many Americans whose achievements were likely unknown to you before reading this essay. Why, do you think, have you not been taught about these Americans in the history courses you have taken? What sort of history do you think Kazin would argue should be taught to schoolchildren and college students? Compare and contrast this approach to history with the one William J. Bennett argues for in the following essay, "A Nation Worth Defending."

4. **Write an essay** in which you evaluate Kazin's techniques for defining patriotism. In writing this essay, you'll find it useful to study Chapter 10, which focuses on evaluative arguments, and Chapter 9, which focuses on definitional arguments. (The "Guide to Writing" at the end of each chapter should prove especially useful.) Note that rather than focusing on the value, truth, or correctness of the definition of patriotism Kazin offers, you should concentrate on evaluating how effectively (or ineffectively) he defines the term.

▼ William J. Bennett currently serves as co-director of Empower America, a policy organization based in Washington, D.C. He is also chair of Americans for Victory Over Terrorism and of an Internet-based primary and secondary school. A former U.S. secretary of education during the Reagan era and a philosophy professor, he has written or edited fourteen books, the most recent of which is Why We Fight: Moral Clarity and the War on Terrorism (2002). In this essay, which first appeared in November 2002 in USA Today Magazine, Bennett argues for a particular conceptualization of patriotism, one that subscribes to what Kazin, of the previous essay, would term "American exceptionalism." As you read, consider how Bennett defines patriotism and its functions.

A Nation Worth Defending

WILLIAM J. BENNETT

"American patriotism has always been rooted in love of the principles upon which the nation was founded: liberty, equality, justice, and democracy."

On Sept. 11, 2001, America suffered more civilian casualties than on any other day in its 226 years when terrorists hijacked jetliners and crashed them into the nation's financial and military centers. Only through the heroism and courage of passengers on one plane were they prevented from striking the nation's capital. For many—especially those who lived in the cities struck—the shock and horror of that day remain with them. For others, however, the memory has faded. I recently spoke with a radio station in Portland, Ore., and asked the host how Sept. 11 had affected them. Not much, he admitted: "We think it was more of an East Coast thing."

In one way, this is a great strength of America: We move on. It is also, though, a great weakness, especially at a time like this. As Americans, we must remember more than we do. The U.S. is, indeed, a nation worth defending, but one that, surprisingly, many Americans find themselves reluctant to defend.

I am the chairman of Americans for Victory Over Terrorism (AVOT), dedicated to sustaining and strengthening American public opinion in the war on terrorism. We recently conducted a poll of college students to determine their knowledge of and attitudes about the war. What we found was disturbing:

- Less than half of those we surveyed could name the U.S. Secretary of State.
- About one-third could identify the prime minister of Israel and the U.S. Secretary of Defense.
- Approximately one-quarter could identify the three nations that Pres. Bush identified as the Axis of Evil.
- Fewer than 20% could name the American national security advisor and the United Nations' secretary-general.
- Just 14% could identify the president of Pakistan, even as we rely on that nation's help in the war in Afghanistan.

John Trumbull's Signing of the Declaration of Independence

Moreover, of the 55 highest-ranked colleges and universities in the nation, not a single one requires students to take a course in American history in order to graduate. Only three require a course in Western civilization. This is cause for alarm, but it should not come as a surprise. The recently released National Assessment of Education Progress reveals that 57% of high school students are "below basic" in their knowledge of history. Just 18% of fourth-graders, 17% of eighth-graders, and 11% of 12th-graders score at the "proficient" level, the one at which the National Assessment Governing Board, the administrators of the tests, says all students should perform.

This historical ignorance is not merely of academic concern. It has real-world consequences. Returning to the AVOT poll, more than 70% of college students disagree — and 34% strongly disagree — that the values of the U.S. are superior to those of other countries. More than one-third disagree with the claim that, "Despite its flaws, the United States is the best country in the world." Eighty percent reject the claim that Western civilization, with its unparalleled

Fourth of July parade attendees

From what does this reluctance to defend America—morally and intellectually—arise? I would argue that it stems from a lack of education about America or, in some cases, a historically incorrect education about America, which is even worse. Education ought not be defined narrowly as the accumulation of knowledge; it also entails preparing a future generation of citizens. Education, by its nature, includes civic education. That is why, as the Greek philosopher Plato put it, the fundamental task of any regime is the education of the young. A nation cannot survive if its young are not intellectually and morally prepared to defend it.

What should children be taught about America? They should be taught the truth about it. If we are a nation that was created by a political vision of equality and liberty, our story is the story of the struggle to realize that vision, those ideals. We have had our failures—some of them shameful—but never once have we lost sight of our moral ideals, which is why we have been able to transcend the stains on our record, foremost among them that of slavery. Who else among the world's nations could enter such a claim?

Our country is something to be proud of, something to celebrate. We should not shrink from saying so. A careful and close reading of our history demonstrates that we have provided more freedom to more people than any other nation in the history of mankind; that we have provided a greater degree of equality to more people than any other nation in the history of mankind; that we have created more prosperity and spread it more widely than any other

achievements and human flourishing, is superior to Arab civilization. In what was perhaps the most striking finding, one-third said that they would evade a military draft in the war on terrorism; another third would refuse to serve abroad; and just one-third would willingly go fight overseas.

Ideas, author Richard Weaver° famously wrote, have consequences. Similarly, pernicious ideas have pernicious consequences. The idea that America is no better than any other nation is one pernicious idea; the claim that our values are no better than any other set of values is another; and the pernicious consequence of such ideas is that two-thirds of our college students—the future leaders of America—would refuse to serve in the military [or] in a foreign country during the war on terrorism.

Richard Weaver: a historian of ideas and rhetorician (1910–1963) who argued for keeping education standards high. He saw the importance of education to help people evolve into reasoning individuals.

nation in the history of mankind; that we have brought more peace and justice to the world than any other nation in the history of mankind; and that our open, tolerant, prosperous society is the marvel — and the envy — of the ages.

This is demonstrably true within our own borders. 10 Outside those borders, we have been a beacon of freedom and opportunity to people throughout the world since the day of our creation. When people around the globe demonstrate in support of freedom and liberty, they do so with American icons and documents. I will never forget — *we* should never forget — how the brave Chinese students in Tiananmen Square° faced off with tanks, armed with only a papier-mâché Statue of Liberty and a copy of the Declaration of Independence. Pernicious ideas have pernicious consequences, but good and noble ideas can have good and noble consequences, too.

The noble ideas of America have led to noble consequences and noble actions on our part. For example, in the 20th century alone, as one British columnist pointed out, Americans "saved Europe from barbarism in two world wars . . . [and] rebuilt the continent from ashes. They confronted and peacefully defeated Soviet Communism, the most murderous system ever devised by man. . . . America, primarily, ejected Iraq from Kuwait and . . . stopped the slaughter in the Balkans while the Europeans dithered." This list could be extended tenfold and it would still be incomplete.

Put simply, America is the place people run to when, in hope or hopelessness, they are running from somewhere else. I have devised a simple test to illustrate this, the gates test, as I call it. If a nation were to have entirely free and unfettered, unchecked and unpatrolled borders, would people come in or go out? If the U.S. opened its borders, there would be streams of people trying to enter the country. Even with border patrols and immigration policies, there are people trying to get in. Many of those people — both today and in decades past — have risked life and limb to flee repressive regimes like Cuba, China, and the Soviet Union to enjoy the freedoms and opportunities unique to America.

That these freedoms and opportunities are unique to America is not merely a conservative position. Listen to what former Senator (D.-N.Y.) and Ambassador to the United Nations Daniel Patrick Moynihan has to say on the matter. "Am I embarrassed to speak for a less than perfect democracy? Not one bit. Find me a better one. Do I suppose there are societies which are free of sin? No, I don't. Do I think ours is, on balance, incomparably the most hopeful set of human relations the world has? Yes, I do."

It is starting from this bedrock understanding that an education in patriotism should proceed, for "what is taught will not be forgotten, and what is forgotten cannot be defended," as the American Council of Trustees and Alumni has put it. The job of educators — not just teachers, but parents and politicians as well — in our time is to make sure that these truths are not forgotten, that children learn that their great nation is, as Pres. Abraham Lincoln said, the last best hope of Earth.

Tiananmen Square: located in Beijing, China, the site of a massive demonstration for democratic reform. Chinese students began the protest in April 1989 and were joined by over a million people — workers, civil servants, and intellectuals — all calling for the resignation of key government leaders. On the nights of June 3 and 4, 1989, the government responded by moving into the square with troops and tanks, killing thousands of people and arresting many others.

There is much that can be taught to our children about Sept. 11. On that bloody day, we saw the face and felt the hand of evil, but we saw something else — heroism, courage, and honor.

We saw the firemen who rushed into the burning infernos of the World Trade Center as so many men and women were rushing out. We heard the audiotapes of the struggle on Flight 93, where men and women who expected nothing more than a normal cross-country flight came together to overpower the terrorists and keep that plane from being used as a missile. Today, we see the ongoing bravery of the men and women in our armed forces, risking their lives around the world to protect America and all that she stands for. Children will learn from that.

To learn from it, however, they must be reminded of it. If our children are not reminded of the heroism of Sept. 11, they will not learn to be brave. If they do not learn about the great and noble things our country has done, they will not learn to be patriotic. If they do not learn to be brave and patriotic, our nation is in grave danger. Today's children are tomorrow's soldiers, citizens, and leaders. They will be called on to defend our country — to defend *their* country — in the years to come. They must be prepared to do so.

In order to do so effectively, we must all be able to see through fogs of moral obfuscation and political correctness. The reluctance of college students to state that Western civilization is superior to Arabic civilization is not surprising. A poll of students by the National Association of Scholars found that three-quarters of American college students say their professors teach them that right and wrong depend "on differences in individual values and cultural diversity."

You may recall that, shortly after Sept. 11, Prime Minister Silvio Berlusconi of Italy asserted that Western civilization was "superior" to that of Islam. As you might expect, the guardians of political correctness

15 were up in arms: "Simply unacceptable" and "deeply dangerous rantings," complained the *Washington Post;* other newspapers and international leaders added that the comments were "absurd," "Neanderthal," "disgusting," and "outrageous." Put aside the question of whether or not Berlusconi's remarks were impolite. Let us focus on the simple question of whether they were true. Could it be that Western civilization is superior to Islamic civilization?

20 It is hard to look at the world today and argue otherwise. The Western world has led to a standard of living unprecedented in human history. It has guaranteed a system of rights and liberties for men and women that are all but unknown in the Islamic world. Scientific progress has benefited rich and poor, young and old. Throughout the Western world, there is a degree of human flourishing that is absent from the suffering that characterizes life for so many in the Middle East.

As Berlusconi said, Western civilization "has guaranteed well-being, respect for human rights and . . . respect for religious and political rights"; it is a "system that has as its values understandings of diversity and tolerance." While he was wrong to deny that such "respect for human rights and religion" existed anywhere in the Islamic world, it is all but inarguable that such respect is the rare exception, and certainly not the rule.

Islamic civilization does have a noble heritage of its own. During the Middle Ages, for instance, Islamic scientists and philosophers made contributions that remain valuable even to this day. Yet, for the past several centuries, as historian Bernard Lewis reminds us, Islamic civilization has remained stagnant, while the West has flourished.

I believe that one reason the West has flourished while Islamic civilization has remained stagnant is that the spirit of democracy and liberty in the West encourages questioning, debate, and progress. To learn about the value of capitalism, we read John Stuart Mill° *and* Karl Marx.° To learn about the value of the religious life, we read Thomas Aquinas° *and* Voltaire.° To learn about the ends of politics, we read Aristotle° *and* Machiavelli.° To learn about the value of warfare, we read Homer° *and* Erasmus.° To learn about the worth of sexual fidelity, we read Leo Tolstoy° *and* James Joyce.° Our intellectual tradition is not monolithic; it is, rather, an ongoing conversation.

DIVERSITY AND TOLERANCE

As Berlusconi said, we value diversity — especially intellectual diversity — and tolerance in a way that no

other civilization does. Western civilization demands inquiry and leads to progress at a rate and of a degree previously unknown to mankind. The tradition of liberalism and liberal education in the West has led to human liberation to think, dream, and live.

As political philosopher A.E. Murphy put it many 25 decades ago, "We do not understand the ideals of other cultures better by misunderstanding our own or adequately enrich an intercultural synthesis by offering to it anything less than the best we have. That best is the theory and practices of intellectual, moral, and political freedom, in a form and at a level which neither medieval, Mexican, Manchu, nor Muscovite culture has so far equaled."

John Stuart Mill: economist and philosopher (1806–1873) who argued for the success of capitalism only when combined with a democratic political system.

Karl Marx: philosopher (1818–1883) who criticized the potential downfalls of capitalism, including the dangers of cyclical recessions and depressions, and the ever-widening economic gap between rich and poor.

Thomas Aquinas: a devout Italian philosopher,

theologian, and monk (ca. 1225–1274).

Voltaire: French Enlightenment agnostic, philosopher and author with a rich satirical wit (1694–1778).

Aristotle: Greek philosopher (384–322 BCE) who argued that humans naturally turn to politics as a means of seeking out the ideal end to an ethical existence.

Machiavelli: Renaissance political theorist (1469–1527) whose *The Prince* establishes methods for

achieving and securing political power at all costs.

Homer: Greek poet (likely before 700 BCE) whose epic *Iliad* presents the glory of war through its dramatic depictions of battles and soldiers of the Trojan War.

Erasmus: Dutch humanist, theologian, and Catholic priest (1466–1536) who argued that war might be justified only under extreme circumstances.

Leo Tolstoy: Russian novelist (1828–1910), author

of *Anna Karenina*, in which the title character ultimately commits suicide after leaving her husband for another man.

James Joyce: Irish novelist (1882–1941) and author of *Ulysses*, in which the reader follows Leopold Bloom throughout a day in which he knows his wife will sleep with another man. The novel ends with husband and wife in bed together, their marriage still intact.

I will never forget the scenes that occurred in November, 2001, when the American and British forces liberated Kabul. Burqas were cast off; beards were shaved; and television sets were dug out of the ground. An entire city celebrated the end of strict Islamic rule. This event suggested that cultures and values are not so different after all. Anyone who saw the pictures of people suddenly free to speak, dress, learn, work, and worship as they saw fit would be hard-pressed to deny a universal human longing for freedom.

Simple honesty ought to compel us to state—and to do so proudly—that, while the longing is universal, one particular cultural tradition has most fully nourished it. That tradition is ours, and students ought to be made aware of it and its successes.

Since the beginning of time, political philosophers have recognized the importance of patriotism. One of Plato's first dialogues is the *Crito*, which is subtitled "The Duty of a Citizen." This is an account of a conversation between Socrates and his friend Crito, as the former awaits his execution by the city of Athens. Crito and other friends have devised a plan by which Socrates can escape the unjust sentence handed down. Yet, Socrates demurs. He explains to Crito that the city—even if it has done him harm—has a claim to his loyalty that surpasses even death. The state, Socrates reminds Crito, "brought [me] into the world, and nurtured and educated [me]." Escaping would be nothing more than "running away and turning your back upon the compacts and agreements which you made as a citizen." It would, in short, be a repudiation of his entire life. In his later and more-detailed studies of government—*The Republic* and *The Laws*—Plato spends a great deal of time discussing the moral and civic education of the young, training them to be good citizens. His pupil Aristotle, too, was concerned with these matters, as a cursory reading of *Politics*—and even the *Nicomachean Ethics*—will show.

In modern times, however, that notion of patriotism has been eviscerated. British philosopher Thomas Hobbes, in *Leviathan*, declared that government is simply a construct designed to ameliorate the state of nature—which in life, in his memorable phrase, is "solitary, poor, nasty, brutish, and short." By identifying the fear of death—especially violent, painful death—as man's most powerful passion, Hobbes argued that the state had claim to our allegiance only as long as it preserved our life. Once it no longer could protect us, we no longer were obliged to obey its commands; the paramount right of nature of man is to "preserve his own life and limbs, with all the power he hath." There is no good greater than one's own life; no man can surrender his right to self-preservation. On this theory, then, we would understand it if our troops were to surrender and join forces with the enemy when outnumbered in combat. It would be, Hobbes writes, cowardly—but not unjust.

That is not the understanding of patriotism 30 accepted by our Founding Fathers, though. They created a nation to which they were dedicated, even at the cost of their own lives. It was a concept of a country—and a claim to loyalty—larger than one's own security and prosperity. Indeed, the Founders themselves risked their lives for this nation and its principles long before it ever existed. Many of the signers of the Declaration of Independence lost their homes, property, and fortunes. They were aware of the risk they were taking. As one signer put it, he and his fellow revolutionaries knew they were signing their own "death warrants." Nathan Hale° famously remarked that his only regret was that he had but one life to give for his country—one that had yet to exist.

Still, in an age where so much has been scorned for so long, what does patriotism mean? Do we stand with American naval officer Stephen Decatur when he exclaimed, "Our country, may she always be in the right, but our country, right or wrong!"? Does patriotism mean that we love America simply because it is our country? In a word, no. The American understanding of patriotism has never been as simple as that.

American patriotism has always been rooted in love of the principles upon which the nation was founded: liberty, equality, justice, and democracy. We are, in that sense, unique—our patriotism is not parochial. That is to say, our love for America does not necessarily entail dislike of other countries. Indeed, insofar as those nations share our principles—think, for instance, of Great Britain or Israel—we consider them our friends and allies, not competitors.

Upon the death of Sen. Henry Clay,° Abraham Lincoln said that Clay "loved his country partly because it was his own country, but mostly because it was a free country . . . he saw in [the advancement of his country] the advancement, prosperity, and glory of human liberty, human right, and human nature." American prosperity is not good only for America; it is good for the rest of the world, for the principles of America are good for the rest of the world. That is a lesson that we adults—as much as our children—need to learn, remember, and, when called upon, defend.

Nathan Hale: captain in the American Revolution (1755–1776), an impassioned soldier and one of the earliest patriots, concerned not with himself but solely with how he could help the colonies break free from Britain. He was caught by the British army and hanged at the age of twenty-one.

Senator Henry Clay: politician and unsuccessful presidential candidate (1777–1852), known as the Great Pacificator and Great Compromiser for his work as a negotiator between opposing sides who helped to bring the nation out of stalemates and crises.

What function does the image accompanying the piece (p. 856) serve? Does the image make an argument? Check out Chapter 15 for more on the power of visual arguments.

LINK TO P. 301

RESPOND.

1. How does Bennett define patriotism? Which categories of definition does he give for patriotism (Chapter 9)? How effective is he in constructing a definition of patriotism that will likely appeal to conservative Americans? To all Americans? Why?

2. Bennett places great stock in knowledge of what might be termed current events; indeed, he is quite troubled by the facts American college students do not know. Take Bennett's test (paragraph 3): How many of the items could you answer correctly if you were given the poll Bennett mentions? What sort of causal argument does Bennett construct in paragraph 5 in linking "this historical ignorance" with student attitudes? How valid do you find his argument? Why?

3. Bennett is comfortable claiming that Western civilization is superior to other cultures and civilizations, particularly Arabic and Islamic civilizations, and, more specifically, that American values are superior among Western countries. What evidence does he cite for this position? How does he characterize those who disagree with him? To what does he attribute the stance those who disagree with him take, especially that taken by many U.S. college students?

4. Predictably, Kazin ("A Patriotic Left") and Bennett read American history in different ways. How would you characterize each? How does each, for example, deal with issues of the treatment of African Americans in U.S. history? With which of these approaches to our history are you more comfortable? Why? What strengths and limitations do you see with respect to the approach with which you are more comfortable? With respect to the other approach? Why?

5. **Write a dialogue** between Kazin and Bennett on American history and patriotism. Here are several questions that may help you get started: About what things do these two men agree, and why? What kind of person is a "real American patriot" for each of these men, and why? How does each understand key events in American history? What would each like Americans to know about their history, and why? You may wish to produce a debate-like dialogue or you may wish to produce a more Rogerian argument, focusing on what these two men share.

"Dissent Is Not Disloyalty"

WE'RE ALL AMERICANS...

BUT, WHICH ONE OF US IS A MUSLIM?

We all are...we're American Muslims. It's impossible to make general assumptions about Muslims because we represent more than one billion people from a vast range of races, nationalities and cultures – from the South Pacific to the Horn of Africa. Only about 18 percent of Muslims live in the Arabic-speaking world. The largest Muslim community is in Indonesia. Substantial parts of Asia and most of Africa have Muslim majority populations, while significant minorities are to be found in the countries of the former Soviet Union, China, North and South America, and Europe.

American Muslims are an equally diverse group of people. We're immigrants from across the globe who came here seeking freedom and opportunity. We're the children of immigrant parents, and descendants of Africans who have called America home for generations. We're converts of varied nationalities and ethnic backgrounds. We're doctors, lawyers, teachers, politicians, civil rights activists, mothers, fathers, students... making our homes and raising our families in communities across America.

What we all have in common is a shared faith and a shared commitment to our nation's safety and prosperity. We're Americans and we're Muslims.

WE'RE AMERICAN MUSLIMS

Number one of fifty-two in the *Islam in America* series.
To learn more about the series, visit www.americanmuslims.info

COUNCIL ON AMERICAN-ISLAMIC RELATIONS

◀ "Dissent Is Not Disloyalty" reads a billboard on a busy street in Austin, Texas, as this book goes to press. After months of negotiation— though far too little for many here and abroad—the United States invaded Iraq. In this selection, we present three very different examples of dissent from early 2003. The first, "We're All Muslims," is the initial newspaper ad in a series of fifty-two being produced by the Council on American-Islamic Relations. The second, "A Statement of Conscience," is from a two-page newspaper ad created by an organization called "Not In Our Name"; the version we print here is from the New York Times in early February, though much of this information is posted on the organization's Web site. The third is from the Web site of Veterans Against the Iraq War, which we visited shortly after the United States began bombing Iraq.

As you study each, consider what it is protesting and what kinds of arguments it uses to try to achieve its goal.

A Statement of Conscience

NOT IN OUR NAME

Let it not be said that people in the United States did nothing when their government declared a war without limit and instituted stark new measures of repression.

The signers of this statement call on the people of the U.S. to resist the policies and overall political direction that have emerged since September 11, 2001, and which pose grave dangers to the people of the world.

We believe that peoples and nations have the right to determine their own destiny, free from military coercion by great powers. We believe that all persons detained or prosecuted by the United States government should have the same rights of due process. We believe that questioning, criticism, and dissent must be valued and protected. We understand that such rights and values are always contested and must be fought for.

We believe that people of conscience must take responsibility for what their own governments do—we must first of all oppose the injustice that is done in our own name. Thus we call on all Americans to RESIST the war and repression that has been loosed on the world by the Bush administration. It is unjust, immoral, and illegitimate. We choose to make common cause with the people of the world.

We too watched with shock the horrific events of September 11, 2001. We too mourned the thousands of innocent dead and shook our heads at the terrible scenes of carnage—even as we recalled similar scenes in Baghdad, Panama City, and, a generation ago, Vietnam. We too joined the anguished questioning of millions of Americans who asked why such a thing could happen.

But the mourning had barely begun, when the highest leaders of the land unleashed a spirit of revenge. They put out a simplistic script of "good vs. evil" that was taken up by a pliant and intimidated media. They told us that asking why these terrible events had happened verged on treason. There was to be no debate. There were by definition no valid political or moral questions. The only possible answer was to be war abroad and repression at home.

In our name, the Bush administration, with near unanimity from Congress, not only attacked Afghanistan but arrogated to itself and its allies the right to rain down military force anywhere and anytime. The brutal repercussions have been felt from the Philippines to Palestine, where Israeli tanks and bulldozers have left a terrible trail of death and destruction. The government now openly prepares to wage all-out war on Iraq—a country which has no connection to the horror of September 11. What kind of world will this become if the U.S. government has a blank check to drop commandos, assassins, and bombs wherever it wants?

In our name, within the U.S., the government has created two classes of people: those to whom the basic rights of the U.S. legal system are at least promised, and those who now seem to have no rights at all. The government rounded up over 1,000 immigrants and detained them in secret and indefinitely. Hundreds have been deported and hundreds of others still languish today in prison. This smacks of the infamous concentration camps for Japanese-Americans in World War 2. For the first time in decades, immigration procedures single out certain nationalities for unequal treatment.

In our name, the government has brought down a pall of repression over society. The President's spokesperson warns people to "watch what they say." Dissident artists, intellectuals, and professors find their views distorted, attacked, and suppressed. The so-called USA PATRIOT Act—along with a host of similar measures on the state level—gives police sweeping new powers of search and seizure, supervised if at all by secret proceedings before secret courts.

In our name, the executive has steadily usurped the roles and func- 10 tions of the other branches of government. Military tribunals with lax rules of evidence and no right to appeal to the regular courts are put in place by executive order. Groups are declared "terrorist" at the stroke of a presidential pen.

We must take the highest officers of the land seriously when they talk of a war that will last a generation and when they speak of a new domestic order. We are confronting a new openly imperial policy towards the world and a domestic policy that manufactures and manipulates fear to curtail rights.

There is a deadly trajectory to the events of the past months that must be seen for what it is and resisted. Too many times in history people have waited until it was too late to resist. President Bush has declared: "you're either with us or against us." Here is our answer: We refuse to allow you to speak for all the American people. We will not give up our right to question. We will not hand over our consciences in return for a hollow promise of safety. We say NOT IN OUR NAME. We refuse to be party to these wars and we repudiate any inference that they are being waged in our name or for our welfare. We extend a hand to those around the world suffering from these policies; we will show our solidarity in word and deed.

We who sign this statement call on all Americans to join together to rise to this challenge. We applaud and support the questioning and protest now going on, even as we recognize the need for much, much more to actually stop this juggernaut. We draw inspiration from the Israeli reservists who, at great personal risk, declare "there IS a limit" and refuse to serve in the occupation of the West Bank and Gaza.

We also draw on the many examples of resistance and conscience from the past of the United States: from those who fought slavery with rebellions and the underground railroad, to those who defied the Vietnam war by refusing orders, resisting the draft, and standing in solidarity with resisters.

Let us not allow the watching world today to despair of our silence 15 and our failure to act. Instead, let the world hear our pledge: we will resist the machinery of war and repression and rally others to do everything possible to stop it.

Editor's note: The above statement is accompanied by a list of hundreds of names, representing the most widely recognized of the 45,000 people who had signed the statement.

Veterans Against the Iraq War

MILITARY VETERANS, ACTIVE DUTY, AND FAMILY MEMBERS

Dear Veteran:

With the prospect of a major war looming just over the horizon, and the threats of more suffering from violence growing, the times are a changing—for the worse! If you are convinced that a U.S. invasion of Iraq is wrong, then you are confronted with a choice: You can ignore the growing crisis, dismiss it as another political conflict beyond your influence, or you can try to stop a war. You can band together with other veterans and give voice to what all of us know is wrong: a war with Iraq.

While others pontificate and theorize about war, veterans know about its realities. The present Administration is led by men and women who chose not to go into the military and today have little understanding of war and no comprehension of its consequences. They do not know what you know, or feel what you feel. For all

too many of them, war is little more than an abstract exercise in geopolitics.

Whether you fought in a war, performed your duty in a support capacity or served our nation during a time of peace, it's all the same: America needs you, again! Whether you are liberal, conservative, libertarian, centrist, green or whatever—our country needs you. Once, you put your body on the line in the service of our nation. You can now serve our nation with your experience and your wisdom.

Please read the Statement of Purpose below; if you agree with it, fill out the form and submit. There is a separate form for family members. This Statement with the list of signatories will be delivered to the White House and Congress.

Stewart Nusbaumer
Igor Bobrowsky
Jan Barry

STATEMENT OF PURPOSE

Veterans Against the Iraq War is a coalition of American veterans who oppose war with Iraq.

Until and unless the current U.S. Administration provides evidence which clearly demonstrates that Iraq or any other nation poses a clear, immediate danger to our country, we oppose all of the Administration's pre-emptive and unilateral military and diplomatic activities geared towards provoking or initiating a military conflict with Iraq. Furthermore, we cannot support any war that is initiated without a formal Declaration of War by Congress, as our Constitution requires.

Although we detest the dictatorial policies of Saddam Hussein and sympathize with the tragic plight of the Iraqi people, we oppose unilateral and pre-emptive U.S. military intervention on the grounds that it would establish a dangerous precedent in the conduct of international affairs, that it could easily lead to an increase of violent regional instability and the spread of a much wider conflict, that it would place needless and unacceptable financial burdens on the American people, that it would further divert us from addressing critical domestic priorities, and that it would distract us from our stated goal of destroying international terrorists and their lairs.

Furthermore, Veterans Against the Iraq War does not believe the American military can or should be used as the police-force of the world by any Administration, Republican or Democrat. Consequently, we believe that the lives and well-being of our nation's soldiers, sailors, airmen and marines should not be squandered or sacrificed for causes other than the direct defense of our people and our nation.

Finally, we believe that a pre-emptive and unilateral U.S. military attack on Iraq would be illegal, unnecessary, counterproductive and present a truly dire threat to our vital international interests and basic national security. As military veterans, we have a unique understanding of war and know the many hidden truths that lie behind easy theories and promises, as well as behind the tragic consequences that even victory brings. We therefore call on all like-minded American veterans to join and support VAIW in its efforts to avert a national tragedy and an international calamity before it begins.

5

Each of these texts relies on multiple lines of argument. What sorts of appeals does each piece use? How? Chapter 1 can help you decide.

LINK TO P. 3

RESPOND.

1. What argument is the "We're All Americans . . ." ad making? What sorts of appeals does it use in the opening paragraph? In the second paragraph? In the final paragraph? In the use of visuals and layout? (Visit <americanmuslims.info> to see how this ad compares with others in the series.) Why might the Council on American-Islamic Relations think this ad and fifty-one others are warranted? In other words, how might this ad be seen as a case of dissent or protest?

2. What sorts of arguments are being made in the text of the "A Statement of Conscience" ad? In what ways does it seek common ground? In what ways is it a case of dissent or protest? What does the organization Not in Our Name claim to be against? What does it claim to be for? In what ways is such an organization particularly American?

3. When the two-page "A Statement of Conscience" ad ran, the banner at the top of the ad read "President Bush has declared: 'You're either with us or against us.' Here is our answer:" Beneath this banner was a list of several hundred names, with affiliations, and then the text of the statement itself, followed by information on what readers could do to "stop" the war. What sorts of arguments can we find in such a layout?

4. What arguments are being made in the "Dear Veteran" letter and "Statement of Purpose" from the Veterans Against the Iraq War site? Who are the intended, invoked, and real audiences of these texts? What specific appeals are used to influence readers who are veterans and those who are not?

5. In what ways could each of the groups sponsoring these ads be considered patriotic? How would each define patriotism? What evidence from each of the ads can you offer?

6. One paradox of American life is that Americans take great pride in their freedom of speech, yet in times of potential crisis — especially with regard to America's political role abroad — protest or dissent of any sort is labeled un-American by many and often is greeted with outright hostility. **Write an essay** in which you evaluate one or more of the ads in this selection, or other ads of dissent or protest that you find with regard to this paradox. Are there limits to freedom of speech with respect to patriotism and dissent or protest? Should there be? Who should determine the nature of such limits? How?

▼ *In this essay, which first appeared in December 2002 in the* New York Times Magazine, *Troy Melhus, who served in the Marine Corps from 1987 until 1991 and who is now a writer and editor for the* Minneapolis Star Tribune, *uses personal experience to explore the meaning of courage and cowardice for himself. As you read, note how Melhus creates his own ethos and that of Sam Lwin.*

Quiescent Objector

When my reserve unit was called to duty in the gulf war, I didn't have the courage to just say no.

TROY MELHUS

In 1990, on Christmas Day, I had a peace symbol tattooed on my back, a week after signing my will. I was 22 years old. Three weeks later, I met Sam Lwin. I was a United States marine, a reservist, and I had just been ordered to deploy to the Persian Gulf. Sam was a marine who had refused to fight. He had applied to become a conscientious objector along with two dozen other marines who all ended up with me at Camp Lejeune in North Carolina.

My reserve unit, based in Des Moines, had been called to active duty a day after Thanksgiving, some three months after Saddam Hussein invaded Kuwait. One week later, we flew to Lejeune, and spent December preparing to ship out. The night we arrived, a reservist in nearby barracks tried to commit suicide. We stood silent, listening to his screams at 3 a.m. as the military police struggled to carry him away.

We would be seeing action, our platoon sergeants told us, most likely on the front lines. We could very likely be attacked with chemical or biological gas. We had served under Gunnery Sergeant Brasher for years; he had taught us everything from marksmanship to what to do if there was a chemical attack — and even he was sounding nervous. As members of the infantry, we would be among those at the greatest risk. But that's what you signed up for, our platoon sergeants said.

I joined the Marine Corps in 1986 for some $5,000 in college money and to be one of the few and the proud. I accepted the recruiters' challenges as thousands of 19-year-olds do every year; I wanted to showcase my strength and will. By the end of boot camp, I was at the top of my platoon. As the honor man, I graduated in the coveted dress blues; later, I was recruited to become an officer. I was a living poster of all heroes Marine. But war? I would maybe see war games. Even during Vietnam, my reserve unit hadn't been activated, the recruiters had told me. Seeing action was about as abstract a thought as nuclear war.

No question that I had joined the Marines on that 5 bet. Even by the time of our activation, I didn't expect to immediately see the gulf. Eleven months before, I injured my knee on a weekend drill and was declared unfit for duty. I didn't know it then, but that would

Antiwar rally in Washington, DC

give me an out. My company flew to Saudi Arabia just days after New Year's. I was detached to a medical platoon at Lejeune and told I would rejoin my company when I was fit.

Some 10 days after U.S. forces began bombing Iraq, I was assigned to barracks adjacent to the conscientious objectors' platoon. I was regularly ordered to take head counts of the group while they awaited trials for their military crimes. While it was not a crime to apply to be a C.O., it was criminal to refuse to obey orders—in this case reporting for duty overseas. And Sam Lwin, my new superiors told me, was trouble. When his reserve unit was activated, they said, Sam persuaded four others in his company to follow in his steps. He had a civilian support group ("Hands Off!") and high-profile attorneys and had questioned the authority of corporals like myself.

But over the next two months at Lejeune, Sam and I began to talk and play chess. I didn't see him as a criminal. I saw shades of myself and my doubts. I had heard of conscientious objection only once — the day I joined the corps. All marines, on the day they enlist, must initial a statement swearing that they are not now nor have ever been C.O.'s. A footnote, really.

By February — near the war's end — an orthopedic specialist on the base gave me a choice. I could remain indefinitely on active duty with the medical platoon. Or I could end my service now. On March 21, 1991, in a small ceremony in front of my medical platoon, I was honorably discharged. I flew home to Iowa City the next day. Two months later, Sam was convicted of unauthorized absence and missing a troop movement. He was sentenced to four months in the brig.

We were cowards. That's the only way you'll ever hear it. That's the only way it will ever be told. We walked away when we were called to fight. I was given a choice, and I chose to excuse myself. Some marines understood. Others thought I should have swallowed the pain or at least stayed, even if it took months for my knee to heal. But Sam had no choice. He followed his conscience. I am now 34, though some days I hardly feel like a man. I hate myself for feeling manipulated; I hate myself for joining the Marines; and I hate myself for feeling like I chickened out.

My family and friends may think I'm a coward 10 because I didn't fight. I think I'm a coward because I couldn't refuse. To this day, Sam tells me that he doesn't regret what he did. But I'm not so sure about myself. More than a decade ago, I didn't have the courage to be a conscientious objector. I was afraid — afraid to kill, afraid to die. I had the same feelings as Sam; I just couldn't speak them aloud. But I knew. I wear the reminder every day on my left shoulder blade.

RESPOND •

1. What features of an evaluative argument does Melhus's essay include? What criteria form the basis for his evaluation? Are they implicit or explicit? Do you agree with his criteria? With the evaluation that results from applying these criteria to the situations he presents?

2. This essay may be divided into two parts structurally: the facts and descriptions that lead up to the two final paragraphs, and the two final paragraphs themselves. What are the functions of the two closing paragraphs? How have the facts and descriptions of the earlier paragraphs set us up, as readers, for what occurs in the two closing paragraphs? Do you find this organizational pattern effective in achieving Melhus's goals? Why or why not?

3. In what ways might this essay by Melhus be termed *risky*? What sorts of personal risks is he taking? What values (and arguments about values) might lead him to take these risks? To what extent do you think they are justified? Why or why not? How do they contribute to the ethos Melhus creates?

Among the elements in Melhus's article are definition arguments exploring the meanings of *patriotism* and *cowardice*. See Chapter 9 for more on making definition arguments.

LINK TO P. 147

4. Faced with Melhus's situation of remaining on active duty indefinitely with the medical platoon or taking an honorable discharge, what do you honestly believe you would have done? Why? Had Melhus continued to serve with the medical platoon at the base, given his own changing feelings about military service, would he have been more or less of a patriot? Why? By whose criteria?

5. **Write an essay** in which you evaluate Melhus's and Lwin's behavior in terms of the limits of patriotism. Which of the two is the greater patriot? Whose behavior is more honorable? Why? How would each man define patriotism? What criteria should be used in evaluating these men's changing understanding of patriotism?

▼ *Robert Scheer is a syndicated columnist who has spent more than three decades as a journalist, including five years in Vietnam as a correspondent during the war there. He is also the author of several books, including* With Enough Shovels: Reagan, Bush and Nuclear War *(1983) and* In Search of an Enemy: Wen Ho Lee and the Revival of the Yellow Peril *(2004). As you read this essay, which appeared as a syndicated column in a number of American newspapers in January 2003, try to evaluate the effectiveness of the comparison Scheer makes between Americans' attitudes toward football and war.*

Between Football and War

There's something perverse about a nation engrossed in football while the drums of war beat persistently in the background.

ROBERT SCHEER

As an unabashed, nail-biting Oakland Raiders fanatic who sits in the nose-bleed seats and who just bought my grandson pajamas and a dishware set emblazoned with the team's infamous pirate logo, I still must admit that there is something unsettling about this year's whirlwind of playoff and bowl games.

Isn't there something perverse about a nation completely engrossed in football while the drums of war, a deadlier game, beat persistently yet quietly in the background?

While the symbols of patriotism are everywhere — from the ubiquitous military recruitment ads to the stars and stripes affixed to referee uniforms at the Orange Bowl — television news anchors chirp about the latest troop movements and "incidents" in the "no-fly" zone. And for many Americans huddled around the tube in midwinter, knocking off Saddam Hussein is an easy sell, offering as it does a cheap thrill demanding less sacrifice than that needed to acquire playoff tickets — and less angst over the outcome.

However, the viewing public doesn't seem to understand that what is being planned by our president is not Gulf War II — a swift punch in the mouth to our old ally Saddam — but rather a multiyear occupation by the United States of an independent, powerful and modern Muslim nation rife with ethnic tension.

If people think the invasion of Iraq 5 is something that can fit neatly in the slot between the Super Bowl and spring training, they ought to read Monday's New York Times report that the "final plans for administering and democratizing Iraq . . . amount to the most ambitious American effort to administer a country since the occupations of Japan and Germany at the end of World War II."

The Times' Sunday magazine cover story was even more explicit: "The American Empire: Get Used to It," challenged the headline. History tells us that wars of empire are wars without end, as nationalism is a force that never can be truly suppressed — just ask the relatives of those killed in the latest suicide bomb attack in Tel Aviv how well Palestinian dreams of statehood are being managed.

Is the United States ready to be fully responsible for the future of Iraq's stateless Kurds and its repressed Shiite population? Some U.S.-based corporations will make out like bandits in a post-occupation Iraq, as a Western power again attempts to bring enlightenment to the region while ripping off its oil. However, U.S. taxpayers and soldiers and, most of all, Iraqi women and children will ultimately suffer the consequences.

It seems clear that if Americans were to devote the same seriousness of thought to the consequences of invading Iraq that they have to evaluating the pros and cons of the controversial computerized ranking system of college football teams, we would not be on the road to "preemptive" war on the other side of the world.

Sports—stats, video replay, expert commentators—are discussed with a blend of logic and fact that we don't get but should demand in discussions about Iraq. But the war debaters on talk radio and cable news shows manage to meld the mindless partisanship of fans with constant obfuscation, macho posturing and a rattling of credentials all designed to intimidate war skeptics.

Meanwhile, like a character in Alice's Wonderland, the president insists facts that challenge the administration's position don't matter. That U.N. inspectors have found nothing alarming during uninhibited visits to more than 200 suspected Iraqi weapons sites is simply spun by the White House as another example of Iraq lying. Never mind that polls show the majority of Americans want proof that Iraq has weapons that actually threaten us before they will support war. Once the troops land, patriotism will trump our common sense.

With no draft and a completely dominant military, most Americans have come to view war as something akin to the dark twin of the Olympics: an international test of strength accompanied by big opening-night fireworks over the host city.

Despite the rampant use of war metaphors in sports, however, war is no game. The whistles are not blown in time, there are no penalties for unnecessary roughness and those risking their lives are never paid the big bucks.

Unfortunately, for those of us sitting safely in the good seats, it can be a heck of a show—just like the Roman circus.°

10

How is Scheer's article an argument based on values? What shared values does he focus on? See Chapter 5 for more examples of arguments based on values.

⋯⋯⋯⋯⋯⋯⋯⋯ LINK TO P. 78

the Roman circus: arena in which gladiator death matches, wild beast fights, and chariot races were held, dating back to the sixth century BCE. Their popularity was encouraged by the Roman emperors because such events served to divert energy and attention away from social and economic conditions leading to popular civil unrest.

RESPOND.

1. What is your response to this essay? To Scheer's comparison of war and football? To understand more analytically the nature of the comparison (in fact, an extended analogy), make a list of all the similarities and differences Scheer notes between football and war. How effective are the specific points of comparison in his essay in supporting his analogy? His overall argument? Scheer also compares war and the Olympics (paragraph 11). How effective is this comparison?

2. Scheer contends that "[o]nce the troops land [in Iraq], patriotism will trump our common sense" (paragraph 10). What does he mean by this claim? How does he seem to be defining patriotism in this essay?

3. Scheer is ultimately quite critical of Americans in this essay. What, specifically, are the grounds for criticism? Could such critique be considered unpatriotic? Why or why not?

4. One of Scheer's complaints is that whereas Americans take sports very seriously, we pay precious little attention to international politics, foreign affairs, or politics in general. Rather than seriously and critically evaluating the consequences of these issues, we settle for far less. **Write an essay** in which you evaluate the consequences of this situation for Americans and for the rest of the world's citizens. If you disagree with Scheer's claims, then explain why he is wrong and evaluate the consequences of that situation for Americans and for the rest of the world's citizens.

▼ *This commentary was first published in the New York Times Magazine the Sunday following the U.S. invasion of Iraq in March 2003. As reporters embedded with troops in Iraq and surrounding countries offered Americans a "reality TV" version of soldiers' experiences there, reporters in the United States and elsewhere around the world brought news of massive demonstrations, the local targets of which included the war; President Bush; America and those fighting alongside it, especially Britain and Australia; the West in general; Arab governments that were not intervening on behalf of Iraq; globalization; and antiwar demonstrations (at least in the United States). This essay, which appeared in the weekly "The Way We Live Now" columns, was written by Michael Ignatieff, a contributing writer for the Magazine, professor at the Harvard Kennedy School of Government, director of the Carr Center for Human Rights Policy there, author of numerous books, and winner of many prizes and awards. In this essay Ignatieff seeks to reframe debates about patriotism by comparing and contrasting current protests with those of the Vietnam War era and by offering a novel perspective on assent and dissent. As you read, note the reader that Ignatieff invokes in this text and the ways in which he creates that reader as uniquely American.*

I Am Iraq

Which side you are on is not about who you are or the company you keep. It's about what you fear, and hope for.

MICHAEL IGNATIEFF

Back in the 60's, when I marched against the war in Vietnam, I learned that it is a mistake to judge a cause by the company it makes you keep. I slogged through the streets with Trotskyites° who thought America was an evil empire, and I chanted slogans under banners that called for socialist revolution in Brooklyn. I stood arm in arm with pacifists, who made me wonder whether they would have fought Hitler. Since I was anti-Communist, I actually had more in common with the liberal hawks who thought they were defending South Vietnam against advancing Communist tyranny. But I believed nothing could save the weak and corrupt South Vietnamese government. This time, over Iraq, I don't like the company I am keeping, but I think they're right on the issue. I much prefer the company on the other side, but I believe they're mistaken.

I don't like the president's domestic policies. He should be helping state and local governments maintain jobs and services, especially for the poor. His attack on affirmative action turns back decades of racial progress. The tax breaks for the rich are unjust. His deficits are mortgaging the future. It's wrong to lock up so-called unlawful combatants on Guantánamo and in military brigs, denying them due

Trotskyite: supporter of the theories of Communism described by Leon Trotsky (1879–1940), who believed that socialism should be established throughout the world through revolution.

Like the people who wear them, these buttons represent various—often seemingly incompatible—causes.

process. The president's attorney general is dangerously cavalier about the civil liberties he is supposed to protect. The bullying tone the president adopted in his diplomacy at the United Nations diminished his chances of U.N. support. But I still think the president is right when he says that Iraq and the world will be better off with Saddam disarmed, even, if necessary, through force.

A lot of my friends think that supporting the president on this issue is naïve. The company you keep, they argue, matters in politics. If you can't trust him on other issues, you have no reason to trust him on this one. If he treats freedom at home so lightly, what makes you believe that he will say what he means about staying the course to create freedom in Iraq?

My friends also imply that the company I am keeping on this war is a definition of what kind of person I am. So where we all stand has become a litmus test of our moral identities. But this shouldn't be the case. Opposing the war doesn't make you an antiglobalist, an anti-Semite or an anti-American, any more than supporting the war makes you a Cheney conservative or an apologist for American imperialism.

In fact, the debate over war is not so much a clash   5
of competing moral identities as a battle within each of us to balance competing moral arguments. Sometimes it is easier to see this in the positions of the other side than in your own.

Recently, 14,000 "writers, academics and other intellectuals"—many of them my friends—published a petition against the war, at the same time condemning the Iraqi regime for its human rights violations and supporting "efforts by the Iraqi opposition to create a democratic, multiethnic and multireligious Iraq." But since they say that "the decision to wage war at this time is morally unacceptable," I wonder what their support for the Iraqi opposition amounts to. One colleague refused to sign the petition because he said it was guilty of confusion. The problem is not that overthrowing Saddam by force is "morally unjustified." Who seriously believes 25 million Iraqis would not be better off if Saddam were overthrown? The issue is whether it is prudent to do so, whether the risks are worth running.

Evaluating risks is not the same thing as making moral choices. It is impossible to be certain that improving the human rights of 25 million people is worth the cost because no one knows what the cost will be. Besides, even if the cost could be known, what the philosophers call "consequential"° justifications—that 25 million people will live better—run smack against "deontological"° objections, namely that good consequences cannot justify killing people. I think the

---

consequential: arguing for the potential effects of the proposed action. In this case, whether the actions could be justified because of the consequences they will bring about.

deontological: from the Greek word *deon*, meaning "duty"; arguing whether the proposed action will violate the foundational duties or moral obligations of all humans.

consequential justifications can override the deonto-logical ones, but only if the gains in human freedom are large and the human costs are low. But let's admit it, the risks are large: the war may be bloody, the peace may be chaotic and what might be good in the long run for Iraqis might not be so good for Americans. Success in Iraq might win America friends or it might increase the anger much of the Muslim world feels toward this country.

It would be great if moral certainty made risk assessment easier, but it doesn't actually do so. What may be desirable from a moral point of view may be so risky that we would be foolish to try. So what do we do? Isaiah Berlin° used to say that we just have to "plump" for one option or the other in the absence of moral certainty or perfect knowledge of the future. We should also try to decide for ourselves, regardless of the company we keep, and that may include our friends, our family and our loved ones.

During Vietnam, I marched with people who thought America was the incarnation of imperial wickedness, and I marched against people who thought America was the last best hope of mankind. Just as in Vietnam, the debate over Iraq has become a referendum on American power, and what you think about Saddam seems to matter much less than what you think about America. Such positions, now as then, seem hopelessly ideological and, at the same time, narcissistic. The fact is that America is neither the redeemer nation nor the evil empire. Ideology cannot help us here.

In the weeks and years ahead, the choices are not 10 going to be about who we are or whose company we keep, or even about what we think America is or should be. The choices are about what risks are worth running when our safety depends on the answer. The real choices are going to be tougher than most of us could have ever imagined.

Although Ignatieff's essay is ultimately philosophical, he relies heavily on personal experience. See Chapter 18 for ideas about how to evaluate the use of personal experience as evidence.

LINK TO P. 375

Isaiah Berlin: Russian-born English philosopher, political theorist, and historian of ideas (1909–1997); among the foremost liberal theorists of the 20th century, he wrote insightfully about the meaning and consequences of freedom.

RESPOND ●

1. Do you agree or disagree with Ignatieff's claim that "the debate over war is not so much a clash of competing moral identities as a battle within each of us to balance competing moral arguments" (paragraph

5)? Why or why not? (Note that Ignatieff is making a claim about a specific war, but this question asks you to consider war more broadly; certainly, the war in Iraq would be an important case to consider.) Ignatieff lists two sorts of competing moral arguments that each of us must seek to balance—consequential and deontological. How are they relevant to those who initially supported or didn't support the war in Iraq? To those who might support or oppose the idea of war more generally?

2. In what ways is Ignatieff's essay a definitional essay? What things, specifically, are being defined? How? How do you think Ignatieff would define patriotism? Why?

3. Would you say that Ignatieff's essay is primarily about the past (forensic), the present (epideictic), or the future (deliberative)? Why? Which features of each do we find in this essay? Which concerns predominate?

4. In his evaluation of his opposition to the Vietnam War (paragraph 9), Ignatieff claims that the positions of Americans at the time were "hopelessly ideological and, at the same time, narcissistic." What does he mean? To what extent do you believe Ignatieff felt the same way about the United States at the beginning of the war with Iraq in 2003? Why? What does Ignatieff mean by his closing paragraph?

5. The lead-in to this essay notes, "Which side you are on is not about who you are or the company you keep. It's about what you fear, and hope for." We can use this comment as the basis for thinking about patriotism by examining the relationships among which side you are on (or feel you should be on), who you are (or feel you should be), your fears, and your hopes. Use these ideas in order to **write a definitional essay** about the meaning of patriotism in time of war. Although your essay is definitional, it will likely have elements of evaluation and causation; it may even offer a proposal.

6. The essays in this cluster have considered aspects of patriotism in the United States since the events of September 11, 2001. **Write an essay** in which you describe and evaluate your changing understanding of patriotism. The best essays will likely be those that appreciate that any notion of patriotism—love of one's country, most generally— must be general enough to apply not just to the United States but to any country. Topics to consider could include what children are taught about their country as they grow up, how dissent and protest relate to patriotism (especially in a country like the United States), and how and why Americans might think about patriotism in the particular ways that they do.

accidental condition in a definition, an element that helps to explain what is being defined but is not essential to it. An accidental condition in defining a bird might be "ability to fly" because most, but not all, birds can fly. (See also *essential condition* and *sufficient condition*.)

ad hominem **argument** a fallacy of argument in which a writer's claim is answered by irrelevant attacks on his or her character.

analogy an extended comparison between something unfamiliar and something more familiar for the purpose of illuminating or dramatizing the unfamiliar. An analogy might, say, compare nuclear fission (less familiar) to a pool player's opening break (more familiar).

anaphora a figure of speech involving repetition, particularly of the same word at the beginning of several clauses.

antithesis the use of parallel structures to call attention to contrasts or opposites, as in *Some like it hot; some like it cold*.

antonomasia use of a title, epithet, or description in place of a name, as in *Your Honor* for *Judge*.

argument (1) a spoken, written, or visual text that expresses a point of view; (2) the use of evidence and reason to discover some version of the truth, as distinct from *persuasion,* the attempt to change someone else's point of view.

artistic appeal support for an argument that a writer creates based on principles of reason and shared knowledge rather than on facts and evidence. (See also *inartistic appeal*.)

assumption a belief regarded as true, upon which other claims are based.

assumption, cultural a belief regarded as true or commonsensical within a particular culture, such as the belief in individual freedom in American culture.

audience the person or persons to whom an argument is directed.

authority the quality conveyed by a writer who is knowledgeable about his or her subject and confident in that knowledge.

background the information a writer provides to create the context for an argument.

backing in Toulmin argument, the evidence provided to support a *warrant*.

bandwagon appeal a fallacy of argument in which a course of action is recommended on the grounds that everyone else is following it.

begging the question a fallacy of argument in which a claim is based on the very grounds that are in doubt or dispute: *Rita can't be the bicycle thief; she's never stolen anything.*

causal argument an argument that seeks to explain the effect(s) of a cause, the cause(s) of an effect, or a causal chain in which A causes B, B causes C, C causes D, and so on.

ceremonial argument an argument that deals with current values and addresses questions of praise and blame. Also called *epideictic,* ceremonial arguments include eulogies and graduation speeches.

character, appeal based on a strategy in which a writer presents an authoritative or credible self-image to dispose an audience to accept a claim.

claim a statement that asserts a belief or truth. In arguments, most claims require supporting evidence. The claim is a key component in Toulmin argument.

connecting (1) identifying with a writer or reader; or (2) crafting an argument to emphasize where writers and audiences share interests, concerns, or experiences.

connotation the suggestions or associations that surround most words and extend beyond their literal meaning, creating associational effects. *Slender* and *skinny* have similar meanings, for example, but carry different connotations, the former more positive than the latter.

context the entire situation in which a piece of writing takes place, including the writer's purpose(s) for writing; the intended audience; the time and place of writing; the institutional, social, personal, and other influences on the piece of writing; the material conditions of writing (whether it is, for instance, online or on paper, in handwriting or print); and the writer's attitude toward the subject and the audience.

conviction the belief that a claim or course of action is true or reasonable. In a proposal argument, a writer must move an audience beyond conviction to action.

credibility an impression of integrity, honesty, and trustworthiness conveyed by a writer in an argument.

criterion in evaluative arguments, the standard by which something is measured to determine its quality or value.

definition, argument of an argument in which the claim specifies that something does or does not meet the conditions or features set forth in a definition: *Affirmative action is discrimination.*

deliberative argument an argument that deals with action to be taken in the future, focusing on matters of policy. Deliberative arguments include parliamentary debates and campaign platforms.

delivery the presentation of a spoken argument.

dogmatism a fallacy of argument in which a claim is supported on the grounds that it is the only conclusion acceptable within a given community.

either-or **choice** a fallacy of argument in which a complicated issue is represented as offering only two possible courses of action, one of which is made to seem vastly preferable to the other. *Either-or* choices generally misrepresent complicated arguments by oversimplifying them.

emotional appeal a strategy in which a writer tries to generate specific emotions (such as fear, envy, anger, or pity) in an audience to dispose it to accept a claim.

enthymeme in Toulmin argument, a statement that links a claim to a supporting reason: *The bank will fail* (claim) *because it has lost the support of its largest investors* (reason). In classical rhetoric, an enthymeme is a *syllogism* with one term understood but not stated: *Socrates is mortal because he is a human being.* (The understood term is: *All human beings are mortal.*)

epideictic argument see *ceremonial argument.*

equivocation a fallacy of argument in which a lie is given the appearance of truth, or in which the truth is misrepresented in deceptive language.

essential condition in a definition, an element that must be part of the definition but, by itself, isn't enough to define the term. An essential condition in defining a bird might be "winged": all birds have wings, yet wings alone do not define a bird since some insects and mammals also have wings. (See also *accidental condition* and *sufficient condition.*)

ethical appeal see *character, appeal based on*, and *ethos.*

ethnographic observation a form of field research involving close and extended observation of a group, event, or phenomenon; careful and detailed note-taking during the observation; analysis of the notes; and interpretation of that analysis.

ethos the self-image a writer creates to define a relationship with readers. In arguments, most writers try to establish an ethos that suggests honesty and credibility.

evaluation, argument of an argument in which the claim specifies that something does or does not meet established criteria: *The Nikon F5 is the most sophisticated 35mm camera currently available.*

evidence material offered to support an argument. See *artistic appeal* and *inartistic appeal.*

example, definition by a definition that operates by identifying individual examples of what is being defined: *Sports car — Corvette, Viper, Miata, Boxster.*

experimental evidence evidence gathered through experimentation; often evidence that can be quantified (for example, a survey of students before and after an election might yield statistical evidence about changes in their attitudes toward the candidates). Experimental evidence is frequently crucial to scientific arguments.

fact, argument of an argument in which the claim can be proved or disproved with specific evidence or testimony: *The winter of 1998 was the warmest on record for the United States.*

fallacy of argument a flaw in the structure of an argument that renders its conclusion invalid or suspect. See *ad hominem argument, bandwagon appeal, begging the question, dogmatism, either-or choice, equivocation, false authority, faulty analogy, faulty causality, hasty generalization, moral equivalence, non sequitur, scare tactic, sentimental appeal,* and *slippery slope.*

false authority a fallacy of argument in which a claim is based on the expertise of someone who lacks appropriate credentials.

faulty analogy a fallacy of argument in which a comparison between two objects or concepts is inaccurate or inconsequential.

faulty causality a fallacy of argument making the unwarranted assumption that because one event follows another, the first event causes the second. Also called *post hoc, ergo propter hoc*, faulty causality forms the basis of many superstitions.

firsthand evidence data — including surveys, observation, personal interviews, etc. — collected and personally examined by the writer. (See also *secondhand evidence.*)

fisking a term invented by Glenn Reynolds to describe a line-by-line refutation, usually online, of an argument that the writer finds inaccurate or rhetorically suspect.

flashpoint see *fallacy of argument*.

forensic argument an argument that deals with actions that have occurred in the past. Sometimes called judicial arguments, forensic arguments include legal cases involving judgments of guilt or innocence.

formal definition a definition that identifies something first by the general class to which it belongs (*genus*) and then by the characteristics that distinguish it from other members of that class (*species*): *Baseball is a game* (genus) *played on a diamond by opposing teams of nine players who score runs by circling bases after striking a ball with a bat* (species).

genus in a definition, the general class to which an object or concept belongs: *baseball is a* sport; *green is a* color.

grounds in Toulmin argument, the evidence provided to support a claim or reason, or *enthymeme*.

hard evidence support for an argument using facts, statistics, testimony, or other evidence the writer finds.

hasty generalization a fallacy of argument in which an inference is drawn from insufficient data.

hyperbole use of overstatement for special effect.

hypothesis an expectation for the findings of one's research or the conclusion to one's argument. Hypotheses must be tested against evidence, counterarguments, and so on.

immediate reason the cause that leads directly to an effect, such as an automobile accident that results in an injury to the driver. (See also *necessary reason* and *sufficient reason*.)

inartistic appeal support for an argument using facts, statistics, eyewitness testimony, or other evidence the writer finds. (See also *artistic appeal*.)

intended readers the actual, real-life people whom a writer consciously wants to address in a piece of writing.

invention the process of finding and creating arguments to support a claim.

inverted word order moving grammatical elements of a sentence out of their usual order (subject-verb-object/complement) for special effect, as in *Tired I was; sleepy I was not.*

invitational argument a term used by Sonja Foss to describe arguments that are aimed not at vanquishing an opponent but at inviting others to collaborate in exploring mutually satisfying ways to solve problems.

invoked readers the readers directly addressed or implied in a text, which may include some that the writer did not consciously intend to reach. An argument that refers to *those who have experienced a major trauma,* for example, invokes all readers who have undergone this experience.

irony use of language that suggests a meaning in contrast to the literal meaning of the words.

line of argument a strategy or approach used in an argument. Argumentative strategies include appeals to the heart (emotional appeals), to values, to character (ethical appeals), and to facts and reason (logical appeals).

logical appeal a strategy in which a writer uses facts, evidence, and reason to make audience members accept a claim.

metaphor a figure of speech that makes a comparison, as in *The ship was a beacon of hope.*

moral equivalence a fallacy of argument in which no distinction is made between serious issues, problems, or failings and much less important ones.

necessary reason a cause that must be present for an effect to occur; for example, infection with a particular virus is a necessary reason for the development of AIDS. (See also *immediate reason* and *sufficient reason.*)

non sequitur a fallacy of argument in which claims, reasons, or warrants fail to connect logically; one point does not follow from another. *If you're really my friend, you'll lend me five hundred dollars.*

operational definition a definition that identifies an object by what it does or by the conditions that create it: *A line is the shortest distance between two points.*

parallelism use of similar grammatical structures or forms for pleasing effect: *in the classroom, on the playground, and at the mall.*

parody a form of humor in which a writer transforms something familiar into a different form to make a comic point.

pathos, appeal to see *emotional appeal.*

persuasion the act of seeking to change someone else's point of view.

precedents actions or decisions in the past that have established a pattern or model for subsequent actions. Precedents are particularly important in legal cases.

prejudices irrational beliefs, usually based on inadequate or outdated information.

premise a statement or position regarded as true and upon which other claims are based.

propaganda an argument advancing a point of view without regard to reason, fairness, or truth.

proposal argument an argument in which a claim is made in favor of or opposing a specific course of action: *Sport utility vehicles should have to meet the same fuel economy standards as passenger cars.*

purpose the goal of an argument. Purposes include entertaining, informing, convincing, exploring, and deciding, among others.

qualifiers words or phrases that limit the scope of a claim: *usually; in a few cases; under these circumstances.*

qualitative argument an argument of evaluation that relies on nonnumerical criteria supported by reason, tradition, precedent, or logic.

quantitative argument an argument of evaluation that relies on criteria that can be measured, counted, or demonstrated objectively.

reason in writing, a statement that expands a claim by offering evidence to support it. The reason may be a statement of fact or another claim. In Toulmin argument, a *reason* is attached to a *claim* by a *warrant,* a statement that establishes the logical connection between claim and supporting reason.

rebuttal an answer that challenges or refutes a specific claim or charge. Rebuttals may also be offered by writers who anticipate objections to the claims or evidence they offer.

rebuttal, conditions of in Toulmin argument, potential objections to an argument. Writers need to anticipate such conditions in shaping their arguments.

reversed structures a figure of speech that involves the inversion of clauses: *What is good in your writing is not original; what is original is not good.*

rhetoric the art of persuasion. Western rhetoric originated in ancient Greece as a discipline to prepare citizens for arguing cases in court.

rhetorical analysis an examination of how well the components of an argument work together to persuade or move an audience.

rhetorical questions questions posed to raise an issue or create an effect rather than to get a response: *You may well wonder, "What's in a name?"*

ridicule humor, usually mean-spirited, directed at a particular target.

Rogerian argument an approach to argumentation that is based on the principle, articulated by psychotherapist Carl Rogers, that audiences respond best when they do not feel threatened. Rogerian argument stresses trust and urges those who disagree to find common ground.

satire a form of humor in which a writer uses wit to expose—and possibly correct—human failings.

scare tactic a fallacy of argument presenting an issue in terms of exaggerated threats or dangers.

scheme a figure of speech that involves a special arrangement of words, such as inversion.

secondhand evidence any information taken from outside sources, including library research and online sources. (See also *firsthand evidence*.)

sentimental appeal a fallacy of argument in which an appeal is based on excessive emotion.

simile a comparison that uses *like* or *as*: *My love is like a red, red rose* or *I wandered lonely as a cloud*.

slippery slope a fallacy of argument exaggerating the possibility that a relatively inconsequential action or choice today will have serious adverse consequences in the future.

species in a definition, the particular features that distinguish one member of a *genus* from another: *Baseball is a sport* (genus) *played on a diamond by teams of nine players* (species).

spin a kind of political advocacy that makes any fact or event, however unfavorable, serve a political purpose.

stance the writer's attitude toward the topic and the audience.

stasis theory in classical rhetoric, a method for coming up with appropriate arguments by determining the nature of a given situation: *a question of fact; of definition; of quality;* or *of policy*.

sufficient condition in a definition, an element or set of elements adequate to define a term. A sufficient condition in defining God, for example, might be "supreme being" or "first cause." No other conditions are necessary, though many might be made. (See also *accidental condition* and *essential condition*.)

sufficient reason a cause that alone is enough to produce a particular effect; for example, a particular level of smoke in the air will set off a smoke alarm. (See also *immediate reason* and *necessary reason*.)

syllogism in formal logic, a structure of deductive logic in which correctly formed major and minor premises lead to a necessary conclusion:

Major premise	All human beings are mortal.
Minor premise	Socrates is a human being.
Conclusion	Socrates is mortal.

testimony a personal experience or observation used to support an argument.

thesis a sentence that succinctly states a writer's main point.

Toulmin argument a method of informal logic first described by Stephen Toulmin in *The Uses of Argument* (1958). Toulmin argument describes the key components of an argument as the *claim, reason, warrant, backing,* and *grounds*.

trope a figure of speech that involves a change in the usual meaning or signification of words, such as *metaphor, simile,* and *analogy*.

understatement a figure of speech that makes a weaker statement than a situation seems to call for. It can lead to powerful or to humorous effects.

values, appeal to a strategy in which a writer invokes shared principles and traditions of a society as a reason for accepting a claim.

warrant in Toulmin argument, the statement (expressed or implied) that establishes the logical connection between a claim and its supporting reason.

Claim	Don't eat that mushroom;
Reason	it's poisonous.
Warrant	What is poisonous should not be eaten.

ACKNOWLEDGMENTS

Chapter-Opening Art

Barbie doll: the first Barbie doll produced in 1959, Barbie Doll Museum, Palo Alto. Photo © Neema Frederic/CORBIS; Seal of the President/United States: Photo Joseph Sohm/Photo Researchers; White dove: Photo © Roger Tidman/CORBIS; 4×4 on Road: Photo Getty Images/Antonio M. Rosario; Cell phone: Rick Rusing/Getty Images.

Texts

Marjorie Agosín. "Always Living in Spanish." Translated by Celeste Kostopulos-Cooperman. "English." Translated by Monica Bruno. Both reprinted with the permission of the author.

Sherman Alexie. "The Exaggeration of Despair." From *The Summer of Black Widows* by Sherman Alexie. Copyright © 1996 by Sherman Alexie. Reprinted by permission of Hanging Loose Press.

ASPCA screen shot. Copyright © The American Society for the Prevention of Cruelty to Animals. Reprinted with permission of ASPCA. All Rights Reserved.

Christie Balka and Andy Rose. "Journey toward Wholeness: Reflections of a Lesbian Rabbi." From *Twice Blessed* by Christie Balka. Copyright © 1989 by Christie Balka and Andy Rose. Reprinted by permission of Beacon Press, Boston.

James Bandler. "A Long Journey Home." From *The Boston Globe*, May 19, 1999. Copyright © 1999 The Boston Globe. Republished by permission of *The Boston Globe* in the format textbook via Copyright Clearance Center.

Dave Barry. "How to Vote in One Easy Step: Use Chisel, Tablet." Excerpt from *The Miami Herald*, September 13, 2002. Copyright © 2002 Dave Barry and The Miami Herald. Reprinted by permission of the author.

Siobhan Benet. "Where We Once Roamed." From *Black Enterprise*, September 1, 2002. Copyright © 2002 by Siobhan Benet. Reprinted with permission of RSI Copyright, for the author.

William J. Bennett. "A Nation Worth Defending." Originally published in *USA Today*, November 2002. Reprinted by permission of the author.

Ira H. Berkow. "Rower with Muslim Name is an All-American Suspect." From *The New York Times*, February 21, 2003. Copyright © 2003 by The New York Times Company, Inc. Reprinted by permission.

Derek Bok. "Protecting Freedom of Expression at Harvard." First published in *The Boston Globe*, May 25, 1991. Reprinted with the permission of the author.

Madeleine Brand. "Schoolchildren debating what it Means to Be a Patriot." © Copyright NPR® 2003. The news report by Madeleine Brand was originally broadcast on National Public Radio's "Morning Edition®" on February 6, 2003, and is used with the permission of National Public Radio, Inc. Any unauthorized duplication is strictly prohibited.

Matthew Brzezinski. "The Homeland Security State: How Far Should We Go?" From *The New York Times Magazine*, February 23, 2003. Copyright © 2003 by Matthew Brzezinski. Reprinted by permission.

Thomas R. Burnett. "Promoting an Extreme Case of Sharing." From *The Atlanta Journal-Constitution*, May 20, 1999. Copyright © 1999 by the Atlanta Journal-Constitution. Reprinted by permission of the Atlanta Journal-Constitution in the format textbook by Copyright Clearance Center.

Deborah Kovach Caldwell. "A Hindu Renaissance." From *The Dallas Morning News*, February 20, 1999. Copyright © 1999 by The Dallas Morning News. Reprinted with the permission of the publisher.

Lan Cao. "Relocating One's Roots." From *Monkey Bridge* by Lan Cao. Copyright © 1997 by Lan Cao. Used by permission of Viking Penguin, a division of Penguin Group, (USA) Inc.

David Carr. "On Covers of Many Magazines, A Full Racial Palette Is Still Rare." From *The New York Times*, November 18, 2002. Copyright © 2002 by The New York Times, Inc. Reprinted by permission.

Damien Cave. "File Sharing: Guilty as Charged?" From *Salon.com*, August 23, 2002. Copyright © 2002. Reprinted with the permission of Salon.com. www.salon.com.

Mona Charen. "We Should Relinquish Some Liberty in Exchange for Security." November 25, 2002. Copyright © 2002 Creators Syndicate, Inc. Reprinted by permission.

Sandra Cisneros. "I'd Never Made Love in Spanish Before." From *Woman Hollering Creek* by Sandra Cisneros. Copyright © 1991 by Sandra Cisneros. Published by Vintage Books, a division of Random House, Inc., New York and originally in hardcover by Random House, Inc. Reprinted by permission of Susan Bergholz Literary Services, New York. All rights reserved.

Dana Cloud. "Modified Pledge of Allegiance." Originally published in *The Daily Texan* July 1, 2002. © 2002 Dana Cloud. Reprinted by permission of the author.

Jessica F. Cohen. "Grade A: The Market for a Yale Woman's Eggs." Excerpt from article published in *The Atlantic Monthly*, December 2002, 74 & 78. Reprinted with the permission of the author.

Randy Cohen. "The Ethicist/Between the Sexes." From *The New York Times*, October 27, 2002. Copyright © 2002 The New York Times Company. Reprinted by permission.

Ruth Conniff. "Title IX: Political Football." Copyright © 2003. Reprinted with permission from the March 24, 2003 issue of *The Nation*, March 24, 2003.

Michelle Cottle. "Turning Boys into Girls." Reprinted with permission from *The Washington Monthly*, May 1998. Copyright by Washington Monthly Publishing, LLC, 733 15th St. NW, Suite 520, Washington, DC 20005. (202) 393-5155. Web site: www.washingtonmonthly.com.

Catherine Crier. Excerpt from the Introduction in *The Case Against Lawyers* by Catherine Crier. © 2002 by Catherine Crier. Reprinted with the permission of Broadway Books, a division of Random House, Inc.

Margaret Curtis. "Kings Don't Own Words." From *The Atlanta Journal-Constitution*, May 20, 1999. Copyright © 1999 Atlanta Journal and Constitution. Republished with permission of the Atlanta Journal-Constitution in the format of Textbook via Copyright Clearance Center.

Craig R. Dean. "Legalize Gay Marriage." From *The New York Times*, © 1991 by The New York Times Company. Reprinted with permission.

Alan Dershowitz. "Testing Speech Codes." From the *Boston Globe Index*. Copyright © 2002 by Globe Newspaper Company (MA). Reproduced with permission of Globe Newspaper Company (MA) in the format of Textbook via Copyright Clearance Center. "Why Fear National ID Cards?" From *The New York Times*, October 13, 2001. Copyright © 2001 by The New York Times Company. Reprinted with permission.

Ariel Dorfman. "If Only We All Spoke Two Languages." From *The New York Times*, June 24, 1994. Copyright © 1994 by The New York Times Company. Reprinted with permission.

Caryn James. "It's All in the Mix: A Plastic Surgery Reality Show." From *The New York Times*, December 11, 2002. Copyright © by The New York Times Company, Inc. Reprinted by permission.

Kaiser Family Foundation. "2002 National Survey of Latinos." (#3301). This information was reprinted with permission of the Henry J. Kaiser Family Foundation. The Kaiser Family Foundation, based in Menlo Park, California is a nonprofit, independent national health care philanthropy and is not associated with Kaiser Permanente or Kaiser Industries.

King Kaufman. "Tiger's Burden." From *Salon.com*, November 27, 2002. Copyright © 2002. Reprinted with the permission of Salon.com. www.salon.com.

Michael Kazin. "A Patriotic Left." © 2002 Foundation for Study of Independent Ideas, Inc. Reprinted with the permission of the author.

Aisha Khan. "The Veil in My Handbag." From *The Guardian*, June 18, 2002. © 2002 The Guardian. Reprinted with the permission of the publisher.

Martin Luther King, Jr. "I Have a Dream." Copyright 1963 Dr. Martin Luther King Jr. Copyright renewed 1991 Coretta Scott King. Reprinted by arrangement with the Estate of Martin Luther King Jr., c/o Writers House as agent for the proprietor, New York, NY.

Georgia Kleege. Excerpt from *Sight Unseen* by Georgia Kleege. Copyright © 1999 Georgia Kleege. Reprinted by permission of Mildred Marmur Associates, Ltd. On behalf of the author.

Gina Kolata. "$50,000 Offered to Tall, Smart Egg Donor." From *The New York Times*, March 3, 1999. Copyright © 1999 by The New York Times Company. Reprinted with permission.

Michael Lassell. "How to Watch Your Brother Die." (one stanza). Copyright © 1995 by Michael Lassell. Reprinted with the permission of the author.

Chang-rae Lee. "Mute in an English-Only World." From *The New York Times*, April 18, 1996. Copyright © 1996 by The New York Times Company. Reprinted with permission.

David Lefer. "An Ad for Smart Eggs Spawns Ethics Uproar." *The Daily News*, March 7, 1999. Copyright © 1999. New York Daily News, L.P. Reprinted with permission.

John Leo. "Fu Manchu on Naboo." From *U.S. News & World Report*, July 12, 1999. © 1999 U.S. News & World Report, L.P. Reprinted with permission.

John Levesque. "Sitcom dads rarely know best, study of TV laments." *Seattle Post-Intelligencer*, June 10, 1999. Copyright 1999, Seattle Post-Intelligencer. Reprinted with permission.

James Lindgren. "Fall from Grace: Arming America and the Bellesiles Scandal." Reprinted by permission of The Yale Law Journal Company and William S. Hein Company from *The Yale Law Journal*, Vol. 111, pages 2195-2249.

Andrea Lo. "Finding Myself through Language." Reprinted with the permission of the author.

Joe Loconte. "Hospice, not Hemlock." From *The Journal of American Citizenship*, March/April 1998, published by the Heritage Foundation. Copyright © 1998 by the Heritage Foundation. Reprinted with permission.

Peter Mandaville. "Digital Islam: Changing the Boundaries of Religious Knowledge?" From *ISIM Newsletter*, No. 2, 1999. Copyright 1999. Reprinted by permission of International Institute for the Study of Islam in the Modern World.

Charles C. Mann. "Who Will Own Your Next Idea?" First published in *The Atlantic Monthly*, September 1998. Copyright © Charles C. Mann. Reprinted by permission of the author.

Dennis Preger. "Divinity and Pornography." *The Weekly Standard*, June 14, 1999. Copyright © 1999 News America Incorporated. Reprinted with permission of the publisher.

Bill Rankin. "King's Speech: Who Owns Soul Stirring Words?" Copyright 1999 by *The Atlanta Journal-Constitution*. Reproduced with permission of The Atlanta Journal-Constitution in the format Textbook via Copyright Clearance Center.

RANTS website. PatrickRuffini.com website. www.patrickruffini.com. Reprinted by permission.

Jonathan Rauch. "The Fat Tax: A Modest Proposal." First published in *The Atlantic Monthly*, December 2002, p. 32. © 2002 by Jonathan Rauch. Reprinted by permission of the author.

Deborah Rhode. "Tea Time for Equality." From *The National Law Journal*, October 7, 2002. Copyright © 2002 NLP IP Co. Reprinted with permission. All rights reserved.

Adrienne Rich. Excerpts from "What Does a Woman Need to Know?" From *Blood, Bread, and Poetry: Selected Prose 1979-1985* by Adrienne Rich. Copyright © 1986 by Adrienne Rich. Used by permission of the author and W.W. Norton & Company, Inc.

John R. Rickford. "Commentary: Suite for Ebony and Phonics." From *Discover* 18.12, December 1997. Copyright © 1997 by John R. Rickford. Reprinted by permission of the author.

Steve Rushin. "Hip Unchecked." From *Sports Illustrated*, June 21, 1999. Reprinted courtesy of SPORTS ILLUSTRATED. Copyright © 1999 Time, Inc. All rights reserved.

Robert Scheer. "Between Football and War." Published January 2003. Copyright © 2003 Robert Scheer. Reprinted with the permission of Creator's Syndicate.

Win Schwartau. "What Counts as Evidence." From the book *Information Warfare* by Winn Schwartau. Copyright © 1994, 1996 by Winn Schwartau. Appears by permission of the publisher, Thunder's Mouth Press.

Janny Scott. "Foreign Born in U.S. at Record High." From *The New York Times*, February 7, 2002. Copyright © 2002 by The New York Times Company. Reprinted with permission.

Sean Jean website screen shot. Reprinted with permisson.

Michael Sokolove. "Football is a Sucker's Game." From *The New York Times*, December 22, 2002. Copyright © 2002 The New York Times Company. Reprinted by permission. Stanford Study of Writing website screen shots. Courtesy of Stanford University.

James Sterngold. "Able to Laugh at Their People, Not Just Cry for Them." From *The New York Times*. Copyright © 1998 by The New York Times Company, Inc. Reprinted by permission.

Welch Suggs. "Colleges Consider Fairness of Cutting Men's Teams to Comply with Title IX." From *The Chronicle of Higher Education*, February 19, 1999, p. A53. Copyright © 1999 The Chronicle of Higher Education. Reprinted with permission.

Andrew Sullivan. "Lacking in Self-Esteem: Good for You!" from *Time*, October 11, 2002, p. 102 and "My America." From *The Sunday Times of London*, November 24, 1996. Reprinted with the permission of The Wylie Agency, Inc.

Margaret Talbot. "Men Behaving Badly." From *The New York Times*, October 13, 2002. Copyright © 2002 Margaret Talbot. Reprinted by permission.

TalkLeft website. www.talkleft.com. Reprinted with permission of Jeralyn Merritt, Owner, Talkleft: the Politics of Crime.

Amy Tan. "Mother's Tongue." Copyright © 1990 by Amy Tan. First appeared in *The Threepenny Review*. Reprinted by permission of the author and the Sandra Dijkstra Literary Agency.

Deborah Tannen. "Teachers' Classroom Strategies Should Recognize That Men and Women Use the Language Differently." From *The Chronicle of Higher Education*, June 19, 1991. Copyright Deborah Tannen. Reprinted by permission.

David D. Troutt. "Defining Who We Are in Society." From *The Los Angeles Times*, January 12, 1997. Copyright © 1997 by David D. Troutt Reprinted with the permission of the author.

Dennis Tyler website and resume. Courtesy of Dennis Tyler.

"Vacation Days" screen shot. © USA TODAY. Reprinted with permission of Usatoday.com.

"Statement of Purpose." Reprinted with the permission of Veterans Against The Iraq War.

Thad Williamson. "Bad as They Wanna Be: Loving the Game is Harder as Colleagues Sell Out . . ." by Thad Williamson. From *The Nation*, October 17, 1998. © THE NATION. Reprinted by permission of the publisher.

Women's Sports Foundation. "Title IX Facts Everyone Should Know!" and "Women at Augusta National Golf Club." Courtesy of www.WomensSportsFoundation.org.

Louise Young. "Cosmetic Surgery." From *The Guardian*, January 13, 1997. Copyright © 1997 by The Guardian. Reprinted with permission of the publisher.

Cartoons and Advertisements

Pat Byrnes. "This Diaper Makes My Butt Look Big" © The New Yorker Collection 2000 Pat Byrnes. From cartoonbank.com. All Rights Reserved.

Johnny Hart. B.C. cartoons. By permission of John L. Hart FLP, and Creators Syndicate, Inc.

Jockey International ad. Copyright © Jockey 2003. Reprinted with the permission of Jockey International Inc.

Jimmy Margulies. "Elian Gonzalez" cartoon. © 2000 The Record, New Jersey. www .bergen.com. Reprinted with the permission of Jimmy Margulies.

Bill O'Reilly photo. © Marc Asnin/CORBIS SABA.

Gary Trudeau. "Sho' Nuff" and "Intellectual Property" *Doonesbury* cartoons. © 2000 G. B. Trudeau. Reprinted with the permission of Universal Press Syndicate. All Rights Reserved.

Jack Ziegler. "Wow, Thanks. I'm a big fan . . ." © The New Yorker Collection 2000 Jack Ziegler. From cartoonbank.com. All Rights Reserved.

Illustrations

Abbr.: GI = Getty Images; AP/WW = Associated Press/Wide World Photos. Pg. 4 (bot.), courtesy, claudeataylor@yahoo.com; Fig. 1.1, cover, DAVE BARRY HITS BELOW THE BELT-LINE by Dave Barry, © 2001, used by permission of Random House, Inc.; Fig. 1.2, Georgia O'Keeffe, "White Flower on Red Earth" (1943), oil on canvas. Collection of the Newark Museum/Art Resource. Permission granted by the Artists Rights Society; Fig. 1.3, facsimile of stained glass window from St. Etiene-Bruge, Alan Baker, Oxford, England; Fig. 2.1, John J. Ruszkiewicz; Fig. 2.2, Texas Dept. of Transportation/Sherry Matthews Advocacy Marketing; Fig. 4.1, image courtesy of www.adbusters.org; Fig. 4.2, Doug Mills/AP/WW; Fig. 5.1, Miss America Organization; Fig. 5.2, Albuquerque Journal; Fig. 6.1 (a), Susan Meislas/Magnum Photos, (b) Marta Lavandier, © Kim D. Johnson, (d) Pablo Martinez Monsivais, (all) AP/WW; Fig. 6.2, Chris Pizzello/AP/WW; Fig. 7.1, Sam Mircovich/AP/WW; Fig. 7.3, © 2003

USA TODAY. Reprinted by permission. Usatoday.com; Fig. 9.1, InstaPundit.com; Fig. 10.2, Chris Pizzello/AP/WW; Fig. 10.3, courtesy, American Honda Models; Fig. 10.4, Scott Frances/ESTP Photographics; Fig. 11.3, Seth Perlman/AP/WW; Fig. 12.1, courtesy, Americans for the Arts; pg. 256, Bedford/St. Martin's photo; Figs. 13.1, 13.2, reprinted with permission of *The Onion*, © 2001, © 1998 by Onion, Inc. www.theonion.com; pg. 265, reprinted by permission from American Family Life Assurance of Columbus (AFLAC), Columbus, Ga.; Fig. 13.3, Todd Nienkerk, TEXAS TRAVESTY, The University of Texas at Austin; Fig. 14.1, photo by Carl Van Vechten/The Granger Collection; Fig. 14.2, *Doonesbury* © G. B. Trudeau. Reprinted with permission of Universal Press Syndicate. All rights reserved; Fig. 14.3, Ric Feld/AP/WW; Fig. 14.4, Reprinted by permission of *The Ironic Times*; Fig. 15.1, courtesy, Mercedes-Benz, USA; Fig. 15.2, courtesy, Viking/Penguin Publishing Co./Coral Graphics, Inc.; Fig. 15.3, "The Chinese Horse" Lascaux Caves, France/Art Resource; Fig. 15.4, Paul Schutzer, LIFE Magazine, TIMEPIX/Getty Images; Fig. 15.5, Bridget Besaw Gorman/AP/WW; Fig. 15.6, Joe Rosenthal/AP/WW; Fig. 15.7, Marty Lederhandler/AP/WW; Fig. 15.9, © 2003 Benetton Group S.P.A.; Fig. 15.10, courtesy, United Nations World Food Programme, www.wfp.org; Fig. 15.11 (a), AP/WW, (b), courtesy, McDonald's Corp., ©, courtesy BMW of North America; Fig. 15.12, Reprinted with permission of Dennis Tyler; Fig. 15.13, Reprinted with permission of Dennis Tyler; Fig. 15.15, Reprinted by permission of Google; Fig. 15.18, J. Scott Applewhite/AP/WW; Fig. 15.19, NASA/AP/WW; Fig. 15.21, courtesy, Brown Lenox Co. Ltd.; Fig. 16.1, Reprinted with permission of Patrick Ruffini; Fig. 16.2, Reprinted by permission of Jerlyn Merritt; Fig. 16.3, copyright © 2003 The American Society for the Prevention of Cruelty to Animals. Reprinted with permission of ASPCA. All rights reserved; Fig. 16.4, reprinted by permission of the Foundation for Individual Rights in Education; Fig. 16.5, Reprinted by permission of Google; Fig. 17.1, AP/WW; Fig. 17.2, © 20th Century Fox/Photofest; Fig. 17.3, Andrew Dalmau/EFE/AP/WW; Fig. 17.4, AP/WW; Fig. 18.1, Michael Caulfield/AP/WW; Fig. 18.2, the Federation of Gay Games, Inc.; Fig. 19.1, Ed Sirrs/Retna; Fig. 19.2, courtesy, World Wildlife Fund; Fig. 19.3, © Jimmy Margulies. Reprinted by permission; Fig. 20.1, courtesy, U.S. Copyright Office; Fig. 20.2, © Garry Trudeau. Reprinted with permission of Universal Press Syndicate. All rights reserved; Fig. 20.3, Janet Hostetter/AP/WW; Fig. 21.1, © 2003 PEOPLE Magazine, photo: Craig DeCristo/L2 Agency, (inset) Matt Jones, (top) Ramey Photo, (cent.) Gary Caspry/Reuters, (bot.) Lester Cohen/WireImage; Fig. 21.2, courtesy, ZYZZYVA, San Francisco; Fig. 21.3, Jack Kutz/Image Works; Fig. 21.4, Dennis Brack/Bloomberg News/Landov; Fig. 22.1, courtesy, The Modern Library Assn.; Fig. 22.2, © 2001 by the American Psychological Association. Courtesy, Naylor Design. Reprinted with permission. Pg. 463, Alex Ramey/Stock, Boston; 467, Archive Photos/GI; 475, Agence France-Presse/GI; 478, Reed Saxon/AP/WW; 481, © ABC Photo Archives; 484, (l.) Bettmann/CORBIS, (r.) Chris Rainier/CORBIS; 487, courtesy, *Men's Health*; 492, Ted Russell; 496, illustration by Hal Mayforth/Gerald & Cullen Rapp, Inc.; 497, (l.) Photofest, (r.) Bettmann/CORBIS; 498, (l.) Bettmann/CORBIS, (r.) Photofest; 500-506, Photofest; 504, AP/WW; 511, Chris Pizzello/AP/WW; 526, illustration by Marcy Mullins from USA TODAY, April, 1999. © 1999, USA TODAY. Reprinted with permission; 529, courtesy, Boston Women's Health Book collective; 536, Culver Pictures; 540, AP/WW; 544, Everett Collection; 547, Stone/GI; 556, Michael Sypniewski/AP/WW; 560, Robert Pavuchak/Pittsburgh Post-Gazette; 564, Reforma Archivo/AP/WW; 574, AP/WW; 581, IT Stock Int'l/Index Stock; 585, illustration by Robert Grossman; 592, Dennis Drenner; 598-601, illustrations by Julie Delton; 611, Roberto Borea/AP/WW; 612, (top) AP/WW, (bot.) AP/WW; 618, John Biever/SPORTS ILLUSTRATED; 619, (top) © AFP/CORBIS, (bot.) Hulton|Archive/GI; 623, INP/CORBIS; 625, AP/WW; 630, Craig Jones/GI; 638, Mark Hall/AP/WW; 651, Susan Watts/NY

DAILY NEWS; 654, engraving by Gustave Dore, courtesy of The NY Public Library - Picture Collection; 662, Joel Gordon; 670, Eddie Moore/Albuquerque Journal, © 1999; 675-677, illustrations by Theo Rudnak Studio/www.rudnak.com; 683, AP/WW; 684, Stephen Marks/GI; 688, courtesy, American Learning Institute for Muslims; 690, © AFP/CORBIS; 694, Bettmann/CORBIS; 697, Joe Marquette/AP/WW; 704, (l.) Photofest, (r.) Ed Bailey/AP/WW; 708, illustration by Tim Bower; 715, Zefa Visual Media, Germany/Index Stock; 720, Library of Congress; 721, photo by Carl Van Vechten, reprinted with permission of his estate; photo courtesy of the James Weldon Johnson Memorial Collection, Beinecke Library, Yale University; 724, illustration by Christian Clayton;www.claytonbrothers.com; 732, illustration by Christophe Vorlet; 737, illustration by Dan Picasso; 742, courtesy of the Ellis Island Immigration Museum, National Park Service/USDI; 751, Jeremy Woodhouse/Photodisc/GI; 761, David Wells/The Image Works; 769, Joel Gordon; 788, EvolveFish.com; 790, Randy Grothe/The Dallas Morning News; 796, Engraving by Gustave Dore, courtesy, NY Public Library - Picture Collection; 807, Bettmann/CORBIS; 811, AP/WW; 821, David J. Sams/GI; 824, Bob Strong/The Image Works; 832, Donna Day/GI; 837, Ron Edmunds/AP/WW; 843, AP/WW; 847, cartoon by Shannon Wheeler/TMCM.com; 855, CORBIS; 856, © Tim Rasmussen/The Hartford Courant/The Image Works; 863, courtesy, Council on American Islamic Relations; 867, courtesy, VAIW.com/vet; 872, Agence France-Presse/GI; 876, Network Productions/Index Stock; 878, © Bettmann/CORBIS; 879, Herbert Orth/TimePix/GI.

INDEX